THE BIN LADENS

Oil, Money, Terrorism and the Secret Saudi World

STEVE COLL

PENGUIN BOOKS

PENGUIN BOOKS

Published by the Penguin Group
Penguin Books Ltd, 80 Strand, London WC2R 0RL, England
Penguin Group (USA) Inc., 375 Hudson Street, New York, New York 10014, USA
Penguin Group (Canada), 90 Eglinton Avenue East, Suite 700, Toronto, Ontario, Canada M4P 2Y3
(a division of Pearson Penguin Canada Inc.)
Penguin Ireland, 25 St Stephen's Green, Dublin 2, Ireland (a division of Penguin Books Ltd)
Penguin Group (Australia), 250 Camberwell Road, Camberwell, Victoria 3124, Australia
(a division of Pearson Australia Group Pty Ltd)
Penguin Books India Pvt Ltd, 11 Community Centre, Panchsheel Park, New Delhi – 110 017, India
Penguin Group (NZ), 67 Apollo Drive, Rosedale, North Shore 0632, New Zealand
(a division of Pearson New Zealand Ltd)
Penguin Books (South Africa) (Pty) Ltd, 24 Sturdee Avenue, Rosebank,
Johannesburg 2196, South Africa

Penguin Books Ltd, Registered Offices: 80 Strand, London WC2R 0RL, England

www.penguin.com

First published in the United States of America by The Penguin Press, a division of
Penguin Group (USA) Inc. 2008
First published in Great Britain by Allen Lane 2008
Published in Penguin Books 2009

1

Printed in England by Clays Ltd, St Ives plc

978-0-141-03648-9

www.greenpenguin.co.uk

Penguin Books is committed to a sustainable future
for our business, our readers and our planet.
The book in your hands is made from paper
certified by the Forest Stewardship Council.

CONTENTS

PART TWO:
SONS AND DAUGHTERS
September 1967 to May 1988

PART THREE: THE GLOBAL FAMILY
June 1988 to September 2001

PART FOUR: LEGACIES

September 2001 to September 2007

AUTHOR'S NOTE

Two journalists now on the staff of the *Washington Post* made extraordinary contributions to the research for this book. Robin Shulman conducted interviews and dug up documents in Egypt, Lebanon, Israel, Spain, France, and the United States. Her persistence, empathy, and eye for detail have made the book immeasurably stronger. After I drafted the manuscript, Julie Tate recontacted my interview subjects to deepen the research and recheck facts and interpretations. Her attention to detail and nuance, her passion for the subject matter, and her astonishing work ethic made an enormous difference.

THE BIN LADENS

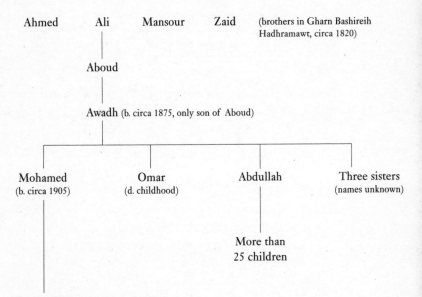

Ahmed   Ali   Mansour   Zaid   (brothers in Gharn Bashireih Hadhramawt, circa 1820)

Aboud

Awadh (b. circa 1875, only son of Aboud)

Mohamed (b. circa 1905)   Omar (d. childhood)   Abdullah   Three sisters (names unknown)

More than 25 children

The 54 children of Mohamed Bin Laden

Born from mid-1940s to 1950:
SONS: Salem, Ali, Thabit, Mahrous, Hassan, Omar, Bakr, Khaled, Yeslam, Ghalib, Yahya, Abdulaziz, Issa, Tareq
DAUGHTERS: Aysha, Fatima, Sheikha, Su'add, Tayyeba, Wafa, Nour

Born from 1951 to 1959:
SONS: Ahmad, Ibrahim, Shafiq, Osama, Khalil, Saleh, Haider
DAUGHTERS: Salma, Zeenat, Ruqqueiya, Randa, Zubaida, Najiah, Samiah, Muna, Saleha, Mariam, Fowziyah, Raja, Huda, Seema

Born from 1959 to 1967:
SONS: Saad, Abdullah, Yasir, Mohammad
DAUGHTERS: Raedah, Eman, Aetedal, Sahar, Ilham, Sana'a, Malak, Muneera

A NOTE ON TRANSLITERATION

THERE IS NO uniform system for transliteration between English and Arabic. The spellings of Arabic-originated place- and proper names relied upon in these pages are to some extent arbitrary, typically chosen to employ the simplest or most common forms. Occasionally, to avoid changing the original text in a quoted document, names may be spelled inconsistently. The Bin Ladens themselves offer an acute case. It is not unusual for family members to render their names in two different spellings in the same English-language document, even in official court filings. "Binladin" has been one common formulation; it is the preferred English spelling for the family's flagship company, the Saudi Binladin Group. Yet "Binladen," "Bin Ladin," "Bin Laden," and even "Benladin" are sometimes employed. I chose "Bin Laden" as the primary form because that is most familiar to American readers and also because when the family's name is written in Arabic script, it appears as two words. For the first names of Mohamed's children, I relied upon the spellings in English-language shareholder documents submitted by the family to a U.S. federal court.

PROLOGUE:
"WE ALL WORSHIP THE
SAME GOD"

October 1984 to February 1985

LYNN PEGHINY played piano most mornings at the Hyatt Regency Grand Cypress Hotel in Orlando, Florida. She was twenty-four, dark-haired, slim, and spirited. She had grown up in Melbourne, on the Atlantic coast, and studied music at the University of Central Florida. She was drawn to the piano and made a living at it, if barely. The breakfast shift in the Hyatt's cavernous atrium was normally subdued—sleepy tourists fortifying themselves for a day at Disney World, businessmen murmuring about real estate. One morning in October 1984, however, a middle-aged man with bright eyes and a mop of black hair walked over and asked in an unfamiliar accent if she would play Beethoven's *Für Elise*. He listened appreciatively, then handed her a twenty-dollar tip. "Do you play private parties?" he asked.

They exchanged business cards. His name was Salem Bin Laden. He had a house just west of Orlando, he told her, not far from Disney World, and he happened to be entertaining some visitors from his native Saudi Arabia who were members of that oil-endowed country's royal family. He owned a piano and hoped she would play at an evening party. A few days later, she drove out State Road 50, which ran due west through miles of orange groves toward Lake County. Salem's home, near the decaying railroad town of Winter Garden, turned out to be an ochre-walled five-acre estate with horse stables, a tiled swimming pool, weeping willows, and palm trees. The main house, a Mediterranean Revival built during the 1920s, had russet Spanish-tile roofing, cupolas, and arched, shaded walkways; it rested on a knoll above a sparkling lake.

"Leeen! Leeen!" Salem exclaimed when she arrived, waving her into the dining room, where his guests were taking breakfast at four in the afternoon. "Come, come," he said. "Sit with us."[1] He placed her next to his guest of honor. Abdul Aziz Al-Ibrahim was a brother of Princess Jawhara Al-Ibrahim, the fourth and reputedly the favorite wife of Saudi Arabia's King Fahd. The Ibrahims had ascended from obscurity after Fahd fell for Jawhara; she left her husband for the king and gave birth to a son, Abdulaziz, upon whom Fahd doted. Princess Jawhara's place at the king's side created opportunities for her brothers. They became influential businessmen, exciting jealousy and gossip in royal circles; they had recently started to invest in Orlando real estate.[2] Salem Bin Laden, whose family's construction firm relied upon access to the king's court, cultivated the Ibrahims' friendship.

Lynn chattered freely; Ibrahim ate vigorously, but in silence. Salem leaned over and whispered, "You're not allowed to speak directly to him." Mortified, she fell silent; she wondered what she had gotten herself into.

Salem took her outside to show her the grounds. He was a slight man in his late thirties, about five feet and seven inches, slim but soft from a life without much exercise. He smoked cigarettes continually, and dark bags had formed beneath his eyes. Yet he radiated a magnetic energy that seemed, along with his money, to immediately attract people and hold them in his orbit. He was a skilled pilot who spoke passionately about flight; he mentioned that one of his brothers had recently injured himself in a crash near the lake. He seemed restless, in perpetual motion, yet also sweet and trustworthy. Gradually that afternoon Lynn came to understand that she had been invited into some sort of rolling intercontinental party over which Salem presided, a party that had no particular beginning or end. He told her that he would be leaving soon on his private jet for California; he had a meeting there, he said, about a possible movie project involving the actress Brooke Shields.[3]

As evening fell the estate began to fill, mainly with Saudi men who appeared to be on vacation. There were also a few middle-aged American women who were friends of Salem's, or seemed to be in business with him. Lynn found a Yamaha upright piano in the living room and began to play. Eventually Salem told her that she should come back the next day; the party would carry on. "Bring your sisters! Bring your friends!" he urged. "We need girls!"

When Lynn did return with a girlfriend and two of her sisters, she found a band in the living room. Salem decided amid some fanfare to organize a talent show. He promised five thousand dollars in cash to whoever won first place, and he appointed himself the sole judge. One of the American women played piano and sang, the band ran through some numbers, and Lynn took a turn at the Yamaha. Lynn's girlfriend, however, had no particular musical talent. She decided, instead, to expound to her Saudi audience about her recent experiences of giving birth and of divorce.

Intimate monologues about a woman's pain and the miracle of life were not often heard in the male-segregated sitting rooms of Saudi palaces or merchant houses, and the quiet that followed her presentation, it seemed to Lynn, was a little awkward.

"I feel really bad," Salem told Lynn afterward. He liked her friend, he said, and he felt bad about her divorce. He peeled off about a thousand dollars in cash. "Please, give this to her."

At one point, one of the American women who seemed to work with Salem in Orlando pulled Lynn aside. "You know, Salem really likes you," she said.

"Romantically?"

As Lynn Peghiny recalled it years later: "She said—and I'll never forget it—she said, 'Lynn, this is a great opportunity for you. You're young. You're unattached . . . You know, he'll show you places and take you places, and if I were you, I'd just go for it.'"[4]

SALEM BIN LADEN was a favored customer of AlamoArrow, a retailer outside San Antonio, Texas, of ultralight sport aircraft. The previous Christmas, he had turned up at the store unexpectedly on a Friday evening and purchased much of its inventory—planes and accessories—and asked that it all be delivered to the airport and loaded onto his private BAC-III twin-engine jet. A few weeks later he returned to buy more ultralights, including a camouflaged former military prototype that had once been equipped to shoot missiles. Its armor had been removed, but "he thought that was pretty cool," recalled George Harrington, one of the store's sales associates.

Ultralights are small open-air hobby planes that are usually flown a few hundred feet high at speeds of about forty miles per hour, powered by a single engine roughly the size of that on a motorcycle. Salem loved them; like gliders, another of his passions, they offered the sensation of flying like a hawk, free and buffeted by wind. They were banned from Saudi Arabia on security grounds, so Salem stored the planes at his various refuges outside the kingdom.

During the last months of 1984, he collected the latest models, called Quicksilvers, because he was outfitting, for early in the New Year, an elaborate Saudi royal hunting expedition to Pakistan that Salem seemed to envision as a blend of *Arabian Nights* and Dr. Seuss. Salem explained to the AlamoArrow managers that he and his Saudi guests, who were princes in the royal family, would camp in the desert and hunt by falconry in the traditional way, but they would also equip themselves with flying toys. He asked George Harrington and his colleagues to buy and prepare a twenty-foot Wells Cargo trailer so it could haul the ultralights across

Pakistan's rough roads and desert tracks. Salem had also ordered a hot air balloon from a champion balloonist in Florida; it came with a plaque that read "Custom Built for Salem Bin Laden." He purchased a Honda mini-trail motorcycle and a red Chevy Blazer light truck outfitted for desert travel with high-beam lights and enormous tires. He installed a high-frequency radio in the truck so he could call out to the nearest Pakistani city if he were lost or stuck in the sand. In Germany he bought a four-wheel-drive air-conditioned Volkswagen camper with a shower and a kitchenette and stuffed it with "every gizmo he could get," as Harrington remembered. They towed the American-made equipment to South Carolina, where the Bin Laden family worked with a freight-forwarding company that could ship the goods to the United Arab Emirates, a small kingdom on the Persian Gulf, and from there to the Pakistani port city of Karachi.[5]

Salem liked to have musicians in his entourage; Harrington played the guitar, so Salem arranged to hire him to travel to Pakistan, where he could help oversee the ultralight flying by the royal guests. A few days before Christmas, Harrington, a genial, big-boned Texan who had never traveled abroad previously, found himself jetting to London in the company of an American pilot, Don Kessler, who worked for Salem and who also played the drums.

They all stopped initially at Salem's estate outside London, and then, on Christmas Eve, they flew to the south of France, and after that, to Salzburg, Austria. They unloaded their luggage and drove to the ski resort in Kitzbühel. Of course, they had no ski equipment with them, as the decision to fly to Austria had been made only hours earlier, so Salem led the group into a shop and bought everyone skis, boots, parkas, and pants. They hit the slopes and then accepted an invitation to a party at the local villa of Adnan Khashoggi, the well-known Saudi arms dealer.

Khashoggi's home had a discotheque with a stage. The room that night was loud, dark, and teeming with Saudis and Europeans. Salem took the microphone and announced that he intended to perform. He and George Harrington took steel-string acoustic guitars onto the stage and struck up the folk and bar band classic "House of the Rising Sun."

There is a house in New Orleans
They call the Rising Sun.
It's been the ruin of many a poor boy,
And God I know I'm one . . .

"He was a half-assed guitar player, and even less qualified as a vocalist, but you couldn't embarrass him at all," Harrington recalled. "So we played that night for a packed house."[6]

They flew next to Marbella, Spain, and then on to Cairo for New Year's Eve. They stopped for a while in Jeddah, Saudi Arabia, and then traveled to Dubai.

At the Hyatt hotel there Harrington met Salem's new girlfriend from Orlando: Lynn Peghiny. They became instant friends, two Americans caught up in an unexpected adventure, hopping from one country to the next, unfamiliar with their surroundings. Lynn had flown in from New York to join the upcoming expedition to Pakistan. ("I look back and I'm astounded at what I did at twenty-four," she said in hindsight.) Salem put her in a hotel suite with a grand piano. They listened to her play Chopin.

A FEW DAYS LATER, Salem packed Lynn and George into his Mitsubishi MU-2, a stubby, short-haul turboprop airplane. An elderly Bedouin aide carried aboard a hooded hunting falcon. George took possession of a briefcase containing at least $250,000 in cash and traveler's checks; he had come to understand that one of his jobs was to keep track of Salem's travel money. Also along was Bengt Johansson, a shaggy-haired, chain-smoking Swedish flight mechanic who was one of the longest-serving European members of Salem's entourage. They roared down the runway, bound for Karachi. "It was so loaded down and they took off and everybody just applauded that the thing got up in the air," Lynn recalled, "and I'm like, 'Why are y'all taking chances?'"[7]

In Karachi, Salem met with a Saudi diplomat; he often dropped in on his country's ambassadors when he traveled the world. His entourage checked into the Sheraton, a concrete-and-glass fortress that passed as the city's finest hotel.

At the Karachi seaport, Salem discovered that the Pakistan Army would not permit either ultralights or hot air balloons into their country. On its eastern frontier, the Pakistan Army faced Indian military forces in a continuous state of alert; to the west, it was embroiled in a secret guerrilla war in Afghanistan against Soviet forces, who occasionally conducted raids inside Pakistan. Saudi princes flying around in uncontrolled small planes and balloons seemed to the army's officers a prescription for disaster. Salem argued, and fumed, and tried to pull strings, but the Pakistani authorities stood firm; they told him to send his airborne toys back to Dubai.

In the midst of these frustrations Salem summoned George Harrington and Bengt Johansson one morning and announced that they would all fly in the Mitsubishi up to Peshawar, the Pakistani city that served as a staging area for the Afghan war. Initially, Salem explained only that he had an errand to run. As it turned out, it involved his half-brother Osama.

"I said, 'Why?'" as Harrington recalled it. Eventually, "he explained that Peshawar was apparently the base for rebels . . . I had never heard of Peshawar. World politics were not on my radar screen. He said that Osama was up there and he was the liaison between the U.S., the Saudi government, and the Afghan rebels," as Harrington remembered. "Salem needed to make sure that Osama was getting what he needed. The Saudi government was funneling stuff to Osama; Salem said he needed to go up and check with his brother to make sure . . . things were going well."

The trio flew up that same afternoon and landed on a dirt strip—

Harrington could not tell if it was a road or a runway. Osama and some of his aides came out to greet them. "I remember being struck that he was so much taller than Salem."[8]

He was then about twenty-seven years old. In addition to his height, his bushy dark beard made a striking impression; it poured down his cheeks and gathered below his chin, elongating his thin face. His brown eyes were bright and communicative, but his manner was reserved. Osama visited Pakistan regularly from his home in Jeddah, Saudi Arabia, but he had not settled down on the war front; he was a philanthropic commuter, encouraged by his religious teachers to fund charities and Arab volunteers who had just begun to arrive to join the fighting.

Salem made formal introductions to his American and Swedish companions. Osama wore robes and a flat Afghan cap; he was reticent around the foreigners, but he shook Johansson's hand respectfully. Bengt had learned over the years that all of Salem's younger siblings treated their eldest brother with unquestioning respect, and that this respect extended by rights to Salem's friends, no matter how indecorous they might appear in Saudi eyes.[9]

They drove to Osama's office and sat in a circle. The two half-brothers spoke together in Arabic for about two hours. A modest lunch appeared. It was typical of Salem to bring his Western friends into settings where they might not otherwise be welcomed, but no one openly questioned their presence, and in any event, neither Harrington nor Johansson could understand much of what was being said.

After lunch Osama led them on a tour of the charitable and humanitarian work that he was supporting in the Peshawar region to help the Afghans. They visited refugee camps where Afghan civilians and fighters displaced by Soviet bombing lived in primitive tents or shelters. They visited a hospital "with people with amputated limbs," and Harrington was amazed to hear tales of terrible atrocities carried out by the Soviets, and how, nonetheless, the wounded rebels "wanted to go back and fight for Afghanistan." They visited an orphanage where, as Johansson recalled it, the children lived in "small blocks . . . concrete blocks, and they were sleeping on the floor." The children gathered together and sang songs for Osama's visitors.[10]

Salem recorded these scenes with a personal video camera, a large and awkward handheld device that he had brought with him. He appeared to be making a home movie to publicize Osama's work and to raise funds. It was "a fact-finding mission," Harrington remembered. "The camera was to show what was going on. Nothing militaristic . . . It was more about money."

AFTER SOME additional adventures in Pakistan, Salem's entourage flew back to Dubai; Salem announced that he had to make an unexpected business trip, and that he would be gone for about a week.

The American balloon champion who was a part of the entourage took George and Lynn on a soaring flight above the emirate's sand dunes. Gulf breezes and desert winds blew them accidentally over a local emir's palace. The emir's guards pointed their automatic weapons angrily at the billowing red and yellow dirigible. "This is it," Harrington remembered thinking. He would end his life as "just a bloodstain on the ruler's lawn." Fortunately, the guards held their fire.[11]

They heard nothing from Salem for a while, but Harrington knew where he had gone, because Salem had told him of his destination: Washington, D.C.

King Fahd of Saudi Arabia was preparing that early winter of 1985 for a summit meeting and state dinner with President Ronald Reagan. "For some reason," as Harrington recalled it, "the king wanted Salem" in Washington. Salem flew off immediately. This was hardly an unusual diversion. As Salem's friend Mohamed Ashmawi, a wealthy Saudi oil executive, put it: "He used to go and visit the king wherever he is."[12]

Secrecy and complexity governed the relationship between King Fahd and Ronald Reagan. That winter of 1985, apart from Great Britain, there was perhaps no government with which the Reagan administration shared more sensitive secrets than it did with Saudi Arabia. Unbeknownst to the American public, for example, Reagan had authorized an attempt to free American hostages held in Lebanon by selling weapons to the kidnappers' sponsors in Iran; Adnan Khashoggi, who worked closely with the Saudi royal family, was centrally involved in those secret transactions. Also, the previous June, after a request by Reagan's national security advisor Robert McFarlane, King Fahd had secretly agreed to funnel $1 million per month into a Cayman Islands bank account in support of Nicaragua's anti-communist rebels, known as the Contras; this contribution allowed President Reagan to evade congressional restrictions on such aid. Saudi Arabia had no particular interest in the Nicaraguan cause, according to the kingdom's longtime ambassador in Washington, Bandar Bin Sultan ("I didn't give a damn about the Contras—I didn't even know where Nicaragua was," he said later). However, according to Bandar, McFarlane claimed the aid would help ensure Reagan's reelection in November by preventing trouble in Central America. The Saudis contributed the money and, as it happened, Reagan won in a landslide.[13]

Early in 1985, King Fahd notified the Americans that he would now double his off-the-books contributions to the Cayman Islands account. Favor begat favor between these two governments during the late Cold War, and secret begat secret, a pattern of conduct that required an unusual measure of personal trust and understanding at the highest levels. Fahd's visit to Washington was therefore of timely significance. Reagan was a master of the theatrical and ceremonial aspects of his office, and he prepared to put on a show.

Up the White House driveway they strolled on the chilly night of February 11—Yogi Berra, the New York Yankees manager; Vice President George Bush; Linda Gray, star of *Dallas*, the television series about oil barons; Oscar Wyatt, the genuine Texas oil baron; the actress Sigourney Weaver; and Donald and Ivana Trump. "It's exciting. It's Americana. It's Ronald Reagan," joked *Saturday Night Live* comedian Joe Piscopo, who was also on the state dinner's guest list. "The king of Saudi Arabia came here to see how a real king lives, I suppose."[14]

Saudi royals do not travel on official business with their wives, so the king escorted Abdulaziz, his eleven-year-old son by Princess Jawhara Al-Ibrahim. They arrived at the White House in traditional Saudi robes and red-checked headdresses. Now in his early sixties, Fahd had become an obese man, and his legs could barely carry him, but his double-chinned face still had a gentle, boyish quality. Back home, Fahd was so devoted to Abdulaziz, who seemed likely to be his last son, that he spent vast sums to ensure that in each of his luxurious palaces, the boy's room was outfitted with exactly the same toys, wallpaper, and bed silks, so that he would never feel that he was away from home. Reagan doted on the child, too, posed for a photograph with him, gave him a private tour of the Oval Office, presented him with a model of the Space Shuttle, and seated him next to Sigourney Weaver at the state dinner. Abdulaziz confided to the actress that when his father's work in Washington was completed, he hoped to visit Disney World.[15]

Salem Bin Laden's activity in Washington around the summit is difficult to pinpoint. A French intelligence report later claimed that Salem was involved in "U.S. operations" in Central America during this period. The American government has not declassified many of the records describing Saudi Arabia's secret aid to the Nicaraguan Contras, but those available provide no evidence of Salem's participation. (Like Bandar, the Saudi ambassador, Salem "had no idea where Nicaragua was," said a European friend who worked with him on arms deals in other parts of the world.) An attorney who represented the Bin Laden family in a Texas civil lawsuit some years later recalled possessing a photo of Salem standing with Ronald Reagan, but that evidence file had been destroyed during a routine archive cleaning, and the photographs taken by White House staff during the Fahd summit show no trace of Salem. He was the eldest of fifty-four children, the leader of the sprawling Bin Laden family, the chairman of several multinational corporations, and a genuine friend to King Fahd, but Salem was also decidedly the king's subordinate; he might just as well have been called to Washington to organize a night on the town as to participate in clandestine statecraft.[16]

There was one portfolio of secrets binding King Fahd and President Reagan that winter that unquestionably involved Salem Bin Laden, however. These concerned the covert aid provided by the United States and Saudi Arabia to anti-communist rebels fighting Soviet forces in Afghanistan. The United States and Saudi Arabia each had already channeled several hundred million dollars in cash and weapons to the Afghan rebels since the Soviet invasion in 1979. It seems probable that when Salem reached Washington that winter, he would have passed to King Fahd, if not directly to the White House, the video evidence he had just gathered documenting Osama's humanitarian work on the Afghan frontier. As he welcomed Fahd to the White House, Reagan took pains to acknowledge Saudi Arabia's particular efforts to support Afghan refugees on the Pakistani frontier: "Their many humanitarian contributions touch us deeply," Reagan said. "Saudi aid to refugees uprooted from their homes in Afghanistan has not gone unnoticed here, Your Majesty."

That February of 1985, in Pakistan, the leading Saudi provider of such assistance was Salem's half-brother, Osama. Reagan's language suggested that he had been given at least a general briefing about Osama's work.

"We all worship the same God," Reagan said. "The people of Afghanistan, with their blood, courage and faith, are an inspiration to the cause of freedom everywhere."[17]

YEARS LATER, as he grew into middle age, Osama Bin Laden gradually abandoned the sources of identity that were his birthright, and which had heavily influenced his early life—his membership in the wealthy Bin Laden family, and his privileges as a subject of the kingdom of Saudi Arabia. He eventually declared himself at war with Saudi Arabia's royal family, and by doing so placed himself in violent opposition to his own family's interests, a posture that was apparently so fraught for him that he very rarely spoke about it in public. When he did, he blamed the Saudi royals for trying "to create a problem between me and my family." He has never denounced or openly repudiated his own family, and he has explained their occasional statements repudiating him as merely the product of heavy pressure brought to bear by the Saudi government.[18]

After September 11, it became commonplace to trace the sources of Osama's radicalism to the Islamic political revival that swept the Middle East after 1979, and also to his experiences as a jihad fighter and organizer during the anti-Soviet Afghan war. These were crucial influences on him, but to focus on them exclusively is to risk passing over the complexity of Osama's relationship with his family and his country, the sources of attraction and repulsion these ties created in his life, and their influence on his character and ideas. These latter subjects are ones that the Bin Ladens and the Saudi royal family have tried to keep as private as possible.

The extraordinary story of the Bin Laden family's rise during the twentieth century is compelling even where it does not touch upon Osama at all. For many of the Bin Ladens of Osama's generation, family ties proved to be changeable and, above all, complicated. Theirs is a story of modernization and power in Saudi Arabia, a young and insecure nation where the family is by far the most important unit of politics. "The Arabia of the Sauds," as the country's name signifies, accurately conveys the ruling Al-Saud family's conception of its power. In their country, political parties are banned, even social clubs are frowned upon, and tribes are relatively weak; family and religious faith offer by far the most legitimate sources of public identity. Within the business community to which they belonged, the Bin Ladens were by no means the kingdom's most significant family, but across decades they built a unique and important partnership with the Al-Saud, anchored by the Bin Laden family's role, from the 1950s onward, as the official building and renovation contractors of the Islamic holy cities of Mecca and Medina, and, for a time, Jerusalem.

The family generation to which Osama belonged—twenty-five brothers and twenty-nine sisters—inherited considerable wealth, but had to cope with intense social and cultural changes. Most of them were born into a poor society where there were no public schools or universities, where social roles were rigid and preordained, where religious texts and rituals dominated public and intellectual life, where slavery was not only legal but openly practiced by the king and his sons. Yet within two decades, by the time this generation of Bin Ladens became young adults, they found themselves bombarded by Western-influenced ideas about individual choice, by gleaming new shopping malls and international fashion brands, by Hollywood movies and alcohol and changing sexual mores—a dizzying world that was theirs for the taking, since they each received annual dividends that started in the hundreds of thousands of dollars. These Bin Ladens, like other privileged Saudis who came of age during the oil shock decade of the 1970s, became Arabian pioneers in the era of globalization. The Bin Ladens were the first private Saudis to own airplanes, and in business and family life alike, they devoured early on the technologies of global integration. It is hardly an accident that Osama's first major tactical innovation as a terrorist involved his creative use of a satellite telephone. It does not seem irrelevant, either, that shocking airplane crashes involving Americans were a recurrent motif of the family's experience long before September 11.

The Bin Laden family saga also provides a particularly consequential thread of the troubled, compulsive, greed-inflected, secret-burdened, and, ultimately—to both sides—unconvincing alliance between the United States and Saudi Arabia during the oil age. Until Osama announced himself as an international terrorist, his family was much more heavily invested in the United States than has generally been understood—his brothers and sisters owned American shopping centers, apartment complexes, condominiums, luxury estates, privatized prisons in Massachusetts, corporate stocks, an airport, and much else. They attended American universities, maintained friendships and business partnerships with Americans, and sought American passports for their children. They financed Hollywood movies, traded Thoroughbred horses with country singer Kenny Rogers, and negotiated real estate deals with Donald Trump. They regarded George H. W. Bush, Jimmy Carter, and Prince Charles as friends of their family. In both a literal and a cultural sense, the Bin Laden family owned an impressive share of the America upon which Osama declared war, and yet, as was true of the relationship between the Saudi and American governments, their involvement in the United States also proved to be narrow and brittle. This made both Osama's anti-American ideology and his family's response to it all the more complex.

The Bin Laden family's global character owes much to the worldwide shape of the oil market and the wealth it created after 1973, but it is rooted, too, in an age before combustion engines. Osama's generation of Bin Ladens was the first to be born on Saudi soil. Their father, Mohamed, the gifted architect of the family's original fortune, migrated from a mud-rock fortress town in a narrow canyon in the remote Hadhramawt region of Yemen. He belonged to a self-confident people who were themselves pioneers of globalization, albeit in a slower-paced era of sailing ships and colonial power. Mohamed Bin Laden bequeathed to his children not just wealth, but a transforming vision of ambition and religious faith in a borderless world.

PART ONE
PATRIARCHS

1900 to September 1967

1. IN EXILE

THE TROUBLE STARTED when an ox died.

The ox belonged to Awadh Aboud Bin Laden. Around the turn of the twentieth century, he lived in the desert village of Gharn Bashireih, in a deep canyon called Wadi Rakiyah. The gorge cut a path of fifty miles through a region of southern Arabia, in modern Yemen, called the Hadhramawt, which means "Death Is Among Us." It was an accurate name; the land was mostly sand and rocks, baked by cyclical droughts. Barren clay bluffs rose on each side of Rakiyah's chasm. Camels, donkeys, and goats strayed among thornbushes and scrub trees. There were perhaps forty villages scattered in the canyon's depths; its population was no greater than ten thousand people.[1]

Awadh's house and the small patch of ground he farmed lay near a four-story rectangular turret built from mud bricks by two Bin Laden brothers, Ali and Ahmed, who probably lived during the early nineteenth century, judging by the genealogies kept by their descendants. This Bin Laden family fort rose from the highest point in Gharn Bashireih, shadowed by the canyon's western wall. By Awadh's lifetime, the turret, which had been used as a home by the two brothers, was eroding into a ruin; it looked like a sand castle washed over by the tide. Clusters of newer mud-brick homes encircled the hillside below the tower, forming a defensive apron. Around the village spread ten or twenty acres of flat farmland, divided into tiny plots of about ten yards by fifty yards, which various Bin Ladens owned. Farming was a precarious vocation dependent upon brief seasonal rains. After each storm, villagers rushed out to capture flood-waters and channel them into their fields. If they succeeded, they might grow wheat or other staple crops for a few months. If they failed, they might face famine.²

Awadh Bin Laden made his fateful decision to borrow a plow ox from an Obeid tribesman after one of these cyclical rains. The Obeidis were a powerful clan who patrolled the empty plateaus above Rakiyah's canyon and also farmed in the valley. There was, of course, no system of insurance or collateral associated with such an ox loan. When the animal died suddenly under Awadh's yoke, his creditor, whose name was Bilawal, made what the Bin Laden family's oral history holds to be an outrageous demand: forty silver riyals. This smacked of extortion, but while there were perhaps several hundred Bin Ladens in the village, "they were so poor they could not stand by" Awadh, said Syed Bin Laden, who still lives in Gharn Bashireih.³

The Bin Ladens belonged to the Kenda tribe, which traced its origins to pre-Islamic Arabia and became a powerful federation in southern Hadhramawt by the seventeenth century. It had been known then as a tribe of rulers and sheikhs, but perpetual warfare gradually dissipated its strength and scattered its members. By Awadh's time, the Kenda no longer functioned as an organized group with recognized leaders and armed militias. The Bin Ladens had become merely a family clan of perhaps four to five hundred people, clustered defensively in an ancestral fortress-village, struggling for survival. They were in no position to sustain warfare against rival groups.

The Bin Ladens divided themselves into four branches, each of which traced itself to the generation of the turret builders, Ahmed and Ali, who were two of four brothers, the others being Mansour and Zaid. Each of these brothers fathered a line of descendants who, by Awadh's lifetime, acted together as an extended family within the wider Bin Laden clan.

Awadh belonged to Ali's branch. The family's oral genealogy holds that Ali was Awadh's great-great grandfather. Little is recalled about the intervening generations except that Awadh was the only child of his father, Aboud. He therefore inherited all of Aboud's land in Gharn Bashireih. This proved to be a very meager estate, however, and as it turned out, it was not enough to help Awadh forestall his ox creditor.[4]

At first, in lieu of forty silver riyals, which he did not have, Awadh negotiated to provide Bilawal with a lien on the several acres he farmed. Bilawal agreed to accept half of the profits from Awadh's harvests until the debt was paid. If the rains had returned, Awadh might have worked himself out of difficulty and the subsequent history of his branch of the Bin Laden family might have turned out quite differently. As it happened, however, a drought hit Rakiyah. Awadh could offer his creditor no profits in the ensuing months, which angered Bilawal. By one Bin Laden family account, Bilawal threatened to kill Awadh unless he either came up with the cash he owed or turned over full title to his land.[5]

Awadh decided to abandon his ancestral village. He was a bachelor, free to travel. The drought had deepened steadily since the ox's demise. Emigration was a common survival strategy in the Hadhramawt, even without the spur of a tribal death threat. Awadh packed his belongings and set out across the high plateau for a neighboring canyon known as Wadi Doan, about a day and a half's ride by camel or donkey. There he would begin again.

SHEER CLIFF WALLS of nine hundred feet or more plunge to the floor of the Wadi Doan, seventy miles inland from the Arabian Sea. Dark green date palm trees nourished by a riverbed cover the canyon's floor. A race of giants hewed the chasm's stones until God took umbrage at their arrogance and destroyed them with a sandstorm, according to local legend. This may explain the stunning architecture: Stacked against the rock walls rise the giant skyscrapers of fortified castle-villages, each town a gated, vertical redoubt against its neighbors. For purposes of defense there are no windows on the houses' lower floors, and the slits higher up are designed for shooting.

To Europeans of the time, the canyons of the Hadhramawt seemed remote and filled with dangerous xenophobes; they were a "parallel, interior world . . . a blank on the map." In truth, the Hadhramawt was not isolated at all, but its deeply religious inhabitants, although capable of gracious hospitality, did not always take kindly to unannounced Christian visitors. For several thousand years Hadhramis had been migrants, travelers, traders, and entrepreneurs, sailing out in wooden dhows from the port of Mukalla to the East Indies, Zanzibar, Abyssinia (modern Ethiopia), and up the Red Sea to Mecca and Cairo. For a time, centuries ago, they and their Sabean kings enjoyed enormous wealth as caravan monopolists in the global trade in myrrh and frankincense, drawn from the gum of Arabian trees. In pharaonic Egypt and during the Roman Empire, incense burned from costly frankincense and even more expensive myrrh transformed these oils into two of the most precious commodities on earth. In Rome, no god could be worshipped properly, no funeral commemorated, no respectable marriage bed entered, without the smoke of frankincense swirling through the room. Only as its empire dissolved and austere Christian preachers denounced incense as a perfume of blasphemers did the trade decline and Hadhramawt fall back into poverty. With Islam's arrival in the seventh century, the men of the canyons sailed again as soldiers in proselytizing Muslim armies. They stayed on in the lands they conquered as bodyguards, traders, and, eventually, political notables. They remained devoted to their homeland and by the turn of the twentieth century, many prosperous Hadhramis had carried their colonial-era trading wealth back to the canyons to build retirement homes and family compounds. So many returned from Asia and Africa that when a British officer carried out the first formal survey of the gorges during the 1930s, he discovered Swahili and Malay among the local languages.[6]

At the time of Awadh Bin Laden's arrival, Britain claimed Doan as part of its Aden Protectorate, a political entity that was more wish than fact, one in a chain of loosely governed coastal territories the empire's strategists had stitched together in Arabia to protect India's shipping lanes from Turkish and German scheming. The local instrument of British control was the Sultan of Mukalla, who ruled from a compound of whitewashed palaces on a rock outcropping beside the Arabian Sea, protected by a personal bodyguard of African slaves. The sultan's family had earned its fortune as mercenaries for the Nizam of Hyderabad, in India; by the early twentieth century, they preferred to spend their time in Hyderabad's luxurious courts. In Mukalla, they left in charge a succession of *wazirs*, or ministers, from the Al-Mihdhar family, which hailed from the Wadi Doan. One of these deputies, Sayyid Hamid Al-Mihdhar, was recalled by a British visitor as "a smooth, oily character, outwardly jovial but with unsmiling eyes," who used his office "to ensure preferential treatment for his fellow Doanis."* The Mukalla sultanate was far from a model government; to the extent it controlled the interior canyons, it did so by taking hostages from prominent local families.[7]

The real powers in southern Doan at the time of Awadh's arrival were not the British or the Mukalla sultans, but a family of local sheikhs called the Ba Surras, who ruled from a mud-brick castle named Masna'a. The Ba Surra governor at the time Awadh Bin Laden arrived took ten wives during his lifetime and suffered from blindness. He ruled the canyon with a firm hand. "Murder cases are now practically non-existent," a British agent reported with satisfaction to London. "Murderers are executed with a dagger plunged into the supra sternal notch."[8]

Doan had about twenty thousand inhabitants, by the Ba Surras' count. They were succored by nearly two hundred mosques, but only two small schools, in which the curriculum was the Koran. None of the women the

---

*Decades later, Osama Bin Laden recruited Khalid Al-Mihdhar, a member of this well-known Wadi Doan family of sayyids, or descendants of the Prophet Mohamed, as a hijacker in the September 11 plot; Al-Mihdhar piloted the plane that crashed into the Pentagon.

English traveler Freya Stark met during the early 1930s could read. Palm trees from the riverbed were harvested for profit, and a few wealthier traders kept bees on their terraces, extracting an export crop of aromatic honey known as an aphrodisiac, particularly if eaten with meat, "something that only men may do, as it is thought inadvisable to excite women too much," the traveler Doreen Ingrams noted.[9]

Awadh Bin Laden chose Doan as a sanctuary from the Obeidis because it enjoyed a reputation for peace and order under the Ba Surras that was then rare in the Hadhramawt, according to some of Awadh's descendants. He settled a few miles from the Ba Surra fortress, in Rabat Bashan, a town stacked up against Doan's southernmost wall, surrounded by palms on the valley floor. Eight hundred men owning one hundred rifles lived there, according to the British survey conducted in the early 1930s. Awadh seems to have had few firm connections when he first arrived in Doan; he relied instead on the region's reputation for hospitality, and his own willingness to work. The evidence about Awadh's circumstances after his arrival in Rabat is sketchy, as he was now separated from the family group in Rakiyah that has kept what oral history survives. He is said to have worked as a wage laborer on local small farms. He did well enough to marry a woman in the town; she was from the Al-Madudi family.[10]

Awadh and his wife had three daughters and three sons. The boys were Mohamed, Abdullah, and Omar; the latter died in childhood, a common fate. (The names of the daughters are not recalled; in Arabia then, as now, the stories of a family's women were rarely told.) The year of Mohamed's birth is sometimes given as 1908, an approximation at best; the celebration of birthdays is not an Arabian tradition, and there was barely a government in Doan then, never mind a birth registry.[11]

Once he settled into his Rabat exile, Awadh Bin Laden worked hard and died young. Indeed, he seems to have died before his two surviving sons, Mohamed and Abdullah, had reached adolescence.[12]

As was true elsewhere in the Hadhramawt, Doan's economy relied upon the persistent willingness of local boys and young men to sail away to foreign jobs, work for years at a time in difficult conditions, and remit money home. Some left at very early ages, as young as six or seven years old. It was also common for local men to marry in their teens, emigrate to Ethiopia or Somalia or Egypt, and stay away for as long as two decades, taking other wives while abroad. For most young men in Doan the question was not whether to leave, but where to go. They depended upon informal employment networks sponsored by Hadhrami traders who had business interests in particular ports abroad. The loyalty of one Hadhrami stranger to another was extraordinary, and by the early twentieth century this ethic had created a thriving diaspora from the Levant to Southeast Asia. In one letter discovered from the early twentieth century, a father writes instructions to two of his young boys about how they should make their way from Hadhramawt to Singapore—he provides lists of trusted contacts in four different port cities and urges the boys to send many postcards home. Young men from the northern Hadhramawt valleys generally emigrated through these kin networks to Southeast Asia; from Doan, they went primarily to Africa or up the Red Sea coastline.

Emigration would have seemed a natural choice for fatherless Mohamed and Abdullah Bin Laden. As they considered their destinations they were probably advised by their mother's family and by other townspeople concerned about their welfare, now that Awadh was gone. The richest man in Rabat was a descendant of the Prophet Mohamed named Sayyid Muhammed Ibn Iasin, a Red Sea cotton dealer with a "long face and large pleasant mouth" whose household kept bees and Ethiopian slaves.[13] The Iasins had connections in Massawa, the main Eritrean port. Another prominent family in the canyon, who lived about a mile or two away, had relatives in Addis Ababa, and had made a small fortune trading skins there. It was likely through one of these contacts that Mohamed

Bin Laden, the eldest of Awadh's sons, but a boy of less than twelve years old, first climbed the canyon walls and joined the camel caravans for the walk to the port of Mukalla.

He sailed to Africa, survived the voyage, and found work somewhere in Ethiopia. But his journey ended in disaster. The Bin Laden family's oral history contains at least two versions about what happened to him. In one, Mohamed was working as a sweeper in a store or small business. According to what his brother Abdullah later told the family, his boss was a disagreeable man with a fierce temper who kept a ring of keys fastened to his belt; one day, annoyed at Mohamed, he hurled the keys at the boy and struck him in the face. The injury was so severe that Mohamed lost his eye. A second version, told by some of the Bin Ladens who remained in Yemen, holds that Mohamed was working on an Ethiopian building site when an iron bar dropped accidentally from a high building, hit the ground, bounced up, and struck his eye. In any event, Mohamed Bin Laden would grow into adulthood with a right eye made of glass.[14]

Mohamed returned to Doan after his injury. A massive earthquake destroyed the Abyssinian port of Massawa in 1921, devastating the region's economy; this may also have been a factor in his retreat. Townspeople in Rabat say it was 1925 when Mohamed left again. This time he traveled with his younger brother Abdullah. It would be about twenty-five years before the brothers returned. Their mother later died in Doan, according to Bin Laden family members who stayed in Yemen; it seems doubtful that the boys ever saw her again.

They aimed now for the eastern coast of the Red Sea. In the port of Jeddah, the gateway favored by Muslim pilgrims traveling to the holy city of Mecca, there was a sizable community of Hadhrami merchants and laborers, including some from Doan; other Hadhramis resided in Mecca itself.

At the time the Bin Laden boys embarked on this journey, Abdullah was only about nine or ten years old; Mohamed was perhaps fourteen or fifteen, according to what Abdullah later related to his family. The journey Abdullah remembered was inflected by magic, miracles, and religious portents. They found their way aboard the overloaded wooden dhows at Mukalla, sailed around the Arabian Peninsula, then up the Red Sea, as far as the port of Jizan, nearly four hundred miles south of Jeddah. From here they began to walk. They became lost in the desert; they were hungry, nearly starving, and thought they might die. A fierce storm blew in on them, and when it cleared the boys found a farm, and in the irrigated fields they found a watermelon. They ate it and were revived.[15]

They walked on and finally reached the stone and coral walls of Jeddah, a fetid city of perhaps twenty-five thousand beside the Red Sea.[16] Perhaps only a teenager who had known the deprivations and perpetual warfare of the Hadhramawt could regard this claustrophobic, disease-ridden port without a single paved street as a place of opportunity. Yet Mohamed Bin Laden had seen in Doan the proud mud skyscrapers, with their painted doors and complements of slaves, which had been built by Hadhramis who had earned their fortunes in all sorts of unlikely places, through luck and faith and hard work. He possessed the drive to seek a fortune of his own.

THE AIR WITHIN Jeddah's protective walls "held a moisture and a sense of great age and exhaustion such as seemed to belong to no other place," wrote T. E. Lawrence, better known as Lawrence of Arabia. There was "a feeling of long use, of the exhalations of many people, of continued bath-heat and sweat." Temperatures rose well above one hundred degrees Fahrenheit in the summer, and salty Red Sea winds stifled breath. "Newspapers flop into rag, matches refuse to strike and keys rust in the pocket," a British visitor complained. Each day about five thousand camels moved through the city, dropping what Jeddah's mayor estimated to be more than thirty thousand pounds of manure. "The goods on display in the market are covered with so many flies that you cannot tell the color of the goods without chasing them away," the Persian pilgrim

Hossein Kazemzadeh wrote. "In the evening, when the shops close, the flies go, like the merchants, to private houses to seek their prey."[17]

For more than a thousand years Jeddah had served as the gateway to Mecca. Through the city poured pilgrims bound for the annual Hajj festival—one hundred thousand of them each year by the early twentieth century. They were Muslims of every hue and background, from Africa, Southeast Asia, India, and Europe. They came, too, for lesser pilgrimages throughout the year; rowboats called *sambuks* ferried the new arrivals from ships anchored in the port's deep water. At the pier porters and guides hustled them to crude barracks where they were segregated by national origin. Many of these pilgrims stayed on in Jeddah after they had offered their devotions, and their descendants had transformed the region, known as the Hejaz, into a polyglot, a "hodge-podge of humanity which Islam brings together from every corner of the earth," as the pilgrim Amin Rihani wrote in 1922. In Jeddah there were extremes of wealth and poverty, observed Kazemzadeh: "You see rich people who will pay several pounds for a flacon of perfume, pour it all out on their heads and walk off . . . On the other hand, there are wretches in a state of total privation, lying nearly nude along the road, seeking some relief in the shade of the bushes." Wealthier families lived in tall Turkish-style town houses fashioned from coral dug from the shoreline and covered in slatted wooden shutters that cooled the interiors and kept women invisible to passersby. The poor wrapped themselves in cloth and slept in Jeddah's sandy lanes.[18]

Cholera epidemics swept through the city. Europe's nascent public health authorities recognized the global migration to and from the Hajj as a potential source of pandemics. The colonial powers struggled to create a workable system of quarantine. An Ottoman doctor summoned to treat one cholera scourge around the century's turn found Jeddah "a vast cemetery" teeming with "dead bodies that filled the caravansaries, mosques, cafes, houses and public places"; he was haunted by "the cries of men, women and children mixed with the roaring of the camels."[19]

Harry St. John Bridger Philby, a British adventurer who would soon play a remarkable role in the city's growth, arrived in Jeddah during the 1920s, around the same time as Mohamed Bin Laden. Philby encountered a

jumble of wealth and poverty; great mansions of the captains of commerce and enterprise, with their solid coral walls and wide expanses of woodwork tracery, side by side with hovels broken and battered with age; mosques great and small, with pointed minarets tapering skyward... Everywhere a contrast of light and shadow, splendor and squalor, dust and dirt; and above it all flew the flags of many nations, Great Britain, France, Italy, and Holland, amid the countless emblems of a united Arabia.[20]

The city's economy turned on pilgrims, who paid taxes amounting to about 3 million British pounds each year in this period and generated another 4 to 5 million pounds in commercial profits for the merchants, camel owners, tour guides, and hoteliers who competed for their purses. The greed and carnival-barking style of Jeddah's hospitality industry was legendary; the medieval traveler Ibn Jubayr noted skeptically that even before the arrival of Islam, the city fathers had raised "an old and lofty domed shrine" to attract tourists; "it is said that this was the resting place of Eve, mother of the human race ... God knows best about all that."[21] The opening of the Suez Canal in the late nineteenth century transformed the Red Sea into a colonial bazaar where European steamers, African traders, and Arabian middlemen competed for profit and influence. By the time Mohamed Bin Laden arrived, Jeddah was a citadel of hustlers.

He began as a porter in the pilgrim trade; a leather satchel he used to haul goods and luggage hung later in one of his offices. He and his younger brother were so poor during their first days in Jeddah that they slept in a ditch they dug in the sand, and covered themselves with bags, according to Nadim Bou Fakhreddine, who worked for the family years later. Early on, Mohamed opened a small grill stand in the Nadha market on the Jeddah seafront, "a small shop with one or two big dishes" for cooking, recalled Hassan Al-Aesa, who worked as a laborer with Bin Laden in Jeddah during the 1930s. An account of Bin Laden's origins written by a British diplomat several decades later reported that he had sold "fruit off a donkey" in these early years, an assertion that may have been more metaphorical than factual.

He saw that the housing industry offered promise. He began to look for odd jobs in the building trade. The coral and sediment paste used in the walls of Jeddah's multistory town houses crumbled easily and required continuous patching and repair. Particularly during the late 1920s, when the city's economy enjoyed a brief period of relative prosperity, there were opportunities for young men to work in the coral quarries or as crude masons and small-time contractors. In 1931, Bin Laden founded his own small company.[22]

He was an attractive man with even features and coffee-colored skin. His wandering glass eye distracted some who met him, but he had a natural lightness and bounce about him. He was not an imposing man— about five feet eight inches tall—but he was a natural organizer, a good-natured practical joker, and a man who thrived in the company of others. He and his brother found their way into Jeddah's tight-knit Hadhrami community and joined in its traditional entertainments, particularly the dances and group songs, called *zomals*, which reminded the men of home. Al-Aesa recalled watching Mohamed and Abdullah dance and sing in the Jeddah night: "They were very humble." There was one *zomal*, traditionally sung with pistols in hand, punctuated by celebratory shots fired into the sky, which the two Bin Laden brothers used to belt out with gusto:

Today my school is finished
And my watch is gold
And my pistol with six bullets
Did not answer my salam aleikum[23]

Bin Laden had a gift for sensing the qualities of people around him, and for retaining their loyalty, recalled Gerald Auerbach, an American pilot who later worked for him. "He knew how to get people who could do the job. He knew how to tell when they were doing the job and when they weren't. He had a better feel for engineering by birth, or accidentally, than many people that I've known have on purpose after they go through a lot of schooling." As Al-Aesa put it: "Because he was so good and so kind, all the chief craftsmen used to work with him willingly."[24]

Abdullah Hashan ran Jeddah's lucrative foreign-exchange markets, where Maria Theresa silver thalers and gold coins traded amid wild swings of prices. He handed Bin Laden his first major job in the old city, "doing maintenance and renovation," on a grand town house he owned that served as a part-time courthouse for some of Jeddah's Islamic judges, as Al-Aesa recalled it. Bin Laden "made some arches and fixed things" in a modest renovation project. "It was pure luck." But not luck alone: he had the ability to build and perform contracting work quickly, and in a manner that pleased the whimsical, demanding personalities of Jeddah's wealthy. The Hashan job set him on his way. Mohamed and Abdullah moved into a very small house on the city's north side.[25]

As the Great Depression settled in during the early 1930s, however, global travel and tourism collapsed, and along with it the Muslim religious pilgrimage to Mecca. The number of annual pilgrim arrivals in Jeddah fell precipitously, as did other Red Sea trade. Jeddah sank into a period of torpor and hardship. Mohamed Bin Laden soon found that his business in Jeddah was not enough to sustain him. He took to the road to find a paying job, across the vast and empty desert steppes that rose to the east, beyond Jeddah's walls. Fortunately for him, profound political and economic changes had begun to sweep across the Arabian Peninsula. Oil was at the heart of this transformation—along with the extraordinary king who owned it.

2. THE ROYAL GARAGE

ABDULAZIZ IBN SAUD walked out of Kuwait in 1902 with a sword, some camels, and a small band of followers to reclaim, in his family's name, the mud-walled town of Riyadh in the central Arabian plateau, and the paltry realm it oversaw. The Al-Saud had twice ruled this scorched, lightly populated emirate in recent centuries, overthrown each time by Egyptian and Ottoman enemies. Abdulaziz fought more than fifty-two battles across an expanse of hundreds of square miles in his quest for restoration. The battles were often little more than a massed, screaming charge on camels and foot by one malnourished band of rifle-toting Bedouin into the encampment of another, but they could take a toll; by 1932, when Abdulaziz announced at last the formation of the new Kingdom of Saudi Arabia, he bore slashing scars on his arms and body, and he limped from a war wound in his leg.

The king was about six feet three inches tall, broad-shouldered—visible on camelback from across a wide valley. Standing in his majlis court, he towered over many of his subjects and slaves, but he ruled as much by charm as by intimidation. He told visitors that he was like the Prophet Mohamed in that there were "three things in the world" that he truly loved: "Women, scent and prayer." He kept a vial of perfume in his robes and doused his hands when greeting visitors, so he might pass along his aroma. He possessed a magnetic and persistent smile, and seated on his throne he would launch into meandering monologues filled with metaphorical desert proverbs about treacherous foxes and venomous scorpions. Yet he was a skillful, pragmatic, cold-eyed politician, able to grasp and manage his peninsula's tribal, religious, and colonial-era complexities better than anyone had done before. "I am not a man of imagination," he told a visitor. "I am a man of actual fact—that is all I have."[1]

His conquest of Hejaz, the western region of the Arabian peninsula, and of its city of Jeddah, had been the last phase of his campaign, and when he completed it in 1926, it delivered him the greatest prizes he had yet known—sovereignty over Islam's holiest cities, in Mecca and Medina, as well as the vast tax revenue from pilgrims arriving there, and in addition, access to Jeddah's Red Sea port. Yet Abdulaziz recognized wisely that his austere army of illiterate plateau warriors and Islamic proselytizers would not be much welcome in worldly Jeddah, so he tried to co-opt the city's businessmen rather than confront them militarily. He laid a one-year siege at Jeddah's walls, which reduced the city's residents to even more desperate poverty than they already knew; the campaign ended when Jeddah's merchant notables handed him the keys. Still, he kept his distance; as long as the tax revenue flowed, he much preferred the isolated comfort of Riyadh in central Arabia, and he felt more secure there. Hejaz and the Red Sea's coast, in Abdulaziz's assessment, was a zone of treacherous British and Italian intrigues.

The collapse of the Ottoman Empire after the First World War had left Europe's colonial powers in competition for Arabia, a contest slowed by the terrible losses of the war but compelled by the inexorable logic of empire. The interior Arabian Peninsula had never been invaded by a European army—it seemed too barren and remote to bother about. To thwart the Turks, the British had subsidized Abdulaziz until 1925, but they never embraced him fully and he never trusted them, because they also propped up his rivals in Mecca, the Hashemite Sharifs. He felt about the British, he said, "like a father when cross with his son, wishing him dead—but the same father would immediately strike dead whomever said 'Amen' to this sentiment." He wanted the Americans to protect him from British intrigues, and he was also fascinated by the rise of Nazi Germany. He had a crude, often xenophobic view of Christians, and even more so of Jews. "Praise be to God, for fourteen hundred years there have been no Jews in my territory," he told one foreign delegation; so far as he knew, he had never set eyes on a Jewish person. As Israel's creation was debated, he was passionate and unyielding in his opposition. "My honor is involved in this matter," he declared. He assumed that all non-Muslims were unreliable. He asked one Christian visitor with cheerful curiosity, "You drink whiskey, you play at cards, you dance with the wives of your colleagues?"[2]

Sex seemed to be the greatest joy in his life, or at least the greatest compulsion. In 1930 he told the Englishman Philby that he had married one hundred thirty-five virgins and about one hundred other women to date, but that he had decided to limit himself to just two new wives annually for the remainder of his years. He bent the Islamic law that permitted four wives at a time by marrying and divorcing rapidly, and by keeping additional retinues of concubines and female slaves. There was a political and even a military aspect to his carnality: "The Saudi state was consolidated by marriage," as the historian Madawi Al-Rasheed put it, and Abdulaziz often "married the ex-wives or daughters of his ex-rivals and enemies."[3]

Estimates of the number of slaves in his kingdom ran from several thousand into the tens of thousands; several hundred served openly in the monarch's Riyadh palace. When a slave concubine gave birth to a son, she received her freedom, and in a few rare cases, her son was acknowledged as legitimate. Abdulaziz ultimately recognized about forty-five legitimate sons, who became his royal heirs; the number of his daughters and other children is unknown.[4]

For all of his seeming profligacy, the king maintained an austere and pious lifestyle. He did not drink or smoke or permit his aides to wear silk; he prayed five times a day; and in his court the dominant sound from day to day was the quiet clink of coffee cups and the rhythmic chanting of Koran readers. He never doubted that God had called him to rule his desert kingdom; he would do his best to answer this call, and to conform to Islam's laws, but the rest was in divine hands. The form of Islam he had been taught was severe and intolerant. In the Hejaz, there were Shias and Sufi mystics, and scholars from every historical school of the Sunni tradition. But in the Riyadh court of Abdulaziz there was only the simple and insistent creed of Mohamed Abdul Wahhab, an eighteenth-century desert preacher who had rejected virtually all adornment, art, music, and technology as blasphemy. In the isolated high desert of central Arabia, as the Jeddah architect Sami Angawi put it, "you have either day or night, you have cold or hot. You don't have these shades. Even the music is only one string . . . It's either black or white. It's either you're with me or against me."[5] Yet the religious passion of the king's Wahhabi followers caused him continual trouble—particularly the Ikhwan, or "Brotherhood," a militia of unbending radicals Abdulaziz created to conquer his enemies. When the Ikhwan threatened to revolt against Abdulaziz because they felt he was not religious enough by their exacting standards, the king turned his guns on them. At the same time, to hold his throne, he had to continuously appease his court's Islamic scholars, the ulema.

He debated with these ulema about the attractions and dangers of modern technology. Through his contacts with the British, Abdulaziz came to understand the outlines of Europe's industrialization and the dizzying array of products and comforts it had created. He had no desire at all to adapt to European civilization, but its gadgets intrigued him greatly. He never left the Arab world and he mocked English finery and pomposity. During a desert meeting with a British officer, he strode into an elaborate colonial tent outfitted with plush chairs, and announced, "Here we are in modernity! Bring tea, boy!" He urged his robed Bedouin retinue to join him on the carved chairs: "Let's be modern!" He mocked, but he also imitated: By the 1930s he had ordered his own European furniture for his Riyadh majlis.

He particularly liked radio sets, through which he could follow European news without ever leaving his palace. The Marconi wireless network he began to build on the Arabian Peninsula during the early 1930s also offered an important, even revolutionary means for Abdulaziz to monitor and control events in his own kingdom. He set up radio stations in major cities and a central operations room in Riyadh from where he could track potential rebels on the periphery of his domain and dispatch orders or units of his army. He struggled to persuade Riyadh's deeply suspicious Islamic scholars that these radio devices were permissible; among other things, the scholars strenuously objected to the music that came on to signal BBC news bulletins. Because it was impossible to anticipate exactly when this music would appear, Abdulaziz persuaded the scholars that the fault was with the radio knobs, not the radios or broadcasts. He also sought to persuade his religious scholars that the telegraph was not a form of sorcery.

Businessmen in Jeddah plied the king with Ford and Chevrolet automobiles, which he used to hunt gazelles in the desert. He would race along in the front seat beside his Bedouin driver, chasing his hunting falcons as they plunged to attack the fleeing antelopes, pecking out their eyes before the men completed the ceremonial kill. Thundering through the rough desert, Abdulaziz ground his cars down quickly and often left them to rust. In 1927 his royal garage had 250 Fords and Chevrolets, and it grew ever larger.[6]

The business agent who supplied Abdulaziz with Fords and Marconi radios, and who increasingly infiltrated his court and provided it with an air of burlesque intrigue, was Harry St. John Philby. He had graduated from Cambridge University with a First Class degree in Modern Languages, joined the Indian Civil Service, and later worked in Iraq, but he quit Britain's colonial service and became increasingly bitter about his government. Still, he desperately wished to be recognized in England as the foremost Arabian geographer and traveler of his time. During the 1920s he attached himself to Abdulaziz as an informal adviser and converted to Islam; the king endowed him with the new name of Abdullah. He was a "stocky, bearded figure in Arab dress, fiercely and fearlessly argumentative, unalterably British and yet more Arab than the Arabs," one acquaintance wrote. Yet for all his airs, he was "neither a soldier nor a poet . . . the kind of man who is always out of step." When not attending the king's Riyadh court, Philby lived in a comfortable house in Jeddah, where he set up his Ford dealership and collected baboons.[7]

Perhaps because Philby was so skeptical about the British government— he was ultimately arrested during the Second World War for promoting the causes of Nazi Germany—Abdulaziz came to rely upon him for independent advice in his dealings with Europeans and Americans. He presented Philby with a slave girl as a gift, and granted him permission to travel across the peninsula, documenting its flora and fauna for books and lectures Philby delivered to English geographers. And it was Philby who controlled the crucial negotiations during the 1930s for mining and oil concessions.

Winston Churchill had converted Britain's navy from coal to oil during the First World War and by doing so helped usher in the oil age. Britain had locked up supplies in Iran and Iraq, but American explorers had begun to poke around the Middle East as well. An American oil company, SOCAL (Standard Oil Company of California), had the insight to put Philby on its payroll; the company paid him $1,000 a month and promised a bonus of $10,000 if it won a concession from the Saudi king, plus an additional $50,000 in royalties if significant amounts of oil were discovered and exported. Abdulaziz had run up huge debts to Philby by purchasing cars and radios from him, and an oil deal with SOCAL offered not only cash in Philby's pocket, but a potential revenue stream from which the king could pay off his debts. Philby seemed determined to keep Britain out of Saudi Arabia. The deal he helped to broker, signed with SOCAL in 1933, provided Abdulaziz with 50,000 British pounds' worth of gold, and the promise of an equal amount if oil was discovered in commercial quantities, plus additional royalties.[8] The king displayed little personal interest in oil; he was much more interested in parallel explorations for minerals and especially water. But to finance his enormous family, to quell the peninsula's tribes and other political rivals, he desperately needed gold.

As soon as he had it, Abdulaziz began to spend it. Like many of the newly wealthy, he and his sons decided that they would enjoy a bigger and finer place to live, and so in Riyadh and just outside its walls, a palace building boom began. At the same time, to the east, along the shores of the Persian Gulf, the Americans had arrived to begin drilling for oil; they began to construct houses, schools, offices, and warehouses.

It was an excellent time and place to be an enterprising young man in the building trades.

A CONSORTIUM called the Arabian American Oil Company, or Aramco, formed to manage the oil rights SOCAL had won. American geologists, drilling engineers, and construction managers settled at Dhahran, about three hundred miles to the east of Riyadh, near the sandy mounds beneath which, it was hoped, the largest oil reserves might lie. The Bedouin nomads who moved through the desert in loose bands, scraping their living from caravan trade and animal husbandry, disdained manual labor. Some did take oil jobs, but they kept their distance from Aramco's settled camps. Hundreds of other Arabs—local Shia who faced discrimination from the Bedouin, and poor foreign migrants like Bin Laden—eagerly accepted the Americans' salaried work.

Mohamed Bin Laden traveled to Dhahran from Jeddah and found work with Aramco as a bricklayer and mason. He excelled. His supervisor, a "redneck mason" from the United States, decided that "this guy's really good," according to Tim Barger, whose father was an Aramco executive. In a matter of just weeks, Aramco promoted Bin Laden to be foreman of a bricklaying crew. A few months later, they promoted him again to supervise several crews. "He had what it took," said Barger, who recorded his father's recollections and later worked in Saudi Arabia. "He was blind in one eye but he knew how to supervise people and get jobs done. Then after a long time—maybe a year or a year and a half—he went to Aramco and said, 'I want to start my own business.'" It was difficult to bring in Americans to Saudi Arabia to do every little job, from catering to fence repair; therefore, Aramco supported any Arab who showed promise as an independent contractor. "They said, 'Go on out, get started, we'll give you some jobs. You can always come back here.' He got his contracting job going well enough so that he could go to Riyadh and hang out for days and days." A profile of Bin Laden assembled several decades later by the American government reported that he struck out on his own from Aramco in 1935.[9]

Building contracts in Riyadh depended upon the favor of King Abdulaziz. It was easy enough for a man like Bin Laden to connect with the ruler: he could attend his majlis, a daily session in which anyone could sit in the king's throne room and wait for the chance to petition him for work.

The Riyadh where Bin Laden arrived during the 1930s was still a walled city-fortress similar to those he had known as a boy in Wadi Doan. The Saudis constructed castle-fortresses on their flat desert plateau by encircling the towns with mud-brick walls twenty-five feet high. Palm groves surrounded Riyadh, and townspeople came and went through its gates to harvest timber or collect water during the day. At night and during prayer time the gates closed shut. Riyadh's wall, wrote Philby, was "surmounted by a fringe of plain shark's tooth design at frequent intervals. Its continuity is interrupted by imposing bastions and guard-turrets." Inside, thick-walled houses stacked up on top of one another along twisting lanes, which helped to create shade; there were also market squares, jumbled trading stalls, and, of course, a grand mosque built by the king.[10]

Because of his conquest of the Hejaz and his new contracts with American oil companies, Abdulaziz no longer feared that his enemies might raid Riyadh unexpectedly, and so in 1934, he began for the first time to build outside the city walls. He hired a local contractor to oversee a large new family palace compound where the king could hold his majlis sessions, install his new Marconi wireless radios, and accommodate at least some of his enormous family. As his sons married, Abdulaziz added to this construction plan by commissioning homes for them in the new complex. He named his new palace Al-Murabba, or "The Square," and when it was finally completed in 1939, the main building was an impressive two-story edifice constructed around an open courtyard, where a tall date palm rose to the open sky. The majlis rooms were on the second floor, flanked by rows of offices for the king's political aides, coffee servers, slave bodyguards, religious scholars, and keepers of the treasury. The entire project, including garages for Abdulaziz's expanding fleet of automobiles, required the construction of dozens of buildings in a barren region that barely had enough timber to support the population's daily requirements. The king and his advisers asked their new American friends for materials and construction help, but Aramco and the companies it had invited to Saudi Arabia, led by the Bechtel Corporation of San Francisco, were busy constructing infrastructure for the new oil economy; they did not want to get tied up by the king's personal palace projects.[11]

In this gap Mohamed Bin Laden saw opportunity. He "had a vision," recalled Mohamed Ashmawi, a friend of the family. "He could foresee you could gain a lot by being helpful to the royalty members, especially the most important ones . . . He started building homes for some of the royalty." Exactly when and how Bin Laden first met Abdulaziz is not known, but soon "many royal orders entitled him to establish projects at Riyadh," according to a Saudi account of his early work. The most important of these was the first palace in Riyadh built entirely from stone; this led to many other contracts in what became known as the Murabba Quarter. Hadhramis, like their more sophisticated Lebanese counterparts, already enjoyed a reputation for entrepreneurialism. They were known as people who would push the limits to get a job done, even if they did not quite know exactly how to do the job in the first place. The plateau around Riyadh is called the Nejd, and the native Nejdis had a saying about Yemeni hustlers like Bin Laden: "If you want him to be a baker, he'll be a baker; if you want him to be a road builder, he'll be a road builder." Bin Laden's strength in these early days, according to the Saudi historian Fahd Al-Semmari, was that he was "always available ... and he would bring many people to do the job. He made many messes but he learned how to do work quickly. If he needed ten people, he would bring one hundred."[12]

Oil royalties had seen Abdulaziz through the Great Depression, if barely. The Second World War, however, shut down international shipping just as Saudi Arabia prepared to deliver its first sizable oil exports. This did not stop the king from building palaces or importing luxuries, but he did not have adequate stores of gold, and he began to run up debts to private merchants. As submarine warfare in the Atlantic and elsewhere crippled British fleets, food supplies to Saudi Arabia grew erratic, and famine haunted its interior desert, where many people lived on the margins even in the best of times.

Churchill's government had many more pressing priorities, particularly during the war's desperate early years, but London resumed subsidies to Abdulaziz early in 1940 in order to dissuade him from exploring an alliance with Germany. Britain ultimately gave the king the equivalent of $38 million during the war to keep him loyal; the American government, starting in 1943, contributed an additional $13 million in lend-lease aid. As Germany's eventual defeat seemed assured, American planners eyed the kingdom as a convenient, uncontested transit point for pushing people and equipment to the Asian front. A top-secret State Department memo to Roosevelt dated December 22, 1944, laid out the case for a new and more committed partnership with Abdulaziz:

A strong and independent Saudi Arabian Government in the Near East ... is less likely to fall victim to war-breeding aggression than a weak and disintegrating state vulnerable to economic and political penetration. The vast oil resources of Saudi Arabia, now in American hands ... should be safeguarded and developed ... The military authorities urgently desire certain facilities in Saudi Arabia for the prosecution of the war, such as the right to construct military airfields . . ."[13]

This thinking spurred Roosevelt to meet Abdulaziz aboard the USS *Quincy*, afloat in the Red Sea, in February 1945. Eight sheep and forty-two courtiers followed the king aboard the American warship. Roosevelt was charming and empathetic; he and Abdulaziz bonded immediately over wonders of the wheelchair, and the president presented one of the latest models to the king as a gift. On the main issues—"oil, God and real estate," as Rachel Bronson has put it—they also fell into easy, warm agreement.[14]

The Americans who began to travel to Riyadh afterward to consult with their new ally found the king admirable, if picaresque and at times puzzling. In the main, they were attracted to his land because, as a secret State Department cable put it, "Saudi Arabia may be likened to an immense aircraft carrier lying athwart a number of the principal air traffic lanes of the world."[15]

Japan's surrender opened the kingdom's oil spigot; exports grew from 30,000 barrels per day to 476,000 barrels by 1949. The aging Abdulaziz was now rolling in gold and silver, and he and his sons and advisers embarked on a spending spree. Mohamed Bin Laden returned to Jeddah, summoned by the king's closest financial adviser, Abdullah Suleiman, who invited him to work on a new royal palace, called Al-Khozam, which the king had decided to build outside of Jeddah's old city walls, about three miles from the sea. It was a grand two-story coral stone and wood-beam building with twenty-foot ceilings, stained-glass windows, and dual staircases ascending to the majlis rooms on the second floor. Abdulaziz was by now in his late sixties and relied increasingly on his wheelchair. At the Al-Murabba palace in Riyadh, his advisers installed an elevator to lift him to the majlis floor—the problem facing his Jeddah contractors was that the king could not walk with dignity up the grand staircases they had designed. Mohamed Bin Laden helped to invent an ingenious solution: a circular stone ramp that ran from the driveway of the palace up to the second floor. It was wide and sturdy enough so that Abdulaziz could ride in one of his Fords directly into his majlis, descend from the car, and take his throne.[16]

Jeddah remained a city that "clamored and howled and brayed and snarled with a bedlam of animal noises, with once in a while a midnight shot as some irritated Englishman potted a prowling pariah dog," wrote Wallace Stegner, a visitor in these years. Yet the city also underwent a "phenomenal building boom," as an American diplomat reported. "Foundations, at least, if not the completed structures, mushroomed overnight. Contractors complained bitterly of their inability to obtain sorely-needed building materials."[17]

Bin Laden and his brother moved into a multistory compound on Jeddah's north side, where Mohamed met each day with subcontractors, haggled over purchases and debts, and assembled his workforces. He was now becoming so prosperous that he bought his first automobiles, yet he remained a hands-on foreman who sang with his men at job sites and did not hesitate to work alongside them. The volume of contracts he won meant that he had to devote himself increasingly to management, which required him to hire clerks and transcribers, since Bin Laden could barely read and could not write. "There were a lot of architects and staff coming in and out of the house," recalled Hassan Al-Aesa, who worked for him during this period. "It became very busy." The city's building trades were divided into guilds, each overseen by a sheikh who controlled the labor supply and apprenticeships. Bin Laden bargained with all of them. "There was work for everyone," recalled Al-Aesa. "Carpenters, plaster, steel, blacksmith—every craft." There was little cement in the city in this period; the dominant building material was coral, harvested from four or five quarries along the sea. Bin Laden purchased one of these quarries, leased it to a partner and used it to deliver reliable supplies to his building sites.[18]

For the first time Mohamed Bin Laden felt secure enough to marry.

He was in his late thirties when he took his first wife during the Second World War; she gave birth to a daughter, Aysha, in about 1943. Bin Laden took a second wife, Fatimah Ahmed Mohsen Bahareth, who was about nineteen years old and belonged to a prominent family in Mecca who had migrated to Saudi Arabia from the Hadhramawt. When Fatimah gave birth to a son in 1944 or 1945 (the year is not certain), Bin Laden named the boy Salem, after his closest friend in Jeddah, Salem Bin Mahfouz.[19]

Bin Mahfouz was a fellow Kenda tribesman from the Hadhramawt. He was born in 1906 to a poor family in the village of Khraikher in Wadi Doan, on the north side of the canyon, about thirty miles from Mohamed Bin Laden's hometown of Rabat Bashan. At age six he traveled by foot to Mecca in the company of his brothers, a journey that lasted six months. He moved to Jeddah during the 1930s and entered into a lucrative foreign-exchange dealership. By the time of the building boom, Bin Mahfouz served as Bin Laden's banker—a loose term in a kingdom that then had no formal banks, where all transactions were conducted in cash, where there were multiple coins and currencies and where savings took the form of personal hoards of gold. As a symbol of their friendship and business bond, not only did Mohamed name his firstborn son after Salem, but Bin Mahfouz named his first son Mohamed.

The young Bin Laden patriarch began to travel, overseeing simulta-neous palace-building jobs in Riyadh and Al-Kharj, an experimental, ir-rigated farming community founded by Abdulaziz south of Riyadh. His projects brought him into increasingly close contact with the king. A mud-brick house on Bin Laden's job site in Al-Kharj collapsed one day and killed one of his workers; the victim left a widow, a son, and a daugh-ter. Bin Laden carried the infant son to the king's majlis in Riyadh, en-tered with the boy on his shoulder, and presented him to Abdulaziz, according to Al-Aesa, who remained close to the victim's family for years afterward. "This is from my responsibility in front of God to yours," Mohamed said. Abdulaziz handed the boy back and instructed him, "Go and buy a house for them in Mecca." Bin Laden made the arrangements; the widow moved in and received a royal stipend for the rest of her life.[20]

Bin Laden was not only the king's contractor; he was also among his creditors. By 1949 rough estimates of the royal family's debts to merchants and palace builders ran between $20 million and $40 million. Saud, the eldest son of Abdulaziz, reportedly ordered a $250,000 American kitchen for his new palace in Riyadh that year. Suleiman, the finance minister for whom Bin Laden worked, embarked for Paris on a medical leave with a $600,000 budget. The royal family was spending more than 400,000 British pounds sterling per month during 1949, the British ambassador estimated, and "construction projects more ambitious than economic absorbed much of the revenue ... In general it cannot, however, be said that the country's real needs in regard to development had been properly considered." Indeed, the royal family's projects were "often of doubtful value and managed by incompetent individuals." Particularly objectionable were "the building of palaces at Riyadh, Mecca and elsewhere for the King's enormous family."[21]

The postwar boom might not benefit Saudi Arabia's impoverished subjects, but it had presented Mohamed Bin Laden with opportunity—and he would seize it.

3. SILENT PARTNERS

ABDULLAH SULEIMAN had become the second-most powerful man in Saudi Arabia next to the king, and he had grown wealthy beyond imagining. His was an accidental fortune. He had journeyed as a young man from an oasis town on the Nejd plateau to Bombay, where he worked for an Arab merchant. He later failed in business in Bahrain and returned home to aid his uncle, a merchant who looked after King Abdulaziz's finances. When his uncle died suddenly, Suleiman became the king's minister of finance, an exalted title for a man whose main job in those days, before the oil wealth, was to look after a tin trunk that contained whatever gold and silver coins the king possessed. Suleiman eventually oversaw Abdulaziz's royalty receipts and palace expenditures, but his highly personal accounting methods never changed. He was a "frail little man," according to Philby, "but with something of the inspiration of the prophets in his soul." He "knew no fatigue," wrote the Dutch diplomat and traveler Daniel Van der Meulen, and he was "endowed with the genuine Arab gift of accommodating himself to all circumstances of life, but he was not strong enough to withstand two enemies who unexpectedly came his way: money and whisky."[1]

By late 1949, Suleiman was at least as important to Mohamed Bin Laden's prospects as the king himself was. He was "reputed to be a silent partner in Bin Laden's construction company," according to a later U.S. State Department report. He commissioned Bin Laden to build what would become a $3 million palace along the Red Sea, in which Suleiman intended to live; the minister also controlled or influenced access to scores of other construction projects, funded by an annual building budget that totaled about $100 million. Apart from his construction work with Suleiman, Bin Laden had a second connection to this endowment: Suleiman's secretary, Mohamed Bahareth, a fellow Hadhrami to whom Bin Laden was now related by marriage. Through these ties Bin Laden adapted to a system of contracting that American and British diplomats in the kingdom referred to as graft, but which the Saudis who benefited from it regarded as an entirely proper form of business in a country where all the land, all the natural resources, and all the power to dispose of them were vested in the estate of the royal family.[2]

During the Second World War, Suleiman had recruited as an aide a Lebanese Druze named Najib Salha, and the two built what an American government report described as "sizeable personal fortunes" by "misappropriating shipments" of trucks and other equipment from the British lend-lease program of military aid to Saudi Arabia; the pair sold the diverted goods to wealthy Saudis. When the British complained, Abdulaziz fired Salha; by that time he had amassed assets in Egypt alone worth 2 million pounds sterling. The king could not bear to get rid of Suleiman, however. Even though his adviser facilitated "rampant graft and corruption," which the king knew about, Abdulaziz was so dependent upon him to keep track of money matters that "it was unlikely in the extreme that anything could be done which would in the slightest way prejudice" Suleiman's position, "so long as the King lived," as a British official judged it.[3]

Suleiman owned a transport business that profited from the pilgrim trade to Mecca. He owned land across the kingdom and after the war he began to develop hotels. He planned one for Dammam, near the American-run oil fields, which he hoped to endow with a bar and movie theater, plans that proved too ambitious, since Islamic scholars in the kingdom had decreed movies illegal—along, of course, with alcohol. He entered into partnerships with many Saudi merchants; his partner in one

Jeddah firm, named Ibrahim Shakir, who imported Dodge cars and trucks, became "one of the wealthiest private citizens in Saudi Arabia, beneficiary of many fat government contracts," according to an American cable. Suleiman acquired farms and irrigated them with scarce water supplies, and he protected his land from encroachments—when the Saudi government sought to improve Jeddah's sanitation by piping fresh water from one of Suleiman's estates, he shut the project down. Alcohol exacerbated the effects of age and an itinerant life without modern medical care. Suleiman fell out of sight for months at a time; he typically said he was fishing in the Red Sea. The American embassy feared that the minister was losing his grip and "hitting [the] bottle" at an "increasing rate."[4]

King Abdulaziz never cared about money as much as his sons and advisers did, but when he occasionally ran out, he became annoyed. In December 1949 the king demanded 10 million riyals from Suleiman to provide wedding gifts to some of his sons and daughters who were soon to be married. When Suleiman told him that the treasury was empty, Abdulaziz was apoplectic. In a supposed move toward reform, the minister of finance summoned from Cairo Najib Salha, his wartime profiteering crony. Having been taken once, the British government was "not particularly hopeful . . . that the Augean stables of the Saudi Arabian Ministry of Finance will be any cleaner for his arrival."[5]

Nor were the Americans. They increasingly regarded the self-dealing and commissions that Suleiman oversaw as an obstacle to Washington's plan to secure its alliance with Saudi Arabia by promoting rapid economic and social progress in the kingdom. The king's budget allocated five times more for palaces and support of the royal family and its allies than it did for the embryonic Ministry of Health.[6] Royal excess and social inequality might make the Saudi population vulnerable to the utopian appeals of the international communist movement, some American officials feared.

As oil flowed during the late 1940s, the Bechtel Corporation negotiated a cost-plus contract with the Saudi government to undertake an ambitious plan, influenced by Washington, to help lift the kingdom into the modern capitalist age. Bechtel's imported bulldozers demolished Jeddah's old city walls and plowed the sand to build piers, ports, airports, and an asphalted road that could speed visiting pilgrims from Jeddah to Mecca. Saudi princes, however, criticized Bechtel's profits as excessive and impossible to police. For its part, Bechtel discovered that Suleiman, the king, and his sons expected the company to be on call around the clock to repair broken refrigerators, air conditioners, or even automobiles at their private palaces. The royal family ordered Bechtel's bulldozers and earthmovers diverted from roads and airports to such work as the digging of a sunken garden at the palace of Prince Faisal, the king's second son. Moreover, Suleiman fell behind on the government's payments to Bechtel; by the summer of 1950, the Saudis owed the company $2 million. Stephen Bechtel told the State Department that "the headaches" of his company's Saudi work "far outweighed the advantages."[7]

Abdulaziz's sons and advisers were divided by factional feuds that proved impossible for Bechtel's executives to manage. When the electricity went out at the huge Riyadh palace of the king's eldest son, Saud, the prince became furious at Bechtel. At the same time, Saud complained that his brother Faisal was spending royal funds too freely, a rich gripe coming from him. Suleiman threw up his hands and said the boys were beyond his ability to control. Abdulaziz was by this time largely oblivious. His legendary energy had drained away with age, and he napped through his days, encased by his many wives, bodyguards, and slaves. He suffered from cataracts in both eyes, one of which drooped in near blindness. Simply moving the king from one palace to another had become an epic production: when Abdulaziz shifted himself and his entourage from Riyadh to Taif in the summer of 1951, it required fifty-five flights over three days and the diversion of every aircraft in the young fleet of Saudi Arabian Airlines.[8]

Bechtel's failure to adapt to the royal family's way of business created openings for Mohamed Bin Laden. The Americans obsessed about the timeliness of hard currency payments to their New York bank accounts; Bin Laden relied upon a much more flexible network of Hadhrami moneylenders based in Jeddah. The Americans wrung their hands over the excesses of Suleiman and the Saudi princes; Bin Laden saw Abdulaziz and his heirs as faithful Muslims ordained by God to rule over Mecca and its environs, and he skillfully cast himself as their obedient and enterprising servant.

Around this time Bin Laden began to prove himself, too, to the committees of Islamic scholars appointed by Abdulaziz to oversee public works in Mecca and Medina. The scholars awarded him contracts to build mosques in the Hejaz, and as the postwar boom gathered momentum, the scale of Bin Laden's contracts for religious works increased. In earlier periods, Egyptian and Lebanese firms had won much of the repair and renovation work in the Islamic holy cities; these companies had connections with the previous Ottoman regime and they employed European-trained engineers. But Abdulaziz found it useful to have a favored contractor of his own. Like Mecca's guardians before him, the king took great pride in sponsoring improvements that would impress pilgrims visiting from around the world. At his instruction, Mohamed Bin Laden traveled to Beirut in 1949 to purchase tents that could shield worshippers from the sun as they prayed at Mecca's grand mosque. When the Lebanese businessman who made the tents, Ahmed Fathalla, flew to Mecca to install them, King Abdulaziz happened to arrive to wash the Ka'ba, the holy black cube that is the focal point of Muslim prayer. Among the king's entourage was Mohamed Bin Laden, Fathalla recalled; Bin Laden and Abdulaziz were "always together, side by side." The next year, Bin Laden was appointed to build a series of dams and reservoirs, at an estimated cost of $1 million, which could pipe fresh water to Mecca from a newly discovered well twenty-eight miles away. A Belgian company provided Bin Laden with an experienced engineer, as well as high-grade piping from Germany. The mason from Wadi Doan was building an international network of Arab and European business contacts and partners.[9]

The king ratified Bin Laden's rise by issuing a Royal Order on May 24, 1950, which appointed Mohamed "Director-General of Construction Works of King Abdulaziz"; he was assigned to work under Suleiman and now had a title to wave around when he needed one. To the consternation of Bechtel executives, Bin Laden moved the company's heavy equipment from the Jeddah-Mecca road so he could use it "for grading around the new residence" he was building for Suleiman by the Red Sea. (Bechtel and State Department correspondence recording this diversion of construction equipment, dated January 17, 1951, apparently marks the first time that the Bin Laden family name appeared in an American government document.)[10]

The boom in palace construction in which Bin Laden specialized had now become influenced by Western notions of luxury, as an American cable from that winter reported:

Various members of the Royal Family, Government dignitaries, and rich merchants lavished vast amounts on the construction of quasi palaces, each endeavoring to outdo the other in size, expense and design of their future homes. In many instances Parisienne "interior decorators" were employed to buy expensive materials and oversee their installation.[11]

Saudis increasingly traveled abroad and saw for themselves the industrialized world's wealth; they carried its aspirations and tastes home. The Meccan newspaper *Al-Bilad Al-Saudiyah* published a travelogue in the summer of 1952 by a Saudi writer, titled "With the Americans in Their Country"; the writer described Times Square as "like a bright flame or a diamond necklace . . . Luxury is visible everywhere, in restaurants full of all kinds of meat placed in lines in glass show cases." Most marvelous of all was the sanitation:

Rarely will you find an insect in New York and months will pass before
you catch sight of a fly . . . People do not speak there about insects or
flies. Years have passed, and now they speak about television and the
atom bomb and the new invention for curing TB . . . .The civilized countries, especially the western nations, respect a country according to its
cleanliness and organizations. The Americans even go further for they
respect a country according to the number of pipes she possesses. This
should not be a surprising fact to the reader, for pipes play an important
part in the cleanliness of a country, because water runs through them and
is consequently free of insects and dirt.[12]

It did not require a trip to New York for many Saudis to see that their
royal family seemed deeply involved with its own luxuries yet lacked any
similar devotion to public welfare or even basic national infrastructure.
"Our poor are of families who are not of the habitual beggar type," a
Saudi writer complained in *Al-Bilad*, in a rare public expression of dissent. "Hardly able to walk, they aimlessly roam the streets . . . They are
starved; they have not tasted even bread for two or three days. There is
no exaggeration in this . . . Our misfortune is the creation of our wealthy
people, who are too greedy to try and do anything for the people."[13]

Neither the king nor his sons nor Suleiman seemed able to take control of the kingdom's finances. Fed up with late payments and the mis-
use of its people and equipment, Bechtel finally abandoned its Saudi
public works contracts. Najib Salha, the deputy finance minister, diverted
$400,000 to his own account as part of the final settlement, according to
a Bechtel executive.[14]

Suleiman brought in another American contractor, Michael Baker Jr.,
Inc., of Pittsburgh, to replace Bechtel, but they, too, soon departed, frustrated by late payments and demands for ad hoc palace repairs. The
British mission in Jeddah noted that Mohamed Bin Laden appeared "to
be interested in ousting Bakers and, while there is little hard evidence for
this, it is clear that [Bin Laden's] firm is taking an increasing part in

Government constructional works." Next arrived a German company called Govenco, which was rumored to have paid Bahareth, Suleiman's secretary, a reported $100,000 to help win business in the kingdom, but Govenco abandoned its public works contract even faster than the Americans had done, and for similar reasons.[15]

The American and European companies left behind unfinished infrastructure projects that involved complex engineering challenges. Mohamed Bin Laden rapidly recruited his own engineers—Italians, Lebanese, Palestinians, Iraqis, and Egyptians—and he convinced Suleiman that he could oversee this work, even though he had no background in it. He was once again persuasive; a new Royal Order issued by King Abdulaziz in June 1951 granted Bin Laden a lucrative concession "to build a power station at the city of Jeddah."[16]

One more unlikely expansion now augured a feat of self-invention that would secure Bin Laden's legend and his family's fortune.

THE ONLY PAVED ROADS in all of Saudi Arabia at this time were a few that Aramco had laid around the eastern oil fields and a single ribbon of badly engineered asphalt between Jeddah and Mecca. Ships continued to unload hundreds of automobiles, trucks, and buses at the Jeddah port, but these vehicles had to navigate the kingdom's deserts along crude, flood-ravaged tracks and riverbeds. Abdulaziz and his eldest son, Saud, seemed to have little interest in paved highways; they saw railroads as the epitome of industrial achievement, and they pressed the American government for loans to build a rail network in the kingdom. The Americans, however, resisted; the railway age was receding, they impressed upon the king, and the era of automobiles and asphalted highways had arrived.

The Hejaz pilgrim trade in particular suffered from the lack of even a rudimentary road network to support religious tourists. Medina, the second city of Islam, was situated a forbidding distance from Jeddah, to the northeast. It was possible to bump and slide across the rock and sand

to Medina in a car or bus, but a smooth paved road was desperately
needed. Harry St. John Philby, the English adventurer now back in the
kingdom after his wartime detention for pro-Nazi oratory, saw in this
problem a business opportunity. He wrote to Abdulaziz arguing that
Saudi Arabia's honor would suffer in the world's eyes if it did not start
paving decent roads for pilgrims to the holy places, and he won the
king's support for a plan to pave a 350-mile road from Jeddah to Medina.
Massive overspending on palaces and gifts meant the royal treasury could
not be relied upon to fund this project, however, and there was, as the
British embassy noted, "a marked reluctance on the part of all concerned
to undertake the unenviable and difficult task of explaining to the King
that the extravagances of himself, his family and his Ministers have
brought the Government heavily into debt . . . The King's elder sons are
understood to have claimed that the King's health might suffer from the
shock." Philby contracted with two British road-building companies and
negotiated for export insurance from the British government, so the
companies would not have to depend entirely on the royal family for
payment.[7]

The Jeddah-to-Medina road, via the Red Sea port of Yanbu, was the
most ambitious public works project yet undertaken in the kingdom, estimated to cost about 4 million British pounds. A sun-soaked tea party
at the side of the roadbed eight miles outside of Jeddah, hosted by the
British embassy and attended by a dozen princes and ministers, formally
launched the undertaking on December 11, 1950. The principal British
contractor was Thomas Ward, Ltd., of Sheffield, England. Its local manager, Robert Donald, expounded at the launch party on his plans: He
would build scores of culverts and bridges, and gird the road with a nine-
meter foundation. Its surface of bituminous macadam would be six meters across. Donald was cautious but optimistic about the timetable for
this work. He had no inkling of the disaster that awaited him.[18]

Building an asphalt road in the Saudi kingdom was difficult even in
the best of circumstances. The terrain was rocky and mountainous in

some places, and sandy and unstable in others. The soil composition varied; it might be a shifting, wind-blown mix of sand and clay, or a blend
of granite gravel and sand, or a bog of brown limestone silt. The ground
was often soft, the wind was unrelenting, and periodic storms unleashed
destructive flash floods. Aramco manufactured asphalt from its oil fields,
but other materials were scarce, and the sandstorms damaged mechanical equipment. For all of these reasons, in the months after the tea party,
Thomas Ward's work on the road north from Jeddah and west from
Medina proceeded slowly. As ever, the Saudi government fell behind on
its promised payments, and the British insurance plan proved inadequate
to prevent losses from accumulating on Thomas Ward's books. In August
1951, the company's chief road engineer in the kingdom died in an automobile collision. The following January, Robert Donald and his wife per-
ished in a second car crash. By the summer of 1952, at the "end of a long
chain of misfortunes," the company at last gave up, and its executives approached Suleiman to negotiate a settlement that would allow Thomas
Ward to leave the kingdom and abandon the road.[19]

Once again, Mohamed Bin Laden stepped forward as a Western contractor retreated. The royal family had gone on a car-buying binge; eight
hundred automobiles were handed out as gifts to family members,
friends, and government officials in April 1952. The princes were revved
up, but they had no place to drive. In November, Crown Prince Saud
traveled from Jeddah to Medina, and as he sped across the partially completed road's smooth surface, he had a revelation about the glories of asphalt. Soon Saud announced that it was of vital importance that the
Medina highway be finished. "Happily presiding over the arrangements
for the Crown Prince's sojourn in Medina was Mohammed bin Ladin,"
the American ambassador reported to Washington. Bin Laden convinced
Saud that he could handle the job, and had "already approached his
new task with great display of energy and enthusiasm, however misguided."[20]

Bin Laden ordered twenty-one thousand tons of asphalt from Aramco

and opened negotiations with Thomas Ward to purchase their abandoned road-building equipment. It turned out that the British machines
would not work with the type of asphalt Aramco manufactured, so the
oil consortium sent Bin Laden an engineer to help him. Thomas Ward
prepared to leave, "about half a million pounds out of pocket and in a
very ill humor," as the British embassy put it. American officials, after
years of frustrating efforts to support Bechtel and other companies, were
resigned to Bin Laden's attempt to take over the Medina road contract.
As the ambassador explained in a dispatch to Washington,

> As this is the Government's first venture into a major construction proj-
> ect not directly supervised or carried out under the auspices of a foreign
> firm, its success or failure may be of considerable significance to future
> operations . . . As the project is so heartily sanctioned by the Crown
> Prince and the Ministry of Finance, Bin Ladin will not be hindered by
> lack of funds or the restrictions of a fixed-fee contract which have proved
> to be the undoing of many a foreign firm.[21]

To overcome his complete lack of experience in road building, Bin
Laden sought out an Italian company that had previously constructed
roads and dams in Sardinia; he offered them work as his subcontractor.
The Italians, however, took "fright on realizing the full extent of the
shabby deal meted out to Thomas Ward . . . and the enormous capital
which will be necessary to do the job," the British embassy reported. Bin
Laden did seem to enjoy impressive access to the king's treasury—he
made a hard currency payment of 328,000 pounds at the scheduled time
to Thomas Ward, to pay for their equipment—but the slow pace of Saudi
reimbursements and other troubles hindered his attempts to make much
progress paving the highway. Throughout 1953, Bin Laden "[had] been
given impossible tasks of constructing roads at short notice without any
idea where payment [was] to come from." Still, he managed. His great

Hadhrami friend Salem Bin Mahfouz had that same year founded the National Commercial Bank, so Bin Laden could more easily draw upon sources of finance outside of the Saudi government.[22]

MOHAMED BIN LADEN was now becoming rich, but money could not change his social identity in Arabia. The Al-Saud royal family and the tribes on the Nejd desert plateau were extraordinarily concerned about the purity of their tribal and family bloodlines. Nejd families kept careful track of their genealogies, and for a price, an enterprising tribal leader might be persuaded to "discover" a respectable lineage for a family whose past ran, say, to slavery. To the self-conscious Nejdis, a hardworking Hadhrami immigrant like Bin Laden, even one as full of ambition and surprises as he was, only conformed to a cliché of their racial stereotyping: the Hadhramis, everyone in Nejd knew, were frugal, avaricious, enterprising, yet also unusually honest and reliable. A prince of the Al-Saud royal family might admire these qualities in a man like Mohamed Bin Laden, but he certainly would never allow Bin Laden to marry one of his daughters. In the Nejd heartland, where political power in Saudi Arabia was concentrated, the Bin Ladens would always be foreigners who had embedded themselves in the mongrel Hejaz. The attitude toward Bin Laden among even a poor but proud Nejdi tribal family, to say nothing of the Al-Saud royal family, was akin to that which a 1950s-era WASP bank executive in New England might hold toward a darkskinned, grade-school-educated entrepreneurial Sicilian who built his lakeside summer cottage—charming fellow, but keep him away from the girls.

The Muslim sheikhs and kings Bin Laden had known since his childhood in Wadi Doan inspired his emerging vision of his own family life. All the rulers he had ever encountered had not just the four wives permitted at any one time by Islamic law, but many more. Wealth might not buy Bin Laden entry into Nejdi families, but in Jeddah and Mecca it instantly transformed him into a sheikh—a loose title of respect, and one that he had more than earned by 1953 through his association with the king, as well as his business accomplishments. He offered a desirable match for any family with eligible daughters that might be attracted by the business and employment connections that Bin Laden could provide. Beginning in the late 1940s, Bin Laden began to imitate his mentor, Abdulaziz, by marrying a succession of young women who caught his eye, or who were offered by fathers in business with him. Between his first marriage in about 1943 and his final takeover of the Medina road contract from Thomas Ward in the autumn of 1953, Mohamed Bin Laden married at least nine times, and he fathered at least fifteen sons and nine daughters, according to records later produced in a court case by the Bin Laden family. Some of the women Bin Laden married during this time stayed with him for many years; others he divorced very quickly. Fatimah Bahareth, for example, enjoyed a privileged position as the mother of Salem, his eldest son, and her marriage endured and proved bountiful— she gave birth to two additional sons, Bakr and Ghalib, as well as three daughters, Su'aad, Zeenat, and Huda. Like Bahareth, some of Bin Laden's early wives were from Hadhrami immigrant families like his own. One early wife, who was of Iranian origin, would bear three sons; she gave birth to the eldest of them, Yeslam, in Mecca on October 19, 1950. Khalil and Ibrahim followed, as did a daughter, Fowziyah. A number of Mohamed's wives were foreigners: one was Egyptian, another Palestinian, and another from this period may have been Ethiopian. The family Mohamed Bin Laden was creating with such vigor looked very much like the Hejaz itself—a polyglot, bound by Islamic faith.[23]

In the manner of every sheikh and prince in Arabia, Bin Laden installed his wives in his Jeddah compound, each with a household of her own but segregated from contact with men other than him or the wife's relatives. Sometimes his ex-wives stayed on at his compound after their divorce. It was customary for wealthy moguls like Bin Laden to ensure that women he divorced had ample means. In some cases this might be accomplished by arranging for the divorced woman to marry a new husband with a steady job. If a wife gave birth to a son, Islamic law ensured that the boy would eventually inherit a share of his father's wealth, and the boy, in turn, was expected to ensure the welfare of his mother. In any event, by the autumn of 1953, Bin Laden had more than enough money to support his expanding family. He was never extravagant or particularly acquisitive in his personal habits, except when it came to women. The family compounds he built, while comfortable, were not as opulent or garish as many of the palaces he built for the royals. He did not seem to have time for indulgences. Mohamed Bin Laden appeared to enjoy work above all, and his ambition was far from sated.

THE AMERICAN EMBASSY supplied Abdulaziz with aphrodisiacs to curry favor with him, but in his last years blindness and impotency deprived the king of the pleasures so long at the center of his life. He withdrew into his court and his harem. Saud, his heir, was fifty years old, but the king still treated him and his other older sons like children, insisting, for example, that they stand in his presence unless he invited them to sit down. Some of his adult sons disappointed Abdulaziz; Mishairi, at about twenty years old, disgraced the family by drinking himself into a rage and shooting to death a British diplomat, Cyril Ousman, whom Abdulaziz had known and liked. Only afterward, in late 1952, did the king impose a formal ban on alcohol in Saudi Arabia.[24]

There was no single Bedouin tradition of succession, but a common practice held that new rulers should be chosen by consensus, on the basis of their ability to lead, and not strictly by primogeniture. Abdulaziz had long before arrogated the decision about succession to himself, however, and he had designated Saud as his political heir, despite Saud's manifest indiscipline, which by the early 1950s included heavy drinking. The king did sense that the crown prince would need help, and so he cultivated an uneasy partnership between Saud and Faisal, his second son, born to a different mother. Faisal was an austere and enigmatic man who seemed more suited for leadership than Saud. To cement this arrangement, and to overcome the tension that was palpable between his two sons, Abdulaziz declared that succession would pass laterally, from Saud to Faisal, rather than through Saud to his own eldest son.

In October 1953, Abdulaziz fell gravely ill at his palace in the mountain town of Taif, a retreat from the humid coastal air of Jeddah. On November 8, as the king's condition worsened, Saud flew to Jeddah, where a military band and a parade festooned him. Word came to him the next morning that his father had arrived at his last hours; Saud rushed to Taif, but too late—Abdulaziz had died that morning in Faisal's arms. Scores of family members had assembled around the king's body by the time Saud arrived. To dispel the uncertainty that hung over them all, Faisal pulled a ring from his dead father's finger, approached Saud, and presented it to him in obedience. Saud handed the ring back and announced that Faisal was his heir and crown prince.[25]

Faisal accompanied his father's body on an airplane to Riyadh, where in the Wahhabi tradition, which rejects the adornment of gravestones and other memorials to the dead, Abdulaziz was loaded onto a truck and buried in an unmarked desert graveyard.

Saud remained in Jeddah. He sensed that his life was about to change profoundly, and that somehow he needed to address the financial chaos and social inequality in the kingdom he had inherited. On the day after his father's death, he met with the American chargé d'affaires and asked to discuss a "private and secret matter."

The new king lamented his land's low standard of living. He pledged to begin a "war against widespread poverty, ignorance, and disease," and said he was "determined to emerge victorious from this war." He would build schools, hospitals, military bases, and highways. He said he was "sickened" by the unsound financial practices in the kingdom. He recognized, he said, that efforts to eradicate "corrupt practices" would have to "begin with himself."

He had just one request, he continued: The kingdom was broke, and he wondered if the United States might lend him $300 million.[26]

4. THE GLORY OF HIS REIGN

A T THE TIME of Saud's ascension to the throne, American oil companies paid about $20 million each month to the Saudi treasury. Mohamed Bin Laden received a fixed percentage. He appears to have been the only person, apart from Suleiman and the royal family, who had direct access to Aramco payments during this period. In theory, his allowance would ensure that he could finance the many building projects he was assigned, whether these were palaces or highways, as the British commercial secretary J. M. Heath wrote in a confidential dispatch to London. In practice, however, the kingdom's state of "administrative chaos" meant that Bin Laden, despite having "influential connections," was nonetheless "obliged to take on all manner of work whose cost, had it been fully carried out, would have far outrun his resources (which, as it is, may well be over-strained)." Bin Laden's work had fallen to a standstill, apart from those jobs he could pay for with his Aramco installments. Overspending on palaces and luxuries had left the royal treasury, once more, facing an "extreme shortage of cash."[1]

In late 1953 Bin Laden decided to reorganize his company, which was known in Jeddah by the same informal title he had given it when he arrived from Wadi Doan more than two decades earlier: Mohamed and Abdullah, Sons of Awadh Bin Laden. He assigned this task to Fuad Zahed, an Iraqi engineer trained in the United States. Zahed decided to turn Bin Laden's "amorphous organization" into professional departments—one for administration, another for construction projects, and a third for new industries. Zahed hoped to persuade the new king to build a cement mill, a tile factory, an iron foundry, a pottery factory, and an aluminum plant. He also wanted to pursue agencies for the exclusive import of industrial equipment from Europe and the United States. Like his employer, Zahed harbored "ambitious plans," Heath concluded.[2]

American advisers told King Saud that he could not expect anyone to lend him money until he put his financial affairs in order. Throughout 1954, Saud's first full year in power, "royal expenditures were immense," the discouraged American embassy in Jeddah reported:

> The King, visiting neighboring countries with his heavily spending entourage, exhausted the state treasury during the spring of the year. While reports of the largesse he dispensed abroad filtered back to Jidda, salaries of Government employees were delayed because of insufficient funds. The Government's debts to merchants were ignored. A palace building program was begun, and its cost was heavy. Conservative estimates ran from $30 million to $50 million. Others were higher. In the midst of this spending orgy, a few voices could be heard calling for responsibility in high places. But for the most part, those who could lined their pockets.[3]

Mohamed Bin Laden, of course, stood near the head of this queue. He managed to hold his place despite a major palace shake-up. Encouraged by his half-brother Faisal, Saud forced Suleiman into retirement in the summer of 1954. Yet Bin Laden remained the king's favored builder; he had an uncanny sense of how to maneuver among the factions of the royal family and its retainers, and he had already distanced himself from Suleiman by the time of his mentor's fall.

Bin Laden became preoccupied by a frantic attempt to improve electricity supplies in Jeddah. The problem was that when King Saud brought his train of wives, concubines, and slaves to visit his Red Sea palaces, the lights and air-conditioning sometimes flickered out; this greatly annoyed the king. Early in 1954 Bin Laden joined with Mohamed Alireza, patriarch of Jeddah's oldest and most influential merchant family, to buy shares in the newly formed National Company for Electrical Power, Ltd., under a license granted by Saud. The company raised about 2 million pounds sterling and inherited some Swiss turbines from the government, but its board of directors couldn't decide on a plausible plan. When Saud and his family camped in Jeddah during the summer of 1954, his household sucked up so much of the city's electricity that more than half of the town had to go without for twelve to sixteen hours each day. Bin Laden turned to an American firm, Burns and Roe, headquartered on lower Broadway in New York City; its engineers promised to ease the crisis by installing the mothballed Swiss generating equipment. The Burns and Roe engineer who flew to Jeddah found Bin Laden "instrumental in winning over the doubtful shareholders" in his electric company—and anxious to see the city's supply improved before the king returned in the summer of 1955 and ran all of his air conditioners again.[4]

Mohamed succeeded. Evidently pleased, the king issued a royal decree on July 22, 1955, which named Bin Laden a state minister of the Saudi government. It was not an administrative position, as Saud barely possessed a functioning cabinet, but it did signal Bin Laden's increasing influence. The contracts he now controlled were large and varied. The West German embassy reported at the end of 1955 that the annual revenue of his enterprise was about $200 million. That may have been an overestimate, perhaps a considerable one—if true, it would have meant that Bin Laden had access that year to the equivalent of more than half of the kingdom's oil royalties from Aramco. Like the Saudi princes who patronized him, Mohamed Bin Laden possessed a wealth of assets, but he did not always have a lot of cash; princes demanded that their palaces be finished very quickly, but afterwards, they turned into sullen deadbeats. In some seasons, documents depict Bin Laden scrambling to obtain local bank loans of just several million dollars, but in others, he was able to deliver large hard currency payments to foreign accounts. His accounts receivable department always looked good on paper, but his cash

holdings were volatile. Still, the $200 million West German revenue es-
timate certainly reflected the scale of Bin Laden's visible activity in the
kingdom at this time. In addition to his many palace projects and the gar-
gantuan undertaking of the Jeddah-to-Medina road (which proceeded
slowly under the twin burdens of poor conditions and late payments), Bin
Laden built a water pipeline into Medina, installed electric generators in
that holy city, built a new headquarters for the Ministry of Foreign
Affairs, paved streets in the eastern city of Dammam, and ran a marble
factory. He hired American engineers to survey a gypsum deposit where
he hoped to build a $1.5 million factory. By now he was also doing so much
business with the United States that he retained an American agent to coordinate his purchasing and contracts in that country: International
Development Services, Inc., of New York, New York.[5]

Bin Laden and his brother Abdullah had by now become legends in
their hometown of Rabat, in Wadi Doan; they were the latest of the
many Hadhramis who had walked out from that region's canyons in
sandal-clad poverty to earn a fortune that would allow them to return in
glory. The brothers flew together during 1956 in a special Saudi government plane to visit Hadhramawt. Increasingly, however, they had diver-
gent views of the future. Mohamed's drive seemed unbounded, but
Abdullah, who married at least nine times during his lifetime, increasingly felt satisfied with what they had already achieved. He was drawn
to the idea of returning to Rabat to enjoy semiretirement and engage in
charitable works. The brothers soon decided to go their separate ways;
in 1957 Mohamed bought out Abdullah's share of their company, twenty-
six years after they had founded it together. "Mohamed was more ambitious than Abdullah and that's why they split," said Khalid Ameri, one of
Abdullah's grandsons. "Mohamed wanted more."[6]

Abdullah moved home to Yemen not long after this separation. He
brought his wives and children with him. His decision reflected a degree
of nostalgia that was not unusual among Hadhrami merchants in Jeddah.
Many had secured Saudi citizenship through their endeavors, and they

enjoyed great wealth, yet they remained foreigners in the kingdom, their sons and daughters excluded from prestigious marriages. There was a sense among many, too, of religious and charitable duty toward the poor kin they had left behind in Hadhramawt's stark canyons.

Salem Bin Mahfouz, founder of Saudi Arabia's National Commercial Bank, opened a school in his Hadhrami hometown during this period. Mohamed Bin Laden paid for a water project in his father's home region of Rakiyah a few years later, although he never visited the place, according to the Bin Ladens who still live there. Abdullah constructed Rabat's first drinking water supply soon after he arrived in Rabat. He walked through the barren hills with Bedouin guides until he found a suitable spring. He then called in one of the Bin Laden firm's Italian engineers. He supervised the piping project and also built for his family a new seven-story house with a modern plaster facade. His showy new compound rose on a slope near the center of the village of his birth.[7]

Mohamed preferred Saudi Arabia, which offered him renown and relative luxury. His Jeddah garage filled up with the gleaming accessories of his success: ten 1957 Packard convertibles imported from the United States. He and his two Hadhrami banking associates, Bin Mahfouz and H. A. Sharbatly, president of the Riyadh Bank, "are known as the 'Three Great Illiterates' of Saudi Arabia," wrote the West German ambassador in September 1957. "Due to his energetic and determined character and a mixture of shrewdness and honesty, he has a good reputation." A second West German report the following summer described Bin Laden's firm as "the richest company in Saudi Arabia . . . whose assets and wealth are said to exceed by far those of the entire state," buoyed by "some sort of monopoly for state orders" granted by King Saud.[8]

As his prominence grew, so did the risk that he might become ensnared in the factionalism and rivalry that constituted politics within the Saudi royal family. There were more than forty Al-Saud brothers who were nominally heirs to the throne, plus scores of mothers, wives, and former wives, all competing for access to the treasury; the potential for an outsider like Bin Laden to err was very great. If he did so, he could lose his contracts, his company—or perhaps his freedom. Shortly after Saud became king, he and his brother Faisal sought to involve Bin Laden in a dispute between them, according to a Lebanese friend of Bin Laden. Mohamed responded by pretending to be ill for a month. He summoned doctors to treat him and hid in his compound until the royal feud had passed. He explained his fears to this friend: "They are King Abdulaziz's sons—whatever happened, they will not hurt each other. But I am not. My head could go." Deference and obedience, expressed in florid Arabic, were Bin Laden's chief political tactics, the balm he applied to soothe royal egos. As a Yemeni of relatively low social status, he did not represent a political threat to the Al-Saud, and so the wealth he accumulated, besides confirming the local cliché of Hadhrami entrepreneurialism, was not particularly relevant in Riyadh. Still, Bin Laden was careful to continually remind the royal family that he knew he served at their pleasure, that he was merely an executor of their decisions. "He told us not to get involved in politics," his son Yeslam recalled. "We are a construction company. We are businesspeople. We do what we are told to do . . . This was our upbringing."

When he did express political opinions, they mimicked those of the royal family. During 1956, when the Al-Saud was locked in a border dispute with Britain over the obscure Buraimi oasis, Bin Laden let it be known to the American embassy that he resented U.S. policy, which he interpreted as insufficiently supportive of King Saud. For the most part, however, he kept his head down.[9]

Perhaps he could sense that the reign of King Saud had become untenable. Increasingly, Faisal emerged as the figure many within the royal family wished to invest with power. As this struggle unfolded, Bin Laden's challenge was to please both men—a difficult feat, for they were two very different leaders, with distinct ideas about what direction Saudi Arabia should pursue.

SAUD LOVED being king—traveling from palace to palace, presiding over sumptuous feasts, handing out money, and retiring to bed with one of his wives or concubines. He had inherited his father's height, and he could project regal dignity even as he became obese. Yet he lacked his father's intelligence and his grasp of international politics. Saud had become heir apparent after the eldest son of Abdulaziz died in the flu pandemic of 1919, but the king had poorly prepared Saud for the throne. His boyhood education was limited to Koran memorization and the desert arts of horsemanship and falconry, at which Saud proved less than outstanding; he had weak eyesight and fallen arches, so he peered through thick eyeglasses and walked awkwardly. He reached adulthood as an illiterate and did not travel to the West until he was in his forties. Abdulaziz assigned him to serve as his principal deputy in Riyadh, but rather than absorbing the subtleties of his father's statecraft, he was drawn instead to the example of his marriage bed; Saud ultimately fathered just over one hundred acknowledged children by an unknown number of wives.[10]

Apart from his automobiles and radio sets, Abdulaziz had mainly ignored Western ideas about modernity, but his eldest son became enamored of consumer luxuries and, gradually, also became addicted to alcohol. Aramco and American government officials initially encouraged Saud's fondness for baubles and modern conveniences. They saw him as crucial to their access to the country's oil, and they sought to impress him with the material benefits of an American alliance.

When Saud first traveled to the United States as crown prince in 1947, he rolled into New York on a private railway car. In the observation tower of the Empire State Building, he told his hosts, "I thought my brothers were exaggerating when they told me about New York, but they didn't tell me half enough. Such a city cannot be real." Thereafter he peered out his limousine window, pointed at cars, and asked, "Cadillac? Buick? Chrysler?" At a gala dinner at the Waldorf-Astoria hotel, the oil men sat

Saud at a table decorated with an elaborate scene of a wintertime New England village, replete with a Texaco filling station and a miniature train rolling through cotton "snow"; the train's controls were at Saud's place setting, and he spent the evening blowing its whistle and making the engine issue puffs of smoke. Eight acts of entertainment followed dessert, including Chinese dancing girls, magicians, and tumblers, which Saud seemed to particularly enjoy. Aramco's goal had been to establish a lasting connection with the crown prince; they did this, but they also helped to fire the imagination of a naive man about how a proper, modern king with a large bank account might display the glory of his reign.[11]

With Mohamed Bin Laden's help, Saud constructed a $200 million palace called Nassiriyah, outside Riyadh's old city walls. The compound became an emblem of Saud's vulgarity, a vast campus of pink and green buildings, with soccer fields and imported American cows. A guest at one of the king's outdoor feasts watched as Saud issued an order at sunset and beamed in satisfaction as "hundreds of colored electric bulbs burst into light . . . The minaret suddenly rose up flood-lit out of the dark . . . in all colors: blue, yellow, green and red; the palace walls were in orange."[12]

His health deteriorated as his drinking increased, and when he became concerned about his sexual potency, he surrounded himself with European quacks who sold him pills and poked him with needles. American and British diplomats clicked their tongues at Saud's indiscipline and bad taste, but some of his impoverished subjects reveled in his seeming generosity, and they particularly appreciated his habit of tossing gold coins from his car as he drove past crowds of onlookers. Two-thirds of Saud's subjects remained nomads or semi-nomads, and less than one in ten school-age children attended a classroom. There were less than a dozen native college graduates in the kingdom and not a university to be found, apart from the centers of Islamic scholarship in the two holy cities.[13]

Saud appeased the tribes by showering them with subsidies, but he proved inept at managing his authority within the royal family. He failed to build alliances among his half-brothers and placed his unqualified sons in positions of military command, exacerbating his relatives' fear that he might use his large brood to usurp the planned succession to Faisal.

Saud's reign coincided with the rise of Gamal Abdel Nasser, an army officer who seized power in Egypt and called for revolution and unity in the Arab world, appeals that won him popular acclaim. Nasser's propaganda attacked the former European colonial powers and their reactionary clients; King Saud seemed to be a conspicuous example. Saud dodged a Nasser-inspired coup in 1955; the foiled conspiracy was a shocking event in politically quiescent Arabia. The king grasped that he had to respond to Nasser's popularity, but he lacked the necessary insight and skill. He veered erratically, embracing Nasser at one point but later participating in a botched conspiracy to murder him.[14]

In Washington, President Eisenhower and his aides set out to make Saud into a staunch anti-communist ally. After Nasser nationalized the Suez Canal with Saud's vocal support, Britain and France responded with an ill-judged invasion; after their defeat, Eisenhower saw a vacuum in the Arab world that American power might fill. He particularly coveted the use of an air base near the Saudi oil fields. In 1957 he invited King Saud to America once again, and while the dancing girls were not so conspicuous this time, the thrust of American flattery was the same; Eisenhower met the Saudi regent at the airport and escorted him beneath a banner strung across Pennsylvania Avenue: "Welcome King Saud!"[15]

Yet the king's spending careened even more out of control. His yacht was impounded in Europe over unpaid bills owed to an Italian palace architect.[16] The Americans might tolerate such embarrassments, for the sake of oil and air base rights, but increasingly the king's relatives felt they could not. Their impatience was sharpened by the presence in their midst of an obvious alternative—Saud's frugal, taciturn half-brother.

Faisal had been born at nearly the same time as Saud, in 1905, but to a different mother, a daughter of the Al-Shaykh family, descendants of

Abdul Wahhab, the austere desert preacher of the eighteenth century whose creed had so influenced the peninsula. By the early twentieth century, the Al-Shaykhs had become Nejd's most prestigious family of religious scholars. Faisal came of age studying religious doctrine and law under the tutelage of his family's conservative but learned scholars. He acquired the same skills of horse riding and falconry as his brother, but proved to be a more convincing and committed military leader. He was small, thin, with a prominent nose and hooded eyes, which struck visitors as those of a hawk.

Abdulaziz decided as early as 1919 that Faisal was best suited to represent the king in the distant capitals of Europe. Under Philby's escort he traveled to England as a teenager on a long, damp winter tour that left him with early lessons in formal diplomacy, as well as powerful memories of sea lions at the London Zoo. He represented his father at the Versailles Conference, where the treaty ending the First World War was signed. Back home, Abdulaziz placed him in charge of the Hejaz, but Faisal often seemed indifferent about governing and withdrew into palace and family life. Amid the challenges of the postwar oil boom, however, he came into his own. He served as the kingdom's representative at the infant United Nations and toured America in a style considerably more mature and businesslike than Saud. At this time Faisal was not abstemious, and he could be a lively companion ready for a practical joke, but he was never remotely as undisciplined as his half-brother. As the years passed, he became increasingly austere and religious, his demeanor dampened by chronic intestinal ailments that left him dyspeptic and gaunt.

He retained strong convictions about the Islamic faith and desert culture he had been taught as a young man. He was a fervent anti-communist and a devoted subscriber to Zionist conspiracy theories. He was also open-minded about how Saudi Arabia might adapt its traditions as it pursued a program of national development. Faisal was innately conservative, in the sense of being cautious, "an unbelievably patient individual," in the words of the Saudi diplomat Ghazi Algosaibi. "He felt that many problems could be safely left for time to solve." To the American officials who pressed him for change, he quoted Arab proverbs about the dangers of haste; he told them "he was anxious for the country to go ahead, but to go ahead slowly."[17]

His brother Saud's reign appeared to require urgent attention, however. By late 1957, when yet another crisis caused by overspending left the kingdom teetering near bankruptcy, the royal family moved to install Faisal as prime minister. Reluctantly, Saud agreed. The implicit arrangement was that Saud could indulge himself, within the limits of an allowance, as a figurehead king, but Faisal would run economic and foreign policy, to restore the treasury and protect the Al-Saud from Nasserism.

Saud retreated temporarily, but he chafed at his half-brother's ascension. This gathering contest between two regents presented Mohamed Bin Laden with a problem of rich complexity after 1958. He owed his fortune to Saud's patronage and palace-building sprees, yet Faisal's habits of piety and work lay much closer to his own. As Bin Laden reportedly told a colleague, "My pocketbook is with Saud, but my head is with Faisal."[18]

FROM THE EXAMPLES of his rulers, Mohamed Bin Laden discerned that multiple marriages could provide not only an outlet for a wealthy man's lust but also a means to build up political and economic alliances. Increasingly, Bin Laden's projects took him to corners of Arabia where he had few acquaintances. There he had to win support from local sheikhs. To do so Bin Laden sometimes married the daughter of a desert tribal leader or town mayor, provided her with money and an impressive house, hired her male relatives onto his project, and then, a year or so later, when his work was completed, left her with a generous financial settlement and perhaps a child as well. "He was very canny politically" in some of these marriages, said Nadim Bou Fakhreddine, a guardian of some of Bin Laden's sons.[19]

The full inventory of the approximately twenty-two wives who ultimately bore children with Bin Laden is unknown. Of the marriages that can be at least partially identified, some suggest a traditional arrangement between two Hadhramawt families; some suggest examples of Bin Laden's tactic of building alliances useful to his construction projects; and others suggest a purely sexual motivation.

Multiple divorces and remarriages of the kind Bin Laden carried out were not unusual in some parts of the Nejd, but social mores in Arabia were changing during the 1950s, particularly in cities such as Jeddah. The practice of taking four wives simultaneously, and of serially divorcing to acquire even more partners, was increasingly seen as backward and anachronistic. Monogamy was modern, and modernity was in vogue. Yet the Hejaz easily accommodated the profligacy of a wealthy Hadhrami immigrant like Bin Laden, in no small part because of the examples of Abdulaziz and Saud.

The Koran's verses about multiple marriages can be interpreted as discouraging or even prohibiting polygamy. The verses emphasize fairness. A married man should declare his intention to divorce, allow a waiting period to pass, and then confirm his decision: "When you divorce women and they have reached their set time, then either keep or release them in a fair manner."[20] The evidence available about Bin Laden's marriages suggests that he mainly followed these principles, yet inevitably, some of his wives enjoyed more favor and longevity than others, and some fared better after divorce than others.

During the early years of King Saud's reign, Bin Laden traveled around the Levant to buy materials and find subcontractors, and during these trips he appears to have married a number of young Arab girls. He had already taken on one Syrian wife by the time he arrived in that country's coastal city of Latakia in the summer of 1956 and was introduced to the Al-Ghanem family, who were poor and not particularly religious. How Bin Laden met the Al-Ghanems, and why they offered their fourteen-year-old daughter, Alia, to him is not known. Bin Laden took Alia with him back to Saudi Arabia and within a year she was pregnant. During the Islamic year of 1377—corresponding to a period from July 1957 until June 1958—Alia gave birth in Riyadh to a son, Osama.[21]

At the time of this marriage, Mohamed Bin Laden was in a particularly active phase of sexual partnering and fatherhood. He remained married to a woman whom he had taken as a wife more than a decade earlier; she was already the mother of one son, and she gave birth to two more sons in the same Islamic year of 1377, according to records supplied to an American court by the Bin Laden family. Besides this wife and fourteen-year-old Alia Ghanem, at least two other of Bin Laden's wives gave birth to sons during that Islamic year. Altogether, according to the family records, Mohamed Bin Laden fathered seven children during the year of Osama's birth—five sons and two daughters. Osama later said that he believed he had been born in the Islamic month corresponding to January 1958. If so, he was apparently one of two sons born to Mohamed by two different wives during that month—the other son, Shafiq, later reported in British corporate records that he was born on January 22, 1958.* It would be difficult for any of the children of Mohamed Bin Laden from this time to be entirely confident of their birth dates or even necessarily of the month of their birth; it was not something that Saudis typically kept track of then, and there was no system of government record keeping, either.[22]

Alia's family came from a city heavily populated by the Alawite religious sect, whose members would later dominate the top echelons of the Syrian army and government. The Alawites adhere to an obscure Islamic

---

*On the morning of September 11, 2001, Shafiq Bin Laden was attending an investors conference at the Ritz-Carlton Hotel in Washington, D.C., when the attack launched by his half-brother struck the Pentagon.

creed passed along by oral tradition, one that is regarded as heresy by Muslims from mainstream traditions. The Al-Ghanems later denied that they were Alawites and said they adhered to orthodox Sunni beliefs, but these claims were issued at a time when it would have been dangerous for the family to admit to an Alawite heritage, so the matter seems uncertain. During the 1950s, Syrian Alawite girls from poor families sometimes worked abroad as maids or even were sold as concubines, and this later produced speculation that Osama's mother might have been such a consort. It seems possible, but there is no evidence to support this speculation. Even if Bin Laden did acquire Alia initially as some sort of temporary wife, he recognized her as legitimate once she had a son, and she retained this status within the Bin Laden family for decades afterward. Osama enjoyed legitimacy as a male heir to Mohamed throughout his life, and in legal and business matters, he was not treated as if he belonged to a lesser birth category than Bin Laden's other younger sons. Still, it is clear that Alia Ghanem did belong to a group of wives who gave birth to a single son or daughter and were then divorced by Mohamed within a relatively short time. Some of these wives quickly remarried, and some drifted from the family's inner circle. Those wives who were the mothers of Mohamed's elder sons or who stayed married to him for longer periods might feel superior to wives like Alia, but the advantages these senior wives enjoyed, at least during the 1950s, were mainly of pride and social perception, and were unrecognized by Islamic law, to which Mohamed Bin Laden hewed.

The husband these women shared was on the move continually, and during the late 1950s he diluted the prestige of any one mother by embracing new ones. His family grew to the size of a small village. Osama would later be described in numerous reports as Mohamed's seventeenth son, but this would mean that he was the first of the five Bin Laden boys born in the Islamic year 1377, and it is not clear how accurately the mothers kept track of such rankings. It seems safest to conclude that Osama arrived among the Bin Ladens as somewhere between son number seventeen and son number twenty-one. Certainly he had to compete for attention. By July 1958, according to the family records, Mohamed Bin Laden had become the father of forty-one children—twenty-one sons, and at least twenty daughters. Nor was he finished.[23]

AS HE TOOK CONTROL of the Saudi government in 1958, Faisal discovered that his kingdom was $500 million in debt. The central bank's vaults had virtually no cash holdings from pilgrim taxes. The government's accounts at Jeddah's commercial banks were overdrawn and myriad lenders were owed monies. Since the royal treasury received ever-larger monthly payments from Aramco, if Faisal could settle some of these debts and cut down on royal spending, he might emerge from this crisis fairly soon. To do this he required help from creditors like Mohamed Bin Laden and a dramatic change in behavior by King Saud.[24]

Saud agreed to the sale of royal property around the kingdom. He surrendered his private office in Jeddah and many of his palaces and guesthouses, and he even conceded that the lights at Nassiriyah should be turned off during daytime hours.

Faisal called in Bin Laden and began negotiations that would last throughout 1958. The crown prince had no cash, so he offered hard assets. Faisal wanted to unload some government-owned enterprises that he felt should be operated by the private sector. To settle debts owed by King Saud for construction work at Nassiriyah, Bin Laden accepted title to the Al-Yamamah Hotel in Riyadh. (Bin Laden later leased the hotel to the U.S. military.)[25] Bin Laden may also have helped Faisal fund the government payroll temporarily during this period. This purported assistance by Bin Laden would become part of the family's legend in Saudi Arabia, quietly promoted by his sons, but contemporary diplomatic records make no reference to such a loan from Bin Laden. If it occurred, the records suggest, it was one piece in a mosaic of barter trades and financing arrangements negotiated between Bin Laden and the crown prince. In any event, Saudi government employees were well accustomed to late paychecks.

At Faisal's urging, Bin Laden also took on a twenty-year concession to manage a royal farm at Al-Kharj, sixty miles south of Riyadh, where American farmers on King Saud's payroll raised livestock and grew wheat, oats, vegetables, and even watermelons. Abdulaziz had founded the farm in 1941 with help from American oil companies, and by 1958 it cost about $1 million a year to run. It showed a small paper profit from the sale of produce, milk, and eggs back to the royal family, but Faisal wanted Bin Laden to assume the operating costs. The crown prince offered him favorable terms on its machinery and agreed that the royal family would continue to buy its produce. Bin Laden had as little experience as a farmer as he had had as a road builder when he took on the Medina highway project five years earlier, but he agreed. He promptly neglected Al-Kharj, cut off supplies to save money, and soon told the American employees that he would have to let them go when their contracts ran out. He replaced them with relatives of some of his foreign wives. "The in-laws are a mixed group of Syrians, Egyptians and Palestinians, with no apparent agricultural experience," reported Sam Logan, the Texas farm manager who was being sent home—an inventory of nationalities that suggests the family of Alia Ghanem, Osama's mother, may have been among the replacement employees.

Logan felt that he and the other Americans at the farm had been fired purely because of the kingdom's financial crisis "and that there was no anti-American sentiment behind this action. Bin Laden treated the Americans very fairly and lived up to all agreements, a rare thing in Saudi business dealings." In Logan's judgment, Bin Laden had taken on the farm "knowing he would lose money on it, on the condition that he be given certain privileges by the government in some other fields of endeavor."[26]

Indeed, Bin Laden's Al-Kharj agreement coincided with a much more lucrative deal he struck with Faisal in the late spring of 1958. Bin Laden formed a joint venture with two Italian brothers named Roma who gave the impression—incorrectly, as it turned out—that they had financial support from one of Italy's largest construction companies. Faisal offered a twenty-year barter plan in which Bin Laden would carry out highway construction and other work in exchange for natural gas from the American-run oil fields. At this time, Aramco flared off the gas from its fields because it was difficult to transport and market; the consortium's priority was oil. The Roma brothers believed they could sell the kingdom's gas in Europe, generating enough money to profitably finance Faisal's planned infrastructure projects. These included more than fifteen hundred kilometers of highway construction that would link Riyadh to Jeddah, and Jeddah to the southern port of Jizan, as well as a new university in Riyadh.[27]

The deal proved to be contentious. Aramco executives believed the natural gas belonged to them; Faisal argued that the kingdom owned it. The Roma brothers feared the dispute would jeopardize Bin Laden's highway contracts, to which they had pledged $5 million in financing.

In September, Faisal summoned Bin Laden and the Italians to his Taif palace. Bin Laden and Faisal spoke at length in Arabic, after which Bin Laden turned to the Romas to assure them that the crown prince was convinced the natural gas was his, and that "Aramco could not impede [the] completion [of] needed public works, providing jobs [to] many workers," as would be made possible by Bin Laden's deal.[28]

Bin Laden and Faisal needed each other. There were other merchant families in the kingdom who were building up experience in construction and light industry, but if the crown prince were to make a convincing start on a national development program, he needed Bin Laden's large store of construction equipment, his army of semiskilled and unskilled laborers, and his irrepressible habit of saying Yes, Your Majesty, it can be done. For his part, Bin Laden had no choice but to adapt to Faisal's priorities and terms. The crown prince's fiscal austerity drive had ended the palace and housing boom in Jeddah by 1959. Thousands of

Yemeni laborers left the city in search of jobs elsewhere as a local recession took hold; local merchants grumbled that Faisal's reforms might be "good for the country, but not for a merchant class brought up and nourished on the lush profits of 'the good old days.'" Bin Laden, however, evaded the brunt of this downturn. As before, he had adapted as required to serve the royal family; if highways and infrastructure were now the priority of the day, then they would become his priority, too.[29]

He was cushioned as well by another patron. By the late 1950s, Mohamed Bin Laden was not only Faisal's favored contractor. In the three holiest cities of Islam—Mecca, Medina, and Jerusalem—he was also blessed, as he put it, by the favor of God.

5. FOR JERUSALEM

T HE DECLINE of the Roman Empire produced as much disarray in the deserts of Arabia as it did in the barbarian-ravaged forests of Europe. Rome's late emperors promoted Christianity as a universal creed, but their decrees proved unconvincing along the camel caravan routes to the east. In the late fifth century A.D., religious faith in Arabia had evolved into a vibrant plurality. There were Jewish and Christian communities, but many Bedouin worshipped portable idols, trees, and stones. A family in an oasis town might rely upon any one of several hundred deities to bless its endeavors; there were moon gods and travel gods and swirling narratives of celestial deities. One organizing force was the entrepreneurialism of religious festival sponsors, particularly those around Mecca, which lay about halfway along one of the great camel routes of the frankincense and myrrh trade. Meccan impresarios divined that a single unified religious fair held once a year, at which all gods would be welcome, might attract more attention—and produce more income—than a looser system of seasonal events. The annual ritual that became the Hajj after the birth of Islam began as a raucous devotional attraction involving hundreds of gods.[1]

At the time of the Prophet Mohamed's birth, in 570, the Ka'ba, or "Cube," then a flat stone structure with no roof, served as a temple for some of the more popular deities. It contained "pictures of trees and pictures of angels," according to the Meccan historian Al-Azraqi, as well as a drawing of Jesus and his mother, Mary, and an image of Abraham as an old man. At the annual Mecca festival, pilgrims who worshipped diverse gods joined in a ritual walk around the edifice. One of the deities then recognized in the Hejaz—a god of gods, not represented by a fixed idol—was named Allah. Even before he received the Koranic revelations, Mohamed developed a conviction that Allah was the one true God, and that the hundreds of other idols worshipped locally were false.[2]

In Koranic tradition, Abraham is credited as the Ka'ba's creator. In this account, while visiting his son Ishmael in Mecca, God ordered Abraham to build a temple devoted to His oneness. As Mohamed received his revelations, he preached for the restoration of Abraham's plan. His sermons provoked resistance from Meccan tribal leaders and elders, who seemed to view the Prophet, himself an active businessman, as a sort of anti-capitalist spoiler, one whose ideas could, in particular, ruin their lucrative festival. Meccan opposition forced Mohamed into exile, to the town later named Medina, where he found political support. He prevailed in a series of battles and returned to Mecca in triumph. He entered the Ka'ba and, according to Al-Azraqi, "he asked for a cloth which he soaked in water, and ordered all the pictures to be erased." With this act Mohamed created an Islamic aesthetic rooted in the eradication of the multihued religious images of his Meccan youth. In the last years of his life Mohamed also announced the detailed new rules of the Hajj, one of the five pillars of the religion that Allah had revealed to him; this annual ritual's crushing crowds, drawn from around the world, would soon belie the earlier skepticism of Mecca's festival merchants.[3]

Islam expanded from Spain to Indonesia; a succession of dynasties ruled Mecca. Egyptian and Ottoman princes took the Hejaz and managed the Hajj after the thirteenth century. They often did so in a style that recalled the pre-Islamic festivals—there were marching bands and opulent parties, and a conspicuous emphasis on profiteering, which caused the reputation of Meccan merchants to fall so low that fleeced pilgrims referred to them as "the dogs of the Hejaz." When the Wahhabi movement first rose in the Nejd desert in the late eighteenth century, its warriors saw themselves as purifiers in Mohamed's name; as the Prophet had done, they would rescue Mecca from idolaters. Theirs was a desert world of parched deprivation and intense kin unity that had rarely been penetrated by other cultures. They shocked Mecca's cosmopolitan pilgrims:

> You must imagine a crowd of individuals, thronged together, without any covering than a small piece of cloth around their waist . . . being naked in every other respect, with their matchlocks upon their shoulders, and their khanjears or large knives hung to their girdles. All the people fled at the sight of this torrent of men . . . They had neither flags, drums nor any other instrument or military trophy during their march. Some uttered cries of holy joy, others recited prayers in a confused and loud voice.[4]

The Wahhabis destroyed every dome and tomb in the city; their scholars regarded much existing Islamic architecture as heretical, apart from the flat-roofed Ka'ba and mosques constructed in a similar design. Egyptian soldiers eventually drove the Wahhabis away and destroyed their featureless capital in Riyadh, but under the more durable leadership of Abdulaziz, the Islamic militias returned to Mecca in 1924. Again they tore down domes and attacked foreign pilgrims who lingered too long at decorated historical shrines, which the Wahhabis regarded as false temples.

Abdulaziz sought Mecca for its tax receipts and its prestige. He adhered to Wahhabi precepts, but he had no particular interest in the endless scholarly arguments in Riyadh about the status of every last curved roof and revered historical tourist site in his expanding kingdom. As with other aspects of his statecraft, Abdulaziz sought a synthesis: he appeased the Islamic radicals who gave him soldiers and legitimacy, yet he tried not to alienate the Ottoman subjects whom he had inherited. The king's Wahhabi militias, for instance, wanted to tear down the Prophet's Mosque in Medina, where Mohamed had preached during his exile; they saw it as a kind of heretical tourist trap. Abdulaziz recognized that its destruction would be deeply unpopular and would also crimp the pilgrim trade. He settled on a compromise in which the Wahhabis were allowed to take off the mosque's dome but were otherwise required to leave it be, and to accommodate its thronging crowds. As a contemporary traveler put it, the king gained credit from the Wahhabis "for having allowed the dome to be demolished, and credit from the foreign Hajjis for protecting the place from complete demolition."[5] This would become a basis for Saudi management of Mecca and Medina in the ensuing decades. The Wahhabi aesthetic would predominate, but it might, at times, be bent grudgingly to accommodate Islam's global diversity, particularly in pursuit of pilgrim revenue.

With ownership of the Hejaz came responsibility for the civic upkeep and improvement of Mecca and Medina. Abdulaziz carpeted the Holy Mosque in Mecca in 1928 and paid for a new gold-plated door in 1944, but otherwise, during the sparse years of the Great Depression and the Second World War, he could afford only light renovations. Amid the postwar boom, however, as the number of pilgrims arriving in his kingdom swelled, the king allocated larger sums. His objectives were not decorative but practical: Both the Medina and Mecca mosques were too small to accommodate the number of pilgrims they now attracted, particularly during the peak Hajj season. Jumbled town houses, market stalls, and twisting lanes surrounded both mosques, preventing their expansion. Encouraged by his sons Saud and Faisal, Abdulaziz agreed to remake both the old towns—Medina first, then Mecca.[6]

By September 6, 1949, when Abdulaziz published an open letter announcing his redevelopment plan for Medina, Mohamed Bin Laden had established himself as the king's principal builder. Mecca's and Medina's mosques and sacred sites were organized as Islamic trusts, or *waqfs*, overseen by boards of scholars and Hejazi notables, but a construction contract of this size was the king's decision, abetted by Suleiman. Bin Laden was their man. He was invited to run the entire Medina project, a lucrative grant that would include the demolition and construction work around the mosque itself, and also a new electrical grid, waterworks, and an airport. An official Bin Laden history, as well as contemporary diplomatic correspondence, suggests the Prophet's Mosque expansion and renovation project alone cost about $19 million during the early 1950s, not counting the even larger sum spent on compensation to landowners whose property was seized and cleared.[7]

The Medina project marked the beginning of the profound architectural and design influence that the Bin Laden family would have on the two holy cities for many years to come. Mohamed Bin Laden brought to the renovation a "modern architectural style," as his company's official history put it, involving the heavy use of reinforced concrete and decorative black marble. The brass lamps might be gaudy and the concrete oppressive, but both were certifiably up to date, and thus, during the 1950s, praiseworthy. And not only in Saudi eyes: one contemporary Lebanese visitor called the architecture Bin Laden oversaw "an impressive and luxurious piece of work." When his redesign was completed in 1955, about two years after the death of Abdulaziz, Bin Laden had constructed more than seven hundred new pillars in the Prophet's Mosque, as well as a similar number of concrete arches. He had added nine gates, two gravel squares for worshippers, and forty-four windows; altogether, he had expanded by 60 percent the area where pilgrims could mingle and pray.[8]

Because he could not read very well, Bin Laden could not deliver his own speeches in public, and so, in late October 1955, at the celebration called by King Saud to mark the project's completion, Bin Laden asked a substitute to read out a speech. It is the first known text attributed to Mohamed Bin Laden, a florid symphony of piety and flattery. He told the king:

> God wants you and your father to have this honor and God gave you the
> success to establish this historic building. And your names will be

recorded in glorious history and everlasting light. Your name will be within the everlasting light of those who built this mosque in different epochs since the time of the Prophet. I congratulate you on achieving this everlasting honor. Praise be to God alone that this construction was completed in your age.[9]

Bin Laden was not so humble as to avoid any reference to his own role. He listed painstakingly all the improvements he had overseen as he expanded this "very strong and fascinating building." He emphasized the jobs that the royal family had helped him to create in the Hejaz by financing new factories for carpet making. He highlighted the huge sums spent on compensation for landowners, and he praised the king's decision "to increase the salaries of the workers of the two holy mosques, so as to provide them with money which made them work honestly—you did not leave any door to reform unopened." As he neared the end of his exegesis, Bin Laden recounted the work he had done to support both modern and traditional transportation to Medina:

You ordered us to build an airport, which is one of the biggest airports. Large airplanes could use this airport; it is about to be finished. You ordered us also to build the road from Medina to Jedda, which is about to be finished. Also, we built an area for camels to gather and rest . . . You purchased the land which lies to the east of the Holy Mosque, and you made it a place for camels to rest for the benefit of Muslims . . . Your Majesty, God's grace is looking after you.[10]

The truth about Saud was less uplifting. In managing public religion, as in so many other areas, the new king struggled to sustain his father's canny balancing act. Saud's "enjoyment of movies, music and vaudeville, and his interest in promoting education for girls, sports, and other pursuits, are deviationist from the Wahhabi point of view," the American embassy noted. To compensate, Saud repudiated in public the conduct he embraced in private. In an open letter, he denounced as "evil" those who listen "on the radio to songs and music; this causes corruption of the soul and morals and keeps people away from God and prayer . . . Another evil thing is that women are dressing extravagantly and going out of doors with full make-up, some of them without veils; this is the worst of evils and a major cause of corruption and destruction."[11]

The king sought to stave off rumors of his impiety by showering the kingdom's holy sites with conspicuous renovation budgets. As soon as the Medina work was finished, Saud directed Bin Laden to start work on an even more expensive project in Mecca, one that would increase the capacity of the Holy Mosque surrounding the Ka'ba from about fifty thousand worshippers to four hundred thousand. Saud declared in public speeches that his budget for the Mecca and Medina projects totaled more than $130 million. The West German embassy estimated that the real figure was closer to $60 million, but as its report noted, "Even this sum seems to be tremendous in Western terms." The Mecca project proceeded slowly, crimped by Faisal's budget tightening after he became prime minister, but it provided Bin Laden a steady supplement to his highway and industrial work.[12]

Between 1956 and the mid-1960s—including the first seven or so years of Osama Bin Laden's life—a principal aspect of Bin Laden's Mecca renovation involved demolishing buildings. Bin Laden had undertaken some demolition and clearing work in Medina, starting in 1951; he brought in explosives to knock down houses and markets in the old city, and the following year, he began to cart away the debris. Mecca's urban clearance project was considerably more ambitious. Ultimately the Saudi government spent more than $375 million on eminent domain payments to Meccan property owners and shopkeepers. Mohamed Bin Laden sometimes brought his young sons to his work sites in these years, and what they saw, there beside the holy Ka'ba, was a succession of controlled explosions and falling buildings, scenes that would thrill many boys. How much of this demolition Osama witnessed is not known, but in later years, he spoke admiringly and accurately, in general terms, about his father's renovation work in Mecca and at other religious sites during this period. Through 1962, the last year for which statistics are available, Mohamed Bin Laden used explosives to blast away eighty-six thousand cubic meters of mountains and rocks in and around Mecca. He and his engineers also demolished 768 houses in the city, along with 928 shops and stores.[13]

FAISAL WAS DEVOUT. He believed that he could defeat Nasser and exclude communism from Arabia by promoting Islamic values; this was a pillar of both his foreign and domestic policies. He supported Bin Laden's work in Mecca in part because it promoted Saudi Arabia's credentials as a steward of Islam. In 1958, shortly after he became prime minister (a professional-sounding title in a thoroughly unprofessional government), Faisal seized on another renovation project that promised similar visibility and prestige, one that appealed in addition to Faisal's fervent anti-Zionist convictions: the refurbishment of the Dome of the Rock in Jerusalem.

The Haram Al-Sharif, or "Noble Sanctuary," is a large raised area at the southeastern corner of Jerusalem's walled Old City. The platform is regarded as the third holiest site in Islam. It contains two important buildings, the Al-Aqsa Mosque and the Dome of the Rock, built in the late seventh century. The Dome's gold-colored cupola soars ninety-eight feet above the sanctuary's esplanade, atop what Jewish tradition identifies as a wall of the First Temple built by King Solomon a thousand years before Christ.

The Dome of the Rock's place in Islamic tradition is more allusive and mystical than the historical narratives of war, politics, and law provided in the Koran about Mecca and Medina. Koranic verses and later interpretations by Muslim scholars hold that the Prophet Mohamed visited the rock outcropping beneath the Dome while on a "Night Journey" on a winged horse from Mecca to Jerusalem, then onward to heaven and finally back to Mecca. After Mohamed's death, Jerusalem became the site of continual conflict among Jews, Christians, and Muslims; as the centuries passed, the Night Journey narrative, and the Dome itself, attracted powerful allegiance from Muslims worldwide. The more Jerusalem became a locus of religious war, the stronger this allegiance grew. European crusaders captured the Dome in 1099 and turned it into a church before the Muslim hero Saladin retook Jerusalem and restored the site to Islam. Much later, Jewish projects to recognize the site's ancient temples, some of which dated to the earliest Jewish kingdoms, drew fierce resistance from Muslims.[14]

By the early 1950s, the Dome of the Rock had sunk into disrepair. Tiles were damaged or missing altogether, its roof was sagging, and its interior required fresh paint, carpentry, and metalwork. The Kingdom of Jordan then controlled the sanctuary, the Old City, and East Jerusalem. Young King Hussein, who had taken the throne after the assassination of his father, announced a pan-Islamic campaign to renovate the Dome in 1952, a project that had political as well as religious appeal amid the anti-Zionist feeling prevalent in the Arab world. Saudi Arabia and Egypt pledged financial support, but the project languished.

Four years later, Nasser announced his own plan to refurbish the Dome, and later that year, with Jordan's agreement, he dispatched engineering and architectural experts to Jerusalem to prepare for contracting bids. Nasser's initiative seems to have galvanized Faisal, for as soon as the crown prince took power in 1958, he worked to ensure Saudi influence over the project. His government backed Mohamed Bin Laden in the bidding. As Bin Laden prepared to make a proposal during the spring of 1958, he was buoyed by financial guarantees from Riyadh.[15]

Seven Arab-owned companies submitted bids by the May deadline—two from Jordan, four from Egypt, and Bin Laden's. He passed an initial cut down to three bidders, but his submission was not initially the lowest in price. Bin Laden corresponded with the decision-making committee about switching materials so as to reduce his bid further. "First, this is a sacred Islamic project, and I am very pleased to participate in the construction of this holy Muslim site," he wrote on July 8, 1958. He pledged to work "at any cost and provide any materials in order to do this great and honorable service to the Muslim community." To ensure success, Bin Laden provided an aide with power of attorney and sent him to Jerusalem for the last round of negotiations. He dropped his bid further to ensure that his was the lowest. His final submission was for 276,990.2 Jordanian dinars, just below the 278,225.5 dinars proposed by the Ali Abrahim Company of Egypt. The narrow margin suggests that a decision to favor Bin Laden might have already been made privately. Bin Laden later said that he had deliberately accepted a loss on the contract, as an act of personal religious charity, so it is also possible that he was determined, on his own, to win the honor. In any event, on July 17, 1958, the committee announced that Bin Laden had won.[16]

"Your highness, Sheikh Mohammed Bin Laden, it is my pleasure to inform you that the Committee for the Reconstruction of the Dome of the Rock and the Al-Aqsa Mosque has awarded the work of the construction . . . to your company," the committee's Supreme Judge wrote. "I am hoping this work will be completed in accordance with God's expectations, and I hope God will help us preserve this Islamic treasure."[17]

For the next nine years, Mohamed Bin Laden oversaw construction and renovations at the sanctuary, first on the Dome of the Rock and the grounds around it, then on the Al-Aqsa Mosque and elsewhere in Muslim areas of Jerusalem's Old City. He emphasized that the project was an act of personal devotion. "It is well known, Your Highness, that I care a great deal about the Dome of the Rock project," he wrote to the Supreme Judge in 1959 while bidding on a contract for lighting and electrical work. "I will execute the plan . . . at my own expense. In addition, I will submit receipts without including any service or labor costs . . . This is not for financial gain, but for its religious significance."[18]

Bin Laden's Jerusalem workforce was multinational and multireligious; it included Italian marble specialists, Armenian Christians and Palestinian Christians, as well as Palestinian Muslims. When the call to prayer rang out, Bin Laden would join the Muslim workers in prostrated worship, but the Italians would carry on or take a coffee break. "We learned a bit of Italian," recalled Nadir Shtaye, a workshop supervisor. "They learned a bit of Arabic." Bin Laden imported aluminum and marble from Europe, sand and cement from Jordan, wood from Lebanon, and tiles from Turkey, all trucked in from the Jordanian port at Aqaba. He won popularity by sometimes tipping workers on top of their salaries— ten dinars per man. A photograph shows him standing near a bank of microphones at a Jerusalem press conference in the late 1950s; he is dressed in a long white Saudi robe and a fashionable pair of dark sunglasses, carrying a modern briefcase. Photographs taken by his American pilot toward the end of the project show an enormous crane rising above the sanctuary's esplanade; nearby are turbaned workers hammering to repair the outdoor plaza, amid piles of white sand.[19]

King Hussein called for a celebration at the sanctuary after the first round of work was finished. Bin Laden flew into Jerusalem on his own private airplane on August 5, 1964, accompanied by a Saudi cabinet minister and notables from Medina. The Jordanian governor of Jerusalem and his military commander met Bin Laden at the airport. About five hundred Arab dignitaries crowded onto the sanctuary platform the next morning under a hot sun. A Koran reader sang out verses, and King Hussein presented Bin Laden with a medal honoring him for his work on Jerusalem's behalf. As was by now a ritual of public Arab oratory, the king pledged to reclaim Palestine from Israel: "Let me emphasize that the actual renovation of the Mosque and the Dome of the Holy Rock assumes significance far beyond the physical repair work," the king said. The renovation project had also advanced the cause of "complete restoration of our full rights in our usurped land."[20]

Bin Laden asked the Saudi minister who had accompanied him to read out his speech. He began with quotations from the Koran and a disquisition on the Prophet's Night Journey. He lavishly praised King Hussein and his family. Bin Laden then moved on to the subject of himself:

> God has also honored me, as I carried out the construction project at the two great mosques of Mecca and Medina, the two holy sites which God bestowed upon the Saudi Arabian government ... [They] contracted me to undertake this project and thus I was granted the honor of developing the three great mosques in Islam, which draw pilgrims from near and far. This is truly a great privilege from God, who gave it to whom He chose.[21]

He told the audience that the final cost had been about 516,000 dinars, or roughly $1.5 million at contemporary rates of exchange. Bin Laden paused to "point out here the generous, large contribution made by the Saudi Arabian government," which had covered about half the budget. He then advertised his own charity rather conspicuously:

> I wish Your Majesty to know that Yours Truly sacrificed an amount of no less than 150,000 dinars, which was spent willingly for this project, without concern about the material losses. I donated for this blessed work without any thought of the losses, but rather, my goal was spiritual gain, which for me is more important than hundreds of thousands of dinars.

He told the audience that King Hussein still owed him 167,000 dinars, but that he would renounce this debt as an additional act of charity—"my contribution to this great duty." He said that as he now moved on to work on the Al-Aqsa Mosque, he intended to build a large ten-acre garden nearby, from his own funds, and he asked for God's help.[22]

Bin Laden bought a house in East Jerusalem around 1963 or 1964. It was a spacious, white-stoned, red-roofed building of the sort that sprouted all around the city during the 1950s and early 1960s. It had a spectacular view of Jerusalem in the distance, as well as sandy ground and white-stone buildings nearer at hand. The cease-fire line then prevailing between Israel and Jordan was just a short walk down the street. To the east was Mount Scopus, a U.N.-controlled no-man's-land, and to the south lay the Israeli neighborhoods of Givat Ha-Mivtar and Ramat Eshkol. Jerusalem's old Qalandia airport was a short drive away, from where Bin Laden could fly directly to Jeddah, Mecca, or Medina on his private plane.

Bin Laden may have married at least one Palestinian wife during the years he worked on the Jerusalem project, but he stayed in his Jerusalem house mainly on short-term visits; it was otherwise occupied by his servants, company aides, and a guard who kept watch over his cars, according to the house's current owner, a Christian Arab who is a citizen of Israel and a former owner, a retired Israeli naval officer.[23]

Israel seized East Jerusalem from Jordan in the 1967 Arab-Israeli war; after that, Bin Laden never returned. The home was renovated and expanded. For a time, a Palestinian consul of Spain leased a unit. Years later, the house fell under the administration of an Israeli government department that managed land abandoned by Arab owners because of the war. The house was transferred formally to the Israeli government, sold to the naval officer, and later sold by this officer to the current owner. Throughout this time, the Bin Ladens remained firmly and prosperously centered in Jeddah, but in a practical and material way, the family could trace its history to the resonant cause—and perhaps even the unresolved legal claims—of Palestinian refugees from the 1967 war.

6. THE BACKLASH

GERMAN ENGINEERS and Turkish laborers laid the Hejaz Railway, linking Damascus to Medina, between 1900 and 1908. It sped Muslim pilgrims more than eight hundred miles to the two holy cities, with the additional and not incidental capacity to carry the fading Ottoman Empire's Turkish troops. As the First World War descended into trench slaughter in France, T. E. Lawrence and his colleagues in British intelligence seized upon the early stirrings of Arab nationalism to organize a guerrilla campaign against Turkish outposts, which included a garrison of eleven thousand soldiers at Medina. Bedouin militia repeatedly tore up Hejaz Railway tracks during the early months of 1917. Lawrence of Arabia enjoyed himself thoroughly: "This show is splendid: You cannot imagine greater fun for us, greater vexation and fury for the Turks," he wrote to a colleague.[1]

The main railway lay unusable for decades afterward and became, in Arab eyes, a symbol of colonial-era interference with the Islamic pilgrimage. The newly independent governments of Jordan and Syria, along with Saudi Arabia, pledged a restoration. From Riyadh, Abdulaziz expressed a particularly romantic view of railroads; they were the "only medium, by God's willingness, whose full advantage will prevail," he had cabled to President Harry Truman in 1946. His son Saud felt as strongly and later helped to organize the remnants of the Hejaz Railway as a formal religious trust. Its executive committee in Damascus spent several million dollars on engineering studies during the late 1950s; they showed that repairs would cost tens of millions of dollars. European and American officials refused financial support, arguing that modern highways and airports would make a better investment. Yet the American embassy in Jeddah recognized that the project held "much emotional appeal in certain Saudi quarters," and it feared accusations of interference with Muslim prerogatives if it objected too strenuously. Finally, in 1960, in the midst of Crown Prince Faisal's campaign to promote Islamic projects as an antidote to Nasser, Saudi Arabia, Jordan, and Syria revived their plan to repair the damage Lawrence and his Arab Revolt had done.[2]

As he had in Jerusalem, Mohamed Bin Laden emerged as an instrument of a religious-minded Saudi foreign policy project. He partnered with a Japanese firm, Marubeni, to bid for the railway repair contract: Bin Laden would undertake the civil engineering work, such as blasting tunnels and building culverts, while his Japanese partners, supervised by West German engineers, would lay the track. An American who worked for Bin Laden in Jeddah reported that the Japanese government, hoping to establish a business foothold in Arabia, had promised to underwrite all Bin Laden's costs. Bin Laden and his aides shuttled to Damascus. The contract "was Bin Laden's for the asking," boasted his American employee.[3]

A delegation of thirteen from the Hejaz Railway Executive Committee flew into Saudi Arabia late in October 1961. Bin Laden hosted them in Riyadh and Taif, taking them on a tour "to show off some of the roads, mosques and other projects" he had built, the American embassy reported. It looked as if the fix was in: Bin Laden enjoyed "extremely good connections with the Saudi Government and Royal Family and is a figure to reckon with in most public tenders involving construction work." The railway contract was likely to be awarded under a Saudi system that a separate cable described as "opening the locked stable after the horse is stolen." Saudi government employees would often trade information about a bid until "the contract is then awarded to the firm assisted by the 'insiders' with handsome bonuses going into the appropriate pockets." A later British government report asserted: "We have good evidence that contracts for this project were allocated on grounds that could not be considered strictly commercial." Among other things, according to British reporting, "King Saud apparently insisted that Bin Laden" win the bid.[4]

Whatever the reasons, Bin Laden and his Japanese partners did indeed win the contract; on November 14, 1961, they were awarded a $25 million deal. They signed a commitment the following summer, yet no work began. The Japanese proved unable to post a bond. Frustrated, the executive committee turned to a British company with proven railway experience, Thomas Summerson & Sons, to join Bin Laden in a new partnership. Two Summerson executives flew in to negotiate and joined British ambassador J. C. M. Mason in his Damascus apartment on the evening of February 18, 1963. "I spent some of the evening as Devil's Advocate," Mason recounted. Among the problems he cited were "the temperamental idiosyncracies of Bin Laden."[5]

The Saudi construction magnate had annoyed the railway committee, whose chairman said "that Bin Laden was now fairly unpopular." Syrian and Jordanian members seem to have resented how Bin Laden pulled Saudi royal strings and then underperformed on the work he won. He had become too powerful to challenge, however. The British executives were "quite prepared to ditch" Bin Laden, but they feared "the effect on eventual work in Saudi Arabia of making an enemy of him." For his part, Bin Laden reportedly claimed "that Saudi support would be withdrawn from the project unless he had a share in it."[6]

THE RAILWAY PROJECT fell apart a few weeks later. Crown Prince Faisal, too, appears to have been fed up with Mohamed Bin Laden; he pulled the contract from him "under severe reproaches," according to a West German assessment.[7] The Hejaz Railway was far from the only cause of Faisal's frustration with Bin Laden. There was a sense emerging in at least some sections of the kingdom that Bin Laden promised too much, did shoddy work, and too often failed to finish on time. His wealth and privileges had also become exceptionally conspicuous. He owned three Beechcraft propeller aircraft as of March 1961—more than any other individual in the kingdom outside the royal family. He hired American pilots to fly him from one job site to another, sprawling encampments of laborers in the deserts over which he ruled. He worked energetically, but his improvised methods increasingly drew questions and complaints from the international consultants who were attempting, at the urging of Crown Prince Faisal, to inject the best modern engineering standards into Saudi building projects.

For the first time in Bin Laden's long career, he had become a public figure of controversy, within the bounds of the kingdom's heavily muted politics.

"We read on every occasion that construction projects in our country are opened up for bids—that Bin Laden's office had a 'lesser bid' and got the project," wrote Ahmad Mohamed Jamal in a front-page column in the Meccan newspaper *Al-Nadwa* on November 15, 1961:

> This at a time when observers are screaming at that office's slowness in carrying out the projects it had undertaken two, three or more years previously. They also scream to high heaven at the dispersal of the efforts of [Bin Laden's] engineers, workers and equipment among numerous projects in distant cities and roads far apart in the kingdom. They scream, too, complaining about the lack of quality of the work, faulting engineering and inefficient organization of most of the asphalting operations.[8]

The larger problem was "the practice of giving the road projects in the whole of our country to one contractor." Ultimately, Jamal concluded, the problem was not only the quality of Bin Laden's work but also the quality of Saudi Arabia's government:

Have mercy upon us, you responsible officials of the Ministry of Communications. Have mercy on our country; have mercy on our projects. Spare our roads from the sole contractor, from him of the "lowest bid," from him whose previous project commitments are also paralyzed. Have mercy upon us, so that God may have mercy upon you.[9]

Accusations that pungent did not typically appear in Saudi Arabia's heavily censored newspapers without government sanction. Faisal and his allies were one possible source of backing for this criticism; Saud had temporarily pushed Faisal out of the cabinet, and at the time the article appeared, the crown prince was fighting to restore his authority. His allies promoted him as a cure for government inefficiency and corruption. A new minister of commerce, Ahmed Jamjum, from a merchant family that competed with Bin Laden, sought to break the stranglehold on contracting at the self-dealing Ministry of Communications. Yet there was more to this than factional competition: the public criticism signaled a broad discontent with the quality and pace of the kingdom's road-building program.

Highways in the early 1960s were a potent symbol of modernity. America's interstate highway plan was now much advanced, and the big-finned Cadillacs and convertibles that streamed along those freeways from coast to coast seemed to epitomize American individualism and prosperity. John F. Kennedy, hatless and handsome, waved to crowds from an open sedan; in Hollywood films and television shows, the convertible was cool. The notion that a national highway network could speed up modernization had particular appeal in Saudi Arabia. For the kingdom's heavily nomadic population, so long accustomed to freedom of movement, the automobile beckoned. The kingdom's population was small—only about 4 million—and dispersed over vast desert territory. Highways were not only exciting; they were essential.

Faisal's austerity budgets cooled the economy, but oil revenue continued to rise. By 1961 the government could afford a leap in highway construction—if only it could figure out how to build the roads efficiently. The kingdom announced plans for a network of highways totaling more than two thousand miles, but its bureaucrats fought to a standstill over how to let the contracts. An American road engineer, Harold Folk, hired as the kingdom's chief development adviser, recommended European consultants who could oversee work by local builders to ensure it met international standards. Faisal returned to the cabinet in the spring of 1962 and embraced Folk's goals, but he balked at the Europeans' fees. Apart from his innate parsimony, Faisal shared the widespread fear within the Saudi royal family, grounded in experience, that Western consultants often jacked up their rates unscrupulously when they did business in the kingdom. "One Roadblock After Another" was the title of a confidential U.S. embassy report on the accumulating fiasco. Privately, Faisal pressed American officials for help. He wanted his government to create a proper highway department that would own a fleet of road-building machinery so that it would not be so dependent upon private contractors like Bin Laden. He appreciated all the consultants, he said, but the "problem was not finding out what needed to be done," which he already knew, "but getting it done quickly."[10]

Faisal also pressured Bin Laden. During the summer of 1962, he revoked Bin Laden's dormant concession to mine gypsum north of Jeddah. The contractor had a "duty not to delay," Faisal's published royal decree declared, yet Bin Laden had nonetheless "shirked" his responsibilities.[11]

The most visible example of Bin Laden's failure to deliver was his performance on the forty-five-mile mountain road linking Mecca with the resort town of Taif, a magnet for royal family vacationers. The road rose from the sandy flatlands near the Red Sea, twisting through steep, treeless, crumbly mountains, climbing almost five thousand feet. For decades the only way to traverse this distance had been on donkeys and camels; this was how Faisal and his royal train had often traveled it during the reign of Abdulaziz. By one contemporary Saudi account, it was Faisal's idea to pave the road. West German engineers pronounced it a formidable job—about thirty tunnels would have to be blasted through the mountains, great mounds of debris removed, and difficult problems of grading overcome. The Germans wanted the work but feared losing out to "dumping bids" by a local contractor who would blithely underestimate the costs and degree of difficulty.[12]

Their worries were justified. Bin Laden, as ever, insisted that he could do the job, and he won a deal worth more than $10 million in 1959; he pledged to finish the work by early 1961. He missed that deadline, however, and when a Swiss television crew turned up late that summer to film his work, they found Bin Laden and his workers stuck at a particularly steep section of the escarpment twelve miles west of Taif. Italian and Egyptian crew chiefs roared away atop German and American graders and bulldozers, but it was obvious that they were a long way from finishing. Months passed, and still Bin Laden could not complete the road. Great stores of dynamite were exhausted to dig tunnels and blast away the mountainsides. The road lay a short distance from Jeddah; for Mohamed's young boys, it was another site of thrilling explosions, in this case to move mountains.[13]

Three years later, Bin Laden was still at it. Occasionally he would host Saud or Faisal at roadside banquets, where he would pull out maps to describe the wonder of engineering that he was attempting, but the plain fact was that Bin Laden was far behind schedule, and nobody could be sure what quality of road he would finally deliver.

By one account, Faisal and Bin Laden argued about the project, with Bin Laden insisting that it was a matter of personal pride that he should finish what he had begun, even if he had to pay for it out of his own pocket. This has a slight ring of mythmaking, but there can be no doubt that there were strains between Faisal and Bin Laden at this time, and Bin Laden may have had to bear substantial losses because of his delays. He had first established himself with the royal family and its retainers by handing out commissions and sharing revenue. With Faisal, who was the least corruptible of senior Saudi princes, perhaps by many orders of magnitude, what mattered was not money, but Bin Laden's dependability, recalled Hermann Eilts, who knew both men when he served as American ambassador to the kingdom during the 1960s. Faisal knew that Bin Laden was not always as precise as his German or Swiss counterparts, yet he had been working in the kingdom faithfully for a long time, and "the point was, the roads were there." Then, too, Faisal felt a "certain amount of national pride" that for all of the enormous technical challenges on a project like the Taif road, "a Saudi firm was doing it." Faisal and Bin Laden were each pious workaholics devoted to Saudi Arabia's advancement. The trouble between them would pass, and their alliance would only deepen as Faisal consolidated power during the 1960s.[14]

Bin Laden's loyalty to Saudi Arabia was particularly at issue after late 1962, when Nasser inspired an Arab nationalist revolution in Yemen and then intervened in that country with tens of thousands of Egyptian troops, igniting a proxy war with Saudi Arabia. Nasser cranked up his propaganda broadcasts attacking the Al-Saud, launched aerial bombing raids on Saudi territory, dropped more than one hundred pallets of weapons along the Red Sea coast to encourage revolt, and conspired with sympathetic Saudi princes to overthrow the government in Riyadh. The years-long crisis that unfolded after Nasser's intervention in Yemen was the most serious external threat yet faced by the modern Saudi kingdom. As he fashioned a survival strategy, Faisal would once again employ Bin Laden's company and its vast fleet of construction equipment as instruments of Saudi defense and foreign policy—as the kingdom's Halliburton.

PRESIDENT JOHN F. KENNEDY initially regarded Nasser as a modernizer who might lift Egypt out of poverty without succumbing to Soviet communism. Kennedy doubled American aid to Nasser's regime, and even after Egyptian troops poured into Yemen and bombed Saudi towns, he urged Faisal to be patient as America tried to negotiate a compromise. This was a risky and even myopic strategy, as the Saudi government seemed to be cracking under Nasser's pressure. King Saud, more erratic than ever, flirted with Moscow. The CIA reported that Saudi merchants were shifting money to Lebanon to protect themselves against a crisis. A group of self-styled "free princes" led by the influential Talal bin Abdulaziz decamped for exile in Beirut, where they held a press conference to announce that they were freeing their household slaves; the princes tacitly promoted themselves as a progressive Saudi government-in-exile. A desperate Faisal launched a publicity drive in the kingdom to improve his government's image. He banned slavery and released his own household servants; Mohamed Bin Laden did the same, allowing the Saudi government to compensate him for their release. Faisal staged a rally in Jeddah and drove along its main streets in an open convertible. The crown prince presided over a festival of singing and dancing, and even seized on a campaign-style slogan: "We are your brothers!"[15]

Reports reached Faisal in early 1963 that Egyptian planes had dropped poison gas on Saudi-backed opposition forces in Yemen and on the Saudi town of Nejran, near the Yemen border. The Kennedy administration still counseled patience. Faisal blew up at a delegation from Washington. "He is evil," Faisal declared of Nasser. "His desires are evil." The Saudi royal family "opened our accounts in Swiss banks and others and gave him permission to take out any amount in dollars and sterling," Faisal said, but still Nasser was unsatisfied:

> What more does the man want? Obviously not our oil, as some people say; nor our money, because when he was a friend, he had easy access to it. Therefor it is obvious that he wants to satisfy his evil nature, his wicked instinct—to crush us . . . You are greatly mistaken to think you can subtly or gently guide Nasser back to the path of reasonableness or wisdom.

The only way you can make Nasser listen to you or come around to your path is by sheer force ... I know Nasser more than you do. I was his closest friend.[16]

Kennedy would eventually come around, but in the meantime, Faisal turned to Bin Laden to shore up his kingdom's southern border. That autumn he pulled road-building and infrastructure contracts out of the highway department and handed them directly to Bin Laden; Faisal said he would "personally take care" of building roads in the war zone, with Bin Laden's assistance. When Saudi inspectors flew down to look at Bin Laden's work, they found it wanting, but he told them that "he and not the Road Department would decide" how to proceed. The department's chief engineer regarded his work on the Yemen border as "a repetition on a smaller scale of the road fiasco that occurred in constructing the two modern highways leading north and southwest of Medina," but there was nothing he could do about "royal intervention."[17]

Faisal, the American embassy believed, had turned to Bin Laden "to ensure fast action on what he probably considers to be an urgent project for the defense of Saudi Arabia."[18] Also, with personal ties to Yemen, Bin Laden would be a credible figure locally as he raised a labor force and supervised construction. It was the beginning of a series of private contracts in which Faisal asked Bin Laden to build infrastructure to defend Saudi Arabia against the spillover from Yemen's guerrilla war. Bin Laden's laborers had to work at times in areas under direct bombardment. Later Bin Laden was joined in the region by the U.S. Army Corps of Engineers, which delivered American and British missiles and military infrastructure to the southern frontier. This was a role that the Bin Laden family would play for the House of Saud, in collaboration with the United States, for many years to come.

7. A MODERN MAN

THE FINAL ACT of Faisal's conflict with his half-brother Saud was inflected with macabre farce. Alcohol had ravaged Saud's stomach and produced episodes of internal bleeding, yet he could not stop drinking. His aides used a forklift to carry him onto his royal plane, a de Havilland Comet. The king and his entourage embarked on a tour of American and European hospital suites—cataract and stomach surgery in Boston, for which Aramco advanced $3.5 million; then further treatment in Lausanne, Switzerland; recuperation in Nice; and a long stay in a Vienna hospital. Periodically Saud would become coherent enough to plot a return to power. Faisal became so furious he could no longer speak Saud's name. Saud decided to arm himself, and smuggled weapons into the Nassiriyah palace to equip his sons and bodyguards, but Faisal rallied the National Guard and the army against him. The rest of the family agreed that with an undeclared war against Egypt on their hands, Saud's conniving and decadence could no longer be tolerated.[1]

As ever, the Al-Saud relied on the kingdom's Islamic scholars, or ulema, to provide them with legitimacy as they prepared to make their move. On November 3, 1964, the ulema issued a fatwa on Radio Mecca deposing Saud and naming Faisal his successor. It took months for Saud to accept his fate and go into exile, initially to Greece, and then subsequently to Egypt, where he joined with Nasser against his homeland. His disappointment over his forced abdication was presumably assuaged by his bank account: the American embassy, citing sources in the Saudi central bank, estimated Saud's wealth in exile at $100 million in cash and $300 million in invested securities.[2]

Years later, some members of the Bin Laden family quietly circulated stories suggesting that Mohamed Bin Laden had played an important role in persuading Saud to give up his throne. This looks clearly to be a case of mythmaking. The notion that Bin Laden played any role at all in Saud's abdication "is not the case," said Faisal's son Turki. "The man was a worthy man . . . But he was always the construction man. When there was a job to be done, Bin Laden would do it, and he did it at the orders of whoever was king." As a 1965 American assessment put it, Saud's overthrow "involved a surprisingly small number of decision makers." These were "certain princes of the House of Saud and a few ulema; no other estates had won the right to be consulted." As for businessmen like Bin Laden:

> Economic power with a limited degree of political influence is enjoyed by the large merchant families concentrated in the Hejaz. These merchants have no present prospect of joining the ranks of the king makers and for the present feel a near complete identity of interest with their rulers . . . To ensure this identity of interests, a leading merchant family either stations one of its members in Riyadh to stay abreast of government contracts or even details one of its own to watch over its interests . . . through having royal partners, as well as by bribery where necessary.[3]

Faisal's power was now uncontested, but the kingdom he had inherited languished in poverty and backwardness. Despite almost two decades of steadily rising oil revenue, the Al-Saud had done little to improve the lot of their subjects. Literacy rates were no higher than 10 percent, and the great majority of school-age children went uneducated. The few schools that functioned still concentrated on Koran memorization and the other religious texts through the third grade; Faisal opened the kingdom's first vocational academy only in 1962. Disease and poor sanitation remained prevalent; clean drinking water was not widely available; and four out of five Saudis were believed to suffer from trachoma, the eye disease that had afflicted King Saud.[4]

The kingdom's Bedouin population disdained manual and technical office work, preferring the freedom of self-employment as truck and taxi drivers; as a result, the kingdom suffered from a basic labor shortage, even amid high rates of unemployment. (This was the gap that Bin Laden's vast desert camps of multinational immigrant workers helped fill.) Faisal sought to follow an Islamic version of the modernization drives championed by Nasser and India's Jawaharlal Nehru, but he lacked the educated classes of civil servants, military officers, and technocrats that the British Empire had bequeathed Egypt and India. For the foreseeable future, foreigners like Bin Laden and the Lebanese builder Rafik Hariri would play major roles, along with a few Nejdi families who were moving into construction.

After six years of effort, Bin Laden at last finished the treacherous road between Mecca and Taif. During the first days of June 1965, King Faisal, senior princes, diplomats, and Jeddah dignitaries gathered under tents at a scenic way station to celebrate Bin Laden's achievement. Reporters for government radio interviewed Bin Laden, and the king "formally inaugurated" the mountain road with "considerable fanfare," as one guest described it.[5]

War emergencies and his own persistence had rehabilitated Bin Laden's public reputation. He was once more indispensable. Like his new king, the third he had served, he would strive to be a pillar of Islam and a modern man.

BIN LADEN wanted for his sons, but not for his daughters, the formal education he had never enjoyed. On his business trips to Lebanon, Syria, and Egypt, he visited the advanced boarding schools of these postcolonial Arab societies. He decided as early as the 1950s that he would use his wealth to educate many of his sons outside of Saudi Arabia. The boys' mothers had a role, too, in deciding how ambitious their education would be, and where they would enroll. By the mid-1960s, Mohamed had more than twenty young sons scattered with their mothers in households from Cairo to his own walled compound in downtown Jeddah. The Egyptian mother of Mohamed's sons Khaled and Abdulaziz enrolled her boys in Cairo schools. Several of his other boys—Bakr, Omar, and Yahya— attended school in Syria. The largest group, however, attended boarding school in Lebanon.[6]

Yeslam, one of the Lebanon contingent, recalled being placed aboard an airplane from Jeddah to Beirut at age six without understanding why he was being sent away from home. He screamed in panic on the flight and didn't see his mother again for a year, a separation that would leave him susceptible to panic attacks and a fear of flying throughout his adult life.[7] Mohamed arranged a guardian for the boys in Lebanon, Nour Beydoun, who ran a small travel agency. The children attended several different schools. Many ended up initially at a boxy stone high school, Upper Metn Secondary School, in a sedate Druze village removed from Beirut's temptations.

Tuition was about fifteen hundred dollars per boy for nine months' full boarding, plus an additional fee for summer terms, an exorbitant amount by Saudi standards of the day. The school's principal flew to Jeddah several times a year to pick up his fees in cash. He remembered that Mohamed "wanted someone to teach them religion," which was not a notable feature of Lebanese schools, so the principal specially recruited a Syrian Islamic teacher to provide Koranic instruction. Mohamed Bin Laden also wanted to avoid giving them "much money, so they will be spoiled." He instructed the principal to buy clothes as necessary and to dole out a small allowance, but not to indulge the boys. The school did provide them with a taste of Lebanon's pleasures, however, including weekend trips to stock car races in Beirut and summer outings to beach resorts.[8]

The boys knew their father as a distant, stern, even regal figure. Mohamed gathered his sons together several times a year, when they were home from school. In the style of the royal family, and of many other Saudi dignitaries, he received the boys in informal *diwaniyahs*, a courtlike gathering in which everyone sits around the edges of the room, usually propped up on pillows on the carpeted floor. Mohamed took a place of primacy and the boys sat obediently around him, pouring coffee for adult guests or presenting themselves to their father for inspection or instruction. "Most of us were afraid of him, I would say," Yeslam recalled. "He would punish us. He would lock somebody up, maybe."[9]

Bin Laden placed a heavy emphasis on frugality, work, religious piety, and self-reliance. Yet he wanted his boys to prepare themselves to inherit his business, and he understood that they would require more technical training than he had received. He "brought us up in a conformist way [but] with more concentration on education" than he had known, his son Abdullah recalled.[10]

Mohamed was not rigid or humorless. When his young son Shafiq impertinently spoke up to demand his allowance money, his father praised his spiritedness. He took the boys to his desert camps and allowed them to drive his wondrous big machines. He impressed upon them, too, the rituals and the glory of Islam. Mohamed prayed faithfully and expected the boys to do the same. Each year, at the Hajj, he proudly hosted scores of prestigious guests in an elaborately provisioned family tent. The scene was a Saudi version of that later found at Western sports events, where corporate executives hosted clients and friends in stadium luxury suites. Mohamed's boys often joined their father in Mecca for the Hajj, a large brood of handsome and growing sons circulating through the family hospitality tent, their presence at Mohamed's side reflecting honor on the patriarch.

Mohamed gave particular attention to his older sons. Succession in a business family like the Bin Ladens worked in a way similar to that in the royal family in the sense that there was a presumption that older boys would be favored, but there was also some flexibility, so that the most capable person might be placed in charge. During the 1960s, two of Mohamed's sons, Salem and Ali, seemed to be the most favored by their father. Ali was the only son of an early wife, and he did not enjoy the fancy boarding school educations of his half-brothers—his father seems to have designated him as the son who would work most closely by his side on field operations. As the war-related infrastructure projects near Yemen grew in size, Ali ran the company's regional office in Taif, an important role. He was a thin, dark-skinned young man who did not spend much time with his brothers. But if Ali seemed to be positioned by his father to become a sort of chief operating officer of the company's vast labor and construction camps, there was no question about whom Mohamed was training to become the firm's eventual chairman and chief executive, the heir to Mohamed's crucial political and marketing role of cultivating favor within the royal family. This was Salem, Mohamed's eldest son by Fatima Bahareth.[11]

During the late 1950s and early 1960s, it became fashionable in certain progressive branches of the House of Saud to dispatch sons to America and Britain for high school and university educations. Faisal sent his boys to Princeton, Georgetown, and elsewhere. Bin Laden could see that the future of Saudi Arabia lay with Faisal. If his family were to keep up, his own sons would have to be comfortable in a Riyadh court influenced by Faisal's English-speaking, university-credentialed boys. Bin Laden himself could speak only a few words of English, and while he traveled frequently to Arab capitals, he seems to have rarely, if ever, visited Europe. He preferred to keep most of his boys in Arabia or the nearby Levant, where there were guardians and mothers and other loyal relatives near at hand. For Salem, however, he made an exception. He dispatched his heir apparent to boarding school in England, to endow him with a proper British education.

In doing this, Mohamed Bin Laden initiated his Arabian family's integration with the West.

AN ELDERLY London resident of subcontinental origin, Rasma Abdullah acted as Salem's guardian in England and arranged for his schooling there. Salem seems to have arrived in Britain during the late 1950s, at about age twelve or thirteen, and to have initially enrolled at the elite English boarding school in Somerset, Millfield School. Salem's principal memory of Millfield, as he described it to a friend and business partner years later, was of a female choirmaster who taught him Christian hymns, which Salem referred to as the "group sing." Not surprisingly, given his lack of preparation, he did not stay at Millfield long. Sometime around 1960, Salem moved to Copford Glebe, a much smaller and less well-known private boarding school for boys in Essex, near the town of Colchester. He stayed here for several years. He came of age in an environment far removed from the milieu of work and Islam presided over by his father back home.[12]

The school lay at the end of a curved stone driveway amid rolling green fields. It had once been a minister's parish home, and the main building was a handsome white three-story Georgian, surrounded by smaller cottages and some trailers hauled in to serve as classrooms. There were only about forty boys during the years Salem attended—about half from overseas, the other half refugees from the better English schools. Salem's classmates included a relative of the deputy chief of the Iranian secret police, a scion of the founder of Liberia, a wealthy boy from Istanbul, and the heir to a great Portuguese arms-trading fortune. Rupert Armitage, a classmate who had transferred from Eton, found the place an "amazing sort of pastiche of an English school . . . with this ridiculous overtone of chaos, because, I mean, there were all of these crazy people there."[13]

The boys lived in small old dormitories in groups of four or five. Salem shared a dorm with a few other wealthy boys from Islamic countries. They had a small stove on which they occasionally cooked eggs stolen from the headmaster's coop. Salem smoked a pipe—Flying Dutchman was his tobacco brand—and later took up cigarettes. The days began with a miserable run, rain or shine, around the playing fields; Salem was usually in a state of comical disarray, staggering out in mismatched shoes and socks. The boys changed into blue blazers, ties, and slacks for classes, then endured another round of athletics in the afternoon. Salem's closest friend was a big Turkish boy named Mehmet Birgen, whom Salem nicknamed "Baby Elephant," and whom he occasionally goaded to fight rival boys on his behalf. It was an awkward time for many of them, particularly those, like Salem, who had no prior experience of the West. Salem amused his English friends by climbing up on the toilet seat to squat on his haunches, as he was accustomed to doing at home. He was not athletic but he was popular nonetheless—full of adventure and mischief, and particularly devoted to chasing after the residents of the nearby all-girls boarding school. Occasionally they would arrange dates with these girls to go bowling or to the movies in Colchester, and afterward they ate hamburgers at Wimpy's.

Salem's father seems to have authorized a more indulgent budget for his eldest son's British education than he did for his boys in Lebanon—or else Salem's mother figured out how to outwit her husband; in any event, Salem had considerably more pocket money than some of his Copford Glebe classmates, and even more important, he had a car, an ancient German DKW. His car was a semisecret, not officially authorized by the school, and Salem kept it hidden on a lane outside the grounds. He and his friends would sneak out on weekend nights and drive into London, where they sometimes searched for sex, but all that happened each time, according to one of his coconspirators, was that club bouncers and bartenders lightened Salem's wallet.

The Beatles and the Rolling Stones ruled England, and at Copford Glebe, Salem's friends formed "The Echoes" to chase their own rock-and-roll dreams. There was some genuine talent in the group—Rupert Armitage later became an accomplished classical guitarist, and another member, Paul Kennerley, would enjoy success as a singer-songwriter-producer and marry the multitalented Emmylou Harris. Salem was never a formal band member, as he did not have that sort of ability, but he played the harmonica at jam sessions and begged for guitar lessons. He did not have the patience for sustained study, however. He just wanted to rock.

8. CROSSWIND

BY THE MID-1960s, Mohamed Bin Laden flew around Saudi Arabia in his seven-passenger Twin Beech propeller plane the way other businessmen might travel to sales calls in a shiny Lincoln. On a typical morning a driver picked him up at his Jeddah compound at daybreak and took him to the city's airport, not far from Abdulaziz's old Khozam Palace, with the conspicuous car ramp Bin Laden had built long ago. The airport served as a base for several dozen American pilots who flew for Saudi Arabian Airlines under a contract managed by the American carrier Trans World Airlines. Bin Laden had arranged for TWA to maintain his aircraft and to supply him with pilots. The tail number of his principal Twin Beech was HZ-IBN, which incorporated the international code for Saudi Arabia. The plane was designed for a single flier, with no copilot, but it had a passenger seat up front, and this was where Bin Laden liked to sit, staring out the cockpit window with a cup of Arabic coffee in his hand. He sometimes enjoyed frightening the aides and drivers who would fly with him to his job sites by grabbing the airplane's wheel during flight and shaking it.[1]

Bin Laden got along well with his American pilots, but working for him was not a particularly popular assignment. He often flew out from Jeddah in the mornings to one of his desert sites and then spent the whole day there, meeting with engineers or walking along a highway under construction, talking with his crews. His pilot would have to wait for hours in a trailer or tent, and then fly back to Jeddah at sunset. "It was completely boring," recalled Stanley Guess, who flew the Twin Beech during the mid-1960s. Sometimes there were small enjoyments, such as flights to Jerusalem or Beirut. Bin Laden would at times take one or two of his wives to his desert camps; on those mornings, he would escort the women, covered head to toe in black, into the rear of the Twin Beech, and then pull black curtains across the cabin to protect their modesty.[2]

His camps lay spread across the desert like the oasis dwellings of nomad clans. At some, Bin Laden worked in a trailer office powered by a small generator, with an air conditioner blowing. In the cooler mountains of Asir, his aides drove stakes into the sand and erected large white canvas tents. On the floor they laid out richly colored carpets and cushions, on which the boss could sit and receive visitors like a proper desert sheikh. Outside these tents, in addition to the occasional herd of camels, stood some of Bin Laden's fleet of red Ford pickup trucks.

Bin Laden sometimes held a morning majlis in his tent, where workers or local tribes petitioned him for aid or asked him to settle disputes. "He was the law," Guess recalled. "Sometimes he'd give out some money or whatever it took to make everyone happy. They looked to him for judgment." Afterward he might settle down for a cup of coffee and a smoke from one of his four-foot-tall, elaborately painted water pipes. At some of his camps he kept green webbed-plastic lawn chairs of the sort then sprouting on the patios of American suburban homes; photographs from this period show Bin Laden relaxing at his camps on these, his water pipe in his mouth, his head draped in a traditional red-checked headdress. His body had begun to thicken and his goatee was flecked with gray. His wandering dark glass eye made him appear slightly inattentive. He dressed in a one-piece tailored robe that fell to his ankles—sometimes the traditional Saudi white, other times a slightly more fashionable design with checks or a hint of color; he strapped a fancy metal watch on the outside of the sleeve. On his feet he wore white socks and brown leather loafers. When he wasn't smoking, he calmed himself by fingering a string of worry beads.[3]

He had plenty to be anxious about; he was again overstretched during 1966 and early 1967. Faisal had given him a lucrative contract to lay a highway from Taif nearly 500 miles to the capital of Riyadh. At a place called Kilo 170, on a featureless desert plain 170 kilometers from Taif, Bin Laden built a large engineering camp with a depot of Caterpillar bulldozers, graders, and asphalt trucks. There were crews of drivers and mechanics, and hundreds of migrant laborers who slept in tents nearby. He had to tend his workers as if they were a militia camping between battles; cooks prepared meals, and truckers hauled in water from distant towns. There was no airport nearby; Bin Laden's pilots landed the Twin Beech on sections of asphalted highway or on a leveled desert strip marked with rocks.[4]

In this period, Bin Laden also regularly flew hundreds of miles east to the United Arab Emirates, along the Persian Gulf, where King Faisal had once again hired him to implement a Saudi foreign policy project—this time to build a sixty-mile, $6.7 million highway with Saudi government funds, to advance Saudi influence in the smaller Gulf kingdoms, from which the British were withdrawing. Bin Laden struggled with this Gulf highway; the site was too far for him to reach easily with his fleet of construction equipment. He formed his first foreign subsidiary in the port city of Dubai to carry out the project, but he worked slowly, and then, after missing some announced deadlines, he turned the entire job over to a local subcontractor.[5]

Bin Laden's greatest preoccupation by far, however, lay in the southern province of Asir, along the border with Yemen. Early in 1966, he was formally awarded a $120 million contract to build a difficult highway, designed by German consultants, from Taif down through the mountains to Abha, the provincial capital of Asir. One spur would then drop down a steep escarpment to the port of Jizan on the Red Sea, where Bin Laden and his brother Abdullah had first landed in Saudi Arabia as immigrant boys many decades earlier. Another road would wind east through rugged mountains to the border town of Nejran. The project was the most lu-

crative announced contract of Bin Laden's long career, and by one account he pledged not to take on any other new highway work until it was
discharged. His crews worked on the main road from both ends. His son
Ali oversaw the portion that extended south from Taif, while other crews
worked in the Yemen border and coastal areas, attempting to cut a track
up the steep cliff sides from the sea, which involved feats of blasting and
engineering similar to those that had earlier daunted Bin Laden on the
Taif road.[6]

Asir's tan-and-black volcanic mountains rose sharply from the Red
Sea beaches, soaring nearly ten thousand feet high. Its slopes and plateaus
could be barren and featureless, like a moonscape, but some of its highest peaks were flecked with pine trees; they sheltered grassy valleys where
settled tribes harvested crops of date palms, squash, melons, and grains.
The population was poor, physically isolated, habitually rebellious, and
deeply religious. Asir's political history was complex and obscure; it had
suffered through a series of Ottoman claimants before a local saint, influenced by the Shia branch of Islam, briefly established an independent
kingdom at the turn of the twentieth century. During the early 1930s,
Abdulaziz dispatched Wahhabi forces led by Faisal and Saud to conquer
the province and incorporate it into his new kingdom. They succeeded,
but neither the king nor his heir Saud paid the place much attention, preferring to spend their oil royalties at Riyadh, Mecca, Medina, and Jeddah.
After Nasser sought to stir a revolution in Yemen, Faisal recognized an
urgent need to secure the loyalty of Asir's border tribes by connecting
them to Saudi markets and promoting local development. He also embarked on a campaign of defense spending in the region. Bin Laden's
highway contract in Asir was the overt side of a multifaceted arrangement
in which Bin Laden also helped to build air force bases, garrisons, and
other secret military infrastructure around the Asiri towns of Abha and
Khamis Mushayt, and the town of Nejran.

Mohamed Bin Laden worked side by side on these classified projects
with the American and British militaries. By 1966 American attempts to

appease Nasser had yielded to a policy of arming Saudi Arabia against Egyptian incursions from Yemen. Washington signed a Military Construction Agreement with Faisal under which the U.S. Army Corps of Engineers pledged to design and help build about $100 million worth of military facilities near the kingdom's borders, including in Asir. Flight logs documenting Bin Laden's private trips during 1966 and 1967 show that he occasionally gave rides to U.S. Army personnel. In this same period, Britain agreed to sell Saudi Arabia jets, missiles, radar, and electronic warfare equipment. London supplied thirty-four Lightning jet aircraft, twenty Jet Provosts, as well as Hawk and Thunderbird missiles and related radars. The missiles were installed secretly at Khamis Mushayt, Jizan, and Nejran, where Bin Laden was simultaneously at work on roads and airfields. Faisal, in effect, employed Bin Laden as the Saudi civil engineering arm of a covert program, bolstered by British and American arms supplies, to defend the kingdom in a guerrilla war against leftist revolutionaries. It was precisely the sort of alliance that the Bin Laden family would participate in later in Afghanistan.[7]

Faisal's massive construction program in Asir reflected the degree of nervousness the king and his Western allies felt about Nasser's continuing drive to overthrow the Al-Saud. Faisal supplied money and arms to royalist Yemeni forces opposed to the Egyptians. Nasser replied by sponsoring terrorist attacks inside Saudi Arabia. On November 18, 1966, a cell of Yemeni infiltrators set off bombs at the Riyadh palace of Prince Fahd, then the Saudi interior minister. Eight days later, three more bombs exploded, including one at a hotel used by American soldiers. The next month infiltrators bombed the home of a Saudi religious leader in Nejran. Faisal's security police made arrests and concluded that the terrorists were Yemeni nationals who had been trained by Egyptians. The king launched a crackdown to prevent what a then-classified British report called "terrorist infiltrators and saboteurs" from disrupting the annual Hajj pilgrimage. The Saudis forced several Yemenis to read out confessions on national television, one of the earliest political uses of the

Saudi broadcasting network, which had only recently been inaugurated by Faisal.[8]

The thousands of Yemeni laborers in Saudi Arabia became a suspect class because of these terrorist attacks. Many fled or were deported. It was a measure of his full incorporation into the Saudi kingdom that despite his deep Yemeni roots, Bin Laden was not only regarded by Faisal as an entirely loyal subject, but was trusted to build facilities designed to defend his adopted country against his native one.

IN LATE 1966, Mohamed Bin Laden joined the jet age. To fly the international distances that his work now required, he purchased a Hawker Siddeley twin-engine jet aircraft. It cost more than a million dollars but would allow him to travel more easily to Dubai or Jerusalem. Around this time he also broke ground on a new compound of houses on the refurbished highway between Jeddah and Mecca, where he owned acres of open land in a section of Jeddah's suburbs that was then most fashionable. At Kilo 7, seven kilometers toward Mecca from the Red Sea, Bin Laden designed what would become, in effect, a small subdivision of suburban homes, one for each of his wives and some for his ex-wives and their children, along with a mosque and business offices. Bin Laden still worked hard, but he was spending some of his wealth to live and travel in finer style.[9]

The private-jet purchase proved complicated, however. Bin Laden had to locate pilots who could be trained and certified on the Hawker in England and who would then be willing to work for him in Jeddah. Also, since the new jet could not land on the desert airstrips that Bin Laden visited frequently in Asir, he would need to expand his roster of pilots, so that one might be available to fly the desert-capable Twin Beech while another flew the Hawker jet.

In the summer of 1966, Gerald Auerbach, a veteran of the United States Air Force who had flown B-47s for the Strategic Air Command, the American reconnaissance and nuclear bombing force, temporarily joined Bin Laden's crew. (A former U.S. Navy pilot named Tom Heacock had fallen ill and returned to the United States.) Auerbach was a meticulous pilot who enjoyed flying Mohamed around the desert. Bin Laden asked him to stay on as one of his permanent pilots. Auerbach's TWA supervisor told him the change would be okay but that he would lose seniority, because it was TWA's policy not to pay Bin Laden's pilots as much as those who worked commercial flights. Auerbach told Bin Laden about the problem, but Mohamed declined to make up the difference in his salary. It would prove to be a fateful decision.

In June 1967, a new American pilot turned up in Jeddah—Jim Harrington, a former fighter pilot in the U.S. Air Force, a sandy-haired man around forty years old. Auerbach decided to leave Bin Laden but agreed to train Harrington. "I took him out to some of the nastiest strips that we went into," Auerbach recalled. These included "dry riverbeds" and other makeshift landing areas in Asir with nothing but sand and rows of rocks to mark the runway.[10]

Harrington hadn't flown for several years and he "was rusty." Auerbach told their mutual supervisor: "I'm a little worried about him. This isn't routine flying." But the supervisor checked Harrington out and declared him ready to go, Auerbach recalled. In July, Harrington took over the Twin Beech and began shuttling with Bin Laden to and from Asir. Auerbach returned to Saudi commercial work.

Bin Laden was at work on the highway extension from Abha to Nejran, a road that climbed through high elevations before falling back down to a desert plain just above the Yemen border. His crews had cut the road about forty miles toward Nejran, and they had set up work sites at a small town called Oom. This was where Harrington landed the Twin Beech when Bin Laden flew down from Jeddah.

Gerald Auerbach bumped into Harrington that summer and asked how he was doing. Harrington said that everything was fine but that Bin Laden had "built a strip up in this Oom area and it's really hard. It's high elevation and it goes up a hill. It's not really good." Bin Laden's crews had used their bulldozers and graders, and cleaned off a section of desert about a thousand yards long, not a particularly long runway. The strip was on a ridge shaped like half of a bowl, so it was difficult to bank or turn to the sides while descending or ascending; you had to fly straight in and straight out, and you had to land uphill and take off downhill. The higher elevation also was an issue because in thinner air, less oxygen ran to the aircraft's engines, which could cause them to lose power.

"Well, just tell him," Auerbach told Harrington, as he later recalled it. "You're in charge. You pick a place and say I want the runway here, and he'll do it for you. He'll do it that way. Tell him this is not safe."

"Oh, I can do it," Harrington said, meaning he could handle the landings at Oom. "I can do it."[11]

On September 3, 1967, one of Mohamed Bin Laden's long-serving drivers, Omar, rode out to the airstrip with a car to await his sheikh's arrival. He saw the Twin Beech descend in clear daylight. As it made its approach over the landing area, about 150 feet in the air, a heavy crosswind blew. Harrington probably found his plane pushed out of alignment with the makeshift runway and then tried to pull up at full power, to ascend out of the bowl and go around to try again, according to what Gerald Auerbach later concluded. Auerbach, who led a team of investigators to examine the site, described what probably happened that morning after Harrington pulled back hard on the Twin Beech's throttle: "The ground is climbing. At his speed, to keep flying at that altitude, he would have had to be able to climb four or five hundred feet a minute to get out. He couldn't turn . . . The airplane didn't have that climb capability, and he ended up stalling it." Because of the thin mountain air, his engines couldn't deliver full power; this exacerbated the chance of a stall. Additional gusts of wind may have made matters worse.

The Twin Beech fell toward the desert, tilted to one side, bounced once, crashed, and burned.

The impact crushed the cockpit, where Harrington and Mohamed

Bin Laden sat. The force was so great that the front end of the plane bore a hole in the desert two to three feet deep. Both men died from the impact. Fire raced through the wreckage as Omar looked on helplessly. Two passengers in the rear cabin may have survived the initial crash but were trapped inside by a chain lock on the cabin door. They burned to death.

In an instant, Mohamed Bin Laden was gone. He was about sixty years old. The investigators identified him by his shiny watch.

PART TWO
SONS AND DAUGHTERS

September 1967 to May 1988

9. THE GUARDIANS

THE PRINCIPAL at the school in Lebanon where Mohamed had sent many of his sons called nine of the boys into his office after he received the news. "You have to be practical and logical," he recalled telling them. "All people die." He flew with three of the older boys—Hassan, Yeslam, and Mahrouz—to Jeddah. Their half-brother Ali, the eldest of Mohamed's sons then living in the kingdom, met them at the airport with a car and driver. In concert with Saudi tradition, their father had been buried quickly in an unmarked grave; the family chose Jeddah's most prestigious site, where religious pilgrims had once worshipped the tomb attributed to the biblical Eve. Days of mourning followed. Family, employees, Jeddah merchants, and princes enveloped the boys at the Bin Laden compound. Islamic and Hejazi rituals of death and remembrance, so often required in harsh Arabia, emphasized the comforts of crowds. Each evening between the sunset prayer and the final daily prayer, the Bin Laden men gathered to receive long lines of sympathetic visitors. (Mohamed's daughters and wives received visitors separately during the afternoon.) This grieving assembly offered a rare public display of family unity. Rhythmic chanting of Koran readers rang out in the humid night air.[1]

It took Salem a few days to reach Jeddah from London. After boarding school he had moved into a flat in Gloucester Place, north of Marble Arch. He had enrolled in a local college, but the friends who visited him found him less than devoted to his studies. His apartment was often filled

with young men in black leather jackets, cigarette smoke, and the occasional amateur strains of Salem's guitar.[2]

He boarded a commercial flight to Jeddah wearing jeans and a T-
shirt, his hair falling toward his shoulders. When he stepped off the plane,
his locks were shorn and he wore a white Saudi *thobe* and headdress. He
was a little older than twenty-one, suddenly and unexpectedly heir to the
largest construction firm in the kingdom. He knew little of engineering
and had only a passing acquaintance with King Faisal. He had not even
met all his half-brothers and half-sisters; some were introduced to him
for the first time at his father's funeral.[3]

Mohamed's sudden death raised immediate fears that the Bin Laden
business empire would collapse. The primary concern was that
Mohamed's many young sons and surviving brother might prove unable
to forge an orderly succession. A cable to Washington dispatched by
American ambassador Hermann Eilts on the day after Mohamed's death
summed up Jeddah's anxiety:

> Death of Mohammed Bin Laden, sole proprietor of largest construction
> company in Saudi Arabia, has caused immediate concern in both SAG
> [Saudi Arabian government] and local business circles. Under Islamic
> lawn [*sic*] assets could conceivably be divided among Bin Laden's 40
> [*sic*] sons, move which could destroy organization. However, as Saudi
> contractor displaying enough energy to handle major public works, Bin
> Laden was well established as SAG avorite [*sic*]: King, Finance Minister,
> and others aware of importance organization to Saudi economy, and re-
> ported determined it shall somehow continue.[4]

Eilts thought he saw an opportunity: a merger between the Bin Laden
organization and a major American construction company:

> One suggestion emerging in private discussions is possibility SAG will
> seek qualified foreign firm to provide management team to run organi-

zation. Company, which is financially sound, normally employs between 4 and 5 thousand workers . . . As Bin Laden operated enterprise single-handedly (to the extent even of signing all checks), need is for team not only experienced in construction operations but also competent create and impose new administrative structure. In embassy's view, this could be excellent opportunity for American firm.[5]

The ambassador suggested that Morrison-Knudsen, an American construction giant that was already working with Bin Laden on a bid to build a military cantonment near the Yemen border, might be an excellent candidate. The Americans might have to move promptly, however, as Bin Laden's technical staff was dominated by Italians and this "may encourage preference for Italian management unless other proposals advanced promptly."[6]

Mohamed Bin Laden had left twenty-five sons. (The youngest, Mohamed bin Mohamed, was born after his death and was named in remembrance.) The potential for disarray or conflict was considerable.

Abdullah, his only surviving brother, no longer had any share in the company and no longer even lived in Saudi Arabia, having moved back to the Hadhramawt with his family seven years earlier. However, harassed by rival militias engaged in Yemen's deepening civil war, he returned to Saudi Arabia not long after Mohamed's death. The Moscow-backed government of South Yemen later confiscated his house, and Abdullah never returned—a bitter end to his nostalgic homecoming. Abdullah now had his own sons and investments to look after. He had no formal claim to leadership in the company he had founded with Mohamed thirty-six years before.

Salem and Ali were the only two sons of Mohamed who had reached adulthood. But while Ali had helped oversee some of his father's road-building operations, he was far from qualified to manage the entire enterprise. Salem had been groomed for leadership by his father, but he had even less business training.

Islamic inheritance law, derived from passages in the Koran, is quite specific: It establishes conditional classes of heirs and lays out the exact percentages of the estate each class shall receive; these entitlements are seen as God's mandate and cannot be altered by a will. One Koranic principle is that sons receive twice as much as daughters. Some Westerners might regard the system as unfair or inflexible, but it has girded social cohesion and family unity in the Muslim world for centuries by removing the whim and intrigue of inheritance that often sunders families in other cultures. A wealthy Muslim man has no way to disinherit sons he does not favor; he may therefore be more inclined to encourage cooperation among his children. There is also no way to change the allocations from an estate by writing a last-minute will and testament. Written wills are permitted but only to designate up to one-third of the writer's estate for charities or other beneficiaries. There are many detailed provisions of this kind; as with prayer and the annual calendar of faith, it is an area of Islam rich with rule making and nuanced interpretation.[7]

Mohamed Bin Laden had a will written on his behalf before his death, according to the account of a Saudi researcher, Adel Toraifi, who said he had read a copy of the document. It was reported to be about eleven or twelve pages, by his account, and was primarily devoted to issues involving Mohamed's religious trust, or *waqf*. It also reportedly contained instructions on how his heirs should carry on with his charitable construction and public works in Mecca, Medina, and Jerusalem, such as those he announced in his Jerusalem speech in 1964.[8]

The principal asset of Mohamed's estate, however, was the Mohamed Bin Laden Organization itself, the family company in which Mohamed was the sole shareholder. Under Islamic law, his heirs automatically received fixed percentages. His four wives at the time of his death split one-eighth of the shares. (Former wives had no entitlement to inheritance; their children were expected to take care of them.) Nearly all the remaining shares were divided on a two-to-one basis among Mohamed's twenty-five sons and twenty-nine daughters. Each son, including Osama, inherited 2.27 percent of the company's shares, and each daughter received just over 1 percent, according to documents later filed in an American divorce case. In rough terms, then, Mohamed's sons wound up sharing ownership of just over 50 percent of the company; his daughters shared ownership of just under 30 percent; and his widows owned most of the rest. There is no evidence that any of these heirs received large cash distributions at the time of Mohamed's death; it is unlikely that he kept much of his wealth in bank accounts, and even less likely that he invested in securities. His heirs would have received his houses and his land and his cars, which they seem to have managed largely as communal holdings. Salem and Ali soon went on the company's payroll, but the great majority of his other children had not yet reached adulthood, and it would be Salem, as eldest son and head of the family, overseen by the company's board of trustees, who would determine the siblings' stipends.[9]

There is no known record of the size of Mohamed's estate at this time, nor would it have been easy to craft an estimate that would pass muster with Western accountants. Michael Pochna, an American investment banker who became a business partner of the Bin Ladens during the mid-1970s, said family members told him the estate was worth about $150 million at the time of Mohamed's death. Gerald Auerbach, the pilot who worked with Mohamed in his last years, said he was told the Saudi government owed the Bin Laden company more than $100 million when Mohamed died. These appear to be reliable indicators of the estate's approximate size, but unlike a fortune invested in stocks or bonds or actively traded real estate, Mohamed's holdings could not be easily valued. He owned a great deal of Saudi land, some of which had been given to him as payment for past contracts, but the true worth of these tracts would have been difficult to determine. His company had some hard assets, mainly tractors and bulldozers and the like, but the firm's value at the time of his death was inseparable from the massive government contracts it had recently been awarded, particularly the road from Jeddah to the

Yemen border and related defense work. If the company failed to finish these projects profitably, its finances might decline. More broadly, Bin Laden's fortune depended almost entirely on the patronage of the Al-Saud royal family; if this support disappeared, so would most of his firm's income.[10]

The king called in some of the older Bin Laden sons and told them, "I am going to be your father now."[11] Saudi Arabia was in the midst of an undeclared war, and the Mohamed Bin Laden Organization was an important part of the kingdom's defense capability. Faisal pledged to appoint several trustees to operate the family firm. This would guarantee the company's continued access to government contracts, and it would also assure Faisal that work on his crucial infrastructure projects in Asir would proceed.

Faisal issued a Royal Ordinance in mid-September announcing these new arrangements. Bin Laden's fortune "was mostly in equipment and in knowing that he could get the job done, because he had the equipment there, and he had the engineers," recalled Faisal's son Turki. The trust Faisal established would ensure "that the companies did not dissolve or go bankrupt or something, until they grew up and started taking over." The length of this interregnum was not spelled out; the decision to hand the company back to the family would be made by Faisal, or his successor, when the time seemed right.[12]

The American government continued to try to convert Bin Laden's death into a business opportunity for a U.S. company. The Commerce Department in Washington contacted major construction firms. A vice president of Brown and Root arranged to fly to Jeddah to open negotiations about a possible merger with the Bin Laden group, but the embassy waved him off, reporting that the "legal situation [is] not completely settled." Still, the State Department remained alert: Bin Laden had run his company "in an entirely personal and centralized manner. The management vacuum created by his death may make it necessary for the heirs to bring in foreign management in order to keep the company going."[13]

King Faisal asked Anwar Ali, the Pakistani-born governor of the kingdom's central bank, to provide financial and management advice to the Bin Laden trustees, a relationship that guaranteed that the company would not falter for lack of government funds. The king also designated Mohamed Bahareth, a Jeddah businessman who operated mainly in the food industry, as the company's leading trustee; Bahareth was a cousin of Salem's mother, Fatima Ahmed Bahareth. His appointment ensured the primacy of the Bahareth cluster within the larger family clan, led by the matriarch, Fatima, a senior widow of Mohamed, and her three sons, Salem, Bakr, and Ghalib.[14]

As a PIPE-SMOKING erstwhile rock musician in his early twenties, Salem was hardly the prototype of a Saudi authority figure when he returned from London, but he did not lack confidence or ambition. He was appointed, along with his half-brother Ali, to the board of trustees governing the family company, and he was given a title, managing director. From the start, however, he struggled with Ali and chafed at the committee's authority. "He wanted very much to get back and get control of the trust," recalled Francis Hunnewell, an American banker who became a partner of Salem's a few years later.[15]

In the evenings, at his house in Jeddah, Salem held court for local Bedouin, to entertain grievances and claims as his father had done before him. Some petitioners had complaints involving land. Mohamed had marked the boundaries of his various land grants as best he could, but his decisions sometimes conflicted with grazing rights or other claims by nomads. Salem found himself besieged by Bedouin bearing obscure slips of paper purporting to document their rights. Some of his friends who visited from Lebanon or London watched in amusement and admiration as Salem gradually adapted to the role of Bedouin land judge, listening patiently in his formal desert dress, trying to render decisions in the idealized manner of a fair-minded but strong-willed sheikh. One of his friends recalled that admiring petitioners nicknamed him "The Gate of Justice." Salem had few pretensions, and he embraced Arabia's egalitarian rituals, joining his brothers cross-legged on the floor for family meals.[16]

He tried to take stock of his company's road building. His father's shadow hung over everything; the remains of the plane in which he had died were placed on display at one of the company's Jeddah compounds. Salem was never much for the desert fieldwork and motivational speeches at which his father excelled. He stumbled in his early attempts at deal making. The Bin Laden organization failed to win the bid on a military cantonment in Asir that it had submitted in partnership with Morrison-Knudsen; the Saudi government now seemed uncertain about whether the firm could finish the job on time. The road the company was trying to finish in the United Arab Emirates proceeded slowly. Salem claimed his father's Hawker jet and flew off to Dubai in the spring of 1968 to inspect the work.[17]

He made no secret of his love of flying. Faisal, however, perhaps sensing Salem's impetuousness, decided that he could not abide the loss of another Bin Laden in a plane crash. Around the end of 1968, the king ordered Salem to sell the Hawker and the company's other propeller planes on the basis that they were too dangerous. The family was grounded, at least when it was in Saudi Arabia; when he was in Europe, Salem sometimes found a way to rent a plane and train as a pilot.[18]

Salem's struggle for power with his half-brother Ali deepened. Ali was tall, sensitive, and without a boarding-school education. He would later become a passionate gardener and photographer. He felt entitled to more authority than either the king's trustees or Salem would permit. Fed up, he asked the trustees to allow him to sell his share of the company and to go his own way. The trustees could not decide what to do, so Ali wrote a letter to King Faisal asking for permission to separate. Faisal granted his request and the trustees worked out a deal in which Ali was paid about $1 million for his holdings, according to the later estimates of family members. (If accurate, and if Ali received full value for his shares, the payment would suggest that the total fair market value of the company at the time was judged to be less than $50 million.) A few years later, Ali moved to Lebanon and then to Paris; he would have nothing to do with the family's business again. Salem and his full brothers were now firmly in charge.[19]

Salem married Sheikha Al-Attas, the daughter of a wealthy and prominent Hadhrami family that managed a Dutch-connected bank; the match signaled Salem's rise into the ranks of Jeddah's international merchant class. Sheikha was about as tall as Salem, slim and impressive. She had grown up in Indonesia, and she spoke, in addition to Arabic, English, French, and Dutch. Salem struck some of his friends as too young and restless to be a reliable husband, but she was a prestigious woman, and she shared Salem's taste for European travel and culture.[20]

Salem sought to prove himself to King Faisal, who would decide his future. They were far from a natural pair—one was young and irreverent, the other aging and cerebral. Whether because he doubted Salem and the viability of succession at the Bin Laden company, or because he was impatient to see his Asir projects finished, Faisal concluded within a year of Mohamed's death that the Bin Ladens should sell a large minority share of itself to a foreign partner, preferably American.

Anwar Ali, the Saudi central bank governor, led these negotiations. He made it clear that a sale would enjoy the king's favor. Ali felt the "management vacancy" left by Mohamed Bin Laden made such a merger imperative, even though it would change the character of the company. Increasingly, the kingdom turned to foreign contractors for major public works, partly to ensure higher quality materials and engineering; in that respect, a merger would help to draw the Bin Laden firm into the kingdom's modernization drive. Anwar Ali and the company trustees held discussions with German, Italian, and Dutch construction companies, but their principal target was the American consortium Morrison-Knudsen, for whom the Bin Ladens acted as agents in Saudi Arabia.[21]

Early in 1970, Anwar Ali proposed a joint venture, in which the Bin Ladens would hold 60 percent and the American company 40 percent. Morrison-Knudsen would contribute cash—half of which, more than $2 million, would be lent by the Saudi central bank. Ali flew to the United States to meet with Morrison-Knudsen executives, and he dangled a prospective contract to build a new airport in Jeddah, which would become one of the largest construction deals ever handed out to a foreign firm. But the parties bickered over how to divide responsibility in the new venture.[22]

Morrison-Knudsen proposed taking majority control of the Bin Laden company, but Ali told State Department officials this would be a "difficult ownership set-up to sell" to Faisal and the royal family, as there was "opposition to joint enterprises with majority foreign ownership." The American embassy in Jeddah, anxious to beat out European companies, wrung its hands over Morrison-Knudsen's reservations. Twenty years earlier, Bechtel had walked away from similar royal family entreaties, clearing the way for Mohamed Bin Laden's rise. Now another American construction giant was threatening to walk away from a chance to buy into the position Bin Laden had established as the kingdom's leading contractor. Yet despite Faisal's interest in the deal, Morrison-Knudsen executives felt "uneasiness over the capability to do business with somewhat unorthodox Ben Ladin organization," as one American dispatch put it.[23]

Hermann Eilts, the U.S. ambassador in Jeddah during the early stages of these negotiations, recalled that the American executives were put off "first of all" by the "disarray that was in the family," and the unwieldy system of management by its board of trustees. In addition, Eilts said, Morrison-Knudsen "was asked by some members of the Bin Laden family for bribes" to secure their agreement to a merger. "Now, it's not that Morrison-Knudsen hadn't been accustomed to that sort of thing," but in the circumstances, it helped tip their decision.[24]

Ultimately, the merger talks failed. The Bin Laden sons would have no foreign partner to ensure the viability of the company they had inherited; they were on their own.

Increasingly they seemed determined to go their separate ways. Tareq Bin Laden, a half-brother with whom Salem was particularly close, formed his own construction company and advertised in the international business press in 1970. To prove that he could handle sizable contracting jobs and perform on time, Salem and six of his brothers and half-brothers formed a separate company, Bin Laden Brothers for Contracting and Industry, two years later. The worried forecasts that had immediately followed Mohamed's death still seemed plausible: his business empire was splitting gradually because of the centrifugal ambitions of his many sons.[25]

EUROPE, Lebanon, and Jeddah were the three main venues of Bin Laden family life during the early 1970s. Mohamed's fifty-four children ranged in age from toddlers to young adults; the majority were teenagers. In many cases, they were just getting to know one another. Salem increasingly asserted himself as the family's new patriarch; it was he who handed out allowances, made decisions about schooling, and organized family gatherings and vacations.

In Jeddah there were three centers of family activity—the offices of Mohamed's old company, the new downtown offices of Bin Laden Brothers for Contracting and Industry, and the suburban housing compound at Kilo 7, on the Mecca Road, where Mohamed's widows and other family members lived. Salem moved among all these places, holding court with employees, brothers, and sisters, and paying respectful calls upon his mother on Fridays when he was in town. The minarets of a family mosque, constructed as an act of religious charity by Mohamed, loomed above the compound's flat-roofed houses. Nearby were the whitewashed, walled enclaves of Mohamed's other wives and some former wives; the women shared their homes with whichever of their sons and daughters were not away at school. The widows were generally relaxed in one another's company. "What surprised me," recalled Carmen Bin Laden, who came to live with them during the mid-1970s, "was that they were all very close to each other . . . I thought, there will be rivalries, they will not talk to each other." Instead, they treated one another as sisters.[26]

On the outskirts of Jeddah sprawled the larger compounds of their father's old company, with its vast yards of Caterpillar equipment and its ranks of Arab and European engineers and accountants. The trustees mainly ran the firm with the help of the executives and technicians who had been in place when the father died. The boys had relatively little to do with it in these years.[27]

Many of the Bin Laden boys, and some of the girls, still attended boarding school outside of Saudi Arabia. At some point after Mohamed's death, after Faisal began to oversee the children's educations, a large number of Bin Laden boys were enrolled in the elite Brummana High School in a Christian resort town nestled in the hills north of Beirut. Lebanon, then untouched by civil war, was the most sophisticated, modern country in the Arab world, religiously diverse and heavily influenced by Europe. Brummana had about seven hundred students. It accommodated primary school children as well as teenagers preparing for college. European Quaker missionaries founded the school during the early 1870s, and its main buildings, made from local stone and red tile, dated from that period. The school admitted girls from its beginning, and in 1902 it became one of the Arab world's few fully integrated coeducational schools. It later found patronage from the British royal family; the Duke of Edinburgh inaugurated a new dormitory in 1967. New science labs and a health center opened a few years later. The curriculum was mainly in English; students included members of the Saudi and Jordanian royal families, but also European teenagers whose families worked in Lebanon. There was an active athletics program and a particular emphasis on volleyball and basketball, which suited two of the taller Bin Laden boys then in attendance, Saleh and Khalil.

Their volleyball coach, Joe Ashkar, a Lebanese Christian, opened a music shop down the street from the school. The Bin Ladens "liked what we called 'underground music,'" he remembered. "The Beatles, Chicago, Jimi Hendrix, Mick Jagger." They listened, too, to mournful Arabic pop music about separation and longing. Sometimes they drove down to Beirut and went to the movies—"Elvis, Bruce Lee. No Arabic movies." They dated European girls. One of the brothers, Khaled, who lived in Egypt, married a young Danish woman during this period. Saleh ended up in a long relationship with an English girl who boarded at Brummana, but his conservative Syrian mother would not allow him to marry her; only a local girl would do.[28]

The boys were attracted to fashionable clothes, cars, and airplanes. Bakr, Salem's full brother, kept a prized Oldsmobile in Beirut. Salem hired friends to fly to Europe and drive more new cars back to Lebanon or Saudi Arabia. "They wore really wide bell-bottoms," remembered Saleh's girlfriend, Shirley Bowman. "They were just outlandish. They did it to provoke comment, really. They all had Afro-style frizzy hair, which they grew very long. Shirts open to the belly button. Beirut was the place to be." For the first time, some of them began to spend lavishly. Saleh bought expensive gifts for Bowman's mother in England, which upset her father because he couldn't afford such luxuries. Saleh "never quite understood the etiquette of Europeans," she said. Still, "he had a really good heart, and he would do anything for anybody."[29]

Authority in the Bin Laden family seemed diffuse. "The family dynasty hadn't really evolved," Bowman said. "It was the older boys who were dictating everything and keeping an eye on the sisters. Some of the sisters were allowed to study abroad, some weren't." Saleh, for his part, "was very proud of his sisters. They were all gorgeous, really. They spent thousands on clothes."[30]

Salem organized family travel to England and Sweden. He had already taken freewheeling road trips to Sweden with boarding-school friends, and he seemed drawn to Scandinavia. In September 1971, Salem organized a family trip to Falun, Sweden. "Arab Celebrity Visit" was the headline in the local newspaper:

> Salem Bin Laden visited Falun on a combined business and pleasure trip through Europe. He was accompanied by twenty-two members of his family . . . He has visited the Club Ophelia in Falun. The young sheikh is reportedly a big fan of discos and has visited the discos of Falun at various times in the past.[31]

"They were so elegantly dressed," recalled Christina Akerblad, who ran the modest hotel where the family stayed. "We saw they used the extra bed in their rooms to lay out their clothes. They had lots of white silk shirts packaged in cellophane."[32]

A photographer persuaded twenty-one members of the family to pose together, leaning against a wide-finned American sedan. The boys wore colorful bell-bottoms, low-slung belts, and brightly patterned shirts. Eleven girls or young women appeared in the picture; they looked to be in their teens or early twenties. They all wore pants, not skirts, but only one of the girls covered her hair. They laughed joyously.

Years later, one of the boys in the photograph, the second from the right, would be routinely identified in media accounts as Osama Bin Laden. There is certainly a resemblance, but Bin Laden family members said emphatically that this was a case of mistaken identity—Osama did not travel to Sweden with the group and was not in the picture. The family's testimony seems convincing, as it comes from varied sources, including some, such as Carmen Bin Laden, who have been adversaries of the family.

In any event, by the early 1970s, Osama's education had begun to take a very different course from that of most of his brothers and sisters. It was increasingly difficult to imagine him in bell-bottoms.

10. YOUNG OSAMA

OSAMA BIN LADEN'S MOTHER, Alia Ghanem, was about fifteen at the time of his birth. Mohamed Bin Laden divorced her soon afterward, probably before she was eighteen. The boy was her only child at the time. Naturally, they clung to each other during this period of change. Later, as a teenager, Osama "would lie at her feet and caress her," said Khaled Batarfi, a neighbor and friend of Osama's. He "wouldn't sleep if he knew she was upset about something."[1]

Alia was handed off from one husband to another; Mohamed arranged for her to remarry a midlevel administrator who worked at his company. This was Mohamed Al-Attas, from the prestigious family of Hadhrami descendants of the Prophet Mohamed. By the account of Batarfi, who knew him well in later years, Al-Attas was a gentle man, and he became a reliable husband and father; he and Alia eventually had four other children and incorporated Osama into a conventional Saudi household. The evidence about Osama's earliest years is thin, yet surely the inauguration of Alia's second marriage must have been a time of some uncertainty. Alia and Osama moved out of the bustling Bin Laden family compound in Jeddah, with its many wives and factions and servants, and into a more modest household with her new husband. Osama's place in this new suburban home was unusual. In one respect, he was the odd boy out, the only child of an absent father, a conspicuous stepbrother. Yet as Mohamed Bin Laden's male heir, Osama was the sole source of his new family's wealth and access to Bin Laden family privileges. The emotional complexity of his position as a young boy who was both excluded and essential, marginalized and powerful, can be readily imagined, but the truth of it is unavailable and the subject lies entirely in the realm of conjecture.

Alia remembered Osama as "a shy kid, very nice, very considerate. He has been always helpful. I tried to instill in him the fear and love of God, the respect and love for his family, neighbors and teachers." All the available testimony about Osama's early childhood emphasizes his shyness and placidity. Each summer, beginning in the late 1950s and continuing into the early 1970s, Alia and Osama, later accompanied by Osama's three stepbrothers and stepsister, traveled from Jeddah to Alia's hometown of Latakia, on the Mediterranean coast, where they stayed with Alia's family. Relatives there remembered Osama as calm and extremely quiet, to the point of timidity. He preferred to be alone, was not particularly social with his cousins, and had trouble communicating at times. Still, he was not a cause of trouble, and he did not shutter himself inside, by their account; they recalled that he particularly enjoyed swimming, hunting, and horseback riding.[2]

The Ghanem family could barely make ends meet; this may have been the reason they turned young Alia over to Mohamed Bin Laden in the first place. One section of the family cultivated fruit trees in a nearby village under a grant from the Syrian government. "If there was no agricultural reform," which provided them with this subsistence orchard, "we wouldn't have had anything," Hosam Aldin Ghanem said years later. By comparison, Osama's stepfather in Jeddah enjoyed a decent salary, and Osama may have received occasional gifts and allowances from Mohamed during his boyhood. Yet he was not so wealthy that his mother could shower her Syrian relatives with money. As the years passed and his own financial circumstances improved, Osama could seem oblivious to the economic differences between himself and his mother's less prosperous Syrian relations. There was a little island in a small lake near Latakia that Osama used to visit with his cousins. "I used to love it a lot," one of them, Soliman Ghanem, recalled. "He asked me if he could buy it to live there."[3]

Mohamed Bin Laden was a distant figure during Osama's boyhood but apparently an inspirational one. Most of the reliable evidence about Osama's relations with his father's side of the family dates to the period after his father's death, but the information available suggests that Osama was always a fully recognized member of the brood of sons that Mohamed periodically called together for inspection and religious instruction. Osama himself has spoken of knowing his father as a boy, of reciting poetry to him, of joining his work sites, and of being uplifted by his example. "He considered him as a model," said Osama's college-era friend Jamal Khalifa. "He was not with his father much" but he "heard a lot" about him. In particular, Osama absorbed the idea that his father "was not a person who sits down behind the desk and gives orders." Rather, Mohamed Bin Laden worked with his own hands in the desert, offering direct leadership to his ethnically diverse employees. This, of course, would become Osama's style of leadership as well.[4]

There is virtually no specific evidence available about which of Mohamed's work sites Osama visited as a young boy or what he saw his father doing there, other than Osama's own occasional oblique references to the Saudi holy cities and his detailed awareness of his father's work in Jerusalem. Osama would have been between six and ten years of age when Mohamed was engaged in massive demolition and urban clearance work in Mecca, quite near to Jeddah; it seems virtually certain that Osama would have visited the city at this time, during the Hajj and on other occasions. Particularly after 1965, Mohamed's other major concentration was Asir, to which he flew back and forth almost every week. His company maintained a large work camp just south of Taif, only a few hours' drive from Jeddah, as well as other camps around Abha that could be reached only by plane. Even if Osama never saw these sites, with their lava boulders and cragged peaks, where new roads were being hewed by his father's Yemeni and African workers, he would certainly have known of the breadth and importance of his father's projects along the southern border. And, of course, like everyone else in his family, Osama learned in 1967, when he was about nine years old, that his father had died in a plane crash in Asir—and that he was killed because of an apparent error by his American pilot.*

The evidence available about Osama's primary-school education is also fragmentary. It seems clear that, as with all his half-brothers, his father ensured that he was enrolled in school steadily. His mother's truncated statements suggest he probably received Koranic instruction of the sort typically given to young boys in Saudi Arabia. Yet like his half-brothers, he seems from the start to have been in schools influenced by Western curricula and culture; there is certainly no evidence that he was ever educated full time in a religious madrassa.

By the time he reached eighth grade, he was a solid if unspectacular student. He seems likely to have received some of his primary schooling in Syria, probably in connection with his mother's frequent sojourns in Latakia. His mother remembered him as "not an A student. He would pass exams with average grades. But he was loved and respected by his classmates and neighbors."[5]

Around age ten—the same age when a number of his half-brothers had been dispatched to boarding schools in Lebanon and Syria—Osama, too, enrolled briefly as a boarder at Brummana, the elite Quaker school north of Beirut. Five former students and administrators at the school, including the head of Brummana's primary school, recalled in separate interviews that Osama was enrolled there during the mid-1960s but that he withdrew and went home after less than one year. None recalled, or

---

*Five of the hijackers who crashed planes into American targets on September 11, who were recruited by Osama Bin Laden, came from Asir. There is a striking symmetry in these air crashes involving Americans and Asiris, which took place during two Septembers thirty-four years apart.

would say, why his short experiment with living away from home had failed, but it was evidently not because of bad behavior or poor grades. Renee Bazz, who was on the school's administrative staff, recalled that Osama had attended another primary school in Lebanon before his arrival at Brummana.

Emile Sawaya, the head of Brummana's primary-school section during the 1960s, remembered that Osama was about ten years old when he arrived, and that several of his half-brothers were already boarders. "He was quiet, calm, and very polite," Sawaya said. "He was obedient. He worked hard."[6]

Osama may have been in Lebanon when his father died. Sawaya recalled that Salem arrived to visit not long after Mohamed's passing. Sawaya asked another school administrator whether Salem was now the boys' guardian and was told, "No, it was the king ... King Faisal, who was their official guardian." Salem met with his brothers, Sawaya remembered. "The strange thing was that he didn't know them—we had to introduce them. When he came into the reception room, they kissed his hands." The housemaster for the primary school "introduced Osama and his brothers."[7]

Osama's stepbrother, Ahmed Mohamed, recalled visiting Beirut with him when Osama was about twelve. "He used to take us to the movies ... Cowboy, karate movies."[8] After he became notorious, rumors circulated that Osama had enjoyed Beirut's sybaritic nightlife as a teenager, but there is no evidence to support this. These rumors may have conflated Osama's presence in Lebanon as a boy with the lifestyles of some of his older half-brothers during the early 1970s.

After Osama withdrew from Brummana, he seems to have spent some time, immediately following his father's death, in his mother's hometown of Latakia. An English teacher there, Suleiman Al-Kateb, recalled that he was "affected by the death of his father; he was very solitary." By the following September, he had moved back into his mother's home in

Jeddah. After Mohamed's passing, "She was all that was there," Khaled Batarfi recalled. "He was so obedient to her." Batarfi felt that Osama grew close to his mother "maybe because he wasn't close to his father."[9]

Alia enrolled him in an elite local private school in Jeddah, the Al-Thaghr Model School, which prided itself on its modern curriculum— it was the only school in Saudi Arabia that could even begin to compare itself to a place like Brummana. Osama entered in 1968, about one year after his father's plane crash, when he was probably in either the fifth or sixth grade. He was on the cusp of puberty, and roiled, presumably, by his father's loss. He enjoyed a comfortable home and a mild, reliable stepfather, but as Mohamed's heir, he stood apart from his stepbrothers in his mother's second household: Osama was, in both a biological and a financial sense, a special case. It seems safe to assume that he was in search of guidance. In any event, the father figure he would soon encounter at Al-Thaghr would change his life.

AL-THAGHR sat on several dozen arid acres lined by eucalyptus trees, whose branches were twisted by winds from the Red Sea. The campus spread north from the Old Mecca Road, near downtown Jeddah. The school's main building was a two-story rectangle constructed from concrete and fieldstone in a featureless modern style. Inside, hallways connected two wings of classrooms; there was a wing for middle-school students, where Osama began, and another for the high school. Between them was a spacious interior courtyard, and from the second floor, students could lean over balcony railings and shout at their classmates below, or pelt them with wads of paper. Like Osama, most Al-Thaghr students were commuters, but there were a few boarders; they lived on the second floor, as did some of the school's foreign teachers.[10]

The Saudi government funded and staffed Al-Thaghr, and during the 1960s and early 1970s, the school had the reputation of a private enclave for the sons of businessmen and the royal family. Mohamed Bin Laden had periodically visited the school during the mid-1960s when it was a site for fundraisers to help found Jeddah's first university, which became King Abdulaziz University, where Osama later enrolled. Al-Thaghr offered rigorous entrance exams that any Saudi could take, and some working-class students who managed to pass attended the school along with the wealthier boys.[11]

Al-Thaghr—the name means, roughly, "The Haven"—was founded in the early 1950s in Taif by Faisal, but the school came into its own when he established its large campus in Jeddah, in 1964, and began to fund it annually with several million riyals from the national budget. Faisal's Turkish father-in-law, Kamal Adham, took an interest in the project and traveled to Britain, where he met with government officials to seek support; he told them that he thought the school should be modeled on the British-influenced Victoria College in Khartoum, Sudan. By the time Osama arrived, Al-Thaghr Model School, as it was formally called, was a showcase for Faisal's modernization drive, and particularly for his interest in science and Western methods of education. It was the only school in Jeddah with air-conditioning during the 1960s, and it hosted some of the kingdom's first classroom computers in later years. Students did not wear the national dress of a *thobe* and cloth headdress, but, rather, a uniform that imitated the styles of English and American prep schools: white button-down shirts with ties, gray slacks, black shoes and socks, and, in the winter months, charcoal blazers.[12]

Each year's graduating class numbered about sixty boys. Every morning, the students would assemble in rows for a military-style call to order; on a stool to one side sat a schoolmaster with a cane, ready to discipline boys who misbehaved by beating them on the soles of their bare feet. The school's curriculum included English-language instruction given by teachers from Ireland and England, and demanding courses in mathematics. At the same time, as with all institutions in Saudi Arabia, Al-

Thaghr adhered to Islamic ritual and included religion as an essential aspect of instruction. At midday, students would kneel together for the *zuhr*, or noon prayer.[13]

When Osama entered the school, he stood out because he was unusually tall, but he was a reticent personality. He sat by a window in a back corner of the classroom, overlooking the playground. In an intermediate-English class, recalled Brian Fyfield-Shayler, a Briton who taught at the school, "I was trying to push the spoken aspects of the language. To succeed, the student needs to be prepared to make mistakes. They need to make a bit of an exhibition of themselves, and Osama was rather shy and reserved and perhaps a little afraid of making mistakes." He was also "extraordinarily courteous . . . more courteous than the average student, probably partly because he was a bit shyer than most of the other students." Seamus O'Brien, an Irishman who taught English at Al-Thaghr, remembered Osama as "a nice fellow and a good student. There were no problems with him . . . He was a quiet lad. I suppose silent waters run deep." Another teacher, Ahmed Badeeb, remembered Osama as "in the middle" academically, an assessment that accords with the account of Osama's mother.[14]

Around 1971 or 1972, when Osama was in the eighth or ninth grade, he was invited to join an after-school Islamic study group led by one of Al-Thaghr's Syrian physical-education teachers, who lived on the second floor above the courtyard. In that period at Saudi high schools and universities, it was common to find Syrian and Egyptian teachers, many of whom had become involved with dissident Islamist political groups in their home countries. Some of these teachers were members of, or were influenced by, the Muslim Brotherhood, an Islamist organization founded in Egypt in 1928 by a schoolteacher, Hassan Al-Banna. The Brotherhood was initially a religious-minded movement opposed to British colonial rule in Egypt; later, its leaders continued their struggle against Nasser. In his approach to the Brotherhood, Nasser alternated between periods of accommodation and brutal crackdowns. Some of the Brotherhood's organizers were forced into exile, and they began to form new chapters across the Muslim world. Their aim was to replace secular and nation-alist Arab leaders with Islamic governments, and they often operated clandestinely. The movement typically recruited its members from elite, well-educated families. Its goals included the imposition throughout Muslim societies of Koranic law and the empowerment of Islamic schol-ars as cultural arbiters and dispensers of justice. Over the years, the Brotherhood operated both in the open and in secret, through peaceful political campaigning and through support for violence.

King Faisal regarded the Brotherhood with some suspicion; certainly, he and others in the royal family were wary of its penchant for political organizing across national boundaries. Still, in his campaign to outflank Nasser through appeals to Islam, Faisal found the Brotherhood's exiled teachers a useful resource. He wished to see the Saudi population edu-cated as rapidly as possible, and he had no indigenous teachers to rely upon. Brotherhood-influenced teachers were a significant grouping, par-ticularly among those educators from Syria and Egypt.[15]

In recruiting candidates for his after-school Islamic study group, the Syrian physical-education teacher at Al-Thaghr appealed to five or six boys, enticing them with promises of extra credit and organized sports. The teacher was "tall, young, in his late twenties, very fit," recalled a schoolmate of Osama's who was also a member of the study group. "He had a beard—not a long beard like a mullah, however. He didn't look like he was religious . . . He walked like an athlete, upright and confident. He was very popular. He was charismatic. He used humor, but it was planned humor, very reserved. He would plan some jokes to break the ice with us.[16]

"Some of us were athletes, some of us were not," the schoolmate re-called of the group's initial membership, which, besides Bin Laden, in-cluded the sons of several prominent Jeddah families. The Syrian "promised that if we stayed we could be part of a sports club, play soc-cer. I very much wanted to play soccer. So we began to stay after school with him from two o'clock until five. When it began, he explained that at the beginning of the session we would spend a little bit of time indoors at first, memorizing a few verses from the Koran each day, and then we would go play soccer. The idea was that if we memorized a few verses each day before soccer, by the time we finished high school we would have memorized the entire Koran, a special distinction.

"Osama was an honorable student," the schoolmate remembered. "He kept to himself, but he was honest. If you brought a sandwich to school, people would often steal it as a joke and eat it for themselves if you left it on your desk. This was a common thing. We used to leave our valuables with Osama because he never cheated. He was sober, serious. He didn't cheat or copy from others, but he didn't hide his paper, either, if others wanted to look over his shoulder."

At first, the study group proceeded as the teacher had promised. "We'd sit down, read a few verses of the Koran, translate or discuss how it should be interpreted, and many points of view would be offered. Then he'd send us out to the field. He had the key to the goodies—the lockers where the balls and athletic equipment were kept. But it turned out that the athletic part was just disorganized, an add-on. There was no organized soccer . . . I ended up playing a lot of one-on-one soccer, which is not very much fun."

As time passed, the group spent more and more time inside. After about a year, Bin Laden's schoolmate said, he began to feel trapped and bored, but by then the group had developed a sense of camaraderie, with Bin Laden emerging as one of its committed participants. Gradually, the teenagers stopped memorizing the Koran and began to read and discuss hadiths, interpretive stories of the life of the Prophet Mohamed, of varied provenance, which are normally studied to help illuminate the ideas imparted by the Koran. The after-school study sessions took place in the Syrian gym teacher's room; he would light a candle on a table in the middle of the room, and the boys, including Osama, would sit on the floor and listen. The stories that the Syrian told were ambiguous as to time and place, the schoolmate recalled, and they were not explicitly set in the time of the Prophet, as are traditional hadiths. Increasingly the Syrian teacher told them "stories that were really violent," the schoolmate remembered. "It was mesmerizing."

The schoolmate said he could remember one in particular: It was a story "about a boy who found God—exactly like us, our age. He wanted to please God and he found that his father was standing in his way. The father was pulling the rug out from under him when he went to pray." The Syrian "told the story slowly, but he was referring to 'this brave boy' or 'this righteous boy' as he moved toward the story's climax. He explained that the father had a gun. He went through twenty minutes of the boy's preparation, step by step—the bullets, loading the gun, making a plan. Finally, the boy shot the father." As he recounted this climax, the Syrian declared, "Lord be praised—Islam was released in that home." As the schoolmate recounted it, "I watched the other boys, fourteen-year-old boys, their mouths open. By the grace of God, I said 'No' to myself ... I had a feeling of anxiety. I began immediately to think of excuses and how I could avoid coming back."

The next day, he stopped attending. But during the next several years, he watched as Osama and the others in his former group, who continued to study with the gym teacher, openly adopted the styles and convictions of teenage Islamic activists. They let their young beards grow, shortened their trouser legs, and declined to iron their shirts (ostensibly to imitate the style of the Prophet's dress), and increasingly, they lectured or debated other students at Al-Thaghr about the urgent need to restore pure Islamic law across the Arab world.

By the time of Osama's high school years, Al-Thaghr had become something of a hotbed of debate, within the limits of Saudi Arabia's dull political culture, involving Nasser-influenced students who advocated pan-Arab nationalism, and Brotherhood-influenced students who argued for a restoration of Islam in Arab politics. Osama was clearly in the latter camp; he "joined the religious committee" at the school, recalled Ahmed Badeeb. "He was a prominent member," remembered

Khaled Batarfi. "That group was influenced by the Brotherhood. He was influenced by this philosophy." Batarfi's account is corroborated by Jamal Khashoggi, who knew Bin Laden during the 1980s; he said Osama "started as a Muslim Brother," meaning that he was formally recruited into the movement during his adolescent years or soon thereafter.[17]

The Brotherhood, to which Khashoggi also belonged for a time, "is a membership," he said. "Usually you will be selected." Recruits "go through different stages." Weekly meetings and religious instruction might unfold for two years before a recruit is invited to "more exclusive meetings . . . And they will say, 'Do you want to be a part of the Muslim Brotherhood?' Mostly he will say 'Yes,' because he will have felt that it is coming . . . And he will become part of the movement." Brotherhood recruiting is often secretive, and its classes of membership have varied over time and from country to country. There is no specific evidence available about when or in what way Osama formally joined, but the Brotherhood normally takes only adults into full membership, so it seems most likely that his schoolyard activism served as a sort of apprenticeship for more formal participation in the movement after he reached university.[18]

The Brotherhood's Egyptian roots and emphasis on political activity would have an influence on the course of Osama's life once he reached adulthood. In high school, however, its precepts were probably difficult to distinguish from the general emphasis on Islamic piety that Faisal promoted in Saudi Arabia as an antidote to Nasserism. Largely because of the Saudi royal family's repression of political organizing in the kingdom, religious scholars usually tried to avoid overt politics, preferring instead to concentrate on the theological topics of prayer, Islamic rituals, and a Muslim's private conduct. Bin Laden's group at Al-Thaghr, Khaled Batarfi said, was influenced to some extent by this emphasis on the search for a truly Islamic life, but it also adopted "a more activist or a political agenda" drawn from the Brotherhood. Saud Al-Faisal, a son of the king who would become foreign minister of Saudi Arabia, complained years later that Islamist teachers from Egypt and Syria had "misused" the hospitality offered them by preaching politics. "We dealt with them honestly, and they dealt with us underhandedly."[19]

In June 1973, when Osama was finishing tenth grade, the British ambassador to the kingdom composed a confidential report for the Foreign and Commonwealth Office titled "The Young People of Saudi Arabia." His findings suggested that Osama's education, while perhaps more ideological than that of some of his peers, was hardly unusual. The ambassador wrote:

> The Royal Family are alive to the dangers to their position that education could represent if modern ideas were allowed to flow so freely in schools ... that they challenged traditional beliefs and customs. Thus the study of Islam features very heavily ... Prominent families will admit that in choosing to send their children to school abroad, for example to the Lebanon, they are influenced not by any lack of quality in teaching of the best local private schools, but the fact that the syllabus is so taken up with religious instruction and study as not to leave enough time for the children to reach normal proficiency in other subjects.

The report described how teenagers in these local elite schools were taught to understand the place of Saudi Arabia and its holy cities in the wider world:

> That God should have endowed his Holy Land with the means to finance it by the accident of oil is seen as a natural part of His plan for a world Islamic revival. Islamic maps in local classrooms show Saudi Arabia at the centre of the world, with two concentric circles drawn around Mecca. The Arab and other Islamic countries are coloured bright green, and countries with Muslim minorities ... in gradually paler shades of green. Most other parts of the world are not even named.[20]

. . .

A FEW YEARS AFTER he enrolled at Al-Thaghr, Osama moved with his family into a comfortable new suburban house in the Al-Musharifah neighborhood of Jeddah. At the time it was one of the city's newest residential areas. The local roads were not asphalted, and patches of open desert wasteland separated the houses, where neighborhood boys played soccer and other games. The ground was slightly elevated, and it was possible on some days to see the Red Sea in the distance. The house Osama shared with his mother and her four other children by Mohamed Al-Attas was spacious but not luxurious—two full stories, with four bedrooms, one of which Osama occupied by himself on the ground floor. As is common in Saudi Arabia, walls and iron railings surrounded the house; it had a garden but no swimming pool.[21]

Osama was a fan of a professional soccer team in Jeddah, Al-'Alim, and he played on a boys' team captained by his neighbor Khaled Batarfi. "He was tall, and so I would put him in front to use his head," Batarfi remembered. "Sometimes I would put him on defense." Once, when they were playing in another area, a boy on the opposing team became angry at Bin Laden and seemed as if he was about to hit him. Batarfi pushed the boy out of the way, but Osama told him, as Batarfi recalled it, "I was going to resolve this peacefully." Batarfi said that years later, he and Osama used to laugh about the incident's irony—"Osama the peaceful negotiator," as Batarfi put it.[22]

After he became immersed in Al-Thaghr's student Islamic movement, Osama could be a stickler on matters of religious conduct—quiet, usually, but insistent. He prayed five times a day, called other boys to join him, and insisted that they wear long pants on the soccer field, as Saudi religious teachers said was proper. "His younger stepsiblings respected him very much," Batarfi said. "He was older. He was tough on them on religious issues, on not mixing with girls, on being modest around women.

When a female servant came into the room, he would duck his head modestly and not look at her."[23]

Batarfi said he and Osama watched television together—soccer games, both Saudi and international, but also American family fare such as *Bonanza*. Osama was a particular fan of action films and Westerns, especially those with prominent roles for horses. Batarfi recalled that they watched the American television series *Fury*, which was made between 1955 and 1960, and then was syndicated around the world, usually under the title *Brave Stallion*. The show was about a troubled orphaned boy named Joey who goes to live on the Broken Wheel Ranch with a man who has lost his own wife and son in an automobile accident. The boy learns to tame wild horses and becomes particularly close to Fury, a black stallion; through this relationship, the wounds of Joey's earlier life are gradually healed. The sources of appeal in this narrative for Osama are not difficult to imagine; in any event, as he grew up, he became passionate about horses. His father had left a family farm—more of a desert ranch—outside of Jeddah, a place that was shared by his sons and daughters after his death. Osama spent weekends there with half-brothers from his father's side of the family and learned to ride and handle horses. Later he acquired his own ranch, south of Jeddah, where he ultimately kept as many as twenty horses.[24]

Many years later, some members of the Bin Laden family, in seeking to distance themselves in public from Osama, emphasized that he had grown up in a separate household and did not have much contact with his half-siblings while he was in high school. It was certainly true that he lived away from the principal family compound with his stepfamily, but he seems to have had at least as much contact with his father's children as did other similar "singleton" boys without full brothers or sisters. Batarfi remembered that Osama would "visit his Mohamed Bin Laden brothers on weekends and such." Moreover, some of these half-brothers were enrolled with him at Al-Thaghr; the teacher Fyfield-Shayler recalled that "several" of Osama's half-brothers were students at the school during various periods when Osama was also there. He seems clearly to have had a sense of himself as one of his father's heirs and to have harbored ambition to work in the family construction firm; his cousins in Syria and his mother all recall his interest in the company, and one cousin remembers him speaking of his aspirations to leadership there. As Salem gradually established his grip on the family during the early 1970s, Osama was far from isolated.[25]

It was Salem, in his role as overseer of his siblings' education, who first brought the family into contact with Pakistan and Afghanistan. Late in 1973, Salem decided to enroll two of his half-sisters at a boarding school in Peshawar, a Pakistani city on the Afghan frontier. At the time, Pakistan and Afghanistan were enjoying periods of relative quietude. The chief engineer at the Mohamed Bin Laden Organization, as it was still called, was a Jordanian whose wife happened to be the daughter of the governor of Pakistan's Northwest Frontier Province, of which Peshawar is the capital. Salem flew to Peshawar on a private airplane with his wife, Sheikha, his two school-aged sisters, the Jordanian, and his wife. The local stores were poorly provisioned, and in those days, Kabul, the Afghan capital, was a relatively prosperous town with thriving markets. Salem decided to fly his sisters there to shop for supplies for their school year ahead—pots, pans, dishes, and the like. Once in Kabul, Salem met the Saudi ambassador to Afghanistan and disappeared on business; he sent his sisters into the city's markets with the American pilot who had flown in with them. Later they all flew back to Peshawar and settled the girls into school. So far as is known, it was the first visit by members of the Bin Laden family to Peshawar. There would be many more.[26]

11. REALM OF CONSPIRACY

THE TENETS OF Osama Bin Laden's education were inseparable from the national ideology promoted by King Faisal in the late years of his reign. Al-Thaghr was not idly named a "model" school; it was a conspicuous example of Faisal's program of modernization without secularization. The Muslim Brotherhood's revolutionary goals made the king uncomfortable because they challenged the authority of the Al-Saud family, yet Faisal's own vision of a politically conscious Islam echoed the Brotherhood's call for action against enemies of the faith. After the 1967 Arab-Israeli war, for example, Faisal spoke repeatedly of a jihad to retake Jerusalem. His speeches denouncing the Israelis as an "impudent gang" bent on the "desecration" of Islam were not just designed to pander to Arab popular opinion; they were deeply felt, voiced by the king as forcefully in private as in public. As a young and increasingly active Saudi subject at Al-Thaghr, Osama identified with Faisal's campaign against Israel—after all, his father had been the king's emissary to Jerusalem before the 1967 war. Osama's radicalization during high school did not, then, carry him into a state of opposition toward the Saudi government; in some respects, it deepened his alignment with Faisal's foreign policy.[1]

Faisal was a popular king because the synthesis of Islam and modernity he called for was consistent with the choices he made in his private life. There was no free press or political opposition to investigate and expose the hypocrisy of the Saudi royal family's irreligious self-indulgence, yet through rumor, informal observation, and Western press reports that filtered in, Saudis knew well enough which princes drank or gambled or extorted commissions from business contracts. By these channels they learned, too, that Faisal was exceptional. He refused to move into a garish palace built for him in Jeddah, preferring a suburban-style compound on a busy road. He had long ago given up alcohol. Operations on his digestive tract had left him able to tolerate only a bland diet of grilled meat, boiled vegetables, and rice. He worked several hours each morning at his palace office, prayed, held a working lunch, meditated privately, and then returned to his office for a second shift. At sunset each day he drove in one of his American sedans to the edge of the desert, sometimes taking his sons along, where he prayed alone in the sand. He returned yet again to his office to work into the night.[2]

For years Faisal had talked about transforming Saudi Arabia into a modern country but had delivered little. That had changed by the late 1960s. Gradually the Saudi state became a pervasive force in its subjects' lives—an employer, an issuer of identity cards and passports, and a repository of commercial records. The long and troubled national highway program slowly linked the kingdom's disparate regions. A few schools and universities opened. The ministries of Faisal's government were far from efficient, but they now employed large numbers of Saudis, and in contrast to previous decades, they often issued their paychecks on time.

Faisal's marriage to Iffat bint Ahmed Al-Thunayan, who became known as Queen Iffat, offered the most inspiring example—at least for women—of the king's modernizing impulses. He had not always lived monogamously, but Iffat had been his only wife since about 1940, and by the 1960s, she had become an archetype of progressive womanhood, in a Saudi style. She had been raised in Istanbul to a Saudi father and a Hungarian or Circassian mother, and she was influenced by Turkish secularism as she came of age. She and Faisal had nine children. Iffat adhered to Wahhabi rules, never accompanying her husband on state visits or appearing unveiled before the Saudi public, yet she managed nonetheless to campaign on women's issues. As early as 1955, she founded a school for orphaned girls, and supported girls' education even in the kingdom's most conservative regions.

She also traveled widely, shopped for modern clothes in Paris and San Francisco (only her husband and other women would see her wear them in Saudi Arabia), and promoted the business endeavors of her half-brother Kamal Adham, who became conspicuously wealthy. Adham served as one of Faisal's most trusted emissaries, delivering cash subsidies to favored Arab leaders. In the early 1970s, Faisal appointed him as the first director of Saudi intelligence.[3]

The king did need someone to watch his back. Nasser had been weakened by his failure in the 1967 war against Israel, yet his pan-Arab nationalist movement, and its offshoots, such as Baathism, still threatened the Al-Saud. In 1969 the Saudi government arrested several hundred Saudis, including sixty to seventy military officers, whom Faisal suspected of plotting to kill him or overthrow his regime. The detentions quelled dissent, reported the bureau of intelligence and research at the U.S. Department of State, and yet "the basic causes of dissatisfaction remain. The process of modernization is creating a new middle-class elite in the military, bureaucratic and commercial fields. Many of the new elite are antagonized by the concentration of power in the Saudi royal family [and] they chafe at the narrow limits on social freedom and political expression."[4]

Nasser died in 1970, succeeded by Anwar Sadat, with whom Faisal developed an alliance and a friendship. They were both cautious men, yet they shared a desire to avenge past losses to Israel. Faisal was profoundly anti-Semitic. From boyhood he had been instructed in a school of Islamic scholarship that cast Arabia's Jews as treacherous betrayers in the narrative of war that culminated in the birth of the Prophet Mohamed's new religion. As king, Faisal subscribed wholeheartedly to conspiracy theories about secret Jewish power. He regarded communism as a clever plot by Jews in their quest for world domination. During meetings with foreign visitors, he would often turn to his chief of protocol and ask, "Have they got the book?" The king was referring to *The Protocols of the Elders of Zion*, a notorious forgery about Jewish plotting, copies of which Faisal kept in a bookshelf outside his reception room, so they could be handed out as gifts.[5]

A pointed British memo summed up the tensions eating at the Saudi king during these years:

He is formidable if over-bearing in argument . . . The effect of sickness and advancing years has been to make him tetchy, opinionated and impatient of contradiction . . . He has in his recent years been almost obsessed by an apocalyptic vision of the forces of religion and morality (conveniently identified with his regime) being sapped by atheism, communism and Zionism. He has made his choice between the political west and east, but he is disenchanted with the west for its lack of support for him and his causes.[6]

Richard Nixon, better qualified than some world leaders to recognize a man with paranoid and anti-Semitic tendencies, remembered that Faisal "even put forward what must be the ultimate conspiratorialist notion: that the Zionists were behind the Palestinian terrorists." Nixon's Jewish national security advisor, Henry Kissinger, endured several of Faisal's long harangues on the "dual conspiracy of Jews and communists," which tested the diplomat's patience considerably.[7]

Faisal's theories might disappoint London and Washington, but ultimately, in an indirect fashion, his convictions helped to enrich Saudi Arabia beyond the king's imagining. When Sadat told him early in October 1973 that Egypt and Syria had prepared a surprise attack against Israel, Faisal unhesitatingly pledged his support. The war that followed, although it proved another disappointment for Arab forces, led to a prolonged international oil embargo imposed by Arab producers, of which Saudi Arabia was the largest. The embargo was designed in part to punish the United States for its airlift of military supplies to Israel. For a time, the Nixon administration was so infuriated that it developed contingency plans for an invasion of Saudi oil fields. Faisal, however, sensed just how far he could go, and he bent just enough to keep the Americans at bay—he secretly allowed oil sales to support American forces fighting communists in Vietnam, for example, and he also agreed to pour billions of dollars from the embargo's cash windfall into U.S. Treasury bonds.

The embargo was not a Saudi initiative, but it did more to transform the kingdom than any event since the discovery of oil itself. Faisal was arguably the 1973 war's biggest winner.

The price of Saudi crude soared sixfold by early 1974 and kept rising. The kingdom's gross domestic product quadrupled between 1973 and 1975. Its oil revenue had been about $4.3 billion in 1973; it now zigzagged upward each year, to a peak of $102 billion by 1981. This gusher of cash stimulated a new boom in construction and luxury imports that exploded so quickly it choked Jeddah's ports; ships lined up for weeks to unload or pick up goods. Hotel lobbies teemed with frustrated salesmen unable to find a vacant room. In Jeddah a new Safeway opened, its shelves stocked with Jell-O and Campbell's soups. Queen Elizabeth flew in for a visit and commented, "I've never seen so many cranes in my life." Faisal's grandson Amr remembered that "you'd go away for a summer holiday, and you'd come back, and you'd get lost . . . Things that would normally have taken twenty years to do were done in a few months. And it made people a little bit crazy."[8]

The boom seemed only to deepen the frugal Faisal's dour mood. He particularly deplored the cultural styles of his kingdom's nouveaux riches. "In one generation we went from riding camels to driving Cadillacs," he commented. "The way we are spending money today, I fear we will soon be riding camels again."[9]

Faisal bin Musaid, a nephew of King Faisal, was a failed graduate student in political science who had pleaded guilty to conspiring to sell LSD while at the University of Colorado and then had been sent home

from the University of California at Berkeley. In 1965 his brother had
been shot dead by Saudi police during a protest against the kingdom's television studio in Riyadh; the protestors feared that television would undermine Islam. Musaid, who apparently lived in a chronic state of
intoxication, decided to avenge his brother's death.[10]

King Faisal held open majlis receptions about twice weekly, and on
March 25, 1975, Musaid followed an old acquaintance, the Kuwaiti oil
minister, into the palace hall, shielding himself behind the minister's
girth. He pulled out a .38-caliber pistol and fired three shots at Faisal,
striking him in the throat. Guards wrestled Musaid to the floor as aides
rushed the king to the Central Hospital in Riyadh, one of the monuments
to Faisal's development campaigns. A blood transfusion and heart massage failed, however, and Faisal died that afternoon. The king was sixty-
nine years old. Mourners hoisted his body, wrapped in brown cloth, onto
a gurney and carried it through the streets of Riyadh to the royal family's burial ground. Three months later, twenty thousand Saudis watched
an executioner behead Musaid in a public square.

Faisal's murder deprived the Bin Laden family of its patron and pro-
tector, and it marked the end of a long and extraordinary partnership between the king and the family, in pursuit of Saudi modernization. If the
alliance was to continue, it would require a new understanding among
the next generation of leaders—for the Bin Ladens, Salem, now about
thirty years old, and for the Al-Saud, Crown Prince Fahd, who took the
reins of government after Faisal's death.

Faisal and Mohamed Bin Laden had forged a bond because they had
compatible values and work habits. Salem and Fahd would prove compatible as well. The values and habits they shared, however, were notably
less pious.

FAHD BIN ABDULAZIZ had reached his early fifties at the time of
Faisal's assassination. He was a tall man whose body seemed to spread out

around him a little more as each year passed. He sported a thin goatee on his round, double-chinned face, which had a placid aspect. His dark, hooded eyes could seem sad and withdrawn. Fahd had been raised along with many of his brothers and half-brothers in the informal schools of the premodern Riyadh court. He was distinguished from an early age, in the judgment of his family, by his interest in affairs of state. He watched attentively his father's decision making and he seemed naturally intelligent. For these reasons he was promoted early on as a candidate to run ministries and to join the royal line of succession. He served first as education minister and then as interior minister, an important security post, and began to travel abroad during the 1960s. He was attracted to the West but showed little capacity for self-discipline when confronted with its entertainments and temptations. Beginning in the mid-1960s, he began to spend several months each year in Europe and America, drifting with his entourage from luxury hotel to luxury hotel. He gambled conspicuously and rotated his wives whenever the whim struck him, which seemed to be quite often. Among his more notorious mistresses was a Palestinian Christian woman known as "Miss Arabia," so called because that was the name of the fashion boutique she ran in Jeddah.[11]

Fahd was the eldest of a group of seven full brothers within the royal family who possessed unusual influence because of the sheer size of their clan, their relative seniority, and the competence in office several of them displayed. They were sometimes referred to as the "Sudayri Seven" because their mother came from the Sudayri family. Fahd appointed or reaffirmed several of his full brothers in key security positions—Sultan, as defense minister; Nayef, as interior minister; and Ahmed, as deputy interior minister. In addition, his full brother Salman served as governor of Riyadh. Their personalities and political outlooks varied, but the seven brothers were, overall, a relatively liberal group with a taste for wealth and luxury that was notable even by Al-Saud standards. This was particularly true of Sultan and Fahd.

As Fahd became obese, his sojourns in the West were increasingly taken up by visits to hospitals, where he was treated for heart and other disorders aggravated by his weight. Eventually he found it difficult to climb stairs or to walk more than a short distance. He found that Western governments were eager to ensure that he received the very best care available. The United States, in particular, pegged Fahd as an up-and-comer in the Saudi royal family, a man whose extravagant habits and accommodating personality seemed to promise a more pliant partnership than had proved possible with Faisal.

In 1969 the United States invited Fahd on the first of a series of private visits, during which he was flattered by a personal audience with President Nixon and flown by the Pentagon to Cape Kennedy, where the National Aeronautics and Space Administration laid on a private tour. In private conversations with American and British officials, Fahd did not hesitate to repudiate Faisal's anti-Zionism, and he hinted that when he attained power, he would be willing to recognize Israel if a broader peace were agreed. He felt that only the United States could guarantee that no rival power would steal Saudi Arabia's wealth, and so he was willing to go further than some of his brothers to win American military protection. Unlike Faisal, however, Fahd did not have a particularly activist or global vision of his own or his kingdom's role in the world. He wanted as a general matter to be left alone, so that he could enjoy himself, and he wanted Saudi Arabia to be somewhat more influenced by European culture. He announced plans to build the Riyadh Opera House—its acoustics were superb, and it would probably have been the finest concert hall in the Middle East, though it never opened due to objections from religious scholars. The episode was typical of Fahd—he was at once bold and timid, but under pressure, he usually reacted more as a caretaker than a leader.[12]

He strained against Wahhabi convention. Faisal rebuked Fahd over some of his more outrageous behavior, such as his loss of millions of dollars in casinos in the south of France in 1974. Perhaps it was Fahd's irritation with his older half-brother's holier-than-thou attitude that led him to think about how he might carve a little breathing space and variety into Saudi culture. In a private meeting with an American official in the summer of 1972, during one of his long respites abroad, Fahd described Islam as

> a stable but flexible framework within which and under whose guidance the needs of the future can be met. But there is no requirement for growing Islamic societies to abide indefinitely by the strictest Islamic tenets. Prevailing views of 80-year-old religious leaders need not be meticulously observed ... Somehow a more progressive outlook needed to be imparted to judges and religious lecturers who do so much to determine the characteristics the Saudi hierarchy represents to its own people.[13]

Fahd did not immediately become king upon Faisal's death. The crown fell instead to Khalid bin Abdulaziz, who was ten years older than Fahd and came from a different branch of the royal family. Faisal had chosen Khalid as his heir in 1965; his rectitude and unassuming manner made him a natural choice after the traumas inflicted by King Saud. Khalid was a lightly educated, pleasant man who displayed no interest in government, politics, or foreign affairs. He dropped out of public life from time to time to devote himself to farming and ranching; he was one of the first princes to establish country estates in the deserts surrounding Riyadh, and he prided himself on the dairy cows and other animals he kept there. To fund his bucolic leisure, he started a number of businesses. "He has been described as a known percentage maker on governmental contracts," a classified American biographical sketch noted.[14] This was not a notable source of distinction among Saudi princes, but it indicated where Khalid's priorities lay after he became king. By his own inclination and with consensus support from the family's senior brothers, Khalid turned management of the Saudi government over to Fahd and retired to enjoy the pleasures of being a figurehead farmer-king.

Fahd's sudden rise to power within the royal family in the summer of 1975 coincided with Salem Bin Laden's restlessness. His family's main company was still overseen by the trustees appointed by Faisal eight years earlier. The post-embargo oil boom had created rich opportunities for Saudi construction companies, yet the Bin Ladens, with their dissipated leadership, were in danger of missing out on many of the larger contracts. They required Fahd's patronage, and to attain it, they had to build deeper personal connections with the new crown prince and his six full brothers. This became Salem Bin Laden's mission. He would woo Fahd and the Sudayris as his father had charmed their predecessors.

12. THE RISING SON

SALEM BIN LADEN had a guileless quality, a giddy and childlike joyousness that allowed him, even as he reached his thirties, to get away with outrageous stunts and pronouncements. The Saudi royal family enforced an acute culture of decorum; like the fool in a Shakespearean court drama, Salem entertained them by violating their etiquette without giving profound offense. He had a particular habit, remembered by many of his friends and employees, of speaking frankly about the gas he passed. Once, in the company of the august governor of Riyadh, Salman bin Abdulaziz, Salem noisily let himself go. This was as taboo in Bedouin culture as in a French drawing room. Prince Salman asked Salem what had happened. "I just farted, Prince," he answered. "Don't you fart sometimes?" He once offended a minister by turning up late and poorly dressed to an important meeting. "I thought you were a man," the minister said angrily. "Who told you I am a man?" Salem replied. "I am a kid!"[1]

His father had cultivated the royal family by attending religious ceremonies in Mecca and Medina, or by leading tours of his construction sites. Salem took other approaches. Many of the younger royals were contemporaries who had traveled abroad and shared his appetite for adventure and experimentation during the late 1960s and early 1970s. Other important princes, like Fahd, were older, yet they delighted in Salem's enthusiasm for Europe, women, fast cars, and private planes. Salem's challenge was to develop genuine friendships with these royal decision makers even while assuring them, too, that he knew his rank. Speaking of Fahd, Salem once told a friend, "He can break me or he can make me—one word out of his mouth."[2]

Each winter many of the senior Al-Saud princes drove out in convoys from Riyadh or Jeddah to camp for several weeks in the desert. The weather was cool and it rained occasionally. Flowers and green grasses blossomed amid the cacti and thornbushes. The trips offered a chance for a prince to return to the land, reaffirm his Bedouin identity, and relive memories of his youth. The expeditions were also good politics, the equivalent of a Western politician's bus or railroad tour through the heartland. Bedouin gathered for feasts with the royal campers, and they would line up to receive cash gifts or to petition for local development projects.

One February afternoon during the mid-1970s, a German pilot and writer named Wolf Heckmann landed a novelty glider at an airstrip in the northern Saudi desert, near the pipeline that transported Saudi crude west from the Persian Gulf to Jordan and Syria. Heckmann was attempting to set an informal world record by flying his plane, OSKAR, which had a small sixty-horsepower engine, about ten thousand miles from Dachau to Australia. As he was refueling, a "thin man, looking like a teenager, in Arabic clothing, dagger and pistol in his belt," approached him. This was Salem Bin Laden. When Salem learned about Heckmann's adventure, he could barely contain himself. He dragged the German into his room in a guesthouse. "Until three in the morning, we talked about adventures in the sky," Heckmann recalled.[3]

Salem said he would be visiting two princes, Nayef and Ahmed, who were full brothers of Fahd, at their winter desert hunting camp the next morning, and he invited Heckmann to join him. The princes had pitched their tents across the border in Iraq, then ruled by Saddam Hussein, but Salem said they would have no trouble crossing into Iraq's police state, since they were guests of Saudi royalty.

Salem climbed into an American-made Jeep the next morning with several aides and six hooded hunting falcons. Heckmann took the wheel of a second vehicle. "The Sheikh drove with hell-like speed," he later wrote:

> Sometimes we followed the traces of other cars, but in most cases, Sheikh Salem would just drive cross-country like a maniac. The area was full of biblical thornbushes, which had strong roots in the sandy soil. In front of each of these, the ever-blowing wind had created little dunes. The Sheikh's soft-spring mounted Jeep drove over those like a ship in a storm . . . Sometimes we would shoot over waves like ski jumpers—only the landing wasn't as elegant.[4]

The Arab passengers in Heckmann's vehicle shook his hand in admiration when they stopped. "A brutal iron foot on the accelerator was apparently seen as the highest driving skill," he noted correctly. He and Salem joined Nayef and Ahmed in a tent heated by a fire pit fueled with smoky wood from thornbushes. Prince Ahmed coughed and commented acidly, "Central heating wouldn't hurt."

Salem unpacked his falcons and hunted with the two senior Sudayri princes, one of whom, Nayef, was about to become the kingdom's powerful interior minister, with Ahmed serving as his chief deputy. Heckmann observed the ease with which Salem crossed from one world to another: "There Sheikh Salem was sitting, his long legs crossed as if he had spent his whole life sitting around a fire basin in a desert hunting camp, when, in fact, he also had completed all-round studies in London, was leading a construction empire, and was able to develop intelligent and even inventive thoughts about economic and political subjects."[5]

Crown Prince Fahd's camps, by comparison, were not plagued by wood smoke. He typically drove out four or five hours from Riyadh in a convoy of fifty or sixty Mercedes trucks and well-appointed trailers; his winter camp came to include a mobile hospital suite staffed by rotating American doctors. Fahd seemed to enjoy being away from Riyadh and the pressures of office; he would sometimes remain in the desert for five or six weeks. The sojourns attracted a swarm of camp followers who pitched their own tents nearby and tried to spend as much time in His Majesty's presence as possible. Salem was often a part of Fahd's invited entourage, and he set up his own site of four or five tents about ten miles from his patron. He brought with him a camp manager, often one of his European employees, plus a mechanic and a cook. He would stay for two or three weeks at a time, riding over to Fahd's camp each day in a dune buggy or some other adventure vehicle that had recently caught his eye. In the evenings he would join a hundred or more male guests at the feasts Fahd hosted. These were egalitarian affairs undertaken in the efficient Bedouin style—the food was spread out on the ground and consumed as quickly as possible, with no time wasted on toasts, speeches, or, for that matter, digestion.[6]

Salem behaved outrageously around Fahd. Once, he arrived back at his own camp in the company of security guards who seemed to be escorting him away from the ruler's section, one of his camp guests recalled. Salem said he had been sitting around in the royal tent when Fahd complained, "*Wallah*, Salem, I am so tired of these Bedouins. They come to me, and I don't mind giving money, but then there are hundreds of them, kissing my hand, giving money, kissing my hand, giving money. It tires me—and I come to rest here in the desert."

"I can solve this problem," Salem replied. "You let me know one day before, and all day long I'll eat food. Some dark beans. You put me in the front of the queue, and I'll start farting, and all the Bedouins will disappear."

Fahd laughed so hard that his doctor feared he might have a heart attack, so Salem was hauled away. "Everybody was always bowing down" to Fahd, the guest recalled. "But Salem was like a friend. He would crack jokes." Fahd, for his part, "loved that casual way of Salem. Of course, he was a lunatic. If a normal person would do this, they would chop his hand off. But because Salem was a bit on the loony side, it was accepted."[7]

Salem finally won permission to buy a private plane. He began to replace his father's fleet, which had been sold off after Faisal's earlier order that no more Bin Ladens should fly. As his first purchase, rather than a fancy jet, he chose a Mitsubishi MU-2 turboprop, a six-passenger propeller plane that could land on short runways. During the late 1970s, Salem began to fly the MU-2 into the desert to join Fahd's encampments. His aides would build a makeshift runway marked by strobe lights and burning tires. Salem could not resist the temptation to buzz Fahd's tent. Versions of this incident vary from teller to teller; in some, Fahd's bodyguards raise their weapons at Salem's plane, while in others, Salem brazenly puts the plane down on a road near where the king is staying. In any event, Jack Hinson, a pilot who worked with Salem during this period, recalled that Salem often recited what Fahd had told him afterward: "You are crazy, and you are going to get killed one of these days."[8]

Salem's zest was genuine, of course, but he also mustered it cannily to ingratiate himself with Fahd and his brothers on business matters. Like a sales manager, Salem assigned each senior Saudi prince to one of his brothers or half-brothers; each Bin Laden's mission was to cultivate a personal relationship with his prince and win contracts. "The question was, 'Who is your prince?'" recalled Rupert Armitage, who ran a business division for Salem in Jeddah during this period. Salem took on Fahd himself; he assigned his full brother Bakr to cultivate Abdullah bin Abdulaziz, who was in line for the throne after Fahd. Salem's strategy was to sniff out upcoming contracts through contacts with civil servants inside key government ministries, and then to seal the deals with the princes. "Some of these were just enormous carve-ups and so you were part of the carve-up as long as you could do the job" and were in the good graces of the royal family, Armitage said.[9]

The desert camping trips also offered a chance to collect on past-due bills. Salem would sit at Fahd's side day after day, gently mentioning what he was owed, until a royal accountant finally arrived with a check. Bengt Johansson, who worked as Salem's chief airplane mechanic for at least fifteen years, remembered him returning from Fahd's tent on one occasion, waving a check in the air. "We've gotten paid, guys! Let's go!" They packed up their tents and departed immediately.[10]

By the late 1970s, Salem had won enough contracts to begin to add Learjet and other luxury business aircraft to his private fleet. He used these planes for his own leisure travel overseas but also to cultivate ties with the royal family. If a prince called and asked to "borrow" one of Salem's Lears, he often felt he had no choice but to turn the plane and its crew over for a weeks-long shopping spree to Europe. This was part of his unwritten bargain with the royal family. Johansson remembered Salem dodging telephone calls from certain princes who were particularly active plane borrowers. "He tried to avoid that, but if they get in touch with him and they put the question directly to him, he has to say yes."[11]

Such favors, combined with the royal family's unreliable accounts payable departments, as well as the normal purchasing and payroll demands of the contracting industry, put heavy pressure on Salem's cash flow. Salem's father had managed his own version of this problem through the support of his great Hadhrami banking friend Salem Bin Mahfouz, after whom Salem had been named. Salem Bin Laden developed a similar friendship and business partnership with Khalid Bin Mahfouz, an heir to his own father's fortune who had been sent to school in England as Salem had, and who, by the mid-1970s, had begun to play an increasingly important role at his family's National Commercial Bank. Khalid was a much quieter personality than Salem, but they became fast friends and close business partners. During the 1970s, they were both still trying to establish themselves as young executives in their own right.

Salem and Khalid each acquired a small fleet of private planes in the first years of the oil boom. They hired American, Pakistani, Afghan, Egyptian, and other pilots, and opened an aviation department at Jeddah's airport. One of the department's missions was to move cash around. Banking in Saudi Arabia remained in a relatively primitive state, with few reliable electronic or computer systems. Cash reigned. Salem often used his private planes to transport bags of money between NCB branches. In his pilots' logbooks, these flights were sometimes listed simply as "money runs." A run would typically begin at NCB headquarters in Jeddah, where trusted expatriate Yemeni workers would load five-foot-tall burlap sacks bulging with riyals and topped with lead seals into a convoy of Honda pickup trucks. Without guards or gunmen, the couriers would roll to the airport and hoist the cash into Learjets, filling all the passenger seats. Two pilots then flew the planes to Dhahran or Riyadh or Hail or some other Saudi city, where the money would be unloaded and transferred to a local NCB branch to fill up its vaults. On other trips they flew cash to Bin Laden desert campsites and doled it out to migrant construction workers. Once in a while, without explanation, the Yemeni couriers loaded a plane with bars of gold bullion, which were then flown to Bahrain, London, or Switzerland. As the years passed, the American pilots who flew on these money runs found the cargo and destinations increasingly intriguing, although they never saw indications of anything illegal.[12]

AT SOME POINT during the mid-1970s, Salem decided that he wanted to become a medical doctor. According to his friend Mohamed Ashmawi, he asked Fahd for permission to study in Cairo; the crown prince looked up at him and said, "Salem, grow up."[13]

Undeterred, Salem asked his family doctor in Jeddah, an American named Terry Bennett, if he would write reference letters. "It was the scheme of the month," Bennett recalled. "He had the attention span of a flea."[14] Salem was a quick study, however. He had become an excellent pilot without rigorous formal training, sometimes by asking more experienced fliers to accompany him to a few required classes. He seemed to believe he could pick up medicine by the same method. In any event, he was absolutely determined, in the manner of patriarchs throughout time, that someone in his family should become a doctor.

He spent increasing amounts of time in Cairo. It lay a relatively short distance from Jeddah, close enough for a weekend commute by air, and its culture was much more vibrant and open than anything in Saudi Arabia. Salem's father had married at least two Egyptian women, and the offspring of those unions lived in and around Cairo. Mohamed had left three children from one marriage to an Egyptian—two sons, Khalid and Abdulaziz, and a daughter, Mona—as well as a singleton daughter from a second marriage, Randa.

Randa was twelve or thirteen years old when Mohamed Bin Laden died, and she first met Salem at the memorial service. Salem told her, "Don't worry, don't worry. I will always take care of you." There was "an immediate bond" between them, recalled an American friend, Gail Freeman. Salem discovered that Randa and her mother, who had remarried, were living in far from comfortable circumstances. He gave them money and bought them a three-story town house near Cairo's colonial-era Shooting Club. Salem stayed on the ground floor when he was in town, Randa had an apartment above him, and her mother lived with her new husband on the highest floor. By the mid-1970s, Randa was becoming known to everyone in Salem's entourage as his favorite sister. She was a slim, coffee-colored, dark-haired woman with an open personality. He doted on her, spoke to her frequently on the telephone, took her shopping in Europe, and traveled regularly to visit her in Cairo. The connection between them grew so intense that it seemed to approach romantic love. None of Salem's close entourage ever thought that anything inappropriate passed between him and his half-sister; nonetheless, they marveled at the open passion in their relationship.[15]

Salem decided that Randa should also become a doctor, and he announced that he would study alongside her at Cairo University. "He pushed Randa to do it," recalled Sabry Ghoneim, a family employee in Cairo.[16] She studied hard. Salem paid for professors to come to her apartment and tutor her privately. He tried to attend these lessons, too, flying back and forth from Jeddah. He ordered his pilots to help Randa shop for supplies, and on at least one occasion, he flew in skeletons from Saudi Arabia in one of his private planes to aid their cram sessions.[17]

Inside Saudi Arabia, it was no longer unheard of for a woman to go to college or even to medical school, although if a woman studied in the kingdom, she did so in an environment of strict gender segregation. Salem encouraged many of his sisters and half-sisters to attend school. He enrolled his full sister Hoda in art school in Paris at the same time that he underwrote Randa's medical education in Cairo. He placed two of his half-sisters in boarding school in Pakistan. Others applied to universities and design academies in the United States; several became interested in interior decorating, a profession they could profit from in turnkey palace-building projects for the family firm. Many of Salem's half-sisters wore Western fashions and traveled without covering when they were outside Saudi Arabia. At the same time, Salem seemed fiercely determined to protect what he imagined to be his sisters' honor. He discouraged any of the younger pilots who flew for him from even speaking with any of his sisters or half-sisters. Only the fatherly Gerald Auerbach was trusted as an escort.[18]

Salem did not live extravagantly when he visited Egypt. There were cooks and servants in the town house he shared with Randa, but it was not a palace. He wore blue jeans and T-shirts, and he drove an old Spanish car or a motorcycle. He opened an office at 14 Al-Thawra Street, hired a few Egyptian aides, and began to explore ambitious land and development deals in Cairo. "Salem dreamed of building residential towers and malls along the Nile," Ghoneim recalled.[19]

By the late 1970s, he knew Cairo's landscape better than most developers because he spent hours swooping above it in the air. Salem might fantasize about becoming a doctor, but he already was a pilot. It was the one passion in his life that never seemed to bore him.

SALEM PURCHASED a Cessna-172 single-engine propeller plane in the United States during this time and had it flown into Cairo. He kept it at a small airport on the city's outskirts, Imbaba, which had been built in 1947 and was mainly used by recreational pilots. Among other things, he used the Cessna to tow his two-seat, German-made glider up to five thousand feet or so, from where it could be released for a meandering flight back to Imbaba—twisting down the Nile, out to the Pyramids, across dusty slums and arid parks, with only the sound of wind rushing across the wings. He reveled in the romance of these flights above the Pyramids. When he courted a new girlfriend (he was still married to Sheikha, but they were drifting apart), he often flew the woman to Cairo and took her aloft in his glider at sunset. With fellow pilots, he trained in acrobatics— loops, rolls, and flying upside down above Imbaba. Later he purchased a pair of ultralights. If there were enough pilots around, he would arrange an evening expedition to the Pyramids; his friends flew behind him in formation, creating a phalanx of toy aircraft.[20]

Wayne Fagan, an American lawyer who visited Salem in Cairo, remembered being invited into the back of one of these planes as Salem gunned the engine and roared down the runway while trying to light a tobacco pipe, all the while "pulling back on the throttles with his elbows." They flew out over the desert in the evening light and circled the Pyramids. Salem had promised Fagan a flight in the glider, but it wasn't available, so on the way back, he shut down his plane's engines and drifted on the currents. "And he says, 'Look, Wayne, we're gliding.' And I said, 'That's great, Salem, thanks a lot. You can start up any time now.'"[21]

On one courtship glider flight with an English girlfriend, Caroline Carey, he miscalculated wind and altitude, and seemed headed for a crash. Caroline became so frightened as they plummeted that she promised to convert to Islam if they somehow survived. Salem steered hurriedly toward a field at the Shooting Club, near Randa's apartment, slipped the plane over high trees, and pulled up in time to stop before striking the club's wall. "When I saw what Salem did, I said, 'My God, any other pilot would crash it,'" recalled Anwar Khan, a Pakistani pilot who flew for him. Club security rushed up; Salem climbed out, helped his girlfriend to her feet, and joked: "Sorry, I'm not a member of the club—but my brother is a member." Caroline kept her promise and became a Muslim.[22]

He employed his acrobatic skills to shake money from his debtors. "People were forever owing him money, so he would offer them rides," recalled Rupert Armitage. Once in the air, "he'd say, 'Look, you owe me two hundred thousand dollars. I want you to write out a check now.'" If they declined, he would threaten to take the plane's controls and roll it upside down. If they still refused, "he'd start doing it . . . and then, 'Okay, okay, I'll sign it!'"[23]

Under Salem's enthusiastic guidance, the Bin Ladens gradually became a family of pilots. Flight logs show no fewer than seven of Salem's brothers and half-brothers taking lessons on his private planes during the 1970s. Several of his half-sisters also trained to fly. Osama, however, was apparently not among this group; he did later acquire private airplanes of his own, and may have taken some informal instruction, but he does not seem to have flown often during the 1970s. His relative youth appears to have been one factor; the brothers who took lessons were older, while Osama remained in high school, increasingly concerned with religious issues.

Flying lessons reinforced the boundaries of an inner circle of Bin Laden brothers around Salem, led by his full brothers Ghalib and Bakr, and including some older half-brothers, such as Omar, Issa, Yahya, Tareq, and Yeslam. They were an eclectic group—some devout, some more secular—tied together by their dependency on Salem's leadership. To taste the pleasures Salem expounded upon, and to win his favor, they followed him into the sky.

The American, Egyptian, and Pakistani pilots who flew with Salem, many of whom were veterans of their respective air forces, genuinely admired his skill. He had excellent reflexes, a natural feel for an aircraft in flight, and a strong enough mind to recall the subtle differences in the control panels of the various models of aircraft he accumulated. He was weak on technical issues and not the most meticulous of checklist followers, but he usually kept a skilled copilot on board to watch after such details. On a typical flight, he would take off and land but let his copilot handle the long cruise at altitude while he snoozed in the back or canoodled with one of his girlfriends. He reveled in "the sensation of speed, man over machine," said one of his instructors, Don Sowell. His skills were "excellent" and he was "never reckless," and yet, "Sheikh Salem was one who lived on the edge, bordered on the edge." He never seemed to be concentrating because he always seemed to be doing more than one thing at a time—patching through phone calls to girlfriends on his high-frequency airplane radio, joking with control towers, and yet, all the while, recalled Anwar Khan, he would be "making a perfect, perfect approach" using only his instruments.[24]

He was not much interested in formal licensing or aviation rules. If a trained copilot was unavailable for a particular flight on a plane that required two pilots, he would ask one of his untrained school buddies or business partners to sit in the jump seat and sign the flight plan so that he could take off. His friends learned to behave nonchalantly in these situations, because if Salem smelled fear in a passenger or putative copilot, he would mercilessly roll or spin the plane to exacerbate their discomfort, laughing all the while. On a long flight to Cairo, he drafted as his copilot Robert Freeman, an American business partner who had not a single hour of flight training. Freeman asked what he should do if Salem fell ill or blacked out. "That would be the end for both of us," he answered matter-of-factly.[25]

Despite Mohamed Bin Laden's fatal accident, Salem ensured that the risks of private aviation became an increasingly pervasive part of the Bin Ladens' family life and conversation. His unconventional habits led to a succession of crashes and near misses from the mid-1970s onward, each of which was circulated and discussed within the family. Salem's full brother Ghalib wrecked a Piper airplane by spinning it out during a landing. A family Learjet returning from Medina fell mysteriously out of the sky, killing the two expatriate pilots. Salem himself skated near disaster. He had trouble managing his MU-2's de-icing equipment when he flew to Europe in winter; if the system was mishandled, the plane would stall. Once, climbing out after takeoff, his engines died at a dangerously low altitude. "I was telling God, 'You can have all my airplanes. You can have all my money. Just give me one little engine,'" he recounted, according to Bengt Johansson. His plea was answered.[26]

By the late 1970s, he was buying more planes than he was wrecking. He purchased a Fokker-27 turboprop, mainly to fly to construction work sites in the desert. He bought a Learjet 25-D and took an interest in more advanced models; he loved the Lears, and he often wore blue jeans with a little Learjet sewn into them. He also bought a Hawker-125, the same model jet that his father had purchased before his death. His friend and banker Khalid Bin Mahfouz added even more extravagant aircraft to their Jeddah department, including a Boeing 707 with a customized interior. Each plane had a unique tail number, and Salem often chose initials drawn from family names.

He played his harmonica over the radio to entertain air traffic controllers. In his Lear, he only had to announce himself on approach— "Hotel Zulu Bravo Lima One"—and controllers in Cairo or Beirut would call out in welcome, "*Ahlan*, Sheikh Salem!" Above all, his planes gave him freedom—to live as he wished, to go where he pleased. As one of his Lebanese friends summed it up: "Salem believed in his Learjet and his MU-2 and his jeans and guitar and harmonica."[27]

IT WAS AN APPEALING CREED, but an expensive one. To live this way, Salem needed to adapt his family's strategy to better profit from the new economy of the oil boom. European and American corporations swarmed into Saudi Arabia during the 1970s. They hawked televisions, telephones, fancy cars, air conditioners, and dishwashers—all the badges of modern consumerism. Saudi law required these firms to sell through local agents. Saudi merchant families competed to sign up agencies with the most desirable brands, a pathway to instant profits. Like his father, Salem had mixed feelings about this approach; he preferred to act as a principal, and where it was desirable to work with foreign companies, to form partnerships, rather than to simply rake off commissions from overseas agencies. He did sign up some agency deals, such as those with the German automakers Volkswagen and Porsche, but he preferred joint ventures involving big construction contracts, and he preferred to concentrate on industries where his family had already built up credibility and expertise. Either way, during the oil boom of the 1970s, the Bin Ladens required, as they never had during Mohamed's lifetime, a spokesman and deal maker who could represent the family successfully in Europe and the United States. This became Salem's role. He was an ideal intermediary—fluent in English, fun to be around, energetic, mobile, and equally at home in Jeddah and London.

He used his uninhibited personality to disarm and manipulate Western executives during negotiations. Flying into Stockholm for a meeting with officials at AVB, one of Sweden's largest construction companies, he asked his Swedish mechanic Johansson to meet him at the airport. Johansson drove down from his home on the coast in a corroded old Volkswagen Golf, while Salem flew in from Cairo. When Johansson arrived at the private aviation terminal, he saw AVB executives in business suits lined up in stiff formation beside a convoy of limousines, waiting for the sheikh. Salem landed, descended from his jet, shook hands with the lead AVB executive, walked past the limousines, and insisted that the Swedish executive cram into the backseat of the Golf, so they could ride into town with Salem's disheveled friend Bengt. Salem wore his usual uniform for trips to Europe—jeans, a T-shirt, a leather jacket, and a ten-dollar plastic Casio watch.[28]

Salem worked most of his overseas deals through Bin Laden Brothers, the company he and some of his brothers had started to prove themselves and to escape the control of the older Saudi trustees, appointed by King Faisal, who still ran the sprawling Mohamed Bin Laden Organization.

Salem opened a shabby office off an alley near the old souk in downtown Jeddah; the suite was crowded with clerks and accountants who labored amid blue clouds of cigarette smoke. In the style of a palace *diwan*, sofas and chairs ran around the outer edge of the reception room, where businessmen pitching deals or younger Bin Laden boys seeking an allowance payment would sit for hours waiting for an audience with Salem or a senior brother. Inside, the older brothers who were partners in the company—Salem, Bakr, Yahya, Hassan, Ghalib, Omar, and perhaps two or three others—had private offices. Salem rarely used his, preferring to work out of his bedroom at home, but most of the other brothers kept regular hours. A visitor would stride in with a bulging armload of traveler's checks, and a boy at the reception desk would size him up and say simply, "Come in the back." There were "loose ends all over the place," recalled Armitage, who worked there. There always seemed to be a scramble under way to get some signature on a document. "It was constant chaos ... of a small, needling nature." Still, the larger problems were managed well, Armitage thought, and his overall impression was that the Bin Laden brothers were learning in these years to work successfully "as a family, together."[29]

There was no question about who was in charge, however. Salem presided over his younger brothers and half-brothers in the manner of an Arabian patriarch. They responded with obedience. They called him "Sheikh" and they were "very subservient to him, very respectful of him as an elder. He was like the king," recalled his pilot Jack Hinson. Bedouin servants brought him tea and coffee. His brothers would ask Salem's European friends and pilots if they would please arrange audiences for them with the boss; they were very reluctant to walk in on him unannounced. Salem alone decided how much money the brothers received in allowances, what schools they attended, what projects they might work on, and how much salary they would earn. He made these decisions confidently, with an air of entitlement to authority, and he did not hesitate to slap or strike a younger brother lightly if he was particularly displeased. He rewarded the engineers and hard workers, such as Bakr, Ghalib, Yahya, and Omar: among other things, they could relieve Salem of day-to-day responsibilities on construction contracts. Not even they enjoyed much autonomy, however. "No one did anything without Salem's approval," said David Grey, another of his pilots. On the phone or in business meetings, Salem would announce forcefully, "I will determine who will get what money, and no one will get anything until I decide," as Grey recalled. "I've heard him use those words time and time again."[30]

His new business was becoming steadily more complex. A profile of Bin Laden Brothers prepared by Aramco's political office in 1979 lists more than a dozen partnerships or companies Salem had organized with foreign firms. These included joint ventures with large American and European building companies, such as Lozinger in Switzerland and Kaiser in the United States, as well as companies that made windows, prestress concrete, air-conditioning systems, kitchens, doors, and accessories for highway construction. Salem could pick and choose as he pleased from the scores of unsolicited proposals he received from visiting Europeans and Americans seeking to cash in on the Saudi boom. The ideas submitted to him by Western suitors had a random, comical diversity—plastic bag manufacturing one day, aeronautical lubricants the next. For the most part, Salem stuck to industries he knew, and he sought out prestigious corporations. He formed a shareholding partnership with General Electric during this time, one that would allow him to develop deals in Saudi Arabia across all GE's lines of business, from medical technology to power generation. Particularly with American businessmen, who were relatively informal, "He was perfect with people," said the investment banker Francis Hunnewell, a partner of Salem's during this period.[31]

Bin Laden Brothers continued to work as a subcontractor for his father's former company. By the late 1970s, Salem had become chairman of the old family firm, and he gradually wrested complete control from the trustees—they formally stepped aside at some point around 1978 or 1979.

The Mohamed Bin Laden Organization still drew much of its revenue from big defense and infrastructure projects. It continued to build roads and other facilities in Asir; it worked on a military garrison project in northern Al-Jouf, alongside the U.S. Army Corps of Engineers; and in the vast Empty Quarter, the desert along the kingdom's southern frontier, the company built roads and an airstrip. Salem occasionally flew out for inspections as his father had so often done, but he was not a hands-on engineer who walked the roads or argued over decisions about tunnels or grading. Indeed, he seemed increasingly to avoid that sort of responsibility. He ordered his two younger full brothers, Bakr and Ghalib, to enroll in civil engineering courses in the United States, and he told his half-brothers Yahya and Omar to do the same. He knew the Bin Ladens would require civil engineering expertise over the long run, but he had no interest in acquiring such knowledge himself.

He spent more and more time in Britain and Europe. On May 18, 1975, Salem's wife Sheikha gave birth in London to their first child, a daughter, Sara. A little more than two years later, also in London, she had a son, Salman.[32]

During these sojourns, Salem met Ian Munro, a tall, elegant, white-haired Scotsman who had served in Britain's famous Black Watch regiment; he had fought with the regiment to put down the Mau Mau rebellion in Kenya during the 1950s, and later he served with the Air Wing of British security forces in Kenya. After leaving the military, Munro went into business in London. He had a sonorous voice and an accent that betrayed little of his Scottish heritage. He was a member of the Naval & Military Club, a flag-draped bastion of fireplaces and leather chairs in Piccadilly. Munro was a reliable, fatherly figure whom Salem decided he could trust to help organize his affairs outside Saudi Arabia. The two registered a company in London for aviation-related ventures named Salian International, a combination of their first names, as well as a British division of Bin Laden Brothers, which later evolved into Bin Laden London. Munro opened a small office in Park Lane.[33]

Salem decided to buy a proper English mansion near London, but he could not be bothered with real estate shopping. He told Munro that he was sure that whatever Ian liked, he would like, too. Munro chose a manor estate built in the early 1920s in a village called Offley Chase, a short drive from the Luton airport, north of London, which was often used by private pilots. The estate conformed to some of the expectations that foreigners bring to English country homes—it was heavily bricked and somewhat gloomy. On a rainy night, it seemed like an ideal setting for a parlor murder. In the years ahead, Offley Chase would be the scene of some of the most dramatic events in Salem's eccentric life.[34]

13. DISCOVERING AMERICA

T HE SOWELL FAMILY ran a flight school in Panama City, Florida, a town of about thirty-five thousand in the state's western panhandle, where the pace hued to the milky rhythms of the Deep South rather than to the samba beat of distant Miami. Downtown held a brick courthouse and a jail, and along the nearby streets, there were Baptist churches, bait shops, and gun stores. White beaches stretched out to the west on sandbars in the Gulf of Mexico. There was an air force base nearby. Weathered roadhouse bars and a few tattoo parlors lined the beach road. Sowell Aviation occupied several hundred acres to the north of downtown. During the 1970s, Don Sowell was preparing to take over the business from his father. Their school offered piloting lessons, aircraft maintenance, charters, sales, and leasing—a typical array of private aviation services. The Sowells had gotten to know the former California governor Ronald Reagan a little, through friends and by attending fundraising events. They attracted international students to their school from Asia, Europe, and South America, so it was not a surprise when one of Don Sowell's pilot contacts from Texas, Jim Bath, invited him to dinner with a Saudi client who was buying up Learjets in the States and who said he might be interested in lessons, for himself and perhaps also for one of his sisters. "I have a baby sister," Salem Bin Laden explained, "and she would like to learn to fly."[1]

Without boasting, exactly, Salem made it clear over dinner that he had a great deal of money and that he was looking for partners in America who could provide a wide variety of services—not only piloting lessons but also business services, particularly the acquisition of cars and consumer goods for the royal family in Saudi Arabia. Afterward, Don Sowell told Jim Bath, "It's either an Alice-in-Wonderland thing, or it may be the biggest opportunity of a lifetime."[2]

The oil embargo transformed America into a shopping mall and vacation resort for many wealthy Saudis. Europe might be fine for skiing, yachting, jewelry shopping, and haute couture, but if you wanted to play in open spaces and find the latest in electronics and toys, there was no substitute for America. Salem, of course, did not initially know—and as the years passed he would never seem to care—that Panama City was not a particularly fashionable destination. If anything, he seemed drawn to its lack of pretension. After his dinner with Sowell, he flew into town regularly. He leased houses at Bay Point, then the region's only luxury resort, located on a peninsula of pine trees and sand along the intercoastal waterway. About a year later he brought Randa from Cairo and installed her in a Bay Point home. He told Sowell that he wanted his sister to take flight lessons until she was certified on a Cessna. He said she would require a cook, a female chaperone, a driver, and a car. Sowell usually sent a Lincoln.

They all adapted to Salem's demands and to his nocturnal schedule. He rarely turned up for flight lessons before late afternoon, and by the time he figured out what he wanted to do for fun each evening, most of Panama City's restaurants and stores had already closed. The city had but one enclosed shopping mall—a modest place downtown at the corner of 23rd Street and Highway 231, anchored by JCPenney, Sears, and Dillard's department stores. Sowell paid store owners to remain open after hours. It was, he reflected, the sort of thing "you would hear about with Elvis Presley." Each Monday, Randa went shopping. On one occasion, Sowell watched Salem hand her twenty-two thousand dollars in traveler's checks for a trip to the mall.[3]

Salem found at the mall a piano and organ store that particularly attracted him. Jack Pizza managed the place along with his wife, Anita Pizza, who was an accomplished pianist. Jack called Don Sowell one night, reporting breathlessly that there was a Saudi in his store who was using Sowell as a reference. The customer wanted to buy thousands of dollars' worth of pianos and other musical instruments, and he wanted them shipped immediately to a home at Bay Point. Pizza asked if there was a dollar limit on how much he should agree to sell. "No, there isn't," Sowell recalled telling him. "Whatever he wants, you send it."[4]

It was the beginning of a long and unlikely friendship between the Pizzas of Panama City and the Bin Laden family of Jeddah. Jack Pizza dabbled in computers and tried to sell the latest models to Salem. Anita proved to be a graceful accompanist for Salem's singing ventures, as well as a faithful companion to Randa.

They hosted dinner and song parties at Bay Point, where royal visitors from Saudi Arabia sometimes mingled with wisecracking pilots from Panama City and Houston. Salem was not a heavy drinker, but he developed a sipping taste for Dom Pérignon champagne, which he insisted should be served chilled about two minutes after opening—not too bubbly, not too flat. For one party, Sowell bought up all the Dom Pérignon in the Panama City region but ran out nonetheless. Salem "sent myself, and my Lear, and my pilot, and we flew to Columbus, Georgia, and loaded the airplane with cases of Dom Pérignon, and flew it back," he recalled. Soon Salem insisted that Sowell and the Pizzas fly with him around the world, particularly so that he and Anita could perform together in restaurants and at parties.[5]

Salem learned in these years that he could buy his way onto just about any stage where he wanted to sing. He paid a bandleader at an Academy Awards party in Los Angeles hundreds of dollars to let him sing "House of the Rising Sun" in seven languages. At an Oktoberfest in Germany, he handed audience members occupying a table in front of the stage two thousand German marks to make room, bought a video camera from another audience member, and spent more still to persuade the bandleader to let him take the stage and belt out a Bavarian folk song; its title, roughly translated, was "On the Green Meadow, the Rabbits Eat the Grass."

There was an undercurrent of mutual contempt in these episodes—Salem's contempt for normal protocol and his insistence on purchasing entry, matched by the growing contempt among some Westerners during the 1970s toward showy Saudis who had become rich from rising gasoline prices. And yet, between Salem and his European and American friends, this taint, while an occasional source of discomfort, was almost always washed away by Salem's innocent exuberance and his transparent need to be adored.

He liked the Beatles, but also traditional sing-alongs, such as "On Top of Old Smokey," or its children's parody, "On Top of Spaghetti." No setting was too august for him, no audience too prestigious. In Cairo, he forced his friend Rupert Armitage to play the guitar while he sang badly at the wedding of Egyptian president Anwar Sadat's daughter. However mortified they might feel, his friends learned to go along, because, as was true with his piloting antics, any expression of resistance or fear only encouraged Salem to go further. His voice never improved, but after he met Anita Pizza in Panama City, her skill at the piano elevated his recitals to a greater level of tolerability.[6]

America became a place for singing, flying, and, above all, shopping. Salem ordered Cadillacs for the Saudi royal family and had them fitted with armor so that they could repel machine-gun fire. With Sowell's help, he also ordered about a dozen Lincolns and shipped them over to the kingdom from New Orleans. He ordered five thousand cases of Tabasco sauce and flew it to Saudi Arabia—he said he liked the taste. Coca-Cola was subject to the Arab boycott against Israel, so Salem discovered an alternative soft drink called Mello Yello and had it shipped home in vast quantities. He found a small plastic airplane toy that tickled him and he bought thousands to take home as gifts. To decorate the desert gardens of a palace his family firm was building for Crown Prince Fahd, he shipped home in refrigerated containers what seemed like a substantial portion of the vegetation of the American Southwest: 481 large American cacti, 360 small cacti, 485 mixed cacti, 100 yucca trees, 625 orchids, and more than 5,000 other desert plants, bushes, and trees.[7]

Salem invited Fahd himself to Panama City, according to Sowell. The crown prince landed his customized Boeing 707 at the city airport; at the time, it was the largest plane ever to have touched down there. Sowell leased extra houses at Bay Point for Fahd's armed bodyguards. It was an "interesting ordeal," he remembered. Fahd's entourage "played bumper cars with the golf carts," and they damaged about half a dozen of them so badly that Sowell had to pay for replacements. Robert Freeman, another of Salem's American partners, remembered that the cost of the broken golf carts was about fifty thousand dollars. Sowell said he sent the bill to Jim Bath, Salem's business partner in Houston, since it involved Salem's relationship with Fahd and the crown prince's private travel in the United States. Bath, Sowell said, "handled all those arrangements."[8]

JIM BATH had grown up in Louisiana. He studied journalism and then became an air force fighter pilot; later he joined the Texas Air National Guard as a reserve pilot. When he was still a young man, he and his wife, Sandra, loaded their belongings into a car and moved to Houston, where Bath went into business as an airplane broker and, eventually, a real estate developer and eclectic international entrepreneur. He was a tall, slim man with a rich southwestern accent, who seemed determined to live by a certain male Texas creed—think big, take risks, seek riches, live freely, and do some hunting and fishing along the way. He undertook some of his early carousing with George W. Bush, whom he befriended around 1970 when they were both pilots in the Texas Air National Guard. This was before the future president attended business school, a period when Bush was drinking and, by his own indirect admission, may have indulged in illegal drugs. In any event, Bush would remember Bath as "a lot of fun," although eventually the relentless questions about their relationship would drain the subject of mirth. By the mid-1970s, partly through Bush, Bath had gotten to know a number of significant figures in Texas politics, such as Bush's father, George H. W. Bush, who became director of the Central Intelligence Agency in 1976; Lan Bentsen, a son of the longtime Democratic U.S. senator and eventual vice presidential candidate Lloyd Bentsen; and James A. Baker, a Houston lawyer who would later become U.S. secretary of state.[9]

At this time, Bath's principal business was JB&A Associates, his aircraft brokerage. In 1975 he was trying to sell a Fokker-27 propeller plane owned by a tobacco company in North Carolina; the plane was outfitted with a small bedroom in the cabin. Salem Bin Laden was looking for a plane to support his company's road-building work in the Saudi deserts. They made a deal, and Bath accompanied the plane to Jeddah. Like just about every American entrepreneur who could find the Middle East on a map, Bath seemed determined to cash in on the Saudi oil boom. He didn't just want to make a few commissions from airplane sales; he wanted to develop deeper partnerships with the rising younger generation of Saudi sheikhs, to help them invest their money profitably in the United States. "He talked a mile a minute," remembered Rupert Armitage, who was working in the Bin Laden Brothers office when Bath turned up. Still, Salem found Bath entertaining. Salem "loved larger-than-life people," said the Houston lawyer Charles Schwartz. Jim Bath "was a wheeler-dealer, and Salem just loved that kind of stuff."[10]

American promoters and deal makers besieged Salem; he learned to be cautious. He rarely committed large sums of money to their care, unless it was to buy something concrete, such as an airplane or a house. Yet, at the same time, for work and play, Salem began to acquire offices, residences, and agents in more and more cities around the world. In each place, he chose a primary representative or partner—someone who could help him confidentially entertain visiting Saudi royalty, host Bin Laden family members when they traveled for school or vacation, and assist in business deals. Bath became Salem's agent and partner in Houston. In a sense, Bath opened a service bureau for Salem in Texas, so that Salem, in turn, could extend his global service bureau for the Saudi royal family, particularly in the field of aviation, where Salem was now establishing himself as an in-house expert for the Al-Saud by helping them make smart decisions as they spent more and more of their windfall on private jets.

Bath made his money from airplane commissions and by channeling Saudi investors like Salem into real estate or other business deals, where Bath took a 5 percent piece of the action for his efforts. He operated out of offices in the Fannin Bank Building in Houston, and he registered Salem Bin Laden's new Texas businesses at that address. He created a vehicle called MBO Investments, Inc., named after the Bin Laden family firm in Jeddah. Bath's authority was established in a "trust agreement" signed by Salem on July 8, 1976, and filed with the Texas secretary of state. Salem provided Bath "full and absolute authority to act on my behalf in all matters relating to the business and operation of Bin Laden-Houston offices," which included "full authority to disburse funds for Company, or Bin Laden family expenses." Bath maintained a revolving line of credit for the Bin Laden family that amounted at one stage to about $6 or $7 million, according to Bill White, who was a business partner of Bath's after 1978.[11]

As his Saudi contacts grew, Bath moved into international aircraft leasing. This was a complex business in which, at the time, American tax and export laws made it particularly attractive to finance aircraft sales to overseas customers. Bath opened offshore corporations in Caribbean tax havens to facilitate such deals. He established a Cayman Islands corporation called Skyway Aircraft Leasing, Ltd., whose ownership was Saudi, according to White and other accounts.[12]

Bath also opened offshore companies for Salem. On July 5, 1977, he incorporated Binco Investments, N.V., in the Netherlands Antilles. Its parent company was SMB Investments, apparently in reference to Salem's initials; it was also located in the Netherlands Antilles. Documents Bath filed with the state of Texas reported that the main purpose of these companies was to hold real estate. Binco Investments, for example, became a vehicle for Bath's purchase around this time, on Salem's behalf, of Houston Gulf Airport, a small field outside the city that Bath hoped would grow into a profitable feeder airport—a hope that was never realized.[13]

Bath's deals with the Bin Ladens appear to have involved smaller amounts of money than those he developed with other Saudis, particularly Salem's friend and banker Khalid Bin Mahfouz. In 1977, for example, Bath invested in the Main Bank in Houston; his partners included Bin Mahfouz, the wealthy Saudi businessman Gaith Pharaon, and former Texas governor John Connally. Salem invested with Bin Mahfouz in the Saudi Bank of Paris but apparently did not join his Texas banking deals.[14]

Bath's Saudi clients, his politically connected friends in Texas, his offshore corporations, his freewheeling lifestyle, and his forays into international aviation all contributed to a growing air of mystery. Bath himself seemed to relish the intrigue. He flew back and forth to Caribbean tax havens, sometimes with hundreds of thousands of dollars in cash aboard the planes; he told his wife, Sandra, that the cash was needed to pay for fuel and contingencies. Sometimes the Saudis who traveled with Bath carried diplomatic passports, which allowed them to bring their briefcases through U.S. Customs without being inspected; on some occasions, according to a pilot who worked with Bath, the cases contained very large sums of cash.[15]

SALEM LED a family migration to America during the 1970s. As his brothers and sisters finished secondary school in Lebanon, Egypt, and Jeddah, he encouraged many of them to enroll in college in the United States. Like many Saudis, they gravitated toward Florida and California, where the weather felt like home. Salem's youngest full brother, Ghalib, studied civil engineering at the University of California at Berkeley. His half-brother Abdulaziz, from Cairo, enrolled at the University of San Francisco, where he earned a master's degree in business administration in 1978. Two other half-brothers, Shafiq and Saleh, and a half-sister, Raja, also enrolled at USF. Yeslam, Khalil, and Ibrahim, a cluster of full brothers by an Iranian-born wife of Mohamed Bin Laden, studied at the University of Southern California in Los Angeles. Other family members enrolled in colleges or design academies in Miami and Houston. School records and interviews show that more than a quarter of Mohamed Bin Laden's fifty-four children studied in the United States at some point, primarily during the 1970s and early 1980s.[16]

Osama, of course, was part of the larger group that enrolled in Saudi or other Arab universities. Salem traveled frequently back and forth between Jeddah and the United States, zipping from city to city in his jets, organizing vacations, and handing out allowances. He was the family leader who kept track of everybody, no matter where they went to school. He carried one of the first portable phones, a bulky model as big as a brick, so that his brothers and sisters could reach him at any time. Mohamed's children were now mainly teenagers or in their twenties, and they constantly had decisions to make about school, jobs, and even marriages. All came to Salem for consultation or permission.

His half-brother Yeslam and his stunning Iranian-born wife, Carmen, provided one harbor for the family in Los Angeles. Yeslam had drifted through Europe after high school. He took race-car driving lessons in Sweden, considered a plan to breed Doberman pinscher dogs in Saudi Arabia, and lodged for a time in the Royal Hotel in Geneva, Switzerland. While leasing an apartment in Geneva with his family in the summer of 1973, he met Carmen, the daughter of the apartment's owner. Her father was Swiss; her mother Iranian. She spoke French and Persian, was twenty-two, extraordinarily beautiful, and fiercely ambitious. Yeslam, also twenty-two, found himself swept away by Carmen. He was a mild, reticent, sensitive young man prone to anxiety attacks. She felt that Yeslam nonetheless had the intelligence to lead his family's international business one day, to bring it into the modern era. "Carmen was very anxious for Yeslam to do well," recalled Mary Martha Barkley, who befriended the couple through her husband, who oversaw international students at USC, where Yeslam enrolled to study business in late 1973. "She had great ambitions for him."[17]

They married the following summer and bought a house on Amalfi Drive in Pacific Palisades, a wealthy neighborhood near the ocean. Yeslam took flying lessons and purchased a twin-engine propeller plane for weekend trips to Santa Barbara and Arizona; his wife drove a Pontiac Firebird. Yeslam's great passion, apart from Carmen, was his rather unfriendly Doberman, Khalif.[18]

Salem flew into Los Angeles periodically and organized family expeditions to Las Vegas, where the Bin Ladens stayed at Caesars Palace. He gambled the way he drank—lightly, and to pass the time. He once wandered over to a Vegas blackjack table while waiting for his traveling party to organize themselves in the hotel lobby. Soon he built up a pile of chips worth more than a thousand dollars. He joked with the female card dealer, and when it was time to go, simply shoved all his winnings over to her with a shrug. He reveled in the thrill that ordinary Americans and Europeans, particularly women, would express when he unexpectedly handed them large amounts of cash; he seemed to enjoy those exchanges more than some of the luxuries his money could buy.[19]

Salem never seemed to doubt himself or to question his identity as a Saudi who traveled widely in America. Some of his brothers and half-brothers, however, found themselves unsettled by the adventures he led them on.

The older boys, in particular, had all known their father in his prime. They had been instilled, naturally, with pride in the family's achievements as Muslims, Arabs, Yemenis, and Saudis. This pride was not only a matter of family honor or some vague sense of national or religious belonging; it was inseparable from the detailed Koranic instruction the boys had received from an early age—the verses memorized and recited, the laws listed and observed. It was part and parcel, too, of the scenes they had enjoyed and the prayers they had offered on frequent visits to Mecca and Medina. Their father's religion was not that of an ardent proselytizer; among other things, in his long association with American, Italian, and Lebanese Christians, he displayed little of the xenophobia sometimes exhibited by Saudi clerics. Yet his devotion lay at the core of his own identity and that which he hoped his sons and daughters would embrace. His adherence to Islamic ritual and values, the prayers he gave five times each day, the many Hajj pilgrimages he hosted in his carpeted tent, the fasts he adhered to during Ramadan—it would be difficult for any son of Mohamed's to blithely set all this aside, even if Salem seemed at times to provide an example of how it might be done.

During Ramadan's long afternoons, when he was supposed to be fasting and abstaining from tobacco, Salem chain-smoked and asked his younger brothers to serve him food and coffee. He rarely prayed when traveling in Europe or America, and he ate pork without hesitation—he thought it was delicious. In Saudi Arabia, he did attend mosques, but he was more likely to poke his friends in the belly while standing in a prayer line than to prostrate himself in humble supplication to God. He had a spiritual side—he talked about time travel, and infinity and the shape of the universe, questions that seemed to encroach upon him during his long hours in the sky. Islam did not seem to press upon him, nor he upon it. His more religious brothers would gently encourage him to find his way a little closer to God's well-marked path, but the culture of deference to the family leader within an Arabian clan like the Bin Ladens was so strong that not even the most devoted of Salem's younger siblings dared to challenge him severely about his lapses. Perhaps more important, their faith, as they understood it, taught that judging sinners was God's business, not mortal man's, as long as the sinner in question did not renounce Islam altogether. "No sin besides that of unbelief makes a believer step outside his faith, even if it is a serious sin, like murder or drinking alcohol," Osama Bin Laden would say years later. "Even if the culprit died without repenting of his sins, his fate is with God, whether He wishes to forgive him or to punish him."[20]

America during the 1970s, roiled by its recent cultural and sexual revolutions—not to mention its garish hairstyles and clothing—continuously demanded an answer of each young Bin Laden who lived there: Are you a Muslim, and if so, how will you practice your faith? Many of Salem's siblings found that they could not shrug off the question, as he seemed to do, and they tacked back and forth, searching for a comfortable answer. Carmen, who lived as a secular European, saw this when Yeslam's brothers came to visit from San Francisco or Jeddah. "You never knew which brother would turn very religious," she recalled. "Even if you had seen them very young, and being very open . . . The men, they used to go out. They go to the movies. They go to bars. And you think they are Westernized. And suddenly small things make you realize: No." Her own husband, she gradually came to realize, "was not as Westernized as I thought he was. They cannot cut that bond that is embedded in them."[21]

An American businessman recalled visiting Yeslam's brother Khalil in Los Angeles on the day Khalil decided to dump out all the alcohol in his house. "That's it," Khalil declared, as this person recalled it. "We're not doing this anymore." Afterward, Khalil still joined his brothers and university friends at the private clubs in Beverly Hills where they often went on Fridays and Saturday nights to dance and search for girls. Khalil would pay the maître d' for a table but preferred to sit soberly and watch. Some of his brothers danced and caroused, but others let their beards grow and ensured they made time for evening prayers. For many of them, this was not a search for religious or personal identity that had a fixed destination; it was a journey of continuous motion, changeable at any time and place. One of the most striking examples involved Salem's half-brother Mahrouz. He initially married a Frenchwoman; at his home, recalled a business partner of the family who visited him, he kept a globe that opened up to serve alcoholic drinks. Rupert Armitage remembered him as "kind of a party animal." But suddenly, during the 1970s, "he turned." Mahrouz rededicated himself to Islam. He eventually took four wives, grew a long beard, moved to Medina, and began to wear clothes thought typical of the Prophet's lifetime. He built a large housing complex with a home for himself and his mother at the center, and homes for each of his four wives at equal distance, around the points of a square.[22]

These questions and struggles involving Islam and identity were hardly unique to the young Bin Ladens. When they traveled or attended school in the West, young Saudis often had a sophisticated, self-conscious sense of their own dilemma. They did not carry themselves around America as disoriented victims, but rather as experimenters in accommodation. Gradually, wrote Peter Theroux, who lived in Riyadh during this period, this kind of private bargaining drove many Saudis back toward Islam, even those who were not necessarily prepared to live fully by its precepts:

> It was common in Saudi Arabia to look down on Europeans and Americans for selling sacreligious pleasures, then making illogical laws against drugs, drunk driving, and roughing up women. They could not keep track of that pesky line between what was licit and what was not. They often thought that the Manichean, if hypocritical situation imposed by Islamic law, which they so often violated, was saner than the West's compromise with vices, regulating and tolerating them within limits.[23]

THE BIN LADEN WOMEN encountered contrasts in America that were even more extreme than those known by their brothers. Salem urged them to broaden their horizons—literally, in some cases, by learning to fly—yet he remained acutely conscious of Arabian decorum. It did not bother him in the slightest if his sisters wore jeans and let their hair flow freely outside the kingdom; indeed, he preferred it. When it came to dating and marriage, however, he enforced a transparent double standard. Salem had many American and European girlfriends, particularly after his divorce from Sheikha in the late 1970s. One of his half-brothers married an American, Mahrouz married a Frenchwoman, and a third married a Danish woman—unions that all ended in divorce. Yet when one of his half-sisters, Salah, fell in love with an older Italian man, it created a firestorm within the family; the episode seemed to stretch the limits of Salem's tolerance, although he did finally bless the marriage, which turned out to be a long-lasting success.[24]

He presided over these issues as an Arabian patriarch—authoritarian, but eager to maintain balance and consensus. "It was just a really hard, really tough job," recalled Gail Freeman, an American who befriended and worked with some of Salem's sisters on palace design projects in Saudi Arabia. "The phone was always ringing." Salem would cradle the phone under his chin and issue a stream of advice about love and marriage, recalled Peter Blum, a German who traveled as Salem's personal valet for several years. "You have a wife," he would say, or "You have enough headaches," or "Listen, wait for a half year and then we can talk about this again." He was not harsh in his judgments, Blum said, but "always like a diplomat." Salem sometimes seemed to spend more time on "the family problems," as Freeman put it, than he did on business deals.[25]

Salem often hid his American and European girlfriends from his sisters and half-sisters, fearing their disapproval. He applauded when his sisters drove fast on American freeways or flew airplanes around California, but he did not want them running about unsupervised with American or European men. His attitudes reflected an uncomplicated sexism, but also a strain of male Saudi pride; Western women might be conquests, but Arab women never would. In the spring of 1978, while at home in Saudi Arabia, Salem punched one of his American pilots after the man spoke to one of his sisters without his permission. The pilot quit immediately. That night, he called Salem in Riyadh to ask for his paycheck and an exit visa, which was required if an American employee wished to leave Saudi

Arabia. This maelstrom involving male honor and the virtue of Bin Laden women seemed to draw out Salem's dark side. He launched into a tirade on the telephone, recalled Francis Hunnewell, an American banker who was with him; Salem said he would not allow the pilot to leave the kingdom until he publicly apologized, and if he refused to work, Salem promised to "have him thrown in jail."[26]

Salem himself preferred intelligent women. His main American girlfriend during the late 1970s was a young doctor serving in the U.S. military, Patty Deckard, who practiced at a hospital in San Antonio. Salem visited her parents in California and talked seriously about their relationship. "He always said, 'I love myself,' . . . but he probably came as close to really, really caring for somebody with her," said his pilot Jack Hinson. "But she wouldn't marry him." She concluded that she could not convert to Islam or endure the role expected of her in Saudi Arabia, said a second employee of Salem's who spent considerable time with the couple during these years. The pair traveled periodically around America and overseas for several years before the affair ended and Deckard married another man.[27]

It was difficult for any woman, including Salem's former wife, Sheikha, to compete with his relationship with Randa. "It was just always 'Randa, Randa, Randa, Randa,'" said Gail Freeman. In the same period when Salem installed Randa in Panama City for flight lessons, he also helped her enroll in medical school in Canada, and he would fly up to visit and deliver supplies. "I think most of the sisters were jealous of Randa."[28]

To win her pilot's license, Randa had to complete a cross-country solo flight, navigating on her own in a Cessna hundreds of miles across Florida to a designated airport, in this case, one near Palm Beach. The day of her big flight arrived in late September 1978, but Salem was very nervous. He called Don Sowell at the flight school and told him, as Sowell recalled, "I really don't want her to go by herself. If something should happen, I really don't want her by herself." There was no legal way for Sowell to

certify Randa as a pilot, however, if he allowed an instructor into the
cockpit with her for the cross-country flight. So they agreed that Salem
would pay for an instructor to fly behind her in a chase plane, just
in case.[29]

Salem's prescience was extraordinary: somewhere over central
Florida, smoke billowed into Randa's cockpit from some sort of engine
or electrical malfunction. Fortunately, she had a trusted pilot nearby to
speak with on the radio. But the smoke was so bad that it quickly became
clear to both of them that she was not going to be able to reach an airport. The instructor told her to prepare to crash-land in a field.

Salem's mobile phone rang at the Palm Beach airport, where he was
waiting for Randa. "She's gone off the radar—we can't find her," the
caller said, according to Gail and Robert Freeman, who were with him.
Salem "went berserk," Gail remembered. "He went crazy running around
the airport, screaming." He cried out again and again that his sister was
dead. "She crashed! She crashed!" Don Sowell had flown to Palm Beach
to receive Randa at her moment of piloting triumph, and the family's
longtime pilot Gerald Auerbach, the air force veteran, was also present.
They tried to calm Salem down, but he lashed out at them angrily, almost
to the point of striking blows, and demanded that they do something.
Salem and the two pilots took off in his Hawker jet for the area where
Randa had apparently gone down. They found an airport nearby, but its
runway was much too small for Salem's plane. Salem insisted he would
land anyway. "Over my dead body," Sowell told Auerbach, as he recalled
it, because, as Sowell put it, "I felt that was a possibility." Finally, he appealed to Salem's common sense; no matter what had happened to Randa,
he pleaded, it was not going to help if Salem got himself killed trying to
rescue her.[30]

They landed safely at a larger airport and at last they got Randa on
the phone. She was crying—but she was fine. She had fought through the
smoke, and with the help of Sowell's instructor, she had found a field
where she could put the Cessna down. She landed roughly but did no sig-

nificant damage to the plane and none at all to herself. It was a remark-able feat for a student pilot. "She had plenty of guts," Sowell said.

Now Salem was as ecstatic as he had been distraught. He asked the Freemans to help him organize a grand party at the Breakers Hotel in Palm Beach, to celebrate Randa's heroism and survival. "Call up every-body you know!" he said. "Call up your friends in a fifty-mile radius!" In the end, some of the guests flew in all the way from New York and Houston. Once more, aviation and its perils had been the source of great drama for the Bin Ladens. That night at the Breakers, Salem hired a band, and his guests danced and sang. The next day, they all went to Disney World.[31]

14. THE CONVERT'S ZEAL

OSAMA BIN LADEN moved freely as a teenager through overlapping worlds. He joined the Bin Laden family on outings and was a visible presence at its two main companies, Bin Laden Brothers and the larger Mohamed Bin Laden Organization. He played soccer and rode horses with local boys from his suburban Jeddah neighborhood. Each summer, until about 1976, he traveled to the more secular Syrian sphere of his mother's family, on the Mediterranean coast, where he hiked in the mountains and apparently fell for a younger cousin, whom he had known as an unveiled girl since childhood. All the while, he immersed himself in Islamic study groups—at Al-Thaghr, his elite high school, and also at a special religious school in Mecca, Thafiz Al-Koran Al-Kareem; he continued this study after he matriculated at Jeddah's King Abdulaziz University in 1976. In all, between the ages of sixteen and twenty-one, Osama managed to integrate his deepening religious faith with his enthusiasm for business administration and the outdoors, as well as his desire for sexual companionship. He accomplished this, after 1973, in a posture of ardent Islamic devotion from which he would never deviate.

Salem, with his rather different synthesis of enthusiasms, was nonetheless "like a father" to Osama in this period, according to Osama's mother.[1] Their relationship was typical of those between Salem and the group of his younger half-brothers who spent their early adulthoods mainly in the Arab world. When he was in Jeddah, Salem shed his jeans and donned his *thobe* and headdress. He chain-smoked cigarettes and was not noted for his leadership at prayer time, but he conducted himself nonetheless as a Saudi. He maintained some distance from his brothers and half-brothers. There were a few half-brothers, such as Tareq and Shafiq, with whom Salem seemed to share a genuine friendship. Mainly, however, Salem drew his friends and international entourage from outside the Bin Laden family—from Lebanese, Turkish, European, and American schoolmates, or from pilots and musicians he met on the road. These foreigners were playmates or aides-de-camp who depended on Salem financially or simply enjoyed his company. With them, he was free from censure and complications. With his family, he tried to be a judicious ruler.

Salem had no qualms about smuggling some of his non-Muslim friends or girlfriends into sacred Mecca or Medina, a practice that annoyed Osama when he learned about it. For their part, some of Salem's friends learned to be wary of Osama's piety. An Arab friend who was not particularly religious recalled meeting Osama in Medina: The muezzin sang out a call to the first of Islam's two evening prayers, which usually take place about one and one half hours apart, and Osama insisted on leading his visitors into the Prophet's Mosque. Salem's friend waited in the car, and he wound up stuck there for much of the evening—Osama insisted, the friend recalled, that the entourage "pray and pray and pray." The others in his group eventually returned shaking their heads. "They were complaining very much. I said, 'Thank God I didn't go inside with you. At least I'm in the fresh air outside, smoking.'"[2]

Osama was "perfectly integrated" into the family during this time, recalled Carmen Bin Laden. Beginning around 1974, while he was still in high school, he received enough money from his allowances, as well as from his work at the family companies, to buy a succession of fancy cars—a Lincoln or a Chrysler, and later, a gray Mercedes sedan, according to his neighbor and friend, Khaled Batarfi. He drove his cars very fast and wrecked at least one of them, in Batarfi's recollection. He also had access to four-wheel-drive Jeeps and trucks from the family firms, which he drove to work sites and into the desert for weekend relaxation with his friends and his beloved horses. Riding horses, he would say years later, was his "favorite hobby," and he prided himself on his ability to ride for forty or more miles at a time. He favored modest outdoor clothing, yellow work boots, and a Swiss Army watch.[3]

He turned up periodically in the smoke-filled reception room of Bin Laden Brothers, where, sometimes in the company of other younger brothers, he would wait patiently for his allowance or for some check or document to be signed. "I remember him only as a sort of supplicant, presumably for some extra cash," Rupert Armitage recalled. Salem's longtime mechanic and friend Bengt Johansson remembered him as "just another kid brother." He had grown into a tall, thin young man, and as he let his beard come in, it sprouted at first in light tufts, and later to a full, dark thickness. He remained quiet and deferential. Many of his half-brothers possessed a similarly restrained demeanor; Salem's continual displays of raucous energy were exceptional. The younger sons of Mohamed "floated" into the Bin Laden Brothers offices during school breaks, Armitage remembered, and quietly lined the chairs around the outer edges of the office. They usually needed something, but they learned to be patient. Every action in their lives, it seemed, required a "bloody signature," which often proved complicated to obtain.[4]

During Ramadan, on weekends, and other holidays, the Bin Ladens entertained themselves at communal properties in Jeddah and its environs. There was a barren desert "farm" in Al-Bahra, between Jeddah and Mecca, where Osama fenced off a small ranch for about twenty horses. There was a large bland summerhouse in Taif, constructed during the 1950s or 1960s, where family members sometimes retreated during the hot season. Along the Red Sea there were family "beach houses," which were little more than concrete sheds where a person might change into swimming trunks or find a little shade. By the standards of the day in Jeddah, these vacation properties were symbols of the family's wealth and privilege, but they were not particularly opulent. Osama seems to have enjoyed all of them, although as he became more and more of a believer, he could be a pain, particularly at the beach.

He was self-conscious about his own conversion experience, aware that in some sense he was special or separate because he had been born again. In later years, he referred to 1973 as the year his "interaction" with Islamic groups began, when he was fifteen. He seemed to interpret—or was taught to interpret—his own conversion or recruitment into the Muslim Brotherhood at that age as the natural passage of a true Muslim: "As is known," he once said, "from birth to fifteen years of age people do not look after themselves, nor are they really aware of great events ... If we're really honest, we find that this section, between the ages of fifteen to twenty-five, is when people are able to wage jihad."[5]

The intensity of Osama's conversion experience in his after-school study group had been unusual, but it was not so unusual that it marked him as some sort of cultish outsider. No young man devoted to Islam in Saudi Arabia would feel that way, or would be seen as such by his family and peers—and certainly not a young Bin Laden, whose father had been a steward of Mecca and Medina, and an emissary to Jerusalem. For many hours each week, state television broadcast scenes of thousands of pilgrims clad in white cloth circling slowly en masse around the Holy Ka'ba in Mecca; it was like having an entire network devoted to perpetual scenes from a religious aquarium. At prayer time, loudspeakers rang out in every town and city with the call to worship; shops and supermarkets closed immediately and *mutawawa*, or "religious police," patrolled the streets with sticks to enforce compliance. The art hanging on Jeddah's office walls, the books on living room shelves, the buildings on every other street corner, the calendar of public life, the speeches of public figures, the rituals of birth, seasons, and death—all of these drew heavily, if not exclusively, upon the idioms of Islam. Religion in Saudi Arabia was like gravity; it explained the order of objects and the trajectory of lives. The Koran was the kingdom's constitution and the basis of all its laws. The kingdom had evolved into the most devout society on earth, not only in its constitutional and legal systems but also in the rhythms of its households, schools, and circles of friendship. The influx of European and American businessmen and advisers during the 1970s, and the widespread introduction of consumer technologies, did not alter Islam's central place in the daily lives of the great majority of the kingdom's subjects. Nasir Al-Bahri, a Yemeni who grew up in Jeddah and later served as Osama Bin Laden's bodyguard, recalled that particularly for those teenagers, like Osama, who were attracted to religious teaching

> [t]he Islamic climate was everywhere in Saudi Arabia, and the Islamic spirit was in everything: in the councils of scholars and in religious gatherings . . . The entire society there was one fabric. It was impossible to find a house without the fragrance of Islamic trends, in any form. Thus if a household did not have a young man who observed the faith, it had a young woman who observed the faith. If it did not have a young woman who observed the faith, the household perhaps had an Islamic tape or an Islamic book.[6]

Osama offered one such touchstone of religious devotion to the extended Bin Laden family. His family saw him—some with skeptical tolerance, others with unequivocal admiration—as their clan's remarkably committed young preacher and prayer leader. Just as European aristocratic families of past eras considered it a matter of course for one or two sons to join the priesthood, while others became officers in the military or advisers at court, so did the Bin Ladens regard it as unremarkable for some of their sons and daughters to answer Islam's call. This choice did not in itself make Osama a particularly prestigious Bin Laden son— certainly not under Salem's leadership. Business, aviation, engineering, interior design, and Salem's desire for someone in the family to become a medical doctor all competed with Koranic education in the family's informal honors lists during the 1970s. And yet, of course, the Bin Ladens regarded themselves as an Islamic family, and so Osama's idealism and commitment were respected, even when he grated.

Carmen Bin Laden saw Osama, with his gangly height and insistent religiosity, as a "minor figure" hovering censoriously on the family's periphery. He was "more literal, more fundamentalist" than even some of his colleagues in the Muslim Brotherhood, said his friend and fellow adherent Jamal Khashoggi. He seemed particularly drawn to teachings that a righteous Muslim should imitate the dress and customs that prevailed during the Prophet's lifetime. Osama scolded his friend Khaled Batarfi for wearing shorts to soccer games, which violated an obscure tenet of theological rule making. He seemed bent on finding a personal state of purity, and to achieve this, he insisted upon introducing Islamic precepts into even the most casual everyday encounters. As his Syrian brother-in-law Najim put it: "He often used to tell us what he had learned about religion."[7]

Osama's early involvement with the Muslim Brotherhood meant that from the very beginning, his understanding of Islam was inflected by messages of political dissent. The Brotherhood's Islam was not passive; its members advocated a journey toward a righteous Islamic government. Lectures by its members were informed, too, by the Brotherhood's recent history of anti-colonial violence in Egypt and the exile to Saudi Arabia of many of its activists. Scholars and writers influenced by the Brotherhood offered varying ideas about how a righteous Islamic government should be pursued, and when, for instance, violence or open political organizing might be justified. They were unified, however, in the view that preaching and teaching should be a bulwark of their campaign. A good Muslim should not only seek out his own state of grace; he should teach others. Brotherhood political precepts might make the Saudi royal family nervous, but this proselytizing vein fitted with the Salafi school of thought that dominated the kingdom. The term "Salafi" refers to the Prophet's earliest companions, whom Salafi believers are taught to imitate. Mohamed Abdul Wahhab, an influential source of this doctrine in Arabia, emphasized that a man should literally model his life on that of the Prophet and his companions. In this school of thought, the purpose of studying the Koran and the hadiths involved a search for literal truths—facts and laws—which had been made available during the seventh century with the Prophet's revelations; these pieces of a righteous life could then be adopted and assembled by any Muslim who wished to please God on Judgment Day.

Years later, after he had declared war against the United States, Osama said that even as a young man, he had been fired by anger over America and its conspiracies with Jews and Christians to destroy Islam. "Every Muslim," he said, "from the moment they realize the distinction in their hearts, hates Americans, hates Jews, and hates Christians. This is a part of our belief and our religion. For as long as I can remember, I have felt tormented and at war, and have felt hatred and animosity for Americans." In fact, prior to 1979, there is not much evidence that Osama was especially political. He seems to have concentrated in these years mainly on learning how to define and live an Islamic life, as outlined by the mentors and scholars he followed in Jeddah and Mecca. He certainly listened to speeches and read books containing anti-colonial and revolutionary political views, particularly the influential works of the hanged Egyptian Islamist Sayid Qutb, whose exiled brother, Mohamed, lectured at Osama's university in Jeddah. According to his friend and university classmate Jamal Khalifa, Osama read Qutb's *Signposts* and *In the Shade of the Koran* for the first time around 1976 or 1977; the books expounded on provocative theories for offensive action, including violence, to protect Islam from imperialists and nonbelievers. In later years, Osama often cited approvingly the works of Taqi Al-Din Ibn Taymiyya, a thirteenth-century theorist of violent jihad against apostate "occupiers," and he cited a particular book by Mohamed Qutb, *Concepts That Should Be Corrected*, which had helped him understand that impious rulers of Islamic countries were "incapable and treacherous, and they have not followed the right path of

Islam, but have followed their wishes and lusts—[and] this is the reason for the setbacks in the nation's march during the past decades." When he first heard these lectures and read these texts in the late 1970s, however, he had no practical way to consider their calls to political action, and no evident desire to take the political risks they urged upon him.[8]

He talked with his friends during this time about the problem of Palestine, according to Batarfi, but his views were unexceptional. In the aftermath of the 1973 Arab-Israeli war, in which American military support for Israel figured prominently, Osama would have heard many anti-American and anti-Semitic harangues in Jeddah's mosques, classrooms, and salons. These themes would also have been an aspect of his formal religious study. The Koranic narrative of Islam's birth and spread is one of territory and warfare, a story in which the supposed treachery of Arabian Jews figures significantly. In later years, Osama would connect his anti-Semitism, which he attributed to Koranic teaching, with his outrage over American support for Israel:

> It appears to us, from the writing of the Prophet, that we will have to fight the Jews under his name and on this land [Palestine] . . . And the United States has involved itself and its people again and again . . . and dispatched a general air supply line in 1973 during the days of Nixon, from America to Tel Aviv, with weapons, aid, and men, which affected the outcome of the battle, so how could we not fight it? . . . Any nation that joins the Jewish trenches has only itself to blame.[9]

It would be a mistake to attribute statements Osama made in his late forties to his state of mind three decades before, yet there is continuity in his opinions. His repeated references to 1973 as a turning point in his own life and as a touchstone of his anti-Zionist and anti-Semitic viewpoints suggest that year's resonance in his life. Still, in Saudi Arabia during the mid-1970s, for an eighteen-year-old to describe Americans and Jews as enemies of Islam was little more than an expression of conventional wisdom. The testimony about him from contemporaries emphasizes other aspects of his religiosity—his insistent piety and his search for a life that was well rounded and pure.

A biography later published by his media office, drawn from the observations of an aide who knew him at a time when Osama was still interacting with the Bin Laden family, tried to inventory the sources of influence in his outlook and character. It read like the comment section in a schoolteacher's report card:

> Raised by his father, Bin Laden became used to responsibility, confidence, generosity, and modesty . . . It is known that he is also shy and taciturn, usually appearing serious, though trying to appear friendly, and avoiding raising his voice, generally, or laughing excessively . . . Osama is quite intelligent, confident, and observant, but also somewhat hesitant in making decisions and taking control, which has sometimes hurt him . . . One of the contradictions within Osama is his emotion and tenderness on the one hand, and his strength and stubbornness on the other hand. He loves to read, and does so frequently, and has an unusual passion for going through information, documents, and archives, as well as following the press.[10]

Some of his most uncompromising conduct involved women. Dating among suburban Jeddah teenagers was a difficult, risky, and frustrating endeavor even among relatively secular families, and for a young man as devout as Osama, it was just about out of the question. He was notably attracted to girls, however, according to Batarfi; by his account, Osama decided to marry at seventeen essentially because he wanted to have legitimate sex. The female cousins he saw in Syria in the summers did not veil or segregate themselves as rigorously as young women in Jeddah did. During his sojourns there, he had gotten to know Najwa, a daughter of his mother's brother. Marriages among first cousins were commonplace in Arabian families; Osama's mother and family may have encouraged and even arranged the match. Najwa's brother, however, has suggested that the initiative came from Osama, and that he asked formally for his cousin's hand. She was fourteen.[11]

Initially they lived with Osama's mother and stepfamily in Jeddah; Najwa became pregnant and gave birth to a son, Abdullah. The marriage bed seems only to have sharpened Osama's conviction that a righteous Muslim man should not cast his eyes even in passing on women other than his legal wives and his mother. He did not permit his wife to meet strangers. He averted his eyes from the family maid. When he made social calls on his brothers, he would back away and cover his eyes if an unveiled woman opened the door. He would not shake hands with any woman.[12]

Osama graduated from Al-Thaghr in 1976. The class photo depicts several rows of boys and teachers in ties and blazers, but Osama is not in the picture. By then, photography was one of the innovations that he rejected—photographs drew faithful eyes to false idols, to human imagery that competed with God's oneness. Around this time he rejected secular music as well, because, as his teachers would have explained, it had not been a part of the Prophet's life and it competed with the sacred sounds of Koranic recital and prayer. Osama did not smoke. He condemned gambling. His only conspicuous pleasures were sex, cars, work, and the outdoors. If he sometimes imagined himself as living in his departed father's image, as some of his friends have suggested, he did so with considerable faithfulness.[13]

An exception was his view of polygamy. He talked with his friend Jamal Khalifa about the serial marriages their fathers had each undertaken, apparently from sexual motives. They felt this was "not the Islamic way at all." They believed that there were more women then men in society, and so for that reason, multiple marriages were desirable, since they "solved a social problem," Khalifa recalled. Yet, according to Islamic teaching, "you have to be fair, you have to give equal justice between all of them, and you have to divide the time, to give each of them what is enough for her." They pledged to handle their married lives more responsibly—they might take the four wives permitted, but they would not divorce frivolously, and they would concentrate on the issue of equity.[14]

As his house filled up with young children (Najwa's intervals between her pregnancies were short), he banned videotapes of Disney cartoons or *Sesame Street*. He rejected most television for the same reasons that he rejected photography and music; it coursed with blasphemous imagery. He did watch news programming, but he trained his children to stand by the television when the news was on, so they could turn down the volume knob when pulsing music announced a broadcast's introduction.

He seems to have derived his early ideas about fatherhood in part from the lessons about self-reliance, faith, and parsimony imparted by his own self-made father. He took his young children camping in the desert. He taught them to ride horses, to sleep in the open, and to cover themselves with sand if they needed warmth. "He did talk a lot about how we lived in luxury, and how we would have to toughen up," Batarfi recalled. "He wanted them to grow up tough—they would practice hunting and shooting." He would not let his children drink from a straw, because these had been unknown in the Prophet's lifetime; on one particularly hot family outing, Carmen Bin Laden watched, appalled, as Osama's wife, draped in black, tried to hydrate her sweating children by spooning water into their mouths. The other Bin Ladens present, she felt, were "simply awed by Osama's zeal, intimidated into silence." Yet others who knew him then have said that while he could be severe with his children about Islamic precepts and instruction, he could also be playful and warm, particularly on family camping trips to the desert.[15]

In the physical world, liquids and gases swirl or condense when temperatures and densities rise and fall. A similar convection of cultures molded Osama's late adolescence. He stood one degree separated from Mecca and two degrees from Las Vegas. And yet, in his own way, he seemed as comfortable with the presence of those competing densities as was Salem; he just managed their demands and temptations differently. Osama, in any event, was hardly the only Bin Laden of his generation to adhere strictly to Islamic teaching. In addition to his half-brother Mahrouz, two of his sisters, Sheikha and Rafah, became particularly devout in this period; they started a religious school in Jeddah for young family members. A number of his other brothers studied Islam formally and circulated in religious circles in the Hejaz. Among other things, religious credibility remained an imperative of the family business— Islamic scholars on urban planning committees in the two holy cities influenced contracting and real estate development decisions, as they had in Mohamed's time.

Osama did not appear in the famous Swedish family portrait, but he certainly knew Europe. According to Batarfi, he visited London at age twelve, with his mother, to receive medical treatment for an eye condition; he stayed for at least a month and did some sightseeing. On a second trip, as a teenager, Bin Laden joined some friends and relatives on a big-game safari in East Africa. According to Batarfi, he also made one trip to the United States. Walid Al-Khatib, Osama's supervisor at the family construction company, has also said that he "went on trips to the U.S. and Europe." In Batarfi's account, the visit to America came about because he and his wife sought treatment for a medical problem of one of their sons.[16]

Only one aspect of the journey made a particularly strong impression, according to Batarfi. On the way home, Osama and his wife were sitting in an airport lounge, waiting for their connecting flight. Najwa wore a black abaya, a draping gown, as well as the full head covering often referred to as hijab. Other passengers in the airport "were staring at them," Batarfi said, "and taking pictures." When Bin Laden returned to Jeddah, he said the experience was like "being in a show." By Batarfi's account,

Bin Laden was not particularly bitter about all the stares and the photographs; rather, "he was joking about it." The provenance of this account of Osama's journey is uncertain; Batarfi is generally reliable, but in this case, his firsthand knowledge is limited. It seems clear that Osama did travel to the West to seek medical treatment for a son during the late 1970s, but he may have gone no further than Britain.[17]

Whatever his itineraries, the same themes prevail: Osama was not a stranger to the West, but he was not radicalized there. Through his own travel and that of his family, he knew something of Europe and America, but by age fifteen, he had already erected a wall against their allures. He felt implicated by the West, and by its presence in his own family, and yet, as he would demonstrate in the years ahead, he lacked a sophisticated or subtle understanding of Western society and history. He used his passport, but he never really left home.

THE AMBITION that most firmly bound Osama to his half-brothers was his interest in the family business. As his generation of Mohamed's sons reached college, some of them drifted away from the prospect of a life in the construction trade—a few of his half-brothers managed to never work a day in their lives. Osama was among the larger group of boys who were strivers. They jockeyed for influence, salaries, and leadership roles. Osama's religious inclinations made him a natural for management assignments involving the family's Mecca and Medina renovation work. Assigning the most ardently religious Bin Laden brothers to work on projects in the holy cities would become a pattern as the family allocated management roles over the years.

Walid Al-Khatib, a Palestinian who supervised Osama in the Mecca office when he was still a teenager, remembered him as "serious for his age, and from the first day, I noticed his interest in small details. We operated heavy equipment, and soon this tall skinny boy was driving them all. His technical ability was impressive."[18]

There were two main educational pathways for those brothers interested in a career at the company—engineering and business administration. The former was demanding academically and required a willingness to attend university abroad, as Saudi universities were not adequate. Between his religious studies and his swelling young family, the prospect of four or more years in Cairo or the West may have seemed undesirable to Osama. Whatever his reasoning, after Al-Thaghr, he enrolled as a business administration student at King Abdulaziz University, a sprawling white-walled campus built less than a decade earlier along the Mecca Road, near the Bin Laden family's main compound at Kilo 7. It was a private university founded by Jeddah merchants who wanted a place to train their sons for business. Abdullah Suleiman, the former finance minister who had helped make Mohamed Bin Laden's fortune, donated the land on which it stood, and had been among the Jeddah moguls who funded its creation during the 1960s.[19]

Years later, in an interview, Osama would boast that he balanced his academic studies with his assignments at the family company more successfully than any of his brothers. This was not only immodest, it was wrong. He apparently sought to leave university early to take a supervisory job in Mecca but may have changed his mind because of his mother's pleadings. He implied in the interview that he had completed his university education, but according to Khalifa, he never earned a degree. A brief résumé prepared by Bin Laden or his aides in 1996 stated only that he "studied management and economics" at the university. In any event, he certainly fell well short of the achievements in academics and business management of a number of his older brothers.[20]

Osama was appointed as a manager in Mecca after he left university, according to Al-Khatib. The Bin Laden firms were responsible for a number of renovation projects in the area during this time. They built a new staircase at the Zamzam well, the Haram's ancient source of sacred water; they demolished buildings to expand platforms and roads around the Mosque; and they restored walls and gates. Al-Khatib remembered

Osama as stingy about distributing cash bonuses but fastidious about conserving food and handing out leftovers to the workers. Like his father, Osama prided himself on his ability to think through complex problems of demolition or engineering, even though he lacked the requisite formal training. As Al-Khatib put it: "He liked to solve technical problems by himself."[21]

15. WIRED

FRANCIS HUNNEWELL grew up in a stone hilltop mansion above a lake; he belonged to a Massachusetts family who traced their lineage and landholdings to the period of America's founding. Michael Pochna's father had been a legal adviser to J. Paul Getty. They were both Harvard men, class of 1960. Later they moved to Paris to seek their fortunes in private finance. They made lists of contacts from family, schools, sports teams, and social clubs, and then started calling around, looking for deals—an attractive line of work if you had the right lists, spoke French, and could raise some stake money. By the early 1970s, they operated a boutique merchant bank. Headquartered in Paris but registered in the Bahamas, it was called Lansdowne Ltd.; it engaged in the kinds of financings that would later be commonly known as venture capital and private equity.[1]

The multiple economic upheavals of 1973 and 1974—the Arab-Israeli war, the international oil embargo, inflation, and stagnating economic growth in America and Europe—forced them to rethink. Liquidity, a banker's synonym for ready cash, was draining rapidly out of Europe and toward the oil regions of the Arab world. Hunnewell, Pochna, and their third active partner, Jan Baily, decided to relocate to the Middle East. Beirut and Cairo seemed the most appealing places for a new headquarters; they flipped a coin, and it came up Cairo. Pochna moved there, equipped with new lists of contacts. Hunnewell's brother-in-law was an influential banker at Credit Suisse. He suggested that they call on a young Saudi he had met, Sheikh Salem Bin Laden.

Hunnewell arranged an introductory meeting and flew into Jeddah. He was a tall, athletic man in his thirties who projected the languid confidence of old money. Salem had grown used to these solicitous bankers who wanted a piece of what they presumed to be his outlandish fortune. He judged them not by the services they offered, about which he was generally indifferent, but by whether they enjoyed his sort of fun. He hosted lunch and then suggested they all ride out to the desert to see some of the Bin Laden horses. He had just bought a new dune buggy, a motorized contraption with a Volkswagen chassis and tires that could roar through soft sand. He loaded Hunnewell and Jan Baily into the passenger seats and began speeding at sixty miles an hour through the open desert, bouncing across dunes. One of the vehicle's wheels soon fell off. Salem stopped and rounded up Bedouins who happened to be walking nearby and forced them to search for the missing wheel. They found it and a few of its nuts and bolts. Salem had no wrench, however. Hunnewell lifted the entire buggy into the air while Salem held a Bedouin's hand in the position of a wrench, twisting it, which Hunnewell imagined must have been very painful for the volunteer. Baily tried to put the wheel back on. It worked, sort of, and Salem was impressed. For years later he would tell the story about how Hunnewell had lifted up the car like a superhero. He seemed to decide then and there that he would do business with them. They got back in the buggy and wobbled on; Salem sped almost as fast as before. What industry they might enter, how, and by what plan—those were details for another day.[2]

Michael Pochna flew out a few weeks later to try to put something specific together. He suffered through the usual long waits and chaotic scheduling before he received an audience with Salem. He pitched a Swiss company that could set up a factory in Saudi Arabia to manufacture pre-stressed concrete and modular housing, which could then support the Bin Ladens' construction projects.

"Well, I'm not interested," Salem said. "What else have you got?"

A silence followed, Pochna recalled, as he tried to come up with another idea. Salem then spoke.

"I think the future is telephones," he said.

Pochna readily agreed, even though he had not previously given the subject any thought. They talked some more. Pochna made some calls to one contact he had in the American telephone industry. It became clear that Salem was thinking very ambitiously. He wanted nothing less than to win a contract from the royal family to build the kingdom's first modern telephone network.

"My father built the roads," Salem said. "I will build the telephones."[3]

His vision was rooted in his global lifestyle. Salem and his generation of Bin Ladens were innovators of the jet age; they hopped effortlessly from Jeddah to Cairo to Corfu to Paris to New York and back again, sometimes in the course of just a few days. The more they moved around, however, the more they wished to stay connected. Salem lived at the center of a spinning family wheel, perpetually in motion. He could not bear to be out of touch—with Randa, or his European and American girlfriends, or his pilot friends, or his mother, or his brothers and sisters, or his royal patrons, or, if it was truly necessary, his business partners. In the 1970s, his and his family's need for telephones with global reach far outpaced the technology's development. Telephone service was particularly dire inside Saudi Arabia, where there were only a few tens of thousands of unreliable phone lines. When he was grounded in Jeddah, Salem resorted to flirting with his overseas girlfriends by telex from his Bin Laden Brothers office.

The idea that the world economy might be rapidly connected together and speeded up by affordable, border-crossing voice communication was barely understood or discussed in this divided era of the late Cold War. Russia and its East European clients lay firmly isolated behind the Iron Curtain. China was cut off and staggering after its dark period of Cultural Revolution. Even in the West the development of international satellites and telephones had only begun. Science fiction writer Arthur C. Clarke's pioneering essay "Extra-Terrestrial Relays," which first imagined the possibility of global satellite communications, had been published just three decades earlier, in 1945. *Sputnik*'s launch inaugurated the military satellite age in 1957, but missile and space races between the United States and the Soviet Union dominated the technology's initial evolution. Governments and sclerotic monopolists controlled the major phone companies in America and Europe. There were no cell phones yet, and the only mobile satellite phones available to consumers were bulky and difficult to operate. The few global phones available usually required a user to identify his location and then call through a patchy private network. These devices improved incrementally every few years, but only a very passionate and very wealthy user (and Salem was both) could find them at all appealing.

It was often easier in these years for Salem to chat with friends and family while he was flying his airplanes than when he was moving around on the ground. Salem installed high-frequency radios in his private planes, at a price of about thirty thousand dollars each—these radios enhanced safety during transatlantic flights, but they also allowed him to connect to various telephone networks while he was up in the air. In Europe, he would call in from the cockpit to a company called Stockholm Radio. For a steep price, its operators would then route him into the Swedish phone system, through which he could connect to just about anyone in Europe. Salem so often called Stockholm Radio—and a similar firm in Houston, Texas—that the operators often just asked him for the name of the friend or sister he wanted to reach, since they already had all his numbers on hand. While flying over San Antonio or Houston, Salem would call down to friends in their houses below and tell them to come outside and look up in the sky. He would flash his jet's lights and shout into his mobile telephone: "Do you see me? Do you see me?" On gliding trips in Europe, he would call his favorite sister in Montreal: "Randa! I'm over the Alps at twelve thousand feet! Do you believe this?"

Flying between European capitals at night, he would talk for hours with his girlfriends while the Stockholm operators listened in sympathetically. If he was bored and his friends were asleep, he would call the Stockholm operators from his plane and play songs on his harmonica.[4]

"There's a lot of money in phones," Salem told his German friend Thomas Dietrich. He knew this because he and his family spent such vast sums of money on international phone calls. When he checked out of European hotels, he usually owed more for his phone bill than for his room and meals. He would call at night just to talk "and he would fall asleep, on an international call," Dietrich recalled. "And when you hang up, he calls back and says, 'Why are you hanging up?'" Dietrich learned that even if they were staying in the same hotel, it made much more sense to call Salem on the phone than to try to visit his room "because when you visit him, he sits in front of the TV and talks on the phone—he will not talk to you . . . In the day, he slept and was on the phone. And in the night, he was on the phone."[5]

SALEM FOUNDED Bin Laden Telecommunications in 1975. He owned 51 percent. Lansdowne Ltd. owned 15 percent; the rest ended up with Salem's bankers, the Bin Mahfouz family. The company operated at first from a modest residential villa in Jeddah. It possessed the air of whimsy that seemed to swirl around Salem like fairy dust.

Although he had virtually no prior experience in business, Rupert Armitage, Salem's guitar-playing schoolmate from Copford Glebe, was soon appointed the company's managing director. Salem and Rupert had fallen out of touch after school until they bumped into each other in the wee hours at a nightclub outside Rome, where Rupert was working as a bar manager and Salem was partying with a son of Lord Carrington, the British politician who was then his country's foreign secretary. They jammed with their guitars that night, and six months later, Salem asked Rupert to come to Jeddah to give him additional lessons. Hunnewell and

Pochna found Rupert to be a bit of an adventurer, and an unlikely telephone company executive, but they thought he was intelligent and reliable, and he was clearly trusted by Salem, so they accepted him.[6]

Their business at first centered on the sale in Saudi Arabia of American-made speed dialers for rotary telephones. These were primitive devices that allowed a user to program the numbers of friends or family and then dial by pressing a single button; they cost about one hundred dollars in the U.S. but sold at a brisk clip for three times that much in the kingdom. Lansdowne won an exclusive agency to sell the dialers in Saudi Arabia, and it turned out that every prince with a palace and a long list of brothers, sisters, aunts, and uncles wanted to have one. They soon branched out into other telephone equipment, such as private exchanges that allowed a palace to have dozens of separate lines. The kingdom still did not have a decent national telephone network, but the royal family wanted the latest and best equipment in their homes, even if the lines crackled or broke off when they punched the blinking buttons.

The biggest problem, Hunnewell discovered, was getting paid. "We were doing compounds in princes' palaces and friends of Salem's," he recalled, and this drew them into the web of informal debts and credits that bound the Bin Ladens to other merchant families and the royal family. They would install an expensive 250-line exchange in a particular palace, only to be told by its owner, "I'm a friend of Salem's, and Salem owes me money over here for this, and so he and I will work that out." Hunnewell would then have to petition through Rupert Armitage to explain, "We're owed 2.5 million by these people, who all say that you owe them money, and who aren't gonna pay us" until Salem reconciled his debts.[7]

The company books were a continuous mess; there were so many claims of credit, debt, and barter exchange between Salem and his customers that it often seemed hopeless to sort out an accurate picture. "There must have been some cash flow problems" among the interlocking Bin Laden companies, and between Salem and his bankers, Rupert

Armitage recalled. Salem "was always saying, 'Rupert! Where can I find one hundred million dollars? I need it by tomorrow!'"[8]

Armitage dealt with much smaller amounts but in an atmosphere of disarray. He would make his way down to the National Commercial Bank "to pick up six hundred thousand riyals in order to pay off some official—and by the way, six hundred thousand riyals is really quite heavy, I can tell you." In the hallways leading to the bank's vaults, he would find "a few Yemenis shoveling out one hundred thousand riyals at a time . . . something huge. Anyhow, that's a lot of money, and there were just blocks of it going off into the distance."[9]

Hunnewell and Baily thought they should try to build a sustainable, organized business as they had tried to do in their previous merchant banking ventures. Hunnewell had contacts at General Electric and tried to deepen GE's steadily expanding partnership with the Bin Ladens. They also tried to find a new source of profit in the Bin Ladens' role as a customer of Caterpillar, the American manufacturer of construction machinery. Hunnewell noticed that there were all sorts of Caterpillar equipment—graders, earthmovers, bulldozers, and so on—just lying abandoned at former Bin Laden job sites. Salem explained that it had been his father's practice to build the price of a new fleet of Caterpillar equipment into the bid of each road or other major project he took on. He would import the tractors, haul them to his job site, use them until the work was complete, and then just leave them. Caterpillar sent out a team to inventory all the equipment scattered around the kingdom. "They found stuff that was buried in the sands in crates that had never been opened," Hunnewell recalled. They counted it up and told the Bin Ladens that they were the largest owners of Caterpillar equipment in the world. They discussed making the Bin Ladens their agents in Saudi Arabia, but Salem wasn't interested. He wanted to build things, not sell somebody else's products, he said.[10]

Salem had his eye on a big prize, a plan announced by the royal family to install about 450,000 new telephone lines in the kingdom, to bring

Saudi Arabia into the modern communications age in a single leap. The contract—always on the verge of being finalized but never quite tangible—was the pot of gold at the end of the Saudi rainbow for many foreign businessmen who had flocked to the kingdom during the mid-1970s. Every Saudi merchant family, courtier, and arms broker in Jeddah and Riyadh, including Adnan Khashoggi, seemed to be angling for a piece of the contract as an agent or partner. With his new telecommunications company up and running, Salem decided to join the game. The American bankers were excited about the potential payoff, but Pochna, in particular, who increasingly found Salem arrogant and frustrating, became skeptical that the Bin Ladens would treat them fairly as partners. Salem, he felt, saw his merchant banking partners as "one of the many Westerners" who provided him with the services he required, "and we were no different than one of his pilots." Pochna particularly resented the long waits he endured in Salem's smoky reception rooms; he got so fed up that he began to bring a deck of cards to pass the time. This was not the way Harvard-educated investment bankers did business.[11]

They all recognized that the monster telephone contract would be won or lost on the basis of private accommodations within and around the royal family that the Americans and Europeans involved in the deal could never fully understand. Salem compounded the mystery of these informal negotiations by speaking about the deal to his partners through "delphic, inaccurate, odd comments," which he then expected the Lansdowne partners to interpret accurately and act upon to strengthen their bid, in Pochna's view.[12]

Saudi Arabia's government-controlled telephone company had announced an exclusive deal with Phillips of the Netherlands, whose agent in the kingdom happened to be Mohammed bin Fahd, a son of the crown prince. The price of this tentative contract was estimated at $6.7 billion, an amount so much larger than the true cost of the system, as calculated by European consultants, that it appeared to involve several billion dollars of very mysterious payments. In 1976 and early 1977, Salem and others in Fahd's circle managed to reopen the negotiations. Logs from Salem's private jets show that he gave several rides to the minister and deputy minister of communications, and their families, during this period; presumably, he was impressing upon them, among other things, the perks of his friendship.[13]

Salem never explained to his American partners how he had worked his way into the contract's new round of talks, or how the deal would finally be decided, but he made clear at a certain point that "this was one of the contracts he would get," Pochna remembered. To succeed, however, Bin Laden Telecommunications needed a capable foreign telephone company as a partner—a company that could actually do the work. Lansdowne had negotiated relationships at Northern Telecom, an affiliate of Bell Canada. Northern's president, Walter Light, flew into Jeddah. Salem threw a party at his house, invited the Canadian ambassador, pulled out his guitar, and sang "She'll Be Coming 'Round the Mountain." He then divided the audience into women and men for a rousing version of "Frère Jacques."[14]

Salem's methods paid off. Despite twists and complications, Bin Laden Telecommunications ended up as Bell Canada's agent for a large portion of the contract, earning a straight cash commission of 1.5 percent of the company's five-year, approximately $1.5 billion deal to operate and maintain the new Saudi phone system. The Bin Ladens also earned a similar percentage of a subsequent five-year Bell Canada contract with the kingdom, plus a large share of $400 million worth of ministry and housing construction contracts that Bell Canada was required to undertake as part of the deal. Almost everyone ended up happy—Phillips and Ericsson won a part of the contract involving equipment sales, and Prince Mohammed bin Fahd reportedly received a commission of about $500 million. Two exceptions were Francis Hunnewell and Michael Pochna. They accused Salem of cutting them out of some of the Bell Canada money and of improperly diverting construction contracts from the deal to other Bin Laden firms. They sued and ended up tied down in Canadian courts for many years.[15]

More and more, in business deals between Saudis and Americans, greed and a competing sense of entitlement became a risk. Each side condescended to the other. Even so, in the late 1970s, there was, it seemed, an almost endless amount of money to go around. Yachts, private jets, palaces filled with new technology, garages stuffed with European race cars—the princes were updating themselves, and a younger and more international generation was coming to the fore around Fahd. Yet the royal family and its courtiers were also drifting back toward the ethos of public luxury and payoffs that had prevailed two decades earlier under King Saud. The relative austerity and the official piety of the intervening Faisal years were receding. With Fahd firmly in control, with his own sons moving boldly into business, with oil prices rising ever higher, with construction cranes towering above every horizon, it was difficult for many privileged Saudis to imagine what might threaten the existing order.

DURING THE LATE 1920s, as he completed his conquest of the Arabian Peninsula, King Abdulaziz faced a Frankenstein problem. He had employed his jihadi militia, the Ikhwan, or "Brothers," to vanquish his enemies and take the Hejaz, but he could not persuade these zealous volunteers that their religious war had reached its end. The Ikhwan protested Abdulaziz's blasphemous embrace of the automobile and the telegraph. Soon they revolted violently. The king showed little mercy; in some battles, he mocked their beliefs by using his Fords as makeshift motorized cavalry to break their ranks. At the same time he sought a broader political accommodation with his enemies. He created oasis settlements for demobilized holy warriors and encouraged them to take up farming and passive religious study. Qasim, a deeply conservative province of rolling dunes and watered oases to the immediate northwest of Riyadh, hosted a number of these villages filled with resettled Ikhwan. Around 1940, a time when the Brothers' memories of their grievances against Abdulaziz and his family remained fresh, Juhaiman Al-Otaibi was born in one such Qasim settlement, called Sajir. As he grew up, he seems to have identified early on with the causes and religious austerity of the Ikhwan and to have felt some nostalgia for their revolt against the royal family.[16]

He joined his tribe's levy, or *mujaheddin*, in the kingdom's National Guard, a paramilitary force that served as a check on the regular Saudi armed services and also as a kind of national employment scheme for restive tribesmen. Juhaiman became a corporal but left his tribe's ranks to take up religious study at the University of Medina during the early 1970s. The university was known for its heavy contingent of exiled faculty who belonged to the Muslim Brotherhood. Its students included exiles from Egypt, Yemen, Kuwait, and Pakistan; there were even some American converts to Islam in what became Juhaiman's Islamic study group. At Medina they studied tenets of Salafi orthodoxy, inherited in part from the beliefs of the Ikhwan, which emphasized the need to withdraw into a state of Islamic purity. These teachings intermingled with the political activism of the Muslim Brotherhood and the specific grievances of expatriate students about their home governments. In all, this blend of Koranic introspection and political dissent, tracing back into Saudi history and connecting outward to pan-Islamic movements abroad, would have seemed quite familiar to Osama Bin Laden and his Muslim Brotherhood–influenced after-school study group at Al-Thaghr, in nearby Jeddah.[17]

Juhaiman was almost two decades older than Osama's generation, but many of his followers at Medina were younger students. They wore short mustaches, long beards, and *thobes* that fell only to the middle of their calfs, styles they attributed to the companions of the Prophet. They rejected photography as a blasphemous innovation, but their views went even further than those of Osama and his schoolmates in Jeddah. Juhaiman echoed the original Ikhwan by attacking modernity as a kind

of grand conspiracy against true believers. After 1974 he and his followers also concluded that the Saudi royal family was illegitimate and corrupt. They withdrew from Medina to form an explicit political conspiracy
to challenge the Al-Saud. Informal circles of study groups and students,
frequently overlapping in their ideologies, were distinguished by intense
and often very subtle debates over theology and the correct course of religious politics. Osama moved in one circle in Jeddah and Mecca;
Juhaiman and his followers occupied a partially overlapping but separate
realm in Medina.

After breaking with his professors in Medina, Juhaiman returned to
Qasim, then moved to Riyadh, where his following grew to about two
hundred. By 1978 they began to print anti-royal pamphlets on presses in
Kuwait. One of the pamphlets was called "Rules of Allegiance and
Obedience: The Misconduct of Rulers." It attacked the Saudi royals and
the officially sanctioned religious scholars who supported them as false
stewards of Islam and its holy places. Some princes were "drunkards" who
"led a dissolute life in luxurious palaces." The royal family had "seized
land" and "squandered the state's money." Commission-laden contracts
like the deal to build a national telephone system were symptoms of a
broader political rot. Juhaiman's fulminations drew the attention of the
Saudi interior minister, who arrested and interrogated Juhaiman and his
followers. They were released in Riyadh after they promised to
quiet down.[18]

In fact, they began to plan for a violent revolt.

IN SEPTEMBER 1979, Salem flew to Washington, D.C., to buy a new
Learjet. He visited his American girlfriend Patty Deckard. The two
picked up Jack and Anita Pizza from Panama City, Florida, then flew to
Europe. They visited Cairo, Jeddah, Dubai, and Abu Dhabi. In early
November, they scooped up two of Salem's sisters, Mona and Randa,
and flew to Athens. They spent a night on the Greek island of Crete, then

they jetted back to Cairo. It was a particularly busy season in Salem's playhouse at thirty thousand feet.[19]

The siege at the Grand Mosque at Mecca began at the call to dawn prayer on November 20, the first day of the portentous Islamic year of 1400. Juhaiman and his followers unpacked weapons they had smuggled in coffins normally carried by worshippers to bless the dead. They seized microphones and announced that among them was the Mahdi—the prophesied redeemer of Islam whose arrival on earth would signal Judgment Day. The purported Mahdi was Mohamed Al-Qahtani, an otherwise undistinguished follower of Juhaiman whose true role had been divined in a dream by another member of the group. As they fired their weapons from the mosque's minarets, Juhaiman's followers announced the start of what they believed would be the last battle known to mortals.[20]

It quickly devolved into a bloody catastrophe. Saudi security forces arrived and tried to undertake a frontal assault on the holy Haram. Floodlights installed by Bin Laden engineers during past renovations, which normally illuminated worshippers and pilgrims in a celestial glow, lit a killing field for Juhaiman's sharpshooters. Scores bled to death on the marble. Salem and his muscular Lebanese aide Mustafa Fathlalla donned military uniforms and drove into Mecca with drawings of the mosque's layout hurriedly pulled from office files.

Salem, Mustafa, and other Bin Laden brothers and employees fought and consulted on the front lines of the Mecca siege for two weeks. Salem's half-brother Yahya, a civil engineer with extensive experience in Mecca, was among those who risked their lives to aid the royal family's increasingly violent assault. Yeslam Bin Laden, another senior executive at the time, "was frantic, dashing from house to office like a man unhinged," his wife remembered. The Saudi forces poured fire at Juhaiman's rebels in the minarets. "Everyone was saying, 'God rest his soul, Mohamed bin Laden,' and at the same time, they were cursing Mohamed bin Laden, because the 106-millimeter cannon could not penetrate the minarets—that was how much steel there was," said a Bin Laden employee who was there. Helicopters swooped in firing machine guns from their open doors.[21]

Juhaiman and his surviving followers soon retreated underground, a maneuver they had evidently planned in advance. Beneath the mosque there were many catacombs and tunnels, some of which carried wiring and pipes to support the mosque; others led to rooms for religious contemplation and retreat. Juhaiman had hidden food and ammunition below during weeks of clandestine preparation; in some cases, he apparently had gained access to privileged Bin Laden company vehicles. Once the rebels slipped into the catacombs, the Bin Ladens' engineering and architectural knowledge became particularly crucial. The employee who was present remembered a Jordanian commander storming through the mosque, calling out, "Where is Bin Laden? Where is Bin Laden?" He found them and spread out the architectural plans, marking an X on every section of the mosque's surface that lay above an underground passage where the rebels might be hiding. "Jackhammer it," the Jordanian ordered.[22]

The Bin Ladens brought in boring equipment to drill holes in the floor of the mosque so that security forces could drop grenades down the makeshift shafts. "They bored all these holes and the sergeant would sit there with his basket of grenades, tea, and cigarettes—drop a hand grenade in the hole," said Tim Barger, who was living in Jeddah and was in contact with participants in the siege. They dropped so many hand grenades into the tunnels during this phase of the assault, said the Bin Laden employee, that up on the surface "we were slipping on the rings of the hand grenades."[23]

Salem seemed thrilled to be involved, but he was also worried. It did not require an advanced degree in political science to see that the Al-Saud was vulnerable to forces of Islamic revolution similar to those that had just toppled the shah of Iran across the Persian Gulf—and if the Saudi royal family fell, so would the Bin Ladens. The brothers moved quickly—and in secret—to create an offshore financial haven. On November 27, 1979, just one week after the Mecca uprising began, lawyers halfway around the world, in Panama City, filed a Notaría Primera del Circuito establishing a new company under Panamanian law: Binladin International Inc. They soon changed its name to the less conspicuous Binar, Inc. Its directors would eventually include the most influential brothers around Salem—Bakr, Omar, Yeslam, Tareq, Hassan, and Khalid. The company's initial share capital was listed at $10 million. The timing of its formation suggests a panicked family hedging its financial bets against the possibility that it might soon face a hostile, postrevolutionary Saudi government. None of the Bin Ladens involved with these Panamanian companies has ever explained their purpose, but family members have acknowledged making a similarly hurried offshore transfer of funds during a later Saudi crisis.[24]

In fact, Juhaiman and his followers were doomed. Saudi and French special forces called in for assistance killed many of the rebels at the Grand Mosque; Juhaiman and sixty-two surviving followers were arrested and beheaded. Still, their bloody revolt did create a profound crisis of legitimacy for the royal family. The rule of the Al-Saud rested on their claims to Islamic credibility, particularly as stewards of Mecca and Medina. They rationalized their assault on the mosque as a regrettable but necessary act of their stewardship, but they were obviously on shaky political and theological ground. As the assault wound down, royal family spokesmen emphasized the rebels' wild claims about the arrival of the Apocalypse and downplayed their more temporal—and threatening—political grievances.

The revolt implicated the Bin Ladens as well. Rumors swirled even as the siege raged that family members must have been involved, for it was their trucks and their Jeeps that had privileges to move freely in and out of the Holy Mosque; surely, the rumors went, some Bin Ladens had aided the conspirators. Mahrouz and a second brother, probably Osama, were arrested briefly during the crisis while driving near Mecca.

According to the Bin Laden employee who participated in the siege, the brothers were mistaken for conspirators because they were using company radios to monitor police communications—only out of curiosity.[25]

When the Bin Laden employee himself drove away from Mecca one night, his clothes bloodied from his involvement in the grenade assaults, a policeman stopped him on the highway. He showed his Bin Laden company identity card, and the officer responded by shoving a gun in his face, announcing, "God sent you to me." The employee said he avoided execution on the spot only by convincing the policeman to consider more than the swirling rumors about the family's role and to check in with his superiors before shooting him.[26]

Years later, Osama criticized then–crown prince Fahd for using indiscriminate force against the rebels. "He could have solved this crisis without a shot being fired, as all sensible people agreed at the time," Osama said. "What the situation needed was some time, especially since those present inside the Haram were only a few dozen. They had only light weapons, mostly hunting rifles, they had few provisions, and they were surrounded." Fahd, he continued—making no reference to Salem or other family members who were involved—"stubbornly fought with them and put bulldozers and armored cars inside the Haram. I still remember the bulldozer's tracks on the paving stones of the Haram . . . People still remember the minarets covered in black after they had been pounded by tanks."[27]

His true attitude toward the revolt at the time it was actually going on is more difficult to discern. Osama was twenty-one years old. The Islamic faith in which he had so deeply immersed himself was stirring suddenly. Beyond the Mecca siege, revolutionaries in Iran had overthrown their corrupt shah. The Muslim Brotherhood was gaining strength and planning revolt in Syria, a conspiracy that Osama would later say he was involved in. Juhaiman and his followers might have been misguided, particularly in their identification of a Mahdi, or divine savior, but their political critique was stimulating, and the royal family's massive counterattack was, at the least, disquieting.

Still, there is hardly any evidence to suggest that Osama was willing to take significant personal risks in the name of rebellion—nor is there evidence that he disagreed at the time with his brothers' cooperation with Saudi security forces. Rather, he seems to have conducted himself as an exceptionally pious, rising construction mogul and family man, an Islamist on the make—a rather common profile in Saudi Arabia. Far from conspiring to revolt, Osama in these years seemed to be exploring how he might have it all—money, multiple wives, children, an ambitious work life, and God's favor. His status as a young Bin Laden son in good standing was a crucial prerequisite.

By early 1980, Osama's tax-free income from Bin Laden sources probably exceeded $150,000 per year and may have been twice that—an income greater than that of many junior princes. In these years, Salem controlled allowances for younger Bin Laden brothers like Osama, and by several accounts from business partners and employees, Salem's system appeared to be arbitrary and inconsistent. By the early 1990s, when dividends were allocated in a more orderly fashion, the minimum amount a son could expect was just under $300,000 annually, according to U.S. court filings by accountants hired to examine Bin Laden finances. It seems safe to assume that comparable allowances were lower a decade earlier. In both periods, the amount a brother received would be greater if he also owned shares in other Bin Laden companies or worked as a salaried executive. Osama's older brother Yeslam, who had earned a degree in business from the University of Southern California, received a salary of about $800,000 per year in 1986, according to an affidavit filed by his wife Carmen. Osama was among those brothers who had ownership in more than one company, and he also took management jobs, although he was more junior than Yeslam and certainly would have earned less in salary. From these fragments of evidence, it is possible to estimate—or guess—that Osama's total annual income from family sources would likely have been around $200,000 during this period. He certainly behaved as if he had money to spare. He bought a small apartment building in the Al-Aziziyah district of Jeddah after he left university and then took a second, and eventually a third, wife, whom he installed in equally sized apartments. These wives were more mature and better educated than the teenaged cousin who had borne his first children—at least one of them had earned a doctoral degree in Arabic or religious studies, according to Osama's later bodyguard. Their qualifications and religious expertise matched his evolving self-image.[28]

At the Bin Ladens' Mecca office, Osama was promoted to supervise Walid Al-Khatib, the Palestinian who had previously been his boss. One of their projects involved routing a new road between the Grand Mosque and a palace, which required demolishing buildings in a densely populated neighborhood—without using any dynamite. Osama worked on detailed engineering questions involving the structural weaknesses of buildings and how these might be leveraged to knock them down. Al-Khatib found Osama "especially effective in liaising with various government departments and smoothing over problems." He worked easily with European and American engineers and spoke to them in English. He was reserved, certainly, and very pious, but in a Saudi context he was a rising young man of the Mecca establishment.[29]

One day a driver came into the office trembling. He showed Al-Khatib a subversive book he had found; it was an underground tract denouncing the Saudi royal family. They searched the place where the driver had discovered the pamphlet and found more than one hundred other such books. Al-Khatib was terrified. "I knew it meant a death sentence, and I didn't want to be associated with it." He called Osama immediately. Bin Laden flipped through the pages and "smiled his famous smile as he turned the pages."

"Will you please call the police?" Al-Khatib asked him, as he recalled it.

"No, you call the police."

Al-Khatib protested; as a non-Saudi, he would be particularly vulnerable to the security investigation that would surely follow. He begged Osama to make the initial contact with the police, but Osama again refused, got into his car, and drove away. Reluctantly, Al-Khatib reported his discovery. The police arrived, and eventually, Al-Khatib "got away with it." The incident changed his feelings about Osama, however. "I didn't like him anymore."[30]

Saudi Arabia's political fabric was stretching. Iran's example seemed to prove that oil money might accelerate dissent rather than quell it. Fearful, Fahd and his brothers hurriedly began to accommodate the kingdom's Islamists, showering them with increased budgets and acceding to the demands by religious scholars for stricter gender segregation and media censorship. Culture and public life in the kingdom grew steadily more conservative. Yet the secular wing of the royal family did not interrupt their lives behind palace walls or in Europe's capitals.

The Bin Ladens remained united, too, after the Mecca uprising. The cultural distance between the secular wing and the religious wing of the family had widened considerably during the 1970s, but Salem's leadership, and his strategy of mutual accommodation and generous financial subsidy, kept the family well intact. Bin Laden identity—and Bin Laden wealth—remained fixed on the same star that had guided Mohamed after his arrival in Jeddah a half century before. Above all else, they depended upon, and loyally served, the Saudi royal family.

16. THE AMUSEMENT PARK

AFTER THE MECCA UPRISING, Salem flew to New York for hemorrhoid surgery. He had put the procedure off for years; when he could delay no longer, he arranged his operation as P. T. Barnum might. He retained an American vascular heart surgeon at New York–Presbyterian; this was considerably more surgical talent than was normally required for such a minor procedure, but Salem said he would pay handsomely. He also announced that he would videotape the event, casting his exposed rear end as the star of the show. The hospital objected, but it did allow him to bring a friend with a Polaroid camera. Afterward, Salem created a multimedia show in which he set to music a medley of photos of his backside. He later showed the pictures at parties and to Saudi royalty, including Crown Prince Fahd.[1]

During his recovery, which he prolonged in a similar spirit of self-dramatization, Salem brooded about his family's vulnerability to revolution in Saudi Arabia. He continued to prepare financial infrastructure that could aid the family if it was ever forced into exile. On January 23, 1980, Panamanian lawyers working for the Bin Ladens established a second company, following on Binar. It was called Saudin Inc., and its directors again read like a roster of the most influential brothers around Salem: Yeslam, Bakr, Omar, Tareq, Hassan, and Khalid. Around this time, Salem told one of his American business partners, Robert Freeman, that he was concerned about what might happen to the family "should there be some sort of turmoil in Saudi Arabia." Salem had his estate near London, but he decided that he should build a larger compound where many of Mohamed's children could also retreat, if it was ever necessary—a place where they could live side by side with their families, as they did in Jeddah.[2]

White, Weld & Co., an elite Boston-based investment bank, had introduced Salem to a property called Oaktree Village, in Orlando, Florida; it was a tract of land that had been divided into 229 lots for single-family homes but had been developed no further. The company that owned Oaktree "was having some cash flow problems," recalled Aaron Dowd, who later managed the property, and it offered the tract for sale for $1.9 million, or about $8,300 per lot. Salem decided to buy. He put down about $380,000 in cash and assumed a mortgage on the rest of the purchase price. It was his first major real estate investment in the United States. He reserved about sixty of the Oaktree lots for the Bin Laden family; each brother or sister who participated would receive two, one for a house and a second for a spacious yard. He decided to create separate corporations, each named after a flower, to hold each family member's property—he bought a book about flowers and paged through it, choosing his favorites. The first flowers went to those closest to him—his devout mother; his full "kid brother," Ghalib; his full sister Mona; his free-living half-brother Shafiq; his half-sisters Raja and Raedah; and, of course, Randa. Salem envisioned that if all remained well in Saudi Arabia, the Bin Ladens would gather at Oaktree occasionally for group vacations around the nearby Walt Disney World resort. If, for any reason, the Saudi kingdom fell apart, they would have a ready refuge beside the Magic Kingdom.[3]

Salem preferred the sprawl and amusement parks of Orlando to Palm Beach, which was favored by some Saudi royalty. He rented limousines and arranged masseuses for visiting princes in Palm Beach but otherwise minimized his time there. He seemed to be put off by its social pretensions. He mocked all snobs. Once, at dinner, an American businessman sampled the wine and haughtily sent it back. Salem excused himself, slipped into the kitchen, and arranged for the waiters to pour the rejected wine into a new bottle. This time, the businessman made a show of being pleased—until Salem announced his prank.[4]

Still, he knew that his royal clients required a grander style than he generally favored for himself. In 1980, as construction began at Oaktree, Salem asked one of his partners if he could locate an elegant mansion in Orlando that might be suitable for rental by a vacationing Saudi prince. There was nothing on the open market, but after some effort, they found a wealthy local businessman named Miller McCarthy, who lived on a multi-acre estate overlooking Johns Lake, to the west of Orlando and not far from Disney World. His stunning Mediterranean main house had been constructed in the mid-1920s by a man named Pratt, a chemist who reputedly derived his fortune from patents on coagulants used in Jell-O. Pratt had taste: He purchased fine materials and commissioned arched walkways and careful detailing. The rear lawn sloped down from the swimming pool to weeping willows and palm groves beside the lake. In later years the property deteriorated, but McCarthy and his wife bought it during the early 1970s and spent about $600,000 on a painstaking restoration.[5]

For a handsome price, the owner and his wife agreed to move out temporarily while Salem's royal friends moved in. The Saudis surrounded the estate with security guards who had been trained by the CIA, or so Salem told McCarthy. They left the place a mess, McCarthy said; he later billed them for $25,000. Still, "the Prince really enjoyed his stay," as Robert Freeman recalled, and "that was good news" for Salem. Afterward, in Salem's "impulsive way," he immediately asked McCarthy if he could buy the entire property. According to Freeman, Salem thought he could use the place "to do some lavish entertaining of visitors from Saudi Arabia."[6]

As they neared an agreement, Salem called McCarthy from Singapore in the middle of the night to bargain. He wanted everything in the house—sheets, pillowcases, even a Chevy van of McCarthy's that had caught Salem's eye because it had a phone inside. When they agreed on terms—McCarthy recalled that the total price was just under $2.2

million—Salem sent an emissary with a $250,000 cashier's check. They closed the transaction in December 1980. Salem's accountants in New York, at Price Waterhouse, set up a Liberian corporation to purchase and hold the estate, apparently as part of Salem's international tax-avoidance strategy. Salem dubbed this offshore holding company Desert Bear Limited. From then on, the Orlando estate became known simply as Desert Bear.[7]

Neighbors around Johns Lake watched in astonishment as Salem and his royal guests transformed the place into a private amusement park. Hot air balloons lifted off the lawns and drifted over Orlando. Helicopters buffeted the palm trees as they landed inside the walls; men in suits climbed out, briefcases chained to their forearms, and jogged to the main house. Salem was friendly to his neighbors, and welcoming, and he tried to keep his parties under control, but the occasional amorous couple did tumble down the lawn, a neighbor said, and according to McCarthy, "they liked to smoke marijuana," and they "did it openly."[8]

When Salem's brothers and sisters visited Desert Bear with their children, the atmosphere calmed considerably. Salem transformed one of the outbuildings into a hangar for ultralight aircraft. He hired a pilot from Texas, Pat Deegan, to assemble his fleet. Deegan walked into the main house one day and found Salem on a couch in the living room, still in his bathrobe, with a large group of Bin Laden children, all under twelve years old, lined up before him. Salem presided over a stack of one-hundred-dollar bills. "Come on up," he told the children, handing out one bill after another. Deegan watched for a while and asked, "Hey, can I get in line?"[9]

By this time, Salem had purchased a seaplane. He kept it in America and used it for family recreation in Florida and Texas. He and Ghalib were among the family's more active fliers during these years; they would zip above Johns Lake and nearby orange groves in ultralights or else haul out the seaplane for takeoffs and splashdowns. "Kid Brother" Ghalib was becoming considerably more religious than Salem, but he was pleasant and adventurous, and he had a growing family of young children who particularly enjoyed Disney World.

Flying ultralights off the back lawn at Desert Bear required some maneuvers during takeoff and landing; there was a fairly tight glide path between orange trees and power lines. Ghalib had flown the route many times without incident, but one day he drifted too close to the power lines. His engine caught one of the lines, and he flipped over and crashed.

He broke his back but he was fortunate; he suffered no permanent damage or paralysis. He was immobilized in the hospital for a time and then recuperated at Desert Bear. It was one more close call in the Bin Laden annals of aviation. It would not be the last.[10]

SALEM OPERATED AN OFFICE in the Olympic Tower on Fifth Avenue, in Midtown Manhattan. His local partner was Robert Freeman, a former investment banker whose father had befriended King Faisal decades earlier. Freeman's wife, Gail, had met Salem's wife, Sheikha, in the first-class cabin of a commercial airliner flying from London to Jeddah. The couples clicked, and they remained close even after Salem and Sheikha divorced. Salem asked Freeman to work for him as his personal financial adviser; Freeman proposed instead that they create a holding company in New York for investments in America. They called their Delaware-registered corporation Amarco—for American Arabian Company. Salem and Khalid Bin Mahfouz each took 40 percent and Freeman took 20 percent. Freeman hoped they would enrich themselves through ambitious undertakings, mainly in commercial real estate; he discovered that Salem was averse to stocks and other intangible assets.[11]

Freeman introduced Salem to Donald Trump. The Bin Ladens owned a vacant tract of land near a royal palace in Riyadh, and Freeman thought the property offered "an excellent opportunity for Donald Trump to build one of his signature buildings, like the Trump Tower in New York." When they met in Trump's office, the developer told Salem that he was intrigued, but he would require $25,000 in cash plus two first-class tickets to Riyadh for himself and a colleague. According to Freeman, Trump explained that given his reputation, he did not feel that he should be spending his own money on "exploratory ventures in faraway places." Besides, Trump continued, if Salem was willing to put up the $25,000, it would show that he was serious about the deal. Salem declined. People were clamoring to do business with the Bin Ladens, he said; they did not need incentive pay. The meeting ended in stalemate, to Freeman's regret. Salem and Trump, he observed, were "very strong personalities, and there was very little give-and-take for either of them."[12] Trump's spokesperson denied that such a discussion took place. Asked to review the author's written source materials describing the meeting, the spokesperson did not respond.

Freeman pitched investment idea after investment idea to his Saudi partners, but Salem rarely expressed interest. He seemed to regard his Manhattan operation mainly as a platform for shopping. When he was in New York, his first priority was to head down to 47th Street, where he expended great energy bargaining for jewelry and consumer electronics with the Hasidim who owned many of the district's retail stores. He bought bags full of diamond necklaces and earrings for Bin Laden mothers and sisters in Saudi Arabia. Other Saudi tourists swaggered around Tiffany's, proud to pay the sticker price and to carry conspicuously the Tiffany's shopping bag, but Salem "was looking for deals," Freeman recalled. He loved haggling with Hasidic retailers but feared losing out, so he ordered Freeman to find an appraiser who could examine particular pieces of jewelry and offer a sense of what he should pay. Freeman located an Italian appraiser with a second-floor office on 47th Street, to whom he could ferry jewelry entrusted to him by the store owners downstairs. He was never entirely sure, however, whether the appraiser was secretly in cahoots with the jewelers. It hardly mattered; Salem relished the negotiations more than the results. He had imbibed the anti-Semitic stereotype that Jews are the world's canniest bargainers; he seemed to regard shopping at Hasidic stores as a feat of daring.[13]

He prowled the nearby electronics stores for the latest portable phones, calculators, cameras, music players, and miniature televisions, all of which he bought in bulk. "He'd buy hundreds of these things for the princes," recalled Gail Freeman. He would walk the aisles and peer through the glass cases, asking "Now, tell me the truth: These are brand new? Nobody's seen them yet, right?" Like a salesman who uses season tickets at Madison Square Garden to cultivate clients, Salem used his mobility and expertise in American consumerism to acquire gadgets that he could use back in Saudi Arabia to ingratiate himself with princes.[14]

Khalid Bin Mahfouz bought two apartments at the Olympic Tower, but he and Salem usually preferred the room service and convenience of hotels; when in New York, they stayed mainly at the Helmsley Palace or the Plaza. Salem threw an extravagant twenty-eighth-birthday party for Randa at the Plaza. Since he didn't know too many people in the city, he asked the Freemans to fill up the private room with friends from their neighborhood in suburban Long Island. Salem sang his usual repertoire of corny folk and Christmas songs. "We were his playthings," Freeman recalled. Salem's lack of interest in ambitious business projects frustrated him—he had, after all, given up a career at a major investment bank.

Still, he tried to live as his partner did. Once, on a trip to Jeddah, Salem ordered Freeman and an Italian associate out of a Jeep at night in the middle of the desert. Salem drove away—Freeman and his colleague had to stumble through the sand to the road, and then hitchhike into Jeddah. When they made it back, Salem was giddy; he seemed to regard his prank as part practical joke, part survival test. Freeman waited patiently for his revenge. One night in New York, when they were all out to dinner with Randa, they discovered that Salem had forgotten his wallet and had no money. Immediately afterward, Freeman drove to Harlem, forced Salem out of the car, and sped away. Randa fretted that Salem would never make it back, but he soon strode into her hotel with two new African American friends. He was, of course, delighted: "Bob, you *do* have a sense of humor."[15]

Freeman needed it. Salem was often so pinched for cash that Freeman had to call Jeddah night after night to plead for wire transfers: "Salem, we've got to have some money—we've got people at our door. We've got to pay the rent . . . What are we doing? Where are we heading?" Salem usually came through with the minimum amounts needed to maintain the office, "but it was always at the last minute." As best Freeman could determine, the Bin Laden companies in Jeddah, which Salem now firmly controlled, had a reasonably steady cash flow, but there were so many calls on that money—employees, equipment, loan repayments, family— that Salem was not able to tap into it very easily for personal projects. Late payments to his construction companies by the royal family drained his liquidity even more. And yet as each year passed, Salem's appetite for private jets and real estate abroad seemed only to grow. Oil prices fell during the early 1980s, but this did not visibly crimp Salem's style. Instead, a pattern set in, according to Freeman and other partners and employees. When Salem needed money, Freeman recalled, "he had to turn to Khalid Bin Mahfouz."[16]

THEY WERE CONTEMPORARIES and best friends, each a scion of a Hadhrami business fortune, each adapting to the international impera- tives of the oil boom. As they reached their thirties and assumed their in- herited responsibilities, however, they exhibited contrasting personalities. When they flew together on their private jets, Salem might joke and sip champagne and play guitar, but Khalid would sit quietly, drinking tea or smoking an Arabian water pipe. He stayed away from Salem's more provocative parties for decadent Saudi princes. He did seem to enjoy Salem and his outrageous antics, but he would often observe his friend impassively, or issue only a slight, crooked smile. He was "a very quiet man, a very private man—very deep in thought," said an employee who spent many hours with the two men. "I think he enjoyed seeing that Salem was not afraid to say or do anything, and I think that he kind of vicariously lived through him."[17]

Khalid was "just as happy to let Salem run the show," said a second employee. Among other things, this meant adapting to Salem's idiosyncratic ideas about when and how to spend his money. Once, on a trip to California, Bin Laden and Bin Mahfouz arranged to meet at the private aviation terminal at Los Angeles International Airport. As they waited, Khalid's aides watched the country singer Kenny Rogers arrive on a private jet and climb with his entourage into stretch limousines. Salem turned up in a cheap rental car—he waved Khalid into the front passenger seat and they peeled out toward the freeway. "Nobody knows who they are and they couldn't care less," recalled the employee.[8]

Some of their American and European colleagues found the friendship and business relationship between Salem and Khalid to be extraordinarily complex. On money matters, Khalid was clearly the senior partner. Yet it was Salem who enjoyed such easy, informal access to Fahd and other royalty; because of his charm and energy, Salem's influence in Riyadh exceeded the size of his bank accounts. One European business partner who knew them both believed that Khalid harbored some quiet resentment about this imbalance. As for Bin Mahfouz himself, some of his partners and employees regarded him as an enigma, a man of many contradictions.

The least complicated thing about him was his wealth; by the early 1980s, it was on full display. Salem had befriended Harry Winston, the prominent New York jeweler, and through him, he and Khalid were invited to the showroom of Hammerman Brothers, a wholesale jeweler in Manhattan. Khalid picked out some exquisite—and very expensive—pieces. Bernie Hammerman pulled Robert Freeman aside and asked if it would be too great an embarrassment to ask Khalid for a credit reference before he walked out with the jewelry. Khalid suggested two names, Freeman recalled: Ben Love, the chairman of Texas Commerce Bank in Houston, and Tom Clausen, the chairman of Bank of America in San Francisco. Hammerman's credit department contacted Clausen, who said he was authorized to clear any check up to $50 million for Khalid Bin Mahfouz. As Freeman recalled it, "This created quite a stir in the showroom."[19]

Bin Mahfouz spent much of his time in America in the Houston area. He had met the aircraft broker Jim Bath around the same time that Salem had, and through Bath and other American partners he purchased private jets and real estate. He bought a large ranch on Houston's outskirts and a mansion in River Oaks, a city neighborhood of oil barons and their retainers who poured their money into antebellum-style plantation houses and columned Georgian estates. The Bin Mahfouz property, at 3800 Willowick, lay just around the corner from Jim Bath's relatively modest pine-shaded home. Khalid's main house looked something like Versailles; in the rear was a swimming pool with an island in the middle that could be reached by a footbridge. Bath called it "the Big House," his partner Bill White recalled. Khalid opened the estate and its guesthouses to the Bin Ladens. Salem's sisters visited and amused themselves climbing trees on the sprawling grounds. Khalid and Salem hosted parties for the Texas notables who promoted and managed some of Bin Mahfouz's American investments. At one point during this period, Khalid noticed that tour buses kept stopping on Willowick in front of his estate. "Why do these people keep coming by?" he asked. One of his employees explained that his home was now on the River Oaks celebrity tour. "The next time they come," he said, apparently quite serious, "invite them in for tea."[20]

John Connally flew on Bin Mahfouz's jets during his 1980 presidential campaign, according to two of Khalid's employees. The oil barons Nelson and Bunker Hunt traveled with him, too, and they tried to draw Bin Mahfouz into their ill-fated attempt to corner the world silver market; one of the employees remembered Khalid complaining that he lost money on the venture. In contrast to Salem, Khalid tracked world financial markets and directed investment strategies in precious metals, foreign currencies, and other volatile instruments. His advisers were so-phisticated about finance, and some enjoyed connections at the highest levels of international politics—in Houston, his attorneys included Baker Botts, the powerful firm that also represented the Bush family.[21]

Khalid was one of several Bin Mahfouz sons who participated in the management of his family's National Commercial Bank; his aging father, Salem, remained chairman. Khalid involved himself in the bank's inter-national transactions. NCB was becoming a formidable global institution; in 1985 it would report that it held more than $1 billion in cash or equiv-alent instruments and more than $6 billion in deposits. As the largest bank in Saudi Arabia, it was inevitably entwined with the royal family and the government. NCB planes sometimes transported payrolls for Aramco, the oil consortium; they carried boxes of brand-new hundred-dollar bills from the Federal Reserve Bank in Dallas, according to pilot David Grey. NCB planes also ferried documents to Baghdad in the early 1980s; the pi-lots who flew this route believed the missions supported Saudi Arabia's quiet liaison with Saddam Hussein during the early stages of the Iran-Iraq war, Grey said. Whatever their role, the flights supported Saudi pol-icy to shore up Saddam, a tilt backed by Washington; Fahd later acknowledged providing $25.7 billion in aid to Iraq, and the kingdom also transferred U.S.-supplied weaponry to Saddam.[22]

NCB's finances were complex, not least because the bank had to hold an unpublished amount of reserves to protect against loans in Saudi Arabia that might not be repaid. Yet the bank's profitability and financial health were never in doubt, and Khalid Bin Mahfouz himself appeared to have no difficulty accessing large amounts of cash. Robert Freeman re-called that Bin Mahfouz protested that some of the real estate invest-ments he proposed, in the neighborhood of $5 million, were too small to be worth his attention. Indeed, in Orlando, separately from Salem, Bin Mahfouz began acquiring land on a larger scale than Salem's family-oriented Oaktree project. In an endeavor code-named "Project Debra," after a waitress who served him while he was discussing the proposal in an Orlando restaurant, Bin Mahfouz and his agents quietly purchased tracts toward what would become an ambitious eighteen-hundred-acre commercial development known as Metro West; it would eventually be worth just under $1 billion. Khalid routinely traveled with $100,000 or more in his briefcase; at the end of a trip, according to his partner Rick Peterson, he would give whatever was left—as much as $30,000—as tips to employees at his Jeddah headquarters.[23]

Salem also traveled with a briefcase full of tens of thousands of dollars, but his underlying accounts appear to have been less secure. Around the time he bought Desert Bear in late 1980, Salem told Miller McCarthy that he and the Bin Laden companies owed Bin Mahfouz and his bank about $220 million. Much of that debt may have involved project loans or letters of credit that would be repaid routinely, but even so, there can be no doubt that Salem lived closer to the financial edge than did Khalid. Robert Freeman was not the only partner of Salem's who sometimes found it painful to extract money from him. Particularly after the fall in oil prices, Salem occasionally struggled to make dollar payments that ran only to six figures. At one point he backed out of the purchase of a $750,000 yacht, pleading depleted accounts, even though it might lead to the loss of a $200,000 deposit, according to his German friend Thomas Dietrich, who was helping him with the acquisition. In 1984, for unknown reasons, he took out a $200,000 mortgage on Desert Bear, according to Florida property records.[24]

These occasional signals of distress usually passed quickly. He stayed close to Khalid, and partly by borrowing, Salem still managed to find cash for one Learjet after another. In any event, it was often impossible to tell when Salem was handling his own money and when he was managing someone else's funds. Some of the cash Salem touched seemed to lie outside of the international banking system. Robert Freeman recalled that Salem once asked him to find a way to surreptitiously deposit—or launder—about $5 million to $10 million in cash into Western banks. Freeman said he refused; he never learned where the money Salem wanted to wash had come from.[25]

Such were Salem's financial dealings in the early 1980s: transnational, but connected with America; impressively resourced; complex; and sometimes mysterious. Those traits also perfectly described the covert war in Afghanistan that was about to alter the Bin Laden family's destiny.

17. IN THE KING'S SERVICE

SALEM'S POLITICAL BELIEFS were vague, if they could be said to exist at all. What the royal family wanted, he wanted. If his friends were in trouble, he helped. When Lebanon cracked up during the 1970s, Salem brought families he knew there to Saudi Arabia and arranged for jobs. He handed cash to a friend who spent time in Beirut during the civil war and told him, "You know what to do with this." His friend used the money to support families in need—"Sunni, Shia, Christians."[1] Such loose charity appealed to Salem's sense of purpose more than, say, political organizing. For a Saudi, he was not a particularly ardent anti-Zionist. He emphatically saw himself as an architect of closer ties between the kingdom and the United States—but if these views were his own, they also coincided with those of Fahd, his royal patron. He did not devour newspapers, and during the long hours he spent propped up in bed, watching television and talking simultaneously on the telephone, he was much more likely to watch action movies than news broadcasts. Yet he loved the rush of adrenaline, and as at Mecca in 1979, he could throw himself into a fight if he had a point of entry.

The events of that year—the Grand Mosque uprising, the Iranian revolution, and in December, the Soviet invasion of Afghanistan—forced all the Bin Ladens to reckon with global politics to a greater extent than ever before. In this, too, they tracked the Al-Saud. Self-preservation motivated both families more than ideology. From the Nasserite revolution onward, the Bin Ladens had often been instruments of clandestine Saudi foreign policy projects whose primary purpose was the protection of the royal family's rule. After the crises of 1979, they were called upon again.

The Al-Saud and the Carter administration both interpreted the invasion of Afghanistan as an initial thrust by Moscow toward oil supplies in the Gulf. This was a misperception of Soviet motives, but Kremlin secrecy made it impossible to know otherwise. Despite their arms purchases and military construction projects during the 1960s and 1970s, the Saudis were hopelessly ill prepared to defend the kingdom from any serious attack; only the American military could do this. Fahd had always leaned toward Washington within the councils of his family; he responded to the events of 1979 by deepening the kingdom's protective alliance with America. He negotiated secret agreements to build oversized military bases in Saudi Arabia that would permit the United States to preposition equipment for a crisis or quickly deploy large forces after one began—this undeclared policy was known in Washington as "overbuilding, overstocking."[2] Abroad, Fahd decided to partner more actively with America's campaign to contain and defeat communism around the world. Ronald Reagan's election in 1980 made such collaboration more palatable to the Saudis; Jimmy Carter's human rights rhetoric and Camp David peacemaking had alienated them. Yet if Fahd embraced Reagan's priorities too openly, he risked angering his kingdom's Islamic activists, whose potency and underground organizing had just been revealed so shockingly at Mecca. The shah of Iran had fallen, in part, because he had come to be seen by ordinary Iranians as a stooge of the Americans. All this argued for yet greater secrecy in U.S.-Saudi collaborations. Here, too, the Bin Ladens had a reliable track record.

Both the Americans and the Saudis were initially cautious about supporting the Afghan *mujaheddin* as the rebels revolted spontaneously against Kabul's new communist government. The Central Intelligence Agency's analysts doubted the rebels could do more than harass the mechanized Soviet occupying army. American policy toward the Afghan rebels during the early 1980s rested not on a premise of future victory but on the notion that providing them guns could raise the cost of the invasion for the Soviets. Fahd agreed to match dollar for dollar the secret U.S. aid budget for the rebels, which initially was in the range of only $30 million annually.[3] For Fahd, the war offered a convenient way to redirect the attention of Islamists outside the kingdom's borders. Even in this era before Al-Jazeera, Afghan suffering had quickly become a celebrated humanitarian cause across the Muslim world. Hundreds of thousands of destitute refugees poured by the month into Pakistan. Soviet planes bombed them as they fled. Fahd organized charitable support for the war's victims; he blessed such donations as official Saudi policy. The Afghan war united in a foreign cause factions of Saudi society that might have been in conflict had they focused solely on domestic matters.

It had the same effect within the Bin Laden family. Through his ambition, force of personality, and control of purse strings, Salem had held the secular and religious wings of his family together. This balancing act became more difficult after the Mecca uprising because the kingdom's Islamist movement acquired new legitimacy and budgets; this revival, often referred to as the *sawa*, or "awakening," emboldened many Saudi believers to assert themselves, including those among the Bin Ladens. "It was not uncommon for a single Saudi family to have its own members divided along these lines," a Saudi writer observed:

> A relative would be labeled *mutawawa* if he internalized the rhetoric and discourse of the new Islamist groups. He would be identified by his constant preaching among family members, listening to religious cassettes, regular denunciation of Western culture, music and luxury goods, and his enforcing of a strict moral code among his female relatives. The era witnessed the emergence of a new generation of self-appointed, literate and articulate *mutawawa*. They coexisted with less conservative members of their families . . . Within families, tolerance and tension progressed hand in hand.[4]

At the periodic family meetings where he reviewed business and financial issues and received requests from his brothers and sisters, Salem
had to manage not only his openly religious half-brothers Osama and
Mahrouz, but other brothers and sisters for whom Islam was an increasingly important part of their young adult lives—and even their political
outlooks. Charity, one of the five pillars of the Islamic faith, offered the
least problematic way to meet such aspirations. The Mohamed Bin Laden
Organization, like every other merchant company in Jeddah, operated a
zakat fund, or family foundation, to handle much of the formal tithing required by Islamic law.⁵ Such routine charity in Saudi Arabia typically
ranged from local mosque construction to feeding hungry orphans
overseas—a range of activities little different from those of churches in
the American heartland. During the first years of the 1980s, organizing
donations to Afghan refugees offered Salem, who was a savvy manipulator, a kind of triple play—it fulfilled his family's tithing obligations, it
supported Fahd's clandestine foreign policy, and it diverted the energies
of the Bin Laden family's religious wing.

Salem had his own connections to the Afghan frontier. He had flown
his sisters to boarding school in Peshawar and visited Kabul. His stable
of pilots, based in Jeddah, included several veterans of the Pakistani air
force, as well as an Afghan pilot named Mohammed Daoud, who had
been forced into exile by the Afghan communists. Flight logs show that
Salem flew into Karachi as early as November 1980. It was around then,
according to his fellow Muslim Brother Jamal Khashoggi, that Osama
took his first trip to Pakistan, announcing himself there as a junior philanthropic activist.⁶

BENEATH A BILINGUAL sign that reads "Al-Thaghr Model Schools,"
Ahmed Badeeb is pictured alongside other teachers in the second row of
the official photograph of the class of 1976, the year Osama Bin Laden
graduated from Jeddah's elite private high school. Badeeb was a full-

faced man with a rakish expression that reflected his profane, unruly, entertaining personality. He was also highly ambitious—an attribute that some who knew him traced to his Yemeni roots. Like the Bin Ladens, the Badeebs had emigrated to Jeddah from the Hadhramawt. By the late 1970s, Ahmed and his brother Saeed, who was studying for a doctorate in political science in the United States, had begun to forge connections to the Saudi government. Ahmed taught biology at Al-Thaghr, where his students included young members of the royal family. He also knew Osama from the school's religious committee and remembered him as "not an extremist at all . . . I liked him because he was a decent and polite person."[7]

After Osama left Al-Thaghr, Ahmed Badeeb came to the attention of Turki Al-Faisal, the youngest son of the late king who, although he was only in his thirties, had recently been appointed by Fahd to succeed his uncle, Kamal Adham, as Saudi Arabia's chief of foreign intelligence. Faisal named Saeed Badeeb as his chief of analysis, and he hired Ahmed as his chief of staff—a job that involved much discreet travel. After 1979, Badeeb became, among other things, Turki's bagman for transfers of government cash to Pakistan. In this role he soon revived his mentorship of Osama.

The official Saudi-American channel for funneling money to the Afghan rebels ran through Pakistan's main intelligence agency, Inter-Services Intelligence, or ISI. By insisting upon this conduit, Pakistan ensured it would maintain secrecy, as well as greater control over how the funds were distributed. One of Badeeb's roles during these early years was to purchase weapons clandestinely on the international market, and then ship them into Pakistan through ISI. From the beginning, Badeeb said, this Pakistan-dominated channel made him uncomfortable; he wanted to develop independent contacts among Afghan fighters. "We cannot depend only one hundred percent on what the Pakistanis give us," he recalled. "We have to know the number of fighters, how many in this organization, how many in that, and how much they received." One easy way to develop such unilateral relationships for Saudi intelligence was to invite particularly important Afghan rebel commanders to visit the holy cities of Mecca and Medina for the minor *umrah* pilgrimage or the annual Hajj. It was an ideal environment for making friends and recruiting clients—on Saudi soil, amid feasts and informal gatherings in the desert evenings, shadowed by the holiest mosques in Islam, at the site of the religion's birth. The visiting Afghans could be showered, too, with cash donations from admiring Saudi businessmen. And who better to help manage such invitations, and to participate in the ensuing charitable and religious festivities, than Osama Bin Laden, a scion of the family that played such an influential role in the holy cities?[8]

He was approaching his midtwenties, married to three wives, with a brood of small children scampering across the floor of the partitioned Jeddah apartment building where his expanding family lived. At his office in Medina he was the boss; he roared around in a desert-beige Land Cruiser and drove bulldozers at job sites, as his father had done. On visits to Pakistan he was a sheikh, deferred to obsequiously because of the cash he carried. On religious holidays at Mecca, he possessed a new aura in the Bin Laden hospitality tents—a righteous activist, a rising son in a respected family. In clandestine meetings of Brotherhood activists in the Hejaz, he may also have joined the movement's planning sessions for violent, secret campaigns in Syria and Yemen; he later said that he was involved, but because these campaigns operated outside the boundaries of Saudi policy, he seems to have participated only quietly and cautiously.

Osama's connections to the Afghan frontier ran through the Muslim Brotherhood, which had recruited him as a teenager. In Pakistan, the Brotherhood affiliate was a political party named Jamaat Islami. When Osama flew to Pakistan for the first time carrying donations for the Afghan rebels, he traveled not to the Afghan border, but to the eastern city of Lahore, where many of Jamaat's senior political leaders were based. Osama "was not trusting ISI," Badeeb recalled. "He doesn't want to give the money to ISI or directly to the *mujaheddin* because he thinks

Jamaat Islami in Lahore can get that money in the hands of the real *mujaheddin*," or those who were truest to the Brotherhood's aims. Bin Laden met two Arabic-speaking Afghan commanders, Burhanuddin Rabbani and Abdurrab Rahul Sayyaf; his trip lasted about a month.[9]

This initial travel signaled a pattern of Osama's relationship with the Afghan war between 1980 and 1983: he was a commuter who did little more than carry cash and hold meetings. He made his contacts in Pakistan through several overlapping networks: his Brotherhood network of religious activists, the charitable circles of Jeddah merchants inhabited by his family, and the Saudi intelligence operation run by Badeeb. "The arrangement" during the early years of the Afghan war, recalled Jamal Khashoggi, was that the Saudi government, through its foreign intelligence service, would "support the military part," while private philanthropists and religious activists would "support the humanitarian and relief work" along with the United States and Pakistani intelligence. These spheres overlapped, however. The donors Osama helped to organize for the Afghan cause included "members of the government," recalled Khalil A. Khalil, a Saudi who tracked Islamic activists for the royal family. Also, Badeeb used humanitarian offices on the Afghan frontier as cover and infrastructure for intelligence operations. Because of Badeeb, Osama developed cordial relations with Prince Turki Al-Faisal, whom he met during Faisal's periodic visits to Pakistan. He also won audiences with the powerful full brothers of Fahd—Nayef and Ahmed, with whom Salem had hunted in the Iraqi desert. Nayef and Ahmed ran the Saudi Interior Ministry, overseeing the kingdom's domestic security.[10]

Because of his rising visibility and contacts with important princes, Osama began for the first time to create value for the Bin Laden family. Nothing was more important to the Bin Ladens than building and revitalizing royal connections. In this new era of Islamic awakening, Osama's role as a courier and religious philanthropist complemented the concierge services Salem provided for Fahd and other secular-minded princes in Europe and America. Osama's work also provided the Bin

Ladens with renewed credibility among the religious leaders who influ-enced contracting in Mecca and Medina. Osama "was a very lovely fig-ure in the family," said Bassim Alim, a relative by marriage who knew him during these years and who traveled occasionally to Pakistan to support the Afghans. "They liked him."[11]

In 1982 Salem appointed Osama as an executive overseeing a new round of renovation at the Prophet's Mosque in Medina—a visible role, and another step in "the training or internship program that his elder brother gives to a younger brother," as Khashoggi put it. Salem also or-dered one of his aides to build a vault in Jeddah where Osama could tem-porarily store gold jewelry and cash donated for Afghans by businessmen and their wealthy wives. These rich Saudis had come to believe "that the Afghans were angels . . . the holy people," recalled Ahmed Badeeb. "Women used to give their jewelry—huge amounts, you could not meas-ure it." The Bin Laden vault was twenty meters by twenty meters, fire-proofed, and bombproofed, recalled the aide who built it.[12]

Osama later conceded that he worked during these years in cooper-ative alignment with clandestine Saudi policy; one of his assignments was to not get caught. "Due to my arrival in Afghanistan," he recalled, "and due to my family's closeness to the Saudi governmental system, a letter arrived commanding Osama not to enter Afghanistan, and to stay with the immigrants in Peshawar, because if the Russians were to capture or imprison him, it would be construed as proof of Saudi backing for the *mujaheddin* against the Soviet Empire."[13]

His ego and his ambitions were swelling, yet he remained a reticent, almost painfully shy man in conversation. Sabry Ghoneim, a Bin Laden executive in Cairo, recalled Osama's arrival in Egypt during this period for a meeting with construction engineers involved in a project Osama was supervising in Jubail, a coastal industrial city in Saudi Arabia. Ghoneim remembered him as "a young man with the attitude of a shy girl. He was always looking at his feet." Nor was he a particularly effective executive. He said little during the interviews with the engineers. Ultimately, according to Ghoneim, the project Osama supervised lost more than $15 million.[14]

He was shy, but he now had several important mentors who decidedly were not: his elder half-brother, his former teacher Badeeb—and increasingly, a Muslim Brotherhood scholar and fundraiser fired by the Afghan war, Abdullah Azzam.

Like Osama, Azzam had been recruited into the Brotherhood as a young man. He was born in a village near Jenin, in the West Bank, and went into exile after Israel occupied the region during the 1967 war. He studied and taught Islamic politics in Egypt and Jordan before his subversive views led him to refuge in Saudi Arabia, where he won an appointment on the faculty of King Abdulaziz University; he lectured at the university when Osama was a student there. Azzam became an elder, charismatic, international figure in the Hejaz circles of the Brotherhood, in which Osama also moved. He was the author of a book about jihad, *Signs of the Merciful*, and he was developing the thesis for what would become an even more influential tract, *Defense of Muslim Lands*.

Like many subversive professors before him, Azzam was burdened by financial debts accumulated during his itinerant and poorly compensated career. Saudi Arabia—and Osama in particular—offered the prospect of financial liberation. There is more than a hint of opportunism in the way Azzam flattered and gradually befriended the high school–educated Osama during the first years of the 1980s, promoting the young philanthropist as a saintly patron of a righteous, assertive Islam. Azzam's wife developed a friendship in Jeddah with Osama's wives. They socialized at Bin Laden farms in the desert. By 1984 their acquaintanceship had deepened into partnership. It was "a meeting of money, will and youth, represented by Osama Bin Laden, and knowledge, direction and experience, represented by Abdullah Azzam," observed Nasir Al-Bahri, Osama's later bodyguard.[15]

Osama Bin Laden "was a soft person, and Abdullah Azzam was empowering him to become a symbol of the Saudi wing of the cause," recalled Khalil A. Khalil. "Azzam saw Osama as a bridge to Saudi Arabia."[16]

Sheltered Saudi teenagers and college students drilled in Islamic ideology but living far from any battlefield embraced the Afghan war as a romantic cause, a weekends-and-holidays rite of youthful passage. Religious students flew on direct Saudia Airlines flights to Peshawar to spend the last ten days of the holy month of Ramadan doing volunteer work or shooting off guns in the hills. Their commitment to the Afghans resembled that of American students who spend a few days a year hammering houses together for the poor. They might be moved by altruism, but they also sought a touch of cool. "When we used to look at the Afghan suits that the *mujaheddin* who returned from Afghanistan wore as they walked the streets of Jeddah, Mecca, or Medina, we used to feel we were living with the generation of the triumphant companions of the Prophet," Al-Bahri remembered.[17] For young Saudis during the early 1980s, the Afghan war was fashion, ideology, a fundraising opportunity, a touchstone of religious revival, a bonding experience—everything but the brutal combat known by the Afghans who actually fought it.

The Saudi religious establishment viewed Azzam as its bridge to Pakistan, which held one of the world's largest Muslim populations and had long been a target of Wahhabi proselytizing. In late 1981, King Abdulaziz University dispatched Azzam to oversee the curriculum at the Islamic University in Islamabad, Pakistan's capital; the campus had been founded recently with $35 million in Saudi funds.[18] Azzam also consulted for the Muslim World League, an arm of official Saudi charity. Peshawar, the frontier city that served as the principal base for the Afghan *mujaheddin*, lay less than two or three hours away by road. Azzam's move to Islamabad created an Arabic-speaking, Jeddah-connected wing of the Muslim Brotherhood through which Osama could channel donations.

THE AFGHAN COMMANDER with the deepest connections in Saudi Arabia was Sayyaf, a white-bearded Arabic speaker schooled in Islamic law who embodied the religious romanticism many Saudis saw in the war. Sayyaf toured Saudi mosques in royal limousines during his periodic fundraising tours in the kingdom; the Saudi government permitted him to open permanent offices to raise money. Badeeb cultivated him on behalf of Saudi intelligence. Increasingly, however, commanders like Sayyaf had to weigh the lure of Saudi money against the headache of hosting teenaged Saudi volunteers on their Ramadan holidays. It was a hassle to provide them guns, light training, and a tour of the battlefield about which they could boast when they went home, but Sayyaf and a few other commanders came to accept their roles as jihad camp counselors—it was a necessary cost of their fundraising operations. In 1984, with Badeeb's support, Sayyaf opened the first formal training camp for Arab volunteers, called Sada, or "Echo." It was an appropriate name—it was a reverberation from the real war. The camp was near the Pakistan border, an easy day trip for Saudi and other wealthy Gulf Arab visitors. "They would watch some militant-inspired plays that would end with the guests donating all the money they had in their pockets," according to one Arab history of the camps. "They would also write down lists of items that must be purchased urgently in order to enable Sayyaf to conquer Kabul."[19]

In 1984 Osama entered Afghanistan for the first time, essentially as a tourist. He may have visited Sada. He witnessed some fighting around Jaji, near the new Arab camp. It was the first time in his life that he had heard the concussive thump of shells or felt the blood-quickening pulse of exposure to war. The experience seemed to thrill him but also infuse him with guilt over the length of time it had taken him to put himself at physical risk in the cause he had espoused with such conspicuous pride. "I feel so guilty for listening to my friends and those that I love not to come here, and stay home for reasons of safety," he told a Syrian journalist. "I feel that this delay of four years requires my own martyrdom in the name of God."[20]

It was a refrain he would repeat for many years, while managing, nonetheless, to persistently avoid what he claimed to welcome. Certainly Azzam wished to keep him in one piece. Osama's fundraising prowess had reached new heights.

Azzam moved to Peshawar in October 1984 to establish the Makhtab Al-Khadamat, or "Services Office," to support Afghan fighters and serve Arab volunteers who traveled to the war. His vision for the office blended Islamic charity and marketing. His projects included *Al-Jihad* magazine, whose first issue, published in December, concentrated mainly on fundraising. The start-up money came from Osama, who provided initial cash infusions at an annual rate of between $200,000 and $300,000. For the first time, too, the Bin Laden family also provided engineering and construction personnel to support the war effort—an Arab volunteer who arrived in Peshawar in 1984 recalled meeting a construction engineer assigned from the Bin Laden organization. During the Hajj pilgrimage of the Islamic year 1405, which took place in June 1985, Azzam lodged for days at a Bin Laden home in Mecca. "The entire Bin Laden family were hosting people. And they had food and busses to take people," recalled Abdullah Anas, Azzam's future son-in-law. A document about Osama's work from that same year describes contributions provided by the Bin Laden family foundation.[21]

Osama associated himself with Azzam's radical voice, yet he remained an entirely orthodox Saudi figure, a minor emissary of its establishment. His volunteerism remained inseparable from his family's identity and its business strategy.

IT WAS AZZAM who first introduced Osama to the concept of transnational jihad. "When the Sheikh started out," Bin Laden said years later, "the atmosphere among the Islamists and sheikhs was limited, location-specific and regional, each dealing with their own particular locale, but he inspired the Islamic movement and motivated Muslims to the broader *jihad.* At that point we were both in the same boat." As an exiled Palestinian, Azzam spoke passionately about his homeland but encouraged his followers to regard the conflict with Israel as part of a larger war waged by unbelievers against Muslims—a millenarian conflict, leading inevitably to Judgment Day, as forecasted in the Koran. Azzam's speeches and books dwelled on the suffering of Muslim innocents. He deified Afghan and Palestinian civilians as victims of aggression and cried for revenge. The women and children dying in Afghanistan under Soviet guns and in Lebanon after the Israeli invasion of 1982 were united by their identity as Muslims. These incursions into Muslim lands gave rise to *fard ayn,* a compulsory duty upon all Muslims to repel them. Azzam's ideas traced to the writings of the thirteenth-century jihadi theorist Ibn Taymiyya, which Bin Laden himself would later quote: "As for repelling the enemy aggressor who corrupts religion and the world, there is no greater duty after faith than uncompromising struggle against him." Azzam argued that Afghanistan was the most pressing theater for such jihad, and that it would strengthen the *ummah,* or "community of believers," for a later war to liberate Palestine. Here the ideological and opportunistic sides of Azzam merged in argument; as a practical matter, in Afghanistan, he could raise money and influence events, whereas in Palestine, at least for the time being, he was a powerless and not particularly influential exile.[22]

The 1982 Israeli campaign in Lebanon lit up the Arab world; it was a televised war filled with infuriating news and images. Osama watched at a time when he was absorbed by Azzam's lectures about jihad and mesmerized by his mentor's stature as an unyielding Islamic activist and an exiled Palestinian. In later years it would become common to describe Osama's overheated rhetoric about Palestinians as little more than media-savvy lip service from a Saudi who pandered to his Arab following. That interpretation overlooks Osama's self-conscious pride about his father's work in Jerusalem, however, as well as his close relationship with Azzam. It also ignores his recollections, which may be suspect in their emphases but are not likely invented. "The events that made a direct impression on me were during and after 1982, when America allowed the Israelis to invade Lebanon," scene of his boyhood schooling, Osama wrote years later:

> I still remember those distressing scenes: blood, torn limbs, women and children massacred. All over the place, houses were being destroyed and tower blocks were collapsing, crushing their residents . . . In those critical moments, many ideas raged inside me, ideas difficult to describe, but they unleashed a powerful urge to reject injustice and a strong determination to punish the oppressors. As I looked at those destroyed towers in Lebanon, it occurred to me to punish the oppressor in kind by destroying towers in America, so that it would have a taste of its own medicine . . . On that day I became sure that the oppression and intentional murder of innocent women and children is a deliberate American policy.[23]

This reminiscence—ideas that "raged inside" and were "difficult to describe"—suggest some of the tension and confusion in Osama's expanding intellectual and political life. Inspired by Azzam, he began in Peshawar to synthesize the banal tasks of organizing and fundraising—forming bureaucratic committees, reviewing publishing plans, creating rules and systems to provide financial subsidies to young Saudi volunteers—with a more mystical and poetical rhetoric of martyrdom. Partly this reflected Azzam's millenarian beliefs, but partly it was a marketing strategy crafted by a money-conscious proselytizer and the former business student who funded him. Their conduct suggests that Osama and Azzam were less interested in becoming martyrs than in creating a movement based on the emotional power of other people's martyrdom. Azzam used testimonials and memorials to sanctify the sacrifices of the first young, poorly trained volunteers who passed through his guesthouses in Peshawar and died in Afghanistan. "Lucky him who is rewarded with martyrdom," Azzam wrote. "Allah rewards him with seventy-two virgins and he can choose seventy of his relatives to join him in heaven." Of the first four committees Osama organized at the Services Office, one promoted media operations and a second promoted education.[24] His instincts were hardly surprising; he had spent much of his early working life in Bin Laden offices filled with glossy brochures and staffed by specialists in advertising and marketing. In his work for the royal family and the religious authorities in Medina and Mecca, Osama had learned that a project was a success only if its sponsors saw it as a success, and to ensure that they did, publishing and advertising had to play a role. He brought some of this modern business ethos to his earliest projects in Peshawar.

It was only about three months after Osama established the Services Office with Azzam that Salem, while on his hunting trip with Saudi royalty in Pakistan, flew into Peshawar with his video camera and his unbelieving entourage, consisting of a Swedish mechanic and an American specialist in ultralight aircraft.[25] Osama seemed to instinctively understand where his own passion for jihad overlapped with Salem's potential interest in the Afghan war—Osama chose to put orphans, not volunteer fighters, on display for his brother's camera. This was mainstream charity marketing on which they could collaborate without any hint of conflict: "God instructs you to treat orphans fairly," holds a Koranic verse. "He is well aware of whatever good you do."[26]

Even now, as he began to think of himself as a war fighter and perhaps, eventually, a martyr in the name of jihad, Osama interacted respectfully with his cigarette-smoking, patently irreligious elder brother. The *sawa*, or religious awakening, in Saudi Arabia might tug at family unity, but Osama also stretched himself to forgive secular-minded siblings, recalled his friend Jamal Khashoggi. What Osama feared more than individual sinfulness was "a mass movement of secularization, mixed schools, top-down changes." Also, recalled Khashoggi, "the Brotherhood emphasized the role of love and care and compassion in reaching out to non-observant Muslims. He had no problem with that, with non-observant Muslims. His method was to be compassionate and patient." Osama regarded his family's contributions to his work as nothing more or less than their duty: "Financial jihad," he would later write, "likewise, is an obligation . . . particularly for those who have the resources, rather than those who don't."[27]

Salem visited Peshawar a second time during this period, according to Bengt Johansson, who accompanied him. They met Osama in a suburban villa, "an Arab office, with some sofas around." They talked together for an hour or two, he remembered. Salem carried a large amount of cash in a case. "I don't know where the money was coming from—if it was from Salem, all this money, because they were sponsored from different people in Saudi Arabia," Johansson said.[28]

By 1985 Salem had learned to serve both Fahd's clandestine foreign policy in Afghanistan and his self-indulgent luxuriating. At the time, these lines of activity did not seem to be burdened by contradictions.

FOLLOWING THE DEATH from heart failure of his placid brother Khalid, Crown Prince Fahd had ascended to become the king of Saudi Arabia. Now that the throne belonged to him, Fahd told Salem he wished to travel in a more regal style. The king wanted a Boeing 747— and not just any one, but the largest model then in existence, known as a 747-300, which had a stretched upper deck, offering the potential for an aerial duplex.

Fahd had become king at sixty-two, just young enough to indulge in one last splurge. His health remained poor and he sometimes had difficulty walking. But he had fallen hard for his new and younger wife, Jawhara Al-Ibrahim, who had left her husband for Fahd and had given him a son, Abdulaziz, upon whom the king doted without restraint. He decorated identical bedrooms for the boy at his various palaces, and he had taken Abdulaziz to the White House to meet Ronald Reagan, early in 1985. Jawhara's brother, also named Abdulaziz, had become one of Fahd's most influential court advisers and had amassed great wealth in a short time. He kept an apartment in London's Mayfair neighborhood, and he purchased his own private planes—a Gulfstream and a DC-8. Salem cultivated a relationship with him; when the king went looking for a 747, his brother-in-law turned to Salem for help.[29]

Fahd knew he wanted something grand, but like a business mogul choosing among architects for a new mansion, he sought several imaginative proposals to which he could react. It would be a demanding, improvisational job to customize a single 747 to Fahd's tastes, however. This was not a project naturally suited for a large company like Boeing, which earned its profits by engineering standardized airline models. Still, to curry favor with Fahd, whose government airline purchased many jets, Boeing developed a proposal for a unique and kingly 747. Its bid for the interior and systems renovations alone exceeded $100 million, however, and the Boeing designs did not excite Fahd's imagination. In fact, the king was unhappy about Boeing's plan, which made his brother-in-law unhappy, which made Salem unhappy.

On his Texas travels, Salem had taken some of his own Learjets to San Antonio for interior renovations, and there he had met a ninth-grade-educated legend of American aviation named Dee Howard, who ran an aircraft service and engineering company at the San Antonio airport. Howard was a compact, fast-talking white-haired man with an intuitive knack for engineering. He lived in a riverside mansion and collected antique cars, but his business rode cycles of boom and bust, and he was always looking for a big score. Salem told him that Fahd's 747 project offered a golden opportunity to move his company into the global business of custom head-of-state aircraft renovation.

"He and I just hit it off real good," Howard recalled. "We liked each other, and he liked the kinds of things I did . . . He insisted that I come over and meet King Fahd and talk about it." Howard was reluctant; his San Antonio hangars weren't even big enough to hold a 747. Salem paid him $60,000 just to prepare a presentation, however. "I was doing Salem a favor."[30]

Salem was right to choose him; he had an instinct for theatrical luxury. Rather than turning to his San Antonio staff for initial designs, Howard hired Syd Mead, a Hollywood illustrator who had recently attracted attention for his work on the futuristic movie *Blade Runner*, directed by Ridley Scott. Mead flew with Howard and Salem to Riyadh to present their ideas to King Fahd. The illustrator dazzled them all by sketching ideas while holding his pad upside down, so that Fahd could see his work more clearly. "Your Majesty, I really want to do this plane for you," Dee Howard told the king. "I'm sixty-three years old, and I'll never get to do another one." Fahd squeezed his hand and smiled, and Howard thought to himself that the king was feeling something similar.[31]

Fahd and Salem engaged in strikingly informal banter; between design sessions, over lunch, they would debate one subject or another in jocular and animated voices, and Salem felt free to shout at Fahd across the table, denouncing the king's opinions. "Some people said, 'Ah you can't say that to the King—you can't,'" remembered one member of the group. "He got away with it—he finally quieted down a little bit, but he got away with it." They spent hours with Fahd working on the 747 designs; this was an aspect of royal life that the king seemed to particularly enjoy. Eventually, after arduous negotiations handled by Ibrahim, which included some unexpected demand, Dee Howard won the contract. It would ultimately be worth $92 million.[32]

The plane would include a number of features not normally found on commercial airliners. Among them was a fully equipped surgical operating theater linked by a private satellite communications system to the Cleveland Clinic, the American medical center. In an emergency, Fahd's surgeons could operate on him while parked on a runway, transmit images by satellite to Cleveland, sedate their patient, then take off and fly to the clinic for follow-up. To protect Fahd from his enemies, Raytheon Corporation installed electronic warfare equipment on the plane, including a system to defend against heat-seeking missiles.[33]

In the absence of medical crises or assassination attempts, the king could expect a comfortable ride. After considerable effort, Howard designed an elevator system that would allow the six-foot-four-inch Fahd to exit his limousine on an airport tarmac, wave to the crowd, and then walk a few steps onto a ground-level lift without any undignified bending of his head. From there, out of view, he would be hoisted into the plane's belly, where he could ascend a second elevator to the upper floor. His majlis contained a chandelier with five thousand unbreakable polycarbonate crystals. Beneath it, on either side of Fahd's throne, these crystals also sparkled in two artificial waterfalls; a Mead-inspired painting of a field of stars spread out on the wall behind. The royal bedroom suite contained a shower large enough to comfortably accommodate the king's girth, as well as a sitting room and a bed billowing with silks. Lest any of this luxury lead the king or his entourage to stray from their devotions, the ceiling of each room contained an electronic compass, linked to a global-positioning satellite system, which pointed continuously toward Mecca.

By 1985 the work on this fantasia was in full swing at the San Antonio airport. As Howard's workers passed certain benchmarks, payments arrived by wire from the royal treasury, sometimes in single increments of more than $10 million. Salem—without compensation, so far as any of his American employees and partners knew—flew in frequently from Saudi Arabia to inspect Howard's progress and urge him toward his deadlines. As Howard recalled it, speaking of Salem, "He was very interested in pleasing the king."[34]

18. ANXIETY DISORDER

BY THE EARLY 1980s, among all the Bin Laden brothers, Salem's only significant rival for leadership was Yeslam, who had graduated from the University of Southern California with a business degree in 1976. He was four or five years younger, but as the eldest of a group of three full brothers born to one of Mohamed's more senior wives, Rabab, a woman of Iranian origin, he had natural allies within the family. He also had friendly relations with some singleton half-brothers who had gotten to know him in California. Yeslam had returned to Jeddah from Los Angeles with plans that seemed to be stoked by his beautiful and ambitious wife, Carmen, the French-speaking daughter of an Iranian mother and a Swiss father. Carmen did not mind saying that she thought Yeslam was the most intelligent of the Bin Laden sons, and that his training and experience in California, where he had dabbled in the nascent personal computer industry, qualified him to lead the Bin Laden companies into modern sectors of international business. By the time Yeslam returned, however, Salem had already established his Bin Laden Brothers incubator; he had sidelined the trustees at the original Mohamed Bin Laden Organization; and, most important, he had made himself indispensable to Fahd. He had also secured the partnership of his own younger full brothers, Bakr and Ghalib, as well as capable half-brothers such as Yahya, Omar, and Tareq, and he had won the contract to participate in the expansion of the kingdom's telephone system, a major business achievement. Yeslam found he had relatively little room in which to maneuver.

He had some advantages, nonetheless: He understood Western stock and bond markets, from which Salem shied away; he spoke excellent French and English; and he had a cosmopolitan, business-minded spouse. Carmen established herself as a hostess in Jeddah's merchant and diplomatic circles. She and Yeslam built a tennis court at their villa along the Mecca Road, and on Thursday nights, the beginning of the Saudi weekend, they hosted tennis parties for young Saudi financiers, socialites, foreign executives, and ambassadors. These were casual events where alcohol flowed freely, steaks were grilled on the barbecue, and English was prevalent—a California-influenced refuge amid the kingdom's Wahhabi awakening.[1]

Yeslam shared Salem's obsession with speed. He had trained as a race car driver as well as a pilot, and over the years he had collected Ferraris, Lamborghinis, and Porsches. His full brother Ibrahim had a fondness for Rolls-Royces. After Yeslam's return to Jeddah, his brother-in-law—the husband of his full sister, Fawzia—suffered fatal brain damage in his Jeddah garage when he snapped his head while backing an imported Formula One racer out of his garage too quickly. Increasingly, among the Bin Laden men, jets and fast cars beckoned as a measure of manhood.[2]

In business, because of his USC classes and his encounters with bankers in America, Yeslam was more comfortable with the complexities of securities markets than were many of his brothers. He imported computers and began to think about how he could build up a modern investment advisory service, run by Saudis for Saudis, to compete with the American and European brokers who flocked to the kingdom to promote stock investments to the newly wealthy.[3]

As his ambitions in this field grew, so did tensions with Salem, who expected utter deference from younger brothers. Yeslam resented being patronized. Still, Salem rewarded him handsomely for his rising contributions. Yeslam earned the equivalent of more than $1 million in 1976, according to filings in a Swiss court by Carmen. Two years later, she reported, he was paid almost $1.5 million in salary and other compensation.[4]

Yeslam and Carmen escaped periodically to Geneva, where they had first met; in 1978, in the suburb of Genthod, at number 1, Chemin de la Petite-Voie, they bought and furnished an old estate. They paid just over 1 million Swiss francs for the property. He lavished her with jewelry—by her count, between 1975 and 1985, he gave her more than $2 million worth of diamond, emerald, ruby, and gold pieces. ("I admit I can be vain," she later conceded.) Her routine spending money sometimes totaled 20,000 Swiss francs per month. They kept a box of cash in their Jeddah home that often contained about $50,000.⁵

Like many of the Bin Laden brothers—other than Salem—Yeslam spoke softly and projected a mild, gentle demeanor. He was a thin, fragile-looking man who had his own streak of vanity—he dressed in fashionable designer brands, and he seemed to favor visible labels. He could seem more at home in Switzerland or California than in Saudi Arabia, and as the months passed after his return to Jeddah, he struggled in his search for a comfortable identity. As he approached thirty, he was rich and successful in business, and a father of two young daughters, but he was plagued increasingly by panic attacks.⁶

He managed for a time to fight through these episodes, but in 1979, that year of multiple upheavals, anxiety finally overwhelmed Yeslam. He "hid himself away in the house," according to Carmen's assertions in court filings. She spent "whole nights trying to give him reassurance." His behavior grew erratic: He "wanted to play backgammon day and night and he was forever waking his wife up and asking her to join in this mania." During the Mecca uprising, Carmen recalled, he dashed "from house to office like a man unhinged." In the aftermath of the violence, "he had nightmares. He was frightened of everything—frightened of dying, especially."⁷

For his part, as his interior struggles deepened, Yeslam felt that his wife was less than understanding. As his attorneys put it in Swiss court filings, "His wife seemed to take a malicious pleasure in aggravating his condition through constant violent scenes, during which she would scream and threaten to commit suicide if her capricious demands were not immediately satisfied . . . Her usual line was that she was going to drive her car into a tree." Carmen denied these allegations; she felt that she had done "everything she could to help him take care of himself and stay in control of his destiny and his business." In any event, unable to cope with either his demons or his wife, Yeslam sought professional help in Geneva, but he found no relief. He flew to Los Angeles for six weeks of medical treatment. According to Yeslam's court statements, this produced some improvement in his condition.[8]

In the midst of these struggles, he decided to lead his family into the international stock and bond markets. He bought computers that could support a stock trading operation, and he opened, in Jeddah, the first Saudi Arabian stock brokerage, designed, as one of its brochures put it, "To dispose of the idea that one has to live on Wall Street in order to make money."[9]

Yeslam quickly emerged, during the early 1980s, as the Bin Laden family's pioneer in global stock trading, syndicated real estate investments, and the use of offshore companies in Caribbean, Central American, and European tax and bank secrecy havens. Bin Laden family charity funds had become entangled with Osama's increasingly disoriented international radicalism; in a similar way, some of the family's investment money would become entangled with Yeslam's global financial vision, his anxiety disorders, and his deteriorating marriage.

AROUND 1980, Yeslam formed a Swiss company that would become the Saudi Investment Company, or SICO. A Cayman Islands corporation called Falken Limited—controlled by Yeslam and his full siblings—owned the firm. Falken also would hold stakes in other corporations; the full rosters of shareholders and activities at these offshore companies are unknown, but some of their names suggest a slightly Gaelic whimsy: Celta Finance S.A., Galway Inc. Some of these offshore companies were formed to manage single investments in commercial real estate projects or private Bin Laden family residences in the United States or Europe; others may have handled import or leasing operations for Bin Laden companies; still others were set up to channel finance for construction work in countries such as Sudan; and some remain entirely mysterious. In 1983 Yeslam formed the Saudi Investment Company Panama Corporation; he served as president, and a Swiss lawyer, Baudouin Dunand, joined him as a director. The next year, also in Panama, he organized a branch of the Mohamed Binladin Organization Incorporated, with Salem as president, Yeslam as treasurer and secretary, and Salem's full brother Bakr as an additional director. The paper residue of these and other Bin Laden–related companies in Panama, the Caymans, Curaçao, the Netherlands Antilles, Liechtenstein, Luxembourg, Switzerland, the Channel Isles, and elsewhere soon extended across oceans and continents. The firms opened and closed, changed names, bought one another out, or lay dormant for years at a time, their bare-bones registrations punctually renewed by family lawyers or accountants based in London and elsewhere. Yeslam appears to have been involved with many of these offshore companies, particularly those directed at real estate projects in the United States.[10]

He hired about a dozen employees at the Saudi Investment Company in Jeddah and held "hundreds of marketing meetings introducing the company to the public," according to a company brochure. In these presentations, Yeslam and his colleagues emphasized the forces of financial globalization: "Since the Kingdom provides much improved communication networks, the information gap to foreign markets is getting very small, enabling us to compete against foreign brokers, and that's exactly what we planned to do when we laid the ground work to cover American stock markets for our customers," the brochure said. Saudi Investment sent several of its brokers abroad to study the operations at foreign brokerages, and it created a department in Jeddah specializing in American and Japanese stock markets. By the end of 1983, the firm claimed to hold more than $10 million worth of stocks for its Saudi customers; it reported annual turnover of almost $200 million. Computer-aided stock trading, which sought to exploit price gaps in markets scattered around the world, and which could increase an investor's speed and volume, was now roiling stock markets in Tokyo, London, and New York; Yeslam, in effect, promised to bring a small piece of the action to Saudi Arabia.[11]

He also developed contacts at Wall Street investment banks. Through one of them—Donaldson, Lufkin & Jenrette—Yeslam arranged to clear trades for Saudi customers in the American stock markets, which made it much easier for them to buy and sell stocks on the New York Stock Exchange and in over-the-counter markets.[12]

Investment bankers at Donaldson, Lufkin introduced Yeslam to Charles Tickle, the chief executive of Daniel Corporation, an American real estate development company. Tickle sought partners who could fund office and residential projects in the United States; Yeslam said he was interested. Yeslam formed another Panamanian company called Saudi Investors, Incorporated, whose shareholders were described in a company document as "Mohamed Binladin Family." In 1980 they joined with Daniel to develop Imperial Plaza, in Richmond, Virginia, a twenty-two-acre adult-residential community with a restaurant, auditorium, barbershop, bank, pharmacy, library, nursing home, and four high-rise towers containing 891 apartments. Three years later, they invested in Woodgate West, a development of 34 two-story apartment buildings in southwest Houston. One of Yeslam's brochures described these deals as "a unique concept of investing in American property." The company expected to have "purchasing power" of $100 million by the spring of 1984.[13]

Charles Tickle, who operated out of Birmingham, Alabama, found Yeslam to be "always very professional . . . well educated, well spoken." Daniel Corporation "never had a bad business dealing with him of any kind." In all, they worked together on about a half dozen commercial real estate ventures in the United States; in each case, Yeslam's firm, Saudi

Investment, was the only investor besides Daniel Corporation. They formed offshore corporations to serve as financing vehicles, with Tickle and Yeslam sometimes named as directors. The only real mystery, Tickle recalled, was whose money Yeslam was actually investing—his, or that of other members of the Bin Laden family, or that of other Saudi investors, or money from some other source. "That was always such a secretive thing," Tickle said. At the time, as a business issue, "We could have cared less." For Daniel Corporation's purposes, all investment funds were the same; Yeslam had access to quite a lot of cash, and there was no reason for Tickle to believe that it was coming from improper sources.[14]

As HE BUILT this global portfolio, Yeslam found it more and more difficult to work with Salem. Yeslam was "now, in effect, the chief financial officer" of the Bin Laden companies, according to Carmen, but his "rise was not welcomed by Salem and Bakr," who increasingly served as Salem's second in command. The pair challenged some of Yeslam's decisions; his resentment deepened. Also, Yeslam and some other brothers "were frustrated by their lack of contact" with the Saudi royal family because "Salem and Bakr guarded their contacts with the princes," according to Carmen. Yeslam was reluctant to openly confront his elder brothers, however. Even in later years, he never spoke in detail about these conflicts, referring only obliquely to "disagreements" and his gradual exclusion from the principal family businesses.[15]

In 1985 Yeslam left Jeddah and moved to his estate in the Geneva suburbs. He distanced himself from his brothers, but he did not break completely with them—Yeslam, Salem, and Bakr remained codirectors of a number of offshore companies for years afterward, and they held business and social meetings from time to time. Yeslam also continued to manage family money, particularly that of his full brothers and sister. He would facilitate Swiss banking and some investments for other halfbrothers and half-sisters as well. Mainly, however, Yeslam hoped, by breaking away from the business scene dominated by Salem in Jeddah, to cultivate his own independent relations with Saudi princes and other wealthy investors who were not already clients of Salem or Bakr—Prince Majid and Prince Mishal, half-brothers of Fahd, were two of his most important contacts during this period.[16]

Yeslam decided to develop the sort of investment firm that would impress Saudis, Europeans, and Americans alike—one that exuded the mahogany elegance of a Swiss bank. For just over 5 million Swiss francs, he purchased and renovated a grand stone building on a corner lot in Old Geneva, on rue François Lefort; it would serve as the headquarters for Saudi Investment Company. From there, Yeslam managed brokerage accounts and international stock trading. A three-page letter to his full brother Ibrahim, written on Saudi Investment Company stationery on March 11, 1985, and later filed in an American court case, offers a snapshot of his trading activity. It refers to an audit by Arthur Andersen of Geneva and then lists Ibrahim Bin Laden's holdings: small positions in gold and silver; several hundred thousand U.S. dollars in cash deposits, apparently to provide collateral for stock trades; and shares or options in eighty-five different corporations, most of them American. Included in Ibrahim's stock portfolio were Anheuser-Busch, the beer company; Bally Manufacturing, a maker of pinball machines; and American Airlines.[17]

It was a heady time to be promoting the stock market, whatever one's strategy. After a severe recession in the United States in 1982, the Dow Jones Industrial Average rose by more than 50 percent over the next three years. Through the summer and autumn of 1985, as Yeslam built up his firm in Geneva, the markets climbed further still; the Dow soon doubled from its 1982 low, and then kept climbing. A mania about stock investing spread across the United States and around the industrialized world; the volume of shares traded daily on the major exchanges skyrocketed, and many middle-class investors who had previously shied away from stocks now dived in.

Carmen felt that a similar craze was overtaking Yeslam. In 1985 "he went through a period of massive and reckless spending, amassing more than 500 pairs of shoes, hundreds of suits and over a dozen luxury cars," her attorneys wrote in Swiss court filings. All the while, he "continued to suffer poor health, phobias and panic attacks." Carmen found him "increasingly intolerant and dogmatic." She sought treatment for her own anxiety and panic attacks. For his part, Yeslam found Carmen increasingly hysterical, and he became exhausted by her repeated threats to kill herself, according to the Swiss court filings by his attorneys. He believed that his wife was involved with another man, that she was "taking him for a ride and that her suicide threats were a pretense." Finally, "unable to stand his wife's scenes any longer," he moved out of their Genthod estate and into his building in Old Geneva. His wife then announced that she was pregnant and gave birth to their third daughter in April 1987.[18]

In the middle of this tumult, Yeslam decided to purchase control of a stock brokerage in London. It was not, perhaps, the most sanguine time in his life to undertake such a complicated investment, but he forged ahead nonetheless. Russell Wood & Company had offices at Southwark, on the south side of the Thames River. George Russell Wood, a British stockbroker, founded the firm with several partners in 1972; it specialized in what was known as the private client business, meaning that it handled stock trading for wealthy individuals. The firm had a seat as a broker-dealer on the London Stock Exchange; this meant it could buy and sell stocks on its own account or for clients without going through any intermediaries—it was a member of the exchange. This allowed it to promote speed, efficiency, and expertise while recruiting wealthy investors. By taking control of the company, Yeslam could bring his firm and the Bin Laden family directly into the international stock markets for the first time. "They wanted to establish themselves as brokers in London because they were brokers in their own country," recalled Auguste Sauter, then one of the firm's partners. Yeslam wanted "to advise all the people in Saudi Arabia with pockets of cash, to invest globally."[19]

Yeslam had brought with him to Switzerland a Tanzanian passport holder named Akbar Moawalla, who had previously worked at an American bank in Saudi Arabia. Moawalla served as Yeslam's chief accountant and manager, and he became Russell Wood's principal contact in Geneva as the acquisition talks unfolded during 1986 and early 1987.

All the while, stock prices went up and up. Trading volume on the major exchanges swelled. By the spring of 1987, they had a deal. The purchase price was not disclosed, but it appears to have totaled at least several million pounds sterling. Yeslam used Falken Limited, his Cayman Islands entity, to take control of Russell Wood. Moawalla became a director. Yeslam brought in one of his stock trading computers to keep track of all the trading by the London brokerage's existing clients and new clients from Saudi Arabia and elsewhere. The computer system was scheduled to take charge of all trading at the firm in late August 1987.[20]

On August 1, at two in the morning, Carmen went to Yeslam's building in Old Geneva and found him with another woman. "The discovery of the affair was a devastating blow for Carmen," her attorneys wrote. She said she wanted a divorce. Yelsam moved to write a separation contract.

On August 17, the Dow Jones Industrial Average reached its all-time high, and then began to fall.

Carmen slipped into a dire emotional state, and a week later, a doctor in Geneva, allegedly anticipating her divorce negotiations with Yeslam, issued a medical certificate indicating that her "anxiety and panic attacks had recently increased" and that "any decision or signature" by her should be "deemed null and void." She was soon hospitalized, suffering from exhaustion.[21]

In London, an accidental power surge of about one thousand volts, originating in the city's electrical grid, "burned all the hard disks" on the Russell Wood computer system, as Sauter recalled it. The surge destroyed all records of stock and option trading by the firm's clients. There were no backup disks, according to Sauter. What happened next is not entirely clear. Sauter recalled that some stockbrokers at the firm had drawn many of Russell Wood's clients into a risky options trading scheme involving the shares of a beer pump manufacturer in Croydon, England, and that suddenly, amid the confusion caused by the computer breakdown, some rival brokers made a run on these shares, causing Russell Wood's positions to collapse. In any event, that autumn, the brokerage's finances declined very rapidly. In October the stock market suffered its biggest one-day crash since the Great Depression of 1929. By the end of the year, Russell Wood had lost £3.5 million sterling, or about $6 million. In filings for British regulators, the firm blamed its trouble on the computer failure, which had led to "a breakdown in accounting controls."[22]

All in all, it had been a discouraging encounter between the Bin Laden family and the forces of globalization. There would soon be worse.

19. THE GRINDER

By the mid-1980s, the twenty-four Bin Laden brothers who owned shares in the main family company resembled a bloc of legislators from the same political party—professional interests bound them, and they often acted with unified purpose, but their membership had distinctly liberal and conservative wings. On the left stood the family's unquestioned leader, Salem, as well as Yeslam and several others who favored Europe and Beirut. Osama and Mahrouz held down the family's fervent, activist religious wing. In between, fashioning more traditional and centrist Arabian lives, were the four rising brothers who had all trained as civil engineers: Bakr, Ghalib, Omar, and Yahya. They were inclined neither to collect five hundred pairs of shoes nor to volunteer as jihadi fighters in foreign wars. They were observant Muslims, but they were notable more for their technical expertise and their willingness to work—they were the grinders among Mohamed's sons, and they invested long hours at the office and on job sites.

Of the four, Bakr, Salem's full brother, who had been born just a year or two after him in Mecca, had emerged as a sort of chief operating officer for the family and its businesses. His title was Field Project Manager for the construction division of the Mohamed Bin Laden Organization; he sat on that company's board of directors, as well as on the boards of several other joint ventures that had emerged from Salem's separate Bin Laden Brothers enterprise. Salem was the one "who got all the business for the Bin Ladens," recalled Mohamed Ashmawi, the Saudi oil executive. "Bakr managed it."[1]

He had the efficient air of a natural bureaucrat; he favored wrinkle-free, white traditional *thobe* gowns, perhaps with a pen or folded business papers in the breast pocket. "Where Salem did everything from the gut," recalled Francis Hunnewell, the investment banker who worked on the telephone project, "Bakr was much more conservative and more process-oriented." Michael Pochna remembered him as "a very intelligent person," but he never heard Bakr say anything in front of his elder brother besides "Yes, Salem."[2]

While his older brother had learned Beatles songs at his Essex boarding school, Bakr had studied in Syria and Lebanon. He spoke some French, but his English was less well developed. After his father's death, Salem decided that both his younger full brothers, Bakr and Ghalib, should pursue university degrees in civil engineering in the United States, so that they could spend their careers running construction projects for the family. Bakr finished high school first, and at this time, in the late 1960s, Salem had very few acquaintances in America. However, his great carousing Turkish friend from boarding school, Mehmet Birgen, known to all of Salem's acquaintances as "Baby Elephant," had moved to Miami. He was a good-looking, loquacious young man with a thick head of black hair. At the time, he was rooming with an American airline pilot, taking a few college classes, and devoting much of his considerable energy to the pursuit of the opposite sex. Salem telephoned and announced that he was dispatching Bakr to attend college in Miami, and he asked Baby Elephant to serve as Bakr's guardian.

This was not a natural match; like Salem, Baby Elephant was less than fully devoted to the traditional precepts of Islam, while Bakr, although young, was nonetheless devout; he had formally studied the Koran. Baby Elephant enrolled him initially at Miami-Dade Community College's North Campus, several miles north of downtown, at 119th Street, three blocks from Interstate 95. He bought Bakr a Vespa scooter, helped him find an apartment, and talked up Miami's many social enticements. He found it difficult to tempt him, with one exception. He invited Bakr to Shorty's Bar-B-Q, on South Dixie Highway, a pungent room where customers sat side by side at wooden tables and doused their ribs with hot sauces squirted from plastic bottles. Baby Elephant ordered a big rack of steaming ribs; when Bakr asked apprehensively if they were pork, his guardian assured him that no, they were beef. Bakr engorged himself, and for months afterward, he returned again and again. Finally, a visiting cousin from Saudi Arabia pointed out that, actually, he had been eating pork ribs all along, in violation of Islamic law. Shocked, Bakr asked a waitress for confirmation, stormed over to Baby Elephant's apartment, and confronted him: "What kind of guardian are you! You knew! You lied to me!" He telephoned Salem and complained, but his brother only replied, "At least he allowed you to discover how good pork ribs actually taste." Shorty's, however, lost a customer.[3]

Bakr polished his English, adjusted to American classrooms, and transferred to the engineering school at the University of Miami, then a sprawl of palm trees and low-slung concrete buildings in Coral Gables. He joined the class of 1973. There were more than four thousand Jewish students at the school, and just over fifteen hundred international students—from Taiwan, Venezuela, Iran, Algeria, and elsewhere. Protests over the Vietnam War roiled the campus. The Republican Party staged its convention in Miami in 1972, and university students joined other protestors in violent battles against police. Three quarters of University of Miami students smoked marijuana, according to a professor's poll. "Three things are essential for a pot party," noted the 1972 edition of the university yearbook, "namely, people, a place and pot."[4]

Bakr joined a clique at the engineering school that seemed oblivious to all this. "We never talked about race or the war," recalled Joaquin Avino, a Cuban American classmate. "The only thing we talked about was graduating, getting a job, becoming an engineer, and making some money." Many of the civil engineering students were second-generation

Cuban exiles; they belonged to "a relatively conservative culture within the university," said John Hall, another classmate. Most commuted to school from their parents' homes. Hall's father was a city fireman; Avino worked part-time as a baggage handler at the airport. Bakr fit right in—quiet, serious, pleasant, a bookworm, with no interest in rambunctious student life. He was particularly friendly with the Cubans, and he partnered with them on lab projects that involved analyzing soil composition and calculating stability and stress in building structures. At exam time, his results were solid but average. He stood out among the twenty to thirty students in the civil engineering course only because he wore silk shirts and drove a Cadillac Seville.[5]

He lived off campus in a suburban rambler with a small swimming pool in the Kendall/Pinecrest neighborhood, just south of Coral Gables. His neighbors included an elementary school and a "Youth For Christ" facility. Family joined him eventually. His half-brother Omar also enrolled in the University of Miami's engineering school, class of 1974, and rented an apartment a half mile from Bakr's house. At one point, Bakr returned home to marry, and he brought his new wife to Miami. She was Haifa Nabulsi, a beautiful Syrian blonde whom he had first met in Damascus when she was about sixteen; she came from an exiled Palestinian family originally from Nazareth. While Bakr completed his studies, Haifa gave birth to two sons, Nawaf and Firas; the Bin Ladens obtained American passports for each of the boys. Bakr would not permit his university classmates to socialize with his wife, and he made a lasting impression on one of them while describing his family when he mentioned that no man in Saudi Arabia bothered to count how many sisters he had. Still, apart from these cultural idiosyncrasies, with his big-finned car, his young boys, his house on a manicured corner lot, and his earnest sense of purpose, Bakr seemed to some of his classmates to be just like them—a young immigrant householder in pursuit of the American dream. As they got to know him better, however, they learned that he would be returning to his family's business in Saudi Arabia after graduation. Bakr offered one Cuban American classmate, Jorge Rodriguez, a job in Jeddah at double the starting salary he could expect to earn in the United States, but Jorge's wife announced, "By no means—I'm staying in America." Bakr departed and they gradually lost touch with him.[6]

In Jeddah he and his family moved into one of the suburban villas at the Kilo 7 family compound. Carmen Bin Laden befriended Haifa and found her "open-minded and lively"; they tanned together beside Haifa's swimming pool and "howled with laughter at how depraved the mothers-in-law would think us if they caught sight of our bathing suits." Carmen found Bakr formal but kind, and unlike some Saudi men, he did not criticize or shun Haifa when she gave birth to a daughter. Bakr was religious but not insistent or strident. He prayed punctually when in Saudi Arabia, but when he traveled to France, he did not search for mosques or carry a prayer rug to business meetings. "He is the type of person who doesn't like to attract the attention of others for things that are not necessary," said a longtime business partner.[7]

At the office, Bakr tried to keep up with Salem's demands and peripatetic deal making. Gradually other brothers returned to the kingdom with engineering degrees to ease some of his burden. Ghalib ran the construction equipment yard, helped to manage procurement from Caterpillar, and supervised projects in the field. Omar supervised complex building projects on his own.

Yahya proved to be a particular workhorse; he was exceptionally well organized and seemed to pride himself on putting in the very longest hours. He made a strong impression on some of the business partners and bankers who met with him. He had always been devout and deeply reflective; asked a question, he might pause for several searching minutes before he answered. He smoked cigarettes from a long plastic holder and had slightly bulging eyes, which created an exaggerated effect when he stared out during these long, contemplative pauses. In a top hat, he would have resembled Penguin from the *Batman* movies.

This engineering coterie spent most of their days concentrating on their work as young construction executives, but as they approached middle age, and as the Islamic awakening spread in Saudi Arabia, their lifestyles became, in some cases, more overtly pious. Non-Muslim partners and friends noted this more explicit religiosity, but they saw, too, that it fell very much within the kingdom's mainstream, which was becoming more conservative. Yahya's wife, who had not previously covered herself, took the veil. Ghalib's did, too. Charity and the Hajj became even more important to family routines. By the mid-1980s, at least one of the Bin Ladens' business partners felt that some of the more traditional engineering coterie—Yahya, in particular—had begun to push Salem to ensure that Osama received all the support he needed as he became involved with the Afghan war. In this partner's analysis, while these brothers did not share Osama's radicalism, they had become very proud, nonetheless, of Osama's charitable work on behalf of suffering Afghans, and they appreciated his ardent commitment to a defining Islamic cause. According to a senior Saudi government official, Bakr accompanied Osama to Pakistan on one of his early visits there.[8]

These were also the brothers who took the lead on construction and renovation work in Mecca and Medina. After he became king, Fahd took a number of steps to enhance his credentials as the regent and guardian of Islam's birthplace. In 1985 he inaugurated an eight-year, multibillion-dollar project to expand, once more, the Prophet's Mosque in Medina, so that it could accommodate almost a half million additional worshippers. The massive spending in Medina helped Fahd to ingratiate himself with the Saudi religious authorities who mistrusted his secular lifestyle, and it increased his visibility across the Islamic world. As Saudi kings had done for four decades, Fahd handed the work to the Bin Ladens—without competitive bidding. The king's decision was consistent with his method for allocating spheres of commissions in government contracting, according to the senior Saudi government official. Fahd identified reliable agents or business families—some Saudi, and some, such as the Lebanese developer Rafik Hariri, who were not—and gave them sole control of a particular sector, such as arms sales, roadwork, or palace construction. In this way Fahd could direct how contracts and commissions would be distributed, and who would benefit from extra payments. The system reinforced loyalty and secrecy. The Bin Ladens had once been dominant in highway construction, but after 1985 their major windfalls came through the huge, exclusive contracts Fahd awarded them in the holy cities—first the Prophet's Mosque renovation in Medina, and then a similar project in Mecca.

The expansion of the Prophet's Mosque contemplated by Fahd was mind-boggling in its scale—a new building of eighty-two thousand square meters, a new plaza and pedestrian spaces of more than two hundred thousand square meters, new and taller minarets, eighteen new staircases, six new escalators, sixty-four new doors and gates. For the Bin Ladens, Bakr played the key role in creating the detailed plans and executing them after approval by Fahd.

The work spoke to Bakr as an engineer, a businessman, a Bin Laden, a Saudi, and a Muslim; the projects became the overriding source of his professional identity and his pride. The work offered a rare and privileged opportunity to leave an authorial mark on the holiest places in his faith. European and Arab architects, designers, and suppliers all contributed to the project over time, but from the beginning, Bakr played a decisive role. He delivered the detailed presentations of designs to Fahd and answered the king's questions, and he drove the golf cart when Fahd visited Medina for an inspection tour. "Many a time he would require us to repeat the plans and the designs, to improve on this side, or develop that side," Bakr later wrote of Fahd. "He used to visit the two projects at various phases and choose the best and most suitable materials with no regard for financial cost." The king even issued "a standing order to establish an open-ended account" to fund the work.[9]

Osama was an executive in the Bin Laden's Medina office at the time this enormous undertaking took shape. He was still commuting from

Saudi Arabia back and forth to the Afghan war. He had deepened his involvement after his brief visit to the fighting front in 1984, but he had not moved his family to Pakistan. He typically stayed in Pakistan for only three or four months at a time.

Fahd's Medina project led to conflicts within the Bin Laden family that may have influenced Osama's priorities, according to a former senior American government official who has discussed the episode with Bakr. The details are unclear, but according to this official, the Medina contract and its many pressures produced a "sort of realignment in the family," which left Osama unhappy about his role. The essential issues were control and authority. "He just basically made a giant pest of himself and everybody wanted him gone," according to the former official. By this account, Bakr and Salem stood on one side of the quarrel, and Osama and some of his more religious half-sisters tried to oppose them. "Salem told me, 'This brother of mine in Afghanistan is going to be our family's big problem,'" said a second business partner who worked very closely with the Bin Ladens during this period. Osama "didn't bother Salem, he bothered all his family." Whatever the nature and extent of this disagreement, it did not result in a full rupture between Osama and his half-brothers, however. Indeed, Salem's risk taking on Osama's behalf would soon increase. But the episode may have led both Osama and his half-brothers to see Pakistan, rather than Medina, as the best outlet for Osama's energies.[10]

EARLY IN 1986, Abdullah Azzam wrote to Osama from Peshawar, urging him to move there. He told his protégé that administrative and financial problems had accumulated at the Services Office, the support service they had founded more than a year earlier for Arab volunteers in Afghanistan. Azzam urged Osama to help put the place in order. Here, at least, was an enterprise that wanted and appreciated Osama fully.

Later that year, Osama moved with his family to a pine-shaded house in the Hyatabad section of Peshawar. In the ensuing months, he would act like an ambitious young man who felt a need to prove himself. He threw himself more actively into the war, and for the first time, he independently sought publicity for his work, to extend his reputation in Saudi Arabia and the Muslim world. Was undeclared competition with Bakr and Salem, now themselves celebrated in Saudi media as the renovators of Medina, one strand in Osama's web of motivations after he moved his family to Pakistan? Even if it was, one constant remained: to achieve his goals on the Afghan frontier, he needed the Bin Ladens.[11]

20. THE ARMS BAZAAR

AROUND THE TIME he moved with his family to Peshawar, Osama made a new request of Salem. This time it wasn't money; he told his brother that he needed weapons, and he specifically asked for portable anti-aircraft missiles.[1]

Osama entered the international arms market because he had decided, for the first time, to create his own jihadist militia. He found the Arab volunteer movement in some disarray early in 1986. Azzam's Services Office, which Osama had funded with about a half million U.S. dollars to this point, was fracturing over petty disputes and prideful slights. As more Arabs arrived, Azzam's inclusive governing system of committees and consultative councils fell under strain. Bin Laden's aide, Abu Haji Al-Iraqi, recalled "an increase of complaints" that led to a decision to "change the administrative staff." Increasingly, leading figures in the group irritated one another and engaged in tedious debates about money and theology. Ayman Al-Zawahiri, an Egyptian doctor who had been tortured in Cairo prisons for his involvement in violent conspiracies, arrived in Peshawar with other radical Egyptian exiles. Zawahiri cultivated a relationship with Osama, motivated as Azzam had been earlier—the doctor was ambitious but poor, and he needed Osama's financial patronage. He stirred bitter disputes in Peshawar salons over jihad strategy. He found Arab allies ripe with grievance. Azzam had promoted the Afghan war as a province of miracles and beautiful sacrifice;

the volunteers summoned up this stairway to heaven found the reality of the war to be cold, brutal, disputatious, and poorly organized.

In April some Arab volunteers participated in a brutal four-week battle at Jawr, a fortified rear base located in high, sandy ridges near the Pakistan border, in an area controlled by a fierce Afghan commander named Jalaladin Haqqani. The fight went badly. Bin Laden decided that the Arabs needed to strengthen themselves in these border areas. He moved away from Peshawar's debilitating office culture and began to build his own brigade of Arab jihadis up in the mountains along the Afghan-Pakistan border. His aim was to participate directly in the war; it was for this that he required his own portable missiles, to challenge Soviet helicopter-borne assault teams.[2]

"It is well known that there are two elements of fighting," Osama said later. "There is the fighting itself and then there is the financial element, such as buying weapons. This is emphasized in many verses of the Koran, such as the following: 'God has purchased the persons and possessions of the believers in return for the Garden.'"[3]

Salem turned to a German friend with an Afghan connection: Thomas Dietrich. They had first met in Cairo; Dietrich was an amateur pilot on vacation, and they fell into a friendship centered on flying. As a boy, Dietrich had lived in Kabul; his father was a West German foreign aid official. He became a fixture in Salem's European entourage. In the mid-1980s, he was enrolled at a university in Stuttgart, but he found time to ski and fly with Salem and some of his brothers and sisters, particularly at resorts in the Alps.

At Offley Chase, his estate outside London, Salem summoned Dietrich to his room. "We need to help my brother," Salem told him, as Dietrich recalled it.

"You've got many of them."

Salem talked about Osama; Dietrich had heard some about him but not a lot. "He is now very religious," Salem said. "He is now in

Afghanistan, and the Russians are there. People are getting killed. And I know that you lived there—and you need to help him." Osama had identified two priorities: missiles that could shoot down helicopters, and equipment that would allow Arab volunteers to manufacture ammunition for AK-47 assault rifles, by filling spent shells with new rounds.[4]

The war was intensifying. After a policy review in the spring of 1985, the United States decided secretly to escalate its support for the Afghan *mujaheddin;* for the first time, the U.S. identified victory over the occupying Soviet army as an objective. The CIA rapidly increased the quantity and quality of the weapons it sent in through Pakistan. The Soviets introduced more aggressive tactics as well, ordering elite helicopter-borne Special Forces units, called Spetsnaz , to Afghanistan; these assault troops flew raids against rebel supply lines and wreaked havoc along the Pakistan border. To thwart the Spetsnaz, the CIA agreed in 1986 to send heat-seeking U.S.-made Stinger missiles to the Afghans; the missiles were particularly lethal against helicopters. The initial shipments occurred during the first half of the year, just as Osama was moving with his family to Peshawar. An Afghan commander fired the first Stingers on the Afghan battlefield in September, at Jalalabad. The missiles destroyed several Soviet helicopters that day, and they quickly acquired an almost mythical reputation for potency among both the *mujaheddin* and the Soviets.[5]

Separately, at some point during this period (it is not clear when), the Reagan administration team supervising U.S. involvement with the Afghan war discussed whether to provide aid directly to the Arab volunteers based in Peshawar. The CIA ran most of the secret war from day to day, but an interagency group at the White House, chaired by Assistant Undersecretary of Defense Michael Pillsbury, decided on the war's broader policies. Twice Pillsbury flew by helicopter to the Afghan frontier to review training facilities and to meet Gulbuddin Hekmatyar and Abdul Rasul Sayyaf, two rebel leaders who were particularly close to the Arabs. During these meetings, Pillsbury asked about the military effectiveness of the Arab volunteers. He concluded, he recalled, that the Afghan commanders didn't want aid or supplies to be diverted to the Arabs; the Afghans saw these relatively small bands of *shaheen*, or "martyrs," as righteous warriors but also as sacrificial pawns of marginal military value. The Afghans wanted all the weapons for themselves.[6]

After he received Osama's requests, Salem made several attempts to contact the Pentagon to see if he could arrange to supply Osama with portable missiles, according to a business partner who participated in these inquiries. Salem tried to locate the right person in the American defense bureaucracy, but he was unsuccessful, the partner said. It is not clear whether the Reagan administration ever made a formal decision to refuse to supply weapons to the Arab volunteers—no such document or account has ever surfaced—but conclusions such as those formed by Pillsbury after his inquiries in Pakistan clearly influenced American thinking about the matter. Pillsbury said he knew of no explicit decision to refuse aid to the Arab volunteers and that he would have known if such a decision had been made; still, they were not a priority.

Salem felt he had no recourse but to use the private arms market, according to interviews with Dietrich and two other individuals in the private sector who joined discussions with Salem about supplying arms to Osama. Salem did receive some financial support from the Saudi government, according to these individuals, but he received no known aid from the United States. As Dietrich recalled it: "The problem was there was no clearance from any of the Western governments" to supply the Arab volunteers "with anti-aircraft missiles."[7]

Dietrich had contacts at Heckler & Koch, the German arms manufacturer. Through them, Dietrich recalled, he arranged several meetings between Salem and salesmen at the firm who specialized in ammunition and rifle manufacturing. A second partner of Salem confirmed these negotiations; the partner said he warned Salem to not get involved, because it was a private transaction of uncertain legality, but that Salem went ahead anyway.[8]

It was not entirely clear to Dietrich why Osama wanted to make his own bullets. Like many of the *mujaheddin*, his volunteers carried mainly Chinese-made assault rifles based on a Soviet design; Pakistani markets were awash with ammunition for these guns. Osama seemed in part to regard remanufacture from spent shells as some sort of virtuous, efficient cottage industry; it was also the sort of technology that was sometimes advertised in the pages of mercenary magazines like *Soldier of Fortune*. Dietrich found an arms salesman who understood the process and flew with him to Dubai to meet with Salem and Osama. "We sat together and said, 'It does not really make sense to refill the bullets there,'" Dietrich recalled. The technical problems were too great. The arms salesman suggested that Osama simply purchase the ammunition he needed from suppliers they could locate in South America.

To discuss buying missiles, Osama flew to London and met with Salem, Dietrich, and Dietrich's contacts in a suite at the Dorchester Hotel on Park Lane, according to Dietrich. They met two or three times at the hotel over a period of six to eight weeks during 1986, he said. Before one meeting, Salem and Dietrich were horsing around in their usual way. As they walked from one room of the suite into a second room, where Osama was waiting, Salem admonished, "Don't do any jokes with my brother. He's very religious."

Ultimately Dietrich heard that his contacts had helped arrange for the purchase in South America of both Russian-made SA-7 shoulder-fired missiles and ammunition for Chinese-made AK-47 rifles; the missiles and bullets were shipped to Karachi. One snag was that Osama's sponsors in the transaction wanted to pay for the ammunition not with cash, but with crude oil. According to Dietrich, they expected the seller to accept "just a tanker offshore, which was not easy to accomplish because a company like Heckler & Koch, they don't want oil, they want money."[9]

Dietrich had "no idea" where the money or oil for these arms purchases originated. The best available evidence suggests it probably came at least in part from the Saudi government. Certainly Salem and Osama were working in concert with official Saudi policy at this time. Also, Osama's arms purchases, as described by Dietrich, seem to fit inside a larger pattern. In late 1985, the Saudi government entered into a multibillion-dollar arms deal with the British government, called Al-Yamamah. The transaction had a number of unconventional aspects. The Saudi government allocated between four hundred thousand and six hundred thousand barrels of oil daily as barter currency to finance the purchase of major weapons systems from British companies. By using oil instead of cash, the Saudis were able to quietly evade official oil production caps imposed by the Organization of the Petroleum Exporting Countries (OPEC), according to an authorized biography drawing on extensive interviews with Prince Bandar bin Sultan, the longtime Saudi ambassador in Washington. According to this account, the financing umbrella arranged for the Al-Yamamah deal also supported a number of Saudi Arabia's covert anti-communist programs, including "arms bought from Egypt and other countries, and sent to the *mujaheddin* in Afghanistan."[10]

Other evidence about possible Saudi government participation in Osama's arms supplies during this period is more fragmentary. Ahmed Badeeb, the Saudi intelligence officer who worked closely with Osama, acknowledged in an interview that he had purchased SA-7 missiles and supplied them to the Afghan fighters, although he did not specify Osama as a recipient. Salem also negotiated during this period to purchase weapons for Osama from South African arms dealers, according to two individuals familiar with those transactions. One individual who participated in these discussions, which were separate from those involving Dietrich, recalled that some of the funding came from the Saudi royal family.[11]

During 1986, in Peshawar, Osama delivered his first known speeches denouncing the United States because of its support for Israel; as Osama later recalled his words, he preached that "Americans take our money and give it to the Jews, so they can kill our children with it in Palestine." It is possible that his hostility toward America, inculcated by Abdullah Azzam, was further inflamed when Salem informed him that his attempt to buy Stingers had been rebuffed at the Pentagon. In any event, by comparison, Osama was fiercely protective of the Saudi royal family during this same period. A Palestinian journalist who worked at *Al-Jihad* magazine recalled Osama lashing out when colleagues suggested during 1986 that King Fahd was not a legitimate Muslim because Queen Elizabeth had presented him a medal that resembled a Christian cross: "For God's sake, don't discuss this subject—concentrate on your mission," Osama said, as the journalist recalled it. "I don't permit anyone to discuss this issue here." He was at war with the enemies of Saudi Arabia, not with its throne.[12]

BEGINNING IN THE SUMMER of 1986, Osama spent more of his time around Jaji, in the Afghan province of Khost, near a protrusion of Pakistani territory called Parrot's Beak. This was an area of increasing strategic importance in the broader Afghan war. A number of important Afghan rebel fighting units with strong Islamist credentials—those led by Haqqani, Sayyaf, Gulbuddin Hekmatyar, and Younus Khalis—operated in this vicinity. They tried to pressure Kabul and its outskirts. Sayyaf, in particular, ran a training facility near Jaji. It was the theatrical site he had used to host Arab donors, but increasingly his camp was situated in a hot battle zone.

Pakistani intelligence officers who directed supplies and tried to manage war strategy on the front lines decided to fortify the border area around Jaji, to preserve their supply lines and protect Afghan fighters from the Soviet raids. Osama joined in this effort. He built infrastructure that served the Islamist Afghan commanders, and for himself, he constructed a new camp near Sayyaf's Jaji facility, which he called the Lion's Den. The number of volunteers who initially joined him there in the autumn of 1986 was tiny—as few as a dozen, many still in their teens.

Abdullah Azzam was uneasy about Osama's solo venture. He was still financially dependent upon his protégé. Among other things, he feared that Soviet troops might kidnap Bin Laden and fly him off to Kabul as a propaganda prize. Azzam sent Arabs from his own nearby camp to join and protect Bin Laden; by the end of the year, the militia at the Lion's Den had grown to about fifty.[13]

Osama built this initially unimposing brigade—barely a platoon, actually—with active support from his family. In addition to helping him buy weapons, the Bin Ladens shipped construction equipment during 1986 to support Osama's projects on the border. Bin Laden company engineers had volunteered in Peshawar earlier, and some construction equipment probably arrived during that earlier period as well. A large batch reached Pakistan between October and December of 1986.[14] Afterward, Osama expanded construction activity around Jaji and built roads north toward the mountain redoubt of Tora Bora, which Pakistani intelligence officers had identified as an area where caves and storage depots could be fortified and defended. None of this support from the Bin Ladens—apart from the missiles and ammunition—would have seemed exceptional; it differed little in character from the defense construction work they had done for the Saudi government for years on the Yemen frontier, among other places. Osama later described the scope of his imports:

> In spite of the Soviet power, we used to move with confidence and God conferred favors on us so that we transported heavy equipment from Saudi Arabia estimated at hundreds of tons altogether that included bulldozers, loaders, dump trucks, and equipment for digging trenches. When we saw the brutality of the Russians bombing *mujaheddin* positions, we dug a good number of huge tunnels and built in them some storage places and in some others we built a hospital. We also dug some roads.[15]

Ahmed Badeeb recalled that Osama was "very professional" as he built these underground fortifications. Indeed, Bin Laden was literally operating at times as a construction professional, under contract with Pakistani and probably also Saudi intelligence. He chose a group of young Saudi volunteers from Medina, the city where he had so recently served as a Bin Laden executive, to work with him. The Bin Laden office in Cairo, in cooperation with the Saudi Ministry of Interior, obtained visas for young Egyptian Islamists who wanted to volunteer in Afghanistan. By one account, Bin Laden companies also contracted to build hospitals and other facilities for Islamic charities in Peshawar. These Peshawar building projects generated several hundred jobs for Arab workers from Egypt and elsewhere, by this account; the workers poured concrete nine to five and some toured the jihad on weekends.[16]

Osama was no longer a tourist to the war, however; he was now shaping the battlefield in a strategically important region at a time of military escalation. His ragtag unit of volunteers might be of little importance, but his construction work was significant, at least in the evaluation of American and Pakistani intelligence officers who monitored the overall war effort. Recalled Milton Bearden, the CIA station chief in Pakistan at the time, speaking of Osama: "He put a lot of money in a lot of the right places in Afghanistan." With his cash and bulldozers, he won allegiance from Arab fighters who saw him as "more practical" than the preachy Azzam.[7]

"HISTORY RECOUNTS THAT AMERICA supported everyone who waged *jihad* and fought against Russia," Osama once noted in passing. It is the only time he is known to have spoken positively about the American role in the anti-Soviet Afghan war. The great majority of his other comments have emphasized American hypocrisy during the conflict and his own staunch independence from the CIA. Even in radical Islamist circles, the canard occasionally circulated that Bin Laden had been a CIA client or paid agent during the 1980s. An Al-Jazeera interviewer once put the question to him directly, and Osama offered a lengthy, defensive reply, one that combined theological and realpolitik justifications for the proximity between his own activities and those of the CIA:

> It's an attempt to distort by the Americans, and praise be to God that He has thwarted their conspiracy . . . As for their claim that they supported the *jihad* and the struggle against the Soviets, well, this support came from Arab countries, especially from the Gulf . . . The Americans are lying when they claim they helped us at any point, and we challenge them to present a single shred of evidence to prove it. In fact, they were a burden on us . . . We were doing our duty, which is supporting Islam in Afghanistan, even if this did coincide with American interests. When the Muslims were fighting the Byzantines, during the fierce war between the Byzantines and the Persians, no one in their right mind could say that the Muslims were fighting as agents of the Persians against the Byzantines. There was merely a common interest . . . Unintended confluence of interests does not mean there is any kind of link or tacit agreement.[18]

There is no evidence from any source—no document, no interview— to suggest that Osama ever met an American intelligence officer. The only American of any kind whom he is known to have greeted personally—apart, perhaps, from Bin Laden family members and other Arab acquaintances who carried American passports—is George Harrington, the ultralight salesman and accidental adventurer from San Antonio who accompanied Salem to Peshawar in early 1985. Nonetheless, whether he was aware of it or not, Osama's logistics and construction work along the Pakistan border, starting in 1986, intersected with CIA programs and funding. The agency's logistics and construction units, working through Pakistani intelligence, provided cement and other materials for the caves and storage facilities that Afghan commanders such as Haqqani and Hekmatyar built along the border during this period. Osama's construction with Bin Laden family equipment certainly complemented these projects, and he may well have participated in them. Moreover, after 1986, Haqqani became what intelligence officers refer to as a "unilateral" asset of the CIA, meaning that he received tens of thousands of dollars in cash directly from CIA officers working undercover in Pakistan, without any mediation by Pakistani intelligence, which normally handled and relayed the great majority of CIA funds to the Afghans. Haqqani had multiple sources of cash but the CIA payments were sizable. Haqqani, in turn, helped and protected Osama and the Arab volunteers as they built their nascent militia. (Osama later referred to Haqqani as a "hero *mujahid* sheikh" and "one of the foremost leaders of the *jihad* against the Soviets.") Haqqani traveled frequently to Peshawar to meet with a Pakistani and, separately, with an American intelligence officer, and to pick up supplies. Osama would have had no reason to know about Haqqani's opportunistic work with the CIA, but he and his Arab volunteers benefited from it. They stood apart from the CIA's cash-laden tradecraft—but just barely.[19]

Osama's contacts with the Saudi government, by comparison, were open and routine. Badeeb maintained offices for the Saudi intelligence service at the Saudi embassy in Islamabad and sleeping quarters in Saudi-funded charities in Peshawar. These charities, in turn, funneled contributions to the Services Office. Azzam's *Al-Jihad* magazine praised the support of seven charities in its December 1986 issue; these included the Red Crescent of Saudi Arabia and the Muslim World League, the large Mecca-based charity. Badeeb visited Pakistan as often as once a month. Prince Turki Al-Faisal, the chief of Saudi intelligence, also traveled there regularly. Their host in Islamabad was Yousef Mottakbani, the Saudi ambassador to Pakistan, a clean-shaven professional who kept a photograph of Gulbuddin Hekmatyar on the wall in his living room. Mottakbani channeled funds from both Saudi intelligence and from private charities to favored Afghan clients, including Haqqani, according to a former American envoy who participated in the covert program. Mottakbani hosted dinner parties in Islamabad at which Osama was a regular guest.

Turki met him at these soirees and in Peshawar. He found Osama "shy, friendly, and almost gentle. He always spoke in a low voice; he was a man of pithy statements."[20]

Turki and other senior Saudi officials, such as Prince Bandar, later said their government had little direct involvement with Osama during this period. Turki characterized Osama as a volunteer from a respectable family who was an "interesting figure" but not an instrument of Saudi tradecraft. By Turki's account, unlike the CIA, Saudi intelligence, which is known by the acronym GID, never deviated from its pledge to funnel money to the Afghans only through the Pakistani intelligence service, known as ISI. "Abdullah Azzam was never supported by me or the GID," Turki wrote later. "GID stuck to its agreement . . . that support for the *Mujaheddin* would be distributed according to their effectiveness, which was measured by the ISI and then evaluated by both the CIA and GID. Sayyaf consistently came in fifth or sixth place."[21]

Turki's account leaves ambiguous whether, separately from Azzam, Saudi intelligence provided direct funding to Bin Laden, particularly after he moved away from Azzam and began to build infrastructure along the Pakistan border. Some of Osama's own followers have said that he did receive direct aid from Saudi intelligence. Abu Musab Al-Suri, a long-time colleague and later an important Al Qaeda ideologist, has written, "It is a big lie that the Afghan Arabs were formed with the backing of the CIA . . . The truth is that Saudi intelligence agencies did have involvement with Bin Laden, and elements of their apparatus did send assistance from Saudi Arabia."[22]

Ahmed Badeeb, the former Al-Thaghr biology teacher and Turki's chief of staff, has provided the fullest inside account of Osama's contacts with the Saudi government during this period:

> He had a strong relation with the Saudi intelligence and with our embassy in Pakistan. The nature of this relation with Saudi intelligence was because the Saudi embassy in Pakistan had a very powerful and active

role ... When persons came from the Kingdom to present assistance, the ambassador would hold dinner parties and invite people, and due to Osama bin Laden's family and personal contacts, he would be invited as well. He had a very good rapport with the ambassador and with all Saudi ambassadors who served there. At times, the embassy would ask Osama bin Laden for some things and he would respond positively ... [Also,] the Pakistanis saw in him one who was helping them do what they wanted done there.[23]

In a broad sense, then, Osama had come to enjoy relations with the Saudi royal family and its intelligence service quite similar to those cultivated with other sectors of the government by his half-brothers: Osama's connections were social, but girded and constrained by his role as a construction contractor; they were respectful and solicitous; and Osama's honorable place at court was reaffirmed periodically in the formal settings of an embassy salon. Unlike his half-brothers, however, he did not return from these rather orthodox Arabian gatherings to a conventional Saudi home, to watch television or smoke a water pipe on the patio. Instead, Osama rolled back down the Grand Trunk Road in his four-wheel-drive vehicles, through Peshawar, and then up rocky roads to the barren encampments, just inside Afghanistan, where he led his small incubating cult of martyrdom.

21. OFF THE BOOKS

BY THE MID-1980S, Jim Bath, Salem's partner in Houston, who had arrived in the city three decades earlier with hardly a dollar to his name, had acquired many of the accessories of a successful Texas adventurer: a pair of .38-caliber Smith & Wesson revolvers, a Westchester high-powered rifle with a scope, a Winchester bolt-action rifle, a BMW 525 automobile, and a Rallye Minerva airplane. He owned interests in a number of residential and investment properties around Houston; these included hotel projects, apartment houses, an airport parking garage, a Denny's restaurant, and a ranch in Liberty County. From offices on several floors of the Fannin Bank Building downtown, he oversaw his aircraft brokerage company, Bin Laden family business entities, his own scattered investments (which included $50,000 he had sunk into an oil-drilling fund run by George W. Bush, his friend from the Texas Air National Guard), and an aircraft leasing company called Skyway Aircraft, which was incorporated in the Cayman Islands and controlled by Khalid Bin Mahfouz. Bath and his wife Sandra still lived immediately behind Khalid's enormous estate in the River Oaks neighborhood of Houston. All in all, Bath presented a grand facade. But it was little more than that; in truth, his life was unraveling.[1]

Bath jetted around the world with his Arab clients and other oil industry friends—to Caribbean tax havens, Europe, Saudi Arabia, and elsewhere in the Middle East. One of the leased oil company jets he occasionally flew on had a bed with a mink throw on it, and it was there that he first met Mary Ellen Lewis, a married air hostess, according to Sheryl Johnson-Todd, an attorney who represented two of Bath's wives in subsequent divorce proceedings. Over the course of their long, tumultuous affair, Bath provided Mary Ellen with a Cadillac, transferred money to her and her husband, and fathered a child with her out of wedlock. After Sandra discovered the relationship, she later testified, anonymous postcards arrived at her home in River Oaks; the cards accused Sandra of clinging to an opportunistic marriage like the fictional one between J.R. and Sue Ellen in the prime-time television soap opera *Dallas*. Ultimately, Sandra learned about Bath's child with Lewis when her husband pulled up to their house one day in a convertible with a little girl asleep in the passenger seat; according to Sandra, Jim Bath asked if she would please raise the child. She filed for divorce instead. Sandra alleged in court filings that Bath abused drugs; he denied her allegations. According to an affidavit by Bath, Mary Ellen Lewis eventually became no happier with him; she "made threats to blow my head off and to kill me."[2]

Bath's affair with Lewis may not have been the only secret he harbored during his last years of working with the Bin Laden family. According to a 1990 court filing by Bath's estranged business partner Bill White, Bath "indicated that he was working as a CIA operative" during a conversation they held in 1982. By White's account, Bath said he had been introduced to the CIA when the elder George Bush was its director, during the late 1970s, and that he had been asked to conduct "covert intelligence gathering on his Saudi Arabian business associates." According to him, Bath said that he had been asked to undertake certain sensitive air-transport operations. After a series of scandals during the 1970s, the CIA had allegedly decided to privatize some of its covert air-transport operations, and the agency had been looking for reliable Americans with security clearances who might take on some of this work under contract. As a former air force pilot who was friendly with the younger Bush, Bath was a natural candidate for such a role, according to

White, who was himself a graduate of the U.S. Naval Academy in Annapolis and a former navy fighter pilot. White came to believe that Bath had used some of his offshore charter aircraft businesses to help ship construction equipment and possibly weapons to Osama Bin Laden on the Afghan frontier during the late 1980s.[3]

Jim Bath has spoken sparsely and infrequently about his business and chartered aviation endeavors during the 1980s. (He declined to be interviewed for this book.) In a court filing from that period, he seemed to mock all White's allegations about their business disputes, arguing that his former business partner suffered from "paranoia" and "demonstrated frequent mood swings." According to Bath, White believed that "those conspiring against him were engaged in 'covert communications' and had 'secret agendas' against him." In 1991 Bath told *Time* that White's account about his supposed intelligence work was "fantasy" and that he was "not a member of the CIA or any other intelligence agency." About a decade later, however, in an interview with the journalist Craig Unger, Bath seemed to suggest that there might be some degree of truth in White's portrayal. Speaking of the CIA, Bath said, "There's all sorts of degrees of civilian participation." He seemed to be referring to the voluntary cooperation sometimes offered to the agency by American businessmen with sensitive foreign contacts. Indeed, the CIA ran a station in Houston to facilitate informal interviews with Americans who worked in the international oil industry. If Bath did have agency connections, it is possible that all he did was report occasionally on what he picked up while consorting with the Bin Ladens, Bin Mahfouz, and other Saudis.[4]

White failed in his lawsuits against Bath and suffered heavy financial losses. He had an honorable military career before his troubles with Bath, but his credibility is difficult to judge. There is no evidence apart from his statements that Bath ran contract operations for the CIA. Nonetheless, for reasons that are not altogether clear, Bath did travel frequently to Caribbean tax havens during this period, according to Sandra's divorce attorney, and he crossed borders carrying large amounts of cash, she said.[5] Bath certainly had the means to support discreet international air operations if he wished, if not for the United States, then perhaps for his Saudi business clients. Salem frequently used his larger private aircraft as makeshift cargo transporters during this period, and it is conceivable, for example, that Salem or Bath might have used one of these planes, or one of the other large jets owned by some of Salem's Saudi associates, to move weapons from South America or South Africa to aid Osama in Pakistan. This is merely conjecture, however; none of the individuals interviewed about Salem's involvement in private arms transactions on Osama's behalf understood how the weapons were to be shipped.

Salem flitted lightly and evasively through these spheres of intrigue, but his style was more Austin Powers than James Bond. Apart from the court filings and statements by White, there are additional fragments of evidence about Salem's possible connections to conservative American political circles that were active in covert anti-communist operations during the 1980s. For example, according to flight logs, Larry McDonald, the Georgia congressman and president of the John Birch Society, flew on one of Salem's private jets in Saudi Arabia just months before McDonald died aboard Korean Air Lines Flight 007, which was shot down on September 1, 1983, after it strayed into Soviet airspace. Jim Bath's connections to the Bush family and other leading figures in the Reagan-era Republican Party in Texas have continued to raise questions about the extent of Salem's relations with these politicians. White, for example, has alleged that Bath used Bin Laden money when investing in Bush's Arbusto drilling fund, a charge that Bath and Bush have adamantly denied. At a minimum—through Jim Bath, Khalid Bin Mahfouz, and the Saudi government—Salem could justifiably regard himself as an ex officio member of the Houston oil and political establishment; he was draped in both its finery and its perpetual culture of mysterious deal making. Vinson and Elkins, one of the city's most prestigious law firms, represented Salem. He owned a private airport in the city. He dined at River Oaks mansions and played with visiting Saudi royalty.[6]

In time, however, Bath's accumulating personal and financial troubles seemed to alienate him from Salem. There were limits to how much craziness even Salem was prepared to tolerate. In 1986 Bath fell into a financial dispute with White involving allegations that he had improperly used a certificate of deposit belonging to Skyway Aircraft as collateral at a Houston bank for a $550,000 personal loan. Later that year, according to White's court filings, the Houston Police Department contacted White and told him they were investigating Bath in an international drug case; no charges were ever brought against him, however. According to Gail Freeman, the Bin Laden family friend and occasional business partner, Salem's beloved half-sister Randa also became estranged from the Baths during this period. She felt the Baths had treated her rudely, according to Freeman, and Randa then seemed to influence Salem's attitude toward his longtime Houston partner.[7]

An era was ending, and Bath's troubles reflected its eclipse. In 1986 oil prices fell to a record low of nine dollars per barrel. The economies of Saudi Arabia and Texas shuddered simultaneously. The real estate boom in Houston gradually imploded. That autumn, as Osama was organizing his first militia training camp on the Afghan frontier, the Iran-Contra scandal broke into the open, and the subsequent investigations dragged some of the uncomfortable history of off-the-books dealings between Reagan and King Fahd into the headlines. The adhesives that had held Salem's multiple worlds together for a decade—spouting oil money, a confident and often secretive alliance between Washington and Riyadh, and an ethos of cultural mobility and play—began to come apart.

OSAMA'S SMALL BAND of fighters suffered through a bitter winter in the high mountains around Jaji. The war usually went into hiatus during the snowy season. When the thaw arrived, so did Soviet soldiers. Osama's rumbling bulldozers had created a provocation in an important battle zone that the Soviets were not about to ignore. Osama's friend and brother-in-law Jamal Khalifa had visited the Lion's Den and found it to be a death trap. That was the point, some of Osama's colleagues told him: "We have plenty of *shaheeds*," or "martyrs,"whose sacrifices would please God. Khalifa said he argued with Osama that this waste of life violated Islamic precepts and that "God will ask you about it in the hereafter." Osama ignored his warning.[8]

The fighting began in April of 1987. Osama's volunteers clashed for a week with Soviet forces; this initial engagement was followed by a longer battle the next month. Bin Laden's positions came under sustained aerial bombardment; the Soviets may have used incendiary weapons similar to napalm. Spetsnaz troops raided Bin Laden's fortified encampments; the Arab volunteers, although lightly trained and little experienced, fought back fiercely in close engagements. Precisely what happened during these battles would become obscured over the years by retrospective accounts from self-mythologizing jihadis; their versions are sometimes contradictory. The earliest known published description, in Azzam's *Al-Jihad* magazine, does not emphasize Osama's role in the battles, but concentrates instead on the heroics of one of his Egyptian military aides; Osama was not even mentioned. He soon painted himself into the picture, however, by giving effusive interviews about his experiences to sympathetic Arab journalists. There is no doubt about the basic facts. The Jaji battles of 1987 were intense, with significant casualties on both sides, but they did nothing to alter the course of the larger war. Osama was present, and he performed honorably under heavy pressure. The battles seem to have left him with two main reactions: they endowed his belief that he had been called to war in God's name with fresh and deep emotion, and they struck him as an outstanding marketing opportunity.[9]

"It was obvious in the way that he was telling stories, that he was trying to create a drive to bring in more, to use the media for attracting more

Arabs, recruiting more Arabs to come to Afghanistan," recalled Jamal Khashoggi, a Saudi journalist who was one of the first to interview Osama after the Jaji campaign. "I liked his enthusiasm." Osama's speaking style in this period was "like a university professor . . . like if he is at the head of the table of the political committee of this party or that party." Yet his memories of the peril he felt at Jaji were florid, infused with a sense of fatalism and surrender to God's will.[10]

"We sometimes spent the whole day in the trenches or in the caves until our ears could no longer bear the sound of the explosions around us," Osama told Khashoggi:

> War planes continually shrieked by us and their crazy song of death echoed endlessly. We spent the days praying to God Almighty. Despite the massive Russian onslaughts, one of us had to come out from our shelter regularly to see the enemy's movements . . . Each time, we were able, by the grace of God, to inflict a crushing defeat on the Russians . . . It was God alone who protected us from the Russians . . . Reliance upon God is the main source of our strength and these trenches and tunnels are merely the military facilities God asked us to make. We depend completely on God in all matters.[11]

Around this time, Osama permitted an Egyptian filmmaker, Essam Deraz, to follow him and document the movement he was building. Deraz helped to crystallize the themes that would later shape Osama's legend— a rich man who lived like the poor, a socially advantaged man who was prepared to sacrifice everything for his religion, a fighter who would not waver in the face of death. "I saw him with my own eyes on the battle-field," Deraz said later. "He was in the middle of the fighting. Being a rich man, no matter what he was like, people of course looked at him as a financier, just a man with money. After the battle of Jaji, he was looked upon as a military man who deserved to be the leader."[12]

This, at least, was the view that filmmaker and the other early Bin

Laden publicists promoted; combined with Osama's quiet charisma, and his ability—common in the Saudi court circles from which he had emerged—to avoid giving offense even to his adversaries, it would prove to be enough.

He was emerging now from the shadow of his mentor, Abdullah Azzam. They quarreled over Osama's plans to group Arabs together in their own separate military encampments; Azzam believed firmly that they should insert themselves into mixed militias, alongside the Afghans, where they could share the war's burdens and proselytize to Afghan fighters whose own religious scholars had been killed off by the communists. "Bin Laden sought to pamper Arab fighters," Azzam's wife later complained. "Even their food was different from that of the Afghan *mujaheddin*. Bin Laden used to bring them special foodstuff in containers from Saudi Arabia."[13]

These tensions complicated Osama's position, but he was careful; he and Azzam remained cordial. By late 1987, their global fundraising and recruitment network included offices in Brooklyn and Tucson in the United States, as well as in Egypt, Saudi Arabia, and elsewhere. As this worldwide retail network spread, it was not in Osama's interest to precipitate a debilitating split.

Osama's own access to money remained unrivaled. His contributors included Salem's friend Khalid Bin Mahfouz. Sometime before May 1988, Bin Mahfouz "was approached for a contribution to the Afghan resistance by Salem Bin Laden," according to a statement by his attorneys. "Consistent with many other prominent Saudi Arabians, and in accordance with U.S. government foreign policy at that time, Sheikh Khalid Bin Mahfouz recalls making a donation of approximately $270,000. This donation was to assist the U.S.-sponsored resistance to the Soviet occupation of Afghanistan and was never intended nor, to the best of Sheikh Khalid Bin Mahfouz's knowledge, [was it] ever used to fund any extension of that resistance movement in other countries." Bin Mahfouz did not donate the money "with the intention" that it be used to purchase

ABOVE: Mohamed Bin Laden at a desert construction camp in the mid-1960s.

LEFT: Bin Laden's offices and work sites were manned by engineers and laborers from dozens of different countries.

RIGHT: The Bin Laden ancestral fort in Yemen.

Mohamed Bin Laden's home in East Jerusalem, purchased during the 1960s and later taken over by Israeli owners after the 1967 war.

Members of the Bin Laden family on vacation in Sweden in 1971. Osama was not on the trip and is not pictured, according to several sources close to the family.

Salem Bin Laden, Mohamed's oldest son, at an English prep school with his childhood friend Mehmet Birgen, who was known as Baby Elephant.

ABOVE: Saleh Bin Laden and his then-girlfriend, Shirley Cottam, at their Quaker boarding school in Lebanon during the 1970s.

LEFT: Salem and his first child, a daughter, Sara, in 1975.

Saleh Bin Laden and some of his half-sisters on vacation at a go-cart track in England during the 1970s.

RIGHT: Salem and Baby Elephant aboard Salem's yacht.

snowmass

Salem skiing at Snowmass during the mid-1980s.

BELOW: Osama Bin Laden in an undated photo from Afghanistan, before the stress of exile turned his beard gray.

FROM LEFT: Sara Bin Laden, Salem's daughter; Salem's second wife, Caroline Carey; his son, Salman; Salem; the sister of Mehmet Birgen; Mehmet; Mehmet's bride, Margarita.

BELOW: The honeymoon party; on the far right is the family's longtime pilot, Gerald Auerbach.

ABOVE, FROM LEFT:
Yahya Bin Laden, Salem,
Bakr Bin Laden, and an
unidentified brother, in
the late 1980s.

Ayman Zawahiri,
Osama's son Mohamed,
and Osama Bin Laden
appeared together in
Afghanistan at
Mohamed's wedding
early in 2001.

Salem Khalid Bin Laden, a member of the family's third generation, at a horse competition in Egypt in 2005.

BELOW: Yeslam Bin Laden, who moved to Geneva and became a Swiss citizen, opened a boutique and launched a line of perfumes and designer goods.

arms, his attorneys said. Osama's fundraising in Saudi Arabia "emphasized the need for humanitarian support (that is, food, shelter, medical supplies) for the Afghan resistance and the Afghan populations under their control that were subject to Soviet attacks . . . The financial needs of the Afghan resistance were, in fact, greater for these purposes than for weapons, which were being freely supplied by the U.S. Government. For the avoidance of any doubt, Sheikh Khalid Bin Mahfouz has never made any donation to Al Qaeda or any organization or person that he knew to be acting on behalf of Al Qaeda or any other terrorist organization."[14]

Osama spread his money and his favor around, some to Azzam, some to the rival Egyptian faction in Peshawar. By this signature method of accommodative Bedouin leadership, he gradually bound a loose coalition of multinational Arab volunteers to his undeclared leadership. As Azzam's son-in-law put it: "I think Osama started to believe in himself."[15]

22. THE PROPOSAL

S ALEM, TOO, dreamed of an idyll. His vision did not revolve around war or martyrdom, however; it involved the women in his life. By 1985, as he approached forty, Salem had approximately five regular girlfriends—one American, one German, one French, one Danish, and one English. He used his money and pilots to weave them in and out of his itineraries. They swirled around Salem and one another like airplanes in an intricate air traffic control pattern; they brushed against one another now and then, but rarely collided. Occasionally he installed girlfriends on two different floors of the same hotel, each unaware of the other's presence. One or two believed they were his only love; the others knew better.

Salem developed a bold plan to resolve this state of affairs. It began as a friendly bet between Salem and King Fahd, Bengt Johansson recalled. Salem told Fahd that he could persuade four young European and American women—"normal family girls"—to marry him simultaneously, as permitted by Islamic law. Fahd said he was crazy, that he could never pull it off. Perhaps the king believed this; perhaps he also understood, as Johansson put it, that if you told Salem he could not do something, "then he was for sure doing it."[1]

Lynn Peghiny, the American pianist from Orlando, had returned to Florida from her adventure with Salem in Pakistan when he called to invite her to London. She flew over, but nobody came to meet her at the airport, so after some confusion, she took a taxi to the Carlton Tower

Hotel in Belgravia. She went shopping, and when she returned, she found a handwritten note addressed to "Lin." It read: "I came by to see you. I feel a little guilty, and I even went looking in the shops for you. I'll call you sometime." It was signed "S."[2]

He did call and arranged to pick her up, but when she arrived at his brick-walled estate at Offley Chase, she found two other young women already there. Lynn knew that Salem dated others, and she had never been particularly put out about it. Still, she was not sure what to make of this. The two other women were both named Caroline; one was French ("Caro*leen*"), the other English ("Caro*line*").

Caroline of France had dark eyes and thickly curled black hair that wrapped around her cheeks. She lived, as it turned out, not far from Cannes, in a house that Salem had purchased for her and her mother. She had been dating Salem for more than a year.

Caroline of England was Caroline Carey, then about twenty-six years old. She had a thin, angular face with high cheekbones, chestnut hair, and a somewhat regal affect. She had grown up in Kensington, London, with her half-brother, Ambrose, and their mother, Anne Carey. Her family lineage touched the English aristocracy, if lightly. Caroline's father, Simon Henry Carey, had not married her mother. Ambrose had also been born out of wedlock, to Anne and David Queensberry, the Marquis of Queensberry. Salem had met Caroline in Hyde Park during the early 1960s, when she was just a toddler. He came to London on school breaks and spotted the Carey family nanny in the park; he thought the nanny was cute and tried to ingratiate himself by playing with the children. Soon he was a regular guest for tea at the Carey residence. As the years passed, he fell out of touch, but he resurfaced during the mid-1980s; when he and Caroline were reacquainted, they began to see each other. Like Salem's other girlfriends, she was his junior by about fifteen years.[3]

Lynn greeted the two Carolines at Offley Chase. She deduced that Salem had convened some sort of girlfriend summit, but apparently they did not yet have a quorum. Anna from Germany had yet to arrive, and Salem asked a pilot friend to take one of his jets, fly over, and bring her back. Lynn decided to go along, to pass the time—"It was like taking a taxi somewhere."[4]

Anna, it turned out, was a very thin, blond woman, even younger than the others, whom Salem had met in a bar at an Austrian ski resort. She had a salaried job near Cologne but traveled often with Salem; he had taken her once to Medina, a city normally off limits to non-Muslims. She was far from imposing in appearance, but when he was with his male friends, Salem sometimes referred to her as his "German tank."

When Anna and Lynn arrived back, Salem settled on a couch in his living room with all four women. He summoned his most earnest demeanor. He explained that since boyhood, he had been raised in a culture where it was common for men to marry several Arabian wives and then live all together on a family compound.

"But that is not my dream," Salem said, as Lynn recalled it. "My dream is to have four Westernized women—that has always been my dream and my fantasy. So I picked you four. You would just make my dream come true."[5]

He outlined the plan he had refined over several months. It was not a coincidence that each girl he had selected was from a different country. Indeed, his vision was to build in Jeddah a new Bin Laden family estate that would resemble the United Nations.

The compound would have four houses. Over one would fly an American flag, over a second a German flag, over a third a French tricolor, and over the fourth a British Union Jack. Each wife would have a car parked outside, a model from her home country—a Mercedes for Anna, a Rolls-Royce for Caroline of England, and so on. They would each have a home in their native countries, too—Salem already owned luxury properties in America, England, and France.

As Salem spoke, Lynn smiled to herself and thought, "I get gypped—I don't want a Corvette or a Cadillac."

Salem kept talking, trying to sell them. He knew they might feel trapped by the prospect of life in Saudi Arabia, so he had come up with an escape clause. He said that if there were children from any of the four marriages, those children would have to remain in the kingdom and be raised there in Saudi tradition. However, if no children were involved, then if any of the women were unhappy after one year, he would give them $100,000 and they could return home. He hoped, however, that they would all be happy together for a long time.

"I would just take turns going from home to home and we would all be friends," he said, as Lynn remembered it.

Lynn found herself thinking, "Hmmm . . . That doesn't sound too bad." But then she would scold herself silently, worrying that if she left after a year no American man would ever marry her, and also, in any event, perhaps "I'd be selling my soul." But then, on the other hand: "What the heck?" She was young and open-minded, and she cared for Salem, who had been very good to her.[6]

The conversation went on for some time. They maintained a civil tone. Caroline of France seemed open to the idea, Lynn thought. Caroline of England—Salem called her "Carrie"—was cool but enigmatic. Anna, however, was clearly unhappy. She rolled her eyes. She seemed the most emotional about the revelation that Salem wanted more than just her. The more upset she became, the more Lynn began to think this wasn't going to work after all. Finally, Anna walked out.

"I'm in trouble," Salem reported when he called a friend in America after the meeting. "They all got mad."[7]

That was an exaggeration. Lynn stayed that night and played Chopin. The French Caroline returned home, but Carrie stayed on, and a few days later, Lynn flew with her and Salem to Cairo on a holiday. They went from there to Saudi Arabia, and then to a Greek island, where they met Salem's two children from his earlier marriage and went sailing on a yacht. Gradually, on this trip, Lynn began to conclude that Salem "favored Carrie . . . They were more connected."

Lynn flew home; some months later, Salem asked her to Jeddah. They spent some time together, and then Salem said what they were both were thinking: "I don't know if this is going to work."

"That's fine," Lynn said. "I've had a wonderful year."

"We'll always be friends," Salem told her. "I'll always keep in touch. I'll always make sure—if you ever need anything."[8]

Lynn admired his generosity but did not want to take advantage of him. People who worked for Salem encouraged her to ask him for a house in Florida—after all, Caroline of France had gotten a house—but she declined.

They went their separate ways. Caroline Carey, Lynn could see, would be the last girlfriend standing.

SOME OF SALEM'S brothers and sisters searched, as he had, for forms of marriage that would synthesize modernity and tradition, but they hewed closer to convention. The beliefs and practices of Mohamed Bin Laden's daughters contrasted almost as greatly as those of his sons; they were just much better hidden from view. In Jeddah, Sheikha and Rafah covered themselves in black abayas, threw themselves into Islamic study, and abjured birthday parties for their children, in the belief that such parties were forbidden by the tenets of their faith—birthdays were a Christian rite, and thus *haram*, or "forbidden." Another group of daughters—Huda, Randa, and Mona—still jetted frequently around Europe to shop or across the Atlantic for spring skiing in Aspen with Salem. If they wanted to consider dating, they had to operate clandestinely and be willing to shoulder considerable risk; otherwise, they could wait for Salem to arrange or bless a traditional marriage to a respectable Arab professional. Like Mohamed's sons, as they reached their thirties, some of these women became more outwardly religious and visited Europe less frequently.[9]

A few followed Randa in pursuit of independent careers. Salem enrolled his half-sisters Raedah and Saleha in American schools specializing in interior design; after they completed their training, he said, they could work on palace projects for the Saudi royal family. None of these women, even the most ambitious, could free herself as easily from Saudi patriarchy as could her brothers, however.

Several of Mohamed's daughters suffered divorces under inflexible Saudi laws that deprived them of the right to live with their children. Najiah, a mother of four, lost custody of her children in Jeddah when her husband divorced her. Carmen Bin Laden once asked Najiah why she didn't fight back; Najiah looked at her as though she were the "village idiot," Carmen recalled. Najiah eventually escaped to Los Angeles, where she took flying lessons, became an accomplished pilot and was noted by some of her American friends for the very high speeds at which she routinely drove on streets and highways.[10]

Randa remained the most untraditional of Mohamed's daughters—now both a licensed medical doctor and a pilot, as comfortable in the Austrian ski resort of Zell am See as in Cairo or Jeddah. Her relatively daring and visible life enjoyed Salem's full protection and oversight, however, and so it carried little risk of censure from the family's conservative wing.

She was approaching thirty. Although it would mean an end to their special relationship, Salem decided it was time for Randa to marry, and he gave his blessing to a suitable Egyptian groom who would later work as a manager for the Bin Laden companies in Jeddah. Salem rented the ballroom of a luxury hotel in Cairo, paid for Randa's American friends to fly to Egypt first-class, and staged a gala celebration. He even flew out the American doctors who had performed his hemorrhoid operation. Before the event, a cluster of brothers and sisters donned blue jeans and joined Randa's American friends on a tour of their half-brother Khalid's Thoroughbred horse farms in the Egyptian countryside.

When the wedding day arrived, laced white tablecloths draped the tables, and the couple sat in fluted, high-backed white chairs. Several of

Randa's half-sisters served as bridesmaids. Some were veiled, others not; they wore peach chiffon dresses and gold headbands. The men dressed in black tuxedos. Osama was not among them. In a bittersweet moment, Salem gave the bride away. A few hours later, on stage, he sang and carried on, exuberant as ever.[11]

AMONG SALEM's half-sisters, it was Saleha, the apprentice interior designer, who most severely tested the family's boundaries of decorum.

Paul Piccirillo was an Italian interior designer and artist, about fifty years of age. He met the Bin Ladens through Salem's New York partner Robert Freeman. Around the time that Saleha, who was about twenty years his junior, completed her studies at a design school in Houston, the Bin Ladens were busy on a number of demanding palace projects in Saudi Arabia; Piccirillo worked on some of these, as well as on the Jeddah home of Salem's former wife, Sheikha. Several involved work on King Fahd's own residences and required extensive travel to inspect and review rare silks for bedding and window treatments at Scalamandre in New York; custom-made furniture in Valencia, Spain; and chandeliers handcrafted in Venice, Italy. Salem did not permit his sisters, even those who were professional designers, to travel abroad without either a female chaperone or one of a several older and trusted male business partners. One night in Paris, however, while on chaperone duty with Saleha, Bob Freeman went to bed early. He failed to notice that Paul and Saleha were paying particularly close attention to each other. While he slept, they "talked all night long and fell in love," as Bob's wife, Gail Freeman, recalled it.

In the ensuing months, Paul and Saleha continued to see each other. Eventually Salem found out; naturally, he blamed Freeman. "We've got to do something about this," he warned. "This is just a tragedy." There were rumors, Gail Freeman recalled, that some of "the brothers were going to go kill" Saleha for dishonoring the family by falling for an older European.[12]

Salem agonized and fumed, and eventually he gave in. He quietly arranged for the couple to marry; they moved to a small town on the Mediterranean coastline. It would take years before Paul was fully welcomed by the family, according to the Freemans, who felt that Paul was conspicuously shunned at Randa's wedding. The couple held together, however, and gradually Bakr and other influential brothers accepted them.

WEALTH, MOBILITY, and Salem's secularism carried the Bin Ladens to far cultural shores, but they remained, at heart, a conservative and Arabian clan. Among other things, their honor was a business imperative; their wealth depended upon the patronage of the Saudi royal family, and so they lacked the political discretion to live entirely as they pleased, as some of the much larger Al-Saud family seemed to think they could do. Indeed, behavior that many Bin Ladens might find racy or challenging, such as Saleha's marriage to Paul, could look timid or downright square alongside the unrestrained European cavorting of some Al-Saud princes—debauchery that Salem and his friends sometimes facilitated, in Salem's role as a royal concierge.

Salem prided himself on never sleeping with prostitutes. This required some fortitude because he arranged periodically for the supply of professional women to entertain Saudi guests at parties he hosted or arranged in England and elsewhere, according to several European friends and employees who were involved. The women were so numerous that they sometimes arrived together on a bus. As cohosts, those in Salem's entourage were charged with promoting cheerful demeanors among the women ("I paid you to smile!"). But apart from their substantial compensation, the girls had little reason to be pleased. The guests could be crude, drunken, and unattractive. Thomas Dietrich recalled one event for visiting Saudis at Offley Chase when he stood eavesdropping on some young German prostitutes who did not know he could understand them as they spoke with one another. "They were bitching like hell" about the guests, he recalled. "'Look at this guy—I hope he doesn't pick me.' I mean, they were just saying what you would imagine they would say."[13]

For many Saudis, Western vice confirmed the precepts of Arabian misogyny, and for many Americans and Europeans, Arabian vices confirmed the precepts of Western racism. "The awe that America commanded, with its skyscrapers, freeways, magnificent telephone system and raw riches, was diminishing as Saudi Arabia casually acquired all of these things with great rapidity," wrote Peter Theroux, an American who lived in Riyadh during this period. "The Saudis saw themselves as our absolute superiors. The secular chaos of America's elections, boisterous press and above all the public sex culture, seemed, except in small doses, to disgust them."[14] It was, in this context, easier and certainly more acceptable for wealthy Saudis to buy sex while visiting the West than it was for them to enter into the mixed marriages and bicultural family life that might produce, over time, integration or even assimilation—as occurred with some frequency, for example, among Pakistani, Iranian, Egyptian, and Palestinian émigrés to the West. The obsession with bloodlines among many Saudis, particularly those from the dominant Nejd region, along with their wealth and deep conservatism, kept them apart. Salem's fantasy of a United Nations (or at least a Security Council) of intercultural marriages was exceptional, and even it presumed the primacy of inflexible and patriarchal Saudi family law.

Whether the subject was sex or shoes, it was almost impossible for a Saudi prince or merchant to travel in the West without being aware, from hour to hour, of the centrality of money in his interactions with Americans and Europeans. Salem managed this by surrounding himself with genuine Western friends who had earned his trust over time; he

provided them with enough money and all-expenses-paid vacations to secure their loyalty, but not so much cash that they would likely consider
leaving his side. Some of those who attached themselves to Salem, such
as the Swedish mechanic Bengt Johansson or the American pilot Gerald
Auerbach, had no great appetite for wealth or what it could purchase, and
they stayed with Salem the longest. Others in the entourage, such as Jim
Bath, seemed much more passionate about making money, and they faded
from the inner circle more quickly. It seemed that just about every
American who won a retainer from Salem soon pitched him on a side
business deal. The ideas came at him like random, subliminal images
flashing on the movie screen of a demented experimental psychiatrist—
a strip mall in San Antonio, a mining deal promoted by the relative of a
powerful senator from Louisiana, a cowboy movie that would be shot in
the Philippines. If a particular proposal appealed to Salem's whimsy, he
might say yes, even if it did not fit in his family's business lines. Salem
told his flight instructor, Don Sowell, for example, that he shared ownership of a luxury apartment in London with the boxer Muhammad Ali.
If the idea bored Salem (as the cowboy movie's story line did), he would
dismiss it with a wave of his hand.[15]

"These people are not great," Johansson recalled telling Salem, speaking about the deal promoters who swirled around him.

"I know, Bengt," Salem answered. "I am stealing more from them than
they are stealing from me."[16]

Once, cruising at forty-one thousand feet in a LearJet above North
Africa, Salem worried aloud about whether his girlfriends cared for him
only because he had money, recalled his pilot Jack Hinson. Salem paused,
and then discarded the conundrum: "As long as I'm happy."[17]

HE COULD NOT BEAR to be alone as he reached middle age. He turned
forty in 1985 or 1986—he did not know either the year or the date of his
birth, and he often used Valentine's Day as a sentimental proxy. His need

for constant companionship grew increasingly awkward. When he used the bathroom, for example, he kept the door open and demanded that his friends sit nearby and talk to him as he sat. If no members of his entourage were around, he called down to the front desk and offered to pay for a maid or maintenance man to come to his room, to sit outside the bathroom and keep him company while he did his business.[18]

His sleeping habits were no less unusual. When he shared a house with his friend Mohamed Ashmawi in Riyadh, he could not bear to sleep alone, and so he would wander in and climb into bed with Mohamed—there was no hint of sexual purpose, just a need for company. When Mohamed had a girlfriend living with him, he would sneak into the room in the night and announce, "I'm going to sleep with you," Ashmawi recalled.

"I said, 'You should be shy—I have my girlfriend.' He said, 'Let her sleep next to you and I'll sleep next to you on the other side—you be in the middle.'"

"No, Salem."

"Let's try it. It might work."

"Go sleep in your room."[19]

He would finally leave, Ashmawi said, but then Salem slept fitfully and with his eyes open. He spent long days and evenings lying in bed, but he often only slept in fifteen- or thirty-minute intervals. He used all his bedrooms as a combination of office, family room, and playhouse. He routinely held meetings with foreign executives from companies such as Firestone while lying in bed; in the middle of a negotiation, he might tuck his head down and nod off, then just as suddenly jerk back awake.

These restless habits took a visible toll on his health. His body grew soft, his legs had atrophied from lack of exercise, and his eyes sagged and darkened so much that he looked at times like a raccoon. He hardly ever walked—cars drove him from home to airport terminal, and then across the tarmac to his plane, and then from his plane to the next terminal, and so on, until he reached his next bed. Bengt worried that Salem's legs would soon fail him altogether, and he tried to implement a regimen of no more car rides between airport terminals and airplanes—if they at least walked across every tarmac, he said, perhaps Salem would gain back some leg muscle strength.

Sleeplessness exacerbated Salem's temper, which could be volcanic. His outbursts usually passed quickly, and left him feeling guilty and sheepish, but particularly as his fatigue accumulated, he could succumb to brief rages. He might wordlessly walk back to the cabin of one of his airplanes and strike one of his brothers, then return and sit down without explanation. He might shout or berate a pilot or even a friend in his entourage, although with them he was very rarely physical. On two or three occasions, according to his friends, he allowed himself to drink beyond his limit and lost all control. Over the course of one particularly memorable and frightening night in Dubai during the late 1980s, Salem smashed up a Sheraton Hotel bandstand, broke a drum over a band member's head, threatened his friends with violence, and created such ugly scenes in the hotel lobby that his friend from boarding school, Mehmet "Baby Elephant" Birgen, finally called a doctor to sedate him. In the morning, Salem said he couldn't remember a thing.[20]

He speculated freely about his own death. In Cannes, around the time that he was developing his proposal to marry his four girlfriends, he sat with his Texas attorney Wayne Fagan and Baby Elephant. Salem mused about how he would react if he discovered that he had cancer or some other serious illness.

"You know what I'd do?" he asked, as Fagan recalled it. "I'd get in my MU-2, and I'd go out and I would find the highest cloud in the sky. And I would climb to the top of that cloud. And I would shut the engines off. I wouldn't have chemotherapy."

The room was silent. Salem looked over at Baby Elephant.

"You're my closest friend, so I'd take you with me—I'm not going alone!"[21]

23. KITTY HAWK FIELD OF DREAMS

IN THE YEARS following his service in Miami as Bakr's guardian, Baby Elephant charmed his way through debutante society in Dallas and Moët-fueled nightlife in Geneva. He moved into the jewelry trade, met the actor Sean Connery, and opened a London store in partnership with him; they called it Bond Street Jewelry. Mehmet chased women even more energetically than Salem, and because of his broad shoulders and his brooding dark eyes, he often had success. He and Salem made a pact that if one ever settled down and married, the other would do so as well, but the agreement never seemed likely to come into force. At one stage, Mehmet considered retiring to his native Turkey to write a book about the art of loving women. Instead, following several heartbreaks and financial reversals, he moved to Saudi Arabia. His work was often an extension of Salem's concierge services. It did have an appealing variety; Mehmet could regale his friends with surreal stories about the whims and peccadilloes of the wealthy Gulf businessmen he looked after during their travels in Europe and America.

In late June 1987, he was in Miami having dinner with the family of his Venezuelan girlfriend, Margarita, when Salem telephoned. As Mehmet later described the conversation for his friends, it went like this:

"This Saturday, I'm marrying Carrie," Salem announced.

"Oh, *mabruk*. Finally, you're marrying—she cornered your ass."

"Yeah, Margarita cornered your ass, too."

"No, nobody cornered my ass."

"I'm telling you, she cornered your ass—because you're going to marry her."

"Come on, Salem."

"No, no, Baby Elephant—you promised me. You're going to do exactly what I tell you. If you don't want to marry Margarita, I have two Egyptian girls here, come and have a look at them. They're not bad. Marry one of them."

Mehmet put the phone down. "Margarita, this Saturday, we're getting married," he said.

They flew the next day to London; Salem sent a car to retrieve them from the airport. When Mehmet hurriedly invited his only sister to the wedding, she asked, "If Salem says you're going to kill yourself, you're going to kill yourself?"[1]

Bin Laden family and friends converged on London from several continents. Salem put his guests up in suites at the Grosvenor House hotel on Park Lane and arranged for limousines to shuttle them to and from Offley Chase. He had chosen July 4, 1987, and as ever, he was fortunate—the skies were clear and the sun shined magnificently through the afternoon. The atmosphere at the estate blended the elegance of a 1930s country house with Ringling Brothers festivity. A line of antique automobiles rolled into the driveway, ferrying the wedding party. In a field beyond the mansion billowed a hot air balloon with green, red, yellow, and purple stripes, its basket open to offer rides to the 250 guests. A helicopter parked on the grass nearby, also available for rides. Clowns, snake handlers, and acrobats wandered among grand white tents pitched on the lawns.[2]

Salem donned a Saudi *thobe* for a brief traditional ceremony, but for much of the afternoon, he and Baby Elephant wore matching black business suits, white shirts, and plain maroon ties. Carrie wore a long-sleeved white bridal gown and a tiara fashioned from white daisies. At dinner, served beneath a white tent, Salem and Carrie sat with Baby Elephant, Margarita, and Salem's two children, Sara and Salman.

Salem's former wife, Sheikha, attended with her second husband, an Austrian diplomat she had met in Jeddah, a match that signaled her modern, independent-minded outlook. Randa, too, arrived with her new husband. All in all, about twenty of Salem's sisters and brothers came, a self-selecting group who were comfortable enough to circulate in England wearing business suits and dresses, in a setting without gender segregation and teeming with Europeans and Americans. The turnout at such an important event—the wedding of the family's leader to an Englishwoman—measured the size of the Bin Ladens' Western-leaning caucus at about half of Mohamed's fifty-four children.

Salem offered a sentimental speech about his friendship with Baby Elephant, and how they had pledged to take this passage into matrimony together. That night, as the music died down, the two betrothed couples climbed into cars and rode a few minutes to the Luton Airport, where they boarded one of Salem's jets and flew to Bristol for a double-dating honeymoon night in a nearby hotel, and then on to the South of France and Germany.

His friends understood, of course, that Salem would never grow up entirely, but after so many years of flying hard on the edge, he seemed at last to be trying to settle and restore himself a little. Among other things, he desired more children. Three months after the wedding, Carrie was pregnant.

SALEM CAMPED in the Saudi desert with Fahd the following winter. The mid-1980s had been a difficult period for the Bin Laden construction business in Saudi Arabia because falling oil prices crimped payment schedules and new project launches. Renovation projects in Medina provided some ballast, but according to Bengt Johansson, the desert sojourn of early 1988 produced a particularly big breakthrough when the king committed to a number of lucrative projects, including a massive renovation in Mecca, to follow on the work in Medina. Another individual close to Salem recalled that he was buoyant about these contracts; he instructed this friend to set up new Swiss accounts to ensure that Salem and his family banked a more reliable share of the proceeds than he had managed to do in the past.[3]

At the same time, however, two individuals who worked closely with Salem recalled separately that he was haunted that same winter by a large international business transaction, involving bartered oil sales in the spot markets, which had gone very badly, causing Salem a substantial loss. One of these people recalled that the deal involved the acquisition by the Saudi government of commercial airliners from Boeing Corporation; the other believed that the deal may have concerned arms shipments to Afghanistan from China and Eastern Europe. In any event, by both of these accounts, Salem felt that he had been let down financially by his partners in the deal, and he was unusually angry and gloomy about what had happened.[4]

In mid-April, Salem vacationed in Greece with Carrie and his two children. A week later, he flew to America with his two half-brothers, Tareq and Shafiq. Salem had purchased a Hawker Siddeley jet, the same model his father had owned at the time of his death two decades earlier. Among other projects, Salem oversaw the remodeling of its interior by an American company. He hopped back and forth across the Atlantic in May.[5] Late that month, he called his former girlfriend, Lynn Peghiny, in Orlando; he had not spoken to her in about a year.

"I'm going to be in Orlando, and I'd love to see you and take you to dinner—and your family is invited," he told her, as Lynn recalled it.[6]

She called up several of her sisters, who all lived nearby, and they met Salem at a little Italian restaurant a few nights later. Lynn learned about his marriage and also that Carrie was pregnant, so far along now that she could no longer travel. Salem and his entourage were all headed for Texas to attend the wedding of Anthony Auerbach, Gerald's only son.

Salem brought his guitar to the Italian restaurant. He ran through his favorites and sang boisterously. He remained enamored of the most familiar American standards. "You Are My Sunshine" was one of his very favorites, and he belted it out that night.

He seemed, as Lynn Peghiny recalled it, "just so happy."[7]

ON SATURDAY, MAY 28, 1988, Salem joined about 250 guests at the Auerbach wedding, which was held at the Officers Club at Lackland Air Force Base, outside San Antonio. The Cone Sisters, three platinum blondes who sang big band standards, provided the entertainment, but of course, when they were on break, Salem and his pilot friend Don Kessler took over their instruments and performed. During the reception, Salem stood before the crowd and ran through a comedy routine that was by now familiar to regular guests at Bin Laden weddings. He announced that he had written a commemorative poem for the occasion. Then he pulled a roll of inscribed toilet paper out of his pocket, explaining that in the bathroom, "I do my best work."[8]

Late the next morning, Sunday, Salem called his friend Jack Hinson from his midmarket hotel along Interstate 410. He was trying to figure out how to spend the day.

"The Thunderbirds are flying," Hinson told him, as he recalled it, referring to the air force's precision-flying demonstration team.

"I've seen the Thunderbirds," Salem said.

Hinson said he was going over to the field where he kept some ultralights, eat a little breakfast, and maybe do some flying.

"What do they have for breakfast?" Salem asked

"They have ham and eggs, fresh ham and eggs, and fresh tomatoes," Hinson said. Teasing, he added, "You don't eat none of that ham."

Salem knew the place; he had flown there several times before. "We're going to come out," he said, according to Hinson. As for the breakfast, Salem joked, "You tell everybody with me it's beef . . . I know I'm going to hell anyway."[9]

The Kitty Hawk Field of Dreams lay about twenty miles northeast

of San Antonio, on the edge of Schertz, an undistinguished town of several thousand people that was being slowly consumed by San Antonio's
far suburbs. A tattooed former U.S. Marine named Earl Mayfield had
created the flying field about seven years earlier. He owned a small
restaurant near San Antonio, took up ultralight flying as a hobby, and decided that he needed some land to fly properly. He bought a plot of fifty-
seven acres off the Old Nacogdoches Road. He cleared the cedar trees
himself with a bulldozer and built a few light metal hangars. One of his
clients was AlamoArrow Ultralights, the local retailer whose salesman,
George Harrington, had accompanied Salem all the way to Peshawar,
Pakistan, in early 1985. AlamoArrow kept some rental aircraft at the field.
It was a relaxed, casual place. In the open grass, Mayfield had built a small
asphalt runway; it was about twenty feet wide. Nearby he had erected a
snack bar with picnic tables and barbecues. The field lay flanked by
scrubland—tall grasses and thorny mesquite trees bent by the wind. To
the south, beyond a line of brush and trees, power line towers shaped like
giant metallic scarecrows traversed a cleared right of way, running west
to east; these towers rose more than one hundred feet into the air.[10]

Salem arrived about two in the afternoon that Sunday with at least
four or five of his traveling party. Ian Munro, his patrician British business partner, was one of them. His half-brother Tareq was also along.
They ate a big breakfast. Hinson drove Salem to his house so he could
wash and use the bathroom. Salem wandered into Hinson's garage and
saw a Yamaha 1500cc motorcycle. He begged to ride back on the bike.
Hinson climbed on and motioned Salem to get on behind him.

"No, I want to be on the front," Salem said, as Hinson remembered it.

"You will kill me! . . . Do you think I'm crazy?"

"I used to own motorcycles—I had Harleys, I know how to ride a
motorcycle . . . I will not show off or do anything."[11]

He kept his word, at least until Hinson climbed off at Kitty Hawk,
after which Salem promptly roared around pulling wheelies out in the
field. Finally he set the motorcycle down, found a dune buggy with big

rubber tires, and raced around in that. All the while, one of the Alamo-Arrow fliers was buzzing overhead in a new single-seater model, called a Sprint, which had just a few hours of flying time on it.

The Sprint came in for a landing and Salem decided to take a turn. A light rain had cleared, and the day had turned bright and sunny, with good visibility. The wind was blowing at about twenty to twenty-five miles per hour, brisk but not fierce. Salem emptied his pockets of coins, keys, and cigarettes, and climbed in.

He was wearing blue jeans and a short-sleeve, blue-and-white striped shirt. He had a pair of sunglasses tied around his neck on a chain, but no helmet or visor. Salem's eyes tended to tear up badly in the wind; according to his friend Thomas Dietrich, he sometimes skied accidentally into trees because the tears would blur his eyesight. He used the sunglasses to protect his eyes, but they were not as effective as a visor. Somebody asked Salem if he wanted a helmet, but he said no; at that time, helmets were not required.[12]

He powered down the runway, tilted back, and climbed to about fifty feet. Then he leveled off and turned toward the power lines. The standard flight path at Kitty Hawk, particularly for new or inexperienced fliers, lay in the opposite direction—a westward turn, and eventually, a loop back around for a landing. It was not unusual for a veteran flier to turn southwest, however, and Salem had done this before, according to Hinson; the alternate path simply required a little more care because you had to climb quickly to an adequate height.

Salem's friends watched him from the snack bar and the picnic tables. One person had climbed onto the cantina roof, from where he tracked Salem's flight with a handheld video camera. The ultralight's engine whined steadily. There were no signs of mechanical distress—no waggling of the wings, no audible change of power, no yaw or struggle to hold altitude. Salem flew straight and level—directly into the power lines.[13]

There was no sound, no pop or crackle, no shower or spark of electricity. The entangled aircraft tilted forward, nose down, as if in slow motion, and then it plummeted to the ground.

Amid stunned shouts and gasps, somebody called 911. It was a few minutes before 3:00 P.M. Earl Mayfield jumped in a golf cart and raced toward the tree line. Hinson and others ran behind him.

When they found Salem, he was strapped into his seat, facing down toward the ground. His eyes were open. Blood trickled from his ears. The engine had struck his head from behind. Both his legs were visibly broken.

They pulled him free, cradling his head. They laid him on the ground and tried to perform CPR while they waited for the ambulance from the Schertz Area Facility for Emergency Services. It arrived in about fifteen minutes. Two paramedics administered oxygen and continued to perform CPR. They loaded Salem into the cabin and drove away, lights flashing and sirens wailing. One of the paramedics scribbled notes: "Unable to find a good airway . . . No change on monitor." The note taker checked boxes on the ambulance run report, indicating the subject's condition: "Convulsing . . . nonreactive . . . critical."[14]

The nearest trauma center was at the Brooke Army Medical Center at Fort Sam Houston, the command headquarters of the Fifth U.S. Army. It was less than fifteen minutes' drive away.

It was there, about an hour later, that American military doctors formally pronounced Salem Bin Laden dead.

PART THREE
THE GLOBAL FAMILY

June 1988 to September 2001

24. WRITER-DIRECTOR-PRODUCER

THE NEWS ARRIVED in Saudi Arabia in the nighttime. King Fahd called Bakr to offer his formal condolences. Some of Salem's friends and relatives had forecasted his death in an airplane crash, but as Mohamed Ashmawi put it, few of them imagined that he would die in a "Mickey Mouse plane." The Bin Ladens, a second person close to them observed, had a way of experiencing such events with particular acuteness, as if they were succumbing to a collective illness. They felt Salem's death as an overwhelming "family tragedy," recalled Abdullah, one of his youngest half-brothers. There was also a pervasive confusion about how such an accident could have happened. Was suicide a possibility? Had he suffered an incapacitating heart attack or stroke while airborne? Had someone drugged or killed him? Conspiracy theories were commonplace in Saudi Arabia, where free discourse was forbidden and history was a narrative punctuated by genuine hidden conspiracies. Even if one presumed an accidental cause, Salem's death marked the second time in two decades that the Bin Laden family had been decapitated by an aviation disaster with an American connection.[1]

After telephone calls between Texas, Jeddah, Riyadh, and the Saudi embassy in Washington, Khalid Bin Mahfouz dispatched his private 707 to San Antonio to retrieve his friend's body. The Bexar County Medical Examiner had taken possession of Salem's corpse after his death; the office was required to perform an autopsy in a case of this type. Tareq and other family members pleaded with their San Antonio friends to call in local favors to minimize the autopsy's visible effects. Once Salem's body was returned to Saudi Arabia, it would be washed, in Islamic tradition, in the presence of Bin Laden brothers and male friends. Gerald Auerbach and Jack Hinson contacted a mortician they knew in San Antonio; he agreed to pick up Salem from the medical examiner and prepare him cosmetically for his journey home.

Family members called Salem's friends and relatives in Europe to say that if they wished to attend the burial and mourning services, they could converge on Geneva, where the Bin Mahfouz plane would make a stopover. When the 707 lumbered into the airport's private aviation terminal above Lake Geneva, Yeslam was waiting, along with Shafiq, another half-brother who spent most of his time in Europe. Baby Elephant and several of Salem's other friends and relatives were there, too.[2]

Yeslam found himself gripped by paralyzing anxiety; he became so concerned about the prospect of flying with Salem's coffin that he was unable to walk up the jet's stairs. His siblings tried to comfort him, but he was stricken. When the plane finally rolled away, Yeslam remained behind.[3]

Ali, Salem's estranged former rival for family leadership, and once a favorite of their father, flew to Saudi Arabia on his own private jet to pay his respects. From Jeddah, a group of relatives and friends drove to Medina to await the arrival of Salem's body. A burial permit for Medina, where the Prophet Mohamed had also been laid to rest, required royal approval, which Fahd's office readily provided. The group waiting at Medina's VIP terminal called up to the air traffic control tower for word about the 707's arrival time, just as they had always done when Salem's private flights were due. They went outside to watch the landing. Salem often kept his friends waiting for hours, and when his jet would finally appear on the horizon, he often teased them with a touch-and-go—he descended until his wheels touched the runway, then pulled up, flew off, circled around, and landed on the second try. That night, his friends watched in astonishment as the Bin Mahfouz plane badly overshot the runway; the pilot had no choice but to pull up, fly around, and land again. The pilot later said it had been a genuine if rare error on his part; Salem's entourage agreed that their friend's spirit had awoken long enough to play one last practical joke on them.

They loaded the coffin into a General Motors Corporation ambulance. The full-bearded Mahrouz was among the brothers who climbed inside; he chanted a prayer for the dead. One of Salem's friends recalled being hoisted into the ambulance by the Bin Laden brothers, so that he could sit beside the coffin. "You haven't left him throughout his life," one of the brothers said. "You're not going to leave him now."[4]

They washed the body at Mohamed Bin Laden's former Medina home. In a gesture of respect, one of the brothers handed Khalid Bin Mahfouz the key to Salem's coffin, so that he could initiate the washing. Afterward they wrapped his body in a shroud of green cloth, the color of dress in Paradise. The only sounds were of grief and prayer.[5]

At the graveyard, in the darkness, mourners in flowing white robes and headdresses swelled and jostled. The outstretched arms of his brothers and friends carried Salem above shoulder height to a sandy ditch. As he was laid in, a man shouted and approached with the shrouded corpse of a very young girl; it was not clear who she was, or how she had died, but she had been chosen to lie in Salem's grave at his feet, to keep him company—her soul was pure and innocent, and would comfort and protect his in the passage to afterlife.[6]

Osama was among the brothers who attended Salem's funeral. It is not clear when he arrived. He continued to travel back and forth from Afghanistan, and it is possible that he was in the kingdom at the time of Salem's death; the Ramadan holiday, a time when the Bin Ladens often gathered together in Saudi Arabia, had ended only recently. If he was present at the burial, he would have joined Mahrouz in the rigorous prayers that believing Wahhabis offer the dead. He was certainly present through the mourning receptions that followed during the next three days. He felt closer to Salem than to any of his other brothers, according to Osama's mother, even though they lived by such different creeds. He had regarded Salem "like a father," she said later. "Salem's death saddened Osama a great deal."[7]

In later years, as he held forth loquaciously about America's alleged crimes against Islam, Osama never spoke about Salem's death on American soil, just as he never spoke about the airplane crash caused by an American pilot that had claimed his father's life. Did he consider the possibility of conspiracies? In Arabia, it would be far more exceptional if he did not. The available evidence about Osama's specific reaction to Salem's accident, however, is virtually nonexistent. His half-brother Ghalib, who visited Osama at least once near the Afghan border, did consider the possibility that a hidden plot might lie behind Salem's death. Later that summer, Ghalib flew to Texas to inspect the Kitty Hawk Field of Dreams. He obtained a copy of the Bexar County Medical Examiner's autopsy report, according to a family business partner. The report found that Salem had no heart disease at the time of his death and had no trace of drugs, alcohol, or other intoxicants in his bloodstream. By the partner's account, Ghalib was relieved at these discoveries, and seemed willing to accept the autopsy's formal conclusion, which read, "Manner of Death: Accident." Jamal Khashoggi, who spoke regularly with Osama during this period, and who shared his Muslim Brotherhood–influenced outlook at the time, said that while he was certain Salem's sudden death "was a big event in his life," Osama never discussed it. Nor, according to the publicly available record, did he discuss it with other friends or journalists.[8]

In Jeddah, as they had two decades earlier after their father's passing, the sons of Mohamed Bin Laden gathered at the family compound, between the evening *mahgrib* and *isha* prayers, for formal ceremonies of condolence. Thousands of mourners flocked to the home Mohamed had built for Salem's mother at Kilo 7 on the Mecca Road, near the headquarters of the family's main construction company.

This time, however, the receptions had a secondary purpose—many of those who had been close to Salem now shuffled forward to swear *bayah*, or fealty, to Bakr Bin Laden as the new head of the Bin Laden family. This ritual was a direct and self-conscious echo of the *bayah* ceremonies in Riyadh that followed the death of a Saudi king. (At the Al-Saud court, the ascending king sits in mourning and receives a line of visitors who demonstrate their loyalty and respect by kissing his shoulder, hand, or cheek.) That it would be Bakr, and not another brother, who received these gestures of obedience was a decision that had accumulated gradually within the Bin Laden family over a period of years. Salem had increasingly designated Bakr as chief of business operations, and Bakr's central role in the Mecca and Medina renovations put him in the lead of the family's two most lucrative and politically sensitive construction contracts. He was not the oldest living son after Salem, but he was among the most senior, and by virtue of his civil engineering degree, also among the most qualified. He was, in addition, Salem's full brother, the guardian of his estate and his legacy, the eldest surviving son of a senior and respected widow of Mohamed. All this made him the natural choice. There is no evidence that Bakr's anointment required any debate or deliberation within the family; it seems, rather, to have been taken more or less for granted.

Heavily pregnant, Salem's widow, Carrie, grieved in the company of hundreds of Saudi women at the separate but parallel female condolence receptions. She staggered through the days, and on June 15, less than three weeks after Salem's accident, she gave birth in Jeddah to a daughter, Sama.[9] More than five years earlier, Carrie had converted to Islam, fulfilling a promise she made to Salem while a passenger in his glider, which she thought was about to crash. Over the years, her decision secured her acceptance by the larger Bin Laden family. She took her new faith seriously. After her daughter's birth, Carrie decided to embrace rather than recoil from her unexpected position as a Bin Laden widow—and she agreed to accept the Arabian and Islamic traditions this position carried.

SALEM HAD BEEN responsible in many important respects for Osama's rise along the Afghan frontier. He publicized Osama's humanitarian work, contributed to his Peshawar treasury, supplied him with construction equipment, procured him weaponry, and cemented his strong relations with the Saudi royal family, which advanced Osama's influence and credibility as a fund-raiser. With Salem's abrupt disappearance, Osama lost an important sponsor. At the same time, he was also losing some of his sense of purpose. The cause that had drawn him to the Afghan frontier was ebbing. The Soviet Union signed the Geneva Accords in April 1988 and announced that all its forces would withdraw by early the following year. The war and the jihad would continue, since Moscow would leave behind an Afghan communist government regarded as apostate by the *mujaheddin*, but with blond Russians no longer pledged to serve in an enemy occupation force, the Afghan war had already drifted from righteous rebellion toward muddy civil conflict. This development had a parallel within the camps of the Arab volunteers: during the first months of 1988, the variety and intensity of disputes among the Arabs increased.

Osama's personality and his habits of mind led him to hold himself above this fray. He followed his father's example. He adapted his work and his attitude to please his mentors, even when they were in competition with one another; simultaneously, as a leader in his own right, he attracted a following that was strikingly diverse.

When Osama returned to the Afghan frontier from Salem's funeral, he shuttled among several homes, offices, and camps. His wives and children lived in Peshawar, and he held meetings there with followers and comrades. He occasionally joined Abdullah Azzam at his Peshawar area preaching and charitable facilities, which still drew upon Osama's financial and rhetorical support, even though differences had arisen between them about war tactics. Osama quarreled with Azzam, but they never broke; early in 1988, the pair formed a joint camp along the Afghan border to train and house Arab fighters. Azzam's rivals, the radical Egyptian military and police exiles led by Ayman Al-Zawahiri, controlled Osama's other camps. He gave this Egyptian faction $100,000.[10] He spread his money around. This was an instinctive tactic of balancing, drawn from the leadership examples of his father and Arabian regents, but it also reflected Osama's embryonic philosophy of jihad—a creed that was not particularly sophisticated but that had an inherent populist appeal. All were welcome. The compulsion of jihad was a matter of individual conscience, not a consequence of group initiation. Osama saw himself as an inspirer of jihad, not a cult leader or a dictator.

In this season of disputation, for example, one of the arguments between Osama and Azzam involved whether they should screen and select among applicants to their cause. "Abdullah Azzam wanted to choose—we do not welcome everybody," recalled Jamal Khashoggi, who was in and out of Peshawar during this period. As an adherent of the Muslim Brotherhood, Azzam sought to recruit elite and talented followers, and train them in the Brotherhood tradition. He felt this method produced more trustworthy and rational volunteers. By contrast, "Osama believed in opening up to everybody—everybody who comes under the banner of jihad is welcome." This disagreement marked the beginning of his formal break with the Muslim Brotherhood, which had been his ideological point of entry to politically aware Islam as a young teenager at the Al-Thaghr Model School in Jeddah. As Osama put it later, he came to think that the true community of believers originates "from many different places and regions, representing a wide spectrum of the unity of Islam, which neither recognizes race nor color; nor does it pay any heed to borders and walls." Here, too, he was emerging into his own, but as his father's son; his camps of racially and nationally diverse volunteers along the Afghan border increasingly resembled the diverse desert camps of olive-skinned and African construction workers he had seen in Arabia as a boy.[11]

His inclusive outlook also compensated in part for his lack of standing as a scholar. He had long been proud and stubborn, and as he gathered confidence, he probably felt the sting of Azzam's condescension. Azzam's widow, reflecting her family's sense of superiority, later noted pointedly that Osama was "not a very educated man. He holds a high school degree . . . It is true that he gave lectures to *ulema* and *sheikhs*, but he was easy to persuade."[12] Such attitudes had long hovered just below the surface of Azzam's patronage. With equal subtlety, Osama now began to assert himself in reply, through his pronouncements about diversity and equality, and also by his decision to spread his financial contributions around, to include Azzam's rivals among the Egyptians. These Egyptians had already broken with the Brotherhood, which they regarded as too cautious. In critiquing Azzam and his philosophy, they emphasized the doctrine of *takfir*, by which Muslims judged to be apostates could be excommunicated or even exterminated.

Salem's death coincided with these changes in Osama's world on the Afghan frontier, and it added to the void created by the ebbing of Azzam's mentorship. In Peshawar that summer, the Egyptians, in particular, saw an opportunity to ingratiate themselves by acting as his publicists. Osama "liked the media spotlight," recalled a Saudi follower from this period, Hasan Al-Surayhi. "Bin Laden's finances were not a secret to anyone and I think the Egyptians wanted to exploit this angle," according to Al-Surayhi. They connected Osama with journalists in Peshawar. The Egyptian military chief at one of Osama's camps, Abu Ubaidah Al-Banjshiri, who had fought with him at Jaji, explained the Egyptians' thinking: Osama, he said, "has spent a lot of money to buy arms for the young *mujaheddin* as well as in training them and paying for their travel tickets. Now that the jihad has ended, we should not waste this. We should invest in these young men and we should mobilize them under his umbrella."[13]

The meetings that gave birth to Al Qaeda occurred in Peshawar in August 1988, three months after Salem's funeral. Notes taken at the sessions describe some of the tension Osama felt that summer: he wanted to break away from Azzam, but he did not want to expose himself by too openly adopting a leadership role. "I am one person," he said. "We have not started an organization or an Islamic group." The experiments in training and war that he had supported so far had constituted "a period of education, building energy, and testing brothers who came." The most important accomplishments, Osama recognized, had come from marketing the jihad: "We took very huge gains from the people in Saudi Arabia. We were able to give political power to the *mujaheddin*, gathering donations in very large amounts."[14]

At a second meeting, held at Osama's house, a note taker recorded that in considering a new approach, Osama was motivated by "the complaints" about Azzam's organization, which he had done so much to fund and shape, particularly its "mismanagement and bad treatment." His emphasis now would be on training a separatist Arab militia, of the kind Azzam opposed, initially numbering about three hundred men. As Banjshiri had urged, Osama would use the arms he had acquired with Salem's help before they went to waste. The camps where this training would take place would be called Al Qaeda Al-Askariya, or "The Military Base." Al Qaeda would be "basically an organized Islamic faction" and would develop "statutes and instructions," but it would also be a vehicle for more open-ended, nonhierarchical participation in jihad. "Its goal will be to lift the word of God, to make His religion victorious." Recruits would swear by a pledge that made no reference to Osama Bin Laden. They would recite:

> The pledge of God and his covenant is upon me, to listen and obey the superiors, who are doing this work, in energy, early-rising, difficulty, and easiness, and for his superiority upon us, so that the word of God will be the highest, and His religion victorious.[15]

This ambiguity present at Al Qaeda's birth—the sense that it was an organization but that its borders dissolved into a wider movement—

would persist for years because it was fundamental to Osama's own out-look. In his mind, Al Qaeda was merely an incidental means to incite and organize the *ummah*, the community of Islamic believers. Across the years, Osama would struggle at times to remain true to this aspiration, as bureaucracy, factionalism, and petty ambition gnawed at his ideals. Yet he never abandoned his original model. "The situation is not as the West portrays it," Osama would tell an interviewer many years later, "that there exists an 'organization' with a specific name, such as 'Al Qaeda' and so on. That particular name is very old, and came about quite independently of me. Brother Abu Ubaida Al-Banjshiri created a military base to train the young men to fight against the Soviet empire . . . So this place was called 'The Base,' as in a training base, and the name grew from this. We aren't separated from the *ummah*. We are the children of an *ummah*, and an inseparable part of it."[16]

He drew upon a rich heritage of Saudi and Brotherhood-influenced ideology, but he synthesized these ideas with his lessons drawn from his family. In the years ahead, Osama would make three indispensable contributions to Al Qaeda, all derived from his experiences as a Bin Laden: his emphasis on diversity and inclusion, his confidence about money and administration, and his attraction to the technologies of global integration. Indeed, arguably, these family-derived strengths of Osama's would become more important to Al Qaeda's potency than its underlying Islamic ideology, which was commonplace among militant groups.

Ambition, energy, natural talent, and a gift for managing people had made Mohamed Bin Laden wealthy. Reinterpreted by Salem, these characteristics had girded a secular life of singular creativity and financial success. Reinterpreted through a prism of Islamic radicalism by Osama, they would soon prove just as transforming.

IN APRIL 1989, Ghalib Bin Laden flew to the United States with one of the family's Pakistani pilots to arrange for final delivery of the Hawker

Siddeley private jet that Salem had purchased prior to his death. It was a sleek, spacious two-engine executive jet that could carry a dozen or more passengers. Ghalib had the piloting skills to evaluate the plane's readiness, and as Bakr's full brother, he had his trust. He had matured into a smart, sharp-minded administrator who did not suffer fools and who could act decisively, in the judgment of one business partner who worked with him extensively. He had two sons; his wife increasingly kept the veil.[17]

On April 22, Ghalib flew to San Diego, where one of his youngest half-brothers, Abdullah, was enrolled in university. He flew on to Honolulu, then Guam, and reached Hong Kong on the 24th. Gerald Auerbach, the family pilot, had joined the flight, as had a second Pakistani pilot and the mechanic Bengt Johansson. They flew to Kuala Lumpur, and then to Bombay. On the evening of April 27, 1989, they continued on to Peshawar. They checked into a hotel in the city, and Ghalib Bin Laden and one of the Pakistani pilots traveled by road to the Afghan frontier.[18]

According to two people who were on the trip but who did not travel out from the Peshawar hotel, Ghalib carried about fifty thousand dollars in cash. One of these people, Auerbach, recalled that the money was destined for Osama because he was in need of "some cash." The second passenger, Johansson, said that he was told by the Pakistani pilot who went out from the hotel that they sought to distribute the money as a Ramadan gift to poor people living in a refugee camp. By Johansson's account, this act of charity turned dangerous. "They were almost killed there" and "had to jump over some fences" because a crowd of refugees, seeing Ghalib's bag of money, decided to rush him, rather than wait for an orderly distribution of charity. A family attorney said that Ghalib recalled that "the cash which he [Ghalib] took with him from Peshawar was distributed to the poor in refugee camps" and was not provided to Osama; the attorney emphasized that Ghalib had never provided financial or other support for Osama's terrorism and there is no evidence that he did.[19]

At the time of this visit, Osama was suffering through the most trying episode of his Afghan adventure. In March, at the direction of Pakistani intelligence, a large force of Afghan rebels had opened an assault on the eastern Afghan city of Jalalabad, about a four-hour drive away from Peshawar, over the Khyber Pass. The city was defended by a rump force of Afghan communist soldiers who feared they would be executed if they yielded their positions, and, therefore, fought fiercely, supported by clandestine Soviet officers who manned Scud missile batteries. Osama joined the siege campaign, leading a company-sized force of Arab volunteers who had been trained over the winter at the inaugural Al Qaeda camps. He ensured once more that his followers were adequately equipped—among other things, he acquired night-vision equipment. On the Jalalabad battlefield, however, he and his militia failed disastrously. The guerrilla and ambush tactics they had honed in the mountains proved futile during assaults on fortified fixed positions. The terrain favored the defenders. About one hundred young Arab men had died under Osama's leadership by the time the campaign was called off in June.[20]

So many casualties in such a transparently failed effort only exacerbated the factionalism and dispute that surrounded Osama. In July an Afghan faction led by Gulbuddin Hekmatyar, who was favored by Osama, massacred the leaders of a rival faction led by Ahmed Shah Massoud, who was favored by Azzam. These two powerful Afghan militias embarked on open civil war. Behind the lines, Peshawar "became a horrible place," recalled Jamal Khashoggi. "Arabs who don't like each other. *Takfiris.* Tensions . . . Splinters, fanatic groups."[21]

On November 24, 1989, Abdullah Azzam died in a car bomb attack. The crime went unsolved. Egyptian rivals of Azzam, Hekmatyar, Bin Laden, or some combination seem the most likely suspects. Osama later denied any involvement. "At that point, we were both in the same boat, and you are all aware of the numerous conspiracies there were to murder us all," he said. He recalled telling Azzam to stay out of Peshawar. Ultimately, he said, he concluded that Israel "in collusion with some of its Arab agents" had carried out the attack. His declaration of innocence is difficult to evaluate but probably correct. He had no particular need to kill Azzam, and there is no convincing evidence that he had yet participated in any assassination plots.[22]

A few weeks before Azzam's death, Osama moved home with his family. In quick succession, he had lost the two most important mentors in his life. His sponsor in Saudi intelligence, Ahmed Badeeb, his former high school teacher, urged him to leave Pakistan. Badeeb was trying to "thin out" the number of agents and allies he supported in Peshawar, now that the Soviets had withdrawn. He offered Osama business advice. Financial developments within the Bin Laden family may also have speeded his departure. Bakr was about to oversee a major corporate reorganization and inheritance distribution to all the Bin Ladens of Osama's generation; it would behoove Osama to be present in Saudi Arabia as this occurred. It was, in a broader sense, a time to find his bearings.[23]

As he left Peshawar, Osama was driven primarily by a sense of exhaustion and even fear about the divisive course of the Afghan war. He had no coherent plan for the next phase of his life. He left behind some money and technology to keep his Al Qaeda followers going. At camps near Kandahar, they soon installed some Apple computers.[24]

TO THE EXTENT it formally existed at all, Al Qaeda at this stage was as much a fundraising network as a militia. This was an aspect of Osama's leadership that most easily traversed borders. It was also something that could be pursued more readily in Jeddah than in Peshawar. The evidence about the specific reach of Osama's funding network in 1989 is fragmentary, but it suggests, unsurprisingly, that the Bin Ladens and other wealthy Saudi merchants may have been among the most generous contributors. As Azzam put it just before his death, at a 1989 conference, "Saudi is the only country which stood by the Afghani jihad as a government and people ... The Saudi merchants come and establish organizations and give huge amounts—may God reward them." Documents seized from an Islamic charity in Bosnia, which purport to describe a "Golden Chain" of donors from this period, list more than a dozen Saudi businessmen and bankers, including the "Bin Laden brothers." American investigators and prosecutors have asserted that the documents are authentic and credible, and have been supported by witness statements. Federal Judge Richard Casey, however, later concluded that the Golden Chain was "only a list of names found in a charity's office . . . The Court cannot make the logical leap that the document is a list of early Al Qaeda supporters." For his part, in an affidavit submitted to Casey, Bakr Bin Laden did not specifically deny making contributions to charities or causes in which Osama was involved during this period, but he did assert, "I have never made any charitable contributions to any organization I understood to be associated with Al Qaeda or terrorism of any sort." Bakr also said that he was not aware until sometime after 1991 "of any involvement by Osama in terrorist activities of any kind."[25]

It is plain that Osama returned to Jeddah as a Bin Laden family member in good standing. Jamal Khashoggi saw Osama "a number of times" with Bakr, following Salem's death. On one occasion, he stayed with Osama at the Bin Laden villa in Riyadh. Bakr joined them one evening. "We had a casual conversation over Afghanistan and other issues," Khashoggi recalled. "Bakr appeared distracted. He did not get into an in-depth discussion with us . . . They treated each other with great respect, as a younger brother and older brother would."[26]

Osama continued to embrace media projects that promoted him and his followers to Arab audiences; he imagined himself as a writer-director-producer of jihad. He continued to finance the Egyptian filmmaker Essam Deraz, who had followed him onto the Jalalabad battlefield. As warfare, Jalalabad had been a calamity; as propaganda, it could be salvaged. During the battle, Osama had cast himself not only as an Islamic warrior but also as an actor in a movie about Islamic warriors. Back in Saudi Arabia, he experimented as a producer, screening the director's cut for friends who could help him evaluate the film's progress. He invited Khashoggi to a Bin Laden company auditorium at a conference facility in Jeddah and arranged for employees to screen a print of the 16-millimeter film; the audience consisted only of Osama, Khashoggi, and one or two other people. "He wanted my critique of the film, as his journalist friend," Khashoggi recalled. Osama had left his following in Peshawar, but he remained a star of his own narrative, and his return to the kingdom had not left him isolated. Among other things, said Khashoggi, "He had access to whatever the company had."[27]

25. LUMP SUMS

Bakr Bin Laden had reached his early forties. He had grown into a serious, hardworking businessman. He was about the same height as Salem, and he shared many of his features, particularly the soft brown eyes and the smooth, boyish face. The timbre of his voice and the lilt of his accent so closely resembled Salem's that it could be startling, particularly on the telephone; it was as if Bakr's voice could summon Salem's spirit back among the living. In person, however, he did not exude the same irrepressible charm. Bakr kept a mustache, which was not particularly thick, and it added to the slight air of officiousness that he sometimes projected. He was dignified and intelligent, responsible and polite, but he could also be stiff.

His time as a student at the University of Miami had influenced him but it had not shaped him; he had become a much more thoroughly Arabian man than Salem had ever been. Bakr received his five sons in a formal *diwan*, or drawing room, setting at his Jeddah home; they bent to kiss him on the hand or on the forehead. Speaking to the boys, he might drop an edifying quotation from the Koran or make passing reference to a story from the Prophet's lifetime. Bakr had memorized a substantial portion of the Koran during his own religious studies, and when he was in Saudi Arabia, he maintained a rigorous prayer schedule. He did not drink, according to his friends, and after a time he gave up cigarettes. At Hajj he summoned religious teachers to enhance his family's experience and Islamic education. Still, along the Bin Laden family's cultural and religious spectrum, and in the context of puritan Saudi Arabia, Bakr was better described as a centrist than as a conservative. In his dedication to civil engineering and in the time he devoted to construction projects in Mecca and Medina, he had come to model his life on that of his father. He even hired, as his driver in Saudi Arabia, a son of the driver who had been waiting for Mohamed at the desert airstrip where his plane crashed and burned. Bakr reared his children as his father had done, with an emphasis on discipline and self-reliance—he would not let his children fly on private jets and insisted that they take care of their own travel documents, tickets, and baggage. And as Mohamed had been, Bakr was at ease in a business climate of ethnic and religious plurality. He worked in close partnership with Middle Eastern Christians, such as the Sarkissian family, with whom he formed a joint venture for major construction projects in Saudi Arabia. He also relied upon Fuad Rihani, an American citizen of Jordanian origin, a Protestant actively involved with Jordanian churches, who served as an important Bin Laden adviser after Bakr took charge.[1]

Bakr remained something of a workaholic. On visits to Cairo, he would check into the royal suite at the Marriott and work around the clock, napping for a few hours on sofas. "All his life was hard," according to his Egyptian employee Sabry Ghoneim. "He didn't eat much, because he was afraid of getting fat and developing health problems. He would work all the time, but he didn't eat well or sleep well . . . Believe me, he paid for his work with his happiness." Not long after Salem's death, Bakr divorced his first wife, Haifa, an event that Ghoneim blamed on his work habits. "Even when he came back home, he was working—he would sleep in the reception area of his home . . . A woman needs her husband to relax and joke with her, to go out to eat with her. But he was in a bad way after the death of his brother."[2]

Salem's disappearance burdened Bakr with leadership responsibilities that he had never anticipated, but it also freed his considerable ambition. He thrived in business meetings and had a distinctly international outlook. As he gained control of the family during 1988 and 1989, he envisioned diversifying its businesses into new countries and new industries; he started up new divisions in dredging and medical supplies, and made plans to explore new opportunities from Southeast Asia to Europe.

Salem's schooling had made him something of an Anglophile, and his restless free spirit drew him to America. Bakr was more influenced by France. His education in the former French colonial spheres of Damascus and Lebanon, and his first wife's Syrian roots, helped draw him toward Paris, where he bought an enormous apartment on the Quai d'Orsay—although, like many of his half-brothers, he often preferred the easy convenience of luxury hotels, and typically, he forsook his apartment for the Ritz. Bakr spoke some French, but he conducted most of his business in English or in Arabic, and he kept private secretaries to assist him in each language; over the course of a typical day, he would slip frequently and easily between the two tongues. In this he resembled many younger, privileged Saudis who had adapted rapidly to global business idioms in the aftermath of the oil shock.

In some respects, he was unprepared for the leadership role he now occupied. As an engineer and an operations man, as Salem's loyal number two, he had learned to work hard and to concentrate on results, but he lacked a natural touch for the richly diverse human foibles and quandaries that his family members continually presented him. As almost anyone would, Bakr suffered by comparison to Salem. He could seem like a bit of a nerd, eager to imitate the sources of his older brother's charisma and popularity but not always able to pull it off. Some of Salem's friends thought that Bakr carried something of a chip on his shoulder because of these deficits. Yet he seemed to have genuinely admired Salem, and as he explored his new circumstances as the boss of all he surveyed, Bakr tried to live in some ways as Salem had done.

He refused, for example, to back off from the family passion for flying, despite the enormous costs that aviation had exacted. Bakr had at first been a somewhat reluctant pilot. He "used to hate flying, maybe because his father died in an airplane" recalled one of his Egyptian instructors, Yahia El Agaty. "And then in Cairo one day at Imbaba Airport, I was flying the [Cessna] 172 which I bought from Salem. And Bakr came to the airport, and he said, 'Okay, I want to fly.' I chuckled: 'You want to fly, Sheikh Bakr!' He said, 'Yeah.'"

"You're a liar!" Salem had exclaimed when Agaty called to report what had happened, but Agaty was right: gradually, Bakr took instruction and conquered his fear.[3] He eventually became qualified on jets and was regarded by his private pilots as quite a competent and enthusiastic flier. He did not fly with Salem's reckless, showy flair—barrel rolls were not his style—but he did enjoy a few modest demonstrations at the controls from time to time, such as taking off in a Learjet or Gulfstream and leveling at a low altitude, and then suddenly tilting back and roaring upward. He came to talk about planes and private aviation with the same all-consuming hobbyist's passion as Salem had possessed; gossip about new models and nuances of range and performance became for Bakr what baseball or soccer rosters were for other men. His piloting did seem to some of Salem's old friends to be a metaphor for Bakr's relationship with his brother's ghost—he wanted to fly where Salem had been, but he did not embrace the same degree of risk.

AS HE ESTABLISHED himself as the new leader, Bakr decided to clean up some family inheritance issues. At the same time, he set up new business partnerships for the future. Court documents describing this period, while far from fully transparent, provide the most detailed snapshots available of the size of the main Bin Laden company and how its wealth was distributed to the heirs of Bakr's generation after Salem's death. Osama's return to Saudi Arabia in 1989 coincided with this family reorganization, overseen by Bakr; it may even have been a factor in his decision to come home.

Of all the myths that would come to swirl around Al Qaeda, none was greater than the fable of Osama Bin Laden's wealth. His followers (and, later, some of his adversaries) romanticized every aspect of his leadership, but they particularly exaggerated his personal fortune. The unrestrained, poetic language employed by Islamist propagandists to celebrate Osama's battlefield achievements in Afghanistan soon extended to the subject of his bank account. To some extent, their exaggerations are explained by Osama's fundraising achievements; his ability to attract outside donations and government support had made him appear wealthier to his comrades in Pakistan than he actually was. Still, the prosaic truth about his personal finances mattered greatly—because of misreporting about Osama's wealth, his adversaries, particularly those in the United States, would repeatedly misunderstand him.

None of Mohamed Bin Laden's children could easily guess what he or she was worth. The family companies did not trade on any stock exchange, and their web of opaque financial entanglements with the Al-Saud complicated any attempt at financial valuation. At the center of the empire stood the Mohamed Bin Laden Organization, the original construction company founded in 1931. Each of Mohamed's sons—except for Ali, who had sold his shares when he broke with Salem after their father's death—owned 2.27 percent of the flagship company, and each of the daughters owned half of that amount, or about 1.14 percent.[4] After Bakr became the Bin Laden emir, or leader, he approved dividend payments to the family shareholders each year, based at least in part on that year's actual profits. These dividends were separate from salaries that particular brothers might earn, and distinct also from profits that might be distributed from other businesses, such as Bin Laden Brothers. Some of the Bin Laden heirs reinvested their dividends in global stock markets, particularly after Yeslam established his Saudi and Swiss brokerages. Yeslam's full brother Ibrahim, for example, testified in a court deposition that in 1983, in order to raise about $1 million in cash for the purchase of a mansion in Los Angeles, he sold "stocks that I inherited from my father." He borrowed the rest of the purchase price, about $600,000. It seems most likely that Ibrahim actually inherited cash from Mohamed's estate, in the form of dividends, which he then shifted into stocks at Yeslam's direction; his testimony on this point is not precise, but overall, it suggests the scale and fluidity of the inheritance.

The most reliable portrait of the family dividend system comes from an American certified public accountant, Linda Pergament Swift, a specialist in forensic accounting, who examined the Bin Laden family's finances during the early 1990s as part of an American divorce proceeding involving Ibrahim. In 1989, Swift reported to an American court, Ibrahim received two dividend payments from the Mohamed Bin Laden Organization totaling just over $325,000. This appears to be roughly the amount allotted to all male shareholders that year, including Osama. Swift wrote, however, that her investigation revealed a strikingly flexible and informal family system: "Each beneficiary receives allotments, usually from profits of the business, on an annual or semi-annual basis. The family business does not simply distribute a lump sum ... [but] acts as a money manager or clearing house." Each son and daughter was credited his or her share of the annual profits, she continued, and then the company doled out the cash as directed by the heir.[5]

Ibrahim's 1989 take implies that Bakr allotted a total of about $15 million in dividends to family members that year. That is consistent with figures in the 1990 edition of *Top 1000 Saudi Companies*, a business directory published in cooperation with the Saudi Arabian government. It reported that the Mohamed Bin Laden Organization was the twenty-seventh-largest company in the kingdom and had revenue of about $340 million. Assuming a profit margin of 5 to 10 percent, as would be typical at a large construction firm, the company's total annual profit around 1989 would have been in the range of $20 to $30 million—an impressive amount, but hardly the stuff of the greatest global business baronies.[6]

Also in 1989, Bakr oversaw a one-time distribution to Mohamed Bin Laden's heirs from the patriarch's broader estate, according to what the family later told American government investigators. Mohamed's children and the four women to whom he was married when he died had inherited not only shares in his company but also his land, his homes, and his personal property. Initially the trustees appointed by King Faisal doled out allowances and conserved the estate's principal. When Salem eventually gained control, according to the account of one family business partner, he argued with some of his brothers over whether and how to distribute the estate's underlying assets, which were not easy to divvy up, since they included much land and real property. By this account, Salem resisted a straight application of Islamic law, under which each brother would receive one equal share, and each sister one equal half-share, after provisions for charity and Mohamed's wives. Among other things, Salem felt that brothers who worked at the company deserved a larger distribution than those who did nothing.[7] Islamic inheritance law, however, made no such distinction, and it would have been difficult for Salem to sustain his position before a Saudi court if any of his brothers had formally objected.

Bakr resolved the matter within months of Salem's death by endorsing a major distribution under Islamic law. Representatives of the Bin Laden family later told the Federal Bureau of Investigation that heirs could choose whether to take cash or to reinvest in the family companies. For his part, Osama seems to have followed both paths. He took about $8 million in cash, according to what family representatives told the FBI. He also became a shareholder in the new partnerships that Bakr organized as he restructured the family businesses. One of these was the Mohamed Bin Laden Company, successor to the original family firm. The other was a new entity called the Saudi Bin Laden Group (SBG), chaired by Bakr and inaugurated in late 1989. These two companies were entirely independent, Bakr later said in an affidavit. After the reorganization and the cash withdrawals, Osama owned about 2 percent of each firm, and his shareholdings were worth about $10 million combined, according to a valuation made several years later.[8]

According to Sabry Ghoneim, director of communications for the

Bin Ladens in Egypt, Bakr extended himself on Osama's behalf throughout this period. Bakr "respected all the mothers of his brothers like his own mother," Ghoneim recalled. "He always felt that Osama's mother was weak, so as a way to dignify her, he wanted to give Osama one of the bigger projects. This was what he did with all the mothers—offer their sons projects . . . Bakr felt that while all his siblings were educated, Osama didn't get a good education. Osama always felt his mother wasn't with the rest of the mothers, because she was from a lower social class . . . Osama always felt broken and felt he didn't get his share—the siblings got education abroad, and he didn't. He would isolate himself. Bakr was very smart to try to include his brother."[9]

The estimated 1989 distribution to Osama and the rest of Mohamed's sons of about $18 million each—some in cash, some in renewed shareholdings, depending on the choices made by each brother—is largely consistent with several credible accounts of the inheritance. Yeslam Bin Laden later told Swiss television, for example, that "the amount received by each member of the family didn't go above $20 million." Also, Yeslam's own Swiss tax returns, filed between 1989 and 1993, indicate that he may have taken out cash in a manner similar to Osama, around the same time—his declared financial assets suddenly jumped by about 8 million Swiss francs after 1989. In an interview, a business partner briefed by the Bin Laden family, who asked to not be identified, pegged a full share for Mohamed's sons circa 1989 at $26 million, higher than other estimates but in the same general range. Investigators for the 9/11 Commission, drawing upon classified documents later provided to the Treasury Department by the Bin Laden family and its lawyers, estimated that Osama received a total of about $24 million between 1970 and 1993 or 1994; this figure would have included his annual allowances and dividends, and the $8 million distribution of 1989, but probably not the value of his shareholdings. (It is not clear whether the figure also included the salaries he earned when he worked at the family firm as a junior executive.) The 9/11 Commission report implied that Osama received equal annual installments of about $1 million, but this does not appear to be accurate. His annual dividends probably averaged less than half of that amount, supplemented by salaries, work bonuses, and the large one-time distribution in 1989. Despite the variations in detail, all these well-sourced estimates of the Bin Laden inheritance are in broad accord. They underline several points: Osama was wealthy, but not grotesquely so; after Salem's death, he received a particularly large sum of cash, just as Al Qaeda was born; and following receipt of this cash distribution, under Bakr's leadership, he remained a partner in good standing in the most important Bin Laden businesses.[10]

The reorganized Mohamed Bin Laden Company had sixty shareholders—all of Mohamed's sons, except the deceased Salem and the estranged Ali; all twenty-nine of Mohamed's daughters; his widows; and Salem's three children. The new Saudi Bin Laden Group, destined to become an important vehicle for wealth creation under Bakr's leadership, had just twenty shareholders, all of them sons of Mohamed. The shares in SBG were not distributed equally—Bakr, as chairman, owned the most, just under 25 percent. Only four living sons did not initially become shareholders in SBG: Ali, Yeslam, Ibrahim, and Shafiq.[11]

In the same period that he reorganized his father's estate and the Bin Laden businesses, Bakr also tried to clean up Salem's personal estate. Salem had not written a will. This in itself did not present much of a complication, however, because under Islamic inheritance law, the identity of his personal heirs was clear: his mother; his widow, Carrie; and his three children. But Salem had left financial detritus scattered around the world.[12]

On June 4, 1988, Bakr applied to an Islamic court in Jeddah to become the legal executor of Salem's estate; about two months later, a Saudi judged approved his position. The judge found after evidentiary hearings that Salem "had, during his life, made a verbal will appointing and instituting his brother Bakr . . . to be the guardian of his minor children . . . and he maintained such testament until his death." The court issued a series of instructions to Bakr, including that he "be God-fearing . . . in private as well as in public."[13]

Under Islamic law, none of Salem's brothers or half-brothers would inherit from his personal estate. This presented a potentially tricky question for the family, since the lines between Salem's individual wealth and that of the family businesses they owned collectively had never been entirely clear. Salem's private jets belonged to the companies, and Bakr kept them for business use. Salem's estates in Florida and at Offley Chase were deemed to be private assets, however, and Bakr soon put them up for sale. He hired lawyers in Florida, Texas, and Germany to chase down outstanding financial claims that might benefit Salem's heirs.

During these investigations, according to Thomas Dietrich, Ghalib Bin Laden, acting for Bakr, accused Dietrich of mishandling a bank account that he had maintained in Germany to fund Salem's various adventures in Europe. Dietrich argued that the money he had received from the account reimbursed him for legitimate—if at times unorthodox—expenses directly authorized by Salem. He also said that Salem had given him title to a glider they flew together, but that the agreement had not been written up as a contract. Hounded by a German lawyer, Dietrich said, he ultimately settled the dispute by selling the glider and turning the proceeds over to the Bin Ladens; the episode left him with some bitter feelings toward Bakr. Separately, Bakr also agreed to settle, by making a payment of about $1 million, the long-running lawsuit in Canada stemming from the payment dispute with American partners over the Saudi telephone contracts Salem had won. Bakr also hired lawyers in Texas to examine a failed shopping center investment Salem had made with his attorney, Wayne Fagan, but they took no action in that case.[14]

One of the biggest paydays from these investigations came at the expense of Dee Howard, the San Antonio aviation pioneer who had remodeled King Fahd's lavish 747 under the contract obtained through Salem. In a separate deal from the airplane project, Salem had invested just less than 1 million British pounds and had guaranteed an NCB loan of $1 million more to develop with Dee Howard some innovative aircraft-engine technology that could extend the flying range of certain jets. Ian Munro, who had been involved in this project, believed that Howard had profited from the technology Salem funded without properly compensating his partners. Howard denied this. Bakr hired lawyers in Florida to explore the claim, and ultimately they retained Charles Schwartz, a partner at the large Houston firm of Vinson and Elkins, to sue Dee Howard and his company. The case eventually came to trial before a civil jury in Bexar County, Texas. Appealing to the presumed skepticism of Texas jurors toward Saudi millionaires, Dee Howard's attorney missed no opportunity to talk at trial about Salem's riches or to refer to him as "sheikh." Schwartz objected to all the "sheikhs" and tried to counter by emphasizing Salem's reputation as a friend of Ronald Reagan and his success in international business. Finally, after a six-week trial highlighted by testimony from both Ian Munro and Dee Howard (the former speaking with aplomb in his British accent, the latter quarreling impetuously in a Texas drawl), the Bin Laden side won. The jury returned a verdict of $6 million in favor of Salem's estate; the case later settled for just over half of that amount.[15]

To pursue the claim against Howard, Bakr had to submit certain legal briefs to the Texas court system, and in one of them, he referred to the existence, in the Jeddah courts, of an intriguing-sounding document entitled "Financial Position of the Inheritance of the Late Salem Binladin as of February 10, 1990," which was "the only financial document filed with the court here in the Kingdom of Saudi Arabia regarding the financial affairs" of Salem and his estate, according to Bakr. This document did not make it into the public court file in Texas, however. Its scope is unclear, but one lawyer who read it at the time recalled that it estimated the value of Salem's personal estate as perhaps several hundred million dollars, and certainly less than one billion dollars. Even that estimate seems high, given Salem's perpetual cash flow struggles in the last years of his life, although the estimate may reflect the value of his relatively illiquid real estate holdings in Saudi Arabia, Egypt, the United Arab Emirates, and elsewhere.[16]

The question of Salem's personal wealth was also complicated by his debts. He had borrowed large sums from the National Commercial Bank, but it was not always evident, at least to his foreign business partners, when he was borrowing for a personal transaction and when for the Bin Laden companies. According to two individuals close to Salem and NCB, the bank presented Bakr with a demand for repayment after Salem's death, and Bakr worked out a settlement; the amounts involved are unknown, but according to these individuals, they may have been very large. "He didn't always talk about it," Ghoneim recalled, "but I saw he was exhausted. He had to deal with inheritance problems. He was doing his best to pay all the debts."[17]

Bakr's settlement agreements and his methodical pursuit of claims for Salem's estate in Europe and America signaled the family's new direction—more businesslike, better organized, more Arabian. In the absence of a family crisis, it was perhaps a welcome change for some from the volatility and peculiarity of Salem's rein. But the Bin Ladens were not destined to live placidly. Very soon, as the family's troubles deepened, Bakr would confront problems and choices of extraordinary importance and complexity. Was he up to the challenge? Despite all his admirable dedication and hard work, his innate caution framed a question he would never entirely shake: What would Salem have done?

26. AMERICA IN MOTION

T HE IRANIAN REVOLUTION of 1979 cast thousands of privileged
Persians into exile. Many gathered in Los Angeles, where they
poured their agitations into business. First- and second-generation
Lebanese and Armenian entrepreneurs maneuvered among them—
builders, restaurateurs, retailers, developers, and hustlers sui generis.
Some blocks on the west side of Los Angeles already resembled a stucco-
and-Spanish-tile bazaar when the Saudis turned up in numbers, their
pockets bulging after the second oil shock. Young merchant scions from
Jeddah and Riyadh and Dhahran rolled through Beverly Hills in Porsches
and Mercedes-Benzes, their sunglasses just a little too fashionable, their
aftershave a little too pungent—as conspicuous a population of marks as
ever swam in the seas of capitalism. Accountants looked at them and saw
fees; lawyers saw billable hours; stockbrokers saw commissions; jewelers
saw gold. There were plenty of Saudi businessmen who held their own
in America, but many suffered from deficits of guile and ruthlessness.
They were newcomers, flush but lacking in confidence and inside angles,
and they did not have a locally rooted diaspora to protect them, as the
Armenians and Lebanese enjoyed. Their instincts and traditions did not
always serve them well. Arabian elites esteemed dignity, decorum, and
reticence. Americans shouted, shoved, and brawled over money. Arabians
settled disputes discreetly. Americans sued in open court.

Salem had thrived on this frontier, but his death cut the main artery
connecting the United States to the Bin Laden family. Bakr was certainly

interested in business partnerships with American multinational corporations, but he very rarely traveled to the States. By 1989 the most active family investor on American soil was Khalil Bin Laden, who lived in Los Angeles several months each year, usually in the summer, when Jeddah's heat was particularly intolerable. He was a younger full brother of Yeslam, a half-brother of Bakr and Osama. He had come to America with considerable business ambition. Gradually, however, Los Angeles and its lawyers were threatening to strip him of his money and his serenity.

Khalil Bin Laden had studied business at the University of Southern California during the 1970s, but he never graduated. He was a thin, shy man, exceedingly polite, curious about American mores but conservative in his habits of mind. He dressed well but not flamboyantly—he wore Greg Chapman gray flannel suits handmade in Beverly Hills and Bally shoes. For a time he drove a Rolls-Royce convertible; later, as he settled into America, he chauffeured his family in a considerably less conspicuous green Ford minivan with cloth seats. He prayed punctually five times each day and gave up alcohol after a few cursory experiments, according to friends. He could be ruthless at French card games—"In cards, I don't know my own mother"—but he was otherwise gentle and diffident. When he met his future wife in a Beverly Hills nightclub, some of his acquaintances thought she was probably the first woman he had ever dated seriously.[1]

She was a formidable character—Isabel Bayma, a Brazilian who had grown up in poverty in her native country, migrated to the United States, and found her way to Beverly Hills. She had had a child by a previous marriage by the time she met and won Khalil. He adored her, according to people who knew them, and he showered her with luxuries she had never known. Some acquaintances described her as strong and stalwart; others as difficult and demanding. They married at the Riviera Country Club in Bel Air. They started a family, and as their household brimmed with young Saudi-Brazilian-American children, they bought a home in fashionable Brentwood, on Jonesboro Drive, and contracted for a $600,000 luxury renovation.[2]

At USC, Khalil met a Beverly Hills jeweler, Michael Kazanjian, who sold high-end pieces to members of the Bin Laden family. Kazanjian was a client of Alexander Cappello, a young USC business graduate who aspired to build a boutique investment bank with global reach. Cappello was a handsome, dark-haired, Gatsby-esque character from Bakersfield, California, who would become an assiduous collector of Italian Renaissance art and statuary. He met Khalil through the international students department at USC. He operated from well-appointed offices in a prestigious skyscraper in Century City. Initially, he helped Khalil with real estate investments.[3]

Khalil's business goals were vague. "If I don't know what's going on, I just say no," he would explain as he turned down one American promoter after another. He seemed mainly to be hedging his bets against political trouble in Saudi Arabia, trying to build up enough American real estate and business activity to generate a secure $200,000 to $300,000 in annual income outside the kingdom, just in case. He tinkered and continually generated new ideas. He was attracted, as were many in his family, to tangible investments such as real estate and aircraft leasing, but he was also willing to consider some unusual ventures.[4]

Early on, Khalil registered a Delaware company called Kabeltan Corporation, where Alex Cappello served for a time as president, according to company documents. Kabeltan acquired a one-story blond-brick office building in Carrollton, Texas, outside Dallas, about five miles north of the Lyndon B. Johnson freeway. In nearby Garland, at 3737 Dividend Drive, the company bought a light warehouse rented out to industrial tenants. Other investments were more exotic. Through Cappello's firm, Khalil purchased an interest in a loan made to the country singer Kenny Rogers for the purchase of an Arabian horse named Nujad, which was estimated to be worth $10 million to $20 million. The breeder who had sold the horse kept a ranch in Northern California and had agreed to lend Rogers a portion of the purchase price. Later, because he needed to raise cash quickly, the breeder offered to sell Cappello's firm the loan at a considerable discount. Cappello made sure the horse had adequate life insurance, and Khalil agreed to participate in the transaction; his only risk involved the creditworthiness of Kenny Rogers, which proved to be a sound bet. Bin Laden made a profit of more than 30 percent in less than a year from the country singer's loan.[5]

During one of his annual sojourns in Saudi Arabia, it occurred to Khalil and Isabel that the kingdom lacked a proper toy store of the kind they and their children had grown accustomed to in Los Angeles—a supermarket for children, like Toys "R" Us. They decided to launch Saudi Arabia's first large toy store, a somewhat daring venture in a kingdom where many religious scholars regarded dolls as blasphemous idols. Khalil explored the possibility of purchasing a Middle Eastern franchise from Toys "R" Us itself, but the price was too steep. (Companies that issue franchises under a famous brand name can also be sticklers about requiring a franchise owner to perform extensive hands-on work at the business, to ensure its success. The Bin Ladens explored purchasing McDonald's franchises for the Middle East, according to a family member, but learned that owners were required by headquarters to put in long hours frying hamburgers and french fries; there was some joking within the family about which Bin Laden brother could be dispatched to deep-fat-frying school in America, but they ultimately decided to pass.) In the end, Khalil decided to launch his own business, Toyland, in Jeddah. To stock its aisles he hired in Los Angeles an experienced American toy merchandiser, Mark Love, and they used a new company, BIN Corporation, to handle purchasing and shipping between America and Jeddah.[6]

As these endeavors flourished, Khalil slowly became entangled in American legal proceedings. He seemed allergic to property taxes, and over the years he allowed a number of his real estate properties to fall into arrears, which led government attorneys for the State of California and Dallas County, Texas, to file civil cases against him. His Brentwood home-renovation project produced vituperative civil lawsuits between Khalil and his Iranian-owned building contractor in Los Angeles, a dispute that carried particular irony for a descendant of such a famous contracting family.[7] But his greatest trouble began, in the aftermath of Salem's death, as Khalil moved into the novel business of private American prison leasing, through the auspices of a new company he formed called America in Motion Corporation.

America in Motion shared an office suite with BIN at 15260 Ventura Boulevard, a granite-and-glass building more than twenty stories tall in Sherman Oaks, California, in the San Fernando Valley, just over the chaparral hills from Hollywood. When he was in Los Angeles, Khalil worked at the Sherman Oaks office from time to time, but mainly he delegated day-to-day management to his American executives and employees. By the late 1980s, Alex Cappello had faded from the scene. He was replaced by Franklin Frisaura, a real estate broker who was Khalil's brother-in-law—Frisaura had married Isabel Bayma's Brazilian sister, Regina, whom he had also met at a Los Angeles nightclub. Frisaura brought a touch of entertainment-industry cachet to the Bin Laden enterprise. He had grown up in Southern California; his father was a comedian, and his mother, after performing as a young adult in the Ringling Bros. and Barnum & Bailey Circus, had also earned a living as an entertainer. Frisaura had attended junior high school with the sons of Mo Austin, the former president of Warner Brothers Records. The Bin Ladens had accommodated relatives by marriage in jobs at their various enterprises for almost a half century, and Frisaura followed in this tradition; he served as an adviser and manager for Khalil on real estate and other business projects.[8]

America in Motion made an initial foray into tax-oriented aircraft leasing, but this did not turn out very well. One early customer was Steven McKim, the president of a small Northern California company, Magnum Aircraft International, whose investors included Clint Eastwood, the actor then renowned for his *Magnum Force* and other movies. Magnum Aircraft, headquartered near Eastwood's home in Carmel, was involved in research into retractable landing gear for helicopters. For reasons that remain opaque, McKim persuaded Khalil to purchase and lease back to Magnum a vintage 1958 twin-engine Spanish fighter jet, according to court documents. McKim's successor at the company, Darius Keaton, later said that Magnum was "a small corporation located in Monterey with no business outside the state. None of the employees of Magnum did any significant travel . . . The last thing needed was a $225,000 jet."

In any event, soon after its purchase, Magnum stopped making lease payments. America in Motion sued. Khalil Bin Laden's lawyers named as defendants not only McKim but also Clint Eastwood. The lawsuit was ultimately dismissed without a judgment against the actor-director or the payment of any settlement. America in Motion wound up in possession of an old jet suitable for aviation hobbyists.[9]

In addition to his brother-in-law Frisaura, Khalil relied for advice upon Musarrat Ali-Khan, a somewhat mysterious figure with a colonial-era mustache who was described in one court document as "a chartered accountant in Pakistan" who had later settled in Jeddah as an employee of the Bin Laden family. When Khalil first opened his Toyland stores in Saudi Arabia, Ali-Khan worked with him there. Later he moved to Los Angeles to help run America in Motion. Khalil paid him a salary of more than five thousand dollars per month. Ali-Khan looked around for business deals that might interest his employer. During the summer of 1988— in the same months that Osama Bin Laden was secretly forming Al Qaeda back in Ali-Khan's native country of Pakistan—he arranged an unusual investment for Khalil involving some Massachusetts prison facilities.[10]

The deal revolved around a company called Resun Leasing, which was headquartered in the Virginia suburbs of Washington, D.C. Founded in 1986, Resun specialized in premanufactured modular buildings for use by governments, schools, hospitals, and businesses; its projects ranged from small offices for security guards to huge warehouses. To avoid tying

up too much of its cash, the company looked for private investors willing to participate in its leasing contracts. America in Motion purchased
what a court document described as "an undivided one-half interest in
certain prison facilities leased to the Commonwealth of Massachusetts"
in Hampden and Hampshire counties.[11]

The price was just over $500,000. Khalil raised the money by bor-
rowing $770,000 from the Banque Indosuez. Resun then returned the dif-
ference to Khalil—more than $200,000—in a transaction that Bin Laden
referred to as a "rebate," but which Ali-Khan called a "kick back," although it was not clear what he meant by that term. Khalil apparently
used the extra cash to pay down separate debts to Banque Indosuez. His
obligations in Los Angeles were beginning to pile up; for example, his
total debts to Banque Indosuez exceeded $3 million, according to a let-
ter written by Ali-Khan to Khalil in 1989. Khalil eventually went into
technical default on some of this debt; he sought to sell some of his Los
Angeles investment properties to pay off his loans.[12]

In May 1989, America in Motion renegotiated its prison-leasing deal
with Resun. As part of the financial transfers generated by this refinanc-
ing, one of Khalil's attorneys in Beverly Hills, Ron Goldie, accepted into
a trust account a sum of $227,500, according to court filings. Goldie then
agreed to pay $130,000 of this money to Musarrat Ali-Khan, who claimed
it was owed to him as part of oral business agreements he had made with
Khalil. The confusion was compounded by the fact that Khalil was attempting to monitor the prison transactions by fax and telephone from
Jeddah, where he had returned for the winter and spring.

On BIN Corporation and America in Motion Corporation stationery,
Ali-Khan wrote several times to Khalil in Jeddah, providing a history of
convoluted financial transfers that had culminated with his receipt of the
$130,000, which he described as a "loan" that had been made to BIN
Corporation on "my personal guarantee." Khalil faxed back a series of
skeptical questions. "Please provide me with the following details of this
said loan," he wrote, including "the purpose for which we get this loan . . .

actual utilization of this loan ... when we got this loan ... who is the creditor ... If there was a loan agreement, fax me a copy." Ali-Khan tried to satisfy him but failed. In early June, Khalil wrote to him from Jeddah: "The faxes you sent to us ... are still vague and I disagree on many of the contents. Please provide us full details of information especially on the $130,000 loan you said you personally guaranteed."[13]

Khalil flew into Los Angeles, talked to the lawyers and executives involved, and concluded that "the $130,000 was fraudulently taken by Khan," as he put it in a written declaration later filed in court. Ali-Khan stopped coming to work. On September 22, 1989, Khalil Bin Laden drove to the Van Nuys police station in the San Fernando Valley, approached an officer working at the counter, and asked to file a criminal complaint. With this act, he took yet one more step into the mire of the American legal system. Khalil had initially been unsure "if this could be criminal or just civil," that is, a situation where he should just sue Ali-Khan to try to get his money back, rather than going to the police. He had decided, however, that he was the victim of a crime under American law. The police "sent me upstairs, and upstairs they sent me back down," Khalil remembered. Finally, "One of the policemen told me, 'Okay, fill this form.'"[14]

Following an investigation, the Van Nuys district attorney did indict Ali-Khan on charges of felony embezzlement, and the police issued a warrant for his arrest. Prosecutors argued in one court filing that the Pakistani was a "possible international thief ... wanted for bank embezzlement in Paris."[15]

Khalil also sued in civil court. Ali-Khan hired lawyers who summoned Khalil to a conference room in a skyscraper in downtown Los Angeles for five grueling days of deposition testimony in July 1990. Ali-Khan's lawyers grilled Bin Laden about the history of America in Motion, his outstanding loans from Banque Indosuez and other banks, his decision to pursue criminal charges at the police station—they even asked whether Khalil had a vendetta against his former employee be-

cause they had both become interested in the same woman at the
Sherman Oaks office. ("No," he answered.) One of the lawyers involved
in the examination later described, in a written declaration, the scene
that unfolded in the skyscraper's conference room as the interrogation
proceeded:

> At some point, Mr. Binladin claimed that I was asking the same questions
> over and over again . . . and seemed to be becoming agitated. I then asked
> a question and, while pondering his response to it, Mr. Binladin got out
> of his chair and walked around the deposition room to a spot near and
> behind me and then back to the general area where Mr. Finkel [his
> lawyer] was sitting . . . Mr. Grimwade made a comment on the record to
> the effect that the record should reflect that the witness was pacing . . .
> At that, there was a heated exchange . . . Mr. Binladin (at about 1:40 P.M.)
> broke into tears, sobbing, holding his head in his hands, with Mr. Finkel
> claiming on the record that I had "made" his client cry . . .[16]

"The tears in my eyes were real," Khalil recalled. The opposing
lawyers were "disrespectful of both me and my attorney"; they made
"nasty comments" and asked "questions full of innuendo":

> The repeated questioning and harassment finally got to me . . . The stress
> relates not . . . to "kickbacks" or my conduct, but rather, to the continu-
> ing barrages of questioning . . . which are intrusive into my personal
> life . . .[17]

It was enough to make a man nostalgic for shariah courts. Nor had
Khalil yet discovered the limits of his aggravations.

ABOUT SIX WEEKS AFTER Khalil's ordeal by deposition, two officers
from the Los Angeles Police Department, accompanied by a Brazilian

woman, Elizabeth Borges, appeared at the door of the Bin Laden home in Brentwood. The officers asked to speak with Marta Silva and Auria DaSilva, two Brazilian women who worked as maids and nannies for the Khalil Bin Laden family. When the two women appeared, the police asked questions about the circumstances of their employment; Borges translated between Portuguese and English. The thrust of the police questioning, as Borges later put it, involved whether the maids were "unable to leave the [Bin Laden] residence and were being prevented from leaving by threats and demands that they must pay monies" to their employers.[18]

Borges later explained the origins of her visit in court documents. She had been telephoned in June and told that Marta Silva "was being forced to work" for the Bin Ladens "for long hours without days off or relief, and she was not being paid for the work she was performing." Borges agreed to contact the Brazilian consulate in Los Angeles, but when she did, she found they "would do nothing." (In Jeddah, Khalil had been appointed Honorary Consul of Brazil, a position designed to help facilitate business between his wife's native country and Saudi Arabia.) The consulate told Borges to contact the Los Angeles Police if she felt there was a serious problem, and she did. She acted, she wrote in a court declaration, because she believed that the Bin Ladens had "violated the constitutional rights" of their maids "by holding them in their employment against their will." Borges claimed that the maids told her that:

They were both required to work 18 hours a day without any breaks for breakfast, lunch or dinner . . . .They were never given any days off and worked seven days a week. They were never paid directly for their work either by cash or check. The conduct of Isabel Binladin was generally very rude and disrespectful to them . . . Their movement and ability to go outside the family compound in Jeddah or Los Angeles was very limited and restricted . . . [The Bin Ladens] also made statements to Ms. Silva that past employees had tried to escape and leave their job, that they were apprehended and made to pay for it in more ways than just with money . . .[19]

After interviewing the two Brazilian women, however, the Los Angeles Police Department took no action. The two employees left the Bin Laden home the following day; according to the Bin Ladens, Borges agreed to arrange for their immediate departure by air, home to Brazil. Instead, they remained in Los Angeles.

The Bin Ladens said they were outraged by the allegations made against them. They quickly filed a lawsuit against Borges, accusing her of helping the maids escape from their contractual employment obligations and speaking "slanderous" words in the presence of the two police officers. In their complaint, they explained that because Khalil and Isabel

> travel extensively, and because Mr. Binladin has heavy business commitments, it is necessary that they have domestic employees who travel with them to care for their five children . . . Ms. Silva and Ms. DaSilva agreed to accompany [the Bin Ladens] to Saudi Arabia to take care of the Binladins' five children and perform light housework and to cook, respectively, at . . . various homes and vacation locales with the proviso that if they desired to terminate their employ, Ms. Silva and Ms. DaSilva would immediately return to Brazil. In reliance on these promises, [the Bin Ladens] obtained precious Saudi Arabian visas . . .[20]

Under U.S. immigration law, the complaint continued, the Bin Ladens were responsible for keeping track of their maids "at all times." Now that the women had disappeared, their family would suffer because they "may not be able to obtain U.S. visas for their household help in the future." They had suffered "severe emotional distress" from the incident with the police, they wrote, and had agreed to allow the maids to leave and fly home only "in order to defuse the embarrassing situation (which could have adversely affected the Binladin children if it had continued)."[21]

Borges replied that "any statements made by her to the Los Angeles Police Department ... were made to protect the constitutional rights" of the two women and thus were legally privileged.[22]

Borges eventually returned to Brazil; the lawsuit's claims and counterclaims were never resolved, according to the available court file. The Bin Ladens ultimately concluded that they had had their fill of Los Angeles. Khalil agreed to purchase from Salem's estate the Liberian corporation set up to hold Desert Bear, the Spanish-revival estate near Orlando; he paid just under $1 million, according to a person familiar with the transaction.[23] The Bin Ladens sold their Brentwood home. In the future, their family would spend summer months in Florida.

America was at times baffling and annoying, at times intrusive and insulting, but it was now an inexorable part of Khalil's hyphenated family, Saudi-Brazilian-American. They were Bin Ladens, but their children were increasingly American influenced. Managing that balance would prove increasingly difficult.

During that summer of 1990, the season of depositions and upstart maids and door-knocking police in Los Angeles, the allied governments of the United States and Saudi Arabia, rocked by crisis, were discovering something similar, on a parallel plane of foreign policy, oil, economics, and war. Here, too, the integrity and wealth of the Bin Laden family would be implicated—and jeopardized.

27. THE SWISS ACCOUNTS

O N THE NIGHT of August 6, 1990, Secretary of Defense Dick Cheney led an American delegation to King Fahd's seaside palace in Jeddah. Fahd preferred the Red Sea port to Riyadh; among other reasons, one of the astrologers he relied upon had forecasted that he might be knifed in the capital. On this particular evening, Jeddah had the additional advantage of placing the king as far from danger as possible and in position to escape Arabia quickly. Four days earlier, Saddam Hussein's army had invaded and occupied Kuwait; the emirate's small army had collapsed and the royal family had fled into exile. Iraqi units now seemed to be regrouping for a possible thrust at Saudi Arabia's eastern oil fields, the largest of which lay below the Kuwaiti border, on the opposite side of the kingdom from Jeddah.

General Norman Schwarzkopf, the senior American military commander for the Middle East, and Paul Wolfowitz, an under secretary of defense, followed Cheney into the king's reception hall. Fahd sat at the head of the room. Beside him was his half-brother Abdullah, now crown prince, an independent-minded man who prided himself on his warm relations with Saudi Arabia's northern desert tribes. Several other princes and a Saudi general formed a row down one side of the room. Prince Bandar Bin Sultan, the ambassador to the United States, hovered near the king, prepared to interpret between English and Arabic. As the discussion began, Schwarzkopf kneeled on the floor to review satellite photos that showed Iraqi troop dispositions near Saudi Arabia; some of Saddam's units, the general pointed out, were patrolling as deeply as twenty-five kilometers inside the kingdom's sovereign territory.[1]

Fahd's government had showered Saddam with subsidies during the Iran-Iraq war of the 1980s—as much as $26 billion, by Fahd's account, a tilt encouraged by the United States in its attempt to contain revolutionary Iran. All that cash had now proved to be a gossamer defense. Equally, the billions spent by the Saudi royal family on British fighter aircraft and weapons systems in the Al-Yamamah deal (which channeled hundreds of millions of dollars in fees each year to Bandar's Washington bank accounts) had proved worthless; Saudi Arabia lacked the manpower (an army of 70,000, in comparison to Iraqi forces numbering about 2 million) and skill to even blunt, never mind defeat, an Iraqi invasion. Saddam's incursion into Kuwait had starkly exposed the Al-Saud as rulers of a country that lacked the trained population, industrial strength, and military rigor to protect its treasure of hydrocarbons. Cheney said the United States could do the job, but its troops would have to deploy quickly and in large numbers. He promised that American forces would leave Saudi Arabia as soon as the crisis passed, or whenever Fahd ordered them to go. For his part, Fahd said that if the Americans were to deploy to the kingdom, he wanted large numbers and a serious operation. The security bargain that had long lain just below the surface of the U.S.-Saudi relationship, managed as discreetly as possible so that it would not embarrass the Al-Saud before their xenophobic people, had now been pulled into the open for all to see. America was the guarantor of Saudi Arabia's independent existence; without that guarantee, the peninsula was vulnerable to any marauder bold or foolish enough to take it—as had been the case for centuries before the Second World War, when Arabia held no great prize but was periodically conquered nonetheless.

Fahd spoke to Abdullah in Arabic. Bandar stopped interpreting, but Chas Freeman, the Arabic-speaking U.S. ambassador to Saudi Arabia, followed their exchange.

"Don't you think there should be some consultation?" Abdullah asked, referring to the religious scholars and tribal leaders who would surely resent the arrival of hundreds of thousands of Christian and Jewish soldiers to defend the kingdom.

"There's no time," Fahd said, as Freeman recalled it. "If we delay, we may end up like Kuwait. There is no Kuwait anymore."

"Yes, there's a Kuwait," Abdullah said. "There is a Kuwait."

"Yes, and its territory consists of hotel rooms in Cairo and Paris and London," said Fahd.

"I take your point," said Abdullah.

Fahd turned away from his half-brother and faced Cheney. "Okay," he said simply.[2]

American fighter jets and military transport planes thundered onto Dhahran's airfields within twenty-four hours, but throughout August, American commanders later acknowledged, their intervention was something of a bluff; if Saddam had poured south from Kuwait with all his forces, he would have certainly been able to occupy some Saudi oil fields, at least temporarily. For several weeks, the kingdom's fate seemed uncertain.

Awkwardly, Fahd tried to consult with Islamic scholars and tribal leaders, even though it was plain that his decision to rely on Washington for rescue was irreversible. On August 14, the kingdom's blind grand mufti, Sheikh Bin Baz, issued a fatwa officially blessing the arrival of non-Muslim troops as necessary and permissible under Islamic law. It was a document no more convincing than the sheikh's pronouncements years earlier about Earth's place at the center of the solar system. Even Saudis who supported Fahd's decision could see, as Osama Bin Laden put it later, that the royal family was manipulating its salaried religious leaders "to increase its legitimacy" at a moment of crisis. The Bin Baz decree was particularly offensive, not least because it "insulted the intelligence of Muslims."[3]

Osama was certainly among those who were outraged, but his later ridicule of Fahd and Bin Baz belied the complexity of his actions and thinking at the time. He was a Bin Laden and still very much a creature of the Saudi government. He offered no public dissent that summer. Rather, he moved quickly with the rest of his family to protect his personal fortune against the possibility that the Al-Saud regime might collapse. Just as the Americans had been hedging for years against a crisis of this kind, so had the Bin Ladens. For them, too, it was a moment for decisive action, and Osama was a full participant in the family's program of self-insurance.

Omar and Haider Bin Laden flew to Geneva to confer with Yeslam about how to shift more of the family's money to the safety of the Swiss banking system. The Bin Ladens had previously established accounts in a Swiss bank for a family foundation; the purpose of this foundation, established by Mohamed Bin Laden, remains unclear, but its Swiss account may have been a hard currency vehicle for overseas charity or inheritance transfers. With Yeslam's assistance, the brothers now decided to close and liquidate that foundation, and to open a master account at a new bank, the Swiss Bank Corporation. On August 17, Omar, Haider, and Yeslam signed documents at the bank's offices in Geneva to create sub-accounts for virtually all of Mohamed Bin Laden's children. As Omar put it later: "Sub-accounts were set up for the benefit of each of more than fifty heirs of Mohammad Binladin, including one sub-account on behalf of Osama, and these sub-accounts were funded . . . with a portion of the legal inheritance of each heir." The accounts were created, Omar acknowledged, "in response to Saddam Hussein's invasion of Kuwait."[4]

On Osama's behalf, Omar and Haider signed a "Declaration on opening an account or securities account," as required by Swiss law. The two formally declared "as holder of the account" that "the beneficial owner of the assets to be deposited with the bank" was "Mr. Osama M. Binladin." Someone handwrote Osama's name into the appropriate blank. On the second page they chose the foreign currency to be used in Osama's account: "U.S. $."

A second form, signed the same day, provided "full Power of

Attorney" to Yeslam over the account; here the beneficiary was hand-written as "Sheikh Osama Mohamed BINLADIN." The bank's account form offered a choice between a kind of authority that would require Osama and Yeslam to sign all documents jointly, or one where either Yeslam or Osama would be authorized "to act severally and by their sole signature." This latter was the approach they chose—Yeslam would be empowered to control money in the account on his own signature, without written approval from Osama. It was a sign of the coherence and confidence that persisted within the family, even amid the strains occasionally produced by Yeslam's withdrawal to Geneva.

On August 20, Osama's account was funded with a deposit of $450,000—a modest portion of his inheritance, but a comfortable hedge against sudden disaster in the kingdom. That sum immediately began to earn interest at a rate of about $2,500 per month; the amount of monthly interest would vary with market rates.[5]

In his later sermons, Osama equated interest-paying banking practices with usury, and he denounced them as stark violations of Islamic law. Usury, he once observed, "has been forbidden by all the religions," yet in the United States, "you build your economy and investments on usury. As a result of this, in all their different forms and guises, the Jews have taken control of your economy."[6] That summer, however, amid his family's panic, Osama showed no reluctance to earn interest—indeed, in his Swiss Bank Corporation account, he would soon take down more interest in a year than many Americans earned in annual salaries. It was a striking instance of his capacity for hypocrisy—and telling that it involved money.

THERE ARE credible accounts that Osama predicted Saddam's invasion of Kuwait before it occurred. His high school–era friend Khaled Batarfi recalled listening to him speak at an informal luncheon *diwaniyah* gathering at the home of a wealthy businessman in Mecca early in 1990, when

Arab news media were full of stories about Saddam's buildup of troops on Kuwait's borders and his bellicose claims to Kuwaiti territory. Osama urged that Saudis begin to train themselves to fight Saddam, as he and his followers had done in Afghanistan. He told an illustrative story, the thrust of which was, as Batarfi paraphrased it:

> You are sophisticated, you are an engineer, you are a doctor, and suppose you send [your children] to a good school. But it is a tough neighborhood, and there are other kids who are street smart and very tough. Then your neighbor comes to you and says, "Lend me money or I will send my kids after your kids." You know he is never going to pay the money back. There is a limit to what you can give him. So it's about time that you train your kids because you are going to have stand up eventually. Saddam has all these tough kids. He has these soldiers who are poor, unemployed, they are motivated and tough. I'm saying, Let us take advantage of our training in Afghanistan. We have gotten tough. But we have to get ready. We have to go to camps now. We have to get tough now. Otherwise, King Fahd won't be ready.[7]

This was certainly Osama's sense of himself in 1990: An international Islamic guerrilla leader who worked in service of his king—someone so loyal to the Al-Saud that he even tried to think ahead on their behalf. Nor were Iraq and Afghanistan the only frontiers where Osama imagined that he played this role.

Even before his return to Saudi Arabia in late 1989, he had provided money to support Islamist rebels fighting against the weakening communist government of South Yemen, the half of divided Yemen that controlled the Bin Laden family homeland in the Hadhramawt. The political and religious equation in Yemen as the Cold War ended was very complex. Ali Abdullah Saleh, an army officer and Sanhan tribesman who had come to power in a coup, led North Yemen; he received some support from Saudi Arabia—primarily because he was not a communist—

but his relationship with the Al-Saud was not smooth. He did, however, share Saudi Arabia's antipathy toward South Yemen's Soviet-backed regime. As global communism teetered during 1989, confronted by democratic rebellions from China to Europe, South Yemen's government looked vulnerable. From Afghanistan, where he had become close to a number of Yemeni volunteers to that war, Osama saw an opportunity to extend his achievements in jihad. South Yemen's leftist government had stripped a number of previously elite families of land and privileges, particularly in the Abyan Governate, and during the 1980s, some younger members of these families had turned to international radical Islam as an ideology of resistance. One of the Abyan leaders, Tariq Hasan Al-Fadli, founded a group called Al-Jihad. Al-Fadli said later that his South Yemen group "did have external support . . . through the grace of Almighty God and our venerable Sheikh Osama Bin Laden, may God protect him . . . He funded everything." Bin Laden supported other Yemeni Islamists as well.[8]

As had been true of the anti-Soviet war in Afghanistan, Islamist violence in South Yemen advanced both the statecraft interests of the Saudi government and the looser ideology of Bin Laden and his allies. Indeed, Osama may have started his jihad project in South Yemen with encouragement or even direct support from Saudi intelligence, in the same way that he had worked in Afghanistan. Richard Clarke, who later directed counterterrorism programs in the Clinton White House, has written that Prince Turki Al-Faisal "had reportedly asked" Osama "to organize a fundamentalist religion-based resistance to the communist-style regime" in South Yemen. Turki has described the matter differently than Clarke, however; he has said that Osama "came to see me with a proposal" to foment rebellion in South Yemen, and that "I advised him at the time that that was not an acceptable idea."[9]

Whatever the truth, the geopolitical equation changed during the first six months of 1990 in a way that led Riyadh to renounce support for violent rebellion in Yemen. The fall of the Berlin Wall led to Yemen's peaceful reunification and the formal end of the South Yemen state. On May 22, 1990, Ali Abdullah Saleh became president of a united Yemen; as part of the bargain, he tried to co-opt and calm Islamist groups that had previously waged jihad. Osama and other radicals, however, did not see the virtue in this deal, or in a national government that incorporated former communists, and they persisted with their preaching and organizing. According to Ahmed Badeeb, Turki's chief of staff, Saleh eventually called King Fahd to complain. The Saudi government responded by pressuring Osama to quiet himself, and by one account, during the late spring or early summer of 1990, the government raided a Bin Laden family farm that Osama was using to support his Yemen project. Afterward, Osama reportedly wrote an angry letter of protest to Crown Prince Abdullah.[10]

This fracture in Osama's alignment with Saudi foreign policy coincided with his rising irritation, during the autumn of 1990, over Fahd's plan to employ American-led troops in a war to oust Saddam's forces from Kuwait. Increasingly Osama conveyed a presumptuous attitude to the Saudi officials with whom he met. He employed bodyguards. He wrote a sixty-page paper laying out his idea to recruit and lead his Afghan-trained *mujaheddin* on a campaign to expel Saddam from Kuwait and save King Fahd from the dark conspiracies of the American occupation troops. He said it would be dangerous for Saudi Arabia to allow Christian troops to fight its wars. He sought a meeting with Fahd but was deflected to other Saudi officials, including a high-ranking prince at the defense ministry—this person has never been clearly identified, but it appears to have been either Abdul-Rahman bin Abdulaziz, a full brother of the king, or Khalid Bin Sultan, the influential son of the defense minister.[11] Osama also met with Ahmed bin Abdulaziz, Salem's longtime contact, number two at the interior ministry. Osama later described what happened:

I directed my advice straight to the deputy Minister of Defense, informing him of the great sins from which the state should desist, and of the danger of persisting with them, but to no avail. Then I met the deputy director of the ministry for security affairs, who strongly reproached me for advising the deputy Minister of Defense and began haranguing me about exactly the same sins that I had mentioned to the minister. Then he said: "This is well known—we don't need anyone to tell us about it."[12]

His proposals about the coming war in Kuwait annoyed the Saudi government, but they were inconsequential. It seems, instead, to have been his persistent preaching and contact with jihadis in Yemen that eventually led the interior ministry to seize his passport during the winter of 1990–1991. As Prince Turki put it, speaking of his conversations with Osama about jihad in Yemen: "This shy, retiring and seemingly very reticent person had changed."[13]

Osama believed—and said repeatedly—that he was working for the true interests of the Saudi royal family, not against them. His older half-brothers, however, particularly Omar and Bakr, interpreted this long-standing family mandate of fealty quite differently after Saddam's invasion of Kuwait.

Around this time, Bakr got to know Chas Freeman, the U.S. ambassador to Saudi Arabia; Freeman occasionally took private soundings from prominent businessmen in Jeddah. Buoyed by these contacts, in the autumn of 1990, Bakr and Omar led the Saudi Bin Laden Group (in which Osama was a shareholder) to sign contracts with the United States Army to build facilities that would support the U.S. troop presence and the coming war with Iraq. Between September 30 and November 7, the Saudi Bin Laden Group constructed a heliport at the King Abdulaziz Air Base "in support of the United States Army deployed on Operation Desert Shield," according to a "Certificate of Achievement" later issued by Major General William G. Pagonis of the U.S. Army Central Support

Command. Pagonis recognized one Bin Laden executive for his "personal contribution" to the "most successful logistical deployment in support of a combat victory in military history . . . We are proud of your accomplishments and humbled by your sacrifices. We salute and thank you." Bin Laden Telecommunications installed systems for the United States Central Command and the 35th Signal Brigade of the U.S.; its executives were awarded certificates of thanks signed by General Norman Schwarzkopf. They had provided, Schwarzkopf affirmed, "outstanding support" of the American war effort. The Bin Ladens also undertook a project to improve a twelve-hundred-kilometer desert highway "so that U.S. troops could move easily and safely to and from the northern regions of Saudi Arabia," as Omar Bin Laden put it later; Omar personally oversaw the work. Osama surely knew about these construction projects, from which he profited as a shareholder and dividend recipient; he was in the kingdom throughout this period, although he also apparently traveled back and forth to Yemen.[14]

As with the interest accumulating in his Swiss bank account, there is no evidence that he was burdened by pangs of conscience over the profits he earned from his family's wartime work for the Americans, even as he lectured in the Bin Laden mosque near Kilo 7 and denounced American foreign policy. He was flirting with rebellion but was unable yet to embrace it fully. He postured as a dissenter but he avoided the most serious risks. His views were nuanced, changeable, and laced with contradictions.

THE ARRIVAL OF American soldiers in the kingdom in late 1990, at a time when democratic revolutions were erupting worldwide, provoked the most vigorous and open debate about political freedom and identity in Saudi Arabia since the Nasser period. Urban liberals, particularly women, seized upon this seeming Riyadh Spring. In November, forty-seven women attracted worldwide attention—and shocked many

Saudis—by staging a protest in which they climbed into automobiles in Riyadh and drove through the city in open violation of the kingdom's ban on female drivers. In early 1991, forty-three liberal-leaning businessmen, journalists, university professors, and former government officials signed a petition to King Fahd asking for ten political reforms. It was a relatively timid list and stopped far short of demands for a democratic order, but in Saudi terms, it was bold: the petition sought new councils to widen political participation, reform of the religious police, and "greater participation of women in public life, within the scope of the *sharia*."[15]

This modest liberal uprising confirmed the deep-seated fears of Saudi Islamists that the royal family's alliance with America, and particularly its decision to invite American troops into the kingdom, would become a lever for a top-down push by the Al-Saud toward a more secular society. Widely circulated underground tape-recorded sermons and lectures voiced these hysterical warnings throughout that autumn and winter. Two conservative university professors, Safar Al-Hawali and Salman Al-Awda, issued particularly fiery speeches arguing that the kingdom's real enemy was not Iraq, but the West. Another influential voice belonged to Awad Al-Qarni, author of a 1987 book titled *Modernity on the Scale of Islam*, which insisted the royal family and its secular allies were promoting alternative forms of national identity that undermined the Koran. The conservative ferment intensified after the women's driving protest; Islamist leaflets listed the female drivers by name, as well as the names of their husbands, and denounced the women as "communist whores."[16]

The Islamists also gathered signatures for their own petition to King Fahd demanding political reforms. They shared the liberals' desire for greater participation but crafted an agenda to direct reforms toward even stricter adherence to Islamic law.

Abdulaziz Al-Gasim, a conservative judge in the sharia courts and a leader of the Islamist petition drive, who would later go to prison, sought out Osama Bin Laden in Jeddah in early 1991 to persuade him to add his signature to the cause. As the son of a Hadhrami immigrant with no formal education in Islam, Osama was not a significant figure in the Saudi world of dissident Islamist scholarship, but his martial reputation as a *mujaheddin* leader in Afghanistan and his membership in a prominent merchant family made him a potentially attractive fellow traveler. "He apologized and refused to sign," Al-Gasim recalled. "He said he was very busy with Afghanistan and Yemen. He was supporting the ideas [in the petition draft] but he didn't want any conflict with the Saudi government and lose support for his activities. He didn't want to start another war. He was not convinced that these goals could be achieved in a peaceful way."[17] Some Islamists in Saudi Arabia, justifying their meek resistance to corrupt governance by the royal family, had long cited their desire to avoid fomenting *fitna*, or Koranically undesirable internal division within the Islamic community; Osama relied upon the same rationale that winter.

One night, Osama joined a rooftop dinner meeting in Jeddah where exiled Kuwaiti guests talked about their travails and asked for support, recalled Jamal Khashoggi, who attended. When his turn came to speak, Osama voiced a fear that America had a secret plan to use its presence in Saudi Arabia to "secularize Saudi Arabia, and to make a dramatic change in its regime or the way it ruled by imposing a president and ministers who are secular," as Khashoggi recalled it. Osama specifically named Ghazi Al-Ghosaibi, the suit-and-tie-clad Saudi ambassador to Great Britain, as a candidate for this imposed leadership. Al-Ghosaibi, Osama predicted, would reform curriculums in school to spread secular ideas, "encourage women to take off their *hejab*," and "spread corruption through arts and opening up society." By Khashoggi's account, Osama concluded his remarks with a warning:

Be aware. Be careful. We have to be united and rally around the Saudi leadership in order not to be weak against this determined secular campaign, that is no doubt coming with American support, that already has some people and some agents—a fifth column in Saudi Arabia. There are a lot of Saudis who are ready to serve the American alienation project, which will alienate Saudis from their religion.[18]

In one sense, Osama's views remained as they had been since he was fourteen: where Muslims live, they should aspire to a pure society based upon Islamic principles. He remained deeply unsettled, however, about how to chase this ideal within Saudi Arabia. The presence of American troops and presumed secular conspiracies worried him, but his faith in the Al-Saud and his own family restrained him. In communist-influenced lands, such as Syria, South Yemen, and Afghanistan, violent jihad could be embraced because it seemed the only alternative. In Saudi Arabia, the situation looked more complicated. Among other things, Osama continued to accept the essential claim of the Al-Saud that they were righteous and legitimate guardians of Islam's birthplace—the claim from which the Bin Laden fortune was derived.

THE SWIFT and overwhelming rout of Iraqi forces from Kuwait by American-led coalition troops infused King Fahd and the royal family with pride, relief, and confidence. Fahd exacted immediate revenge against those Arab governments and entities that had supported Saddam—particularly Jordan, the Palestinian Authority, and Yemen. Tens of thousands of Palestinian and Yemeni workers were expelled from the kingdom. On the domestic front, amid the general sense of relief that accompanied the war's end, Fahd seemed to have a divided mind; he thought some mild political reforms might assuage his subjects, but he and his brothers also sought to ensure that wartime ferment did not lead to postwar revolution. As the weeks passed after Iraq's surrender, petitioners on both the left and right were fired from their jobs, and some were imprisoned. To all of those who had doubted or needled Saudi

Arabia in its season of crisis, the royal family offered an unmistakable message: we are back with a vengeance.

Osama Bin Laden left the kingdom on May 1, 1991, by his own account, less than two months after the end of the war. The circumstances surrounding his departure remain somewhat unclear. He was not forced out, according to Bakr Bin Laden. Through one of his half-brothers—apparently not Bakr—Osama pleaded to the interior ministry that he needed a one-time exit visa to travel to Pakistan to liquidate investments there. The best evidence suggests that he was genuinely uncertain of his plans—that he wanted to reunite with the Al Qaeda followers he had left in Afghanistan but was ambivalent about returning to the Afghan civil war. While in Jeddah during the war, Bin Laden had dispatched followers from Afghanistan to Sudan to rent farms and guesthouses there. Later, using a donation from an Egyptian lawyer, he bought a farm north of Khartoum for $250,000, according to a Sudanese aide. During the same period, according to Khalil A. Khalil, who tracked Islamists for the Saudi government, Osama "spent some time trying to find a tribe" in Yemen "where he could marry a daughter and win the tribe's allegiance. He worked on this for about eighteen months to establish himself—first in a social context, then to bring his fighters to the south of Yemen . . . There was speculation that he had weapons in the United Arab Emirates and also investments and businesses there. The framework he was exploring was Yemen first, for the jihad army, and UAE as a base for media and economic activities."[19]

Osama's motivations are easier to document than his particular logistical plans. The harassment he faced from Saudi officials over his Yemeni organizing, and the humiliation he felt over their rejection of his wartime advice, left him burning with a desire to be free of the kingdom's stifling repression, to re-create the independence and prestige he had enjoyed during his late years in Afghanistan—preferably without the constant exposure to gunfire, however. He was as exhausted in his own way

by the narrowness of Saudi political culture as were the more secular
members of his family who decamped periodically to Los Angeles or
Orlando or Paris to enjoy some breathing space. As Osama later described his passage into exile during that spring of 1991:

> The Saudi regime imposed on the people a life that does not appeal to
> the free believer. They wanted the people to eat and drink and sing the
> praise of God, but if the people wanted to encourage what is right and
> forbid what is wrong, they could not. Rather, the regime dismisses them
> from their jobs and in the event the people continue to do so, they are
> detained in prisons. I refused to live this submissive life, which is not be-
> fitting of man, let alone a believer. So I waited for the chance when God
> made it possible for me to leave Saudi Arabia.[20]

How did Bakr and his half-brothers regard his departure? The evidence is thin, but it nonetheless makes plain that as Osama left the kingdom, his family made no effort to exclude him from access to his own
money or from participation in new family investments. In July 1991, for
example, Yves Bruderlein, a Swiss lawyer with offices in Geneva, formed
a Cayman Islands company called Cambridge Engineering "to make
and hold investments," particularly "in hedge fund products offered by
major financial institutions, including Deutsche Bank." According to
Bruderlein, Cambridge was "indirectly owned" by the Saudi Bin Laden
Group, and Bakr Bin Laden had signing power at the firm. The Saudi Bin
Laden Group chose the Cayman Islands as its place of organization
"based on the advice of their attorneys," he said later. Its Swiss directors
received "our instructions solely from the Saudi Bin Laden Group." In
the initial period after the formation of Cambridge Engineering,
Bruderlein and other Swiss directors never had contact with Osama, but
nonetheless, Bruderlein said he was aware that Osama was "part of the
Saudi Bin Laden Group" and thus a participant in the hedge fund investments.[21]

Bakr said later that he "never intervened" with anyone in the Saudi government to help Osama leave the kingdom, "nor was I aware at that time of any involvement by Osama in terrorist activities of any kind."[22] He was, he suggests, passive and accepting of Osama's decision. The broader credibility of his assertion may depend in part, of course, on the definition of "terrorist activities." Al Qaeda had been founded three years earlier. Its volunteers still participated in the Afghan civil war; others fought in Yemen or evaded capture by the Egyptian security services from which they had fled. Whether some or all of this violence consti- tuted terrorism lay to some extent in the eye of the beholder. It is also uncertain how much Bakr knew about these militias or Osama's in- volvement with them.

The Bin Ladens continued to facilitate financial transfers to Osama. On October 28, 1991, a sum of $482,034.37—his original deposit, plus ac- crued interest, less banking fees—was transferred out of Osama's sub- account at the Swiss Bank Corporation in Geneva to the custody of his half-brother Haider. The transfer occurred during a period when other subaccount holders among Mohamed's children were taking full control of their own Swiss accounts, now that the war crisis had passed. Osama apparently decided to reorganize his banking within the Islamic world. What became of his dollar deposit after it reached his half-brother Haider is unknown, but there is no indication that it was withheld from Osama. Nor is there any indication that it was used to facilitate terror- ism. The transfer marks Osama's last known use of the Western banking system.[23] With a stubborn attitude, but without a coherent plan, he passed into a new life of voluntary exile. His circumstances were more compli- cated than those of his grandfather Awadh, whose flight from debt almost a century earlier had ultimately birthed the family fortune, but Osama's instinct was the same: he had no choice, he felt, but to start again.

28. A ROLLS-ROYCE IN THE RAIN

I BRAHIM AND CHRISTINE BIN LADEN formally separated on November 22, 1991, after almost five years of marriage. They had a two-year-old daughter, Sibba; Christine moved with her into a Los Angeles–area duplex apartment. She hired divorce lawyers. In February they filed papers in Los Angeles County Superior Court seeking a temporary restraining order against Ibrahim; Christine feared, she wrote in a declaration, that her husband "may become angry with me" over her decision to leave their marriage "and may retaliate by taking my daughter with him to Saudi Arabia."

Christine was then thirty-one years old, about five years younger than her husband. She told the court of her "desperate financial situation." It was a sort of desperation, however, that was peculiar to the west side of Los Angeles. "For many years during the marriage, Ibrahim provided me with a monthly allowance of approximately $15,000," she reported. Yet for January and February of 1992, following their separation, he had provided her only $5,000, which was "woefully inadequate." She had no income apart from Ibrahim's support. Because of her husband's sudden parsimony, she wrote, "our lifestyle has been changed and our living conditions are substandard to those which we had during marriage." She explained to the court:

Ibrahim, my daughter and I lived in our Bel Air mansion at 634 Stone Canyon Road. This was a 7,000 square foot house, on three acres of property, with a seven car garage. The house is presently worth between $8–$10 million dollars. We employed full-time groundskeepers, household help, chauffeurs, and enjoyed private security. We had many cars, two of which were Rolls-Royces. Ibrahim would take my daughter and I on frequent vacation trips. We always flew First Class or on one of the private family jets. We would spend a month at a time traveling in Europe, or skiing in Switzerland, or short trips to Hawaii. This lifestyle also supported me making trips to New York, to go shopping, the opera and the theater. Last year Ibrahim let me buy a $16,000 fur coat on a shopping trip.

Christine inventoried the considerable investments she had made in education and other forms of self-improvement, such as the $3,250 she had recently spent on cosmetic surgery, as well as additional sums on manicures, pedicures, waxing, hair coloring, and haircuts. She had enrolled in private needlepoint classes and took private lessons in English horseback riding, painting, watercolors, sculpture, and Arabic. It was "not uncommon" for her to spend $3,500 on a dress. Ibrahim bought her "furs, jewelry, a $30,000 watch," and a $90,000 diamond wedding ring. She purchased a Steinway piano for their Bel Air home, and they "always ate at the best restaurants," such as Spago and Morton's.

Not that the issues all revolved around her: Christine reported that she also typically spent $3,000 per month on Sibba's and her clothing. It cost her several hundred dollars per month just to buy birthday presents adequate for Sibba to give to her Bel Air toddler friends at parties. The Bin Ladens, she added, did not shirk when it came to their own parties for children. In Jeddah, the previous September, she had spent $7,000 on a party for Sibba that included "a monkey, the rental of five horses, a hot air balloon, a private disc jockey, a photographer and catering, decoration and gifts for our guests."

Christine did not wish to create the impression that she had built this lifestyle on her own. Ibrahim, she reported, also lived well. For example:

He has flown us to Switzerland just for the weekend to see a car show. He has numerous cars: Two Rolls-Royces, a Honda, a Lexus, a Mercedes 500 SEL and a Lamborghini jeep. Ibrahim will, at times, rent a Mercedes at $350 a day so that he does not have to drive his Rolls-Royce in the rain.

His passion for his cars had left her with some resentment. In particular, when she became pregnant with Sibba, Ibrahim had promised "to buy me a Rolls-Royce of my own; however, I only received a Limited Edition Jeep Cherokee." She expected better of him. He was, after all, involved in construction in Saudi Arabia of the two Holy Mosques, airports, highways, military bases, royal palaces, and other large development projects.

The Bin Laden family is worth in excess of $2 billion dollars. This organization employs 17,000 people and has substantial real estate holdings. This family organization also owns a fleet of 8–9 airplanes, with a full staff of pilots and stewardesses. The family just recently purchased a G-4 Aircraft worth approximately $25 million, and a new Learjet.

Christine's declaration offered a hint about how she might be assuaged now that she and Ibrahim were destined for divorce. She had found her previous personal allowance of $15,000 per month, she noted in her court filing, to be "adequate."[1]

THEY HAD MET in Beverly Hills during the mid-1980s, according to Jack Kayajanian, one of Christine's attorneys. Ibrahim was in the company of Dodi Fayed, who later died in a Paris automobile accident with Princess Diana of Wales. (Fayed was the son of a wealthy Egyptian businessman, Mohamed Fayed, who purchased control of Harrods department store in London and the Hotel Ritz in Paris, where members of the Bin Laden family frequently stayed.) Christine Hartunian, as she was then, was a daughter of an Armenian Christian businessman who lived in Orange County, California. At twenty-five, Christine relied upon her father for financial support and had never earned enough money at a job to have filed a tax return. She was tall, slender, dark, and beautiful—"a very attractive, very flashy young lady," as another of her attorneys, Michael Balaban, recalled. One of her favorite nightspots was the Denim and Diamonds bar in Santa Monica, then a fashionable urban cowboy watering hole with a sparkling globe above the dance floor and stuffed heads of moose and deer mounted on the walls.[2]

As Balaban got to know Christine, he found that she seemed to drop the names of a number of celebrities, suggesting that they were her friends. Balaban thought she was "full of crap," as he put it later. One day, however, he was meeting with his client in his Los Angeles office. A partner of Balaban's represented Paul McCartney, the former Beatle, on a copyright matter, and McCartney happened to be in the law firm's waiting room. Christine stepped into the corridor; McCartney saw her and exclaimed, "Christine! How the hell are you?" As Balaban said later: "You don't forget things like that. She knew what the hell she was doing."[3]

Ibrahim Bin Laden was not batting in the same league. He was the youngest full brother of Yeslam and Khalil. He had followed them to Los Angeles and attended the University of Southern California for a year, but he did not share his older brothers' interest in business. He seemed content to drift along on his dividend payments. One of the Americans who occasionally joined him on the L.A. nightclub circuit recalled an evening at a restaurant in Beverly Hills when several of the Bin Laden brothers had come into town and gathered for dinner. It was around the time when Ibrahim fell for Christine. The Bin Laden brothers had a ritual, the American recalled: when the restaurant bill arrived, they would wrestle for control of the check, each more determined than the next to perform the role of host and patron. Ibrahim was the only brother present who did not seem interested in this performance. "In the end, my father is going to pay for this," he explained. Another time, this person recalled, Ibrahim said he did not see the point of working as an executive in the family business. They could never surpass their father's financial achievements. They had more than enough money. What was the point of striving so hard?[4]

Ibrahim was devout. Christine regarded herself as a Christian, without allegiance to any particular denomination, but as she and Ibrahim talked about marrying, she agreed to convert to Islam. There would be no other way to live comfortably as a member of the Bin Laden family. As their wedding neared, however, the couple negotiated over how to synthesize—in the form of a written prenuptial contract—the imperatives of his upbringing in Saudi Arabia with those of her upbringing in Southern California.

A Los Angeles–area attorney, Robert Shahin, drafted a proposed agreement, titled "Antenuptial Agreement Submitting Marriage to Islamic Law." It was an extraordinary document, one that attempted to ensure that Ibrahim was protected by Saudi laws governing child custody and inheritance issues, in exchange for his pledge to Christine to forswear his right under Islamic law to take more than one wife. A draft copy was later filed in court.

It began:

> Whereas the Bridegroom and Bride anticipate moving from time to time from various parts of the world to others . . . The parties agree as follows:
> 1) Islamic Faith. Both the Bridegroom and Bride shall be practicing Muslims during the marriage and the children of their marriage shall be raised as Muslims . . .
> 2) Islamic Law Controls. All incidents of the marriage shall be governed by Islamic law, except as modified herein . . .
> 3) Only One Wife. The Bridegroom hereby waives his right during this marriage to have more than one lawful wife.
> 4) *Mahr* (Dowry to Bride). The Bridegroom hereby pledges a $_____ dowry to the Bride, as her sole and separate prop-

erty ... In the event of divorce, the Bridegroom shall pay the Bride
another $_____ ...

The draft required Christine to give up her rights under California's
laws governing community property; Ibrahim pledged "under Islamic
law" to support any children born to them. A provision captioned
"Equalizing Grounds for Divorce" noted that under Islamic law, Ibrahim
could initiate a divorce virtually at will, while Christine's grounds for divorce were more circumscribed. Therefore, "The Bridegroom hereby
agrees that he will take steps to terminate the marriage upon the Bride's
request if irreconcilable differences arise between them." In the event of
divorce, Ibrahim "shall have custody of the children after their infancy,
as defined by Islamic law."[5]

Christine later said that she and Ibrahim "never could agree" about
all the points in the draft prenuptial contract. They decided to marry anyway. "We were supposed to sign it after the marriage and we still never
agreed," she said later. "So it was never signed."[6]

Their wedding took place at the Beverly Hills Hotel. The betrothal
ceremony consecrated their union under Islamic law. Visiting Bin Laden
family members and other guests lodged overnight in the hotel's pink
stucco bungalows "and the wine and champagne flowed throughout the
evening," recalled Robert Freeman, one of those who attended. Half-
siblings such as Shafiq and Huda were among those in attendance. Salem
was still alive—the wedding took place in January 1987—and he presided
over the reception dinner with his usual songs and jokey monologues.
Christine was "a beautiful bride," Freeman later wrote. Her dress molded
itself tightly around her hourglass figure and spread out in circular
drapes around her ankles. "Her long beautiful flowing red tresses mesmerized the guests ... The top florists must have worked into the night
preparing the stupendous array of beautiful blooms throughout the hotel.
It was an unbelievable sight!"[7]

After their honeymoon, the couple moved into the mansion on Stone

Canyon, across from the Riviera Country Club. Sibba arrived in January 1989. As they had planned, they divided their time between Bel Air and Jeddah. Christine found it difficult to be away from her mother, who lived in California, and to share space with the larger Bin Laden family at Kilo 7, Ibrahim later said. To please her, he said, he bought beachfront land beside the Red Sea and broke ground on what would become a seaside estate worth about $3 million.

It was not long, however, before their marriage slipped into difficulty. Their quarrels persisted, and finally, late in 1991, Christine decided to move out of the Bel Air house and take Sibba with her. Ibrahim hired his own lawyers after she sued for divorce. As his brother Khalil had learned in 1990, when America in Motion had its troubles, Ibrahim was about to discover that American attorneys, once loosed, could rattle even a mellow man's serenity.

"DO YOU KNOW what your assets are worth?"

"No."

"Do you have any idea what your assets are worth?"

"No."

Ibrahim sat in a Los Angeles conference room in the summer of 1992, answering deposition questions from Christine's attorneys. The couple now seemed to be headed for a full-blown Los Angeles divorce trial; among other issues, lawyers for the two sides argued over how much income Ibrahim received, how his fortune might be valued, and what part of it Christine and Sibba might tap as alimony and child support. Christine's lawyers found Ibrahim elusive on the subject of money. He said it was just not something he worried about or understood in any detail.

"Have you made any attempt to find out what your assets are worth?"

"Yes . . . I talked to my brothers who run the company. Nobody—nobody knows."

"Which brothers did you talk to?"

"I talked to Yehia . . . Y-e-h-i-a . . ."

"Where is Yehia located?"

"Saudi Arabia."

"What did you ask him?"

"How much each of them worth. How much each of—each one of us worth."

"And what did he say?"

"It is hard to tell. He doesn't know."

"Did you tell him you needed to have the information to file with the Court in the United States?"

"No. I told that to my brother Khalil, and he told him."

"And what happened?"

"Nobody knows. They don't know."

". . . Mr. Bin Laden, other than what you have already stated, what attempts have you made to ascertain what your net worth is?"

"Just pick up the phone, and I talk to my brother, and to my knowledge, you see, I don't know the work. I don't work with them. I don't know what they have, so what they send me, I assume that is what they—that is what they sent. I don't know . . ."

"Do you know what your income is on a yearly basis?"

"It goes up and down. It is—it depends on the job we get. It is not like a salary, so I don't know."

"What do you mean, it depends on the job you get?"

"Like if the organization this year have jobs from the government, we have more roads. If we are doing good the profit will go up. If we don't do good or if we don't have a job, there is no profits."

"What was your income for 1991?"

"I don't know."

"What has been your income so far in 1992?"

"The what?"

"What has been your income so far in 1992?"

"I have no idea."

Michael Balaban and Christine's other lawyers had particular difficulty believing that Ibrahim did not work at all, as he claimed, and, indeed, had never worked a day in his life. Under California divorce law, it was in Ibrahim's interest to maintain during court proceedings that he did not receive any salary during the period of their marriage; if his income derived from assets he owned before he met Christine, it might be harder for her to win a large settlement.

"Do you know any of your brothers who don't work at some job?" Balaban asked Ibrahim at one point during his deposition.

"Period—they don't work at all, you mean?" Ibrahim asked.

"Exactly."

"Yes."

"Which ones?"

"Myself . . ."

"Well, give me a number, and then we will identify them."

"Myself. Abdullah. Mohammed. Shafig . . . Abdullah Aziz . . . and some I don't keep in contact with. I don't know if they work or not."

Balaban asked about his purchase of his Bel Air mansion during the early 1980s, before he met Christine; the price of the estate had been just over $2 million.

"How much cash did you pay?"

"I don't remember, but some—around one million cash . . . No. More than that. I paid, maybe, one mill, six hundred."

"Thousand?"

"Yeah, dollars."

"Okay, so one million, six hundred thousand dollars?"

"Yes."

"Where did you get the cash?"

"From Saudi Arabia, from my brother, Yeslam."

"Was that a loan?"

"No. He sold some of my stocks."

". . . And whose name was the house put in?"

"My brother in—my brother's name."

"Which brother?"

"Yeslam."

"Why?"

"Because they told me if I put the house under my name, and then here, I have to pay income taxes if I own something."

"Who told you that?"

"Some of my friends."[8]

On and on it went, the lawyers probing, Ibrahim responding in a tone of genial indolence. Following the depositions, as their trial date steadily approached, the estranged couple filed dueling declarations about the collapse of their marriage and their daughter's best interests.

Christine wrote that she felt trapped when she visited Saudi Arabia with Sibba. Ibrahim would disappear and "stay at the beach or go to one of his brothers' houses . . . and if he did come home . . . he would eat and take a nap or eat and leave the house quickly." During her stay in Jeddah during 1991, she wanted to go home to California, but Ibrahim "would not allow Sibba and myself to return to the United States." Ibrahim took her passport and told her "that it was being held at the Bin Laden Organization's office." She needed Ibrahim's signature to obtain an exit visa, and he refused, she wrote, telling her, "If you want to go home, you can go home, but Sibba is staying." She now feared, she told the court, that if Ibrahim was permitted to take Sibba to Saudi Arabia as part of their postdivorce custody agreement, she might never return. During their quarrels, Ibrahim had told her "numerous" times that Sibba "would go to Saudi Arabia no matter what happens and no matter what the court orders." Other members of the Bin Laden family had also told her that if Ibrahim took Sibba to Saudi Arabia, "he would not return her to me."[9]

"I see very clearly the intention of Chris is to punish me by keeping Sibba from going to Saudi Arabia," Ibrahim wrote in reply. He had "never tried to stop her from leaving" the kingdom; in fact, "I helped her to leave . . . One time we had an argument and she wanted to leave and I told her you could do whatever you want, she knows very well she could leave if she wanted to. The law a wife can't leave without a husband's permission applies on the Saudis only. The only time I take her passport is to get her an exit visa . . . She did not need any signature from me for her to leave."

He felt that Christine was deliberately attempting to alienate him from his young daughter. As an example, he reported that he had recently been laughing with Sibba in the car when he asked her if she was happy, and she said she was, and then she asked him, "Are you happy, *Baba*?"

"Yes," he had answered.

"But mom said you are unhappy man."[10]

At a deposition called by Ibrahim's lawyers, Christine described the agreements she and her husband had made about Sibba's upbringing.

"So it would be correct, then, that you and Mr. Bin Laden agreed that she was going to be reared in the Muslim faith?

"Yes."

"And would the child be exposed to, and if possible, learn to speak, read and write Arabic?"

"Yes."[11]

Ibrahim wanted to raise his daughter as a Saudi and as a Bin Laden, he told the court. It was in Sibba's best interest to understand who she was, and to become a full member of an extended family upon which she could long rely:

It is better for her now to know these things and grow up exposed to that culture, because I believe growing up with different "way of life" make you accept them, and it would be harder if she is not exposed to it until later—after she is grown. The other reason I want her to go to Saudi Arabia is to know her other part of the family, to feel their love for her, to be able to speak the language and feel comfortable to pick up the phone and ask any of her family if she needed anything or had a problem.[12]

He was convinced that Christine was using their daughter as a lever to extract money from him. "She only started to give me this trouble when she found out the Court will not give her what she wants from me," namely, alimony of $21,648 a month and an additional $6,188 in child support. He was prepared to offer $3,250 in monthly child support, but as for alimony for Christine, his lawyers asserted, she had "remained with Ibrahim for less than five years, during which she enjoyed the benefits of Ibrahim's family's largesse. She certainly didn't earn a lifetime of such living." She should go out and find a job; she "has been supported long enough."[13]

Their trial was scheduled for June 1993. As it neared, the two finally began to negotiate. On July 6, 1993, they completed a "Final Divorce Judgment" that brought their struggle to an end—or so they believed.

Ibrahim agreed to pay $5,000 per month in child support and $335,000 in a onetime cash settlement payment to Christine, with no additional alimony or attorney fees. He would be permitted to keep his 1977 Rolls-Royce Silver Shadow; his 1983 Rolls-Royce Corniche; his 1992 Hummer; his 1991 Lexus; his 1984 Honda Civic; his 1987 Lamborghini jeep; his 1986 Mercedes-Benz 500 SEL; and his Mercedes jeep, as well as sole title to his real estate in Los Angeles and Jeddah, his bank accounts, and his interest in the Mohamed Bin Laden Company. Ibrahim agreed to spend six months of each year in the United States and to share custody of Sibba during that period.

Christine agreed to enroll their daughter in an Islamic school and to ensure that she received Arabic lessons. Until she was seven years old,

Ibrahim could take her to Saudi Arabia for visits of up to one month; later, the stays could be longer.

It seemed a reasonable if expensively constructed compromise, and, indeed, the divorce decree between Ibrahim and Christine Bin Laden would hold steady for the rest of the decade—until the events of September 11 shattered the bicultural comity on which it rested.

29. THE CONSTRUCTION OF EXILE

BRITISH IMPERIALISTS laid out Port Sudan's geometrical street grid in 1905. Its harbor lay tucked behind coral reef barriers halfway up the Red Sea's western coast, across from Jeddah. In Britain's vision of the coming century, the town would thrive at the head of a rail line linking the Nile River to Europe, via the Suez Canal, but the place was still awaiting its renaissance as the twentieth century neared its close. Postcolonial Sudan's latest leader-for-life, General Omar Bashir, a veteran of brutal wars against African Christians in the country's south, overthrew an elected prime minister in 1989. As he consolidated power, Bashir allied himself with an Islamist coalition led by a Sorbonne-educated, self-impressed Sudanese theoretician of religion and politics, Hassan Al-Turabi. In the usual manner of coup leaders, they promised to revive their country by investing in infrastructure projects that would benefit "The People." In the same year that Bashir came to power, an off-shore company controlled by the senior Bin Laden brothers won a contract to build a new airport at Port Sudan, where the country's modest but economically vital oil exports flowed to market. The government of Saudi Arabia, which sought influence with its Red Sea neighbor, pledged to shoulder most of the $35 million cost.[1]

The project was assigned to the Public Buildings and Airports Division of the Saudi Bin Laden Group. Omar Bin Laden, the University of Miami graduate, was placed in charge. By 1992 construction was well under way.

Omar was not the only Bin Laden who now had occasion to visit Port Sudan. At around the same time that his brothers won the airport contract, Osama provided $180,000 to a Sudanese-born aide, Jamal Al-Fadl, to purchase a salt farm near Port Sudan.[2] It was one of a number of investments in land and businesses that Osama had decided to make in Sudan. He had visited the country from time to time as he wound down his involvements in Afghanistan. It was an unruly, lively, friendly, and deeply impoverished country where a Saudi sheikh could be made to feel very important and where his hard currency accounts could go a considerable distance. After he found himself under pressure at home in Saudi Arabia, Osama came to see Sudan as preferable to either Pakistan or Yemen as a base for voluntary exile. The country's Islamist-influenced government and its freewheeling poor society accommodated two strains of his evolving ambition—his commitment to international guerrilla warfare and his desire to establish himself as the head of his own business complex, in a manner comparable to other semi-independent Bin Laden brothers living abroad, such as Yeslam in Switzerland and Khaled in Egypt.

After he left Saudi Arabia in 1991, although he retained his shareholdings in the two major family firms, Osama seems to have regarded Bakr's leadership of the Bin Ladens with gathering contempt. On some foreign policy issues of the day—the Israeli-Palestinian conflict, the suffering of Muslim civilians in Bosnia and Chechnya—Osama's outlook remained in broad alignment with the conventional wisdom of the Saudi establishment, which his elder brother took such pains to internalize and represent. Osama's tactical approaches to these conflicts were increasingly independent, however. In 1992 the war in Bosnia measured the new equation between Osama and Bakr. Violence erupted around Sarajevo early in the year, and satellite news broadcasters beamed terrible images of Muslim civilian suffering to the Middle East. In July Bakr attended a glittering fundraising dinner at Jeddah's Laylaty Hall, a site of society wedding receptions near the Red Sea. The guest list that night included Saudi foreign minister Prince Saud Al-Faisal. Contemporary Saudi newspaper stories reported that the donors, including Bakr, contributed about $5 million to the Bosnian cause, channeled through international Islamic charities. Osama was stirred by the same television imagery that spring, but his response was of a different kind—from Sudan, he dispatched a team of Afghan veterans to join the shooting war against Croatia's attacking Catholics. "Gifts of charity," Osama later wrote pointedly, "are weak ... Bosnia is in need of men [and] weapons."[3]

He seemed increasingly proud of his martial ambitions, particularly in comparison to the softer, regime-authorized foreign policy work of his brothers. A Bin Laden employee who had helped Osama during the anti-Soviet period in Afghanistan recalled meeting him at the Port Sudan airport construction site, where the employee was overseeing Bin Laden work camps. Osama seemed disappointed in him, as the employee remembered it. "I'm fighting a war here," Osama said, "and you're building an airport."[4]

It would have been natural for Osama to visit the airport site—he was, after all, a shareholder of the Saudi Bin Laden Group, which was carrying out the contract—but whether he participated in that multimillion-dollar project to a greater extent, or profited from it, remains unclear. At some point between late 1991 and mid-1992, Osama decided to move permanently with his four wives and growing number of children to Sudan's capital of Khartoum, which lay about seven hundred miles southwest of Port Sudan. He organized a number of new businesses in the city, with names such as Ladin International Company and Al-Hijra Construction; the latter referred to the Prophet Mohamed's famous passage into exile, from Mecca to Medina. It was a presumptuous self-reference but one that spoke to Osama's rising sense of himself as both righteous and persecuted, a self-image drawn in part from the experiences of his earliest mentors—his exiled prep school gymnasium teacher, who indoctrinated him, as well as the itinerant Palestinian organizer, Abdullah Azzam. As Osama now refitted, he may have imported construction equipment he had previously stored in Pakistan. His early projects in Sudan included some road building, according to Al-Fadl, particularly an eighty-three-mile road in the southwest of the country, near the border with Ethiopia.[5]

Several sources—although not Al-Fadl—have also mentioned Osama's involvement with the Port Sudan airport project. Richard Clarke, the Clinton administration's counterterrorism supervisor, has identified "a new airport" as among Bin Laden's early Sudan projects, which Clarke said were undertaken as "a joint project" with the Islamist leader Al-Turabi. (Hassan Al-Turabi was fast becoming the latest in a succession of older religious intellectuals to mentor Osama self-interestedly, stroking his ego while reaching for his wallet.) Al-Turabi's wife has been quoted as saying that Osama "built the Port Sudan airport." Omar Bin Laden, however, has sworn in an affidavit that "to the best of my knowledge, Osama had no role in the performance of the Port Sudan airport construction project." Omar also denied that the major Bin Laden family firms participated in joint construction projects of any kind with Osama or "with any other company controlled by Osama" while he was in Sudan during the 1990s.[6]

The Port Sudan airport was mostly finished by June 1992. That month, Prince Mohamed bin Abdullah Al-Saqeer of the Saudi Development Fund led an official delegation, including newspaper reporters, to attend a ribbon-cutting ceremony. Omar Bin Laden, dressed in a red-checked headdress, his round face sporting a neatly trimmed mustache, took the podium. He recited statistics about the new airport's size and facilities. "This project has been accomplished by the will of God, and according to the international requirements and specifications," Omar said. "We are happy to participate in this celebration to inaugurate this large cultural edifice and we ask God to bless this project and everyone who participated in it."[7]

An account published in the London-based newspaper *Al-Quds Al-Arabi* almost a decade later reported that Osama was a "guest of honor" at this ceremony and that he sat in the front row. Omar Bin Laden has denied this, writing in an affidavit, "To the best of my recollection,

Osama was not in attendance." Omar produced contemporary Saudi newspaper stories that made no mention of Osama's presence. "I did not see or meet with Osama on that trip or, in fact, on any other trip I made to the Sudan."[8]

Bakr Bin Laden did meet with Osama in Khartoum during 1992. He traveled there "accompanied by other family members," according to a family attorney, "to make a plea to Osama to return to his country, make amends with the Saudi government, and abandon the path of political opposition and exile from country and family on which he appeared to have set." This was Bakr's last meeting with Osama according to Bakr. Other family members and emissaries apparently continued to visit Osama and plead with him to come home. There were "almost nine" such missions, in Osama's oddly phrased counting, and they appear to have lasted at least into 1994. Osama's half-brother Tareq, for example, recalled visiting Khartoum in "late 1992 or early 1993." His purpose, he remembered, was "to convince Osama to abandon his criticisms of the Saudi government and return to Saudi Arabia." It was a short visit; Osama said that "he was happy in the Sudan and did not want to return to Saudi Arabia, as he was focused on building his businesses in the Sudan." Tareq believed that Osama was engaged in legitimate business, he later told an American court. Tareq "did not see or hear anything during the visit suggesting that [Osama] was involved in terrorist or violent activities of any kind. Nor did he express any hostility to the United States."[9]

These missions to Khartoum began when it "became clear to us that he had a hand in one way or another in some of these things, such as terrorist operations in Egypt and Libya," according to Ahmed Badeeb, then chief of staff to the head of Saudi intelligence, Prince Turki. "The King ordered that Osama Bin Laden be called into the Kingdom. He was asked to return in order to discuss some of the things that needed to be discussed, and other things that were harming the Kingdom, but he refused to. He was sent a few messages, and his family was contacted; he continued to refuse to return."[10]

King Fahd ordered Bakr to see Osama and persuade him to come home for consultations, according to two people who have discussed the matter with Bakr. He found Osama stubborn and arrogant. In his own account, Osama has emphasized that he did not blame any of his relatives for their entreaties—he regarded them as victims of King Fahd's pressure, and he believed that his family's dependency on the Al-Saud for construction contracts made them vulnerable to a form of extortion by the Saudi government. "I apologized to my family kindly," Osama said, "because I know that they were driven by force to come to talk to me. This regime wants to create a problem between me and my family in order to take some measures against them."[11]

Some people in and around the Bin Laden family wondered if Bakr was really an adequate match for Osama. Bakr could come across as a less than commanding presence; one person who knew him well said he could seem like the boy on the playground who is often picked last for team games. As the family's Osama problem accumulated during 1992 and early 1993, even some who respected and admired Bakr wondered how Salem might have handled things differently. Salem had been such a forceful whirlwind—he was physical, insistent, and difficult to stop. If he had been alive to undertake these early missions to Khartoum, Osama might have been returned to the kingdom in a burlap sack, tossed into the cabin of a private jet with a pile of Salem's designer-brand luggage. But Salem was gone; Osama seemed to exploit the void.

He seemed also to revel in the attention that came with his family's pleading. "He was out of touch in Sudan," recalled his friend Jamal Khashoggi, who visited him there several times. Bodyguards, acolytes, employees, and volunteer fighters encased him as he moved around Khartoum; the nationalities and occupations of his followers varied, but they all depended on his money and his patronage. He shuffled between comfortable offices on King Leopard Street and a shaded home-office compound in posh Riyadh City. He attended horse races and stabled his own horses on his farms. His grandest business project involved an enormous tract of agricultural land in the southwest granted to him by the Sudanese government, where seasonal Sudanese laborers in his employ harvested oil and seeds from sunflowers; Osama showed off his largest flowers with the pride of a passionate gardener. He was tossing money by the bucketful into new and questionable Sudanese businesses, but in 1992 and early 1993, he nonetheless had plenty of cash to go around— enough to spend $480,000 on the purchase and renovation of a used airplane ferried in from the United States, and enough to meet payroll for several hundred Arab jihadis flown in from Pakistan, as well as the many hundreds of Sudanese laborers at his sunflower farm. Osama seemed to believe during this period that he could have it all in Sudan—wives, children, business, horticulture, horse breeding, leisure, pious devotion, and jihad—all of it buoyed by the deference and public reputation due a proper sheikh. He did not yet seem to grasp that his enterprise, particularly in its support for violence against governments friendly to or dependent upon the Al-Saud, might prove difficult to reconcile with the interests of his family in Jeddah. He could seem oblivious to the fissures opening up around him. When Jamal Khashoggi visited, Osama even spoke at length about his desire to organize an investment drive that would draw prominent Saudi businesses to Sudan, in order to strengthen this important new Islamist-leaning country.

"Osama, don't you realize that people are afraid to be associated with you?" Khashoggi asked. Osama did not answer. He only smiled, Khashoggi recalled, "as if he were happy he was so important."[12]

ON FEBRUARY 26, 1993, in New York, a car bomb detonated in a parking garage of the World Trade Center, killing six people and injuring just over one thousand. Investigators soon identified a fugitive, Ramzi Yousef, a Pakistani raised in Kuwait, educated in Wales, and trained at camps in Afghanistan, as the leader of the conspiracy. Although Osama Bin Laden was not identified as Yousef's direct patron, then or later, in the broader media coverage of transnational jihad that followed the first World Trade Center attack, some journalists and commentators did note Osama's presence in Sudan and described his reported financial handouts to multinational volunteer fighters. For the Saudi royal family, this attention transformed Osama, for the first time, from a discreet domestic problem into a public embarrassment.[13]

Less than three months after the New York bombing, on May 3, 1993, in Riyadh, Mohammed Al-Masari, a professor of physics, and Saad Al-Faqih, a medical doctor, announced the formation of the Committee for the Defense of Legitimate Rights, an organization seeking reform of the Saudi political system. Al-Masari and Al-Faqih were both Islamists; the Muslim Brotherhood, in particular, had influenced Al-Faqih, who came from a well-known Saudi family of doctors who attended to the royals. Al-Masari, for his part, had shown unusual facility as a media spokesman and organizer at a time when unlicensed satellite television dishes and fax machines were proliferating in Saudi households. Both men had been involved in political petition drives and underground sermon distribution after the Gulf war. After two years of organizing, Al-Faqih said later, "Everything appeared to be in place: charismatic preachers, thousands of enthusiastic followers, and a religious public. What was missing was an effective organization to channel this energy and pose a serious challenge to the regime." They prepared carefully for their committee's formal launch. Al-Masari met with diplomats at the U.S. embassy and solicited their support. The BBC, Voice of America, and other global media covered the organization's debut.[14]

King Fahd struck back decisively. Perhaps he felt he had allowed these currents of dissent to drift along for too long. On May 12, the kingdom's official Council of Higher 'Ulema, its supreme body of religious scholars, denounced the upstart reformers, pronouncing officially and pointedly that they had violated Islamic law. Police arrested Al-Masari, Al-Faqih, and other known troublemakers. A broader attack on Islamist dissenters followed.

Osama now became a target; it is not entirely clear why. He is not known to have signed any of the important documents associated with the Al-Faqih–led dissident group, which posed a much more visible threat to the Saudi regime. It is possible that Osama issued tape-recorded or other underground sermons denouncing the Al-Saud during this period, and that the Interior Ministry discovered them. "We were there, working secretly," Khalid Al-Fawwaz, who later served as Osama's spokesman in London, once boasted.[15] It is equally possible, however, that the Saudi government simply decided to include Osama's case in its broader crackdown, given that he had now acquired an international profile in Sudan and that the government's previous efforts to reel him in, through Bakr and other family channels, had failed.

On June 16, 1993, in Jeddah, Bakr undertook proceedings within the Bin Laden family to expel Osama as a shareholder of the Mohamed Bin Laden Company and the Saudi Bin Laden Group. In a later affidavit, Bakr implied that the family took this initiative, but it is likely that pressure from the Saudi government was a substantial cause. Bakr acted, he explained, "because Osama's increasingly vocal criticisms of the Saudi government were harmful to the companies' reputations in the Kingdom and elsewhere in the Middle East, and because Osama had refused to comply with the Saudi government's demand that he return to the Kingdom."[16]

"In the Name of Allah, Most Merciful, Most Compassionate," began the text of one resolution setting forth "the Exit of One Shareholder." The document suggests the family negotiated with Osama before it went forward. For example, Osama designated a "lawful attorney" from Jeddah, Muhamad Salem Al-Yaf'ei, to represent him. Also, Osama specifically assigned all his divested shares to Ghalib Bin Laden, the younger full brother of Bakr and Salem. It was Ghalib who had visited Peshawar, Pakistan, during Ramadan in 1989, at a time when Osama was fighting in the battle for Jalalabad. There is evidence that Ghalib retained an interest in Islamic financial institutions at the time he agreed to accept Osama's divested shares: in late 1993, Ghalib transferred $1 million to a new investment account at Bank Al-Taqwa, in the Bahamas, an offshore bank founded in 1988 with backing from the Egyptian Muslim Brotherhood. Al-Taqwa funded HAMAS in Israel and other Brotherhood-influenced radical groups in Algeria and Tunisia, according to a written assessment by the U.S. Treasury Department. What involvement Bakr Bin Laden had in the Al-Taqwa investment is not known, but Bakr did have signature authority over Ghalib's account, which remained active until at least the late 1990s, according to bank documents filed in a U.S. court, although there is no suggestion that the account was used to support terrorism. Ghalib later sought to withdraw his investment from Al-Taqwa and filed suit against the bank. Through family attorneys, Ghalib said that he had never provided financial or other support for terrorism of any kind and there is no evidence that he did so.[7]

The June 1993 shareholder resolutions initiated a process that lasted until the end of the year, leading to the final disposition of Osama's assets. Its purpose, according to a family attorney, was "to deprive Osama of access to any funds derived from his interests in the family-owned companies." Bakr and other family shareholders "were firmly opposed to any direct or indirect financial support from the family companies." Tareq Bin Laden, a director of Mohamed Bin Laden's flagship construction firm, felt that "Osama's vocal criticisms of the Saudi government were harming the companies' reputations in the Middle East." There were also consultations during this time between the family and the Saudi Ministry of Commerce. The pace apparently allowed additional family delegations to visit Khartoum and plead with Osama to reconsider his position. His mother was among those dispatched. At least one younger brother met with him, according to Jamal Khashoggi, who was present in Sudan during that particular visit. (It was a "brother-to-brother" conversation, said Khashoggi, and he did not join in.) The most prestigious visitor throughout this period was Abdullah Bin Awadh Bin Laden, the legendary brother of Osama's father, who was now near eighty years old. Bakr might be the head of the Bin Laden family for all practical and financial matters, but Abdullah, eldest of the male elders, remained a spiritual and moral leader. That a man of his age would fly to rough Khartoum to plead with Osama signaled the seriousness of the situation. Osama dug in. "With God's grace," as he described it later, "this regime did not get its wish fulfilled. I refused to go back."[18]

His relatives warned him "that if I did not go back, they'll freeze all my assets, deprive me of my citizenship, my passport, and my Saudi i.d., and distort my picture in the Saudi and foreign media. They think that a Muslim may bargain on his religion. I said to them: 'Do whatever you may wish.'"[19]

Osama's shares in the Mohamed Bin Laden Company and the Saudi Bin Laden Group were sold in a transaction designed so that Osama would not profit, yet in a way that would protect the rights of his heirs under Islamic law. The total value of Osama's combined shares was set at about $9.9 million—a strikingly modest sum, but one that is difficult to evaluate, as an indicator of the market value of the Bin Laden companies, because few of the underlying assumptions used to set the price are available. In round numbers, however, the sale price suggests a total valuation of about $500 million for the two main Bin Laden companies combined. After consultations with the Saudi government, the funds generated by the sale of Osama's shares were placed in some kind of special trust and eventually frozen, under court supervision. According to Abdulaziz Al-Gasim, a Saudi attorney who was jailed during the 1990s because of his Islamist activism, a Saudi judge ruled that the government could "take this money, seize it" but that it should not permit it to be distributed "to the other relatives." Under Islamic law, Al-Gasim said, the money should be protected for the possibility of Osama's reconciliation with the kingdom or, after his death, for his heirs. A number of aspects of Osama's shareholding divestment remain unclear, however. For example, it is uncertain whether Ghalib paid cash for Osama's shares, and if so, where he raised the money from. Is there a bank account in Saudi Arabia that has held the $9.9 million in trust ever since the sale was completed? How do Saudi courts assert control over such an account, if it exists? If the sale did not involve a cash payment, but rather a credit of some sort, how was this organized and who has kept track of the proceeds since then? The Bin Laden family has provided little clarity about these details. In any event, Osama was cut off from all dividend and loan payments, according to Bakr Bin Laden. "Osama has not received a penny" from any Bin Laden companies "since, at the latest, June 1993," Bakr wrote in a later affidavit. Moreover, "I have not authorized and, indeed, have forbidden any person" acting on behalf of any Bin Laden firms "to make any payments, do any business with, or otherwise provide any support directly or indirectly to Osama or any of his companies since June 1993."[20]

In February 1994—for the first time—the Bin Laden family publicly repudiated Osama in a press statement. Bakr authorized a short release, which appeared in a Saudi newspaper under the headline "Bakr Bin Laden: All Family Members Condemn Osama Bin Laden's Behavior." The story referred to "reports by the media" about Osama and then offered two sentences from Bakr "to clarify his family's position towards him." Bakr announced:

I myself, and all members of the family, whose number exceeds fifty persons, express our strong condemnation and denunciation of all the behavior of Osama, which behavior we do not accept or approve of. As said Osama has been residing outside the Kingdom of Saudi Arabia for more than two years despite our attempts to convince him to return to the right path, we, therefore, consider him to be alone responsible for his statements, actions, and behavior, if truly emanating from him.[21]

It was a careful formulation, focused on Osama's conduct, not his character, and expressing a whiff of doubt about the reliability of media reporting about him. Two months later, in April, an equally terse statement from the Ministry of Interior announced that Osama Bin Laden had been formally stripped of his Saudi citizenship. The release cited Article

29 of the "Saudi nationality regulation"; it declared that Osama had refused to obey instructions, and that his actions "contradict the Kingdom's
national interest." A Saudi government freeze on the proceeds of Osama's
divested shareholdings also took effect that month. According to attorneys for the Saudi Bin Laden Group, Osama "never had access to these
funds" although they were not placed "in trust outside [his] control"
until 1994, about nine months after the divestment proceedings began.[22]

Osama issued no formal statement of his own on any of these occasions. Instead, beginning in the summer of 1994, he began to behave like
a man who felt, so far as the Saudi royal family was concerned, that he
no longer had anything to lose.

By EARLY 1994, Osama had already secretly dispatched groups of jihad
fighters, arms smugglers, and organizers to Somalia, Kenya, Yemen,
Bosnia, Egypt, Libya, and Tajikistan, among other places, according to
letters and testimony by his followers and allies. Some of these fighters
arrived at their destinations and found that local conditions were not
ripe for warfare. Others, like the Egyptian exiles around Ayman Al-
Zawahiri, organized violent and ambitious conspiracies, such as an attempt to assassinate Egyptian president Hosni Mubarak—the plot went
forward in 1995, when Mubarak was visiting Ethiopia, but it failed.

Al Qaeda persisted as a formal organization during these years; in
Khartoum, steering committees wrestled with drafts of a wordy constitution. Its mission was to seed jihad in Muslim lands seen as under occupation or ruled by apostates. Still, it was a group more characterized
by diversity than discipline. Partly this was because Osama himself remained unsettled about how he would define and organize his own participation in the international jihad—with his loss of citizenship and
family shareholdings, he was in a renewed state of flux. His gifts of fore-
sight and political analysis had always been limited; he now entered a pe-

riod of groping and searching. Yet he made one explicit, forthright decision during the summer of 1994: he openly joined the opposition to the Saudi royal family.

His chief aide in this project was Khalid Al-Fawwaz, who was then in his early thirties. He had been born in Kuwait and studied engineering at King Fahd University in Saudi Arabia; he spoke English well. He had moved to Nairobi, where he dealt in automobiles and was in contact with other Al Qaeda adherents in the country to plan for a violent attack against Western targets. In early 1994, Al-Fawwaz was arrested; afterward he decided to escape from Kenya with his family. He made his way to London.[23]

Al-Faqih and Al-Masari, the Saudi activists arrested the previous spring after unveiling their Committee for the Defense of Legitimate Rights, had escaped to London as well, with help from the Islamist underground. Osama had initially doubted the credibility of Al-Faqih's reform group: "We thought at first that this may be a ploy by the regime to take the wind out of the sail of our movement, but by the time we realized that these were our brothers, they were taken into custody," Al-Fawwaz later explained.[24] Now they were all united in London exile, protected by Britain's asylum laws, which were among the most liberal in Europe. Working from ramshackle houses in North London, Al-Faqih and Al-Masari relaunched their opposition group, which represented the most serious political challenge to Al-Saud rule in Arabia since the Nasser period. Al-Fawwaz shared office space with them. Osama, however, did not wish to formally join. He wanted an organization of his own.

The Committee for Advice and Reform debuted in July 1994 in London. It was Osama's own vehicle for participating in Saudi politics as an exiled dissenter and pamphleteer. It was little more than a musty room and a fax machine, but it described itself as "an all-encompassing organization that aims at applying the teachings of God to all aspects of life." It had four aims: to eradicate all forms of non-Islamic governance;

to achieve Islamic justice; to reform the Saudi political system and "purify it from corruption and injustice"; and to revive the traditional Islamic system by which citizens had the right, guided by religious scholars, to bring charges against government officials.[25]

Osama's committee was born in a period of technological prelude, on the eve of the explosion of the World Wide Web. At the time, fax machines offered the easiest way to send text documents across government borders without the risk of censorship. By the autumn of 1994, Al-Faqih, Al-Masari, and Al-Fawwaz were all blasting faxes from their allied groups to lists of numbers all around Saudi Arabia, the Gulf, and to international media outlets.

In Khartoum, released at last from any constraints of family and national loyalties, Osama sat at his several desks during late 1994 and early 1995 and wrote out lengthy essays, as frequently as once a week. He sent them to Al-Fawwaz, who put them on the blast fax. Some pieces were the length of op-ed articles; others went on for thousands of words, laced with religious quotations. Osama's subject was not so much Islam as Saudi Arabia. His tone about the kingdom, the country his father and his family had done so much to build and legitimize, was often intemperate, impetuous, petty, sarcastic, or unreservedly angry. On September 12, 1994: "Saudi Arabia Unveils Its War on Islam and Its Scholars." A week later: "Do not Give Inferiority To Your Religion." On October 15, referring to the Saudi government's Supreme Council for Islamic Affairs: "Supreme Council for Damage." On March 9, 1995: "Saudi Arabia Continues War on Islam and Its Scholars." On July 11: "Prince Sultan and Flight Commissions."[26]

He denounced by name King Fahd and his full brothers, the so-called Sudeiris, who were now the dominant grouping in the royal family—Nayef, at the Interior Ministry; Sultan, at the Defense Ministry; and Salman, the governor of Riyadh. Osama did not write subtly about them. Nayef, with whom he had met regularly and collaboratively during the

Afghan war of the 1980s, had a "shady history" and was "filled with craftiness towards Islam and hatred for its advocates and religious authorities." These princes were unworthy of their roles as guardians of the birthplace of Islam:

> How could any intelligent person who knows the facts believe that these kinsmen—who corrupt the land and wage war on Allah and His Prophet—could possibly have been brought to serve Islam and Muslims?[27]

Prince Salman, he later wrote, "has a shady past in which he has defrauded Islam and waged war on its people." Prince Sultan was one of the "tricksters" who milked contracts for commissions and helped to drive the Saudi economy into the ground. And over all of this perfidy, greed, and incompetence presided King Fahd, who had impeded God's laws, aligned himself with nonbelievers, and had proved to be "hostile to Islam and Muslims."[28]

To Saudi readers, his explicit attacks on Fahd and his full brothers had an obvious corollary—Osama was silent about the crown prince of Saudi Arabia, Abdullah, who was presumed by many Saudis to be estranged from the Sudeiris and who enjoyed a reputation for relative piety and financial rectitude. It was possible to imagine in 1995 that pressure from Islamist campaigners abroad and jailed religious scholars at home might create a quiet coup among the Al-Saud, favoring Abdullah, similar to that which had brought Faisal to the throne three decades earlier. Osama seemed to be developing this angle in his essays. In one tract, he explicitly listed the late years of Faisal's reign as an exception to his criticisms of royal family rule. From Switzerland, Yeslam Bin Laden predicted that Osama would be restored to power within the Bin Laden family, and Bakr would fade, once Abdullah came to the throne, according to Carmen Bin Laden.[29] Osama did probably fantasize that the Islamists might force Fahd out, and that Abdullah might then welcome him home on terms he could embrace. Who could predict the future? It was in God's hands.

OSAMA'S EXPERIENCE as a businessman in Sudan was similar to that of his half-brother Khalil's in Los Angeles, with America in Motion. His grandiose schemes did not pan out. His mentors took advantage of him. His employees misappropriated tens of thousands of dollars, money he could no longer afford to lose—Jamal Al-Fadl, for example, took Osama for $110,000 in a series of manipulated land and commodity deals. Osama had reorganized his personal banking at the Al-Shamal Bank in Khartoum, but his accounts gradually dried up. In the past, his personal wealth had provided him a financial cushion, but much of the money he spent on jihad came from private donors, charities, or quasi-governmental channels. Now his access to family dividends and loans had been pinched, and, simultaneously, as an enemy of the Saudi state, his charity fundraising had become complicated. As early as 1994 or 1995, "We had a crisis in Al Qaeda," recalled L'Hossaine Kherchtou, one of his adherents. "Osama bin Laden himself said to us that he had lost all his money, and he reduced the salary of his people." He was forced to lay off as many as two thousand workers at his sunflower farm during 1995. It was an extraordinarily fast downturn—Osama had blown through his lump sum inheritance, his dividends, and his charitable funds in just four to five years, a total of perhaps $15 million or more. In his essays, he denounced the Saudi royal family for corruption and financial malfeasance, but he had managed his own funds with all the prudence of a self-infatuated Hollywood celebrity.[30]

He betrayed his desperation in a blast fax he issued on February 12, 1995, titled "Prince Salman and Charity Offerings in Ramadan." He slandered the royal government with typical bombast, denouncing them in particular for new regulations that required annual *zakat*, or "charity," contributions to be routed only through officially approved charities overseen by Prince Salman. "The Saudi regime's previous general history of managing donations has been extremely bad," Osama wrote. "It took popular donations for the Afghani *mujaheddin* as a means to put pressure on them, in order to realize Western and, in particular, American policies." As he went on, however, Osama made clear that his essay was intended less as a critique than as a solicitation. He was worried about his own continued access to the Saudi charity on which he had so long depended:

> We at the Committee for Advice and Reform alert all philanthropists and givers of charity of the danger of submitting any funds or alms to these harmful institutions, bodies and associations which use them to wage war on Allah and His Prophet. We call them to submit funds directly to those who deserve them domestically and abroad. They can also submit funds to religious or custodial persons who can assure that those who legally deserve the funds will receive them without them first being tampered with by the Saudi clan ... There are safe agencies that will transmit funds to those who deserve them such as charitable associations in Qatar, Kuwait, Jordan, Yemen, Sudan and others. To ensure that funds are transferred to the accounts of these associations, we alert you of the importance of transferring outside the Gulf—far from tracking by the regime's spies.[31]

His problems at the office were compounded by his troubles at home. One of his wives, known as Om Ali, or the "Mother of Ali," traveled back and forth between Saudi Arabia and Sudan; she grew tired of Khartoum. She asked Osama for a divorce because "she could not continue to live in an austere way, and in hardship," according to Nasir Al-Bahri, who later served as Osama's bodyguard.

Osama's eldest son, Abdullah, a teenager, also chafed at being cut off from the privileges enjoyed by a Bin Laden in good standing. He had seen enough of his cousins' lifestyles in Jeddah—the slick cars, the Harley motorcycles, the wave runners on weekends in the Red Sea—to know what he was missing. He asked his father for permission to return to the king-

dom and take up a job in the family business. He had already become engaged to one of his relatives "because my father supports early marriage," as he later explained, and in 1995 he pressed his father to return
to Saudi Arabia:

> He would ask me to be patient and wait every time. On one occasion, I
> went into his bedroom when we were in Sudan to wake him up to pray,
> and he said to me with no introductions: "Abdullah, you can go to Saudi
> Arabia if you want." I started crying for joy without saying a word. My
> father smiled calmly and said nothing. On the next day, I called my un-
> cles in Jeddah and they helped in speeding up my arrival there . . . I
> wanted to be independent and build my life on my own, and according
> to my desires.

The defection of his firstborn pained Osama, according to Al-Bahri.
Thereafter he "avoided mentioning Abdullah's name . . . because he had
been hurt by him."[32]

Osama's mother still visited him, but now the Saudi authorities monitored her to ensure she was not ferrying cash surreptitiously. Osama reportedly continued to have contact with some of the religious wing of
the family—his brother-in-law Jamal Khalifa said later that he stayed in
touch. They had been fast friends during the early 1980s, and now Khalifa
found himself in legal trouble over allegations that he supported violent
Al Qaeda–inspired Islamic groups in the Philippines. A second brother-
in-law may also have participated in Osama's campaigns from Sudan.
Yet for the senior brothers in Jeddah who led the Bin Ladens, and who
managed the family's relationships with the Saudi royals, Osama was now
plainly an anathema. King Fahd's court put the senior brothers on notice,
according to a person who worked with them in Jeddah at the time; the
Saudi government made it plain that the Bin Ladens would pay a steep
price if they succored Osama. Nothing got the family's attention like the
prospect of losing its wealth. To ensure there could be no question about

their loyalties, the family decided during this period to donate all of its *zakat* funds directly to the king's charities, according to the person working with them in Jeddah.[33]

Osama could probably sense the change in his family's attitude. In 1995 one of his half-sisters died of cancer; she was the first of Mohamed Bin Laden's daughters to pass away. Her death left the number of his surviving children at fifty-two. From Sudan, Osama telephoned Omar Bin Laden to express his condolences. "That conversation lasted only about a minute, as I purposely cut it short," Omar said later.[34]

Out of money, divorced by one of his wives, abandoned by his eldest son, estranged from his family—a hint of King Lear in the wilderness began to enter Osama's exile. He told a Saudi visitor, "I am tired. I miss living in Medina. Only God knows how nostalgic I am." He was so unmoored during 1995 that he explored the possibility of moving to London. There he would join his colleagues in the self-styled Saudi opposition in a more traditional, more political exile, one that would inevitably reduce his scope for participation in violence. It is easy to imagine the appeal of London: occasional press conferences attended by the international media; long afternoons at the writing desk penning poetry and unrelenting political essays on behalf of a new Saudi Arabia; visits from his son Abdullah and other family; a chance to live by principles, but also amid some of the comfort craved by the middle-aged.[35]

It proved to be a passing fantasy. Saudi Arabia pressured Britain to do something about Al-Faqih and Al-Masari, and the government did initiate deportation proceedings against the latter. It would likely have been impossible politically for Osama to receive asylum by the time he considered seeking it. The complaint involved immigration matters; there was no evidence that Al-Faqih or Al-Masari were involved in terrorism.

In Khartoum he remained surrounded by other wives, children, employees, and followers, and his calendar of business and conspiracy meetings mitigated his isolation. Yet there was now a self-reinforcing quality to the narrative Osama was constructing around his exile. The more pressure he faced, the more readily he compared his circumstances to those of the Prophet Mohamed, who had been driven by political opponents to Medina, where he waged a righteous war and eventually returned home. "Emigration is related to *jihad*, and *jihad* will go on until the Day of Judgment," Osama wrote while in Sudan. It was not the sort of formulation likely to appeal to a restless wife or teenager with memories of Jeddah's better restaurants. Yet there is no reason to doubt that Osama believed precisely what he penned.

Moreover, the wealth and global visibility of his enemies—King Fahd, and his patron, the Americans—only highlighted for him the enduring righteousness of his cause. He even seemed to regard some of the missions undertaken by his relatives as a form of outreach from the United States, the country on which Osama increasingly focused his wrath, particularly after Washington put pressure on Sudan's government to expel him from Khartoum. At first he had regarded his family members as helpless, manipulated agents of the Al-Saud. Now he came to see his exile as a contest of will and faith between himself and the government of the most powerful country on earth. Each iteration of this contest only highlighted for him the significance of his struggle and his leadership. "I tell you that the Americans are bargaining with us in silence," Osama would explain in late 1996. "America and some of its agents in the region have bargained with us discreetly more than ten times, I tell you: [they say] shut up and we'll give you back your passport and possessions, we'll give you back your i.d. card, but shut up. These people think that people live in this world for its own sake, but they have forgotten that our existence has no meaning if we do not strive for the pleasure of God."[36]

30. HEDGE FUNDS

D URING A LONG CAREER as an American diplomat, Philip Griffin became a specialist in the Arab world, and he acquired particular experience in the Persian Gulf region—he served in Kuwait, Abu Dhabi, and twice in Dhahran, the principal city in Saudi Arabia's oil-producing region. He was a mild man with blue eyes and a full head of graying hair; his years in diplomacy and his extended exposure to reticent Arabia had left him with impeccable manners and a habit of speaking in cautious, deliberate, fully articulated paragraphs. In 1989 Griffin arrived in Jeddah as consul general, the State Department's highest-ranking officer in the Hejaz and a liaison to the U.S. embassy in Riyadh.

On his early diplomatic rounds, Griffin met Henry Sarkissian, of the Sarkissian business family, Armenian Christians who had migrated to Lebanon, established themselves in the electrical and industrial air-conditioning field, and then become important partners of the Bin Ladens in Saudi Arabia. Sarkissian introduced Griffin to Bakr Bin Laden, a connection that led to periodic discreet conversations among Bakr, Griffin, and Chas Freeman, then the U.S. ambassador to Saudi Arabia. The two American diplomats used Bakr as a sounding board about goings-on in the court of King Fahd and about the king's private views on issues of the day. They found Bakr to be very careful during these conversations, which usually took place in his Jeddah office; Bakr was far from a natural gossip, and he was protective of the king, but he occasionally passed along a useful nugget or insight.[1]

During the summer of 1992, Griffin's posting neared its end, and he let it be known that he was planning to retire from the diplomatic service; he was then sixty years old. Through Sarkissian, Bakr asked to see him. He did not mention Osama, although by now, the trouble with his half-brother had begun to percolate. Bakr did mention that although the Bin Ladens had enjoyed many business connections in the United States over the years, they had no one person—no brother, no other representative—to oversee their scattered investments in the U.S., or to develop new ones. After this encounter, through Sarkissian, Bakr inquired if Griffin might be interested in opening an office for the Saudi Bin Laden Group in Washington, an office that would be supported partly by Sarkissian's joint venture with the Bin Ladens and partly by the Saudi Bin Laden Group itself. The inquiry Bakr relayed was not specific about the office's writ or purpose, but in follow-up discussions, Sarkissian mentioned that in addition to maintaining ties with existing partners such as General Electric and pursuing new business development in the United States, they would want someone in the capital who could give them access to the American government if it was required.

"Well, that's easier said than done," Griffin responded. "Let me think about it."[2]

He returned to his home in the Washington suburbs, but he stayed in touch as he moved through the State Department's formal retirement process. By early 1993, the Bin Ladens made clear that they wanted to go ahead with the plan, and Griffin decided to come on board. The Bin Ladens agreed to allow him to open an office near his home in Maryland so he would not have to endure a grueling daily commute into downtown Washington. He found an office building that specialized in providing packaged services, such as telephone-answering and conference facilities, to very small companies. On June 16, 1993, in the same week that the Bin Laden brothers were in the midst of their still-private legal proceedings in Jeddah to divest Osama of his shareholdings, Griffin, as "resident agent," incorporated a company in Maryland as the Saudi Bin Laden

Group's new American outpost. The firm was initially called Cromwell Corporation, but it then formally became SBG (USA), Inc.[3] Griffin moved into an office at 51 Monroe Street, in downtown Rockville, Maryland, near Rockville Pike, a cluttered six-lane avenue lined with strip malls, consumer electronics stores, and brightly lit chain restaurants. It was perhaps not the marbled outpost in imperial-tinted Washington that Bakr might initially have imagined, but it was at least a foothold, manned by an experienced American diplomat, in a country that was coming to play an increasingly complicated role in the family's life.

Bakr assigned Griffin's office to his half-brother Hassan, who had been appointed to oversee international business development under Bakr's new management regime. This sounded fairly clear-cut, but the inner workings of the Bin Laden companies remained idiosyncratic. Once, when a non-Saudi executive complained to Henry Sarkissian that he was puzzled about what the Saudi Bin Laden Group actually wanted him to do, Sarkissian quipped, "You'll never learn," by which he meant that vagueness and mystery were permanent features of the corporate culture. Under Bakr, in comparison to Salem's reign, there was a new veneer of professional organization charts, yet Bakr himself made many of his most important decisions not in boardrooms, but while sitting in his afternoon majlis in Jeddah, in the manner of an Arabian sheikh, or while flying from place to place in his private jets. The corporate culture he oversaw remained utterly dependent on the boss, habitually secretive, compartmented, and at times confusing, particularly for outsiders who joined as executives or partners.[4]

During the mid-1990s, Bakr signed a number of lucrative contracts in partnership with General Electric to develop power stations in Saudi Arabia, and he even hosted a celebratory party in the kingdom for GE's famous chief executive, Jack Welch—but none of this U.S.-connected work was routed through or coordinated with the new U.S. office. Also, at the time Griffin set up shop, elements of the family were invested in a number of commercial real estate partnerships in the United States—those developed by the Daniel Corporation of Alabama, whose project money was channeled by Yeslam Bin Laden; those purchased by Yeslam's full brother Khalil, through America in Motion; and another suite of projects overseen by the Sarkissians from an office in New Jersey. These latter developments included commercial properties in the Dallas area; some of those partnerships were named in reference to iconic places or events of the American Revolutionary War period, such as Concord or Bunker Hill. None of these projects was assigned directly to the new American office opened by Griffin, either. If anything, Griffin would be subordinate to the family's real estate partners: listed as directors of SBG (USA) in the official corporate records were Kourken Sarkissian, in Canada, who helped oversee some family investments in North America, and Robert McBride, of Spicewood, Texas, who worked in a similar vein.[5]

The Bin Ladens' business and advisory network in the United States also included an additional outpost, in the person of Fuad Rihani, a businessman who had run a European company that supplied lighting equipment to the two holy mosques in Mecca and Medina. Rihani was originally from Jordan; he was a Christian who was active in that country's Protestant Church circles. By the time SBG (USA) opened outside Washington, Rihani had become a senior and respected adviser to the Bin Ladens; he eventually purchased a home in North Carolina, carried the title of Director of Research and Development for the Saudi Bin Laden Group, and served on the board of a Washington think tank, the Middle East Policy Council, to which the Bin Ladens made donations. Its later chairman was Chas Freeman, the former U.S. ambassador in Riyadh.[6]

These contributions and connections offered the Bin Ladens a way to distinguish themselves from Osama, to deepen their contacts with American and British elites—to construct, subtly but unmistakably, an alternative basis to evaluate the family's attitude toward the West. The more trouble Osama caused, the more Bakr seemed to search for ways to make offsetting donations and financial investments.

ALL OF THE BIN LADEN companies, whether in Saudi Arabia or abroad, operated as privately held entities, so the family was not legally required to disclose its spider's web of global holdings to stock market regulators or public investors or even to their own executives. There was a random and whimsical nature to some of the family's investments. A brother might go on vacation in Eastern Europe, meet an enterprising local man, invest in a travel agency, and then neglect it, until the company's very existence was forgotten. Family firms sold casual wear in London's Covent Garden and in shopping malls in Cairo and Beirut ("tank tops, jogging shorts, jeans, denims . . ."); produced television programming and commercials in a Jeddah photo lab; published children's books in London; and licensed intellectual property in Dubai. The lines between the hobbies of family members and serious businesses were not always easy to discern. Offshore companies would open, fall dormant, and then sit on the books for years, earning fees for the lawyers and accountants who renewed their registrations, but doing little else. By the early 1990s, there were so many small companies and affiliates scattered around the world that at one point, around the time Griffin opened the Rockville office, executives at headquarters retained an American firm just to inventory the family's holdings, according to a person familiar with the study.[7]

The locus of the family's most significant international investments during this period was not Washington but London. As Bakr's control of the family tightened, he worked out an arrangement with Yeslam to transform Russell Wood & Company—the London Stock Exchange broker-dealer that had endured a computer meltdown and other troubles after its initial purchase in 1987—from a brokerage that relied upon outside clients to a more discreet portfolio-management firm that could coordinate Bin Laden family investments in global markets. How this transformation was arranged financially is not entirely clear—for example, the

Cayman Islands parent company of Russell Wood remained Falken Limited, an entity owned by Yeslam and his full siblings, but the firm had booked loans with a number of other offshore companies in Panama, the British Virgin Islands, and the Netherlands Antilles. The changes in management evolved over a number of years, according to company records filed with regulators in London. As late as 1991, Russell Wood's British auditors were still struggling to make sense of records from the 1987 market crash period. "We are unable to form an opinion," the auditors reported "as to a) whether the financial statements give a true and fair view of the state of affairs of the Company . . . and b) whether the financial statements have been properly prepared in all respects . . ." Eventually Britain's Securities and Futures Authority required the Bin Ladens to inject about 4 million British pounds into the brokerage, to cover the earlier losses, according to regulatory records.[8]

Akbar Moawalla, originally from Tanzania, managed the London office. He lived in a large Tudor-style home in suburban Woking, south of the city, and commuted to offices on Berkeley Square in the central Mayfair district, near the Saudi Arabian embassy. Some colleagues found Moawalla particularly secretive, even by the standards of a company that valued discretion. He had a long history with the family and he seemed to know as much as anyone about its finances. Moawalla would sometimes answer a seemingly routine business inquiry from a fellow executive by saying matter-of-factly, "You don't have a need to know." He did not seem to be the architect of family investment strategy, however; rather, he was a reliable and efficient administrator. As the London office settled down after its crises of the late 1980s, John Pilley, an experienced British financial executive, joined Moawalla.[9]

At Bakr's direction, the two men reported to his half-brother Shafiq, who was placed in charge of international financial issues—an assignment designed to complement Hassan's role overseeing international business development. Shafiq spent a great deal of time in Europe, where he still lived exclusively in hotel rooms, such as one in the Noga Hilton

in Geneva. His Quaker-supervised boarding-school education in Lebanon and his college education in America had led him, by his forties,
to a notably Western lifestyle of business meetings and exuberant
nightlife, a way of life that provided a notable contrast to that of his
half-brother Osama—particularly since the two were both singleton
sons of Mohamed's who had apparently been born in the same month of
January 1958. Shafiq remained a quirky character; his hair sometimes
grew out in long tufts and his hotel rooms, according to one visitor, could
be as messy as a teenager's. Yet he had earned a bachelor's degree in
business from the University of San Francisco in 1981, and he was one of
the few Bin Laden brothers who could hold his own in the technical vernacular of finance and investing, a sometimes mysterious realm of puts
and calls, options and warrants, margin calls and vesting dates. In time,
according to a business partner, Bakr chaired an investment committee
consisting of five Bin Laden brothers, and Shafiq became the committee's
chief manager.[10]

For years the Bin Ladens had invested on the obscure margins of the
United States—the odd strip mall or apartment complex, or blue chip
stocks that were very widely held. During the mid-1990s, for the first
time, the family began to make more diverse and sophisticated financial
investments, particularly in firms that had connections to political elites
in Washington and London.

The Carlyle Group operated from majestic offices at 1001
Pennsylvania Avenue, between the White House and the U.S. Capitol. It
was a private equity firm, meaning that its partners raised money from
wealthy and institutional investors, pooled those funds, and then used
them to buy and sell stakes in private companies and other assets. The
partners made their money—considerable amounts—by charging management fees to their investors and by orchestrating profitable deals. The
moving force at Carlyle was a young workaholic lawyer named David
Rubenstein, who had served at a very young age as a domestic policy adviser to President Jimmy Carter. With Stephen Norris, a mergers spe-

cialist, Rubenstein formed Carlyle in 1987; they drew its name from the posh Carlyle Hotel in New York. By 1993 the firm's portfolio of investments had grown to about $2 billion.[11]

Rubenstein had lured Frank Carlucci, secretary of defense in the first Bush administration, to serve as vice chairman; his connections among Pentagon contractors drew Carlyle into the defense arena. Carlucci's success impressed upon Rubenstein the advantages of attracting prominent, connected politicians as partners to the firm—their reputations and fame helped attract investors, and their inside connections led to profitable deals. After Bush's defeat by Bill Clinton in 1992, Rubenstein and Norris visited the White House to meet with outgoing secretary of state James Baker. With the Democrats back in power, Baker was ready to make money. He decided to sign on as a consultant to an upstart energy company in Houston called Enron Corporation. And he agreed to become a partner at Carlyle.[12]

Baker enjoyed an excellent reputation among Arab elites in the Middle East, particularly in the Persian Gulf region, largely because of his performance in the Gulf war. With other partners and promoters at Carlyle, he traveled the Middle East to raise investment funds from wealthy Arab investors. His most important role—and those of other big-name promoters, such as President George H. W. Bush and former British prime minister John Major—was to draw the deepest pockets in Arabia to dinners and private seminars, to impress upon them Carlyle's profitable record and outstanding prospects. The tactic worked: between 1994 and 1996, the firm raised $1.3 billion for an investment fund called Carlyle Partners II. The investors included George Soros—the enormously wealthy currency trader, who put in $100 million—and pension funds, such as the California Public Employees' Retirement System, which put in $80 million.[13]

The Bin Laden family heard Carlyle's pitch in 1995, through its London office. The family agreed to put in at least $2 million. Jim Baker "knew them very well" and was the family's "favorite politician," said

Charles Schwartz, the Houston lawyer who represented Bin Laden family interests in Texas. Shafiq Bin Laden, although an unlikely dinner or hunting partner for the former secretary of state, was appointed by Bakr to attend Carlyle conferences and keep track of the family's investment. It was this assignment that would ultimately carry him to Washington, D.C., on the same day his half-brother attacked the city.[14]

Shafiq also supervised the family's investment in United Press International, the venerable American wire service, which a consortium of Saudi investors, including the Bin Ladens and the Alireza family, had purchased at a bankruptcy auction in 1992 for $4 million. The spread of satellite television dishes on the rooftops of Saudi households during the early 1990s, and the birth of popular Arabic-language broadcasters such as Al-Jazeera, who were hostile or indifferent to the Saudi establishment, had led the Saudi government to encourage the development of Saudi-owned alternatives, such as Al-Arabiya and Middle East Broadcasting. The theory of the UPI purchase seemed to be that its news gathering could support Middle East Broadcasting, although it was never entirely clear to some UPI executives whether families like the Bin Ladens had made this investment on their own accord or as silent partners of the Saudi government. Ahmed Badeeb, former chief of staff to Prince Turki, the head of Saudi intelligence, eventually became chairman of the board. Badeeb had retired and now operated international companies from Paris and Lebanon. Arnaud de Borchgrave, who served for a time as UPI's editor, struggled with him over the company's perpetual financial problems. At one point, de Borchgrave recalled, Badeeb sent him a resentful message: "I don't appreciate your criticism of my business procedure. I'll have you know I've made over $500 million in over thirty-one years of government service."[15]

At the quarterly board meetings, Shafiq sat silently. He seemed to Borchgrave to be "clearly a man who had never done anything with his life—spoiled." The Saudis on the board struggled with one another and tried to forestall bankruptcy; they sold out eventually to business interests controlled by the controversial South Korean church of the Reverend Sun Myung Moon.[16]

AT THE TIME Osama began to publish his first faxes attacking King Fahd's dependence on America, a number of his half-siblings continued to spend lengthy periods of time in the United States. Khalil Bin Laden now summered with his wife, Isabel, and their children at Desert Bear, outside Orlando. They turned the estate, at least initially, into a considerably quieter place than it had been during its earlier heyday as Salem's princely vacation resort. Khalil sat out by the swimming pool in the evenings, overlooking the willow trees and the lake, and puffed tobacco from a tangled Arabian water pipe. He invited the neighbors over for July 4 barbecues, and he occasionally set off fireworks to punctuate his celebrations of American independence. Gaggles of American-accented children belonging to Khalil and Isabel, as well as nieces and nephews visiting from Saudi Arabia or attending preparatory school in the States, occasionally passed through the compound. So did Khalil's half-sister Rajia, who visited from Los Angeles, where she lived for significant periods of time. She was a pilot and a particularly fast driver of automobiles—so fast that some members of Khalil's circle joked that they were frightened to ride as a passenger if Rajia was at the wheel.[17]

The family member with the most embedded life in America was Abdullah Bin Laden, the second youngest of Mohamed's sons. Some of his friends joked that he was a student for life, and there was some literal truth in this assessment. He had attended college in San Diego, studied law in Saudi Arabia, took courses in business and finance, and then applied to Harvard Law School—not to enroll in its rigorous, spirit-breaking program that churned out lawyers qualified to take American bar exams, but rather to earn first a master's degree and then a doctoral degree in the academic study of law or legal theories. This was a track at Harvard Law School that attracted a number of international students. Ultimately, Abdullah Bin Laden would remain at Harvard Law for about eight years, not quite a record for the school, but not too far from one, either, his professors said. His enrollment was not continuous, however. He maintained a small office in Cambridge, Massachusetts, where he worked on his theses and on various family business projects. (In the early 1990s, two of his half-sisters spent time in Boston, and his younger half-brother, Mohamed, whose mother had been pregnant with him when Mohamed Bin Laden died in 1967, also lived in the city.) Among other endeavors, he invested in condominiums along Boston Harbor. Between these siblings and various nieces and nephews, Abdullah found himself acting occasionally as the Bin Ladens' all-purpose guardian in New England. Throughout these years he kept an apartment near Beacon Street, where he lived alone. By the mid-1990s, he had reached his late twenties. He was a man of medium height, slim, with traces of his father's distinctive nose and cheekbones. Like a number of his half-brothers, he exuded rectitude to the point of pathological shyness, yet he could also project an air of regal dignity, and he could be a genial and intelligent companion. He drove a Range Rover, and he favored an Italian restaurant, Papa Razzi, near his flat.[18]

He befriended other students from Arab and Islamic countries at Harvard and occasionally invited them over for dinner; he impressed some by cooking many of the dishes himself, which they knew was an unusual hobby for a Saudi man, particularly a wealthy one. He had no maids or servants on display during these evenings, and he ladled out his Middle Eastern vegetable dishes on plastic plates. He was so reserved and polite that he was a natural target for teasing. One of his most audacious tormentors was Lama Abu-Odeh, a young Jordanian woman with a considerably more exuberant style than Abdullah's. She liked and admired him unreservedly, but "I would tease him a lot about being conservative—make him laugh and blush, laugh and blush," she recalled. "I would try to push him to his edge." The elites in her native Jordan prided themselves on their relatively secular sophistication, and she enjoyed ranting about "how conservative his country was, how Saudis appear to be socially conservative. I would say, 'Behind every plain Saudi is a whiskey addict.' Just to make him laugh." She particularly liked to get on Abdullah about how he was handsome and rich, yet he never seemed to date. In fact, Abdullah deflected friends who tried to fix him up with women by describing himself as someone who was not interested in Western-style dating.

"Abdullah, if you're gay, you can tell me," Lama would announce. He only laughed some more, and then returned to his reserved mannerisms.[19]

By the mid-1990s, many of his fellow Arab students at Harvard—much more so than fellow American students—were becoming aware of Osama's dissident activity and particularly his open defiance of the Saudi government. If Lama was in an especially feisty mood, she would start praising Osama in front of Abdullah and other students. "At least there's somebody who's gutsy in that family," she would pronounce. "You all just want to make money—at least there's someone who's said 'No!'"

Abdullah's reply was succinct, as Lama recalled it: "Shut up," he said.[20]

His academic adviser was Frank E. Vogel, who had conducted his own scholarly research in Saudi Arabia, visiting its Islamic courts and analyzing its approach to legal and religious doctrines. Vogel took an appreciative academic interest in the Saudi system, and he found that Abdullah was interested in questions related to his own research. In May 1992, Abdullah completed a 101-page master's thesis under Vogel's supervision titled "Western Banking Practices and *Shari'a* Law in Saudi Arabia." His paper explored the conflict between the interest-paying practices of the Western financial system and the prohibitions on interest decreed by many Islamic legal authorities, and how these doctrines had evolved through history and from religious text. He strived to find solutions, a synthesis that would allow both modern banking and Islamic law to thrive in Saudi Arabia. "It could well be," he wrote, "that when a society as a whole is operating in full compliance with the *shari'a* code and an Islamic economic system is instituted, that the prohibition of interest would be feasible."[21]

In pursuit of his doctoral degree, Abdullah embarked on a much more detailed elaboration on the same themes—his thesis would ultimately run to 327 pages, bearing the distinctly unglamorous title "Negotiability of Financial Instruments in Contemporary Financial Markets: An Islamic Legal Analysis." Here Abdullah wrestled with how certain instruments of the global markets—such as warrants bonds and profit-sharing contracts—might be accommodated in an Islamic financial system. It was a lucid and richly footnoted thesis, if often arcane, and when it was eventually completed, it marked at least two milestones in the centuries-long history of the Bin Laden family: Abdullah became the family's first academic doctor (alongside his half-sister Randa, the family's first medical doctor) and the holder of the Bin Ladens' first Harvard degree. Intellectually, Abdullah strived to reconcile the two worlds, Arabian and Western, in which the Bin Ladens lived and worked. Vogel respected "the academic seriousness" of his doctoral thesis, "that he really put himself to difficult research, and quite difficult or abstruse text." As for the subject matter, and what it indicated about the Bin Ladens or Abdullah, in Vogel's judgment, "For a Saudi to work on a topic related to Islamic law is not saying very much about whether he's preoccupied with religion." In the kingdom, there simply was no other way to approach economics, he believed.[22]

The fundraising opportunity represented by the presence of a young Bin Laden at Harvard was not lost on the law school's professors. Around 1993—the same year Philip Griffin opened the Bin Laden office outside Washington—the Bin Ladens entered into discussions with the dean of Harvard Law School. "They were interested in the study of Islam, in lots of places," Vogel recalled. The discussions were "extraordinarily sort of low-key." Abdullah indicated to Harvard that Bakr would be interested in making a $1 million donation to the university to support the study of Islamic design, one of Bakr's personal interests, plus an additional $1 million to support visiting scholarships and stipends for students from Arab League countries who wished to follow Abdullah's footsteps and study at Harvard Law. Vogel and the law school dean traveled to Saudi Arabia; they were received by Bakr at the headquarters of the Saudi Bin Laden Group, where they admired the display models of the family's work on the holy mosques in Mecca and Medina. Vogel explained to the family, "One of the purposes of our program is to build links with the Middle East." There was, of course, no discussion of Osama; he was little known outside the Arab world.[23]

During this same period, Salem Bin Laden's oldest son, Salman, enrolled as an undergraduate student at Tufts University, just outside Boston. Abdullah helped to keep an eye on him; Salman struggled at times to manage his money and his friendships. One of his business professors, Andrew Hess, felt that Salman had suffered psychologically because of Salem's sudden death in Texas in 1988. Salman took after his father in some ways, and played the guitar, and he spoke fluent English in a British-inflected accent. But he had his ups and downs at Tufts. He made a personal connection with Hess, who prior to his professorship had worked for many years in Saudi Arabia, in the oil industry. Salman then introduced Hess to his Harvard uncle, Abdullah.[24]

They met several times for dinner at another of Abdullah's favorite restaurants, in Cambridge. It was called Helmand, after a province in southern Afghanistan. It was run by a gregarious, exiled Afghan family— the Karzais.

Over dinners at Helmand, Hess mentioned to Abdullah that he was having trouble raising money to support some of his academic programs. The Bin Ladens were mostly interested in supporting Islamic studies, Abdullah told him. Hess said that if he had enough funding, he could bring in lecturers and speakers from the Islamic world, to address economic and political issues that fit the Tufts curriculum. Abdullah said he would see what he could do.

Later, he delivered a check to Tufts for $350,000.[25]

31. A TROJAN DESK

A CAR BOMB bearing about 250 pounds of explosives detonated in Riyadh on November 13, 1995. It was the worst terrorist attack in the kingdom since the almost-forgotten days of proxy war with Yemen during the 1960s. The targets this time were not Saudis, however. Seven people died, including five Americans, and thirty-four others were wounded. The attackers, soon beheaded, were former Afghan jihadis; one said in a televised confession that they had been inspired by the writings of Osama Bin Laden. From the point of view of the Bin Laden family, it was hard to judge which was the more discouraging possibility—that the terrorist's confession had been authentic, or that he had been encouraged by Saudi interrogators to implicate Osama publicly, in order to discredit him. In an indirect sense, the Bin Ladens had also been on the receiving end of the attack. The targeted building was an American training facility for the Saudi National Guard. One of the facility's principal contractors, a specialist in military training, was Vinnell Corporation, a low-profile company that has been described by a former board member as associated with the Central Intelligence Agency. Several spouses of Vinnell contractors were among the wounded. At the time, the Carlyle Group owned the firm—although not through the same fund in which the Bin Ladens had just invested. The larger point was the same: the family was now officially at war with itself, even if that war was embryonic and in many respects undeclared.[1]

Bakr said nothing in public, beyond the press statements he had previously issued, but in private, he tried to make clear to the Americans and Europeans he knew that he was appalled by Osama's increasingly violent radicalism. Around Christmas 1995, just a few weeks after the Riyadh attack, Bakr flew a number of Salem's old American and British friends to Jeddah, all expenses paid. Salem's eldest daughter, Sara, was marrying a young man from a prominent Jeddah merchant family, one that had a lucrative car dealership. Bakr hosted a reunion of some of the pilots and musicians who had known Salem in the glory days.[2]

The contrasts now accumulating within the family, even at its home base in Jeddah, were startling. Bakr's Red Sea estate lay a few miles south of one of the family's grand real estate projects, the Salhia Lotus Beach Resort. The development was named for Saheha Bin Laden, the half-brother of Bakr who had traveled widely in Europe and the United States. The resort opened as a private beach club with two hundred furnished chalets and studios, located on Jeddah's North Obhur Beach. Security guards carefully checked the names of Saudi members and authorized foreign guests before allowing them behind the resort's walls. Once inside, the reason for such tight security became obvious: there were women in bikinis lounging alongside men in Speedos; Saudis mixing in their bathing suits with foreigners of both sexes; and Lebanese Christians splashing in the swimming pool with crosses and crucifixes dangling around their necks. It was as if the Bin Ladens had built, and were operating for profit, an alternative Saudi Arabia in a wealthy corner of Jeddah's northern suburbs.[3]

Away from the beach club, at Sara's wedding reception, Bakr was his more traditional self; the genders were duly segregated, and there was an emphasis on fruit juice. Bakr invited some of his foreign guests aboard his large, steel-hulled boat and motored into the Red Sea, where he dropped anchor and hosted an afternoon of shipside swimming. Spirits ran high throughout several days of celebration. Anita Pizza, the pianist, and Gerald Auerbach, the American pilot who had flown both Mohamed and Salem, and who was now in his seventies, were persuaded to run through some of Salem's favorite numbers. Auerbach belted out "On Top of Old Smokey," for old times.[4]

THE MUTED OPENING of Osama's war on Saudi Arabia coincided with the end of King Fahd's reign—at least, the end of his ability to rule actively. On November 29, 1995, Fahd suffered a massive stroke. Perhaps the Riyadh bombing and its aftermath raised his blood pressure, or perhaps it was only age or genetics or his untreated obesity. He almost died, but his doctors, so long the beneficiaries of his patronage and largesse, worked to save him. By doing so they inaugurated an Elizabethan-tinged drama of rivalry and succession maneuvering within the Saudi royal family.

The intrigue was more whispered about than witnessed, more presumed than observed, but its outlines were clear enough. As long as Fahd remained technically alive, he would be king, even if he could do little more than nod silently in his wheelchair. The Al-Saud had no precedent for removing an ailing monarch, and after all, the crown prince could govern in his stead. But there was more to this decision than constitutional order. As long as Fahd remained on the throne, his full brothers—Sultan at Defense; Nayef and Ahmed at Interior; and Salman, the governor of Riyadh—might remain unchallenged in their lucrative ministerial fiefdoms, free to supervise their own contracts and to preside over their own patronage machines. Moreover, Fahd's favorite son, Abdulaziz, might continue to enrich himself and those around him. (By 1993 companies controlled by the Ibrahim family, Abdulaziz's maternal uncles, owned real estate in the United States valued at more than $1.2 billion worldwide, including Ritz-Carlton hotels in New York, Washington, Houston, and Aspen; a 23,000-acre ranch in Colorado; the Marina del Rey complex in Los Angeles; and a planned resort community near Disney World.) If Fahd died, Crown Prince Abdullah would take the throne—penny-pinching, provincial, isolated, stubborn, unreliable Abdullah, as the Fahd group tended to see him. In "their heart of hearts," said Wyche Fowler, who served as U.S. ambassador to Saudi Arabia as this narrative unfolded, Fahd's full brothers "were not enthusiastic that Abdullah would be their next king."[5]

Abdullah remained, as a British diplomat had described him several decades earlier, "abrupt, impulsive, but popular."[6] He had little formal education, but his steady contact across decades with tribal levies in the National Guard had attuned his ear to public opinion—or, at least, to the opinions of male soldiers from the major tribes. At the time of Fahd's stroke, Abdullah seemed to grasp, in a way that Fahd's son, full brothers, and brothers-in-law did not, that the kingdom simply could not continue to drift along, ignoring the excesses of the royal family, as it had done for so long. Oil prices fell steadily during the 1990s, eventually touching record lows, if inflation was taken into account. Saudi Arabia's per capita income, which had soared during the initial oil boom period, also declined dramatically—in part because the size of the native Saudi population grew at alarming rates. Yet Saudis remained poorly equipped for the modern workplace, and the kingdom's universities remained dominated by religious curricula. In his seventies, living in his own grand palaces and on his desert farms, Abdullah was no firebrand reformer, but at a minimum, he wanted to bring the most visible excesses and self-enrichment of senior princes under control. He tried after Fahd's stroke to unwind or cancel some of the most egregious contracts, such as the Al-Yamamah deal overseen by Prince Sultan, but he found his anti-corruption drive to be difficult. Among other things, according to Fowler, Fahd's group sometimes evaded his edicts on contracting by routing their business through the untouchable young Abdulaziz—he was, after all, still the king's favorite son. Then, too, Abdullah faced his own family members interested in business opportunities. Some of his own sons were entering into commerce, and one of those sons was a school friend of Abdulaziz. Abdullah might have sound instincts about Saudi Arabia's needs, but he shared power, lacked strong blood allies, and possessed no transformational vision. Political and economic reform in the kingdom, it soon became plain, would be at best an evolutionary project, one where the pace might be barely perceptible to the human eye—nothing like what Osama Bin Laden and his allied dissidents in London had apparently hoped that Abdullah might champion.

As Osama careened toward violence in 1996, his family moved to strengthen its ties to America, and to hedge their bets. The Al-Saud, on the other hand, allowed their alliance with Washington to deteriorate. A shared antipathy to communism no longer bound Saudi Arabia to America. The rise of potent transnational Islamist ideology and jihadi violence, some of it supported by Saudi fundraising, presented a new divide. There were also more particular factors. Fahd's sudden incapacitation was one—he had been the most pro-American king in Saudi history, by a considerable margin. At the Saudi embassy in Washington, Bandar Bin Sultan, the longtime ambassador, had failed to strike up a successful relationship with Clinton; they were similar personalities, and they seemed to annoy each other. Bandar drifted into diplomatic irrelevancy, and his embassy, filled with Saudi bureaucrats from the religious and education ministries who did not speak much English, became an impediment to day-to-day communication between the two governments. In an astonishingly short time, the confident, risk-taking, back-of-the-envelope relationship that had prevailed between Washington and Riyadh during the Cold War and the Gulf war came to an end. In its place rose a muddled, mutually resentful engagement in which the top leaders of the two countries rarely spoke, while midlevel and cabinet-level officials fumed at one another over perceived slights and failures to cooperate.

Early in 1996, alarmed by Osama's support for violent attacks against American and Arab targets, the CIA formed a new unit to track him. Michael Scheuer, its leader, as one of his first tasks, submitted a request to the Saudi government for basic information about Osama Bin Laden—his medical records, his birth certificate, if one existed, and copies of the residence permit and passport the government claimed it had previously seized from him. Scheuer never heard a word in reply. He soon concluded that the Saudi government should be regarded as "hostile" to the United States on the subject of Osama and his Islamist militia. That was the same terminology used at the CIA to describe the intelligence services of Cuba and Iran. "They refused to do anything to help us, or even to provide us the minimal information," Scheuer said later. He and other CIA officers also thought it was possible that Osama had recruited sympathizers or followers inside the Saudi intelligence or security services. Equally, the Saudi services themselves, in Scheuer's analysis, wanted from the very beginning of the violence Bin Laden inspired to protect themselves from American investigations into Saudi Arabia's private collaborations with Osama in the past, dating back to the anti-Soviet Afghan war. "Bin Laden knows so much about who the Saudis dealt with during the Afghan war, how the mechanisms for moving money work," Scheuer concluded. "They were protecting the royal family, they were protecting the skeletons in the closet from the Afghan war." Scheuer also believed, as did Clinton's counterterrorism aide Richard Clarke, that the Saudi government had authorized some of Osama's adventures in South Yemen. This history, too, had to be shielded from the Americans, in Scheuer's analysis.[7]

Scheuer did not want to share sensitive CIA information with the Saudis, for fear it would leak through to Osama. For their part, some of the Saudis felt the same way about the CIA. When they passed on information they regarded as sensitive, they, too, often read it in the American papers or heard it on CNN.

Prince Nayef, the interior minister, presented perhaps the greatest obstacle to trust and cooperation after Fahd's stroke. Nayef was particularly hostile toward the CIA. During the 1970s, the CIA had presented him with a new desk for his office as a gift. Afterward, Nayef discovered a listening device on the desk. He had a long memory.[8]

32. THE AESTHETICS OF WORSHIP

CITIZENS OF SAUDI ARABIA made up a tiny percentage of the world's Muslim population—less than 2 percent by the mid-1990s. The kingdom's influence on Islamic thought, however, had become pervasive. Oil wealth and its missionary purchases—mosques built in poorer Muslim countries, salaried imams of the Wahhabi school to oversee those mosques, pamphlets and textbooks to instruct the young—explained some of its reach. Yet the number of Muslims individually touched even by this expansive proselytizing remained relatively small. Far more important to the lived experience of Islam by its faithful was the annual Hajj. When King Abdulaziz founded Saudi Arabia early in the twentieth century, a busy Hajj season might see fifty thousand pilgrims visiting the kingdom. The jet age, the oil boom, and the growth of middle-class Muslim populations in Asia and elsewhere meant that by the end of the 1990s, a typical number annually was about 2 million. The pilgrims all arrived at the same time of year and all went to the same places, Medina and Mecca, more or less simultaneously. They arrived, too, in a heightened state of spiritual awareness, if not longing or near-rapture. On this heavily preconceived yet richly emotional journey, millions of Muslims discovered and judged modern Saudi Arabia. It was a process about as reliable as the one by which Saudis discovered America through vacations in Disney World and west Los Angeles. But it was no less true or powerful, in either case, for being incomplete.

Well-educated, globally conscious Hajj pilgrims from poorer Muslim countries such as Egypt or India sometimes resented Saudi Arabia for two reasons: its garish, wasteful nouveau wealth, and its intolerant religious orthodoxy. To encounter for the first time the kingdom's pre-stressed concrete modernity and its designer-label greed, all integrated with its insistent theological doctrines, could be unsettling. A pilgrim might approach Saudi Arabia aspiring to inner purity; what he found there could be polluted by banality.

"Through the window, I had my first glimpse of Medina—buses parked in rows and rows as far as the horizon," recalled the Moroccan anthropologist Abdellah Hammoudi, who arrived on Hajj in the late 1990s. He made his way to the center of the city, where he encountered King Fahd's "spectacular renovations" to the Prophet's Mosque, carried out by the Bin Ladens. The floodlights and shiny brass fixtures awed him: "There it was in its immensity, with its minarets like giant chandeliers charging the sky. It seemed for a moment to be floating in the firmament." And yet, when Hammoudi walked through the surrounding streets, in neighborhoods remade by Saudi modernization drives, he saw nothing of Medina's rich architectural or religious history, only "shop windows and consumer displays":

> Carpets, caps, sheets, turbans, sandals, belts, watches, compasses, radios, tea sets, coffee sets, shirts, dresses, blankets, shoes, televisions, VCRs, computers, calculators, perfumes, incense, aromatic plants ... elevators, air-conditioning, restaurants, cafeterias, ice-cream vendors, all American-style: self-service, cardboard plates and cups, plastic forks and knives, menus and prices displayed on neon-lit boards ... "Modernity" ravaged everything.[1]

Inside the mosque, jostling in crowds for a glimpse of the Prophet Mohamed's tomb, which lay in an unadorned chamber, Hammoudi spied the omnipresent Saudi religious police, who patrolled Medina with sticks so they could beat worshippers who dallied too long at the tomb or displayed excessive emotion there—signs of *shirk*, or forbidden worship of idols. Elsewhere in the city, these police patrolled cemeteries, historical battlefields, and Shiite shrines to prevent unauthorized prayers or other displays of fervor by the deviant or the nostalgic. For centuries, under previous dynastic rulers, culminating in the Ottomans, Medina had tolerated and, indeed, cultivated Islam's global diversity of belief and practice; in Saudi Arabia, Hammoudi concluded, the dominant creed was propagated with all the subtlety of a bulldozer:

> They have brought the Koran and the Prophet's example down to the
> level of a recipe book and consigned its implementations to militias . . .
> This was actually a form of modern totalitarianism, far closer to the
> defunct Soviet system than the constitution of Medina or to Bedouin in-
> formality. A merciless formula managed by technocrats with sophisti-
> cated means of communication and espionage, technique for daily
> intimidation, and a propaganda force that could recycle traditions and
> social pressures to its own benefit. In Medina, as elsewhere, it served us
> its exclusive version of the holy city. Its version and no other.[2]

Whose version, exactly? The theological framework belonged to the semi-independent Saudi religious establishment, subsidized by the royal family. Saudi Islamic scholars controlled much—but not all—of the religious rule making around the Hajj. (Left to their own devices, for example, Saudi Arabia's ardently sectarian Sunni scholars would probably ban Shia from attending altogether, but the royal family, wishing to avoid a global confrontation, managed a compromise, under which Shia could come if they accepted certain quotas and constraints.) King Fahd shaped the Hajj's physical environment. The architectural ambition of the two renovated holy cities—bigger, better, shinier, ringed by condominium towers and shopping malls, and under surveillance by security cameras—reflected the same spirit Fahd had brought during the early 1930s to the refurbishment of his Boeing 747. Among other things, his ideas about urban planning seemed to express a "deliberate desire to erase the past," as Hammoudi put it. This was partly another bow to his religious establishment, who tended to view all of the schools of Islamic art and architecture between the Prophet's death and their arrival in the Hejaz in the 1920s as illegitimate. There was also a more general disinterest among the Saudi royal family about historical preservation and archaeology. The design sensibility that evolved during the Mecca and Medina projects of the late 1980s and mid-1990s—one that evoked Disney, Mall of the Americas, and the Ritz-Carlton Hotel chain—originated with Fahd but also came in substantial part from the Bin Ladens, and particularly from Bakr, who looked after the Fahd account in Riyadh and took a close personal interest in the holy city work. Among other compulsions, these renovation projects had become, by 1995, the largest single source of revenue for the Mohamed Bin Laden Company: Fahd's total spending in Mecca and Medina during this period has been estimated at $25 billion. That may have been an exaggeration designed to impress Muslim publics, but the contracting work—all handled on a sole-source, no-bid basis by the Bin Ladens—certainly ran into many billions of dollars.[3]

Before his stroke, when King Fahd visited the construction sites in Mecca and Medina, Bakr steered him around at the wheel of a white golf cart, a form of transport that only reinforced the Florida-derived vision they seemed to share. At the University of Miami during the early 1970s, Bakr had studied basic architecture on a campus full of mid-century white concrete boxes, in a state where the cutting edge of the spectacular tourist destination built for international crowds was Disney's Epcot Center—a place, like renovated Mecca, that advertised itself as a microcosm of global diversity, lit up in floodlights and neon. It was also America, and particularly humid Florida, that pressed upon Saudi elites the apparent correlation between national progress and the spread of air-conditioning, an imperative that Fahd and the Bin Ladens carried at considerable expense to Mecca and Medina.

The renovation projects began in 1985 and proceeded in two sequential phases—Medina first, then Mecca. In Medina the needs were great-est. For all the effort Wahhabi scholars made to discourage the venera-tion of the Prophet's Mosque and other local historical sites, practicing Muslims simply could not be persuaded to forgo the journey to the city of the Prophet's storied exile. Hajj spiritual rituals are entirely centered on Mecca, but most pilgrims, having taken the time and expense to travel to Saudi Arabia in the first place, felt compelled to include Medina as a side journey. The trouble was that the worship area in the Prophet's Mosque was about one-tenth the size of the one in the Grand Mosque in Mecca, and as the number of pilgrims swelled during the 1980s, the squeeze in Medina appeared unsustainable. Fahd embraced an expansion plan that would transform Medina into a viable, if still undeclared, com-panion destination to Mecca. The urban clearance work necessary to ex-tend the mosque's footprint was completed by 1988; at that point, with Salem gone and Bakr fully in charge, renovation of the sanctuary it-self began.[4]

For all of its modernity and scale, and despite its disregard for in-herited architectural diversity, the Bin Ladens' work in Medina did pro-duce some beautiful and striking innovations, such as an array of retractable domes and umbrella-like coverings. The modernized mosque's polish and lighting and soaring minarets, in the clear desert sky, against the silhouettes of barren hills, could produce spectacular visual effects, particularly at night; it could snatch the breath of even a skeptic like Hammoudi. These were achievements in which the Bin Ladens could and did take pride; the truth was, however, that most of their important and impressive work lay hidden from view. The Bin Ladens were not masters of architecture; they were masters of infrastructure.

The Prophet's Mosque, across all its centuries as an icon in the desert, had never, of course, enjoyed air-conditioning. The Bin Ladens, however, had formed a partnership during the 1980s with York International Corporation, of York, Pennsylvania, the world's leading manufacturer and installer of what are known as "large tonnage chillers," industrial systems for cooling very large buildings. York chillers cooled the U.S. Capitol, the Pentagon, the Twin Towers of the World Trade Center in New York, and the Kremlin. The systems typically worked by reducing water to a temperature of about forty degrees and then piping the water through the targeted building; this was the only practical way to distribute cool air through such large spaces. Large and mechanically complex machines cooled the water initially and then expelled its heat into the air upon its return from the building. York manufactured these chiller systems in a 1.5-million-square-foot plant in Grantley, Pennsylvania. The Medina chillers ordered by the Bin Ladens posed a number of unusual challenges. Desert temperatures and the project's enormous size meant that York would have to manufacture a number of its heaviest-duty machine, later dubbed the Titan. Also, because only Muslims are allowed inside the Medina city center, there were questions about how the chillers could be reliably serviced if they occasionally required the attention of a non-Muslim engineer or technician. To address this concern, the Bin Ladens decided to install the principal chiller plant outside the Muslim-only exclusion zone, more than four miles from the Prophet's Mosque; they dug a wide tunnel, big enough for a sport utility vehicle to drive in, between the chiller plant and the mosque, down which traveled trunk cooling pipes and other utilities. By the time the plant was finished, by 1993, it had given the marketing department at York headquarters something new to boast about: the air-conditioning project in Medina had become the largest heating or air-conditioning project of its type in world history.[5]

Anwar Hassan, a York manager who worked on it, was originally from Sudan. On his trips to Jeddah or Medina, the Bin Ladens would invite him to receptions, or to an *iftar* fast-breaking dinner during Ramadan. They projected "a great sense of pride" about their work in the holy cities. Hassan shared their vision that the Hajj could and should be modernized. He felt it was misleading to romanticize the past. He remembered stories he had heard as a child from one of his great-uncles in

Sudan, who recounted how, in the days before Abdulaziz and the birth of Saudi Arabia, if a hundred African-looking Sudanese pilgrims attended Hajj, only sixty or seventy might return—the rest were victims of highway robbers, or disease, or worse. Even during the 1960s, when another of Hassan's uncles undertook the pilgrimage, "He came back appalled at the poor level of hygiene. People would slaughter sheep in the street." By the early 1990s, Hassan could ascend an escalator to stand amid the crowds by the Prophet's tomb, and as he touched his head upon the floor in prayer, he might feel a touch of cool air on the back of his neck. "That's a fabulous transformation," he believed. "You have to appreciate that they did it for the comfort. It's a great thing that they've done."[6]

THOSE WHO THOUGHT otherwise did so at their peril.

Sami Angawi tied his thinning, graying hair behind his head in a ponytail, and he draped himself in undulating Hejazi robes, not the flat white uniform of Saudi national dress. He looked like a Saudi hippie. He adhered to Sufism, a school of Islam that emphasized diversity and individual spiritual experience. He had been born in Mecca to a traditional family of *mutawwafs*, or "pilgrimage guides," an ancient vocation in decline in the age of Hajj package air-hotel tours and Saudi nationalization (by the 1990s, a federal ministry administered most aspects of the pilgrimage). At the University of Texas, Angawi studied architecture and urban planning; he wrote a master's thesis about a possible renovation of Mecca that would emphasize historical preservation, pedestrian zones, and environmental conservation.

In 1975 he returned to Saudi Arabia to form and supervise a Hajj Research Center at King Abdulaziz University in Jeddah. Its goal, approved by the Saudi government, was "to preserve the natural environment as created by God and the Islamic environment of the two holy cities." This was a tricky principle to interpret on Saudi ground, since if

Angawi advocated historical conservation per se, he would run afoul of the religious establishment's opposition to false monuments. Still, he believed that he could see a way forward. Angawi and his staff carried out surveys in Jakarta, Karachi, Cairo, and elsewhere, trying to document the experiences and desires of Muslim pilgrims in all of their heterodoxy. He incorporated this research into his evolving plans for Mecca and Medina. In his vision, influenced by environmentally conscious European urban planning, automobiles and buses would be excluded from the two city centers—vehicles would park on the perimeter, and pilgrims would flood through the worship areas on foot, praying not only at the mosques but also in parks and in traditional, renovated *souks.*[7]

This was not, of course, the image of Mecca and Medina's future that King Fahd or the Bin Ladens had in mind as they undertook their massive renovations. Angawi was not a radical—he tried to work within the Saudi system, and he earned a lucrative living as an architect, enough to design and construct a stunning traditional Hejazi home in a wealthy neighborhood of Jeddah. Yet he had given much of his professional life to the proposition that Mecca and Medina need not succumb to the same soulless sprawl that was engulfing every other city in Saudi Arabia. He tried to suggest the purchase of Westinghouse fast trains that could speed large numbers of pilgrims between Mecca and Medina. He produced a film about the worsening traffic problems in the holy cities.

Angawi emphasized, prudently, that he did not doubt "for a second" King Fahd's good intentions, but he challenged the basic assumptions of the Bin Laden–managed projects. "We keep the foreigners out, but allow everything else you can think of—shopping malls, Kentucky Fried Chicken, McDonald's, neon signs," he said later. "The companies that plan, that construct, that buy the land—you only have one company [the Bin Ladens]. I have nothing against them. But this is the wrong approach. It's a fantastic conflict of interest. The answer is bulldozers and dynamite. Knock it down, build it up, pour it over with marble and decorate it with things that look Islamic . . . If you want to accommodate more people praying, that's one thing. If you want to accommodate more cars, that's another. We ended up with skyscrapers and buildings."[8]

By 1989, because of his dissent, Angawi had fallen under so much pressure from the Saudi establishment that he resigned from his Hajj center. At that point, the Medina renovation was a lost cause—the new mosque and its supporting infrastructure were under construction, and York International had its orders for multiton chillers. In Mecca, however, where the plans for renovation were not yet fully committed, Angawi saw an opportunity to push for at least some historical preservation of ancient monuments and sites. He and the Hejazi intellectuals around him in Jeddah who joined his quiet agitation felt a connection, often through their family histories, to the pre-Saudi architecture of Mecca. In some respects, Angawi's circle in Jeddah—lawyers, architects, writers, business executives—constituted a new generation of globally minded Saudi intellectuals, who had been influenced through travel and schooling by preservation movements elsewhere in the Arab world, as well as in Europe. They understood that in Wahhabi-dominated Saudi Arabia, advocating historic conservation was a dangerous political and theological stance, but they also felt protected by the global respectability of their cause. So they pushed back—not enough to end up in prison, but enough, as it happened, to annoy the Bin Ladens.

The family's renovation work in Mecca during the 1990s was of a different character than its renovation of the Prophet's Mosque in Medina. In Medina a single building had to be expanded and updated. In Mecca the priorities had less to do with the Grand Mosque itself than with surrounding sites visited during the Hajj rituals. Each year, for example, all the pilgrims assembled in tent camps on the plain of Arafat, about nine miles from Mecca city; at a prescribed time, known as the Day of Standing, they stood together in an awesome assembly in the desert, beseeching God. That huge gathering was followed by a mass symbolic stoning of the Devil, carried out by hurling pebbles at certain columns several miles from Arafat. Each pilgrim was also expected to purchase and sacrifice a sheep or other animal, as an offering to God. The logistical and sanitary challenges presented by the occupation of an open desert camp of 2 million people, followed by group rock throwing and animal slaughter, can be readily imagined. Hajj after Hajj, a stampede, fire, collapsing bridge, or other mishap would claim hundreds of pilgrim lives. Even in the absence of such calamities, the heat of a summer Hajj on Arafat could be too much for many elderly pilgrims. Then, too, there was the traffic: "The largest traffic jam I have ever seen," recalled Mark Caudill, an American pilgrim. It took hours to move just a few miles around Arafat, and even after the day's rituals were completed, "The sounds and smells of diesel trucks idling through the night were accompanied by occasional screams of sirens, Saudi traffic police barking admonitions through bullhorns, and the roiling murmur of more than two million souls."[9]

King Fahd, with the Bin Ladens as his instrument, tried to alleviate this traffic-induced suffering. His approach, however, was typical of transportation development approaches popular in the United States: more roads, more parking lots, more tunnels, and more bridges. The Mohamed Bin Laden Company built parking lots at Arafat and elsewhere during the mid-1990s, totaling millions of square feet. Above the Arafat plain, to cool off the faithful during the Day of Standing, they installed an overhead water piping system that spewed out thin jets of water above the pilgrims' heads. They dug new connector roads and flyovers, laid down pedestrian walkways, installed water fountains, and put in 14,200 public toilets. They built a modern slaughterhouse that could accommodate 500,000 goats and sheep, plus another that could handle 10,000 camels and cattle—these facilities supported a new government-run voucher system for the slaughter ritual, whereby pilgrims could purchase a ticket that ensured a Saudi official carried out their sacrifice in a sanitary manner. All this was supported by new security systems in and around Mecca, designed to ensure that the 1979 uprising at the Grand Mosque was never repeated—surveillance cameras were installed copiously, along with command centers, alarm systems, and supporting communications. Here, too, the Bin Ladens were in charge.[10]

Sami Angawi consulted for the governor of Mecca following his resignation from the Hajj center. He tried to keep track of the city's archaeological heritage. There had been a time, he knew, prior to the Saudi kingdom, when pilgrims in Mecca diverted themselves with visits to several hundred historical and mythical sites, much as visitors to Jerusalem and its surrounding areas still do. One semi-mythical site that had been long discussed in Meccan tradition was the Prophet Mohamed's original home, where he lived during his days as a businessman, prior to receiving divine revelations. Around 1991, as the Bin Ladens began to shift their renovation work from Medina to Mecca, Angawi learned from a local preservationist that a site had been discovered that might be the Prophet's house. It seemed to be in the right place. An ancient wall of the structure had been exposed by initial bulldozer work undertaken during Mecca's redevelopment.

"I was told by one of the elders of the city that this place might be destroyed," Angawi recalled. "So I moved in and I tried to use every connection and authority I have." He found a professor at the School of Oriental and African Studies in London to advise his preliminary archaeological work at the site. He began to dig and to inventory carefully what he found. He undertook historical research to explore evidence that could confirm or refute the discovery.[11]

As he worked, the question became whether it might be possible to accommodate both Angawi's vision of Mecca and that of Fahd and the Bin Ladens. Angawi and his allies acknowledged that the renovations had eased the experience of visiting pilgrims. Mecca and Medina could now "accommodate more, and it could accommodate them more comfortably," said a Jeddah professional aligned with Angawi. "But it was done at the expense of other things.

"This is where they used the Bin Ladens," Angawi's ally recalled. "In the Holy Mosque of Mecca, there were columns with engraved inscriptions a thousand years old. And they'd say, 'Wouldn't a marble column be nice here?' And the Bin Ladens would say, 'Sure, we can give you a polished marble column.' And they didn't preserve what they knocked down for a museum, and they did it without any control or supervision ... We have all these slick brass lamps, but no accounting of the heritage."[12]

The Bin Ladens, of course, were considerably more influential than the preservationists. Within forty days after he started working at the presumed site of the Prophet's house, Angawi won the formal attention of the Saudi government: Officials ordered him to stop what he was doing and vacate the place.

Angawi contacted the Bin Ladens, including Bakr. Couldn't they find some way to work around this one particular area of the Prophet's house during their renovation projects? Or could they at least proceed in gradual steps, so he could finish some of his digging and documentation? No, he was told. Either Angawi would get out of the hole or he would be bulldozed over himself, he was told. "We have our orders."[13]

At that point Angawi began to lose some of his equilibrium. "I brought my children out to the site," and he dared the Bin Ladens to start up their bulldozer engines. "They took that in for a couple of weeks," he recalled. "I was really going wild. My mind was fixed."[14]

Gradually the two camps shuffled toward a partial compromise. This was not jihad, after all; it was a struggle over principle and ideology between two wealthy and privileged camps of the Saudi elite, a struggle in which leaders on both sides carried memories of noisy but passive sit-ins at their Vietnam-era American university campuses overseas. In the end, Angawi was permitted to spend some time making a fuller inventory of his dig site—but he was then ordered to stay away from the site for three months. The Bin Ladens moved in and did their bulldozing.

Ultimately, the Bin Ladens installed a sparkling new public toilet facility on top of the ruin that Angawi believed had been the Prophet's home. At times, it seemed, there was something about being a Bin Laden that made it hard to be subtle.

IN 1996 Bakr published a book to celebrate the family's work in Mecca and Medina during the previous eight years. It was titled *Story of the Great Expansion*, and it was intended as a coffee table volume for Bin Laden customers and for the royal family. Bakr dedicated the book, of course, to King Fahd. In the florid and obsequious tones of courtly Arabic, he summarized the history of the alliance between the Bin Ladens and the Al-Saud, from the time of Mohamed Bin Laden until the present:

> It was a dear trust your father, the founder of this great nation that has been built on the cherished principles of love, nobleness and purity, gave to our father, who felt greatly honored by it throughout his life . . . Our father went the way of all mortals, and your brothers followed in the footsteps of their great father. We were young and grew up in glorious and proficient hands. You, my Lord, conferred on us a great badge of honor, for we have been honored to carry out your two most magnificent projects of the Holy Mosque in Mecca and the Prophet's Mosque in Medina . . . Could the Custodian of the Two Holy Mosques please accept this dedication, offered with heartfelt affection and invocation, deep amity and allegiance.[15]

By now, in exile, Osama Bin Laden enjoyed a luxury that Bakr did not: he no longer felt a need to curry favor with the royal family, and also, free from government censors, he could write whatever he pleased. On April 16, 1996, around the same time that Bakr published his self-promoting book, Osama sent out a blast fax from London, titled "The Saudi Regime and Repeated Tragedies of the Pilgrims." It was Hajj season, and as was typical of his essays, Osama played off recent news headlines—a massive tent fire had killed or injured a large number of pilgrims.

He aimed his venom at the Saudi royal family. He never referred to the widely known fact that his own family was responsible for the design and implementation of renovations in Mecca that were supposed to keep pilgrims safer and more comfortable. More than any single essay Osama is known to have written, this one seemed to carry an open subtext of resentment, anger, and disapproval directed at the Bin Ladens, particularly at the senior brothers in charge of the Mecca and Medina renovations. Since they had just forced him out of the family firm, in obedience to Fahd, Osama's anger was perhaps not surprising, and it was telling, as ever, that he could still not express himself directly on the subject of his family. Not all of the criticisms in his essay implicated his brothers; for instance, he argued that the Saudi government's budgeting for Mecca and Medina had been inadequate and that the royals should be spending *more* money on renovations, an argument Osama's brothers might have appreciated, if it were not coming from him. Other aspects of his critique, however, seemed to express Osama's ambition not only to overthrow the Saudi government, but to take charge of the Bin Laden family, perhaps in partnership with a new and improved Riyadh regime:

> It has become very normal for pilgrims to the House of God to be exposed to disasters and tragedies that result in hundreds of deaths and injuries every year ... If we examine the reasons for these disasters, we find that they include: narrowness of the facilities which leads to collision and trampling in the crowds ... negligence in security procedures, poor response to incidents, or neglect of pilgrims by not taking the necessary security precautions.

He turned to the question of who bore responsibility for this pattern of avoidable neglect. The royal family, as ever, was to blame. That he also meant, at the same time, to criticize Bakr and other brothers in the company leadership could hardly be mistaken:

> Preparing, maintaining and equipping the necessary facilities in a sufficient manner and at the level appropriate for the needs of the pilgrims

is supposed to be the responsibility of the rulers of this country, who have massive resources and huge budgets to work with. The facilities they have built and services they have provided thus far do not vouch for them. Experiences and incidents have already proven that these facilities and services are not at the desired and sufficient level.[16]

If only I were in charge. How long had he harbored this thought, behind his passive veneer? Since childhood, when he had mumbled about his ambitions inside the family on summer vacations with his cousins in Syria? Since his return from Afghanistan, when his reversion to the life of junior contracting executive, subordinate to his older brothers, had proved so frustrating? Was family leadership a possibility that he considered only occasionally, a rumination that merely reflected his rising opinion of himself as a business executive and jihad leader? Or was it deeper and enduring? No one could say with any confidence, because Osama never said, certainly not in public. Perhaps he did not know himself.

33. ONE PHONE, ONE WORLD

"IF YOU BELIEVE in God," an executive of the satellite telephone company Iridium said in 1996, "Iridium is God manifesting Himself through us."[1]

At the century's end, of all the developments in technology and culture lumped under the graceless label of globalization, none seemed to inspire more passion—or more hubris—than the familiar telephone. More than a hundred years after its invention, the phone still shined with potential—more mobility, more connectivity, more speed, and more innovation. Among other things, it would no longer be tethered to walls and floors; it would be portable, and oblivious to national borders. This mobility would mirror—and stimulate—an era of global business and society that promised, paradoxically, both greater transience and greater community.

By 1990, particularly in America, there were competing visions—and competing business plans—describing how telephone portability might be constructed in the most practical and profitable way. There were those who believed globally linked cellular towers, erected on the earth's surface, might offer the most efficient path. And then there was Iridium, named for a rare element with the atomic number 77, which was the number of low-earth orbiting satellites the company's founders believed they would need to launch into space to provide worldwide telephonic connections, so that an Iridium owner might use his phone anywhere on the planet, at any time, to dial any telephone number.

In 1945 the budding science fiction writer Arthur C. Clarke, then an electronics officer in Britain's Royal Air Force, published a short article called "Extra-Terrestrial Relays" in a magazine bearing the premature title *Wireless World*. Clarke imagined an array of manned satellites beaming television pictures down to Earth. His was the first outline of integrated global communications enabled by orbiting machines. The launch of the Soviet satellite *Sputnik* in 1957, the subsequent space race between the United States and the Soviet Union, and the worldwide growth of the television industry fulfilled much of Clarke's vision. Yet the commercial satellite industry, shadowed by the Cold War, remained largely a province of government and defense, and its initial market economics favored television, not telephony.[2]

Among the companies experimenting with portable telephones was Motorola Corporation, which manufactured a number of mobile radios that could connect to landline telephone systems. These devices were marketed for use on ships at sea, or by businesses with remote job sites, such as those working along the remote oil pipelines that crossed Saudi Arabia's empty deserts.

Salem Bin Laden's peripatetic life and his love of gadgetry had introduced his family to global telephony long before most American consumers imagined the possibilities. He used Motorola and other radio devices while flying or traveling on the ground—not only for his continent-hopping business and pleasure trips but also for camping and hunting in the Saudi deserts. He positioned himself as an agent for Motorola as he built his own telephone company during the 1970s and 1980s. The kingdom's vast spaces, its weak infrastructure, and its excess cash all suggested Saudi Arabia as a natural marketplace for portable telephones that could function in remote locations.

Around 1987, while conducting experiments in the Arizona desert, Motorola engineers conceived the idea that would become Iridium—a network of satellites that orbited at a lower altitude than most others and that could assume the role normally played in telephony by ground-based switching and routing systems. By 1991 Motorola had developed the outlines of a business plan, one that would ultimately cost more than $5 billion to carry out. The corporation eventually spun off Iridium as a separate business, but Motorola designed and built the satellites it would use, under a fixed-price contract worth about $3.5 billion. It was a grandiose project infused with risk and uncertainty.[3]

Motorola's executives approached major phone companies in Europe and Asia, seeking investors. Iridium's founders were so convinced of the genius of their vision that when they held an initial conference in Switzerland, the legend was that they charged participants $1 million or more just to hear about their business plan—a price that kept many companies away, recalled F. Thomas Tuttle, who later served as Iridium's general counsel. Ultimately, because interest in the venture was not as overwhelming as initially hoped, Motorola had to "drop down a tier or two" and form partnerships with secondary phone companies, Tuttle said. Iridium's idea was to recruit a number of "gateway" investors scattered around the world, each of which would take responsibility for managing its global service in a particular region, such as the Middle East. Since Motorola had a prior business relationship with the Bin Ladens, they were natural targets for Iridium's pitch.[4]

Bakr was interested. He formed an offshore corporation, Trinford Investments S.A., which was later described in U.S. regulatory filings as an affiliate of the Saudi Bin Laden Group. Trinford then purchased an interest in Iridium's gateway for much of the Arab world and Central Asia with the right to appoint two of six directors. In 1993 this company, called Iridium Middle East Corporation, put up $40 million in cash to join the parent consortium, according to a second former Iridium executive involved. The following year, Iridium Middle East put up another installment of $40 million. The Bin Ladens reduced their initial exposure by syndicating some of their investment to other Saudi backers, including members of the royal family, according to the former Iridium executive. Worldwide, Iridium raised about $3.46 billion from gateway partners like the Bin Ladens.[5]

Flush with optimism and cash, the company opened its headquarters in Washington, D.C., at 1575 I Street, N.W. Bakr Bin Laden assigned the investment to his half-brother Hassan, as part of Hassan's international portfolio. (He was already the liaison to the Saudi Bin Laden Group's American office in suburban Maryland, and he also traveled regularly to Texas on assignment, where he helped oversee the refurbishment of Saudi Air Force planes at a U.S. facility.) Iridium Middle East opened a small office in the Georgetown neighborhood of Washington. Two or three young Arabs with backgrounds in economics worked there, keeping in touch with Iridium headquarters as the satellites were built and launched, and as consumer marketing plans developed. Hassan joined the Iridium board of directors and flew to the United States for quarterly board meetings.[6]

He was a clean-shaven, congenial man in his late thirties or early forties who seemed to live nocturnally. He invited some Iridium executives to join him for chain-smoking late-night bull sessions fueled by Johnny Walker. Some of these executives had long worked in Saudi Arabia, and they were accustomed to encountering split personalities among their Saudi counterparts—social drinkers in the West, stern teetotalers at home. Hassan was different: he seemed to party the same way whether he was in Jeddah, Washington, or Beirut. After 1996, one of the former executives recalled, the subject of Hassan's half-brother Osama occasionally arose at their after-hours bull sessions. Hassan practically spit in vitriol. Osama "has been ex-communicated," he said, as the participant remembered it. That was about all Hassan had to say on the subject. He did not talk much about Islam or the sources of grievance in the Islamic world. It would be unusual for a Saudi to expound openly about his religious views with a foreigner. In any event, Hassan, it turned out, was more interested in vintage cars and rock and roll.[7]

. . . .

HASSAN BIN LADEN was a major shareholder in Hard Rock Cafe
Middle East, Inc., the official Hard Rock Cafe franchisee for much of the
Arab world, Greece, Cyprus, and Turkey. More than satellite telephones
or commercial real estate, Hard Rock's music-themed restaurants seemed
to be aligned with his personality. He had spent much of his youth in
Beirut; he could speak in the local urban Lebanese slang, and he seemed
to know every pinball machine in the city. He met his first wife, Layla,
in Lebanon. They lived in hotel rooms, and Hassan collected cars—
Ferraris, Cadillacs, a vintage Chrysler New Yorker, Rolls-Royces, and
Mercedes-Benzes. He entered the import-export business as a young
man, but he seemed to love soccer, music, casinos, and nightlife more. He
was a committed follower of the Jeddah soccer team, Al-Ittihad (rival to
the team Osama had supported as a teenager), and he was such a devoted
fan of the Egyptian singer Umm Kulsum that he would fly to Cairo on
weekends just to attend her concerts. When civil war broke out in
Lebanon during the 1970s, Hassan moved his base to Jeddah, but he returned to Beirut as soon as the city began to revive, in the mid-1990s. It
was a period of great longing among Beirutis for a return to cosmopolitan normalcy, and so even an event like the grand opening of a local
Hard Rock Cafe franchise could seem special.[8]

Fireworks, not shells, burst brightly above the Beirut Corniche,
alongside the Mediterranean, on opening night in December 1996. The
Gipsy Kings, a pop-flamenco band from France, headlined on the restaurant's main stage. Hassan roped off a special seating section for Bin
Laden family members—about two dozen flew in for the occasion, including a number of Hassan's half-brothers, such as Shafiq and Tareq.
It was the sort of night that Salem had once lived for—it was easy to
imagine him seizing the stage and singing off-key with the Gipsy Kings'
rhythm section.

Music paraphernalia draped the restaurant walls: a red shirt with glass stones sewn into the fabric that had once been worn by Michael Jackson; an embroidered silk shirt that had belonged to Elvis Presley; a crêpe de chine shirt worn by John Lennon of the Beatles; a 1958 Fender Stratocaster used by members of the Cars; another Stratocaster, signed by Eric Clapton; the playing surface of a Rolling Stones pinball machine, signed by members of the band; and an Oberheim electronic keyboard used and signed by Billy Joel. Most impressive of all was a sheet of lined paper on which John Lennon, using a black ballpoint pen, had written out the lyrics to his song "Imagine."[9]

A night in late 1996: one son of Mohamed Bin Laden lives in exile, seeking utopia in Islamic revolution, while several others launch a restaurant and bar in an Arab capital promoting reified utopian rock lyrics. Perhaps more striking than the competing content of their dreams was the shared stage: a world in which jihad and emotion-laden Western popular music spoke to young and overlapping global audiences.

IRIDIUM'S BUSINESS PLAN relied on an expansive forecast of the coming wireless world. The company's gateway investors included phone companies that already possessed about 14 million wireless customers, to whom the new phones could be marketed. In its regulatory filings, Iridium estimated that the world's "traveling professional market"—by which it meant employed adults with wireless phones who left their local phone service area at least four times per year—would grow to about 42 million people by 2002. This forecast, if even approximately accurate, suggested that signing up the 500,000 or so customers that Iridium needed to break even would not be very difficult. There were clear challenges, nonetheless. The most obvious was price: Iridium's initial handsets would cost about three thousand dollars each, and international calls would be billed at rates as high as seven dollars per minute. Even in this pre-cellular era when consumers did not know what kinds of prices to expect for portable phone service, those numbers looked steep.[10]

The sheer romanticism of Iridium's plan sometimes seemed to quiet skeptics, however. As if to emphasize its groundbreaking character, the company turned to China to launch its satellites into space, and by early 1997, Long March Rockets, named for the events surrounding the birth of Chinese communism, were blasting into the sky every few months, lifting Iridium's decidedly capitalist machines into position. Al Gore, America's futurist vice president, invited Iridium executives to the White House Rose Garden to celebrate their vision. Gore placed a ceremonial call to a great-grandson of the telephone's nineteenth-century inventor, Alexander Graham Bell. Satellite systems like Iridium's "complete the telephone coverage of the Earth's surface that Alexander Graham Bell began more than a century ago," Gore said when his call went through. "Your great-grandfather would be very proud."[11]

Iridium burned its bankroll at a breathtaking pace as it raced toward its service launch. Its greatest challenge was to win timely government permissions to sell and operate its telephones within the borders of more than 150 different countries. The company had chosen Washington for its headquarters, in part to facilitate this licensing drive through embassies in the capital, and by seeking diplomatic support from the U.S. government. The final responsibility for winning licenses fell to each Iridium gateway operator, however. Iridium Middle East had to secure permission from more than twenty governments in the Arab world and Central Asia—many of these governments possessed corrupt, serpentine bureaucracies, or they barely functioned at all. Lawyers at Iridium headquarters rendered the final judgment about when "permission" from a particular country had actually been obtained. The forms of acceptable permission varied greatly—some governments simply issued a ministerial announcement, while others negotiated a more traditional legal agreement. "I had a Mongolian license on a napkin," recalled one Iridium executive. In some cases, recalled Tuttle, the general counsel, "What we had was basically the country saying, 'Just tell us what you're doing. We don't need an approval.'"[12]

The campaign proved to be slow going, particularly in the Middle East. Hassan Bin Laden and other gateway executives came under intense pressure to secure permissions in their areas of operation. As of July 1997, about a year before the service was supposed to begin operation, Iridium had secured a conditional license to operate in only one country within Iridium Middle East's region, according to regulatory filings. That country was Afghanistan.[13]

Three former Iridium executives involved in the licensing effort, including Tuttle, said they could no longer recall how permission from Afghanistan was secured, when it was received, what form it took, or what Afghan authority granted it. As of July 1997, the Taliban, a radical Islamist militia, controlled the country's government. At the same time, however, a competing faction manned the country's embassy in Washington; it is possible the initial permission was obtained there. According to a Bin Laden attorney, Iridium never acquired a final Afghan license or a single Afghan customer.

The Taliban had already become notorious for their repression of women's education and their bizarre Islamic rule making. That summer of 1997, they also faced criticism because of the radical statements, supporting violence, which emanated from a foreign guest the Taliban's one-eyed leader, Mullah Omar, had decided to embrace: Osama Bin Laden. However, Osama did not play any role in the grant of the initial license for Afghanistan. Nor did anyone try to get him involved in the licensing process. The Bin Ladens' attorney, Timothy J. Finn, later wrote that the family believed that the initial license was obtained by Iridium before the Bin Ladens came on the scene. "Hassan did not have any involvement with this and does not know how it came about," Finn wrote. "Indeed, Hassan does not believe he had any significant involvement at any time with Afghanistan, which was not regarded as a significant market for this high-priced service. Needless to say he never contacted Osama about any aspect of this."

It seems likely that Osama was at least aware of his family's investment in Iridium. He could have offered them a testament supporting their investment gamble; he was learning himself about the powers of a global satellite telephone.

"MOTHERS SUFFER MOST," Osama's mother later remarked, but it was not because her son failed to phone home from political exile. "He used to call regularly" even from Afghanistan. "He would tell me about his and his family's well-being—mother-son talk."[14]

Osama's fealty to his mother had become a greater technical challenge after his departure in May 1996 from Sudan, which had a shaky but functioning phone network, to Afghanistan, where communications were considerably more unreliable. He conceived his exile as an echo of the seventh-century journeys of the Prophet Mohamed; at the same time, he had become a model customer for a twenty-first-century company like Iridium.

He did not go to Afghanistan voluntarily. Sudan's government sought a modicum of international legitimacy; the United States made clear it could not achieve this as long as Osama Bin Laden lived and operated openly in Khartoum. Osama's former mentor, Hassan Al-Turabi, told him he had to go, and then compounded the betrayal, along with others in the Sudanese government, by failing to pay off debts owed to Osama and by taking his businesses at fire sale prices. Osama "sold them all," recalled his bodyguard Nasir Al-Bahri, "for a very cheap price, because he had no other option."[15]

Under financial pressure, less one wife and his eldest son, who had already returned to Saudi Arabia, Osama flew with his remaining family to Jalalabad, Afghanistan, on a chartered jet. He left behind a comfortable urban sheikh's life of air-conditioned offices, horse farms, and business and jihad meetings. In the considerably more unplugged and violent landscape of eastern Afghanistan, he tried to make a virtue of necessity, often lecturing his children about the character-building benefits of an austere lifestyle, such as that endured by the Prophet and his companions. Yet it was plain, from the first weeks after his arrival in Afghanistan, that he did not relish his rough circumstances and that he was feeling a degree of psychological pressure. He fumed with renewed intensity at those who had forced him to endure a return to Afghanistan. Increasingly, in particular, he concentrated his anger on the government of the United States.

While in Khartoum, in his political essays, Osama had directed his incitement and sarcasm at Riyadh. The royal family's failures and depredations were his dominant literary obsession, but he never formally declared war on the Saudi government. His expulsion from Sudan seems to have convinced him once and for all, however, that the Al-Saud were best understood as mere puppets of Washington. In any event, soon after he arrived in Afghanistan, Osama composed a rambling declaration of war against the United States, the first document he ever published that formally and openly endorsed a violent campaign against the West.

Its most striking passages were stanzas of poetry, particularly an autobiographical passage that suggested the anger and defiance building up within him. In these lines, Osama chose words and images associated with insanity or loss of control. He made near-explicit reference to those family members who had abandoned him, and to those he had defied in the name of Islam. He described his burning feelings about the "loss" of the Al-Quds mosque in Jerusalem, which he had never visited, so far as is known, but which he associated with his father in other public comments; perhaps this passage is best read as entirely political, but the possible complementary reading of an unconscious paternal reference is at least notable, particularly since the line is quickly followed by references to death, his mother, and her sanity. Overall, Osama's self-portrait in verse suggested a man grappling with new extremities of personal experience—but while these feelings might be tormenting, he wrote, he retained a faith that they could ultimately be cleansed by righteous violence:

I am willing to sacrifice self and wealth for knights who never disappointed me.
Knights who are never fed up or deterred by death, even if the mill of war turns.
In the heat of battle they do not care, and cure the insanity of the enemy
by their "insane" courage . . .

I rejected all the critics, who chose the wrong way;
I rejected those who enjoy fireplaces in clubs, discussing eternally;
I rejected those who, despite being lost, think they are at the goal;
I respect those who carried on, not asking or bothering about the difficulties;
Never letting up from their goals, despite all hardships on the road;
Whose blood is oil for the flame guiding in the darkness of confusion;
I still feel the pain of the loss of Al-Quds in my internal organs;
That loss is like a burning fire in my intestines; . . .
Death is truth and ultimate destiny, and life will end anyway. If I do not fight you,
then my mother must be insane! . . .

The walls of oppression and humiliation cannot be demolished except in a rain of bullets.
The free man does not surrender leadership to infidels and sinners.
Without shedding blood, no degradation and branding can be removed
from the forehead . . .[16]

Some of Osama's agitation may have been caused by the insecurity of his situation immediately upon arrival with his family near Jalalabad that summer of 1996. Eastern Afghanistan was then in violent flux, and Osama's old Afghan contacts were in disarray as the Taliban swept to power. With a reputation for wealth and little political protection, he was fortunate during these initial weeks not to have become one more collateral victim of the ever-shifting Afghan civil war.

By the end of the year, however, his circumstances had improved dramatically. Bin Laden won an introduction to Mullah Omar and established cordial relations. Omar offered him hospitality in the poor but entirely peaceful southern Afghan city of Kandahar. Osama moved there with much of his large family—at least eleven sons by this point, three wives, and a brood of daughters whom none of his aides could or would try to count.

Even after his world calmed, he remained preoccupied by the United States. He collected and read an odd assortment of books about America, according to Al-Bahri, who later joined him as a bodyguard. These in- cluded accounts of former U.S. secretary of state Henry Kissinger's dis- cussions about the seizure of Saudi oil fields during the 1973 Arab-Israeli war; a book by an American military commander about the use of rapid- deployment forces; and a book of undetermined origin that described a supposed plan by former U.S. president Franklin Roosevelt to control the world.[17] Osama's public comments during this period make clear that, like many Saudis, he subscribed to hoary anti-Semitic screeds such as the Protocols of the Elders of Zion, an invented text about supposed global Jewish conspiracies that had been one of Adolf Hitler's preferred "his- torical" sources. In Osama's spare library, these sorts of tracts lay inter- spersed with traditional Koranic texts, faxed essays from radical Islamic scholars in Saudi Arabia, and bits and pieces from Western media reports. Sitting cross-legged on wool carpets, sharing meals of bread and yogurt, as the electricity flickered on and off, the line between history and fan- tasy would have been difficult to discern, even if Osama had been inter- ested in locating it.

Osama and his colleagues asked, as Al-Bahri recalled it: "What is America?" If they had succeeded in jihad against the Russians in Afghanistan and Chechnya, and against the Serbs in Bosnia, then "America will not be something new." They heard oral reports from vet- erans returning from participating in combat against American troops in Somalia. They heard about the confessions of the bombers who had struck American targets in Saudi Arabia. The United States, they con- cluded, "has become a target for all and sundry."[18]

The broad political-military equation they perceived was sadly familiar, particularly in its fundamental view of Judaism as a fountain-head of evil global conspiracy: Jews and Christians, or "Zionists" and "Crusaders," sought to destroy Islam and seize its lands. This war had been described and forecasted in the Koran, which called upon Allah's followers to resist in His name, to hasten Islam's ultimate victory and the arrival of Judgment Day. Possession of oil was one contemporary object of this contest because God had placed vast oil reserves in Saudi Arabia in order to strengthen those who resided in Islam's birthplace; fearing this, the Jews and Crusaders had conspired to take the oil for themselves, preying on the weakness and infidelity of local Arab rulers. In this light, American manipulations in Saudi Arabia constituted the worst crimes by infidels in more than a thousand years of struggle, Osama wrote in his August 1996 declaration. He included himself among the victims:

> The latest and greatest of these aggressions incurred by the Muslims since the death of the Prophet is the occupation of the land of the two Holy Places. By orders from the U.S.A. they also arrested a large number of scholars in the land of the two Holy Places . . . Myself and my group have suffered some of this injustice. We have been pursued in Pakistan, Sudan and Afghanistan . . .[9]

When at home with his family, away from his fax-writing offices, Osama remained in many ways the same puritan, quirky, middle-aged father he had become in Sudan: he was an insistent scold about the requirements of prayer and self-reliance, but he could also be kind and forgiving, and playful, particularly on outings to the desert. He refused to allow his children to put ice in their water on the grounds that it would soften them, and he banned such indulgences as Tabasco sauce as part of his relentless boycott of American goods. Yet he organized relaxing volleyball games, horseback-riding adventures, shooting expeditions, and family picnics. Armed bodyguards wove constantly among him and his wives; there was no mistaking Osama's importance now, particularly in relief against the poverty and isolation of Taliban-ruled Afghanistan. Even so, there remained something distant, soft, and inscrutable about Osama. He had a flaccid handshake; greeting him was "like sort of shaking hands with a fish," recalled Peter Jouvenal, an English journalist. One of his former wives recalled that after his return to Afghanistan, there were periods when he "did not like anybody to talk to him," and that "he used to sit and think for a long time and sleep very late."[20]

Like many of his half-brothers, Osama preferred to be surrounded by family and followers, he liked to move from place to place, and he craved connections to the wider world. He continued to rely upon his London office. There his colleague Fawwaz stayed in touch with him in Kandahar by trundling down to a small international telephone and fax shop in North London called The Grapevine, where he could exchange written messages with his boss.[21] Yet fax machines were becoming a relatively frustrating and declining technology.

Osama understood the rising influence of global satellite television networks. He saw them as a crucial mechanism for marketing and fundraising. The loss of his personal inheritance, family dividends, and his business assets and savings in Sudan meant that, upon his return to Afghanistan, he needed a strong media profile, primarily to attract donors and volunteers. This had been his essential strategy during the anti-Soviet Afghan war; now, through global television networks, he could update and extend it, by speaking to worldwide audiences previously unavailable. The technology-phobic Taliban generally regarded media as a tool of the Devil, but it was not only crucial to Osama's conception of his jihad operations; it was also something he loved to consume: during his long days in exile, he seems to have evolved into something of a global news junkie.

He granted a series of interviews inside Afghanistan during 1997 and 1998—he gave an early and significant interview to CNN, another a year later to ABC, and he also made himself available to several Arabic language print reporters whose work he respected. He saw early on the power of Al-Jazeera, an independent Arabic-language satellite broadcaster, and in late 1998, he sat for an influential interview that allowed him to speak more directly and more thoroughly to Saudi and other Arab audiences than ever before. He became self-conscious about visual staging: the books that appeared behind him; the assault rifle he propped beside him; the tracer bullets that flew into the sky like fireworks upon his arrival for an interview.

Early in 1998, after a period of separation, Bin Laden reunited with the Egyptian Al-Jihad faction led by Ayman Al-Zawahiri; they announced their new coalition, the International Islamic Front for Jihad Against the Crusaders and the Jews, at a press conference attended by television cameramen and print journalists. Bin Laden and Al-Zawahiri sat a table draped by a banner—they looked like a pair of dubious marketing executives at a small Islamic pharmaceutical firm, announcing their debut of a new product line. The imagery harkened back to Osama's self-produced videos during his late Afghan period.

Rahimullah Yusufzai, a Pakistani journalist who attended, asked Osama about his family's decision to disown him.

"Blood is thicker than water," he answered wryly.

"Are you still a billionaire?" Yusufzai asked. Osama clearly enjoyed the wordplay; he had grown comfortable with the media. "My heart is rich and generous," he said.[22]

Fax machines could distribute his essays, satellite television could convey his presence and his speechmaking, but Osama needed a telephone for more private operations.

On November 1, 1996, just as he was securing his new sanctuary with the Taliban, Osama purchased, through his London office, an Inmarsat Mini-M satellite telephone, a device about the size of a laptop computer. It had a retail price of about fifteen thousand dollars. His office also purchased several thousand prepaid minutes. Inmarsat had begun as a government consortium, but it had more recently been privatized. Its Mini-Ms had beaten Iridium to market, but unlike Iridium, Inmarsat did not target the general consumer. Its phones were intended primarily for businesses with remote job sites. Al Qaeda might not be a conventional company in its market set, but its geography—headquarters in remote Afghanistan, regional offices in Africa and the Arab world—fit the Mini-M niche.[23]

Calling records from Osama's phone suggest that he was something of a chatterbox. The numbers he and his aides dialed between late 1996 and the autumn of 1998 conjure the image of Osama checking in regularly with far-flung publicists, financial aides, and terrorist-cell leaders, then suddenly remembering that he owed his mother a hello. He called his liaisons in Britain most often—260 times, to 27 different numbers. He or his aides placed more than 200 calls to Yemen, 131 calls to Sudan, 106 to Iran, 67 to Azerbaijan, 59 to Pakistan, 57 to Saudi Arabia, 13 to a ship sailing on the Indian Ocean, and 6 to the United States.[24]

From early 1997, the American government listened in. A CIA officer in Europe discovered in January or February that listening systems run by the National Security Agency (America's principal intelligence agency for intercepting communications) were picking up Inmarsat phone calls emanating from Afghanistan. The phone, upon investigation, appeared to belong to Osama Bin Laden, who was by now a formally designated target of CIA intelligence collection. A reports officer in the CIA station tracking Bin Laden from suburban Virginia drew up link diagrams showing the telephone numbers Bin Laden was calling, and in some cases, what numbers those phones dialed in turn. But according to Michael Scheuer, who then ran the Bin Laden tracking unit, the CIA could not persuade the NSA to deliver regular transcripts of the intercepted satellite calls. Frustrated, Scheuer managed to deploy his own interception equipment to the region, but this system could pick up only one side of Bin Laden's conversations—the side emanating from Afghanistan, as Scheuer remembered it. Nonetheless, even with this limitation, throughout 1997 and early 1998, Bin Laden's satellite phone calls generated for the CIA the first truly reliable global map of Al Qaeda's spreading reach.[25]

Bin Laden seemed to be using vague code words during some of his conversations, but the analysts could not sort out his meanings. In the end, so far as is known (the partial transcripts of the calls have never been declassified), the intelligence collected from his phone was not specific enough to save the lives taken by Osama's first spectacular terrorist attack.

For years, dating back to his time in Sudan, Bin Laden had been nurturing a plan to bomb American embassies in East Africa. On August 7, 1998, after a last round of phone conversations with Afghan headquarters, two of Al Qaeda's clandestine African cells struck. Suicide truck bombers tried to ram themselves into American embassies in Nairobi, Kenya, and Dar es Salaam, Tanzania. They detonated near the buildings; they killed more than 225 people and wounded several thousand more.

Osama had used his satellite phone to cross the Indian Ocean and strike American targets by remote control. It was an innovation in global terrorism derived from his instincts and experiences as a Bin Laden: as his half-brothers invested in satellite telephony in Washington, Osama used the same technology to attack Washington's embassies abroad. It was not the last time that he would use technologies of global mobility familiar to his family as a means of brilliant tactical innovation.

That August, in the name of a previously unknown front organization, Bin Laden sent a claim of responsibility by fax, through the North London fax shop, The Grapevine: "The days to come are sufficient for the U.S., God willing, to see a black fate like the one that befell the Soviet Union," he wrote. "Blows will come down on the U.S. one after another from everywhere and new Islamic groups will emerge one after another . . . "[26]

PRESIDENT BILL CLINTON fired cruise missiles at Osama several weeks after the Africa attack. The evidence from Osama's monitored satellite phone, combined with admissions by detained Al Qaeda operatives, left no doubt about Bin Laden's responsibility for the bombings. The intelligence used to target him proved faulty, however, and the missiles failed to find him. Osama realized that his satellite phone might be employed to track him as a target; he turned it off and never used it again.

The retaliatory missile attack instantly elevated Osama's global profile. He was now certified as worthy of the military attention of the most powerful political leader on the planet. That August, televised press conferences in Washington held by Clinton administration officials and generals responsible for the missile strike introduced Bin Laden's name to mass audiences who had never heard of him. Muslims rallied in Pakistan to praise Osama's leadership; his bearded face appeared on posters and T-shirts.

In the midst of Osama's global brand launch, Iridium was itself just weeks away from inaugurating its phone service. "It suddenly occurred to all of us that we had one of these people on our board," General Counsel Tuttle recalled, referring to the Bin Ladens. Iridium executives hurriedly tried to research the Bin Laden family. They inquired about Osama with Hassan in a "dignified and tactful way." He assured them that Osama had been cut off. Iridium's executives decided to issue no formal statement; they did not want to call attention to themselves at such a crucial moment, with $5 billion in investments at stake. When reporters called, a spokeswoman said only that Osama had been cut off from his family and its businesses.[27]

Iridium's executives soon had other problems to worry about. When the company's phones went on sale, it became clear that Iridium was destined not to change the world, but to be recorded as one of the most spectacular bankruptcies in recent business history.

The company had misjudged the price question. It had also been so slow to bring its service to market—more than a decade had passed between conception and launch—that cellular telephone service and the World Wide Web began to overtake its initial vision. Iridium persuaded only about fifty-five thousand people and businesses to purchase handsets and subscribe to its service, about one-tenth of the number required. Motorola ultimately wrote off losses totaling more than $2.5 billion.[28] Iridium filed for bankruptcy in 1999. Its gateway investors, the Bin Ladens among them, lost all of their money.

The company's satellites were soon in danger of falling from the sky and burning up in the Earth's atmosphere. To prevent this, the Pentagon signed a contract to pay $3 million a month for Iridium phone service, to help keep the system operating. A Pentagon spokesman explained that a global phone network offered some unique military advantages. "Iridium provides service to some areas of the world that are very underserved," the spokesman said. For the American armed forces, the network's reach and security "has some operational implications," he added.[29]

They were learning, but not fast enough. Osama Bin Laden had now announced himself as a formal enemy of the United States. The American government knew remarkably little about him or his family, however, and some of the information it possessed—and circulated at the highest levels—was wrong. Investigating the Bin Ladens, however, was proving to be a daunting and complicated task, even for the CIA.

34. LAWYERS, GUNS, AND MONEY

DANIEL COLEMAN, an agent at the Federal Bureau of Investigation, arrived on assignment to the CIA's Bin Laden unit in March 1996. The CIA and the FBI sought to foster cooperation; because of his prior experience with intelligence investigations, Coleman was a natural emissary. He was a bulky, plain-speaking man who had lived for most of his life in New York or New Jersey. The Bin Laden unit was then housed in a suburban office building in Northern Virginia. As Coleman settled in, he immersed himself by reading what is referred to at the CIA as a "201 file," a kind of case history. The Bin Laden 201 ran to thirty-six volumes, although some of it included duplications and repetitions. Remarkably, Coleman noted, there was not a single written record of Osama Bin Laden's involvement in the anti-Soviet Afghan war of the 1980s, a conflict in which the CIA had played such a prominent role.[1]

CIA officers had collected intelligence about Osama from the agency's station in Khartoum; their files, mainly accumulated between 1993 and 1995, contained detailed information about Bin Laden's bank accounts in Sudan and Dubai, his Sudanese businesses, farms, and equipment inventories. Beginning in the summer of 1996, two informants who had worked for Bin Laden, and who volunteered to help the United States, added considerably to this portrait. One of the defectors, Jamal Al-Fadl, described the existence and history of Al Qaeda—it was the first time anyone in the U.S. government had heard the name.

The amounts of money the CIA had discovered in Osama's bank accounts were not very large, but at least they knew where some of his funds were located. The presumption was that he had hidden larger sums in other accounts, possibly in Europe, which had not yet been identified. The CIA's analysts took for granted that Osama Bin Laden was independently very wealthy, as a result of his inheritance. And yet, until 1996, nobody in the United States government had attempted to investigate in depth basic questions about Osama's supposed riches: How much cash had he actually received from his father? How much income had he received from the Bin Laden businesses? Had the family truly cut him off? If he was still receiving aid from Saudi Arabia, where was it coming from? How much cash savings had he retained?[2]

Anthony Lake, national security advisor to President Clinton during the first term of Clinton's presidency, had pushed for the creation of a special Bin Laden tracking unit at the CIA; Lake was concerned about the threat of transnational terrorist financing. The unit was initially referred to as CTC-TFL, which stood for Counterterrorist Center–Terrorist-Financial Links.[3] Its chief when Daniel Coleman arrived was Michael Scheuer, a blunt and aggressive CIA intelligence analyst who had followed the covert Afghan war during the 1980s.

Scheuer was skeptical about the value of investigating terrorist finance, compared to other lines of investigation or covert action; he gradually concluded that following money trails would not reveal very much about Osama's intentions and plans for violent attacks. Nonetheless, toward the second half of 1996, Scheuer and Coleman decided to investigate how many Bin Laden family members were in the United States, what they were doing, and how they viewed Osama. Through formal interviews, they figured, they might learn something useful about Osama's resources and motivations. The CIA was prohibited by law from collecting intelligence inside the United States in many circumstances; that mission fell primarily to the FBI, and so Coleman took on the task of rounding up Bin Laden interviews.[4]

Coleman and another agent in the FBI's Washington field office went to visit with Philip Griffin, the former State Department diplomat who now ran the Bin Laden office in suburban Maryland. Coleman felt the session was not particularly fruitful: "We just got a lecture about how saintly the Bin Laden family was," he recalled. Coleman returned to Rockville a second time and asked Griffin if it would be possible to arrange a meeting with Bakr Bin Laden, since he was the head of the family and would know the most about Osama's history and finances. Griffin said that Bakr traveled to the United States rarely, if at all, and he suggested that the FBI would do better to focus its request on other brothers, such as Hassan or Shafiq, who had senior roles in the company and spent more time in the West.[5]

When Bakr learned of the FBI's interest in the family, he took a direct interest. He held discussions in Jeddah about how to respond; ultimately, Bakr told Griffin that he should not serve as the family's representative in these contacts with the FBI. Bakr contacted James Baker, the former secretary of state, and drew upon advice from Baker's law firm, Baker Botts; Jim Baker's son, a highly regarded attorney, ran the firm's Washington office. Bakr also consulted and retained the influential Wall Street law firm of Sullivan & Cromwell, whose clients included Microsoft Corporation and the investment bank Goldman Sachs.

On April 17, 1997, Daniel Coleman arrived at the Washington offices of Sullivan & Cromwell for an interview with Shafiq and Hassan Bin Laden. They convened in a conference room. As Coleman conducted the questioning, another agent took notes. After conducting interviews for the FBI over many years, Coleman had concluded that the best approach in a situation like this one was to be as informal as possible—no stenographer typing a transcription of the interview, no legal pad on his lap with a written script of questions. He knew the Bin Ladens would feel defensive and anxious, and he wanted them to relax. He preferred to develop a "proper conversation," one in which he would take his time to

learn "what the guy's interested in talking about," and then try to gradually develop mutual confidence.[6]

The lead attorney for the Bin Laden brothers was Richard J. Urowsky,
a Yale Law School graduate and a senior partner at Sullivan & Cromwell
who specialized in litigation. In addition to Urowsky, two other Sullivan
lawyers were present. The interview lasted about two hours and covered
at least a dozen subjects—the shape and history of the Bin Laden family, Osama's relationship with his half-siblings, the number of Bin Ladens
who were in the United States, and inheritance matters. The atmosphere
was subdued but not confrontational. Shafiq and Hassan were responsive
but not loquacious. On the subject of Osama's wealth, they told the FBI
agents that Osama's allowances, salaries, and inheritances ran into the
millions of dollars, but did not amount to hundreds of millions; it is not
clear, however, how specific the brothers were about numbers during
this initial interview.

Coleman felt that Urowsky handled the meeting as if his clients were
criminal suspects, which they were not. Coleman tried to explain that this
was not intended as a confrontational session, but he felt that Urowsky
interrupted him and prevented him from establishing the sort of rapport
he valued with interview subjects of this kind.

After the Washington interview, Abdullah Bin Laden, the half-brother
of Osama enrolled as a graduate student in legal affairs at Harvard
University, received a call from another FBI agent who wanted an interview. Bin Ladens scattered around the United States also received interview requests from agents in local FBI field offices; these approaches
were not coordinated with Coleman. Different FBI field offices were
competing, in effect, to interview Bin Ladens residing in the United
States now that Osama was a subject of interest.

Urowsky telephoned Coleman to report the latest request, and they
scheduled a meeting with Abdullah Bin Laden in Sullivan & Cromwell's
Boston office. Two agents joined Coleman. Urowsky was there again

and "was just horrible," or so Coleman felt. At one point Urowsky accused Coleman of distorting what Shafiq and Hassan Bin Laden had
said during their interview in Washington; it was all Coleman could do
to restrain himself from leaping across the conference table and throt-
tling Urowsky. "Guys like him think they can talk to everybody the way
they do in court," Coleman recalled. "Not to me, you can't . . . He's just
an arrogant jerk." Coleman knew "damn well" that the half-brothers had
nothing to do with Osama anymore. "I was just trying to figure out who
was in his family . . . I just need somebody to tell me who's who. That's
all." But he found it impossible to fight past the posturing by their
lawyers.[7]

After these initial interviews, according to Scheuer, lawyers for the
Bin Ladens contacted the FBI "at the senior level" and told them "you
can't talk to the Bin Ladens like that." One reason cited, as Scheuer recalled it, was that some members of the Bin Laden family had been issued diplomatic passports by the government of Saudi Arabia, which
meant that they could not be subjected to American legal proceedings of
any kind—they enjoyed sweeping privileges under the doctrine of diplomatic immunity, which offers reciprocal protections to diplomats serving on accredited missions. The number of Bin Ladens who had been
issued diplomatic passports is not clear—Coleman recalled that only a
few members of the family had them, and that the rest carried ordinary
passports. In any event, as Scheuer remembered it, the thrust of the message from FBI Director Louis Freeh, as passed through to him, was loud
and clear: No more of that crap. Scheuer recalled arguing in reply: "Well,
listen, these guys are related—it's a big family, it's a lot of money, and we
have a suspicion that some of these guys support Osama." But he was told,
in effect, "No, we don't need that kind of trouble."[8]

Scheuer's frustration accumulated steadily. He saw Osama Bin Laden
emerging as a dangerous adversary of the United States and its allies, particularly Egypt, and he felt that his supervisors at the CIA and the White
House were unwilling to take risks to disrupt Bin Laden's increasingly

violent ambitions. His supervisors, for their part, saw Scheuer as a career analyst, admittedly hardworking and dedicated, but one who lacked the experience and maturity to run risky field operations and who was such a combative personality that he undermined his own work by alienating many of the people he served.

Scheuer proposed a number of intelligence-collection and covert-action plans targeting Osama's money and businesses; all were rejected or aborted. In one operation, Scheuer's unit sought to recruit an agent in Switzerland who could obtain encryption codes necessary to break into Geneva and Zurich banks electronically, to search for Osama's presumed accounts. The CIA's European Division and the Treasury Department both objected, the latter on the grounds that a successful operation might undermine confidence in the global banking system. Scheuer also proposed an operation to steal the relatively small amounts of money identified in Osama's Sudanese and Dubai accounts, but again Treasury objected, according to Scheuer. "They said, 'Yeah, it's evil money, it's bad for Bin Laden to have money, but if the Europeans even found out that we had such a capability, they would not like it, and there would be repercussions in the economic system.'"⁹

Scheuer then tried to target Islamic banks where Bin Laden reportedly did business. He discovered, however, that these banks sometimes routed money through New York, and so Treasury argued they could not be targeted. Finally, after Bin Laden had moved to Afghanistan, Scheuer recalled, his unit proposed, "Okay, let's do it the old-fashioned way: let's burn the bastards down." He proposed the use of covert-action authority to destroy by arson one of the Sudanese banks where Osama still kept money. The CIA could not guarantee, however, that there were no U.S. citizens holding accounts at the bank, and so that plan was also scuttled. Scheuer made a separate proposal to burn or sabotage all the equipment at Osama's large farm near the Ethiopian border. That, too, was rejected, he recalled. In the end, after almost four years of "feckless, and at times, dangerous recruitment efforts and safe-house establishments," as he put it later, he had nothing to show. Osama still had his money—and the CIA still was uncertain about how much he had.[10]

THE AFRICA EMBASSY bombings made it plain that Osama was more than a rich radical who authored threatening essays and poems, and occasionally provided financial grants to violent Egyptian and Central Asian jihadist allies. He had now built an organization that responded to his direct leadership, had declared war against the United States, and could carry out sophisticated attacks across oceans. Osama's understanding of America was fragmentary and distorted, but so was America's understanding of him. In the more urgent atmosphere that followed the Africa bombings, the United States revitalized its attempts to collect intelligence about Osama's biography, his finances, and his relationship with the larger Bin Laden family.

The U.S. ambassador to Saudi Arabia in that summer of 1998 was Wyche Fowler Jr., a former Democratic senator from Georgia. He worked closely with John Brennan, then the CIA station chief in Saudi Arabia, a veteran officer with silver sideburns and a diplomat's demeanor. By the time of the Africa attacks, Bin Laden had been a subject of cable traffic in and out of the Riyadh embassy for several years. Some of it was routine reporting—translations of Osama's interviews on Arabic-language satellite television or in the Arabic-language press. Occasionally Fowler or Brennan would discuss Bin Laden's case with senior princes in the royal family, but these were often general conversations in which the Saudis emphasized their complete repudiation of a man they had, after all, stripped of citizenship.[11]

About six weeks after the Africa attacks, Fowler and Brennan sought a meeting with Bakr Bin Laden in Saudi Arabia, and he agreed. Bakr arrived for the discussion without any lawyers. He seemed eager to reassure the American government that Osama enjoyed no favor in his family. Bakr said the Bin Ladens had nothing to do with Osama, that he had been cut off years ago, and that they were embarrassed and sorry about his recent violence.

The Americans told Bakr that Osama had now been formally charged with crimes under U.S. law. As a consequence, the United States would try to apprehend him in Afghanistan. To do this, they explained, they wanted help from the Bin Laden family. Among other things, they needed to learn more about Osama's financial history and current resources.

"President Clinton has asked me to seek your assistance," Fowler said pointedly.

Bakr said his family would cooperate. He referred the American officials to his half-brother Yahya, who was now functioning as chief of operations for the main Bin Laden businesses. Bakr explained that on financial matters, the family's office in London possessed most of the important records, particularly those concerning international accounts and investments. Shafiq Bin Laden, who oversaw that office, could help answer any questions the U.S. government might have.[12]

Bakr's view of Osama, as he explained it during this meeting and in subsequent conversations with American officials, was that his half-brother had essentially gone off the deep end. Osama's extremism had surprised Bakr in some respects, he said, because as a younger man, Osama had always seemed relatively bookish and thoughtful, and he was certainly very shy. As a younger man, Bakr said, Osama had never really voiced strong political convictions, even when he was active in Afghanistan.

American officials in Saudi Arabia who visited occasionally with the Bin Ladens could see that the senior brothers around Bakr were relatively conservative in cultural terms. For example, at receptions they hosted in private homes in Jeddah, the Bin Ladens did not serve alcohol to Western visitors, unlike some other Saudi merchant families, and they adhered rigorously to Islamic prayer schedules. And yet, in Bakr's view, as he presented it to the American officials he met, there was a bright line between the religious orthodoxy of his family and the violent radicalism now being espoused by Osama. Why Osama had crossed that line remained a mystery. There were theories within the Bin Laden family: some talked about the impact of Osama's participation in the violence of the Afghan war, or about the influence of Egyptian radicals who had ingratiated themselves with Osama over the years. But there could be no certainty or pat explanations.

It remains unclear how much cooperation the Bin Ladens actually provided to the FBI and CIA during the months following the initial meeting with Fowler and Brennan in the late summer of 1998. One former senior American official involved described multiple "depositions" provided by Bin Laden representatives in London and Geneva to the FBI, the CIA, or both. If so, none of this information ever reached the White House's counterterrorism office, or was referred to in public investigations such as those carried out by the 9/11 Commission. Accounts from other former officials suggest that the private cooperation from the Bin Ladens may have been limited. These officials said that while Bakr wanted to be helpful, he also sought to protect his family's wealth and investments. After the Africa bombings, he and his American and British attorneys grew particularly concerned about a scenario in which the Bin Laden family might be formally accused by the United States of aiding Osama. They might be threatened with economic sanctions, asset seizures, forfeitures, or civil lawsuits filed by victims of Osama's attacks. Throughout late 1998 and into 1999, the family and its attorneys proceeded at times with caution in their dealings with American government officials. At the U.S. embassy, Fowler's primary objective was to try to identify Osama's current bank accounts and to discover if any money was still reaching him from Saudi Arabia or elsewhere; in this endeavor, Fowler felt that he received particularly strong cooperation from senior princes in the Saudi government.[13]

For their part, the Bin Ladens and their lawyers feared, Brennan recalled, that even if they provided off-the-record and confidential assistance to American investigators, "they would expose themselves, and that because of the animus to the Bin Laden name, that people in the U.S. government might take advantage of their cooperation to freeze their assets." Considering such risks, as Brennan put it, "Why make yourself vulnerable?"[14]

At the CIA's Bin Laden unit, Michael Scheuer increasingly perceived this caution, and U.S. acceptance of it, as a form of appeasement. Scheuer detected "a decided reluctance to even ask the questions" that might make the Bin Ladens or the Saudi government uncomfortable. Partly, Scheuer believed, this reticence reflected Bakr's skillful management of Fowler, Brennan, and others at the U.S. embassy in Riyadh. "Bakr was very good," Scheuer said later. "He used to go into the ambassador, or he used to go into the consul general in Jeddah on the Fourth of July, or other American holidays, and say, 'What great guys you are—we love to be in America, we love to invest there, and we've divorced ourselves from the black sheep'—very, very good PR work by Bakr and his brothers."[15]

"There was never a reluctance on our parts to ask questions of the Saudis," Brennan said later, responding to Scheuer's criticisms. Added Wyche Fowler, the ambassador: "From the moment Bakr Bin Laden agreed to my request for the family's cooperation, they provided the Treasury Department and the FBI access to their books, family records—and their contract with the U.S. military on its base in Saudi Arabia was not terminated. Further, I never heard a complaint from our government about their lack of cooperation."[16]

Among Scheuer's particular concerns, he said later, were continuing reports he saw that the Bin Ladens' Cairo office, overseen by Osama's half-brother Khalid, provided work and travel visas to Egyptian Islamists who wanted to travel to Afghanistan. Other CIA officials regarded Scheuer's fears as plausible but unproven. Their most widely shared concerns about the Bin Laden family involved Jamal Khalifa, Osama's brother-in-law and former Afghan war comrade, who had been tried and acquitted of supporting terrorist activity by a Jordanian court. During the mid-1990s, through his wife Sheikha, Osama's half-sister Khalifa used the Mohamed Bin Laden Company's travel office to obtain a U.S. visa and for other family travel help. Another concern was Osama's continuing telephone contact with his mother and stepbrothers in Jeddah. CIA officers also tried to get a grip on Osama's own scattered offspring—the wife and sons who had returned to Saudi Arabia, another son who was reported to be living in Karachi, and other family members who reportedly traveled back and forth between the kingdom and Pakistan. The CIA pressed the Saudis informally for intelligence about all these issues but learned little.[17]

There were so many sources of mutual frustration in the liaison between the two governments that it was difficult to separate one source of irritation from another. However, for those in the U.S. intelligence community assigned to the specific problem of Osama Bin Laden and his money, the case of Osama's one-legged former London financial aide was a particular cause of aggravation. Al-Ghazi Madani Al-Tayyib had kept track of some of Al Qaeda's money and businesses during Osama's Sudan years. Exhausted and demoralized by exile in Britain, Al-Tayyib had turned himself into the Saudi authorities. He seemed likely to possess a wealth of knowledge about Osama's personal accounts and, perhaps even more important, about his access to sympathetic religious charities and individual fundraisers. A succession of senior American officials, from the CIA and other U.S. agencies, asked Crown Prince Abdullah, Prince Nayef, and other Saudi officials for the opportunity to meet and question Al-Tayyib directly. The Saudis steadfastly refused.[18]

The ambassador and the CIA station chief also pressed the Saudi government to curtail flights between the kingdom and Afghanistan by the Taliban-controlled airline, Afghan Ariana, which appeared, in the late 1990s, to be operating as Al Qaeda's air-courier service, shuttling guns, money, and volunteers to Osama. On this matter they eventually won greater, if belated, cooperation.[19]

THE CONNECTIONS among Saudi charities, radical Islamist networks, and members of the Bin Laden family were particularly difficult for American investigators to assess. Around 1996, for example, Scheuer and Coleman took an interest in a proselytizing group, the World Assembly of Muslim Youth, which operated an American branch out of modest quarters in Falls Church, Virginia, only a few miles from the offices of the CIA's secret Bin Laden tracking unit. The president of the U.S. branch was listed in public incorporation documents as Abdullah Awadh Bin Laden. It took investigators some time to sort out how Abdullah fit into the Bin Laden family tree, since there were several other prominent Abdullahs in the family, such as the one at Harvard and the family's venerated patriarch, Mohamed Bin Laden's brother. Eventually the American investigators learned that the particular Abdullah running the World Assembly branch was the son of one of Osama Bin Laden's half-siblings—possibly, the son of one of his half-sisters. Osama, then, was one of Abdullah's many uncles.[20]

The World Assembly of Muslim Youth had headquarters in Riyadh and advertised itself as the world's largest Muslim youth group, dedicated to the spread of Islamic ideas, values, and sacred texts; it operated more than fifty regional and local offices on five continents. Abdullah Bin Laden incorporated an American branch in 1992. In a 1997 speech in Riyadh, he described his work: He offered financial subsidies to needy American Muslims wishing to undertake the Hajj; he ran one-week summer camps for Muslim youth in Texas, New York, Florida, California, Ohio, and Washington State; he sought to visit schools, universities, and prisons. His aim, as a journalist's account of his speech put it, was to combat "the deliberate distortion of Islam" by "certain information and media outlets" that sought to "make people hate Islam, and to give Islam the label of terrorism by exploiting certain incidents, such as the explosion at the World Trade Center in New York in 1993." Abdullah Bin Laden was particularly proud of his "good word" project to help converted American Muslims absorb Islamic values and remain on the correct spiritual path. He said that he had created kits of proselytizing materials—a silver kit, a golden kit, and a diamond kit. All the kits contained translations of the Koran and a book by Sayed Abdullah Al-Mawdudi, an early twentieth-century Islamist radical who was one of the intellectual founders of the Muslim Brotherhood.[21]

The materials distributed by the World Assembly of Muslim Youth did not explicitly promote violent jihad in the style of Osama's published essays, but they did contain the sort of vicious anti-Semitic tracts that were all too typical of the publications of Muslim Brotherhood–influenced organizations. In an Arabic-language book titled *A Handy Encyclopedia of Contemporary Religions and Sects*, the World Assembly's authors listed reasons for Muslims to hate Jews, using language that echoed the extermination-promoting tracts of Germany's Third Reich:

> The Jews are enemies of the faithful, God and the angels; the Jews are humanity's enemies; they forment immorality in this world; The Jews are deceitful, they say something but mean the exact opposite; Who was behind the biological crisis which became like brain washing? A Jew; Who was behind the disintegration of family life and values? A Jew; ... Every tragedy that inflicts the Muslims is caused by the Jews.[22]

As part of his inquiries into the Bin Ladens' presence in America, the FBI's Daniel Coleman visited Abdullah at his Northern Virginia office with two other agents from the Washington field office. He found the young man "very friendly," and he seemed as if he "would have been somebody interesting to talk to." Soon after Coleman arrived, however, Abdullah presented him with a Saudi diplomatic passport. The World

Assembly described itself as a nongovernmental organization, but the Saudi embassy had issued its representatives diplomatic passports, as Coleman later confirmed after requesting State Department records. Abdullah was listed as an attaché of the Saudi embassy and had been formally accredited to the United States as a Saudi diplomat. Coleman knew that this legal protection was impermeable; he left Abdullah alone.[23]

In addition to his proselytizing, it later became clear, Abdullah Bin Laden invested $500,000 in U.S. business vehicles controlled by an Egyptian citizen, Soliman Biheiri, who operated a number of investment firms adhering to Islamic principles. Abdullah was joined in these investments by two of Osama's half-sisters, Nur and Iman. These women were among a number of Osama's more religious half-siblings who made investments in Islamic banks or investment firms with offices scattered around the world, including in bank secrecy havens, according to court records and media reports.[24]

One of these entities was the Al-Taqwa Bank, which "has long acted as financial advisers to Al Qaeda," according to an affidavit later filed in an American court by a U.S. government investigator. The bank's chairman and an aide involved in Al-Taqwa operations provided "indirect investment services" for Al Qaeda, which included "investing funds for Bin Laden and making cash deliveries on request." Like the World Assembly of Muslim Youth, Al-Taqwa had historical ties to the Muslim Brotherhood. Its banking and investment entities operated offices in Switzerland, Liechtenstein, Italy, and the Bahamas. In 1999, according to a number of published reports, the FBI obtained a list of about seven hundred investors in Al-Taqwa. Among them were two of Osama's half-sisters, Iman and Huda. The latter had once been a playful member of Salem Bin Laden's European entourage, but after Salem's death, she became more religious. Another Al-Taqwa investor was Ghalib Bin Laden, Bakr's full brother, who had visited Osama in Peshawar in 1989 and who had been selected to receive Osama's shares in family companies when he was forced to sell in 1994. No evidence has emerged to show that Ghalib or Osama's half-sisters supported terrorism. Ghalib's initial deposit of $1 million in an Al-Taqwa investment account in the Bahamas grew to just under $2.5 million by 1997; at that point, losses incurred by the bank and charged to Ghailb's account caused him to seek the return of his money. When the bank failed to satisfy him, Ghailb sued, in 1999, "seeking to put the bank out of business," as lawyers for the Saudi Bin Laden Group put it later. The U.S. government later designated Al-Taqwa as a terrorist entity. A Bin Laden lawyer later wrote: "Any suggestion that the [Bin Laden] family or their businesses were somehow aligned with or supportive of Osama's terrorist activities is completely at odds with the facts."[25]

An offshore entity controlled by the Saudi Bin Laden Group invested $3 million in late 1997 in Global Diamond Resources, Inc., a California-headquartered mining company that owned diamond mines in South Africa. Through a Bin Laden executive, Global Diamond executives met Yasin Al-Qadi, a Saudi businessman in Jeddah who was a wealthy contemporary of the Bin Laden sons. In 1998 Al-Qadi also invested and became one of the mining company's largest shareholders. Al-Qadi was later designated as a terrorist financier by the U.S. Treasury Department, a designation Al-Qadi rejected as untrue and unjust. Blessed Relief, a charity Al-Qadi cofounded, which operated in Bosnia, Sudan, Pakistan, and other countries between 1992 and 1997, was described in a Treasury citation as a "front" for Bin Laden, one that had been used to pass money to him from wealthy Saudis. Al-Qadi denied these accusations, too. He said that he had met Osama at religious gatherings in Saudi Arabia during the 1980s but that these meetings had been casual and inconsequential, and he adamantly denied providing any support to Al Qaeda or other terrorists at any time.[26]

Taken together, these offshore financial connections, while far from offering proof that some members of the Bin Laden family might have found ways to quietly pass funds to Osama after he had been forced to sell his family shareholdings, nonetheless offered fragments of intriguing evidence—strands that certainly demanded further and more rigorous investigation than the American government had yet managed to undertake, at least in the opinion of Michael Scheuer, the CIA's lead analyst. By the end of the 1990s, Scheuer had reached the conclusion, as he wrote, that there was "every reason to believe members of Bin Laden's extended family have ensured that he has gotten his share of family profits."[27]

Osama's relationship with his half-sisters was a particularly murky and frustrating subject. The American ambassador or CIA station chief in Riyadh might be able to meet with senior brothers such as Bakr or Yahya, and they might win limited cooperation from them, but given Saudi Arabia's systematic segregation of women, and the general limitations placed upon American investigators in the kingdom, it was impossible to explore in any depth the finances, attitudes, investments, and travel of Osama's half-sisters. Observations by family members such as Carmen Bin Laden suggest that Osama seemed to have more comfortable relations with some of his half-sisters than with many of his half-brothers. Dominic Simpson, who served as a British intelligence officer in charge of Saudi Arabian matters during the mid- and late-1990s, recalled "lots of talk about odd members of the Bin Laden family" who "still claim to stay in touch with him," reports that raised the possibility of "monies being channeled in some way." The concern within intelligence agencies at the time, Simpson recalled, focused on "particularly some of the sisters—a couple of his sisters." For his part, Simpson saw no convincing evidence that any Bin Laden family members, including these sisters, were "covertly or discreetly funding" Osama "in any way" or that they had allowed themselves to be "used as the channel for others . . . But it may well be that some members of the family were in occasional contact for purely personal reasons. And again, some of the sisters have been named."[28]

Simpson's analysis was that Osama "always got on better with his sisters than his brothers," in part because of the relatively weak status of Osama's mother within the family. "Some of the brothers would sneer, and the sisters would feel sorry for him and pat poor little Osama . . .

Women often like the chance to sort of mother a man, and I think that perhaps that's how they replied to him, slightly . . . But I'm sure there was no institutionalized support for him." American investigators with the 9/11 Commission, who later reviewed the evidence available to U.S. intelligence, reached a somewhat more cautious conclusion: after the Africa embassy bombings, they wrote, the Bin Laden family "generally turned away" from Osama. But these investigators, too, offered no evidence of culpable financial support for Osama.[29]

The U.S. intelligence community simply did not know very much about the Bin Laden family, and an important aspect of what it claimed to know was wrong: even after 1998, the CIA's evaluation of Osama and his capabilities rested on mistaken assumptions about the scale and history of the Bin Ladens' wealth.

ON NOVEMBER 17, 1998, the CIA circulated within the U.S. government an intelligence report stating that Osama had inherited $300 million after his father's death. This estimate did not come from hard evidence, the report conceded; it had probably originated with rumors circulating in the Saudi business community. The FBI had learned in its interview with Shafiq and Hassan Bin Laden that Osama's income and inheritance had been considerably smaller. Yet in its intelligence reports, the CIA affirmed the $300 million figure as a "reasonable estimate" as of the mid-1990s, based on its valuation of Osama's business activities in Sudan and its estimate of the amounts he might have inherited from Mohamed Bin Laden. Analysts felt that Osama could have built up Al Qaeda so quickly only if he had access to a large personal fortune. Other U.S. intelligence agencies circulated similar assessments to Clinton administration decision makers after the Africa attacks. A Defense Intelligence Agency report of October 1998 passed along, without comment, a document that claimed Osama had a fortune of $150 million, with $35 million invested in Sudan.[30]

Richard Clarke, Clinton's counterterrorism czar at the White House, expressed chronic dissatisfaction with intelligence reporting about Osama's finances. In the autumn of 1998, he reorganized the National Security Council's work on Al Qaeda. He summoned a young aide, William Wechsler, who had studied illicit financing and organized crime issues, although never Al Qaeda. Clarke told Wechsler to set up a new interagency working group devoted solely to the subject of Al Qaeda's money. The government's terrorism specialists had neglected the subject, Clarke said, and now they had their hands full with other matters, such as trying to find Bin Laden in Afghanistan and locating other violent cells worldwide.

Clarke and Wechsler designated their new task force the UBL Finances Sub-Group; it would report to the larger counterterrorism group that Clarke chaired. They recruited Richard Newcomb, who ran an office at the Treasury Department in charge of identifying and freezing the wealth of terrorist and drug-trafficking groups. They also brought in an analyst from Scheuer's Bin Laden unit; an analyst from another CIA unit that specialized in black market global finance, called the Illicit Transactions Group; a representative from the Defense Intelligence Agency; and others from the FBI, the State Department, and the National Security Agency.

Wechsler read into the existing intelligence files, particularly those reporting on Osama's inheritance, and he began to ask questions. As a newly assigned, relatively young White House aide, he could get away with posing some basic, even naive queries, such as where the information about Osama's $300 million had actually come from, what efforts had been made to verify it with reliable documentation from the Bin Laden family or the Saudi government, and so on. The answers he received from the CIA were mushy. The FBI seemed to have little hard data, either, or if it did, its representatives were unable or unwilling to share it with the White House.

"This is insane," Wechsler told Clarke, as the latter recalled it. "FBI thinks we should just leave this to them, but they can't tell me anything I can't read in the newspapers. CIA has given us a data dump of everything they have ever come across on the subject, and thinks that answers the question. There are no formal assessments at all, no understanding of the whole picture of where the money is coming from ... The general impression I get out there is that this is all a waste of time because, they keep saying, it doesn't take much money to blow something up and Osama's got all he needs from daddy."[31]

It was Richard Newcomb, the director of Treasury's Office of Foreign Assets Control, who had previously developed sanctions against nations supporting terrorism and against such complex criminal groups as the Cali cocaine trafficking cartel in Colombia, who first asked, during a subgroup meeting, one fundamental question: "What is the theory of the case that we're working on here?" Was it one rich person—Osama—spending his own money? If so, the implication was that they should search for Osama's big pot of money and take it away. And yet as they examined the government's reporting, what they saw was not evidence of a unitary fortune, but continual references to Osama's relations with Islamic charities, donors, and proselytizing networks—a complex, international web of religious and political fundraising. They also confronted the fact that they knew very little about the real state of Osama's investments in Sudan. (The fact that he had been stripped of some of his wealth as he left that country was unknown to the U.S. government at the time.) Above all, the analysts in Wechsler's group realized that they needed greater cooperation from Saudi Arabia.

One problem with asking for help from the Saudis on terrorist finance issues was that the questions were usually lumped into the larger government-to-government agenda, where they had to fight for priority with other subject matter—terrorism prosecutions, regional politics, the Palestinian conflict, oil. Wechsler's group decided to propose a special mission to the kingdom solely dedicated to the exploration of Al Qaeda and terrorist money. Vice President Al Gore agreed to contact Crown

Prince Abdullah—his counterpart under diplomatic protocol—to plead for cooperation.[32]

Abdullah agreed to arrange for a meeting with Saudi counterterrorist police and banking officials. Newcomb led an interagency delegation to Riyadh in early 1999. They flew out by commercial airliner. In the U.S. group, besides Newcomb and Wechsler, were representatives from State, the CIA, and Treasury. They met with their Saudi counterparts at the Ministry of Interior, in a typically ornate and heavily air-conditioned conference room. The Saudis brought senior officers from their domestic security service, the Mubahith, and specialists from the Saudi Arabian Monetary Authority, the kingdom's central bank.

The Americans unfolded a diverse list of agenda items. Some of their issues involved suggestions for new laws or banking rules that might improve Saudi Arabia's capacity to detect and stop illicit transactions. Other agenda items concerned international campaigns to isolate the Taliban, particularly by shutting down Afghan Ariana flights. Finally, there was the sensitive subject of Osama Bin Laden, his money, and his relationship with his family.

Newcomb issued a formal request to meet with members of the Bin Laden family. The Saudi Interior Ministry delegates seemed startled. They were the Saudi equivalent of senior FBI investigators, but such a meeting was not something they could promise, they said—it seemed to be above their pay grade. The Saudi officials emphasized that the Bin Ladens were a respected, law-abiding family. They had ostracized Osama, as had the Saudi government. Why would the Americans need to meet with them?

The Saudis knew, of course, that Newcomb's office at Treasury was in charge of identifying and administrating U.S. sanctions on foreign governments and groups involved in terrorism or other crimes. This may have explained some of their protective instinct. Here was the scenario the Bin Ladens and their lawyers feared: voluntary cooperation with U.S. investigators that might lead to a legal attack on the Bin Laden fortune.

The Saudis told Newcomb and his colleagues that they would have to coordinate his request with Wyche Fowler, the U.S. ambassador. They did so, but members of the delegation had the sense that Fowler was not happy about their intrusion into an area that he had been handling. Nonetheless, Fowler pressed the Saudis and the Bin Ladens to cooperate with Treasury.

Newcomb and his colleagues told their Saudi counterparts that they wanted specific information about the size and disposition of Osama's inheritance. In the meeting, the Saudis did provide an outline of the 1994 forced sales of Osama's shares in the Bin Laden companies, and the relatively modest $9.9 million in proceeds that had been frozen in Saudi accounts. Some of the American delegates were struck by how much smaller this amount was than U.S. intelligence reporting had led them to expect. In any event, the money was out of the Saudi banking system and was not accessible by Osama, the Saudi side asserted.

Were there documents available to describe all this? No, the Saudis answered. How are you sure, then, the Americans asked, that it was all done properly? It's the Bin Laden family, the Saudis answered—of course we are sure.

The Americans mentioned their concern that Osama continued to telephone his mother in Jeddah. Did this suggest continuing relations with his family? "You can never ask an Arab mother not to speak to her son," one of the Saudi officials replied.[33]

Listening, one American in the room found himself thinking: Well, then they're not really separated, are they? And also: *We* would insist that a mother stop talking to her son, if the son were a fugitive accused of mass murder.

CONFUSION PERSISTED at the White House and the CIA about the basic facts of Osama's wealth and inheritance until the spring of 2000.

That March, Richard Newcomb's office telephoned Richard Urowsky, the Sullivan & Cromwell partner, and requested a meeting with Bin Laden family members to discuss financial issues. Urowsky, Abdullah Bin Laden, and Shafiq Bin Laden flew to Washington to meet with Newcomb at the Treasury Department.

Newcomb explained that he and his colleagues were struggling to evaluate reports that Osama had inherited $300 million. The Treasury and the White House wanted to know if this was accurate, and if not, how much Osama had received and when he had received it. They wanted to understand the nature of his income, past and present.[34]

The two Bin Ladens answered Newcomb's questions. A few weeks later, Sullivan & Cromwell forwarded a formal letter to Treasury from the Saudi Bin Laden Group to confirm in writing what Abdullah and Shafiq had conveyed. This document provided—about a year and a half after the Africa embassy bombings—a specific accounting from the Bin Laden family of Osama's inheritance and income. Over his lifetime, Osama had received a total of about $27 million, but never all at once, the letter disclosed. He had received regular dividends and salaries, beginning in the early 1970s and ending in the early 1990s. This income averaged slightly more than $1 million per year.[35]

Even after these formal disclosures, analysts within the U.S. government remained uncertain about a number of questions. Daniel Coleman at the FBI, for example, had been told during his interviews with Osama's half-brothers that there had been a major distribution of perhaps $8 million after Salem Bin Laden's death, when Bakr reorganized the family's finances and businesses. Mohamed Bin Laden's children had the option to take their distribution in cash or to reinvest it. What, exactly, had Osama done? The answer seemed murky—he had taken out a substantial amount of cash, according to Bin Laden family accounts, but he also had remained a shareholder in good standing in both of the major family firms. There were a number of similar issues that seemed confusing;

perhaps they were mere details, but there was a continuing sense among some of the American investigators that they could never quite see the picture in clear relief.[36]

The myth of Osama's $300 million inheritance had at last been punctured—that much was certain. He had enjoyed a healthy bank account, but he had never been among the extremely rich, and at this point, after years in exile, he clearly was not funding his terrorist operations from his inheritance.

It infuriated some officials in the White House counterterrorism office that the CIA never seemed to acknowledge that it had circulated at the highest levels of government such misleading information about such an important question for so long. Rather than admitting error, CIA reporting now took the line that the entire subject was a confounding mystery: "We presently do not have the reporting to determine how much of Bin Laden's personal wealth he has used or continues to use in financing his organization," said an intelligence report circulated in April 2001. "We are unable to estimate with confidence the value of his assets and net worth; and we do not know the level of financial support he draws from his family and other donors sympathetic to his cause."[37]

The FBI's reporting was no better, where it existed at all. Several years later, investigators from the bipartisan 9/11 Commission examined all the classified files on the subject of Bin Laden's wealth and terrorist finance at the CIA and the FBI alike. They found CIA reporting on Bin Laden's money to be beautifully written, elegantly printed, and efficiently distributed within the national security bureaucracy—but it was crafted from thin, poorly audited sources that turned out to be wrong. The FBI's raw files, by comparison, contained accurate and specific data, but the files were scattered loosely around field offices and poorly analyzed. The bureau lacked the culture and capability to pull this information together, synthesize it in writing, and distribute it so that it might aid decision makers.[38] The FBI also never conducted significant physical surveillance of Bin Ladens in the United States or launched a systematic review of their businesses and finances.[39] Throughout the 1990s, any American or foreign citizen could have walked into the Los Angeles County Superior Court, ordered for free archived Bin Laden family divorce files, and read rich details about annual dividends, profits, loans, and business matters—information that would have refuted the CIA's reporting about Osama's $300 million inheritance. Yet this publicly accessible information was probably never examined, and it certainly was never reflected in intelligence reports circulating to decision makers in the Clinton administration as they tried to understand the threat Bin Laden posed to American lives and interests.

The failure to unearth the truth about Osama's finances "hampered the U.S. government's ability to integrate potential covert action or economic disruption" into its attempts to stop Bin Laden before he could strike again, American investigators later concluded. The cost of particular terrorist attacks was low—perhaps $10,000 for the Africa attacks, and several hundred thousand dollars for the more challenging September 11 conspiracy. Yet the financial pressures on Bin Laden as he planned for September 11 were much greater than those numbers would suggest.[40]

To maintain good graces with the Taliban, for example, Osama had to raise about $20 million per year for training camps, weapons, salaries, and subsidies for the families of volunteers. Operations outside Afghanistan cost approximately $10 million more, American investigators later concluded, when they had the benefit of a much richer archive of Al Qaeda documents and testimony. Some of these budgets overlapped with business and construction projects Osama engaged in to please Mullah Omar: a new palace for the Taliban leader outside of Kandahar in 1999, a new mosque in the city, and later, a new covered shopping market downtown.[41] The funds came from sympathetic charities and from individuals who raised funds from rich individuals in the Persian Gulf; some of these donors might know where their money was going, but some might not. By 2000 Osama was running an international Islamist nonprofit whose fundraising and spending cycles looked similar to many other global charities, and whose rising use of the Internet was particularly innovative. He had restored himself to the position he enjoyed during the early 1980s when he first arrived in Afghanistan espousing Islamic charity, and learned how to use the media, the religious calendar, and his own charisma to raise millions year after year. Then, as later, when Osama needed money, he seemed to know how to find it.

35. BIN LADEN ISLAND

B Y THE LATE 1990S, it was common within Bin Laden corporate culture to refer respectfully to each of the sons of Mohamed Bin Laden by the honorific "Sheikh." Its usage was similar to "General" or "Colonel" within the American military—a routine prefix. One day, as Bakr Bin Laden received a rundown of management items, his briefer kept referring to his younger half-brothers in this manner, as in, "Sheikh Shafiq called from London with a question," or "Sheikh Hassan is flying in from Lebanon tomorrow." A person who was present recalled that Bakr waited for a suitable pause and then remarked wryly: "There's only one sheikh in this family."[1]

Osama might wish it otherwise, but Bakr had a point. By the time the Bin Laden name became globally infamous—or celebrated, depending upon the audience—Bakr had freed himself from much of the strain and awkwardness that had accompanied his unexpected transition to family leadership after Salem's death. He was still a very hard worker, and he still did not always seem comfortable in his own skin, but by now, in his early fifties, as the chairman of a diversified business empire, there could be no doubt about his success. The Saudi Bin Laden Group and the Mohamed Bin Laden Company employed many thousands between them. They had expanded their geographical reach: Their international construction contracts at the decade's end included the Cairo International Airport, the Kuala Lumpur International Airport, and the Amman Grand Hyatt Hotel. They had become substantial players in new fields such as the medical industry; the United Medical Group, founded by the Saudi Bin Laden Group in 1990, was growing into a global company with $120 million in annual revenue, more than two thousand employees, and offices in London, Australia, and across the Middle East. Bakr and the brothers closest to him, particularly Yahya, had created this growth despite a series of risky political and business episodes after Salem's death: Osama's excommunication, falling oil prices, King Fahd's stroke, and Crown Prince Abdullah's attempts to exert greater control over the kingdom's contracting system. Any one of these challenges might have set them back, but Bakr had finessed them, and in part because of his strategy of business modernization and diversity, he had emerged with greater wealth and financial independence than either Salem or his father had enjoyed.[2]

He was twice divorced, but his children remained under his roof. He hired guardians and tutors, and if the boys were perhaps more interested in the latest Sony PlayStation games than in their father's ponderous Islamic verses, the generation gap between them seemed of normal expanse. Bakr sent his talented eldest son, Nawaf, an American passport holder, to the United States for schooling, and in the Arabian tradition, he cultivated the boy for a leadership role in the next generation.

When Bakr was at home in Jeddah, his world revolved around his palace near the Red Sea, a campus with a main home, a guesthouse, buildings that served as offices for executive staff, and his majlis, where he received executives and visitors in the afternoons and evenings. He attended banquets and receptions hosted by the Al-Saud, but these soirees often had more to do with attending to his royal clients than with the pursuit of pleasure. He retained a passion for aircraft, and he built out his private fleet of jets; when traveling, he moved in the privileged and luxurious bubble of private aviation—a subculture of exclusive lounges, limousines, and white-glove service far removed from the bus station ambience of commercial aviation. He commissioned a Swedish Egyptian boat builder to construct a 190-foot aluminum yacht with a landing pad for helicopters on its deck, but the project proceeded slowly, so in the meanwhile, Bakr motored back and forth across the Red Sea, between Jeddah and the Egyptian resort at Sharm El Sheikh, on one of several smaller yachts. Once out of Saudi Arabia, his lifestyle was active but restrained. His idea of a night out was ogling jets at the Dubai Air Show or taking in the Ice Capades in Paris. He could be generous, particularly to charitable or educational causes to which he had a personal or family connection, but he generally preferred to act discreetly, all the more so after Osama declared war on the United States.

It was a testament to Bakr's temperament that his employees rarely left him unhappy. He was usually a reasonable boss—respectful and correct. It was difficult to find former business partners or executives who felt badly used by any of the Bin Ladens, although there were some. The salaries paid by Bin Laden companies were not extravagant, but they were in line with international standards, and once housing subsidies and Saudi aversion to taxation were taken into account, a Bin Laden engineer or accountant could do fairly well. As the Bin Laden companies modernized, they took on the trappings of typical multinationals, or at least of those typical in the Arab world: Employees were assigned to various categories, depending on their rank, and issued color-coded badges—red, yellow, or blue. There were regular vacations, home leave, and even a formal severance policy for expatriate employees at the Saudi Bin Laden Group: half a month's pay for each year of service for those remaining less than five years, and a month's pay for each year of service after five.[3]

Those who stayed long and developed personal connections to the family could expect exceptional rewards. A Pakistani on Bakr's household staff in Jeddah had been with him so long it was rumored that he had a net worth of at least several million dollars. Bakr's driver in London, a Pole nicknamed "Martin," had put his children through fine British schools on the money and abandoned luxury cars he had been given by various Bin Ladens over the years. In middle age, Bakr had become something of a health nut, and Martin eventually found a Polish-born personal trainer and masseur who accompanied him on his travels, worked him out, and kept his muscles loose. Perhaps the most remarkable case of an accidental fortune in Bakr's entourage belonged to Nur Bayoun, the Lebanese travel agent who had served as an informal guardian to some of the Bin Laden boys during the early 1960s. After civil war erupted in Lebanon, Bayoun was invited to Jeddah. He won a luxury Bulgari jewelry franchise in Saudi Arabia; the attractiveness of owning such a business in the kingdom can be readily imagined, and Bayoun became exceptionally wealthy. He eventually married a young woman who seemed to be about half his age and who traveled on vacations with the Bin Laden family draped in what appeared to be two to three million dollars' worth of Bulgari jewelry.[4]

Apart from Osama, the primary source of concern in Bakr's world seemed to be his relationship with the Al-Saud. All the confidence and swagger he had built up in the years since Salem's death could vanish the instant a prince walked in the room. In the confines of his own majlis, he was a sheikh among sheikhs, but in the royal courts of Riyadh, he remained just an overachieving Yemeni, vulnerable to the whims of the genealogy-conscious Al-Saud; he could never marry into their ranks or expect their full acceptance. Bakr would leap to open the door deferentially for even a minor royal. He seemed to worry chronically about the disposition of the major Al-Saud on whom his businesses relied—Crown Prince Abdullah, of course, but also Prince Salman, the governor of Riyadh, and Abdulaziz bin Fahd, the son of the disabled king. Abdulaziz had built himself a palace campus along the Red Sea in Jeddah that made Bakr's look cramped by comparison. The Bin Ladens watched after the king's son attentively.

Bakr kept track of the news, and he had some contemporary political interests: For example, he was more interested in environmental issues, such as the health of the Red Sea, than many Arabians. He spoke up with friends and colleagues about the Palestinian cause, and his majlis sometimes filled with the usual Arabian talk about the unseen power of Jews in American government and media. But those who issued these harangues regarded them as commonplace, hardly controversial.

Bakr had become a kind of Babbitt of the Hejaz by the turn of the century, an optimistic embodiment and promoter of the Saudi Arabian mainstream. The question was how durable this mainstream order would prove to be in a world that had lost communism but gained Osama. At the heart of Saudi Arabia's dilemmas—involving national identity, foreign policy, and defense—was its partnership with America, forged at the Cold War's dawn and rarely questioned afterward. By the time of Osama's war declarations, Saudi elites were already searching tentatively for a new direction—one that could accommodate the American partnership (which remained essential to defend the kingdom's oil from predators) but also enhance Saudi pride, room for maneuver, and, of course, the power of its royal family.

IN APRIL 2000, Prince Khaled Al-Faisal, the governor of Asir Province, near the border with Yemen, published a poem in the Jeddah daily newspaper *Al-Medina*. A son of the former king, Khaled was a painter, falconer, and writer regarded as one of the more progressive and effective Al-Saud governors. He traveled; he counted Britain's Prince Charles among his personal friends; and he seemed to reflect the modernizing and internationally minded wing of Saudi royal opinion. His outlook about American and European human rights and democracy campaigning, however, was less than accommodating. Khaled titled his poem "Human Rights":

> *If they accept it or do not accept it,*
> *We have only the rights of our Islam.*

Even if they do not declare it,
We know their goal is to spread vice among us.

Why do we have to accept their lies
And abandon for their sake our traditions?[5]

Two months after he published these lines, Khaled stood with Prince Charles at the head of a reception line in Whitehall, London, the seat of British government. The occasion was the formal launch of "Painting and Patronage," a joint art exhibition of twenty-six oil paintings by Khaled and thirty-five watercolors by Charles. Prince Khaled's work depicted the sunlit contrasts of Asir's barren mountains and verdant watered valley; Charles's included scenes of Balmoral, Scotland, and a few of Asir as well, painted on his periodic private visits to the kingdom.[6]

Bakr Bin Laden arrived at the gala opening, waited in the reception line, and approached the two princes; Khaled introduced him to Charles.

"This is Mr. Bin Laden."

Charles arched his eyebrows. "Not *the* Bin Laden?"

"No, no, it's his brother," Khaled hastened to explain.

The Prince of Wales turned to Bakr and shook his hand. "What's your brother up to these days?" he asked.[7]

Bakr's reply is not recorded. He apparently took no offense; he and Charles soon opened a cordial acquaintance. Bakr even landed on the royal Christmas card list; each December, he received warm seasonal greetings, typically accompanied by a photograph of young princes Harry and William.

Prince Charles took seriously his role as an informal emissary to Saudi Arabia. He had developed a deep and personal interest in the Islamic world. There was something about its suspicion of Western consumerism and media culture that seemed to appeal to Charles's own traditionalism. He sought to promote a more emphatically multireligious Britain; he wished, if he became king, to be called Defender of the *Faiths*.

In 1993 Charles had made these inclinations conspicuous, by becoming a formal Patron of the Oxford Center for Islamic Studies. As he announced this priority, he delivered a prescient speech based upon the premise that "misunderstandings between Islam and the West . . . may be growing." Predictably, he argued for mutual accommodation and respect for peaceful Islamic traditions. More interesting was his personal identification with the sources of Muslim grievance in the era of globalization:

> Some of us may think the material trappings of Western society which we have exported to the Islamic world—television, fast-food and the electronic gadgets of our everyday lives—are a modernizing, self-evidently good, influence. But we fall into the trap of dreadful arrogance if we confuse "modernity" in other countries with their becoming more like us. The fact is that our form of materialism can be offensive to devout Muslims—and I do not just mean the extremists among them . . . Western civilization has become increasingly acquisitive and exploitative in defiance of our environmental responsibilities. This crucial sense of oneness and trusteeship of the vital sacramental and spiritual character of the world about us is surely something important we can re-learn from Islam.[8]

In February 2001, Charles and Khaled brought "Paintings and Patronage" to the Al-Faisaliah Center in Riyadh, a glass shopping mall, office tower, and luxury hotel complex constructed by the Saudi Bin Laden Group. At a celebratory banquet, Charles sat beside Crown Prince Abdullah and Bakr Bin Laden sat at a nearby table. The Saudi press dutifully promoted the works on display and honored the kingdom's distinguished royal guest—there was, of course, no risk of independent-minded art criticism in the newspapers that might irritate either of the royal painters.

Also in attendance that night at the Al-Faisaliah was Sir Mark Moody-Stuart, chairman of the Committee of Managing Directors of the Royal

Dutch/Shell Group of Companies, the international oil giant, a cosponsor of the Riyadh exhibition, along with BAE Systems, the British defense contractor. Their financial contributions to the gala might not reflect the "vital sacramental and spiritual" link between Islam and the West that Charles had earlier emphasized, but unlike his friend Khaled, of course, Charles was only a figurehead prince, an informal ambassador in service of Her Majesty's government, whose elected job it was to attend to more material concerns of British factory workers and automobile owners.[9]

Prince Charles's Christmas cards offered Bakr one additional source of reassurance as Osama's violent ambitions became more visible. Bakr and his brothers actively sought other such contacts in the United States and Europe after the Africa embassy bombings. Philip Griffin, from his office in Maryland, telephoned his former contacts at the State Department, but his connections operated at a lower level than that to which the Bin Ladens were accustomed. The Carlyle Group, where the Bin Ladens had already made investments, offered a more influential pathway: George H. W. Bush, the former American president, traveled to Saudi Arabia in November 1998, three months after the Africa attacks, and again in 2000, to speak at Carlyle events designed to raise money from Saudi investors. He met the Bin Ladens and wrote them gracious thank-you notes for their hospitality.[10]

Former president Jimmy Carter, seeking to raise money for the Carter Center, which promoted human rights and disease eradication worldwide, met with a group of ten Bin Laden brothers during a fundraising campaign in Saudi Arabia in early 2000. The Bin Ladens assured Carter that they had nothing to do with Osama; the former president, in turn, urged them to support his efforts to combat poverty and suffering in the Third World. Perhaps the Bin Ladens realized that at the end of a two-term Clinton administration, with Vice President Al Gore looking like a plausible next president, it would be useful to broaden their political contacts beyond the Republican-heavy, Texas-centric networks offered by Carlyle. In any event, Bakr flew to New York in September 2000, on the eve of the U.S. presidential election, and had breakfast with Carter. It was a very rare effort on Bakr's part—one of only two trips to the United States that he had made since he left the University of Miami in 1973. Bakr pledged a $1 million gift to the Carter Center, to be paid over several years; the initial donation was $200,000. The funds would support Carter's campaign to control and prevent river blindness disease.[11]

INSIDE THE UNITED STATES itself, after 1998, what the Bin Ladens sought most was to avoid attention, but even this did not always prove easy. Bin Laden children continued to attend prep schools, colleges, and universities in the U.S. Khalil Bin Laden's children were among them. Although he had long since abandoned America in Motion, Khalil still visited Desert Bear, the estate outside Orlando. His wife's Brazilian mother often stayed there, as did his wife's sister, Regina Frisaura, and her four daughters. Regina had lived in Jeddah during the mid-1990s, but she had gone through a divorce from her American husband, Franklin Frisaura, and had returned to Orlando. She was a deeply troubled woman, and her behavior increasingly threatened to attract the interest of the police at a time when the Bin Laden family did not need such attention.

On June 11, 1999, Michele Smith, a local Florida police officer, arrived at Regina Frisaura's home, where she discovered the aftermath of a violent argument. Regina's fifteen-year-old daughter, Vanessa, told the policewoman that her mother had beaten her with her fists, thrown a picture frame at her, thrown a skateboard at her three times, and grabbed her by the hair. Vanessa said that "for as long as she can remember, she has been physically and emotionally abused by her mother," according to Smith's police report. Two other daughters joined Vanessa in recounting "numerous acts of violence" over the previous several years.[12]

That police encounter plunged the Orlando outpost of the extended Bin Laden family into the debilitating world of American family court, with its custody struggles, social worker reports, and judicial hearings. A report filed in July 1999 by a county social worker quoted one of the Frisaura girls saying that Regina used drugs, including crack cocaine, and "that the mother would disappear for days when they lived in Saudi Arabia, and the father once found the mother in a crack house." This was only the beginning, it turned out, of a disturbing series of reports filed in an Orange County, Florida, courthouse after 1999, which described abusive behavior by Khalil Bin Laden's sister-in-law toward her own children. Khalil appeared occasionally at Orlando court hearings called to evaluate the best interests of Regina's children. It was a sad and pro- longed ordeal; Regina sometimes disappeared in the night and left her children alone, according to reports filed with the court. Much of her vi- olence appeared to be related to her abuse of crack cocaine, which con- tinued into the spring of 2001, according to a home study filed by the Department of Children and Families.[13]

Addictive drugs ruined lives in Jeddah just as they did in Orlando, and it was hardly surprising that a family as large as the Bin Ladens would be affected. The timing and geography of this particular case was awk- ward, but the Bin Ladens were fortunate: there was no publicity.

BY EARLY 2001, the biggest change occurring in the Bin Laden family was the rise of a large third generation. The older children of Mohamed's fifty-four sons and daughters were reaching their twenties, and a phalanx of teenagers stood right behind them. The sheer numbers were stagger- ing: well over one hundred direct descendants of Mohamed, plus the collateral branch descending from his brother Abdullah Bin Laden's many children, plus dozens more incorporated into the family through marriage. The children of Mohamed still tried to assemble together as a family, particularly in the summer. A number of them gathered each year at a modern, gated seaside resort in Egypt called the Marina, an ar- chipelago of islands fashioned from reclaimed land along a palm-draped shore of the Mediterranean. The Bin Ladens had helped to develop the resort, and they had claimed an island for themselves—Bin Laden Island, as locals called it—where the family had built a ring of stone vacation homes side by side. It was an Egyptian version of the Oaktree family village in Florida that Salem had once envisioned. On their Marina island, the Bin Ladens laid themselves out on the seashore in all of their diversity—women who were fully covered, and women who were not; men who were bearded and prayed conspicuously, and others who strapped on earphones and jogged to contemporary music.[14]

The Bin Laden women were by now just as striking in their diversity as the men; the difference was that they were much better hidden from view. Among Mohamed's daughters, Randa remained an impressive figure, at least to the family's American and European friends. She had retired from medical practice and raised her family in Jeddah. Bakr occasionally drew upon her unconventional life and comfort with the United States by inviting her as a guest at dinner when he hosted visiting American dignitaries, such as the U.S. consul general in Jeddah. One summer, Randa and her husband insisted that their teenaged son take a summer job at a Pizza Hut in Jeddah, so he would know something of ordinary life. In the family's Westernized caucus, in addition to her, there was also Saleha, still married to her Italian designer and living on the Riviera. There was Najiah, who spent much of her time in Los Angeles, where she had taken up piloting lessons at the Santa Monica Airport. That such unconventional Arabian women shared membership in a family—and occasionally, a summer seashore—with much more traditional sisters, draped in their black abayas, was perhaps no more or less striking than the fact that Osama and Shafiq Bin Laden had been born in the same month and had now fashioned such different worlds. Indeed, without Osama, by the year 2001, the Bin Ladens might have seemed no more remarkable than thousands of other Muslim melting-pot families in an age of cultural integration.

As Hadhramis, they came from a long line of confident global travelers. As Mohamed's children, they had inherited a spark of creative genius. As Saudis, they had learned to accommodate contradictions. These qualities described and complimented them; unfortunately, they also described and complimented Osama.

THE "PLANES OPERATION," as it was then being called among the few around Osama who were authorized to know about it, was apparently conceived as a media event.[15]

Its origins are not entirely understood; the only full narrative available is one that was related under American interrogation by Khalid Sheikh Mohammed. He was a Pakistani raised in Kuwait, educated in North Carolina, and radicalized on the Afghan frontier during the anti-Soviet war of the 1980s. He was not particularly close to Osama in those years, but he was an uncle of Ramzi Yousef, who had led the first attack on the World Trade Center. By Khalid Sheikh Mohammed's account, he and Yousef first conceived of using hijacked airliners as weapons while they were in exile in the Philippines during the early 1990s. His nephew was then arrested in Pakistan by a team that included FBI agents and CIA officers. At some point afterward, Mohammed met with Osama to discuss an idea that would offer a spectacular reply.

The initial discussion unfolded like a pitch meeting for a Hollywood fireball thriller. Mohammed proposed hijacking ten airplanes in the United States. Suicide pilots would fly nine of them into landmark targets on the East and West Coast—the Pentagon, the White House, the U.S. Capitol, the World Trade Center, CIA headquarters, FBI headquarters, nuclear power plants, and skyscrapers in California and Washington State. The tenth plane, bearing Khalid Sheikh Mohammed himself, would touch down at an American airport. He would then kill all of the male passengers aboard, alert the media, and deliver a speech denouncing American foreign policy. The pitch was "theater, a spectacle of destruction," American investigators wrote later, but it was one in which Khalid Sheikh Mohammed, not Osama Bin Laden, would be "the self-cast star—the superterrorist."[16]

Bin Laden heard Mohammed out, but he was not enthusiastic. Perhaps it was because, as Mohammed recounted later, Osama saw the first draft of the plan as a bit too ambitious, not practical enough to justify a green light. That was certainly a plausible reaction, and consistent with Osama's history of caution and care in the planning of violent operations. Perhaps, too, Osama preferred a different approach to the casting of the star role.

Late in 1998 or early in 1999, Osama summoned Mohammed back, and they met at the Al-Matar complex outside Kandahar. This time they discussed a scaled-back version of the plan, one with a more manageable budget and supporting cast, and one that would not involve any press conferences presided over by Khalid Sheikh Mohammed. Osama said he would provide the necessary money.[17]

AT THE WEDDING of Osama's second-eldest son, Mohamed, which took place in January 2001, upward of five hundred bearded guests sat cross-legged on the open ground outside Kandahar, lined up as if for prayer. They faced the groom and the groom's father, who sat cross-legged before them, on carpets. The bride was a fourteen-year-old daughter of a former Egyptian policeman, Mohamed Atef, who was Osama's closest military adviser—she was not in sight, of course; this was a male-only affair. The groom appeared to be about nineteen years old. He had a fuzzy, immature mustache. He wore white robes and a white Saudi headdress. Mohamed Osama Bin Laden bore a striking resemblance to his father, having inherited his thin features and flared nose. He had appeared at earlier media events with Osama; he carried an assault rifle and spoke passionately about his commitment to jihad, although he looked so young and frail that the effect was half-comical, like something from a

Saturday-morning adventure cartoon. Now, on the occasion of his marriage, when Mohamed looked into the video cameras on hand, his smile seemed awkward and lacking in confidence. So, for that matter, did his father's smile, as he sat beside Mohamed; despite appearing over many years in self-produced videos, Osama still was prone to self-consciousness when the cameras rolled.[8]

After Osama's son Abdullah had decided to abandon his father to take up a normal Saudi teenager's life in Jeddah, Mohamed had assumed the role of faithful eldest son in exile, and so his wedding was an unusually important occasion. There were other teenagers in Osama's Afghan brood—the Al Qaeda leader had done more than many of his half-brothers to contribute to the swelling size of the family's third generation. His sons alone now numbered about a dozen. In addition to Mohamed, the next eldest, Sa'ad, had been groomed for future leadership. Three other younger boys—Khalid, Hamzah, and Ladin—would soon appear in war-fighting propaganda videos, posing like African or Sri Lankan child soldiers.

Osama seemed to regard Mohamed's wedding as an opportunity to create a video postcard that could be enjoyed by relatives unable to attend, and at the same time, as a chance to contribute a new propaganda piece for Arab television audiences. His aides telephoned the Al-Jazeera bureau chief in Pakistan, Ahmad Zaidan, and invited him to Kandahar. When he arrived, they promised him a copy of the wedding video, so he could arrange for its broadcast by satellite. Osama's team filmed the ceremony with their own cameras, discreetly tucking them beneath robes at times so as not to offend photography-phobic Taliban guests.

Osama was in an expansive mood. Three months earlier, Al Qaeda suicide bombers in Yemen had piloted an explosive-laden skiff into the hull of the USS *Cole*, an American guided-missile destroyer; when the two attackers blew themselves up, they killed seventeen sailors and wounded more than thirty others.

"I will tell you one thing," Osama told Zaidan afterward, as the latter recalled it. "We did the *Cole* and we wanted the United States to react. And if they reacted, they are going to invade Afghanistan and that's what we want . . . Then we will start holy war against the Americans, exactly like the Soviets."[19]

He was not preoccupied only by office talk, however. Osama's mother had flown in from Jeddah, and she had brought along at least two of Osama's younger stepbrothers, with whom he had shared his suburban household after his mother's remarriage. (The Saudi intelligence service, which had been informed of her decision to travel to Afghanistan, still felt that it could not interfere with a mother's desire to see her son, even after the brazen *Cole* attack.) Osama, Zaidan recalled, felt bad that his position among the FBI's Most Wanted had forced his mother to fly commercial and by an indirect route. "I am very much feeling guilty," Osama said, as Zaidan remembered it. "If there is no embargo on the Taliban, I could bring a special plane to take from here to Saudi Arabia." He chastised himself: "I am not so kind to my mother."[20]

The wedding ceremony itself did not take long—perhaps one hour, by Zaidan's estimation, followed by a banquet of food and a dessert course of fruits. Osama decided against a speech honoring his son but chose instead to recite a poem he had written about the USS *Cole* operation. He stood before the assembled and began to recite:

> *A destroyer: even the brave fear its might.*
> *It inspires horror in the harbor and in the open sea*
> *She sails into the waves . . .*

His performance did not go particularly well, however. He stumbled. The crowd shouted *"Allah Akhbar!"* to encourage him. He carried on, but afterward he called Zaidan aside.

"I don't think my delivery was good," he confessed. Zaidan deduced that Osama was "very much caring about public relations—very much caring about how he would appear on the TV."

Osama decided to try it a second time. He went back outside, the cameras rolled, and he recited the poem again:

> *... Flanked by arrogance, haughtiness and false power.*
> *To her doom she moves slowly ...*

He went back inside and looked at the video, reviewing his performances. "No, no, the first one was better," he concluded.[21]

PART FOUR
LEGACIES

September 2001 to September 2007

36. THE NAME

O N SEPTEMBER 13, 2001, Jason Blum, a former police officer who had moved into the private security industry, received a telephone call from Airworks Inc., a New Jersey broker of charter aircraft operations. The company was arranging a charter to carry members of the Bin Laden family out of the United States, its representative said. Given the events of the previous forty-eight hours, Airworks had decided to hire a security guard to protect the airplane's crew—the pilot, copilot, and several flight attendants. Blum, however, would not be permitted to carry a weapon on board; he would have to rely on his wits and his training in martial arts.[1]

Blum asked what the Bin Laden family members would have with them. Any guns? Cash? Had they been cleared to depart by the Federal Bureau of Investigation? These issues would be resolved, the charter representative assured him. Blum agreed to take the job. He was later told to arrive at a private aviation terminal at the Los Angeles International Airport at seven in the morning on September 19.

When the day arrived, Blum dressed in a suit and tie and drove to the airport. Several FBI agents met him; they patted him down and looked through his carry-on bag, and then they escorted him aboard a Boeing 727. The plane belonged to Ryan International, a charter company based in the Midwest. Previously, the Baltimore Orioles baseball team, and more recently, the Chicago Bulls basketball team, had used this particular plane to travel between games. Its cabin was large enough to hold about 180 seats if it were configured for a commercial airliner, but to accommodate the sports teams, it had been outfitted in a more luxurious style. There were about thirty comfortable blue leather chairs and a half-circle wet bar at which passengers could stand and talk.

As Blum stepped inside, he saw there were only two people aboard, both women. One introduced herself as an FBI agent. The other, a woman in her midforties, dressed in the elegant but professional style of an American businesswoman, was Najiah Bin Laden.

The FBI agents all departed, the plane doors closed, and Blum sat down to talk with Najiah. She was "visibly upset," and "just shaking," as Blum remembered it. She described the novel experience of being patted down by the female FBI agent before she came aboard; he told her he had just been through the same procedure, and they chuckled about it.[2]

Najiah said that she had been living in Los Angeles, in the Westwood neighborhood, for years, and that she loved Southern California. She rode horses, played polo, and took piloting lessons, she said, and she did not want to return to Saudi Arabia. She talked about "how horrible this was, and how horrible this was for the name of her family," Blum recalled.

A few days after the attacks in New York and Washington, Najiah continued, she had gone into a large department store in west Los Angeles to purchase some clothing. The cashier looked at her credit card and made derogatory comments, as Blum recalled her account. Afterward, she had begun to fear for her life. FBI agents had visited her at her home on September 17; she told them that she was deeply upset by the suicide attacks because "violence is not the way of Islam."[3]

Najiah told Blum that she had not talked to Osama in thirty years. She could not believe a member of her family had done this.

Maybe it will turn out to be someone else who was responsible, Blum said. He mentioned how after the Oklahoma City terrorist attack in 1995, much of the initial speculation had centered on Muslim extremists, but then it had turned out to be a homegrown terrorist plot.

No, Najiah replied, this is Osama's work.

She held a Koran. As the airplane accelerated down the runway and lifted into the air, she opened its pages and read.[4]

SOMEWHERE OVER ARIZONA, Blum ducked into the cockpit to speak with the pilot, who was in his late forties or early fifties. His copilot was a woman who said that she had previously flown for Southwest Airlines. The captain asked Blum who he was, who he worked for, and why he was on the flight.

Blum explained that he used to be a cop, but that he was now working as a security guard, to protect the airplane's crew.

Why do I need security? the pilot asked. They were just picking up some college students in Florida, he said, and some other college kids in Washington, and then taking them to Boston. Then he asked: Do you have a passenger manifest?

Blum paused. He had one, but it was full of Bin Laden names—obviously, the captain had not been told. He felt it was a bad idea to lie to airplane pilots, however, particularly while they were in the air, so he handed the paper over.

"The guy turned white," Blum recalled, "just absolutely ghost white." He was visibly angry as he handed the manifest to his copilot. They all passed it around. Then they pulled out cigarettes and started chain-smoking. Blum found his Marlboros and joined them.

The pilot and copilot contacted their charter company and issued a series of profane complaints. The crew told Blum that, no offense, but they were a little worried about his ability to control things on his own once the rest of the Bin Ladens came aboard—should something go wrong.

"You've got one woman in her midforties in the center of the plane," Blum said. There was nothing to be anxious about.

Now the flight attendants also picked up on who was on their passenger list. "They started going berserk," Blum recalled. The attendants paced back and forth to the cockpit.

Finally they landed in Orlando. It was late afternoon East Coast time. The charter crew had decided upon their demands: because they were concerned about their safety and also felt they had been deceived, they were not going to fly any farther than Orlando unless they were each paid an additional $10,000.

Blum learned that a TV channel was reporting that a flight related to September 11—the report was sketchy about the nature of the connection—was preparing to take off from Orlando. Great, Blum thought. He started to worry about some nut turning up with a rifle to take pot shots at them on the tarmac or to try to shoot them out of the sky.

He went back out to the 727 to monitor who and what went aboard. Their flight plan was now on indefinite hold because of the crew's demands. Three FBI agents patrolled the tarmac and the terminal.

Blum talked on his cell phone with a manager at Ryan Air: the longer we sit on the tarmac, Blum pleaded, the bigger target we become.

Blum spotted a tall man, perhaps six feet four inches tall, and handsome. He wore a thin mustache. He looked exactly like Osama Bin Laden, Blum thought, except that he wore designer sunglasses and a five-thousand-dollar Bijan suit.

Khalil Bin Laden introduced himself and apologized to Blum; he said he was sorry that Blum even had to be there.

Najiah came out and asked Khalil what the long delay was all about. Blum explained: The flight crew was not made aware of your identities. One problem, he continued, is that they are terrified to fly with you. The other is they want more money.

Give them whatever they want, Khalil said, exasperated. "Let's just get out of here."[5]

ON THE EVENING of September 13, the same day Jason Blum was first contacted about the Bin Laden flight, Prince Bandar Bin Sultan, the Saudi ambassador in Washington, met with President George W. Bush at the White House. They smoked cigars on the Truman Balcony, over-looking the South Lawn. The number of dead was still uncounted—in the thousands, certainly. The televised imagery of the attacks and their aftermath—the helpless office workers leaping to their deaths from the twin towers; the tear-streaked, dust-covered faces of the wounded; the shards of paper and debris; the impromptu bulletin boards covered by photos of the missing—still pulsed through the country like a crackling current. What the events would mean ultimately for the U.S.-Saudi governmental alliance was difficult to predict, but there would obviously be a rethinking on both sides.

Bandar insisted later that he did not trouble Bush that evening with the plans he had been working on at the Saudi embassy to evacuate the Bin Laden family, as well as the several dozen members of the Saudi royal family and their entourages who were scattered around the United States. (One group of royals had come to the country before September 11 to purchase Thoroughbred horses in Kentucky; another had come to vacation in California and Las Vegas.) According to Bandar, he called the FBI directly to obtain permission for the charter flights he organized and to ensure that Saudi nationals were adequately protected from vigilante revenge attacks. "Those people were scattered all over America and with tempers high at that time, rightly so, we were worried that someone getting emotional would hurt them," Bandar said later. He did not say whom he telephoned at the FBI, but he had an excellent relationship with the director, Louis Freeh. After settling things with the bureau, Bandar telephoned Richard Clarke, the counterterrorism director at the White House, who told him, "I have no problem if the FBI has no problem."[6]

About three or four days after September 11, Bandar also called Fred Dutton, a Washington lawyer who had served as a legal and political adviser to the Saudi royal family for many years. Bandar explained that some of Osama's half-brothers happened to be in the United States and wanted to retain legal counsel. "Talk to them and see if you can be of any help," Bandar said. Dutton was reluctant, but he agreed.[7]

Dutton was a white-haired doyen of the Washington bar, now in his seventies, a man who was protective of his reputation and who spoke with precision and care. He drove to the Four Seasons Hotel on the edge of Georgetown and rode the elevator to a two-room suite. There he introduced himself to Shafiq Bin Laden and Abdullah Bin Laden, the Harvard law graduate. The brothers both wore business suits. They all sat down to talk in the living room area of the suite.

Shafiq Bin Laden had been attending a Carlyle Group investors' conference at the Ritz-Carlton Hotel in Washington, near Dupont Circle, when American Airlines Flight 77 smashed into the Pentagon across the Potomac River. Abdullah Bin Laden had been buying a latte at a Starbucks in Cambridge, Massachusetts, when news of the attacks flashed on the television. He had then made his way to Washington to join his half-brother, to assist with the efforts to evacuate his family, and to assess how to manage their legal position.

The brothers asked Dutton for advice on "what to do, how to handle what was obviously a very embarrassing, messy situation for most of the rest of the Bin Laden family," as Dutton recalled it. They said they were estranged from Osama, hadn't seen him in a very long time, and thought he was "a bad apple," as Dutton put it later.[8]

The brothers did not propose retaining Dutton himself, but they asked him if he could recommend the names of some lawyers who might be willing to take the Bin Ladens on as clients. They wanted a law firm that could provide general advice, but that could also assist them on specific legal issues that might arise for the family in the United States in the aftermath of the suicide attacks. Civil lawsuits filed on behalf of the victims were one obvious possibility. The U.S. government would certainly renew its investigations of family finances and related issues. Dutton knew that the Bin Laden family had previously worked with Sullivan & Cromwell, but the brothers did not say whether they had also contacted Sullivan—whose New York headquarters was near the World Trade Center—or what had come of their inquiry if they had made one.

Dutton recalled that he "tried to throw cold water on them," saying that he did not think this was a time when legal representation could be of any real help to the Bin Laden family. It was too early and feelings were too raw. But he agreed to explore the matter.

Over the next day or two, Dutton called a few prestigious Washington attorneys he knew to sound them out. He was not going to put people he did not know well on the spot by making cold calls. He concluded from the conversations he held that "this just is not the right time, and it can't be done."[9]

He called the Bin Ladens back and told them; he said he did not believe there was any merit in even holding exploratory meetings. He suggested that they pull back and "let some breathing space" develop. He also advised them to avoid working with any of the sorts of attorneys who might be willing to take them on in this atmosphere—such lawyers would be grandstanders, and would not ultimately help the family. The entire proposition, Dutton felt, was a "non-starter."[10]

Shafiq and Abdullah also met in Washington during these initial days after September 11 with Chas Freeman, the former U.S. ambassador to Saudi Arabia who had developed an acquaintance with Bakr. After leaving government, Freeman had become president of the Middle East Policy Council in Washington, to which the Bin Ladens had made financial contributions over many years; he also negotiated business deals in Saudi Arabia and elsewhere overseas. The brothers told Freeman they were receiving a stream of terrible threats. They had found the FBI "solicitous and kind," and had tried to be helpful themselves in answering the bureau's questions about family history and Osama's situation within it, but given their circumstances in the United States, those Bin Ladens still in the country felt they were now essentially under the bureau's protection.[11]

They talked with Freeman about the family's public relations problem. After Osama declared war on the United States, the Bin Ladens had retained a former *Wall Street Journal* reporter, Timothy Metz, who had started his own public relations firm in New York, but Metz was mainly just a point of entry for the American media; he relayed inquiries from reporters and passed along clippings about the Bin Ladens from the American press. Freeman advised Shafiq and Abdullah to hire someone with specific experience in crisis communications. He felt that law firms were not the ideal advisers in a situation of this kind; they had a distinct orientation. The Bin Laden brothers said they would consider Freeman's idea. Like many people during those September days, they seemed to be in something of a state of shock.[12]

WHEN THE FIRST PLANE struck the World Trade Center, Yeslam Bin Laden was driving to the airport in Geneva with a friend. His cell phone rang; a second friend, an American investment banker in New York, told him the news. At first Yeslam thought it was an accident, that a plane had somehow missed its approach. His friend called back a few minutes later to report the second strike. Yeslam said later that he knew then it was not an accident, and yet it still did not occur to him to think that his half-brother might be involved. It seemed "too sophisticated" to be Osama's work, he said later. He "never thought" even for "a second" that Osama "could have been alone behind this affair."[13]

Yeslam drove to a Geneva hotel where his mother and his brother Ibrahim were staying for a visit. They watched the news and heard Osama named as the suspected mastermind of the attacks. His mother fell ill from the strain. They had to call a doctor.

The next morning the Swiss federal police telephoned. They asked Yeslam to come for an interview. Earlier, when Yeslam was an applicant for Swiss citizenship, Swiss investigators had interviewed him about family history and his relationship with Osama. Now they wanted to go back through the same questions in greater depth. The session lasted several hours, according to Yeslam. That same day, he decided to issue a written statement from Geneva:

"I am shocked by this criminal attack of terrorism which killed innocent people yesterday," it said. "I would like to express my deepest feelings of sorrow. All life is sacred and I condemn all killing and all attacks against liberty and human values. My thoughts and profound sympathy are with the victims, their families and the American people."[14]

It was the first and most expansive expression of sympathy issued by any member of the Bin Laden family about September 11. It also placed responsibility for the attacks in a generalized context—"all life . . . all attacks against liberty and human values"—and it made no particular reference to Osama.

Yeslam flew to Cannes, France, to meet with Bakr and another Bin Laden brother on the first weekend after the attacks. They discussed "the possibility of bringing everybody back to Saudi Arabia" to regroup.[15]

Bakr's reaction to the attacks seemed to be infused with caution. He did not issue any statement on behalf of the family or provide any media interviews or other public remarks for an entire week. At that point Bakr's office issued a brief written statement on behalf of the Bin Laden family, under the name of his uncle, Abdullah, Mohamed's aged brother. The statement expressed "the strong denunciation and condemnation of this sad event, which resulted in the loss of many innocent men, women and children, and which contradicts our Islamic faith."

Privately, Bakr was more forthright. Sabry Ghoneim, the family's communications adviser in Egypt, recalled that Bakr told him, "This is a criminal act. If America seeks revenge, it's their right, because that's the price of the people who died." This was not unusual language for Bakr to use about Al Qaeda when there was no public audience listening in. Once, after an Al Qaeda–inspired bombing, he telephoned a British friend from his private jet to denounce the "bloody Arabs" and their destructive terrorism. But he never offered such strong language in public.[16]

Instead, the belated statement Bakr authorized followed what had become Saudi government policy. In the initial days and weeks following September 11, Saudi princes and spokesmen denounced the terrible violence of that day, expressed sympathy for the victims, and said that the attacks contradicted the tenets of Islam. But Saudi statements usually made no specific reference to Osama, Al Qaeda, or the Saudi nationalities of nineteen of the September 11 hijackers. Indeed, as late as December 2002, Prince Nayef, the interior minister, who had such a long history with Osama and the Bin Ladens, still refused to acknowledge that the hijackers were Saudis at all; he suggested that September 11 was a Zionist conspiracy concocted to discredit Muslims. Nayef's comments shocked many Americans. Of course, his opinions about September 11—and his beliefs about Zionists and Jews—were quite commonplace in the kingdom. It was just that Americans previously had little occasion to hear such opinions, and certainly not at a transforming moment of national shock and grief. Nayef's words wafted through American political and media circles like a toxic gas released from a long-buried cavern.

There were certainly some Saudis who celebrated the September 11 attacks. Saad Al-Faqih, the exiled dissident, claimed that text messages ricocheted on mobile phones around the kingdom, declaring, "Congratulations" or "Our prayers to Bin Laden," and that sheep and camels were slaughtered for celebratory feasts. Al-Faqih wasn't in the kingdom but others who were there acknowledge that celebration was at least an element of initial popular reaction. This joy mingled with fear of retaliation against Arabs and Muslims, and confusion about how such an ambitious conspiracy could have been carried off by a loose band of individuals based in Afghanistan—the improbability of the attacks was widely taken as empirical proof of Zionist involvement. At the heart of the reaction lay the sense of grievance toward the United States and Israel nurtured by many Arabians, even though most of them had little or no meaningful contact with either country. Arab media and governments cultivated this discourse in part because it deflected anger from local failures. September 11 amplified all these perceptions at least temporarily.

Bassim Alim, an attorney in Jeddah who was related by marriage to the Bin Laden family, summed up the typical Saudi attitude: "Even if I do not condone what Osama has done, I'm not going to cry for the broken hearts of American mothers and American daughters and American fathers . . . Maybe what he did is wrong but it's God's justice, God's way of helping us. Sometimes we have a criminal kill another criminal—it's God's way of having his own justice." After the attacks in New York and Washington, Alim said, he attended "many social events and social gatherings" in Jeddah with "people from different stratas of life and different stratas of society, whether they're extreme liberals or the extreme religious, and you can see this commonality: 'Osama has destroyed our image . . . But you know, at the end of the day, the Americans deserve it.'"[17]

KHALIL BIN LADEN had been vacationing at Desert Bear outside Orlando on the morning of September 11; he and members of his family had watched the attacks unfold on the television news. An FBI agent telephoned Khalil at his estate on September 12; the agent said that the local FBI office had received reports, apparently from neighbors of Desert Bear, of "a large amount of activity" at the estate. Khalil denied that there was anything unusual going on at his home. He said his main concern was "the safety of his family," and he asked the agent if the FBI was aware of specific threats against them. The agent told Khalil to call the Orange County Sheriff's Department if he or his family ever felt threatened.[18]

Khalil called the FBI agent back three days later and asked if it would be possible for him and his family to fly by commercial airliner to Washington, D.C., so they could connect with a charter flight home that was being arranged by the Saudi embassy. FBI agents drove out to Desert Bear to talk it over; ultimately, the charter plane was routed through Orlando.

On September 19, as the plane carrying Najiah and Jason Blum flew toward Orlando from Los Angeles, FBI agents escorted Khalil and his family to the Orlando International Airport. The traveling party included Khalil's wife, Isabel, and their son Sultan. FBI agents interviewed the embarking passengers and looked through their luggage.

Khalil wandered out to the tarmac. There he met Jason Blum and learned of the charter flight crew's revolt.

As they waited, Khalil mentioned that he and his family had started to receive death threats at Desert Bear. Cars were driving by the estate very slowly, checking them out.[19]

Blum wore down his cell phone batteries talking to Bob Bernstein, the Ryan Air executive in charge of the charter flight, as they tried to resolve the crew's demands for extra money. Blum and Bernstein joked on the phone that they were just two Jews trying to get the Bin Laden family out of the country. Finally they resolved the money issue, essentially by giving into the crew's demands, according to Blum.[20]

The pilot and copilot climbed back aboard, the Bin Ladens took their seats, and they lifted off for Washington's Dulles International Airport. At a private aviation terminal they met Shafiq and his London-based financial executive, Akber Moawalla, who had accompanied Shafiq to the United States to attend the September 11 Carlyle Group meeting.

Also boarding the plane in Washington was Omar Awadh Bin Laden. He had apparently once shared an address with the Abdullah Bin Laden who ran the local office of the World Assembly of Muslim Youth. (The office had previously been a subject of FBI inquiries, which had been aborted in part because of the issue of diplomatic immunity.) Of all the passengers on the Bin Laden flight, Omar is the only one known to have even a possible connection to Islamist preaching or organizing. And yet, oddly, Omar may have been one of the few passengers on the charter who was not interviewed by the FBI.[21]

As the number of Bin Ladens aboard the 727 swelled with each successive stop, there was a growing atmosphere inside the cabin of a mournful family reunion, Blum recalled. Some of the Bin Ladens aboard had not seen each other for a long while, and they greeted each other with excitement. Others were crying and visibly upset. Some stood at the bar and sipped tea or soft drinks. Almost everybody smoked cigarettes nervously, it seemed, and the passenger lounge filled up with thick clouds of blue smoke.[22]

As the plane flew toward its final departure from American airspace, there was a sense that the Bin Ladens might now be leaving the United States behind for good, or at least for a very long time. Najiah and Khalil talked with Blum about how they might have to change their name if they ever returned.

In Boston a number of college students from the family's third generation came aboard. One was Nawaf, Bakr's eldest son. Salem's son Salman, the student at Tufts University, was another. Altogether, about a dozen younger Bin Ladens joined the plane in Boston, and many of them looked and sounded American. One of the male students mentioned that he was just starting his sophomore year in college and had finally managed to obtain a fake ID of some quality, so that he could go out to clubs and bars with his friends—this was not going to be of much use in Saudi Arabia, he told Blum ruefully.[23]

The FBI made one last pass through the plane at Logan International Airport in Boston, checking luggage and talking to the passengers. The original pilot and co-pilot disembarked and a new crew took over. Blum was supposed to leave the plane in Boston, too, but Najiah and Khalil asked him to stay all the way to Paris, and he agreed. Finally they lifted off and cleared American airspace. Because of the 727's limited range, they would refuel in Nova Scotia and again in Iceland before they reached France. But the United States was at last behind them.

The younger Bin Ladens chatted and smoked with Blum and a second security guard who had joined them in Boston, Ric Pascetta, who, like Blum, was a martial arts specialist, and two other private security officers who had come aboard. The Bin Laden kids asked the two of them about police work; the students said they were particularly devastated that so many policemen and firemen had died in New York while trying to rescue others. "I was explaining to them that that's what we do," Blum remembered. "It's like a mental defect that we have—instead of running away, we go after it."[24]

Also in Boston, Sanaa Bin Laden, a half-sister of Osama's who spent much of her time in New England, had joined the flight. She had worked on children's cultural exhibitions in Boston. She was about forty years old, one of several middle-aged Bin Laden mothers now on the plane. Blum noticed that the older women tended to dress more conservatively— usually headscarves or something similar. Even more striking, as they neared Paris, all the Bin Laden women, young or old, in Western designer clothes or not, prepared to cover themselves in full black abayas. Blum learned that they would transfer in Paris to a Saudi government plane for the last leg home. When they stepped onto that Saudi aircraft, they would effectively reenter the kingdom; some of the women waited as long as possible, as they crossed the Atlantic, to transform themselves appropriately.

ONE BIN LADEN stayed behind: Abdullah, the longtime Harvard law student who lived in Boston. He was thirty-five years old and had now spent the majority of his adult life in the United States. He retained some faith in the resilience and tolerance of American society. After the attacks, he told his younger nieces and nephews, the ones who had been pulled out of college in Boston, "Believe me, if any society is going to understand your case, is going to differentiate between good and evil, it is here." He later told a reporter, "I'm here, a member of my family is being accused, and still I'm being treated as a human being." In the weeks following the evacuation flight, Abdullah traveled between Boston, New York, Washington, and London, searching for a public relations strategy that might salvage some of their standing in the United States and Europe.[25]

He contacted Steven Goldstein, a communications strategist in New York who happened to be Jewish. They met at a café in New York City. The Bin Ladens had no previous connections with his firm. Abdullah said the family was looking for a way to publicize the fact that they had previously renounced Osama, Goldstein recalled.[26]

He did not know where his half-brother was hiding, Abdullah said. Goldstein asked if Osama had always been "a madman." Abdullah said that while Osama had never loved America, something in the mid-1990s had made him snap.

Abdullah said he regarded Goldstein's Jewish heritage as "a plus." He also asked, according to Goldstein, "Do you know any Jewish lawyers?" Goldstein bristled and tried to keep his composure. Abdullah seemed oblivious to the possibility that his preference for Jewish representation might be offensive. At best Abdullah's approach was naive—an insensitive attempt to associate the Bin Ladens with American diversity and values. Perhaps he harbored less attractive thoughts—that Jews were always for hire at the right price, or that he could leverage their supposedly hidden powers in America to aid his family. In any event, Goldstein turned Abdullah down.[27]

IN AFGHANISTAN, Osama Bin Laden held two lengthy and reflective conversations with sympathetic visitors during the first two months after the September 11 attacks. Both conversations were recorded, although neither was broadcast immediately.

The full transcripts suggest that like his adversaries in America, Osama had spent many hours after the attacks glued to a television, watching news report after news report, commentary after commentary. Osama seemed particularly vulnerable to feelings of aggravation about President Bush's language and attitude. He also apparently was infused by feelings of defensiveness about the accusation, so often repeated in

American and some Arab news broadcasts, that whatever the merits of Al Qaeda's political grievances, Osama had discredited himself by taking the lives of so many innocents.

On October 20, 2001, he sat down with the Syrian-born, Spanish national Taysir Allouni, a reporter for Al-Jazeera. In the first part of their interview discussion, Osama performed in a familiar manner, and he sounded some of his stock themes: America was a paper tiger; its economy and political system would collapse in the face of determined jihad, as had happened to the Soviet Union. He reeled off a series of calculations based on the reported figures of Wall Street stock market losses after September 11. He sounded as if he had recently been sitting in front of his television or his computer, furiously scribbling down numerical estimates:

> According to their own admission, the share of the losses on Wall Street market reached sixteen percent. They said that this number is a record ... The gross amount that is traded in that market reaches $4 trillion. So if we multiply 16 percent by $4 trillion ... it reaches $640 billion of losses from stocks, with God's grace, an amount that is equivalent to the budget of Sudan for 640 years ... The daily income of the American nation is $20 billion. The first week they didn't work at all as a result of the psychological shock ... So if you multiply $20 billion by one week, it comes to $140 billion ... If you add it to the $640 billion, we've reached how much? Approximately $800 billion ...[28]

On he went, swerving between accountancy and the poetical rhetoric of a typical tenor. Then the interview took a striking turn.

"What about the killing of innocent civilians?" Allouni asked.

"It is very strange for Americans and other educated people to talk about the killing of innocent civilians," Osama answered.

"I mean," he continued, "Who said that our children and civilians are not innocents, and that the shedding of their blood is permissible.

Whenever we kill their civilians, the whole world yells at us from East to West, and America starts putting pressure on its allies and puppets . . . There is a strong instinct in humans to lean towards the powerful without knowing it, so when they talk about us, they know we will not answer them . . ."

"So you say that it is an eye for an eye? They kill our innocents, so we kill theirs?"

"Yes, so we kill their innocents—this is valid both religiously and logically. But some of the people who talk about this issue, discuss it from a religious point of view . . . They say that the killing of innocents is wrong and invalid, and for proof, they say that the Prophet forbade the killing of children and women, and that is true . . ."

"This is precisely what I'm talking about!" Allouni interrupted. "This is exactly what I'm asking you about!"

". . . But this forbidding of killing children and innocents is not set in stone, and there are other writings that uphold it."

Now Osama embarked on a different justification, one that seemed to contradict his own argument: He defended himself by saying that he hadn't actually intended to kill people who should be classified as innocents. "[We] didn't set out to kill children," he said, "but rather attacked the biggest center of military power in the world, the Pentagon, which contains more than 64,000 workers, a military base which has a big concentration of army and intelligence."

"What about the World Trade Center?"

"As for the World Trade Center, the ones who were attacked who died in it were part of a financial power. It wasn't a children's school! Neither was it a residence. And the general consensus is that most of the people who were in the towers were men that backed the biggest financial force in the world . . . And those individuals should stand before God, and rethink and redo their calculations."

Immediately, however, Osama returned to his first argument: Even if they *were* innocent, his attack was justified on the basis of retribution: "We treat others like they treat us. Those who kill our women and our innocent, we kill their women and innocent, until they stop doing so." These were the evasions of a man who had apparently not expected to be criticized or questioned on the issue.

A little later, Osama assessed Bush's ill-considered use of the word "Crusade" to describe America's response to September 11: "So Bush has declared in his own words: 'Crusade attack.' The odd thing about this is that he has taken the word right out of our mouth ... People make apologies for him and they say that he didn't mean to say that this war is a Crusade, even though he himself said that it was! So the world today is split into two parts, as Bush said: Either you are with us, or you are with terrorism. Either you are with the Crusade, or you are with Islam. Bush's image today is of him being in the front of the line, yelling and carrying his big cross."[29]

There was something striking and authentic in this entire exchange—perhaps it was the absence of Osama's self-mystifying verses, and the absence, too, of archaic language, Koranic justification, or reference to ancient maps. Here was a well-informed, up-to-date media consumer and amateur political analyst defending the violence he sponsored through straightforward argument, as if he were appearing at a mosque debate or on a televised current-affairs program.

And yet as his exchange with Allouni continued, Osama spoke just as fluidly in the vernacular of a religious cultist—with the seeming flick of a switch, he could find the voice in which he recounted dreams, spoke in Koranic riddles, or expressed his conviction that he and his followers were engaged in a preordained war that would continue until the climax of earthly time—a war that was not a means to a political end, but was rather an expression of God's will, and as such, could offer no peace to the enemies of His true religion.

"What is your opinion," Allouni asked him, "about what is being said concerning your analogies and the 'Clash of Civilizations'? Your constant use and repetition of the word 'Crusade' and 'Crusader' shows that you uphold the saying, the 'Clash of Civilizations.'"

"I say there is no doubt about this," Osama answered. "This [clash of civilizations] is a very clear matter, proven in the Koran... The Jews and America have come up with a fairytale that they transmit to the Muslims, and they've unfortunately been followed by the local rulers and a lot of people who are close to them, by using 'world peace' as an excuse. That is a fairytale that has no substance whatsoever!"

"Peace?"

"The peace that they foist on Muslims in order to ready and prepare them to be slaughtered... Whoever claims that there is permanent peace between us and the Jews has disbelieved what has been sent down through Mohamed; the battle is between us and the enemies of Islam, and it will go on until the Hour."[30]

Several weeks after this interview, a Saudi religious scholar, Ali Al-Ghandi, arrived in Afghanistan on a tour. Near Kandahar, he was granted an audience with Osama. The transcript of their informal conversation is peppered with risible passages, particularly as Al-Ghandi tries awkwardly to flatter Osama: "We don't want to take much of your time... Everybody praises what you did, the great action that you did ... Hundreds of people used to doubt you and few only would follow you until this huge event happened. Now hundreds of people are coming out to join you."

Osama explained how the planes operation had exceeded his expectations, and he referred to his own background in civil engineering and demolition: "We calculated that the floors that would be hit would be three or four floors. I was the most optimistic of them all ... due to my experience in this field. I was thinking that the fire from the gas in the plane would melt the iron structure of the building and collapse the area where the plane hit, and all the floors above it only. This is all that we

hoped for." Osama said he was pleased and surprised when both buildings collapsed entirely.

"By God," Al-Ghandi said obsequiously, "it is a great work."[31]

Osama's sudden popularity among ordinary Saudis redoubled
the complexity of the Bin Laden family's position: Had they brought
shame and disrepute upon the kingdom, or had they nurtured a new
Arab folk hero? It did not require professional expertise in public relations to see the contours of this dilemma as the Bin Ladens searched for
a legal and communications strategy. To please American audiences, the
Bin Ladens would have to seek forgiveness and denounce Osama. To
please audiences in the Arab world, where the family's financial interests
predominantly lay, such a posture would be seen as craven.

It was perhaps unrealistic to expect Abdullah, in Boston, with his diffident personality and his very junior standing in the family, to manage
these questions on his own.

Abdullah joined Andrew Hess for dinner one evening that autumn at
the Helmand Restaurant, run by the Karzai family, whose own exiled
scion would soon be restored to power in their native country, displac-
ing Osama's influence there. Hess was the Tufts professor whose academic program the Bin Ladens had supported during the 1990s. From his
many years spent in Saudi Arabia, Hess had come to think that there was
"a certain posture that Arabs take in cases of tragedy" and that Abdullah
Bin Laden, over dinner, now exuded this posture, which Hess saw as a sort
of burdened fatalism: What can one do?

"He regarded this as a huge tragedy for the family," Hess recalled.
Abdullah took pains to convince him that the Bin Ladens were "hugely
hostile" to what Osama had done, and that they had "no interest whatsoever in supporting anything he's doing . . . that he's receiving no money
from the corporation." Abdullah made this last point more than once.[32]

In December, after flying over to London, Abdullah agreed to meet with Charlotte Edwardes, a British journalist with the *Telegraph*. Bakr had tentatively given Abdullah some scope to humanize his section of the family through occasional contact with the media. Edwardes found Abdullah a sympathetic figure—a "tall, slight foreigner dressed in an expensively cut black overcoat," who worried about his many allergies, and walked somberly through the Mayfair streets, oblivious to Christmas shoppers. Abdullah could barely speak of Osama; he referred to his half-brother as "Mr. O."[33]

He talked to Edwardes about his new life in America and Britain. He used cash as much as possible, to avoid that awkward moment when a clerk might stare down at the raised letters on his credit card. At home in Boston, he had stopped jogging out of doors and had given up private piloting. Flying, he said, "is like nothing else. When I am up there in the plane I feel free," and none of his family's history with tragic aviation events had diminished his passion. And yet, he understood that "it would be an insult for me to pilot a plane in America now."

During one of several meetings, Abdullah sat down with Edwardes at the Four Seasons Hotel in Knightsbridge. Abdullah paid for his Evian water (it was Ramadan, and he was fasting during the daytime) from a wad of fifty-pound notes. As they prepared to leave for dinner, Abdullah asked the hotel waiter if it might be possible to book a table at Nobu, then the most sought-after restaurant in London.

"Sorry, no, not unless you are a name," the waiter said.

For a moment, Edwardes thought, Abdullah Bin Laden "allowed himself the shadow of a smile."[34]

37. PUBLIC RELATIONS

R ICHARD NEWCOMB, the attorney who ran the Treasury
Department's Office of Foreign Assets Control, led a delegation
to Saudi Arabia in December 2001 to speak with businessmen in the kingdom about the problem of terrorist financing. The delegation's
purpose—although its members did not put it quite so bluntly as this
during meetings—was to shake up the attitudes of wealthy Saudis about
their charitable giving and other financial dealings in the Islamic world.
Newcomb and colleagues from the State Department and other agencies
hoped to accomplish this by enumerating for audiences of Saudi businessmen the penalties that individuals and companies could incur under
American law if they passed money to the wrong people. The Bush administration had identified the disruption of terrorist financing as an
important priority after September 11, and Treasury had already designated several dozen individuals, charities, and businesses as supporters
of terrorism, which meant their U.S.-held assets could be frozen.
Newcomb and his colleagues scheduled roundtable meetings with the
Jeddah Chamber of Commerce and other businessmen in Riyadh and
Jeddah. The Treasury team also asked for a private meeting with the Bin
Laden family, and somewhat to their surprise, they learned that Bakr Bin
Laden would meet with them.[1]

The meeting took place in the elegant offices of the Saudi Bin Laden
Group. Shafiq and Abdullah, who had met with Newcomb at Treasury
prior to September 11 to outline the history of Bin Laden inheritances,

joined Bakr in his office. This time, instead of the business suits they had worn to the Treasury Annex in Washington, the two brothers appeared in traditional Saudi robes and headdresses. No one from Treasury had met Bakr before; they were struck by his relatively modest stature, at least in comparison to Osama.

Bakr apologized to the Americans about the September 11 attacks. He said that Osama was no longer considered a part of the Bin Laden family, and that he had been cut off for years. Bakr added that he had no idea where Osama was hiding. He offered the cooperation of his family and his company.

Newcomb and his colleagues walked through their presentation about American terrorist-financing laws. They tried to speak in a diplomatic, nonthreatening tone. They did not go into depth with Bakr about specific Bin Laden family or inheritance issues; Newcomb's office believed the letter sent to Treasury by Sullivan & Cromwell in 2000 had adequately addressed these questions.

The Bin Laden brothers were cordial. Shafiq suggested to one member of the delegation that he come back when he wasn't so busy so they could go fishing together in the Red Sea. In a more serious vein, one of the brothers mentioned that his American Express card had been blocked after September 11—he presumed this was because of the family name on the card. He wanted to go back to America, he said, but he could not do so without a working American Express card. One of the American officials joked that this was a pretty good advertisement for the credit card company.

Back in Washington, in the first weeks of 2002, Treasury officials discussed the credit card matter at the White House, where several interagency working groups convened on a weekly or biweekly basis to review global counterterrorism operations. The Taliban had fallen by now, intelligence operations against Al Qaeda were unfolding in dozens of countries, and preparations had quietly begun for an invasion of Iraq. In this interregnum the Bush administration was also focusing intently on terrorist-financing matters, and its interagency groups on terrorism reviewed many detailed case files. After the mission to Saudi Arabia, a sensitive question arose: Was the Bush administration prepared, at least provisionally, to clear Bin Laden family bank accounts and credit cards, so that members of the family resident in Saudi Arabia and Europe could travel more freely?[2]

U.S. government investigators had learned a great deal about the Bin Laden family in the several months since September 11, particularly about its business history in America. The Federal Bureau of Investigation had carried out much of this work after the attacks in Washington and New York. Dennis Lormel, an agent with a background in financial crime investigations, had been appointed on September 13 to lead a team at FBI headquarters assigned to concentrate on the financial aspects of the September 11 plot, and more generally on Al Qaeda's money trail. The FBI's fifty-six field offices scattered around the United States also carried out investigations into the Bin Laden family, some in cooperation with Lormel's group, others on a more ad hoc basis. On the evening of September 11 itself, for example, agents from the Boston field office turned up at the local condominium where Abdullah and his half-brother Mohamed had owned apartments; the FBI agents started what would become weeks of shoe-leather police work in the Boston area. They interviewed neighbors, investigated nightclubs and bars where younger Bin Ladens were said to appear on occasion, and dug for evidence about family money. Similar investigations, none of them announced to the public, took place in New York, Washington, Los Angeles, Florida, Texas, and elsewhere. Through the autumn, FBI agents gathered an enormous sheaf of files and interview reports about the Bin Ladens, although as ever, the bureau struggled to pull its data together and deliver it in a way that policy makers outside the FBI could use.[3]

FBI agents and investigators from the nascent Department of Homeland Security spent long hours with some of the Bin Ladens' key American business partners after September 11, talking through the minutia of each long-ago business transaction involving Salem, Khalil, Yeslam, and other brothers active in the United States. The agents examined where and how the money had flowed in these deals. The investigators also took flight logs from family pilots and interviewed some pilots at length about Bin Laden family travel history, reaching as far back as the 1970s. The FBI learned, for example, about the flight to Peshawar, Pakistan, by Gerald Auerbach and Ghalib Bin Laden early in 1989.[4]

These investigations amounted to intelligence collection; there were no grand juries convened to consider criminal charges. Some of the work fell inevitably into the gray area between the mandate of the FBI and that of the Central Intelligence Agency. Charles Tickle, who had directed commercial real estate investments in Richmond, Virginia, and elsewhere for Yeslam Bin Laden, telephoned the CIA switchboard on his own after the attacks. He volunteered to the operator, "We had business dealings with the Bin Laden family." They asked a few questions and later called back to say, in effect, "No, everything's good."[5]

All this digging on American soil turned up no evidence of complicity by the Bin Laden family in terrorist violence. Dale Watson, the FBI's chief of counterterrorism in the fall of 2001, concluded that the Bin Laden family "couldn't help us and they were not a threat," as he put it later. Dennis Lormel and his terrorist-finance team reached a similar judgment, although they felt there were a few areas of family activity where it was difficult to be conclusive.[6]

Because he was new to the subject, it took Lormel a while to unravel and move beyond the misleading U.S. intelligence reports he inherited, originating at the CIA, which described Osama's supposedly vast personal fortune. Lormel and his team felt they could not simply accept at face value the Bin Laden family's report, through Sullivan & Cromwell, about the size and timing of Osama's inheritance and dividend payments— that account might well be correct, and the FBI had no specific reason to doubt it, but a letter from a family lawyer hardly counted as definitive evidence in a matter as important as Osama's wealth. Where were the original documents? Where was the evidence that could hold up in a courtroom?

Another area that seemed to require additional investigation was the Swiss and offshore banking and investments overseen by Yeslam Bin Laden and other family partners and aides in Switzerland. After the September 11 attacks, Swiss and French investigators had initiated their own inquiries into Bin Laden bank accounts and investment vehicles in Switzerland and elsewhere. On March 27, 2002, Swiss police raided nine offices and companies connected to Yeslam Bin Laden, including his principal firm, Saudi Investment Company, in Geneva. They hauled away boxes and records, but ultimately filed no charges against him.[7]

Despite these lingering issues, the FBI's counterterrorism investigators felt by early 2002 that they had no reason to argue for the continued blocking of Bin Laden family credit cards and checking accounts in the United States. The final decision, according to one person involved in the discussions, was carefully reviewed by interagency groups run by the National Security Council and approved at a very high level.[8] Such a decision would almost certainly have required President Bush's personal endorsement, although what role, if any, Bush actually played in the ruling is not known. What seems clear is that a specific decision was made at the White House sometime early in 2002: barring the emergence of new evidence, the U.S. government would not sanction the Bin Laden family in any way because of its history with Osama.

An FBI analyst summed up the bureau's assessment of the evidence in a breezy e-mail written in September 2003: There were "millions" of Bin Ladens "running around" and "99.999999% of them are of the non-evil variety."[9]

FBI SCRUTINY of the Bin Ladens had at least one virtue, from the family's point of view—it took place almost entirely in private. Far more painful were the public repudiations of the family by American universities and corporations that had courted them in the past. In the emotional climate that pervaded during the autumn of 2001, some of these institutions felt they had no choice but to end or suspend their dealings with the Bin Ladens. None explicitly declared that the family might still be aiding Osama, but this was a possibility that could be freely interpreted from their decisions to cut ties.

Harvard University, which had accepted $2 million in donations from Bakr Bin Laden, received many calls from people "who were emotional" and who "said it was murder money and we should give to the victims," recalled Peri Bearman of the Islamic Legal Studies program. Harvard soon chose to suspend its Bin Laden fellowships.[10]

The University of Miami, Bakr's alma mater, also backed away from him. Before September 11, university fundraisers had contacted the Bin Ladens, looking to coax funds from their wealthy alumni. Bakr had indicated that he might be willing to fund a research project into the health of the Red Sea's coral reefs, which were under assault from pollution, silt, and too much fishing. John C. McManus, a University of Miami professor who specialized in coral reef management, obtained a Saudi visa and planned to leave for the kingdom to meet with Bakr and others on September 24, 2001. The trip was canceled and the project was abandoned. McManus recalled that the decision was mutual: "The family wasn't pursuing it, so we didn't either." Bakr, however, believed that the university had shunned him because of September 11, and he felt hurt by the episode, according to a person who talked with him about it.[11]

Cadbury-Schweppes, the British chocolate maker, announced that it was breaking ties with a Bin Laden subsidiary. Companies that sold telecommunications equipment through the Bin Laden's company made similar announcements. A few of the family's more prominent corporate partners stood by them. A General Electric spokesman said that it was confident that the Saudi Bin Laden Group "is fully separated from Osama Bin Laden." Chas Freeman, the former U.S. ambassador who now developed business projects in the kingdom, said that "Bin Laden" remains "a very honored name," and he suggested pointedly that American companies that "had very long and profitable relationships" with the family were "now running for public relations cover."[12]

Even after their American Express cards were restored, the Bin Ladens were reluctant to travel to the United States. None of the senior brothers around Bakr was willing to go. The atmosphere seemed too unsettled, too threatening. Saleha, Bakr's half-sister, did go back from time to time with her Italian husband, but she was often detained at U.S. airports for two hours or more, which she found increasingly depressing. "I don't know if we're going to be able to keep this up because we just can't travel this way," she told Gail Freeman.

Europe seemed easier to navigate, particularly since the Bin Ladens often moved in the protective bubble of private aviation and so did not have to worry about alarming fellow passengers on a commercial airliner. Still, they had trouble. Police from Scotland Yard boarded Bakr's private jet at Luton Airport and questioned him before allowing him on his way. A man punched Hassan Bin Laden in the face on the street outside the Inter-Continental Hotel in London in August 2002. In Germany or Austria, a local police chief surrounded a hotel where Bakr was vacationing, apparently in the belief that he was about to write himself into the history books for nabbing the world's most wanted fugitive.[13]

Yasser Bin Laden was a younger half-brother of Bakr who lived in Jeddah and played squash with an English-speaking circle of friends in the city. He also belonged to a local Harley-Davidson motorcycle club. Each summer he and his Saudi friends would roar out on their Harleys on a cross-country road trip. After September 11 they biked through Europe. The other Saudi motorcyclists in the club joked with Yasser relentlessly, saying that his passport was going to cause them nothing but trouble every time they crossed a border. They were right: when Yasser presented his travel documents to British immigration at the entrance to the tunnel that runs beneath the English Channel from France, the British officer ordered Yasser aside, peered out his booth, and waved back all the rest of the motorcycle gang, which had previously been cleared. It took hours to run their names through all the relevant terrorist databases.

The Harley club members decided to bike through Syria and Lebanon on the next trip they took. When they reached the Saudi-Syrian border station, they all started joking with Yasser again, complaining about the trouble they would now endure from the Syrian border officials.

A Syrian guard combed through their passports and then came out to address the motorcyclists. "Where's the sheikh? Where's the sheikh?" the guard demanded.

They found Yasser, but the interest of the police turned out to be of a different sort than that to which they had grown accustomed: when Yasser Bin Laden thundered past on his Harley, the Syrian guards stood and saluted. For them, Osama had turned all Bin Ladens into heroes.[14]

"WHEN 20/20 RETURNS, a family name to be proud of—until September 11th. But what if your last name were Bin Laden now?"[15]

Barbara Walters traveled to Saudi Arabia early in 2002 to produce an ambitious report for the ABC television network's evening news magazine program *20/20.* In setting up the trip, Walters and her producers worked closely with Bandar Bin Sultan, the Saudi ambassador in Washington, and Adel Al-Jubeir, then a political and media adviser in the court of Crown Prince Abdullah. Walters told both of them that she very much wanted to interview a member of the Bin Laden family for her report. Her broadcast would offer an opportunity for the family to humanize themselves before a large American television audience and to emphasize their estrangement from Osama. This in turn might salve some of the wounds in U.S.-Saudi relations, which had become increasingly constrained by the mutually hostile attitudes of the two countries' publics. The Saudi officials Walters spoke with agreed that the program might be helpful. Adel Al-Jubeir, in particular, enlisted the support of

Crown Prince Abdullah, and he met with Bakr Bin Laden and two other members of the Bin Laden family in an effort to persuade them to cooperate. But Crown Prince Abdullah had made clear that he would not order the Bin Ladens to appear on American television; the choice was theirs. Bakr proved reluctant, despite repeated entreaties from Al-Jubeir and other Saudi officials.[16]

The Bin Ladens had by now become a commodity in the media marketplace. According to Khaled Al-Maenna, editor of the *Arab News* in Jeddah and a frequent interlocutor with foreign media, an American media outlet (which he would not identify) telephoned to offer him a fifty-thousand-dollar fee if he could get a Bin Laden family member on camera. As a media strategist, Al-Maenna agreed that the Bin Ladens might have helped Saudi Arabia if a confident, English-speaking member of the family would appear on television, apologize, and try to make themselves accessible to American audiences. Yet the hostility and presumptuous attitudes of the American media offended him and many other Saudis.[17] Pride, resentment, and fear predominated after September 11 in both America and Saudi Arabia. The Bin Ladens—with so much to lose, and in Bakr's evident judgment, so little to gain from media publicity—kept their collective heads down.

They were perhaps unable to conceive, however, of the force of nature that was Barbara Walters. As she traveled in Saudi Arabia early in 2002, conducting a number of interviews with members of the royal family and with families of September 11 hijackers in Asir, she grew increasingly frustrated. She had sought an interview with Crown Prince Abdullah, the most powerful man in the kingdom; this did not materialize. Without a Bin Laden on camera, she told the Saudis assisting her, her trip would be a bust—and the implication was, of course, that she would be very angry. Sensing a public relations fiasco, Bandar and Al-Jubeir concocted a bold ploy to help Walters. As it happened, Bandar owed the Bin Ladens a large sum of money for work they had completed on his palace in Jeddah. The Bin Ladens had been agitating for payment. Bandar proposed inviting Abdullah Bin Laden, the Harvard graduate, to his home, supposedly for a meeting with accountants called to settle the final palace bill. Barbara Walters would arrive—and Abdullah would have no choice but to submit to an interview.[18]

The ambush came off seamlessly. Walters walked in on the business meeting and Abdullah, as Bandar hovered, reluctantly agreed to sit for a few questions. On her broadcast, Walters did not burden viewers with the story of how the interview had come about, but she did note on air, during her introduction, "As we sat down together, he was so nervous—and who could blame him?"

"How difficult has this been for your family?" Walters asked Abdullah in her signature tone of empathy.

"We went through a tough time, it was difficult. But—and we felt we are a victim as well, but no matter what happened to us, it is not—our tragedy is not as bad, or we didn't feel as bad, as those victims, the families and victims in New York. Our tragedy compared to their tragedies—there is no comparison, and we do feel for them."

"Do you have any idea what made Osama bin Laden the man he is?"

"I wish I can answer this question."[19]

38. BRANDS

J ACK KAYAJANIAN practiced family law in Costa Mesa, California, south of Los Angeles. He was a gregarious man who spent some of his spare time at the Del Mar racetrack, where he dabbled in Thoroughbreds and kept his eyes peeled for long-shot winners. He was an active member of the Armenian American community in conservative Orange County, and he regarded himself as a fiercely patriotic American. So when an Armenian friend of his telephoned in the summer of 2002 to say that his daughter, Christine, was having custody trouble with her ex-husband, who happened to be a member of the Bin Laden family, Kayajanian took up the case with some gusto.[1]

After their divorce in 1993, Ibrahim Bin Laden and Christine Hartunian had accommodated one another for eight years without notable difficulty. They cooperated in raising their only child, their daughter Sibba. She lived with her mother and attended school in Southern California but also spent summers and Ramadan holidays with Ibrahim in Jeddah or at his Stone Canyon estate in Bel Air. The rise of Osama Bin Laden during the late 1990s created some tension within the family because Ibrahim started to think that he might not be safe in the United States. "I began to feel uncomfortable in Los Angeles in the summer of 2001," he said later, "as a result of remarks that were made to me even before September 11."[2]

When the Bin Ladens evacuated to Jeddah, Ibrahim took Sibba with him; they had been vacationing in Geneva when the attacks took place. Sibba found the scene in Jeddah somewhat unnerving, according to

Kayajanian: she told family members that some of the young people at the Bin Laden compound openly celebrated the September 11 attacks. Ibrahim enrolled his daughter in the British International School in Jeddah that autumn. Christine Hartunian, now a struggling artist who lived in a gated community in west Los Angeles, did not initially object, but she opposed the idea that Sibba would take up indefinite residence in Saudi Arabia. She was struggling financially; she had little money in her bank accounts and relied on loans from her parents. Christine flew to Jeddah to visit with Sibba at the Bin Laden compound.[3]

By the summer of 2002, her daughter had developed some health problems; these were not life threatening, but they required a specialist's care. Doctors in Saudi Arabia referred her to specialists in Southern California, and Christine took Sibba back to Los Angeles. Ibrahim, however, wanted Sibba to return to live with him and his new wife in Saudi Arabia; he argued that Sibba could get the treatment she required in the kingdom, and that she would be better off attending school there and living among the Bin Ladens. Sibba's parents could not reach an agreement about where she should live, as required by their divorce decree, and Christine believed she was about to lose custody of her only daughter to a Saudi system where she enjoyed few legal rights. She tried initially to represent herself in the court proceedings, but in about August 2002, her family called Jack Kayajanian onto the case.

Kayajanian pored through the old divorce files, rushed to Los Angeles Superior Court, where the original decree had been filed, and won an order that would at least delay Sibba's departure for Jeddah. Ibrahim hired a Santa Monica law firm that specialized in divorce; the lead partner on the case was a woman, as were two of her associates. These lawyers buried Kayajanian with motions and papers—new filings seemed to arrive almost around the clock. Kayajanian decided to concentrate on the medical issue, arguing that Sibba could obtain the care she needed only in the United States.[4]

Ibrahim refused to travel to America for a hearing. Because of

September 11, he feared for "my own safety" because of "the backlash against people of Arabic descent in the United States ... The fear is real and justified, given the notoriety of our last name. I know that our surname triggers very strong reactions in many individuals." Judge Roy L. Paul agreed to permit Ibrahim to testify by live video transmission from a studio in Dubai, in the United Arab Emirates, so that he would not have to travel to Los Angeles.[5]

On October 4, 2002, Kayajanian and Ibrahim's lawyers arrived at a special secure courtroom in Los Angeles known as "the bank," where high-profile cases involving Hollywood celebrities were sometimes convened. Ibrahim appeared on a video monitor.[6]

Judge Paul ordered Ibrahim's testimony to be sealed, ostensibly to protect Sibba from possible vigilante violence. Open court records nonetheless make clear what happened at the hearing: By day's end, Kayajanian had won on the crucial custody question. Judge Paul ruled that Sibba should attend school in Southern California and receive medical treatment in the U.S. The judge ordered Ibrahim Bin Laden to put up a $4 million bond to ensure that he would return his daughter to her mother after summer vacations and religious holidays. For almost a decade, Sibba's custody arrangements with the Bin Laden family in Saudi Arabia had been based on mutual trust. On both sides, that era was gone.[7]

IBRAHIM AND CHRISTINE had their difficulties, but their troubles remained unpublicized, and they paled beside the epic divorce between Yeslam and Carmen Bin Laden. Their lawsuit began in the Swiss courts during the early 1990s, but like many Bin Laden endeavors, it soon hopped international boundaries. Carmen sued Yeslam in Los Angeles, seeking (unsuccessfully) to prove that Ibrahim's Bel Air house should be considered one of her marital assets because it had been purchased in Yeslam's name. She also alleged that her husband had improperly sold jewelry originally purchased in Beverly Hills that belonged to her. Motions, pleadings, and sworn declarations piled up on two continents, but the years passed without resolution. The shock of September 11 seemed only to spur on both sides. After the terrorist attacks, Carmen chose what many Saudis would regard as the nuclear option: she wrote a book.

Inside the Kingdom became an international bestseller. Its tone was often respectful toward the Bin Ladens and even toward Yeslam, but Carmen suggested that the family had probably continued to support Osama long after the time it claimed to have cut him off. Carmen also offered this opinion repeatedly in television and newspaper interviews during her book tours in Europe and America. In addition, she was outspoken about the second-class condition of women in Saudi society, and she criticized the Islamic system of family law that empowered men in custody and divorce struggles. The descriptions in her book of the privileged but suffocating lives of Saudi women—accounts drawn from Carmen's years as a wife and mother in the Bin Laden compound in Jeddah during the 1970s and early 1980s—were particularly powerful.

The book's success exacerbated the strains between her ex-husband, Yeslam, in Geneva and the senior Bin Laden brothers around Bakr in Jeddah. Carmen might not be the world's most compliant woman, but Bakr and the brothers around him tended to blame Yeslam for Carmen's decision to go public. Presumably money had been one motivation in her decision to write the book: Why couldn't Yeslam reach a settlement with her that would satisfy her? Why had he allowed the divorce to drag on for so long? How had Yeslam allowed himself to become estranged from his own daughters—what kind of father would permit this?[8] There had been many divorces among the Bin Ladens, but none with the Dickensian duration or humiliating public profile of this one.

Yeslam and Carmen were both entrepreneurial; in the aftermath of September 11, they competed not only in their divorce litigation but also for control of the Bin Laden brand. Through her book tours, Carmen became the most famous Bin Laden in the world after Osama. Yeslam seemed determined to catch up.

On her side, Carmen had an ally in this contest—her eldest daughter, Wafah, who followed her into the limelight after 2003. Wafah had been a graduate student at Columbia University at the time of the September 11 attacks; she lived in a $6,000-per-month rented loft in New York City's West Village. She was a strikingly beautiful woman in her early twenties who aspired to a career as a popular singer. To promote her first recording, she sat for an interview with Barbara Walters. Wafah seemed to be in search of the marketing equivalent of a jujitsu move, in which a wrestler uses an opponent's momentum as a weapon against him—in Wafah's case, she would flip Osama's notoriety into her own pop music career. She posed for come-hither pictures in a popular American men's magazine, GQ. She changed her surname to Daufour, her mother's maiden name, but Wafah did not shy away from her status as a Bin Laden; this brought the media to her door. And yet, she said, "I feel that everybody's judging me and rejecting me. Come on, where's the American spirit? Accept me. I want to be embraced, because my values are just like yours." She spoke no Arabic and did not carry a Saudi passport. Perhaps her feeling of isolation was genuine, but there was also a hint of rock-and-roll posture in her complaints—she was an ingénue rebel without a culture. Her CD sales proved to be modest.[9]

Yeslam raced to the marketplace ahead of his estranged wife and daughter in one respect: In February 2001 he had applied to trademark "Bin Laden" under Swiss law, through Falcon Sporting Goods, one of his companies. Yeslam planned to develop a line of Bin Laden–labeled clothing, glasses, and perhaps jewelry, bicycles, backpacks, and luggage. After the September 11 attacks, Yeslam's Swiss attorney, Juerg Brand, confirmed their plans to go forward with a Bin Laden clothing line, initially in the Arab world. "The name is one of the most famous names in the world," Brand said. Asked if he also intended to sell the jeans in the United

States, Brand followed one unfortunate phrase with another: "We can't make an immediate jump across the ocean," he said.[10]

Bin Laden jeans might appeal to rebellious Arab teenagers, but Yeslam and his partners did not account for the reaction in Switzerland and the United States. The Swiss Federal Institute of Intellectual Property announced that it would revoke the Bin Laden trademark because it violated "accepted moral standards." Yeslam then said his plans had been misunderstood. He recognized, he said, that selling a Bin Laden–labeled clothing line would be "insensitive." And yet, he declared later, "I am not only a Bin Laden. I am Yeslam Bin Laden. I have my own identity." Osama to him was now only "a name in a newspaper."[11]

Yeslam opened a luxury boutique in a pedestrian square in Old Geneva, where he sold luxury handbags, silk scarves, perfumes, and handmade watches whose faces were engraved with a map of the kingdom of Saudi Arabia; the watches cost upwards of twenty thousand dollars. He settled on a new brand: Yeslam. He spent hours blending the perfumes that bore his name; he sifted jasmine and fruit scents in a perfume he labeled "Passion."

The British writer Marianne MacDonald visited him in Geneva and found him a "shy, quiet man dressed in an Hermès jacket with Dior jeans covering his narrow legs." Yeslam struck her as sensitive; he spoke openly about the anxieties that had bothered him since childhood.[12]

Had Osama ruined his life? Yeslam clasped his hands. "Whatever had to happen, happened," he told MacDonald. "There is nothing I can do. If you say, 'Look what happened to me,' I would only put myself into a depression. If I can do something I love, and create perfume and watches and so on, then I am doing something that's good for me."

He felt that his Yeslam brand could compete successfully for market share with Hermès and Chanel, the Parisian fashion houses. This was an ambitious goal, he acknowledged, "But I am offering better quality, and I hope this will come across."[13]

39. SO WHAT?

SALEM'S ENGLISH WIDOW, Caroline, expressed a desire after her husband's death to remain part of the Bin Laden family. It was not unusual in Arabia for widows to marry a brother of the widow's former husband. When Sama, Caroline's daughter by Salem, was about eight years old, Bakr approached his half-brother in Egypt, Khaled, about taking Caroline as a wife. "She's still young," Bakr said of Caroline, according to Khaled's aide Sabry Ghoneim. "She wants to live in Egypt. If she marries a foreigner, we lose our daughter, Sama. We need one of the family to marry her and be kind with her. We know you are close with her because you were close with Salem, and you will be good to Sama." With his horse farms, his passion for Thoroughbreds, art, and poetry, and his apartment in open-minded Cairo, Khaled presided over a household more suitable for Caroline than any available in Jeddah. Khaled agreed to wed her.[1]

On November 18, 2005, Caroline Carey arrived with her husband Khaled at the El Zahraa Farm, in the desert countryside outside Cairo, for the annual International Arabian Horse Show. She wore white pearl earrings, a white blouse, and tan pants, and she had a sweater wrapped around her waist. She has piercing blue eyes and a strong jaw. She was "Mum" to her daughter, Sama, who was now a spirited teenager with an interest in diplomacy; some in the family describe Sama as an heir to her father's most attractive qualities. She, too, arrived for the horse competition; Khaled Bin Laden had entered a number of his Arabians.[2]

In the entourage as well was Salem, Khaled's son by an earlier wife. He had attended boarding school in Virginia and now worked in one of the family companies. He also has bred his own Arabian horses and has trained to enter Olympic shooting competitions as a Saudi marksman. He wore a black Prada turtleneck, narrow Giorgio Armani jeans, black boots, and reflective sunglasses. The screen saver on his silver Nokia cellular telephone was the Armani logo.

A song played over the loudspeaker: "Barbie Girl." Salem sat in the grandstands, watching stallions prance and trot in the ring below. He smoked fresh green tobacco in a pipe, a habit he picked up in the Gulf.

He entertained a question: Has Osama changed life among the Bin Ladens? "What can we do?" Salem replied. "He is one of us, he has our name. We can deal with it . . . It affects us all. But we are a big family, we can absorb it." The issue passed like a breeze.

His father circulated below among the spectators, trainers, and riders participating in the competition. In his fifties, Khaled was well maintained. He wore stiff blue jeans, a blue shirt, running shoes of a mustard color, and a yellow, blue, and red tie. His receding hair was cropped closely.

"My father sees horses as art," Salem said. "He paints, too. He paints horses."

Khaled agreed to speak for a few minutes, "but only about horses."

The Bin Ladens had amassed a table beneath a tent near the competition ring. Khaled took a seat, pleasant but reticent.

Like so many of his brothers, Khaled had once been a recreational pilot, but he gave up the hobby after running out of fuel one day above Luxor. He enjoys hunting and frequents the colonial Shooting Club in Cairo. He has owned a horse farm in Egypt since 1982 and now keeps about fifty Arabian horses there. The bloodlines of these animals trace to the great Bedouin herds of the precolonial Arabian Peninsula; they were brought to Egypt by Ottoman conquerors of previous centuries. The horses do not race but are bred for show; the competitions revolve around appearance and presentation maneuvers. Khaled selects stallions and mares for breeding on his own Egyptian farm, Rabab Stud. There he also cultivates cactus plants, date palms, and mango trees in the desert. His stables are designed in old Arab and Moorish styles. In the main house there is a photograph of his father, Mohamed Bin Laden, as well as portraits of two Saudi kings, Fahd and Faisal. Khaled says that he has been refining his passion for Arabian horses over a quarter century.

"We make the selection from the stable and see which one is the best," he said. Even anodyne questions about horses seem to pain him, however. Straining to be polite, he conceded that his favorite is named Afrah, or "Joy."

In a pamphlet he has published, which he offers to visitors, Khaled has been more expansive about his passion: "I am trying to create a symphony with the horse," he said. "It is like a composition where you take elements from many sources to form a piece of living art that must be harmonious." The history of Arabia moves through these animals. "You have to see an Arabian horse moving with pride and elegance," he says. "It has to snort and trumpet with the tail flowing and flying over the ground, catching the wind. Then you are seeing what you should."

Khaled's horses have performed well in the competition this day— one first place, two seconds, and a third.

Several middle-aged British women approached his table beneath the tent to offer congratulations. *"Mabruk!"* one of them exclaimed. She leaned down to kiss him on each cheek. Khaled returned the kisses.

He looked over. "So I can kiss like a European," he said.[3]

EGYPT BECAME A LOCUS of recovery and sanctuary for the Bin Ladens after September 11. There was Khaled's farm and his other properties in and around Cairo, as well other town houses and estates owned by other half-brothers and half-sisters of Bakr. There was Bin Laden Island and Bakr's separate resort property at Sharm El Sheikh, on the Red Sea. Like

Beirut, Egypt offered a respite from the puritanical humidity of Jeddah, without the complications that came with crossing borders or using credit cards in Europe or America. It was a lively and welcoming country—a place where the mosque and Hard Rock Cafe wings of the family could each relax.

It also offered the distractions of work. The Bin Laden subsidiary in Egypt employed about a thousand people and won several contracts for airport work in Cairo and Sharm El Sheikh after 2002; the contracts were partially supported by the World Bank, which offered a visible endorsement of the family's continuing business legitimacy. Osama's violence did force one adjustment: The Egyptian government felt that if construction signs scattered around two of its most important international airports advertised the name Bin Laden, this might confuse and worry foreign tourists, and so the local subsidiary changed its name to Al-Murasim.[4]

By late 2005, it was clear that the Bin Ladens would not only survive Osama, but might thrive as never before. The Saudi royal family stuck by them and ensured their continuing prestige as the most important building contractors in Mecca and Medina. King Fahd died in the summer of 2005, but Bakr had already cultivated ties with his successor, Abdullah; the Bin Ladens gathered hurriedly in Riyadh that summer to swear loyalty to the new king. Rather than the dawn of a new period of uncertainty for the Bin Ladens, Abdullah's ascension promised new opportunity. The Bin Ladens suffered from no political backlash in Saudi Arabia. As a large family with its share of black sheep, the Al-Saud acted on principle by supporting them, but Abdullah also sent a subliminal message to the Islamic world—the Saudi royal family might not condone Osama, but they would not seek revenge against him or his family, either, as sometimes happened to the families of dissidents in Arab countries. As ever, the Al-Saud needed the Bin Ladens' expertise. As the war in Iraq deteriorated, oil prices soared above seventy dollars a barrel, and construction boomed in the kingdom and in neighboring Dubai. New condominium and office skyscrapers, shopping malls, freeways, mosques, and airports were announced one after another—even an inexperienced and poorly organized construction company could thrive in this atmosphere, which resembled the 1970s in its indiscriminate showers of cash. The Bin Ladens were particularly well positioned to profit.

The drive to modernize and internationalize the family companies, overseen by Bakr and Yahya, had largely succeeded. The engineer brothers might not be as glamorous or amusing as Salem, but after many years of hard work, they had positioned the Bin Ladens to enjoy sustained and secure wealth, and to successfully pass the family fortune intact through several generations. In his heyday, Salem had paraphrased King Faisal: "My father was riding on a camel. I am flying in jets. My children will fly in jets. My grandchildren will ride a camel again." Bakr and Yahya had not rendered this forecast implausible, but they had certainly reduced its likelihood, with a notable assist from the geopolitical forces that drove oil prices up and up.[5]

Yahya Bin Laden said late in 2005 that he expected the number of employees at the Bin Laden firms to rise from about thirty-five thousand toward about seventy-five thousand during the next decade as oil wealth continued to pour into the Gulf region. He hoped to further diversify the family companies, he said, so that construction contracts of the traditional type might ultimately generate only about a quarter of the Bin Ladens' revenue. He quoted an Arabic saying: The first generation makes the money, the second generation tries to preserve it, and the third generation squanders it. The family could avoid this fate, he believed. His own children and those of Bakr and other brothers had acquired excellent educations at the finest universities in the West, and some were committed to the future of the business. Younger half-brothers such as Mohamed, not yet fifty years old, were proving to be capable and modern executives. But these younger Bin Ladens were not going to spend two weeks sitting around a Riyadh majlis waiting for a moody prince to sign a contract, as Salem and then Bakr had done patiently and obsequiously for so many years. It was imperative to modernize the company and then hope that something similar would happen to Saudi decision making.[6]

The chances of this did not look especially promising. As had been true since the 1950s, the more oil money flowed into Saudi coffers, the less urgent seemed any imperative for change. In an unusually candid soliloquy, Bandar Bin Sultan described the assumptions of the Al-Saud:

> The way I answer the corruption charges is this: In the last thirty years—we have implemented a development program that was approximately . . . close to $400 billion worth. Okay? Now, look at the whole country, where it was, where it is now. And I am confident, after you look at it, you could not have done all of that for less than, let's say, $350 billion. If you tell me that building this whole country, spending $350 billion out of $400 billion, that we had misused or [were] corrupt with $50 billion, I'll tell you, "Yes. But I'll take that anytime." There are so many countries in the Third World that have oil that are still thirty years behind. But more important, more important—"Hey, who are you to tell me this?" What I'm trying to tell you is: So what?[7]

Not long afterward, citing national security concerns, the British government dropped a criminal investigation into the sale of defense equipment to Saudi Arabia during the 1980s and 1990s. According to a British newspaper, as part of the financial arrangements required by the Saudis to consummate these arms deals, hundreds of millions of dollars flowed into bank accounts controlled by Bandar Bin Sultan.[8]

So what? Unlike Bandar, the Bin Ladens lacked the nerve to ask this question out loud, and yet, the more time passed after September 11, the less significance the attacks seemed to hold for the family's future. Lawsuits filed in the United States by families of the victims, consolidated under the title *In Re: Terrorist Attacks on September 11, 2001*, named the Saudi Bin Laden Group, and four Bin Laden brothers—Bakr, Omar, Tareq, and Yeslam—as defendants. One of the lawsuits alleged that, "under Bakr Bin Laden's control," the Saudi Bin Laden group had "provided substantial material support and assistance to Al Qaeda." The Bin Ladens hired Jones Day, a large American law firm whose Washington offices occupied a polished building across from the U.S. Capitol, to handle the family's defense. The legal bills endured by the Bin Ladens in this and related matters quickly exceeded $10 million, according to what Bakr told the Saudi government, but it was money well spent: early in 2005, U.S. District Judge Richard Casey in New York dismissed the individual Bin Ladens as defendants on jurisdictional grounds. He allowed some further investigation of whether the Saudi Bin Laden Group might have been significantly active in the United States to justify its inclusion in the lawsuit, but at the very minimum, it would be several years before the lawsuit considered the merits of the company's history with Osama if it did so at all.[9]

Desert Bear went up for sale in 2004 for about $4 million, more than twenty years after Salem first purchased the estate and began landing his helicopters on the lawn. Since the property was owned and titled in Florida by a Liberian corporation, the purchaser would not be able to buy the land or the home directly, but would have to buy portable bearer shares in the Liberian company and then try to prove ownership to Florida real estate authorities, according to several people who inquired about the property listing. Potential buyers were told that they would have to bring or deliver cash overseas to purchase control of the Liberian corporation; the Bin Ladens did not want to enter the United States to close the transaction. The buyers who persisted through these negotiations planned to subdivide the property and build suburban homes.[10] It was an untidy end to the estate's remarkable history, one that began with a Jell-O patent at the beginning of the twentieth century and ended, in effect, with the September 11 attacks.

As the pressure on the family eased, Bakr flourished. He took as his third wife a much younger woman—she was still in her late teens when he met and married her around 2004. Bakr now wove more leisure into his schedule: he vacationed on a private island in the Maldives, visited a resort in Bali, socialized with other yacht-owning wealthy Saudi businessmen in Beirut, attended air shows in Dubai, and gossiped for hours with colleagues about the latest models of private jets. His sons took up the family passion for fast-moving machines; late in 2006, Abdulaziz Bin Bakr won the U.A.E. National Superstock Bike Trophy.[11] By then, Bakr's confidence seemed to reflect that of Saudi Arabia: The kingdom's tormentor, Saddam Hussein, was headed to the gallows; Osama was in hiding and Al Qaeda's attacks inside Saudi Arabia, while occasionally unnerving, had amounted to little more than a nuisance; oil prices were sky high; Saudi politics and succession plans were stable; and the Americans would surely take care of any future threats from Iran. What was there to fear?

IN MECCA, the heart of Islam and the headwaters of the Bin Laden fortune, York International Corporation of Pennsylvania installed during 2005 a complex of industrial air-conditioning units, or water chillers, on a hilltop of volcanic rock called Jabal Al-Qala, or "Castle Mountain." The units constituted the largest industrial air-conditioning project undertaken by York since it serviced the Prophet's Mosque at Medina in partnership with the Bin Ladens. This time it was not a religious sanctuary that would be cooled in the desert, but a seven-tower condominium and hotel project overlooking Mecca's Grand Mosque. According to a York executive, by the time it was completed, this Mecca condo project would overtake the Prophet's Mosque as the largest air conditioner in the world.[12]

In the latest oil boom, every Gulf businessman with real estate profits or a corporate bonus to spend seemed to covet a condo overlooking Mecca; by 2005, the real estate rush in the holy city rivaled that in Miami's fevered South Beach. The Bin Ladens initially thought they would not bother with the time and expense required to sell individual condo units at Castle Mountain, so they sold an entire tower to Kuwaiti investors. When they learned the soaring retail prices units in the building were attracting, the Bin Ladens "were furious," said Anwar Hassan of York International. The family's executives decided in the future they would "retail every apartment themselves" to maximize profits.[13]

With the Faqih family—another Saudi business group with a black sheep living in exile—the Bin Ladens planned for an even more ambitious condominium tower project on Omar Mountain, overlooking Mecca, a project that would require blasting off the volcanic mountaintop in order to build. This development contemplated the construction of four towers, each about thirty stories high, containing one hundred elevators and a total of more than forty-six hundred apartment units. There would be a five-star hotel, a shopping mall, and parking for two thousand cars.[14] The sprawl-inducing, profit-making commercial evolution of Islam's holiest places had reached its apotheosis, and the Bin Ladens were partners in all of the most ambitious projects.

They were partners, too, in the planned King Abdullah Economic City, announced in late 2005 as oil prices moved above fifty dollars a barrel. The new king commandeered undeveloped land along the Red Sea north of Jeddah and announced a city designed to rival Dubai. Abdullah said the project would cost about $27 billion. He planned a Millennium Seaport to rival the largest commercial ports in the world; high-speed rail and air links to the rest of the kingdom; an Industrial District of petrochemical and other plants; a waterside resort to attract tourists, complete with the kingdom's first world-class 18-hole golf course; a Financial Island topped by two office towers reaching sixty or more stories into the sky; an Education Zone filled with modern universities; and, of course, more condominiums. The project, said a Bin Laden executive, "could either make or break the local economy." For the Bin Laden companies, the construction work alone would be "absolutely huge in scope."[15]

"For the Roads Ahead," was the headline on a self-promotional advertisement purchased by the Saudi Bin Laden Group in the *Washington Post* late in 2005. "Construction may be at the heart of what we do. But our interests also extend into the worlds of media, retail, industrial projects and telecommunications. It's all part of our vision to ensure Saudi Arabia remains a modern and dynamic regional center in the 21st Century."[16]

There seemed to be no aspect of Saudi Arabia's second wave of modernization projects from which the Bin Ladens would not profit handsomely. Even the sometimes shaky security environment in the kingdom offered opportunity. In May 2003, Al Qaeda cells inside Saudi Arabia launched a series of mostly ineffectual attacks against the Interior Ministry, American compounds in the oil zones, and against the U.S. consulate in Jeddah. Osama Bin Laden's son Sa'ad, in exile in Iran, was accused of playing a role in organizing the strikes. Saudi security forces, aided by surveillance technology acquired from the United States, launched violent crackdowns against suspected Al Qaeda sympathizers. Hundreds of Islamists were rounded up and interrogated. The violence soon subsided. In April 2006, the Saudi government announced a fast-track project to build nine new prisons across the kingdom within twelve months. The construction contract was awarded to the Saudi Bin Laden Group; it was valued at $1.6 billion.[17]

40. IN EXILE

THE OFFICES of Fame Advertising are on the second floor of a strip mall in downtown Jeddah, on Palestine Street. The shopping center also houses a Starbucks, a Java Lounge, a Vertigo Music Café, and a Body Master, a massage and health club. Inside the Fame Advertising suite, the ambience suggests a Silicon Valley startup company. There is a juice bar with tall bar stools, and on the wall hangs a large black-and-white photograph of cable cars on an undulating San Francisco street. Impressionist paintings of European café scenes grace other rooms. The furniture is chrome, black leather, and cherry wood; the computers sport the labels of International Business Machines.[1]

This is the realm of Osama Bin Laden's eldest son, Abdullah, who started Fame as an outlet for his entrepreneurial ambitions after he returned to Saudi Arabia, following his separation from his father in Sudan. As of late 2005, Fame enjoyed an association with the larger Saudi Bin Laden Group, and it had about fifteen employees. Unlike many Saudi companies, the firm did not enforce gender segregation within its offices. It produced a stylish Web site, www.fame-adv.com. Its clients included large Jeddah-based merchant groups such as the Jufallis and Western companies such as Phillips, the electronics maker.

The proprietor, now in his midtwenties, often wore blue jeans and a baseball cap. In the spring of 2002, he stunned diplomats at the nearby American consulate by turning up in such an outfit at a July 4–style celebration of U.S. independence (held a little early on the calendar because

Jeddah's weather in July is unbearable). Abdullah vacationed in Europe, and when in Jeddah, he became a fixture at the relatively freewheeling Bin Laden–owned beach club along the Red Sea.

To promote Fame's services, Abdullah created marketing brochures, in the form of small and colorful cards, which could be handed out to prospective clients. A card entitled "Corporate Identity Management" exuded, "At FAME ADVERTISING we believe that the development of a successful corporate identity is essential to any project or business. Our creation of corporate identities is based on extensive research . . . with innovative methods that succeed every time." On the back of the card was a one-word slogan: "Strong." A second brochure was titled "Event Management." It boasted, "FAME ADVERTISING events are novel, planned meticulously and executed with efficiency." The slogan on the back: "Different." If Abdullah was conscious of the way he quoted his father's methodology, he did not extend the parallels too far: colorful balloon displays, rather than simultaneous car bomb explosions, were a typical motif of Fame events, according to the photographs posted on its Web site.[2]

As Osama Bin Laden's exile lengthened after September 11, his own large family, the product of at least five marriages over two decades, scattered and drifted, much as had happened to Osama's own generation after the death of Mohamed Bin Laden. As of 2002, Osama had fathered at least twenty-three children. The great majority of them, apart from Abdullah and a few others, lived with him in Afghanistan during the run-up to September 11. As that attack approached, however, Osama seemed to decide that he would endure the next phase of his banishment without the company of most of his current wives. In the summer of 2001, some of Osama's older sons arranged for at least one of his wives and her children to take shelter with tribesmen along the Afghan-Pakistan border; they later turned her over to the Pakistan government, and after several months, this wife apparently returned to her native Saudi Arabia with some of her children. Two of Osama's earlier wives had already returned to the kingdom. By December 2001, his recent, very young Yemeni wife had also returned home.[3]

Osama's sons divided themselves into two camps—those who stayed to fight with him, and those who returned to Saudi Arabia, where they could enjoy some of the benefits of Bin Laden family membership. Sa'ad, Hamzah, Sayf, Mohamed, Khalid, and Ladin were among the sons who stayed with Osama or devoted themselves to his cause from separate (and ambiguous) exile in Iran. Those who returned to Saudi Arabia, in addition to Abdullah, included Osama's sons Ali and Omar; the latter had decided to leave Afghanistan in 2000, at the age of nineteen.[4]

When Omar reached Jeddah, he found that he lagged behind his peers in the Bin Laden family. "Osama did not educate his children" in conventional schools, explained Jamal Khalifa, Osama's brother-in-law, who came to know Omar after his return. In Afghanistan, he insisted that they only "memorize the Koran . . . So Omar, he was feeling really sorry. He saw the difference between himself and others in the family."[5] Nonetheless, he established himself as a scrap dealer in Jeddah. He married a Saudi woman, developed a muscular physique, donned blue jeans, and trimmed his beard into a fashionable goatee.

In the autumn of 2006, while riding horses near the Pyramids in Egypt, Omar, now in his midtwenties, met Jane Felix-Browne, a fifty-one-year-old grandmother from Cheshire. Omar and Jane fell in love, by her account, and quickly married. She had previously been married five times and had converted to Islam; their romance had to overcome some of the tensions that arose from his father's notoriety. "Omar is wary of everyone," Felix-Browne said. "He is constantly watching people who he feels might be following him. Not without reason, he is fearful of cameras . . . But when we are together, he forgets his life." She said Omar had "left his father because he did not feel it was right to fight or to be in an army," and yet "he misses his father." When news of his union generated sensational headlines in Britain, Omar issued a statement to a Saudi newspaper defending his marriage. He explained that his first wife had agreed to this expansion of their family—"Polygamy is not strange in our Arab and Islamic society"—and he pointed out that the Prophet Mohamed had married his wife Khadjia "when he was twenty and she was forty." There seemed to be some confusion about this issue among his two wives; Felix-Browne soon announced their divorce. She said that she and Omar feared for their lives.[6]

On December 14, 2001, Osama Bin Laden wrote and signed his last will and testament. At Tora Bora, around this time, he had endured heavy aerial bombardment by American-led forces, and now he prepared to die. He opened his will with religious invocations, and then wrote, "Allah commended to us that when death approaches any of us that we make a bequest to parents and next of kin and to Muslims as a whole ... Allah bears witness that the love of jihad and death in the cause of Allah has dominated my life and the verses of the sword permeated every cell in my heart, 'and fight the pagans all together as they fight you all together.' How many times did I wake up to find myself reciting this holy verse!"

His tone, reflecting the military and political setbacks his organization had suffered throughout the autumn of 2001, was thoroughly downhearted:

> If every Muslim asks himself why has our nation reached this state of humiliation and defeat, then his obvious answer is because it rushed madly for the comforts of life and discarded the Book of Allah behind its back, though it is the only one that has its cure ... The Jews and Christians have tempted us with the comforts of life and its cheap pleasures and invaded us with their materialistic values before invading us with their armies, while we stood like women doing nothing because the love of death in the cause of Allah has deserted the hearts ... The prin-

cipal cause of our nation's ordeal is its fear from dying in the cause of Allah . . . Today, the nation has failed to support us.[7]

To his wives, Osama wrote, "You were, after Allah . . . the best support and the best help from the first day you knew that the road was full of thorns and mines . . . You renounced worldly pleasures with me—renounce them more after me. Do not think of remarrying and you need only to look after our children, make sacrifices, and pray for them."

To his children, he wrote, "Forgive me because I have given you only a little of my time since I answered the jihad call. I have shouldered the Muslims' concerns and the concerns of their hardships, embitterment, betrayal and treachery. If it was not for treachery, the situation would not be what it is now and the outcome would not be what it is now."

He explicitly advised his children not to work with Al Qaeda. He cited the story of a Muslim leader, Omar Bin Al-Khattab, who forbid his son from becoming caliph, telling him, "If it is good, then we have had our share; if it is bad, then it is enough . . ."[8]

During his years in Sudan, as his family gradually disowned him, Osama's writings sometimes rang with anger and frustration, but never before had a document attributed to him conveyed such despair and exhaustion. He had apparently assumed that the American military would quickly fall victim to a popular uprising by ordinary Afghans, as had occurred to the Soviet army after its invasion in 1979; instead, his allies in the Taliban had collapsed as the United States and its allies swept into every major Afghan city and town, and a number of his trusted compatriots in Al Qaeda had been killed or captured. If Osama imagined himself as the triumphant leader of a guerrilla vanguard, he now confronted the humiliating prospect of retreat, and the serious possibility that he would be killed or imprisoned.

The winter passed, however, and none of these fears materialized. By June 2002, Osama remained safe, and he had established a network of personal protection stable enough to allow him to return cautiously to jihad publishing and video production. His initial work that spring still expressed an unusual degree of self-pity; a jihadi Web site published a poetic exchange with his son Hamzah, evoking the conditions and causes of their shared exile:

"Oh father!" Hamzah wrote. "Where is the escape and when will we have a home? Oh father! I see spheres of danger everywhere I look. How come our home has vanished without a trace? . . . Why have they showered us with bombs like rain, having no mercy for a child? . . . Tell me, father, something useful about what I see."

"Oh son!" Osama answered. "Suffice to say that I am full of grief and sighs. What can I say if we are living in a world of laziness and discontent . . . Pardon me, my son, but I can only see a very steep path ahead. A decade has gone by in vagrancy and travel, and here we are in our tragedy. Security has gone, but danger remains. It is a world of crimes in which children are slaughtered like cows. For how long will real men be in short supply?"[9]

NOT FOR LONG, as it happened. As the months passed, and still he remained free, Osama's courage and confidence returned. The particular circumstances of his life as a fugitive are, as of this writing, unknown, but the open record of his published statements and recordings from exile during this period—more than a dozen altogether—makes plain the general trajectory of Osama's experience: an initial period of giddy celebration immediately after the attacks on New York and Washington, followed by a rapid descent into desperation, and then a gradual recovery and a reawakened sense of purpose, producing a return to the ambition and boastfulness of his past. Osama's statements make clear, too, that by 2003, at least, he enjoyed regular access to satellite television and the Internet.

Planning for the U.S.-led invasion of Iraq, more than any other event, seemed to draw Osama back to himself; judging by what he said and wrote, the war arrived as a kind of spiritual and political elixir, just when he required it most. The buildup to combat early in 2003 brought forth a burst of lengthy and ambitious writing, essays that harkened to his prolific period of pamphleteering from Sudan. After a period of quietude and anguish, suddenly Osama seemed to have much that he wished to say.

"I am rejoicing in the fact that America has become embroiled in the quagmires of the Tigris and Euphrates," he wrote in October 2003. "Bush thought that Iraq and its oil would be easy prey, and now here he is, stuck in dire straits, by the grace of God Almighty. Here is America today, screaming at the top of its voice as it falls apart in front of the whole world."[10]

Osama saw the Iraq war as "a rare and essentially valuable chance in every sense of the word to mobilize the *ummah*'s potential and unchain it." He urged young volunteers to "take off to the battlefields in Iraq to cut off the head of world infidelity."[11] Many answered his call, particularly from Saudi Arabia.

Osama made no secret of his disdain for Saddam Hussein, but this, of course, could not justify the American occupation, he said: "It is true that Saddam is a thief and an apostate, but the solution is not to be found in moving the government of Iraq from a local thief to a foreign one." When the United States announced increases in the reward money available for his capture or death, Osama retaliated by announcing his own reward schedule, in units of gold, for the murder of Paul Bremer, head of the Coalition Provisional Authority in Iraq, as well as for the deaths of other Americans.[12]

He seemed to particularly cherish the rhetoric of transformation in the Middle East enunciated by Bush and his cabinet. Their formulations about a "new" Arab world, anchored by a secular, democratic constitution in Iraq, confirmed Osama's belief that he was engaged in an epochal conflict. The occupation of Iraq "shows that the struggle is an ideological and religious struggle, and that the clash is a clash of civilizations," he wrote in May 2004. "They are keen to destroy the Islamic identity in the entire Islamic world."[13]

He mocked his Western adversaries for misunderstanding him as a premodern fanatic, a bearded loner in a faraway cave; he saw himself, instead, as a master of global technology and change. Indeed, after 2001, encouraged by Bin Laden's embrace of digital technology, Al Qaeda—now an organization, a movement, and a franchised brand—rapidly adapted itself to the loss of physical sanctuary in Afghanistan by making greater use of the Internet for training, tactical communication, and preaching. When American officials suggested that some of Osama's self-produced videos might contain secret codes to trigger terrorist attacks by sleeper cells, Bin Laden reacted to these fears with contempt. "The Americans have made laughable claims," he said. "They said that there are hidden messages intended for terrorists in Bin Laden's statements. It is as if we are living in a time of carrier pigeons, without the existence of telephones, without travelers, without the Internet, without regular mail, without faxes, without e-mail. This is just farcical; words that belittle people's intellects."[14]

One of his most remarkable essays, published as preparations for the invasion of Iraq were under way, presented a list of grievances—numbered and subnumbered into categories—that described the fullness of his opposition to the United States, its foreign policies, and its national values. The essay suggested that Osama had been perusing American news magazines during the long hours of his exile and had grown frustrated by the typical analysis he read of his motivations. "Some American writers have published articles under the title 'On what basis are we fighting?' ... Here we wanted to outline the truth." He posed two essential questions: "Why are we fighting and opposing you?" and "What are we calling you to, and what do we want from you?"[15]

The answer to the first question, he wrote, "is very simple: 1) Because you attacked us and continue to attack us." He listed the venues where he perceived these attacks: Palestine, Somalia, Chechnya, Kashmir, Lebanon. "You steal our wealth and oil at paltry prices because of your international influence and military threats. This theft is indeed the biggest theft ever witnessed by mankind in the history of the world."

As to the second question, his essential war aims, "The first thing we are calling you to is Islam." Americans should convert to the "seal of all previous religions" in order to rescue themselves from a profound state of debauchery:

> We call you to be a people of manners, principles, honor and purity; to reject the immoral acts of fornication, homosexuality, intoxicants, gambling, and usury . . . You are a nation that permits acts of immorality, and you consider these acts to be pillars of personal freedom . . . Who can forget your President Clinton's immoral acts committed in the official Oval office? After that you did not even bring him to account, other than that he "made a mistake," after which everything passed with no punishment . . . You are a nation that exploits women like consumer products or advertising tools, calling upon customers to purchase them . . . You then rant that you support the liberation of women.[16]

The more idle time Osama spent as a fugitive, the more hours he watched satellite television or perused Web sites for news of the world outside, the more he seemed to internalize and synthesize, in a characteristic fashion, diverse strands of anti-American grievance, whether they had originated with the European left, the Christian right, or the anti-globalization movement. He valued rhetorical effect over consistency of argument. His lines of poetry might be labored and archaic, but from time to time, he could turn a memorable sentence. Describing his impervious defiance in the name of Islam, he wrote: "The swimmer in the sea does not fear rain."[17] When he was not elegant, he was at least clear:

"The freedom and democracy that you call for is for yourselves and for the white race only," he wrote. "As for the rest of the world, you impose upon it your monstrous, destructive policies and governments, which you call 'friends of America.'"[18]

He often blended these secular-tinted criticisms of the United States with the millenarian and anti-Semitic creeds that had long been at the heart of his outlook. Throughout his essays and recordings, like many Arabians, Osama presumed the power and relentlessness of Zionist and Jewish conspiracies.

"America didn't start by taking my money and didn't hurt me personally at all," he conceded, "but it made claims about me as a result of our incitement against the Jews and the Americans . . . The government will take the American people and the West in general into a choking life, into an unsupportable hell, because of the fact that it has very strong ties with and are under the payroll of the Zionist lobby." He described Jews in dehumanizing terms, "the idiots of the age," who, when confronted by righteous Palestinian youth, "have become like agitated wild asses fleeing from a lion."[19]

He rejected the borders of many nation-states as illegitimate lines drawn by pagan colonialists, yet he retained an emotional identification with the particular country of his youth—no longer as a "Saudi," a word that honored the hated Al-Saud family, but rather as a "Hejazi," a son of the land of Mecca and Medina. "I miss my country greatly, and have long been absent from it; but this is easy to endure because it is for the sake of God," he wrote in late 2004. "Love for the Hejaz is deep in my heart, but its rulers are wolves."[20]

By now he forswore almost all his earlier sympathy for Crown Prince Abdullah, soon to become king, although he suggested that Abdullah was a victim, to some extent, of American blackmail. Many had believed, Osama wrote, "that when Prince Abdullah . . . took over management of the country, he would save it from the mires of religious disobedience, and administrative, financial and media corruption . . . and that he would save it from subservience to America. But although people were expecting good to come from him, he brought them evil."[21]

As yet more months passed and he still remained at large, and as Al Qaeda steadily revitalized itself and supported prominent attacks in London and elsewhere, Osama expressed open pride in what he had achieved since 2001. He had long thought of himself not as the general of an Islamic army or the self-anointed ruler of a prospective caliphate, but as the vanguard of a much broader and looser Islamic political resistance, in which his own band of violent operators would play no more than a galvanizing role. The September 11 attacks, he now concluded, had served to "demonstrate the enormous hostility that the Crusaders feel towards us" and had "revealed the American wolf in its true ugliness."[22]

For the future, he promised a patient, long-term guerrilla strategy in Iraq, Afghanistan, and elsewhere, punctuated by occasional "raids," or terrorism, on Western territory: "The balance of terror has evened out." He wanted to "underline the importance of dragging the enemy forces into a protracted, exhausting, close combat, making the most of camouflaged defense positions . . . Further, we emphasize the importance of martyrdom operations which have inflicted unprecedented harm on America and Israel, thanks to God Almighty." He retained a considerable interest in nuclear and other weapons of mass destruction, which he had once referred to as "war winners."[23]

In January 2006, apparently provoked once again by watching Bush on satellite television, Osama issued an audiotaped statement, which would be his last communiqué for a prolonged period.

"I had not intended to speak to you about this issue," he began. "However, what prompted me to speak are the repeated fallacies of your President Bush, in his comment on the outcome of the U.S. opinion polls, which indicated that the overwhelming majority of you want the withdrawal of the forces from Iraq—but he objected to this desire, and said that the withdrawal of troops would send a wrong message to the enemy.

Bush said: It is better to fight them on their ground than they fighting us on our ground." This rhetoric, although mainly intended for domestic political audiences in the United States, plainly infuriated Osama:

Reality testifies that the war against America and its allies has not remained confined to Iraq, as he claims. In fact, Iraq has become a point of attraction and recruitment of qualified resources. On the other hand, the *mujaheddin*, praise be to God, have managed to breach all the security measures adopted by the unjust nations of the coalition time and again. The evidence of this is the bombings you have seen in the most important European countries of this aggressive coalition.

Osama then issued a warning:

As for the delay in carrying out similar operations in America, this was not due to failure to breach your security measures. Operations are under preparation, and you will see them on your own ground once they are finished, God willing.

As for himself, he said, "I swear not to die but a free man."[24]

He fell into a long silence. On the sixth anniversary of the September II attacks, Al Qaeda's revived media operation, Al-Sahab, or "The Clouds," delivered a new videotape in which Osama donned a gold formal robe and read out a political essay to a single fixed camera. The images were blurry, but his eyes appeared a little baggy—hardly surprising for a man now almost fifty years old living under conditions that presumably carried some stress. The most striking aspects of his appearance reflected his unembarrassed middle-aged vanity: Since his last video, he had trimmed his long beard to a rounded shape and dyed its gray streaks black.

His speech again synthesized disparate and not particularly religious anti-American critiques. He managed to praise both Noam Chomsky, the linguist and ardently left-wing intellectual, and Michael Scheuer, the former CIA analyst whose professional life had once been devoted to killing him, because both men denounced in books they had recently published the business-influenced imperial strains in American foreign policy. Osama seemed clearly to be hiding in or near Pakistan, or somewhere else where English books were readily available, as he appeared to be using the considerable time on his hands to read in English, advancing the linguistic training he had first acquired from Irish and British instructors at the Al-Thaghr school. He also seemed, as before, to be watching and reading English-language news. Western media aggravated him: they were often worse "than the condition of the media of the dictatorial regimes which march in the caravan of the single leader," a view that also placed him in the company of many Western leftists.

Yet when Osama watched American or British television, sequestered in his hideaway, he now gazed into a flattering mirror—the media might distort his image, but they also depicted him as one of the most pervasive and powerful political figures on earth. Through the events of September 11, and their cascading aftermath, he now considered himself the author of this singular achievement, as an instrument of Allah. America might be "the greatest economic power" and "the major state influencing the policies of the world," and yet by recruiting nineteen young men to fly as suicide pilots and bodyguards, Osama had achieved the improbable: He had "changed the direction of its compass."[25]

This was Osama in his later exile: A man who, although relatively young, lived continuously close to death, and who worried, considering the short time he might have left, about how he might be remembered. His speeches were political and religious oratory of a now familiar type, but his lines also seemed intended to draft or at least influence the themes of his own posthumous reputation. Osama lacked a valid passport. He spoke in a Saudi accent but had been stripped—and had stripped himself—of conventional Saudi identity, and he was almost certainly living, at least some of the time, in an area of western Pakistan that lacked a recognizable government. In this denationalized condition, he chose wardrobes and props for his video statements that suggested three over-lapping strands of self-imagining: the formal gowns of a religious scholar; the assault rifle of a modern jihadi warrior; and the traditional dagger of his Hadhrami origins.

A century before, British colonial officers had struggled to under-stand the global Hadhrami diaspora from which the Bin Laden family and its wayward son later arose; the Hadhramis' mobile and independent net-works eluded or surprised the empire's census takers because they spilled across diverse political territory, often indifferent to the border posts of imperial mapmakers. Osama constructed his life as a political fugitive after September 11 in territory of just this character—a mountainous moonscape inhabited by tribally organized Pashtuns whom neither British colonial armies nor their Pakistani and American successors could penetrate or subdue. The history of similar exiles in Pashtun territory suggested he would probably face betrayal, eventually, by one of his local hosts. In the meanwhile, each time his audio- or videotapes reached Al-Jazeera or CNN, Osama reemphasized, like a Barbary pirate with a mar-keting degree, the impunity that he still enjoyed, as well as his continuing capacity to plan and inspire mass violence by exploiting the channels and the ethos of global integration.

ACKNOWLEDGMENTS

A large number of collaborators, friends, and generous strangers enabled the research for this book. I am grateful first and foremost to the many individuals who agreed to participate in interviews and reinterviews.

In Saudi Arabia, I owe special thanks to Faiza Ambah, Hatem Mohamed, and Adel Toraifi. The Faisaliyah Center for Research and Islamic Studies generously received me as an unpaid fellow during early 2005; thanks to Dr. Yahya Mahmoud Ibn Juniad, Syed Jameel, and Awadh Al-Badi. Prince Turki Al-Faisal graciously arranged my access to the center. Paul Dresch and Engseng Ho inspired me with their observations about the history of the Hadhrami diaspora and its relations with global empires. Fahd Al-Semmari at the King Abdulaziz Foundation provided valuable access to newspaper archives and research specialists. Erin L. Eddy in Jeddah was exceptionally helpful.

In Yemen, the governor of the Hadhramawt, Abdelqader Ali Al-Hilal, proved a gracious and an invaluable host. I owe thanks as well to Alawi Bin Sumait, Ali Mandanij, Megan Goodfellow, and Thomas Krajeski for supporting my research there.

In addition to Robin Shulman and Julie Tate, four part-time re-searchers made important contributions during the three-year life of this project. In Germany, Petra Krischok's persistence at the Foreign Ministry archives unearthed valuable records. In London, Gita Daneshjoo rein-terviewed overseas sources and provided other careful research. In the United States, Keach Hagey patiently developed and conducted interviews for chapter 36. Mohamed Elmenshawy provided elegant translations and acquired valuable materials during his travels to Egypt.

Thanks also to Sunlen Miller, Sami Sockol, Emily Eckland, Alexandra Coll, Emma Coll, Cynthia Zeiss, and Victoria Green for their research and organizing skills

Bruce Hoffman, Kim Cragin, Daniel Byman, Martha Crenshaw, Rohan Gunaratna, Nadia Oweidat, Sara Daly, Heather Gregg, and Anna Kasupski of the Rand Corporation's Early Al Qaeda History Working Group, where I was an ad hoc participant, provided generous support and inspiring scholarship. Anna Kasupski's work on financial issues proved particularly valuable. In other research forums, Dan Benjamin and Steven Simon made serious discourse unusually enjoyable.

As the source notes reflect, Peter Bergen's journalism and scholarship have been a core resource for this work; his many writings and his oral history, *The Osama Bin Laden I Know,* provide a foundation for any credible work on Al Qaeda's development and Osama's biography. I am even more grateful for his generous friendship. My *New Yorker* colleague Lawrence Wright's brilliant work, *The Looming Tower,* was another core resource, as it will be for many other writers. Peter and Larry graciously read a draft manuscript and offered helpful corrections and observations.

Michael Dobbs transformed my research by guiding me through the National Archives II at College Park. The archives' exceptional professional staff made my weeks there highly productive.

Glenn Frankel took time to read an early draft and provided insightful comment and editing. Other former *Washington Post* colleagues—Phil Bennett, David Hoffman, Len Downie, Bob Kaiser, and Anthony Shadid—helped to steer me ahead. To David Finkel, my unqualified thanks, affection, and admiration.

David Remnick, Jeff Frank, Dorothy Wickenden, Pam McCarthy, Jeffrey Goldberg, Jane Mayer, Alexander Dryer, Annie Lowrey, Virginia Cannon, Raffi Khatchadourian, Nandi Rodrigo, Scott Staton, Tim

Farrington, Allison Hoffman, Mike Peed, and Lila Byock have made my work at the *New Yorker* a rewarding privilege.

Jim Fallows, Ted Halstead, Steve Clemons, Anne-Marie Slaughter, Bernard Schwartz, Eric Schmidt, Sherle Schwenninger, Ray Boshara, Simone Frank, Rachel White, Maya MacGuinness, Len Nichols, Michael Dannenberg, David Gray, and Troy Schneider are among those who have welcomed and inspired me at the New America Foundation.

I am very fortunate to be published by the superb Ann Godoff. Thanks, too, to Tracy Locke, Liza Darnton, Lindsay Whalen, and Hal Fessenden at Penguin Press. Simon Winder at Penguin U.K. was exceptionally helpful. Thanks also to copy editor John Jusino. Melanie Jackson has been my literary agent for more than two decades; I can't imagine my professional life without her.

One of the rewards of this research was the chance to reflect upon the universal grammar of families; in this, I enjoyed the support and teachings of all the Colls, and above all, Susan.

NOTES

THE PRECEDING NARRATIVE is based on more than 150 interviews conducted in Saudi Arabia, Yemen, the United States, Great Britain, Switzerland, Germany, Israel, Egypt, Lebanon, and seven other countries. It also draws upon government and private archives in Saudi Arabia, the United States, Britain, Germany, and Israel, including original correspondence and bid documents that describe Mohamed Bin Laden's work in Jerusalem during the 1950s and 1960s. State Department and British Foreign Office correspondence from Jeddah from the 1940s through the late 1960s also proved to be particularly valuable for penetrating some of the myths and generalities that have surrounded Mohamed's life and work, and for describing with greater specificity the world his children grew up in. For more recent periods, in addition to interviews, the narrative relies extensively upon court and regulatory records, primarily from civil lawsuits in the United States and corporate filings there and in Great Britain. I am also indebted in many important ways to previously published work by journalists and historians, as the notes below describe.

Many of the interviews for this book were conducted on the record. Where an interview subject spoke on condition that he or she would not be named the notes provide as much information as possible, consistent with these agreements. For on-the-record interviews, the date and identity of the interviewer are indicated. Robin Shulman's interviews are identified in the notes by (RS). Keach Hagey conducted several interviews for chapter 36, which are identified by (KH). I conducted all other interviews, supplemented by fact-checking re-interviews by Julie Tate.

In response to numerous requests for interviews over a three-year period, Bin Laden family members offered only very limited cooperation, other than those in Yemen; senior family members based in Jeddah granted no extensive or substantive interviews. In explaining their decision, family members and representatives cited their desire for privacy and also their concerns about civil lawsuits filed in the United States by victims of the September 11 attacks. Nonetheless, after the manuscript was substantially drafted, Julie Tate and I attempted to fact-check material about living Bin Ladens with family representatives. Through their lawyers, the family declined to respond to the great majority of written questions submitted, but the family did offer a few helpful responses, as the text and the source notes reflect.

PROLOGUE: "WE ALL WORSHIP THE SAME GOD"

1. Interview with Lynn Peghiny, February 7, 2006. Description of the estate is from the author's visit, as well as interviews with a previous owner, neighbors, and two members of Winter Garden's historical society.

2. The Ibrahims, their influence in Fahd's court, and their Orlando investments: Jeffrey L. Rabin and William C. Rempel, "Saudis Secretly Bought Stake in Marina Leases," *Los Angeles Times*, November 12, 1989. Also, Michael Field, "Financial Times Survey: Saudi Arabia," p. vi, April 22, 1985.

3. Peghiny interview, op. cit. A spokesperson for Shields said she had no recollection of such a project.

4. All quotations from Peghiny interview, op. cit.

5. Quotations from an interview with George Harrington, February 23, 2006. Also, interviews with Thomas Dietrich, April 12, 2006; Peter Blum, May 5, 2006; and Bengt Johansson, October 3, 2006, all of whom were involved in preparations for the Pakistan trip.

6. Harrington interview, op cit.

7. Peghiny interview, op. cit. "Briefcase containing at least $250,000": Harrington interview, ibid.

8. Harrington interview, op. cit.

9. Johansson interview, op. cit.

10. All quotations from Harrington and Johansson interviews, op. cit.

11. "This is it": Harrington interview, op. cit.

12. "For some reason": Ibid. "He used to go": Interview with Mohamed Ashmawi, November 26, 2005 (RS).

13. For the dates and amounts of Saudi contributions to the Contras, see Brinkley and Engelberg (eds.), *Report of the Congressional Committees Investigating the Iran-Contra Affair*, pp. 49–57. Also, Bob Woodward, *Veil*, pp. 352–53 and 401. "I didn't give a damn": Simpson, *The Prince*, pp. 118–19. That McFarlane said the aid would ensure Reagan's reelection: *The Prince*, pp. 113–14. McFarlane later emphasized in testimony before Congress that the Saudis had volunteered these financial contributions, a claim that Bandar disputes.

14. Guest list and Piscopo: Elizabeth Kastor and Donnie Radcliffe, "Fahd's Night: Fanfare Fit for a King," *Washington Post*, February 12, 1985. Also, Ronald Reagan Presidential Library, White House Photo Collection, contact sheets C27237–C27257.

15. Ibid. That Fahd decorated the boy's palace rooms in matched style: From an interview with two former business partners of the Bin Ladens who worked on palace projects.

16. The French intelligence report was published by the Public Broadcasting System's investigative program *Frontline* and is available on its Web site. The report contains a variety of material about the Bin Laden family, only some of which is accurate. "had no idea where Nicaragua was": Interview with Dietrich, op. cit. Attorney who remembered photo of Salem and Reagan: Interviews with Charles Schwartz, May 12, 2005, and September 20, 2006.

17. Remarks by Reagan and Fahd, February 11, 1985, Office of the Press Secretary, Ronald Reagan Presidential Library, Box 189. The intriguing possibility is that Salem passed the

video he made of Osama's charitable work to the Reagan White House, or perhaps to the Saudi embassy in Washington, as part of the preparations for the Fahd summit. No such material has ever surfaced in previous investigations of Bin Laden's time in Afghanistan or the history leading up to the September 11 attacks, but a great many relevant national security files from the Reagan administration remain classified. The strikingly specific language in Reagan's welcoming remarks to Fahd—"Saudi aid to refugees uprooted . . . has not gone unnoticed here, Your Majesty"—is suggestive but inconclusive. CIA officials have asserted repeatedly that no CIA officer ever made direct contact with Osama during the covert Afghan campaign of the 1980s or afterward, and no evidence has yet surfaced to contradict this assertion.

18. "create a problem": Osama's interview with CNN, March 1977, from Lawrence (ed.), *Messages to the World*, p. 55.

1. IN EXILE

1. Author's visit to Gharn Bashireih, March 18, 2007. Forty villages, less than ten thousand people: *Alyom* (Aden), January 23, 2002, from reporting on Rakiyah by the journalist Alawi Abdullah Bin Sumait. His figures are recent; he cites a population in the entire canyon of seventy-eight hundred in 2002. A ceiling of ten thousand is an approximation supported by the absence of any evidence of dense towns and by earlier British population estimates in nearby areas.

2. Interviews with twelve Bin Laden family members, primarily through their spokesman, Syed Bin Laden, in Gharn Bashireih, March 18, 2007. Their account of Awadh's life, his dispute over the borrowed ox, and his migration to Doan is corroborated by research by two Hadrami journalists, Alawi Bin Sumait and Awadh Saleh Kashmimi. The latter conducted separate interviews for the author with Bin Laden family members and representatives in the Hadhramawt. The author is indebted to the governor of the Hadhramawt, Abdelqader Ali Al-Hilal, for his invitation to visit the region and for his introductions to the Bin Laden family still living in Rakiyah.

3. Interview with Syed Bin Laden, op. cit.

4. Interviews with Bin Laden family members in Gharn Bashireih, op. cit. Those who remain in the family village are descendants of the Ahmed branch. According to them, the Mansour branch of the family emigrated years ago to Jizan in the Asir Province of Saudi Arabia. The Zaid branch migrated to other cities in Yemen, including the capital, Sanaa.

5. The death threat is from Kashmimi's interviews, op. cit. The Bin Ladens interviewed by the author in Gharn Bashireih implied that there had been such a threat, but did not say so explicitly.

6. "parallel . . . on the map": Mackintosh-Smith, *Yemen*, pp. 172–73. Swahili and Malay: W. H. Ingrams, *Report on the Social, Economic and Political Condition of the Hadramaut*, p. 12.

7. "a smooth . . . fellow Doanis": Doreen Ingrams, *A Time in Arabia*, p. 13.

8. "Murder cases . . . sternal notch": Ingrams, *Report on the Social*, op. cit., p. 97.

9. Ba Surra cited twenty thousand in a meeting with the Dutch traveler van der Meulen. *A Time in Arabia*, op. cit., pp. 38–39.

10. Kashmimi interviews, op. cit. Interviews with Gharn Bashireih Bin Ladens, op. cit. The

male Bin Laden family line in Rabat appears to have been broken between the boys' emigration for Saudi Arabia and Abdullah's return in the late 1950s or early 1960s. However, their sisters presumably married and retained connections in the town; as is typical of research in Arabia, it was difficult to learn anything about them. It is possible that Awadh's wife lived long enough to be reunited with her sons when they were wealthy enough to return to Doan after the Second World War, but the Bin Ladens in Gharn Bashireh were emphatic that their mother had died in Doan and had not enjoyed a particularly long life.

11. Omar's short life, three sisters: Kashmimi interviews. Mohamed's birth year: Among others, Wright, *The Looming Tower*, p. 118, uses 1908; it may have been two or three years later, if the reported recollections of his younger brother and the townspeople of Rabat are correct. On the other hand, one well-informed person close to the family cited 1904 as Mohamed's birth year and suggested that he arrived in Saudi Arabia several years earlier than is usually described. Any date from Mohamed's life before 1931, when he founded his company, must be taken as an estimate.

12. Kashmimi's interviews, op. cit., suggest Awadh may have made the Hajj before his death, but this seems dubious and likely crept into oral history to honor his memory. That he died young, probably before his boys reached adolescence, is from both the Kashmimi and Gharn Bashireh interviews.

13. Father's letter for a journey to Singapore: Quoted in Talib, "Hadhramis Networking: Salvage of the Homeland." Iasin's "long face": Stark, *The Gates of Arabia*, pp. 126–27.

14. The version in which the storekeeper hurls keys is from interviews with two people close to the family who asked not to be otherwise identified. The version in which the iron bar strikes Mohamed accidentally is from the Gharn Bashireh interviews, op. cit.

15. This account is from the same two people who recounted the anecdote of the storekeeper's keys, Gharn Bashireh interviews.

16. Hossein Kazemzadeh, a Persian writer who made the Hajj pilgrimage in 1910–11, is the source of this population estimate. Peters, *The Hajj*, p. 286.

17. "held a moisture . . . and sweat": *Yemen*, op. cit., p. 202. "Newspapers flop . . . in the pocket": De Gaury, *Arabia Phoenix*, p. 121. "The goods . . . their prey": Peters, op. cit., p. 287. Kazemzadeh also reports the mayor's manure estimate.

18. "hodge-podge . . . earth": Peters, op. cit., p. 288. "You see rich people . . . the bushes": Ibid., p. 275.

19. Ibid., p. 303.

20. Ibid., p. 288.

21. Ibid., p. 106.

22. Covered with bags: Interview with Nadim Bou Fakhreddine, April 26, 2006 (RS). "a small shop": Interview with Hassan Mahowil Mahmoud Al-Aesa, August 10, 2005. "fruit off a donkey": FO 371/170190, T. E. Bromley, Damascus to London, December 9, 1963. That his company was founded in 1931: Saudi Binladin Group advertisement, *Washington Post*, October 14, 2005.

23. Al-Aesa interview, op. cit.

24. "He knew how . . . schooling": Interview with Gerald Auerbach, March 10, 2005. Al-Aesa interview, op. cit.

25. Al-Aesa interview, op. cit. His account of these years is corroborated by the Jeddah

historian Sami Saleh Nawar, director of Naseef House, who has interviewed other former colleagues of Mohamed Bin Laden from this period.

2. THE ROYAL GARAGE

1. More than fifty-two battles: Al-Rasheed, *A History of Saudi Arabia*, pp. 4–5. De Gaury,
in *Arabia Phoenix*, offers a marvelous account of the Bedouin way of battle, pp. 48–52.
Perfume to visitors: Al-Saleh, "Travels to Arabia During the Reign of King Abdulaziz."
"three things . . . and prayer": *Arabia Phoenix*, op. cit., p. 66. "I am not . . . that is all I have":
Department of State 59/7209 Jeddah to Washington, April 29, 1948.

2. "like a father . . . this sentiment": FO 141/1094, January 14, 1946. "Praise be . . . in my
territory": Ibid. "My honor": DOS 59/7212 Dhahran to Washington, June 14, 1946. "You
drink . . . your colleagues": Van der Meulen, *The Wells of Ibn Saud*, p. 15.

3. What Abdulaziz told Philby: Howarth, *The Desert King*, p. 127. "The Saudi state . . . and
enemies": *A History of Saudi Arabia*, op. cit., pp. 9, 80.

4. One American diplomat in Jeddah estimated in a cable dated April 3, 1950, that there
were "not more than 2,000 slaves" in the kingdom and that Abdulaziz owned "some
200." A second American diplomat, on October 2, 1951, quoted a "reliable" estimate of
50,000 slaves in Saudi Arabia. Those numbers would seem to provide a very rough
boundary of the population; the inherent difficulty of such estimates was compounded
by the ambiguous position of many slaves in Saudi households, where some enjoyed considerable status and were indistinguishable from free servants.

5. Quoted in "The House of Saud," Algeria Productions, 2004.

6. "Here we are . . . be modern": "Travels to Arabia," op. cit. Negotiating with Islamic
scholars about radio knobs: *Arabia Phoenix*, op. cit., pp. 96–97. Royal garage of 250 cars in
1927: Holden and Johns, *The House of Saud*, p. 106.

7. Philby's degree and service: "Travels to Arabia," op. cit. "stocky, bearded . . . out of step":
Howarth, *The Desert King*, pp. 100–101. Baboons: Ibid., p. 179.

8. Philby's contract: *A History of Saudi Arabia*, op. cit., p. 92. The SOCAL contract:
Lippman, *Inside the Mirage*, p. 16.

9. Telephone interview with Tim Barger, March 7, 2006. Barger recorded some of his
father's recollections for a private oral history project; he later worked in Jeddah, where
he became acquainted with Salem Bin Laden. American report, 1935: DOS 59 "The Bin
Ladin Construction Empire," Jeddah to Washington, September 25, 1967.

10. Quoted in Abdulrahman Alangari, *"Mataqat Qasr Alhokm:* The Development of the
20th Century."

11. Materials at the surviving portions of the palace, which houses the King Abdulaziz
Foundation, report that construction began in 1934 and ended in 1939. The Saudi historian Madawi Al-Rasheed writes that the palace was started in 1936 "out of the first
cheque paid by the oil company" and was finished in 1937. *A History of Saudi Arabia*, p. 93.

12. "had a vision . . . the royalty": Interview with Mohamed Ashmawi, November 26, 2005
(RS). "many royal orders": "Mohamed bin Awad Binladen: From a Building Laborer to
the Owner of the Biggest Construction Company in the Middle East," *Transport &
Communications* magazine, August 2002. The profile in this magazine, which appears to
draw upon information supplied by the Bin Laden family, lists Atiaqua Palace, Naseriyah

Palace, Mather Palace, the Guest Palace, the Government Palace, Al-Hamra Palace, and the Mansour Buildings as some of Mohamed's projects in Riyadh, although no dates are given. "always available . . . bring one hundred": Interview with Fahd Al-Semmari, director of research at the King Abdulaziz Foundation in Riyadh, February 9, 2005. He is also the source of the saying about entrepreneurial Yemenis.

13. The figures of $38 million and $13 million are from DOS 59/7207 Murray to Acheson, January 27, 1945. This is the oft-quoted memo laying out American strategy in Saudi Arabia for decades to come; the December 22, 1944, memo quoted here, "A strong . . . airfields," is from 59/7211 and probably was an earlier draft by Murray.

14. Bronson, *Thicker Than Oil*, p. 14.

15. DOS 59/7209 Jeddah to Washington, December 27, 1948.

16. Export figures: *The House of Saud*, pp. 125, 151. Al-Khozam description and history: Author's visit, February 20, 2005.

17. Stegner in *Inside the Mirage*, p. 30. "phenomenal building boom . . . materials": DOS 59/7210 Jeddah to Secretary of State, March 26, 1949.

18. Interview with Hassan Mahowil Mahmoud Al-Aesa, August 10, 2005.

19. Bin Mahfouz biography is from www.binmahfouz.info, the family's official Web site, and from the author's visit to Khraiker, March 17, 2007. Naming compact between Bin Laden and Bin Mahfouz is from an interview with a person close to the Bin Laden family. Documents submitted to an American court by the Bin Ladens in a civil lawsuit show that Aysha was born during the Hijra year 1362, which corresponded almost exactly to the Georgian calendar year of 1943. Salem's Hijra birth year is not given. A longtime friend and employee of Salem's, Bengt Johansson, said that Salem's passport read that he was born in 1946, but that Salem said that his true birth year was probably 1944 or 1945.

20. Interview with Al-Aesa, op. cit.

21. Debts of $20 million and $40 million is from a conversation held by an American diplomat with Sayyid Hussain Al-Attas, a Hadhrami banker in Jeddah DOS 59/7211, August 16, 1949. The $250,000 kitchen and $600,000 trip to Paris: 59/7212, July 30, 1949, citing a conversation with a Bechtel Corporation executive. "construction projects . . . enormous family": FO 371/82638 "Annual Review for 1949."

3. SILENT PARTNERS

1. Suleiman's biography: Al-Rasheed, *A History of Saudi Arabia*, p. 88. "frail little man . . . in his soul": Holden and Johns, *The House of Saud*, p. 107. "knew no fatigue . . . money and whisky": van der Meulen, *The Wells of Ibn Saud*, pp. 189–90.

2. "reputed to be a silent partner": Department of State 59, "The Bin Ladin Construction Empire," Jeddah to Washington, September 25, 1967. Suleiman's palace cost $3 million: DOS 59/5467 Jeddah to Washington, April 12, 1953. Bahareth was Suleiman's secretary: DOS 59/5471 Jeddah to Washington, October 4, 1953.

3. "sizeable . . . shipments": DOS 59/7207 Jeddah to Washington, December 29, 1949. "rampant graft . . . so long as the King lived": DOS 59/7211 Jeddah to Washington, September 6, 1946, quoting the British minister in Jeddah.

4. Pilgrim transport business: Long, *The Kingdom of Saudi Arabia*, p. 100. Dammam hotel with theater and bar: DOS 59/5468 Jeddah to Washington, December 18, 1950. "one of

the wealthiest . . . fat government contracts": DOS 59/7214 Jeddah to Washington, August 14, 1946. Stopped the water project: DOS 59/7209 Jeddah to Washington, August 16, 1946. "hitting the bottle . . . increasing rate": DOS 59/7210 Jeddah to Washington, July 12, 1949.

5. King demanding wedding gifts, treasury empty: FO 371/82664 Jeddah to London, January 12, 1950. "not particularly . . . for his arrival": FO 370/82639 Jeddah to London, January 3, 1950.

6. DOS 59/5469 Jeddah to Washington, July 7, 1951. The budget announced that summer provided for 21 million riyals to the Ministry of Health, and about 109 million riyals on "palaces, princes, Riyadh."

7. Digging Faisal's garden: DOS 59/5471 "Memorandum of Conversation," October 25, 1951. "the headaches . . . the advantages": DOS 59/57/D/298/7 "Memorandum of Conversation," June 14, 1950.

8. King to Taif: DOS 59/5469 Jeddah to Washington, July 26, 1951.

9. "always together": Interview with Ahmed Fathalla, April 23, 2006 (RS). Bin Laden's work on Mecca water project: DOS 59/5467 Jeddah to Washington, April 17, 1951, and FO 371/82657 Jeddah to London, "Jeddah Monthly Economic Reports," July and August 1950.

10. Royal Order: Annual Record, KAA Foundation, May 24, 1950. "for grading around the new residence": DOS 59/5472 Cover letter and memorandum from Bechtel International Corp. to DOS, January 17, 1951. Bechtel reported that it had been promised that Bin Laden would soon give the machinery back.

11. "Various members . . . their installation": DOS 59/5467 Jeddah to Washington, February 20, 1951.

12. Translated in DOS 59/6119 Jeddah to Washington, July 7, 1952.

13. Translated in DOS 59/5468, article dated January 3, 1951.

14. Salha's diversion: DOS 59/5471 "Memorandum of Conversation," April 4, 1952. The Bechtel executive, Mr. English, is quoted as saying, "there was not the slightest doubt in his mind" that Salha had stolen the $400,000, the equivalent of about $3 million in 2008 dollars.

15. "to be interested . . . constructional works": FO 371/104859 Jeddah to London, Jeddah Economic Report, November 1952 to January 1953. Bahareth's $100,000: DOS 59/5471 Jeddah to Washington, October 4, 1953.

16. Royal Order 15/12/5607 dated June 22, 1951. KAA Foundation.

17. Philby writes to the king: DOS 59/5472 Jeddah to Washington, January 12, 1950. "a marked reluctance . . . from the shock": FO 371/82657 "Jeddah Monthly Economic Reports," March and April 1950. Export insurance: DOS 59/5472 Jeddah to Washington, May 27, 1950.

18. Tea party: DOS 59/5467 Jeddah to Washington, December 21, 1950, and January 20, 1951.

19. Soil composition: DOS 59/5472 Survey by W. J. Chalkley of Bechtel, February 6, 1951. "end of a long chain of misfortunes": DOS 59/5468 Jeddah to Washington, November 24, 1952.

20. Eight hundred automobiles: DOS 59/5467 Jeddah to Washington, May 6, 1952. "Happily presiding . . . however misguided": DOS 59/5472 Jeddah to Washington, January 7, 1953.

21. Asphalt order: DOS 59/5472 Jeddah to Washington, January 7, 1953. "about half a mil-

lion ... ill humor": FO 371/104859 Jeddah Economic Report, February 1953 to April 1953.
"As this is ... foreign firm": FO 371/104859 Jeddah to London, January 7, 1953.
22. "fright ... do the job": FO 371/104859, Jeddah to London, January 7, 1953. "has been given ... to come from": Ibid., Jeddah Economic Report, August 1953 to October 1953.
23. Shareholder records submitted by the family in a consolidated series of civil cases arising from the events of September 11, 2001, *In Re Terrorist Attacks on September 11, 2001*, 03 MDL 1570, provide the year of birth, using the Islamic calendar, of each of Mohamed's surviving children, except for Osama and also Mohamed's son Ali, neither of whom was a shareholder in the period described by the records. The numbers of sons and daughters born before late 1953 is taken from these filings; the number of wives that produced these children has been calculated from confidential interviews with family members and business associates of the Bin Ladens, who described which brothers, and in some cases, which sisters, were born to the same mother. That the mother of Yeslam, Khalil, Ibrahim, and Fawzia is of Iranian origin is also confirmed by Bin Laden, *Inside the Kingdom*, p. 17. Yeslam's birth date is from Swiss divorce pleadings translated and filed in *Carmen Binladin v. Yeslam and Ibrahim Binladin*, Los Angeles County Superior Court, BC212648.
24. Aphrodisiacs and forcing his sons to stand: *The House of Saud*, p. 159. Holden and Johns provide a thorough account of Ousman's murder, pp. 170–71.
25. The scene and the king's burial: FO 371/104868 Jeddah to London, November 24, 1953.
26. "private and secret ... begin with himself" and the loan request: DOS 59/5469 Jeddah to Washington, November 10, 1953. The scene was recorded by the American chargé d'affaires.

4. THE GLORY OF HIS REIGN

1. $20 million per month: Oil revenue during 1954 was $234.8 million, Holden and Johns, *The House of Saud*, p. 180. "administrative chaos ... shortage of cash": FO 371/104867 Jeddah to London, October 11, 1953.
2. Mohamed and Abdullah, Sons of Awadh Bin Laden: Ger FM 366, WI 416-80.04-427/59 Jeddah to Bonn, September 8, 1959. "amorphous organization ... ambitious plans": FO 371/104867, op. cit.
3. "royal expenditures ... their pockets": DOS 59/4944 Jeddah to Washington, "Economic and Financial Review: Saudi Arabia 1954," April 7, 1955.
4. The electric company and its problems: DOS 59/5472 Jeddah to Washington, June 12, 1954. Burns and Roe, "instrumental in winning": DOS 59/4945 Jeddah to Washington, January 8, 1955.
5. Royal Order: Decree no. 21/1/138/2265, *Umm al-Qura* Annual Record, KAA Foundation. West German estimate of $200 million: Ger FO 146/97-649/55 Jeddah to Bonn, December 23, 1955. Bin Laden's projects circa 1955: FO 371/114885 Jeddah to London, April 6, 1955. Gypsum deposit: DOS 59/4945 Jeddah to Washington, July 5, 1955. Bin Laden's New York agent: Burns and Roe report, attachment, ibid.
6. Flight to Mukalla: DOS translation of article in *Al-Bilad Al-Saudiyah* no. 2110, March 25, 1956, 59/5371. Bought out Abdullah: DOS RG 59 "The Bin Ladin Construction Empire," Jeddah to Washington, September 25, 1967. "Mohamed was more ambitious ... wanted more": Interview with Khalid Ameri, March 17, 2007.

7. Abdullah's return home: Interviews with Rabat town council members and with Khalid Ameri, March 17, 2007. Bin Mahfouz school: Interview with its principal, March 17, 2007. Mohamed's Rakiyah water project: Interviews with Bin Laden family members in their ancestral village of Gharn Bashireih, March 18, 2007.

8. Packard convertibles: Interview with Nadim Fakhreddine, April 26, 2006 (RS). "are known as . . . good reputation": Ger FM 145/560 Jeddah to Bonn, September 19, 1957. "the richest company . . . state orders": 277/200/WI-416-84-04.461/58 Jeddah to Bonn, July 2, 1958.

9. "They are . . . My head could go": Interview with Fakhreddine, op. cit. "He told us . . . our upbringing": *Dateline NBC*, broadcast July 10, 2004. Buraimi dispute: DOS 59/5371 Beirut to Washington, March 1, 1956. The Americans had hoped that Bin Laden would intervene with King Saud to prevent a construction contract from being awarded to a state-owned Polish communist firm, but Fouad Zahed, Bin Laden's chief engineer, said that Bin Laden would not get involved because of "dissatisfaction United States policy re Buraimi dispute and handling of tank shipment," as the cable reporting on the issue put it. In fact, the United States sided decisively with Saudi Arabia against Britain in this border dispute, according to Bronson, *Thicker Than Oil*, p. 62; nor is it clear from the documents reviewed what "tank shipment" Bin Laden was complaining about.

10. FO 371/114872 Jeddah to London, January 6, 1955. De Gaury, *Arabia Phoenix*, pp. 86–92. *House of Saud*, op. cit., pp. 174–83. Saud's children: DOS 59/2643 Jeddah to Washington, December 16, 1964.

11. Aramco visit and quotations: DOS 59/7208 "Crown Prince Saud's Official Visit to America: Notes on the period Monday, January 13, through Wednesday, January 22, 1947."

12. $200 million palace: FO 371/132661, Minute by J. M. Heath, January 7, 1958. "hundreds of colored . . . in orange": Van der Meulen, *The Wells of Ibn Saud*, pp. 234–35.

13. European quacks: *House of Saud*, op. cit., p. 178. Two-thirds nomads, less than one in ten in school: Vassiliev, *The History of Saudi Arabia*, pp. 421, 433, statistics circa 1956 and 1954, respectively.

14. Saud's erratic conduct: FO 371/132661 Minute of December 1, 1958. Coup attempt: Bligh, "Interplay Between . . . "; Mackey, *The Saudis*, p. 297. Conspiracy to kill Nasser: *House of Saud*, op. cit., p. 196.

15. *House of Saud*, pp. 191–94. "Welcome King Saud!": Footage in "The House of Saud," Algeria Productions, 2004. *Thicker Than Oil*, op. cit., pp. 69–75.

16. FO 371 Letter in reply to British engineer inquiring about National Electricity Co., June 6, 1958.

17. Alireza, "The Late King Faisal." De Gaury, op. cit., pp. 86ff. Field, *The Merchants*, p. 40. "an unbelievably patient . . . time to solve": Algosaibi, *Arabian Essays*. "he was anxious . . . go ahead slowly": DOS 59/4945 Jeddah to Washington, March 5, 1959.

18. Interview with Khaled Batarfi, February 19, 2005. Batarfi's uncle worked with Bin Laden in Mecca, and he is quoting what his uncle recalled.

19. Interview with Fakhreddine, op. cit. Bin Laden's strategy of marrying the daughters of desert leaders and town mayors was described in interviews by several people who worked with him at the time.

20. *Surah* 2, verse 231.

21. Interviews with several people close to the Bin Laden family. The Al-Ghanem fam-

ily provided an account of the marriage, and were described as poor and relatively secular in the Kuwaiti newspaper *Al-Qabas*, November 14, 2001. For other, similar accounts, see also Randal, *Osama*, p. 55; Scheuer, *Through Our Enemies' Eyes*, pp. 80–81; and Wright, *The Looming Tower*, p. 72.

22. *In Re Terrorist Attacks on September 11, 2001*, 03 MDL 1570. Interviews with people close to the family, including Carmen Bin Laden, August 6, 2004, establish that four different wives gave birth to the children listed in the court records as born in 1377. Wright, *The Looming Tower*, cites Osama's 1991 statement to the newspaper *Al-Umma Al-Islamiyya* that he was born in the month of Ragab. Shafiq's birth date is from the 2000 annual report of Symphony Advisers Ltd., Companies House records, London.

23. According to the court records, the four sons born during 1377, besides Osama, were Ibrahim, Shafiq, Khalil, and Haider. The two daughters were Mariam and Fowziyah. However, deposition testimony by Ibrahim and Khalil in other civil lawsuits in the United States confirms that they shared the same mother, so while it is conceivable they were both born during 1377, it is also possible that the court records submitted by the Bin Ladens are inaccurate in at least this respect.

24. $500 million in debt: *House of Saud*, op. cit., p. 199. No pilgrim receipts: DOS 59/4944 Jeddah to Washington, December 4, 1958. Structure of debt, Faisal's thinking: DOS 59/4946 Dhahran to Washington, February 4, 1959.

25. Telephone interview with Mike Ameen, March 1, 2006. Ameen worked in Aramco's political office during this period and knew Mohamed Bin Laden.

26. DOS 59/4945 Dhahran to Washington, May 27, 1959, and "Memorandum of Conversation with Sam Logan," June 23, 1959. All quotations are from the Memorandum of Conversation.

27. The negotiations are described in a series of State Department cables from Jeddah to Washington between June 1958 and November 1958. When American commercial officers checked on the Roma brothers' claims in Italy, they were told that Finmeccanica, the construction company with whom the brothers claimed affiliation, regarded them as "financially and commercially unreliable."

28. "Aramco . . . workers": DOS 59 Jeddah to Washington, October 2, 1958.

29. "good for the country . . . good old days": DOS 59/4944 "Economic Summary, Third Quarter of 1959," Jeddah to Washington, December 15, 1959.

5. FOR JERUSALEM

1. Peters, *The Hajj*, pp. 3–40. Aslan, *No God but God*, pp. 3–18. Caudill, "Twilight of the Hejaz" manuscript, pp. 21–23.

2. *The Hajj*, pp. 40–55. "pictures of trees . . . angels": Ibid., p. 48.

3. "he asked for a cloth": Ibid.

4. "dogs of the Hejaz": Caudill manuscript, op. cit., p. 24. "You must imagine . . . loud voice": The observation is from a man whom Peters describes as a possible Jewish spy of Napoleon disguised as a traveling pilgrim, who went by the name Ali Bey Al-Abbasi. *The Hajj*, op. cit., p. 198.

5. *The Hajj*, p. 359, quoting Eldon Rutter, an English convert to Islam, who visited Medina in 1925.

6. Abbas, *Story of the Great Expansion*, pp. 100–101, 260–61.

7. The official history, ibid., cites a figure of 30 million riyals for construction and 40 million riyals for eminent domain payments. DOS 59/5467 Jeddah to Washington, April 12, 1953, cites a figure of $1.35 million for construction costs in Medina in 1952 alone. Other diplomatic estimates, citing government budget documents and other sources, are similar in scale through 1955.

8. "modern architectural style" and renovation statistics: *Story of the Great Expansion*, op. cit., p. 278. "an impressive . . . piece of work": DOS 59/2810 Jeddah to Washington, June 24, 1961.

9. *Umm al-Qura*, October 28, 1955, KAA Foundation.

10. Ibid.

11. "enjoyment of movies . . . point of view": DOS 59/4946 Jeddah to Washington, March 29, 1958. "evil . . . corruption and destruction": Published in *Al-Yamamah*, March 30, 1958.

12. Fifty thousand to four hundred thousand and $130 million: DOS 59/4947 Jeddah to Washington, July 24, 1956, translation of King Saud's Mecca welcome address. "Even this sum": Ger FM File 145, Jeddah to Bonn, October 2, 1956.

13. Medina demolition and debris removal: *Story of the Great Expansion*, op. cit., pp. 276–77. Osama's account: Bergen, *The Osama Bin Laden I Know*, p. 2, quoting his interview with Al-Jazeera in 1999. Bin Laden's description of his father's bidding for the Jerusalem project, in particular, is somewhat detailed and entirely accurate, documents from the renovation project show. Mecca demolition statistics: *Story of the Great Expansion*, p. 264.

14. Peters, *Jerusalem*, pp. 1–406, is rich with the accounts of travelers and participants in the city's history.

15. Hussein's initiative and the date of Nasser's announcement are from a 1981 Egyptian report reviewing the history of renovations in the site, one in a collection of documents supplied by the *waqf* authorities about the 1950s and 1960s renovation project. The author is indebted throughout this section to the exceptional research in Jerusalem carried out by Robin Shulman, who collected the documents and conducted related interviews. The documents were translated in Washington by Mohamed Elmenshawy; they will be referred to in notes hereafter as "Jer Docs."

16. "First, this is a sacred . . . Muslim community": Jer Docs, MBL to Committee, July 8, 1958, written on stationery captioned "Office of Mohamed Awad Bin Laden, 51-S." To get below the Egyptian bid, Bin Laden cut his proposal by 8,000 dinars in the very last round. The Supreme Judge said in his decision that in addition to price, the committee had been influenced by Bin Laden's willingness to work without certain conditions named by the Egyptian bidder.

17. Jer Docs Letter MH-8-32-169, July 19, 1958.

18. Jer Docs Letter 1390, March 8, 1959.

19. "We learned . . . a bit of Arabic," import details, and tipping: Interviews with Nadir Shtaye, October 31, 2005, and November 6, 2005 (RS). Other Palestinian Muslims who were in Jerusalem at the time confirm the presence of Christian workers on the job site. Late-1950s photograph: *Story of the Great Expansion*, op. cit. The book dates the photo to 1959 but the caption suggests it might have been taken in 1964. Photos from American pilot: Provided by Terri Daley, the pilot's daughter. The aluminum cupola and joists Bin Laden installed on the Dome of the Rock would prove leaky and unreliable, and they

were removed years later, but engineers and architects who later oversaw the mosque said the blame for this lay with the project's oversight committee, which had been dazzled at the time of the original bidding by the promise of "modern" aluminum, about which they knew too little. A UNESCO report written in 1979 by European experts documents the problems in detail.

20. English translation: "Address on the Occasion of the Unveiling of the Restored Dome of the Rock," April 18, 1994, which includes excerpts from the earlier 1964 speech. Accessed at www.kinghussein.gov.jo/94_april18.html.

21. Text reprinted in *Palestine*, August 8, 1964, p. 5.

22. All quotations: Ibid.

23. This account of the house is primarily from an interview with its owner and a tour of the home (RS). Other residents of the area who knew of Bin Laden at this time confirmed that he stayed at the house when he was in town. Two acquaintances said he took a Palestinian wife; one thought the wife was from Gaza, another thought she was from Jenin. These specific accounts could not be confirmed, but they accord with the recollections of other family acquaintances and business partners that Bin Laden had at least one Palestinian wife. Interviews conducted for the author by Israeli journalist Samuel Sockol confirm that Bin Laden owned the house and was not merely a tenant. Sockol interviewed Yehuda Semberg, a retired Israeli naval officer who lived in the house for twenty-five years, and also Aharon Shakarji, a former official of Israel's land authority.

6. THE BACKLASH

1. "This show is splendid . . . the Turks": Mack, *A Prince of Our Disorder*, p. 151.

2. "only medium . . . will prevail": DOS 59/7214, text of telegram, October 3, 1946. "much emotional appeal": DOS 59/3100 Jeddah to Washington, September 28, 1960.

3. "Bin Laden's for the asking": Ibid., Jeddah to Washington, April 5, 1961.

4. "to show off . . . other projects": Ibid., Jeddah to Washington, November 25, 1961. "extremely good connection . . . construction work": Ibid., Jeddah to Washington, November 28, 1961. "opening the locked stable . . . appropriate pockets": Ibid., Jeddah to Washington, October 20, 1960. "We have . . . strictly commercial": FO 371/170324 FO minute, February 20, 1963. "King Saud . . . Bin Laden": Ibid., Memorandum of telephone call, February 8, 1963.

5. "I spent . . . Bin Laden": Ibid., Damascus to London, February 20, 1963.

6. "that Bin Laden . . . an enemy of him": Ibid. "that Saudi support . . . a share in it": FO 371/170190 Board of Trade to Jeddah, December 2, 1963.

7. "under severe reproaches": Ger FO 350/217/63 Jeddah to Bonn, April 3, 1963.

8. "We read . . . asphalting operations": *Al-Nadwa*, November 15, 1961, translated in DOS 59/3100 Jeddah to Washington, November 25, 1961.

9. All quotations: Ibid.

10. "One Roadblock": DOS 59/3567 Jeddah to Washington, May 9, 1963. "problem was . . . done quickly": Ibid., Jeddah to Washington, June 11, 1963.

11. "duty not to delay . . . shirked": DOS 59/2810 Jeddah to Washington, August 1, 1962.

12. "dumping bids": Ger FO 277/564-2912/56 Jeddah to Bonn, July 28, 1956.

13. *Saudi Weekly*, July 24, 1961, describes the Swiss TV crew visit and provides photographs of the construction site near Taif. The clipping is enclosed in DOS 59/2810 Jeddah to Washington, August 14, 1961.

14. That Faisal and Bin Laden argued: Interview with Khaled Batarfi, February 19, 2005. "the point was ... doing it": Interview with Hermann Eilts, March 29, 2006.

15. CIA report: Bronson, *Thicker Than Oil*, p. 83. That Mohamed Bin Laden had slaves, freed them, and was compensated: Interview with Carmen Bin Laden, August 6, 2004. Rally and "We are your brothers!": DOS 59/4033-4 Jeddah to Washington, April 25, 1963.

16. "He is evil ... closest friend": Ibid., Jeddah to Washington, February 18, 1963. Faisal asked the American delegation pointedly, "What are you, our friends, going to do about this? ... We adhered to your advice and fulfilled our promise to 'fold our arms' ... How long do you think we can go on like this ... How long can I face my people with his kind of placidity and inactivity?"

17. "personally take care ... royal intervention": DOS 59/3567 Dhahran to Washington, September 10, 1963.

18. Ibid.

7. A MODERN MAN

1. Forklift: DOS 59/2810 Dhahran to Washington, December 5, 1962. Aramco paid $3.5 million: Holden and Johns, *The House of Saud*, p. 218.

2. Saud's wealth in exile: DOS RG 59/2472 Jeddah to Washington, May 7, 1967.

3. "is not the case ... whoever was king": Interview with Turki Al-Faisal, August 2, 2002. "involved a surprisingly small ... where necessary": DOS 59/2642, "The Power Structure in Saudi Arabia," Jeddah to Washington, March 23, 1965.

4. Al-Rasheed, *A History of Saudi Arabia*, pp. 121–22. *House of Saud*, op. cit., pp. 257–58.

5. "formally inaugurated ... considerable fanfare": DOS 59/2642 Jeddah to Washington, August 31, 1965.

6. Interviews with several friends, employees, and business partners of the Bin Ladens in Lebanon and Egypt, including an interview with Nadim Bou Fakhreddine, former head of Upper Metn Secondary School, April 26, 2006 (RS).

7. From Yeslam's interview to the *Evening Standard* of London, May 26, 2006.

8. "wanted someone ... spoiled": Interview with Fakhreddine, op. cit.

9. "Most of us were afraid ... somebody up, maybe": *Evening Standard*, op. cit.

10. From Abdullah's interview published in Bahrain's newspaper *Alayam*, December 21, 2001.

11. Ali's appearance and role: From several interviews with friends and employees of the family, including an interview with an employee who met Ali in Taif with Mohamed on several occasions during this period.

12. There is some uncertainty about whether Salem attended Millfield before or after he attended Copford Glebe. Several former Copford classmates said in interviews that he attended Millfield earlier, and briefly, but one former business partner thought it was possible that he had attended Millfield later. It is clear, however, that Salem was at Copford for a prolonged period during the early to mid-1960s.

13. "amazing sort of pastiche ... people there": Interview with Rupert Armitage,

September 19, 2006. The portrait of Salem's life at Copford in this section is from Armitage and interviews with two other classmates who asked not to be identified.

8. CROSSWIND

1. Interviews with Gerald Auerbach, March 10, 2005, and April 7, 2005. Other pilots who knew Bin Laden provide similar accounts.
2. "It was completely boring": *Times-Picayune*, October 13, 2001. Flight logs and photographs from the period 1965 through 1967 reviewed by the author document Bin Laden's international travel during this period, primarily to Jerusalem, Beirut, and the United Arab Emirates.
3. "He was the law . . . judgment": Ibid.
4. Kilo 170 is from interviews with Auerbach, op. cit., who flew there regularly.
5. Bin Laden's work on the Trucial coast road from Sharjah to Ras al-Khayma is documented in British and American diplomatic cables during 1966 and 1967. The figure of $6.7 million is from DOS 59/761 Jeddah to Washington, September 19, 1966.
6. Interviews with Auerbach, op. cit. The figure of $120 million and the report that he agreed not to take on additional highway work are from DOS 59/761 Jeddah to Washington, May 24, 1966. The cable calls Bin Laden "The Old Master of Saudi highway construction."
7. The $100 million Military Construction Project: DOS RG 59/2643 Jeddah to Washington, June 2, 1965. British military sales, missile and radar deployments: "At a glance—Saudi Arabia/November 1967," a report then classified secret, in Burdett, *Records of Saudi Arabia, 1966–1971, Volume 2: 1967, Part I.*
8. Sequence of attacks and "terrorist infiltrators and saboteurs": British report of January 12, 1967, in Burdett, op. cit.
9. Hawker Siddeley purchase: Interviews with Auerbach, op. cit. History of Kilo 7 complex: Bin Laden, *Inside the Kingdom*, p. 36.
10. Heacock: Interview with a daughter of the pilot. "I took him out . . . riverbeds": Interviews with Auerbach, op. cit.
11. All quotations in this section are from interviews with Auerbach, op. cit. The author failed to locate any of Harrington's surviving family. Auerbach flew to the crash site with a team of pilots and other personnel on September 4, 1967, the day after the accident occurred. Mike Ameen, then working in Aramco's political department, said he had heard that Bin Laden intended to remarry in Asir at the time of his death. Identified from his watch: Interview with Nadim Bou Fakhreddine, April 26, 2006 (RS).

9. THE GUARDIANS

1. Interview with Nadim Bou Fakhreddine, April 26, 2006 (RS). For a thorough account of Hejazi funeral and mourning rituals, see Yamani, *Cradle of Islam*, pp. 102–10.
2. Interview with Rupert Armitage, September 19, 2006, as well as a second friend who visited Salem at the flat. Armitage recalled that Salem thought nothing about sitting around naked with his male friends and that he had the memorable habit of displaying his erect penis, which he had nicknamed "Lucky."

3. Salem's transformational flight: Interview with Gerald Auerbach, April 7, 2005. That Salem did not know all of his half-siblings and that he met some brothers and sisters for the first time: Interviews with Mohamed Ashmawi, November 26, 2005 (RS), and Robert Freeman, April 27, 2006.

4. DOS 59 Jeddah to Washington, September 7, 1967.

5. Ibid.

6. Ibid.

7. Koranic principle about male and female heirs: *Surah* 4, verse 11. Islamic inheritance law: Interview with a Saudi lawyer who has worked for the Bin Laden family. See also Almidhar, "International Succession Laws."

8. Interview with Adel Toraifi, February 9, 2005.

9. That the boys received 2.27 percent: Declaration of Barbara L. Irshay, January 21, 1993, *Christine Hartunian v. Ibrahim Binladin*, Los Angeles County Superior Court, BD058156. The five heirs other than the children is from shareholder lists submitted by the family in *In Re Terrorist Attacks on September 11, 2001*, 03 MDL 1570. The 9/11 Commission dates Osama Bin Laden's first cash dividend to 1973, six years after Mohamed's death. This would have been a time when more of the boys were reaching adulthood and oil revenue in the kingdom began to boom because of the Arab embargo. Salem was then running his own company and was gaining influence at his father's firm. It is clear that a regular system of annual dividends to all Mohamed's children evolved at some point during this period; the 9/11 Commission's date is drawn from submissions made to the U.S. Treasury Department by family representatives prior to the September 11 attacks.

10. Interview with Michael Pochna, August 31, 2006. Interview with Gerald Auerbach, March 10, 2005.

11. "I am going to be your father now": from Yeslam Bin Laden, quoted by *The Australian*, December 17, 2001.

12. Royal Ordinance: DOS RG 59 Jeddah to Washington, September 25, 1967. "was mostly in equipment . . . started taking over": Interview with Turki Al-Faisal, August 2, 2002.

13. "legal situation": DOS RG 59 Jeddah to Washington, September 22, 1967. "in an entirely personal . . . company going": Ibid., Jeddah to Washington, September 25, 1967.

14. Interview with Bassim Alim, February 21, 2005. Alim is Mohamed Bahareth's grandson. Bahareth died in 2004.

15. "He wanted . . . get control": Interview with Francis Hunnewell, August 9, 2006.

16. Interviews with several friends and employees of Salem who asked not to be identified.

17. The plane on display: Interview with Peter Blum, who later served as Salem's personal assistant, March 5, 2006. Salem's travel to Dubai is from flight logs examined by the author.

18. Interview with Auerbach, op. cit.

19. That Ali wrote a letter to King Faisal: Interview with a person close to the Bin Laden family, who asked not to be identified. Also, on the struggle with Ali: Interviews with Carmen Bin Laden, August 6, 2004, and Fakhreddine, op. cit.

20. Sheikha's appearance, languages: Interview with Auerbach, op. cit. The date of their marriage is uncertain, but it occurred before May 1973.

21. DOS 59/553 Jeddah to Washington, August 30, 1969; September 3, 1969; September 10, 1969; November 5, 1970; March 19, 1971; March 27, 1972; April 7, 1972.

22. Saudi loan, deal terms, Ali to U.S.: Ibid., November 5, 1970.

23. "difficult ownership ... foreign ownership": Ibid., March 27, 1972. "uneasiness ... Ben Ladin organization": Ibid., November 5, 1970. The correspondence also quotes Anwar Ali as emphasizing the Saudi government's need to complete defense and infrastructure projects in Asir on which the Bin Laden company had been at work.

24. Interview with Hermann Eilts, March 29, 2006.

25. The advertisement for "Tarik Mohammed Bin Ladin Organization For General Civil Contracting and Crushing" appeared in a *Financial Times* survey of Saudi Arabia published December 28, 1970. It was filed in FCO 8/1742. A number of employees and business partners date the founding of Binladen Brothers to the early 1970s; an entry in the Graham & Whiteside Ltd. Business database dates the founding to 1972.

26. "What surprised me ... each other": Interview with Carmen Bin Laden, op. cit.

27. Interviews with Hunnewell, Pochna, and Armitage, op. cit., as well as other Bin Laden employees who asked not to be identified.

28. "liked what we called ... Mick Jagger": Interview with Joe Ashkar, April 22, 2006 (RS).

29. "They wore ... anything for anybody": Telephone interview with Shirley Cottam Bowman, April 18, 2006 (RS).

30. Ibid.

31. Bergen, *The Osama Bin Laden I Know*, p. 12.

32. "They were so elegantly . . . cellophane": Quoted in the *Melbourne Herald Sun*, September 25, 2001.

10. YOUNG OSAMA

1. "would lie at her feet ... about something": Interview with Khaled Batarfi, February 19, 2005.

2. "a shy kid ... neighbors and teachers": Transcript of interview supplied by Khaled Batarfi to the author. Excerpts from this interview appeared in several publications under Batarfi's byline. That his Syrian relatives recalled his shyness: Interviews published in the Kuwaiti newspaper *Al-Qabas*, November 14, 2001. Also, "Bin Laden, World's Most Wanted Man, Was a Quiet, Shy Child," Agence France-Presse, November 15, 2001.

3. "If there was no agricultural reform ... anything": In *Al-Qabas*, op. cit. "I used to love it ... live there": Ibid.

4. "He considered him ... gives orders": Bergen, *The Osama Bin Laden I Know*, p. 17.

5. Batarfi interview text, op. cit.

6. "He was quiet ... worked hard": Interview with Emile Sawaya, April 22, 2006 (RS).

7. All quotations: Ibid.

8. "He used to ... karate movies": Interview with David Ensor, CNN, broadcast March 19, 2002.

9. "affected ... very solitary": Agence France-Presse, op. cit. "She was all ... to his father": Interview with Batarfi, op. cit.

10. The author visited Al-Thaghr twice, including once in the company of Osama's schoolmate, who described in detail the school's layout during the late 1960s and early

1970s. The schoolmate's descriptions of the school were corroborated by the accounts of Fyfield-Shayler and Seamus O'Brien, two teachers there during this period.

11. Saudi funding: DOS 59/906 Jeddah to Washington, November 17, 1966, reports on the Saudi national budget and cites a line item of 2.9 million riyals for "subsidy" to Al-Thaghr. Mohamed's appearance at the school for fundraisers: Interview with Brian Fyfield-Shayler, February 23, 2007 (RS).

12. Kamal Adham's discussions about the school with British authorities are described in DOS 59/2813 Jeddah to Washington, November 7, 1962. The school uniform is from photographs and the memories of several former students.

13. These details and many that follow are drawn from a series of interviews with the schoolmate of Osama, who joined his after-school Islamic study group, and who asked not to be identified. The author conducted many discussions and interviews with the schoolmate over the course of two years, and is very grateful for his contributions. The authenticity of the schoolmate's recollections, in the author's judgment, is beyond reasonable doubt.

14. "I was trying . . . making mistakes": Fyfield-Shayler quoted in *Meeting Osama Bin Laden*, WGBH, 2004. "extraordinarily courteous . . . other students": *The Osama Bin Laden I Know*, pp. 8–9. "a nice fellow . . . run deep": Interview with Seamus O'Brien, November 28, 2005. "in the middle": From an interview with Ahmed Badeeb by Orbit Television in early 2002; a tape of the interview was provided by Badeeb to the author, who had it translated by a private firm, The Language Doctors, in Washington, D.C. From his unlikely beginnings as a biology teacher at Al-Thaghr, Badeeb became chief of staff to the director of Saudi intelligence, Turki Al-Faisal, a position that brought him into regular contact with Osama during the war in Afghanistan.

15. The Brotherhood's influence in Saudi Arabia: Interviews with several Saudi analysts who asked not to be identified, and Saudi government consultant Khalil A. Khalil, February 10, 2005. Faisal's skepticism: DOS 59/4944 Jeddah to Washington, May 5, 1959, reports on a meeting of the Muslim Brotherhood in Mecca and notes, "King Saud looks with favor upon the Brotherhood, but Crown Prince Faisal does not." A dispatch the following day on the same subject reported that Saud "possibly contributes to its coffers" and that "Members of the Brotherhood are permitted to travel freely in and out of Saudi Arabia."

16. See note 13. All quotations here and following are from the same schoolmate.

17. "joined the religious committee": Badeeb, Orbit, 2002, op. cit. "He was a prominent member . . . this philosophy": Interview with Batarfi, op. cit. "started as a Muslim Brother": Interview with Jamal Khashoggi, February 2, 2002.

18. "is a membership . . . the movement": Interview with Khashoggi, op. cit. Classes of membership and preference for adults: A research report on Brotherhood recruiting provided to the author by an American government contractor who asked not to be identified.

19. "a more . . . agenda": Interview with Batarfi, op. cit. "misused . . . underhandedly": Quoted in "The House of Saud," *Frontline*, 2005.

20. FCO 8/2122 June 30, 1973, Departmental Series, Middle East Department.

21. Interview with Batarfi, op. cit.; author's visit to the house, in Batarfi's company.

22. All quotations from interview with Batarfi, op. cit.

23. Ibid.

24. Ibid. Also, Batarfi as quoted in *Sunday Mirror*, April 21, 2002. Details about *Fury* and its characters from www.brokenwheelranch.com, examined and typed, March 2, 2007.

25. "visit his Mohamed Bin Laden brothers": Interview with Batarfi, op. cit. "several": Interview with Fyfield-Shayler, op. cit.

26. The trip to Afghanistan is from flight logs and an interview with pilot Gerald Auerbach, April 7, 2005.

II. REALM OF CONSPIRACY

1. "impudent gang" and "desecration": DOS 59/2472 Jeddah to Washington, February 24, 1969. The cable reports: "Faisal said 'Jerusalem cries out for salvation' . . . He called for jihad to liberate holy places." That Osama identified with his campaign: Interview with Khaled Batarfi, February 19, 2005. Bin Laden's mother also reported that Osama frequently spoke about the Palestinian cause as a young man.

2. Faisal's routine: Algosaibi, "Arabian Essays"; Alireza, "The Late King Faisal . . ."; Sheean, *Faisal*; Gros, *Feisal of Arabia*; Holden and Johns, *The House of Saud*, pp. 202–3.

3. Iffat's biography, travels, shopping: DOS 59/2643 Dhahran to Washington, August 17, 1966, "Biographic Information on Wife of King Faysal." Also *House of Saud*, op. cit., p. 203.

4. "the basic causes . . . political expression": DOS 59/2472 Research Memorandum, Director of Intelligence and Research, August 21, 1969.

5. Lippman, *Inside the Mirage*, p. 221.

6. FCO 8/2109 Memo prepared in 1973 for a visit to Saudi Arabia by the governor of the Bank of England.

7. "even put forward . . . Palestinian terrorists": Quoted in *House of Saud*, op. cit., p. 359. "dual conspiracy": *Inside the Mirage*, op. cit., p. 221.

8. Gross domestic product: *House of Saud*, op. cit., p. 390. $102 billion: *Inside the Mirage*, op. cit., p. 160. Safeway: Carmen Bin Laden, *Inside the Kingdom*, pp. 94–95. "I've never seen so many cranes": "The House of Saud," Algeria Productions, 2004. "you'd go away . . . a little bit crazy": Quoted ibid.

9. Quoted in Bradley, *Saudi Arabia Exposed*, p. 215.

10. Musaid: Interviews with two of his former Berkeley professors. LSD conviction: *House of Saud*, op. cit., p. 379.

11. DOS 59/2584 Jeddah to Washington, September 26, 1973, "Prince Fahd, the King, and the Inner Circle"; Jeddah to Washington, April 18, 1973. Miss Arabia: Jeddah to Washington, November 5, 1970.

12. Interview with a former senior diplomat in Riyadh who spoke on condition that he would not be to be identified. Fahd had "a great sense of humor, loved jokes," he said, "and he was a very self-indulgent and ill-disciplined man who never kept to the point. He had a bad habit of rambling on and on and on in meetings."

13. DOS 59/2585 Jeddah to Washington, August 29, 1972, "Discussion with Prince Fahd."

14. DOS 59/2472 Jeddah to Washington, June 12, 1968, "Biographical Sketch of Crown Prince Khalid."

12. THE RISING SON

1. "I just farted . . . a kid": Interview with Mohamed Ashmawi, November 26, 2005 (RS).

2. Interview with a friend and former employee of Salem who spoke on the condition that he would not be identified.

3. All quotations are from Heckmann, *Hai fressen kein Deutschen*, translated for the author by Petra Krischok.

4. Ibid.

5. Ibid.

6. This account of Fahd's winter camps is drawn primarily from three former employees of Salem's who attended or worked in the camps. Two of these people spoke on the condition that they not be identified. The third was Bengt Johansson, interviewed on October 3, 2006.

7. The anecdote about what Salem told Fahd and all of the quotations are from a recorded interview with the person cited in note 2.

8. The date of the MU-2 purchase is from interviews with Johansson, op. cit., and Gerald Auerbach, April 7, 2005. "You are crazy . . . these days": Interview with Jack Hinson, May 10, 2005.

9. "The question was . . . do the job": Interview with Rupert Armitage, September 19, 2006.

10. "We've gotten paid": Interview with Johansson, op. cit.

11. Ibid.

12. The description of the money runs is from flight records and interviews with Auerbach, op. cit.; David Grey, February 21, 2006; and two other former employees of the aviation department who spoke on the condition that they would not be identified.

13. Interview with Ashmawi, op. cit.

14. Interview with Terry Bennett, December 2005 (RS).

15. "Don't worry . . . immediate bond": Interview with Gail Freeman, April 27, 2006. Less than comfortable circumstances: Interview with Auerbach, op. cit. Three-story town house: Interview with Sabry Ghoneim, November 14, 2005 (RS). Their relationship: Interviews with multiple friends and employees of Salem, including Johansson, who said: "It wasn't sexual, but emotional, maybe. She had a very big influence on him, and she was giving him a lot of headache, too." Peter Blum, who later served as Salem's personal assistant, added in an interview, "She was one of the most important persons to Salem . . . like the father and daughter."

16. "He pushed Randa": Interview with Ghoneim, op. cit.

17. Skeletons from Saudi Arabia: Interview with Ashmawi, op. cit.

18. Interviews with pilots Hinson, op. cit., and Grey, op. cit. "He was very protective of his sisters," Gail Freeman said in an interview, op. cit.

19. Interview with Ghoneim, op. cit.

20. Interviews with Auerbach, Hinson, and Grey, op. cit.

21. "pulling back . . . any time now": Interview with Wayne Fagan, May 10, 2005.

22. "When I saw . . . brother is a member": Interview with Anwar Khan, May 6, 2006 (RS). Caroline was the passenger, promised to convert to Islam: Interview with a person close to the family who asked not to be identified.

23. "People were forever . . . I'll sign it!": Interview with Armitage, op. cit.

24. "the sensation . . . on the edge": Interview with Don Sowell, June 2, 2005. "perfect approach": Interview with Khan, op. cit.

25. "That would be the end": Interview with Robert Freeman, April 27, 2006.

26. Piper, Medina accidents: Interviews with Bin Laden pilots. "I was telling God . . . one little engine": Interview with Johansson, op. cit.

27. Plane inventory: Interviews with several pilots who worked at Bin Laden Aviation or for Bin Mahfouz. "Salem believed": Interview with a Lebanese friend who spoke on condition that he would not be identified.

28. Interview with Johansson, op. cit.

29. "loose ends . . . a family, together": Interview with Armitage, op. cit.

30. "very subservient . . . the king": Interview with Hinson, op. cit. "No one did . . . time and time again": Interview with Grey, op. cit. That Salem alone controlled salaries, allowances, and assignments is confirmed by another employee who asked not to be identified.

31. Aramco report: Telephone interview with Mike Ameen, who has retained a copy of the report, March 1, 2006. "He was perfect": Interview with Francis Hunnewell, August 9, 2006.

32. Dates and places of Sara and Salman's births: "Application For Appointment of Administrator," from Ian Munro, April 4, 1991, probate filings of Salem Bin Laden, Bexar County, Texas, 91-PC-1012.

33. Munro's biography: Interview with a former Bin Laden business partner, and interview with Charles Schwartz, May 12, 2005. London companies, dates of formation, address: Filings with Companies House, London.

34. That Salem did not see Offley Chase before he bought it: Interview with the former business partner, op. cit. The estate and village: Author's visit, interviews with numerous other visitors.

13. DISCOVERING AMERICA

1. Interview with Don Sowell, June 2, 2005. Author's visit to Panama City, Sowell Aviation, Bay Point.

2. Ibid. Salem's time in Panama City was also described by several other partners and pilots who visited him and Randa during this period, but the detailed account here is primarily from Sowell.

3. Ibid.

4. Ibid. Jack Pizza declined to be interviewed. Anita Pizza spoke affectionately about Randa Bin Laden and other family members during several brief telephone conversations but ultimately declined to be interviewed.

5. "not too bubbly, not too flat": Interviews with two former employees of Salem and Khalid Bin Mahfouz who asked not to be further identified. "sent myself . . . flew it back": Sowell interview, ibid.

6. Academy Awards party: Interview with Jack Hinson, May 10, 2005, and interview with Dave Whitney, February 20, 2006. Oktoberfest: Interview with Thomas Dietrich, April 12, 2006. Wedding of Sadat's daughter: Interview with Rupert Armitage, September 19, 2006.

7. Armored Cadillacs: Interview with Robert and Gail Freeman, April 27, 2006. Lincolns, Tabasco sauce, Mello Yello, airplane toys: Interview with Sowell, op. cit. Cacti and other plants: *Binladen BSB Landscaping v. M.V. Nedlloyd*, 82 Civ. 1037. The case produced a significant federal court decision involving liability for shipping damages; until 1998, this was the most notable involvement of the Bin Laden family in the U.S. federal legal system.

8. All quotations: Interview with Sowell, op. cit. Fifty thousand dollars: Interview with Freeman, op. cit.

9. Bath's background and appearance: Interviews with seven former business acquaintances or partners. Civil litigation files also provide a rich portrait of his life during these years, particularly *Sandra C. Bath v. James R. Bath*, Harris County Court, 85-046927, its successor, 89-07180, and the several lawsuits between Bath and White, lodged in Harris County, Texas, and in Houston's federal court. "a lot of fun": Quoted in the *Wall Street Journal*, September 28, 1999, citing a 1990 interview with the *Houston Post*. The best published accounts of this period in Texas business and politics are Unger, *House of Bush, House of Saud*; Phillips, *American Dynasty*, and Beaty and Gwynne, *The Outlaw Bank*.

10. Fokker sale: Interview with Gerald Auerbach, April 7, 2005. "He talked": Interview with Armitage, op. cit. "loved . . . that kind of stuff": Interview with Charles Schwartz, May 12, 2005. Bath declined several requests for an interview.

11. MBO Investments, trust agreement: Web site of the Texas secretary of state, examined and typed, September 9, 2005. Revolving line of credit: Transcript of White's interview with Canadian Broadcasting Corporation program *The Fifth Estate*. White confirmed for the author the accuracy of the transcript and its assertions. White claims to have a large archive of confidential documents about Bath's business activities, including deposition testimony that Bath provided in their civil case, but he declined to make these documents available. Some excerpts of Bath's deposition testimony are in public court files, however.

12. White transcript, op. cit. Skyway's history is described in documents and affidavits filed by White and Bath in several lawsuits, but these documents do not make fully clear which Saudis owned the company. White has suggested that Salem Bin Laden may have an interest in Skyway. The *Wall Street Journal*, September 28, 1999, reported that Khalid Bin Mahfouz owned Skyway. Its assertion relied partially on a confidential court document originally cited by the *Houston Chronicle* in a published report. Unger, *House of Bush*, p. 34, also reports that Bin Mahfouz owned Skyway; Unger interviewed Bath, although it is not clear whether Bath was the source of his account.

13. Binco: Texas secretary of state, op. cit. Houston Gulf never generated significant profits: Interview with Schwartz, op. cit.

14. Saudi Bank of Paris: Salem Bin Laden entry in *Who's Who in Saudi Arabia*, 1976–77 edition, and 1978–79 edition, both of which identify Salem as a "founding member" of the bank. Main Bank: Unger, *House of Bush*, p. 34.

15. Interview with Sheryl Johnson-Todd, former attorney for Sandra Bath, September 8, 2005. Interview with a pilot who traveled with Bath during this period and who asked not to be identified.

16. Timothy J. Finn, a Bin Laden attorney, said that Ghalib earned a degree in civil engineering from the University of California at Berkeley, but a school spokesman was un-

able to locate the records of his attendance. Several people close to the family recalled that Ghalib studied at Berkeley, however. USF records: Telephone interviews with Gary McDonald, March 15 and 16, 2006. USC records: E-mail communication from James Grant, March 1, 2006.

17. Yeslam's time in Europe, his anxiety attacks: Affidavits and pleadings from Swiss divorce proceedings, Canton of Geneva, translated and filed in *Carmen Bin Ladin v. Yeslam and Ibrahim Bin Ladin*, Los Angeles County Superior Court, BC212648. "Carmen was . . . ambitions for him": Telephone interview with Mary Martha Barkley, August 27, 2004.

18. Court filings: Ibid. Pontiac Firebird: Bin Laden, *Inside the Kingdom*, p. 47. Khalif: Interview with Barkley, ibid.

19. Caesars Palace: Interview with Carmen Bin Laden, August 6, 2004. Blackjack scene: Interview with Gerald Auerbach, op. cit.

20. "No sin . . . punish him": From Osama Bin Laden's statement of December 16, 2004, as translated in Lawrence (ed.), *Messages to the World*, p. 262.

21. "You never knew . . . embedded in them": Interview with Carmen Bin Laden, op. cit.

22. Khalil and alcohol: Interview with a businessman who asked not to be identified. Mahrouz: Interview with a different business partner who also asked not to be identified. "kind of a party animal": Interview with Armitage, op. cit. Carmen Bin Laden recalled that Mahrouz's French wife also became very religious. She had a daughter from a previous marriage, Bin Laden said, for whom Mahrouz arranged a marriage to a Saudi man when the girl was quite young.

23. Theroux, *Sandstorms*, p. 72.

24. Ibrahim Bin Laden married Christine Hartunian, an American. As a young man, Khaled married a Danish woman. In addition to these examples, Khalil married a Brazilian woman, Isabel Bayma.

25. "It was just a really hard . . . always ringing" and "the family problems": Interview with Gail Freeman, op. cit. "You have a wife . . . like a diplomat": Interview with Peter Blum, May 5, 2006.

26. Hunnewell quotation from Surtees, *Pa Bell*, p. 237. Several pilots interviewed by the author also described this incident; it became part of the indoctrination new pilots received.

27. "He always said . . . wouldn't marry him": Interview with Jack Hinson, May 10, 2005.

28. All quotations: Interview with Gail Freeman, op. cit.

29. "I really don't . . . by herself": Interview with Sowell, op. cit.

30. "She's gone off . . . She crashed!": Interview with Freeman, op. cit. "Over my dead body . . . possibility": Interview with Sowell, op. cit.

31. All quotations: Interviews with Freeman and Sowell, op. cit.

14. THE CONVERT'S ZEAL

1. Transcript of Khaled Batarfi interview, published in *Al-Madinah*, late 2001, translated and supplied to the author by Batarfi.

2. Interview with a friend of Salem Bin Laden who asked not to be further identified.

3. "perfectly integrated": Bin Laden, *Inside the Kingdom*, p. 70. Cars, desert weekends: Interview with Khaled Batarfi, February 19, 2005. Osama's friend Jamal Khalifa, in Bergen,

The Osama Bin Laden I Know, p. 17, recalled Osama as "a very good driver; together we go fast, mostly the two of us, so that made us very close." "favorite hobby": Transcript of Bin Laden's December 1998 interview with Al-Jazeera, in Lawrence (ed.), *Messages to the World*, p. 71. Yellow boots and Swiss Army watch: Walid Al-Khatib, interview in *Sunday Times* (London), January 6, 2002.

4. "I remember . . . bloody signature": Interview with Rupert Armitage, September 19, 2006. "just another kid brother": Interview with Bengt Johansson, October 3, 2006.

5. "interaction" began in 1973: Biography supplied by Bin Laden or his aides to *Nida'ul Islam*, a magazine based in Australia that published an interview with Bin Laden in late 1996, in *Messages to the World*, op. cit., p. 31. "As is known . . . wage jihad": 1998 Al-Jazeera transcript in *Messages to the World*, op. cit., p. 91.

6. Transcript of interview with Nasir Al-Bahri, *Al-Quds Al-Arabi*, March 20, 2005, FBIS translation.

7. "minor figure": *Inside the Kingdom*, op. cit., p. 70. "more literal": *The Osama Bin Laden I Know*, p. 21. Soccer shorts: Interview with Batarfi, op. cit. "He often . . . about religion": Interview published in *Al-Qabas* (Kuwait), November 14, 2001. Translated for the author by Hatem Y. Mohammed.

8. "Every Muslim . . . for Americans": 1998 Al-Jazeera transcript in *Messages to the World*, op. cit., p. 87. "incapable . . . past decades": Statement of January 4, 2004, ibid., p. 229.

9. Ibid., p. 126.

10. Al-Din, *Bin Laden*, pp. 79–82.

11. Interview with Batarfi, op. cit. *Al-Qabas* interviews with Syrian relatives, op. cit.

12. Interview with Batarfi, op. cit. Bergen, *The Osama Bin Laden I Know*, p. 16. Also, interview with Khashoggi, op. cit.; *The Osama Bin Laden I Know*, p. 21; *Inside the Kingdom*, op. cit., pp. 70–71.

13. Class photo: A schoolmate of Osama's showed a copy of the class picture to the author. Jamal Khalifa, who met Osama the year he graduated from high school, and who would marry one of his half-sisters, said that their beliefs meant "no photographs. That's why I don't have any pictures with Osama. I was photographed in high school, but when I became religious, I threw everything away." Quoted in *The Osama Bin Laden I Know*, op. cit.

14. "not the Islamic . . . for her": Ibid.

15. "He did talk . . . hunting and shooting": Interview with Batarfi, op. cit. "simply awed . . . into silence": *Inside the Kingdom*, op. cit., p. 87.

16. Interview with Batarfi, op. cit. Al-Khatib: *Sunday Times*, op. cit.

17. All quotations: Interview with Batarfi, op. cit. Also, Coll, "Young Osama," *New Yorker*, December 12, 2005. Wright, *The Looming Tower*, reports that it was not Abdullah, but rather Osama's second son, Abdul Rahman, who suffered from a birth defect called hydrocephalus and sought treatment in Britain, pp. 80–81.

18. *Sunday Times*, op. cit.

19. University land donated from Suleiman, background of its founding: DOS 59/2643 Jeddah to Washington, August 31, 1965; and 59/2471 Jeddah to Washington, November 6, 1967. Mohamed Bin Laden's contributions: Telephone interview with Brian Fyfield-Shayler, February 23, 2007 (RS).

20. The interview was published in 1991 in *Al-Umma Al-Islamiyya* and is cited in Wright,

The Looming Tower, p. 78. "I recall, with pride, that I was the only family member who succeeded in combining work and doing excellently in school," Bin Laden said. "I decided to drop out of school to achieve my goals and dreams. I was surprised at the major opposition to this idea, especially from my mother, who cried and begged me to change my mind. In the end, there was no way out. I couldn't resist my mother's tears. I had to go back and finish my education." The 1996 résumé was published in connection with his interview with *Nida'ul Islam*, op. cit.

21. Mecca project work: Abbas, *Story of the Great Expansion*, pp. 262–63. "He liked . . . by himself": *Sunday Times*, op. cit.

15. WIRED

1. Interview with Francis Hunnewell, August 9, 2006. Interview with Michael Pochna, August 31, 2006.

2. Interview with Hunnewell, op. cit.

3. All quotations: Interview with Pochna, op. cit.

4. "Do you see me?": Interview with Dave Whitney, February 20, 2006. "Randa! . . . Do you believe this?": Interview with Thomas Dietrich, April 12, 2006. Also, interview with Peter Blum, May 5, 2006; interview with George Harrington, February 23, 2006.

5. All quotations: Interview with Dietrich, op. cit.

6. Rome nightclub, son of Lord Carrington: Interview with Rupert Armitage, September 19, 2006. Also, interviews with Hunnewell and Pochna, op. cit.

7. All quotations: Interview with Hunnewell, op. cit.

8. "There must have . . . by tomorrow": Interview with Armitage, op. cit.

9. All quotations: Ibid.

10. "They found . . . opened": Interview with Hunnewell, op. cit.

11. "one of the . . . pilots": Interview with Pochna, op. cit.

12. Ibid.

13. The initial $6.7 billion contract, Fahd's commission, European consultants' estimate: Surtees, *Pa Bell*, pp. 218–38; Holden and Johns, *The House of Saud*, p. 412. Salem's flight logs examined by the author.

14. "this was one of the contracts" and scene with Walter Light: Interview with Pochna, op. cit.

15. The size of the Bell Canada portion of the contract is difficult to determine precisely. Pochna and Hunnewell, and documents from their litigation, suggest they were owed about $21 million for their 1.5 percent commission during the first five years, which would place the contract value in the neighborhood of $1.5 billion. The total announced value of the contract, including all equipment sales, was more than $3 billion. That there was $400 million in construction contracts in addition: Surtees, *Pa Bell*, p. 231; that these went to Bin Laden interests in the main: Interviews with Pochna and Hunnewell, op. cit. Mohammed bin Fahd's $500 million commission: *House of Saud*, op. cit., p. 414.

16. Juhaiman's origins in Sajir: Al-Rasheed, *A History of Saudi Arabia*, p. 145; *House of Saud*, op. cit., pp. 514–15.

17. *House of Saud*, op. cit., pp. 515–26.

18. "Rules of Allegiance": Ibid. "drunkards . . . the state's money": Vassiliev, *A History of*

Saudi Arabia, pp. 395–96; Teitelbaum, *Holier Than Thou*, pp. 20–21. Quoted also in Coll, *Ghost Wars*, p. 28.

19. Flight logs examined by the author.

20. Mahdi divined in a dream: *House of Saud*, op. cit., p. 520.

21. "was frantic . . . unhinged": Carmen Bin Laden, *Inside the Kingdom*, pp. 123–25. "Everyone was saying . . . steel there was": Interview with the Bin Laden employee, who asked to not be further identified.

22. Gained access with Bin Laden vehicles: *Inside the Kingdom*, op. cit., p. 123. "Where is Bin Laden . . . Jackhammer it": Interview with the Bin Laden employee, op. cit.

23. "They bored . . . in the hole": Telephone interview with Tim Barger, March 7, 2006. "we were slipping": Interview with the Bin Laden employee, op. cit.

24. Binladin International initial filings in Panama, dates, directors, successor corporation names: Documents collected and provided to the author by Douglas Farah and the Nine/Eleven Finding Answers Foundation. In other court documents, the Bin Ladens acknowledged moving money offshore quickly in August 1990, following Saddam Hussein's invasion of Kuwait. See chapter 27.

25. Interview with the employee, op. cit. He did not recall the identity of the second brother. Wright, *The Looming Tower*, p. 94, reports that Osama was with Mahrouz, citing an interview with Jamal Khalifa. *Inside the Kingdom*, pp. 123–24, describes Mahrouz's arrest but does not mention a second brother; it reports that Mahrouz had a pistol in his car.

26. Interview with the employee, op. cit.

27. Lawrence (ed.), *Messages to the World*, p. 266.

28. Osama would also have been able to borrow or obtain much larger sums to make purchases such as the apartment he bought for his expanding family. The apartment building: Interview with Khaled Batarfi, February 19, 2005. According to Nasir Al-Bahri, Osama's later bodyguard, two of the wives Osama took before he moved to Afghanistan had earned doctoral degrees either in Islamic law or in Arabic. Osama seems to have married one of these wives from the Al-Sharif family during the 1980s.

29. "especially effective . . . problems": Randal, *Osama*, p. 64, where Al-Khatib also describes the demolition work and Osama's interaction with Europeans and Americans.

30. "I knew it meant . . . like him anymore": Al-Khatib interview in the *Sunday Times* (London), January 6, 2002.

16. THE AMUSEMENT PARK

1. Heart surgeon: Interview with Gail and Robert Freeman, April 27, 2006. Polaroid: Interview with Jack Hinson, May 10, 2005. Showed it to royalty: Interview with Mohamed Ashmawi, November 26, 2005 (RS.)

2. Saudin Inc. filings and directors: Documents provided to the author by Douglas Farah and the Nine/Eleven Finding Answers Foundation. "should there . . . Saudi Arabia": Robert Freeman, "The Saudi Connection" (unpublished manuscript).

3. "was having some cash flow problems": Telephone interview with Aaron Dowd, February 13, 2006. Price of the property, sale terms: Freeman, "The Saudi Connection," ibid. Book of flowers, who received the first houses: Interview with Gail and Robert Freeman, op. cit.

4. Wine prank: Interview with Anwar Khan, May 6, 2006 (RS).

5. Winter Garden and Desert Bear history: Telephone interview with Rod Reeves, former director of Winter Garden Heritage Museum, February 7, 2006; interview Julie Butler, Heritage Museum director, February 6, 2006. Also, Desert Bear history, McCarthy purchase and restoration: telephone interview with Miller McCarthy, February 10, 2006.

6. Salem told McCarthy: Telephone interview with McCarthy, ibid. "the Prince ... from Saudi Arabia": "The Saudi Connection," op. cit.

7. Telephone interview with McCarthy, ibid. Closing date: Orange County property records. These show the purchase price as $1.61 million. McCarthy's recollection of a higher price may include other contiguous land. The Deed for 17920 West Colonial, the address of the main estate, was purchased by Desert Bear Limited, "a Liberian corporation," according to the Orange County records. That Price Waterhouse arranged the company: Interview with Robert Freeman, op. cit.

8. Interviews with four longtime neighbors who asked not to be otherwise identified. "they liked ... openly": Telephone interview with McCarthy, ibid.

9. "Come on up ... in line": Interview with Pat Deegan, September 8, 2005.

10. Ibid. A number of other friends and employees of the Bin Ladens described Ghalib's accident, but Deegan, who flew ultralights at Desert Bear and visited Ghalib in the hospital after the incident, offered the most specific account.

11. Interview with Gail and Robert Freeman, op. cit.

12. All quotations: "The Saudi Connection," op. cit.

13. "was looking for deals": Interview with Freeman, op. cit.

14. All quotations are from the interview with Gail Freeman, op. cit.

15. "We were his playthings" and "Bob, you do ... humor": Interview with Freeman, op. cit.

16. All quotations, ibid.

17. "a very quiet ... through him": Interview with a former employee of Bin Mahfouz who asked not to be identified. Asked for comment about the profile of Bin Mahfouz and his business activities described throughout this chapter, attorneys for Bin Mahfouz said that he did not ordinarily comment about his family's personal or business relationships, and that he would not do so in this case.

18. "just as happy ... care less": Interview with a second former employee of Bin Mahfouz who asked to not be identified.

19. Hammerman Brothers shopping, "This created quite a stir": "The Saudi Connection," op. cit. Attorneys for Bin Mahfouz said he had no comment.

20. "The Big House": Transcript of White's interview with Canadian Broadcasting Corporation; White affirmed the transcript's accuracy in a telephone interview. "Why do these people ... in for tea": Interview with two former employees of Bin Mahfouz who asked not to be identified.

21. Connolly and Hunt brothers on the plane, Khalid complaining about silver losses: Interview with the two former employees cited in notes 17 and 18. Khalid directed trading strategies: "Whose Rules?" in *The Banker*, November 1, 1990. Baker Botts: White transcript, ibid. Attorneys for Bin Mahfouz said he would have no comment.

22. 1985 cash and deposits: *The Banker*, ibid. Aramco dollars and Baghdad flights: Interview with David Grey, February 21, 2006. Aid to Iraq of $25.7 billion: Al-Rasheed, *A History of Saudi Arabia*, p. 157. Transferred U.S. weapons: Clarke, *Against All Enemies*, p. 42. Attorneys

for Bin Mahfouz said he had no comment. Salem Bin Mahfouz, the founder of National Commercial Bank and Khalid's father, died in 1994. By the end of 2002, according to the Khalid's attorneys, the Bin Mahfouz family had divested the last of its holdings in the bank, which remains one of the largest financial institutions in Saudi Arabia.

23. Five million too small: "The Saudi Connection," op. cit. Project Debra: Telephone interview with Andy Pugh, Metro West, February 13, 2006. $100,000 in cash, $30,000 tips: Peterson quoted in "Arabian Adventure," *Pittsburgh Post-Gazette*, March 18, 2003.

24. Told McCarthy $220 million in debt: Telephone interview with McCarthy, op. cit. Backing out of yacht purchase: Interview with Thomas Dietrich, April 12, 2006. According to Orange County, Florida, records, the mortgage was taken out from Sun Bank on June 4, 1984 and was repaid on August 15, 1988.

25. Asked to launder $5 million to $10 million: Interview with Robert Freeman, op. cit.

17. IN THE KING'S SERVICE

1. Interview with an aide to Salem who asked to not be identified.

2. Clarke, *Against All Enemies*, p. 39.

3. Coll, *Ghost Wars*, p. 65, for the U.S. government's 1981 fiscal year. The brief analysis of U.S. and Saudi governmental attitudes toward the war here and elsewhere in this chapter is drawn from the research for *Ghost Wars*, chapters 1–5.

4. Al-Rasheed, *A History of Saudi Arabia*, p. 155.

5. The company had a *zakat* fund: Interview with Carmen Bin Laden, September 29, 2004. Also, Rand Corporation researcher Anna Kasupski, reviewing materials about the early history of the Services Office in Peshawar, located a 1985 document describing donations from a Bin Laden family foundation. "Rand: Early History of Al Qaeda Working Group, 2006."

6. Pakistani air force veterans, Mohammed Daoud: Interview with David Grey, February 21, 2006. Karachi in November 1980: Flight logs examined by the author. Osama's first trip in 1980: Interview with Jamal Khashoggi, February 2, 2002. It is not clear what time of year he traveled.

7. Class photograph: Author's copy. "not an extremist . . . polite person": Badeeb's 2001 interview with Orbit televsion, supplied to the author by Badeeb, translated by The Language Doctors, Inc.

8. "We cannot . . . they received" and using trips to Hajj to cultivate independent contacts: Interview with Ahmed Badeeb, February 1, 2002.

9. "was not trusting . . . real *mujaheddin*": Interview with Badeeb, ibid. Rabbani and Sayyaf, stayed a month: Al-Din, *Bin Laden*, p. 47.

10. "The arrangement . . . relief work": Interview with Khashoggi, op. cit. "Members of the government": Interview with Khalil Khalil, February 10, 2005. Badeeb used humanitarian agencies as cover, Osama's audiences with Nayef and Ahmed: Interview with Badeeb, and Badeeb Orbit interview, op. cit.

11. "was a very . . . liked him": Interview with Bassim Alim, February 21, 2005.

12. "The training . . . younger brother": Interview with Khashoggi, March 17, 2006. "That the Afghans . . . measure it": Interview with Badeeb, op. cit. Vault for Osama's jewelry donations: Interview with the aide to Salem, who asked to not be identified.

13. Lawrence (ed.), *Messages to the World*, p. 110.

14. "a young ... his feet" and more than $15 million loss: Interview with Sabry Ghoneim, November 14, 2005 (RS).

15. Azzam's debts: Interview with Azzam's wife by Mohammed Al Shafey, *Al-Sharq Al-Awsat*, April 30, 2006. "meeting of money ... Azzam": *Al-Quds Al-Arabi*, April 4, 2005.

16. Interview with Khalil, op. cit.

17. *Al-Quds Al-Arabi*, March 20, 2005.

18. That Azzam arrived in late 1981: Jamal Ismail in Bergen, *The Osama Bin Laden I Know*, p. 26. Saudi funding of $35 million: Piscatori, "Islamic Values and National Interest," in *Islam and Foreign Policy*, p. 47.

19. Badeeb's role in Sada camp: Interview with Badeeb, op. cit. That it was open by 1984: Hutaifa Azzam in *The Osama Bin Laden I Know*, op. cit. p. 28. "They would ... conquer Kabul": "The Story of the Arab Afghans," Anonymous, *Al-Sharq Al-Awsat*, December 12, 2004.

20. Quoted in Bergen and Cruickshank, "How the Idea of Al Qaeda Was Conceived," 2006.

21. Between $200,000 and $300,000: Anna Kasupski, "Rand: Early History of Al Qaeda Working Group, 2006." Construction engineer from the Bin Laden firm: Abdullah Anas, in *The Osama Bin Laden I Know*, op. cit., p. 29, identifies this engineer as Abdullah Saadi and says he was there "to guide the bulldozers. Osama borrowed him from the company." Azzam at the Bin Laden home in Mecca; "The entire ... take people" quoted in *The Osama Bin Laden I Know*, ibid., p. 31. The 1985 document: See note 5.

22. "When the Sheikh ... same boat": *Messages to the World*, op. cit., p. 77. "As for repelling ... against him": Ibid., p. 202.

23. Ibid., p. 239, from Bin Laden's statement of October 29, 2004.

24. "Lucky him ... in heaven": "Early Al Qaeda Working Group," op. cit. First four committees: Gunaratna, "Al Qaeda: Its Organizational Strengths and Weaknesses with a Special Focus on the Pre-1996 Phase," 2006.

25. See the prologue.

26. *Surah* 4, verse 127.

27. "a mass movement ... compassionate and patient": Interview with Khashoggi, March 17, 2006. "Financial jihad ... who don't": *Messages to the World*, op. cit., p. 203.

28. Interview with Bengt Johansson, October 3, 2006.

29. Ibrahim's Mayfair apartment: Interview with Wayne Fagan, former Dee Howard Company general counsel, May 10, 2005. That he bought a Gulfstream and DC-8: Interview with a Bin Laden employee involved in the transactions. On Ibrahim and Fahd, also see the prologue.

30. "He and I ... a favor": Interview with Dee Howard, March 16, 2005.

31. "Your Majesty ... another one": Interview with Howard, ibid.

32. "Some people ... away with it": Interview with a Bin Laden employee who was present. Arduous negotiations: Interview with the Bin Laden employee. Howard and Fagan declined to comment about Ibrahim's specific demands. Several published newspaper accounts place the final value of the contract at $92 million, although Howard recalled that his initial bid was closer to $70 million, and that the price rose through additional changes and orders.

33. Cleveland Clinic and operating theater: Interviews with Howard, Fagan, and the Bin Laden employee, op. cit. Raytheon provided defenses against heat-seeking missles: Dee Howard's 1993 testimony in *Ian Munro v. The Dee Howard Co.*, Bexar County, Texas, 91-CI-00928.

34. Money wired, some increments of more than $10 million: Testimony of Wayne Fagan in *Ian Munro v. The Dee Howard Co.*, ibid. "He was very interested": Interview with Howard, op. cit.

18. ANXIETY DISORDER

1. Tennis parties, Yeslam and his brothers: Interview with Carmen Bin Laden, August 6, 2004, and interview with Terry Bennett, December 2005 (RS). Alcohol and steak: Bin Laden, *Inside the Kingdom*, p. 99.

2. Yeslam's cars: "Justified Statement of Claims" for Carmen Bin Laden, September 8, 2000, Court of the First Instance of the Republic and Canton of Geneva, Case No. 19750/94-11, translated from the original French and filed in *Carmen Binladin v. Yeslam and Ibrahim Binladin*, Los Angeles County Superior Court, BC212648. Ibrahim's Rolls-Royce: *Ibrahim Bin Ladin v. Paul Andrew Richey*, Los Angeles County Superior Court, WEC114264. Fatal brain damage, Formula One incident: *Inside the Kingdom*, op. cit., p. 154.

3. Interview with Carmen Bin Laden, op. cit.; *Inside the Kingdom*, op. cit., pp. 109 and 115.

4. Yeslam's compensation in 1976 and 1978: "Respondent's statement of defense and pleas," Court of First Instance, Geneva, translated and filed in Los Angeles C212648, op. cit.

5. Genthod property and purchase price: "Respondent's statement," ibid. Jewelry inventory: "Complaint for Declaratory Relief," June 28, 1999, Los Angeles C212648, op. cit. "I admit" and cash box: *Inside the Kingdom*, op. cit., p. 150.

6. In his divorce application in Geneva, Yeslam's lawyers describe him as "a very emotional man who is prone to anxiety." Yeslam's own statement in the case refers to his falling "ill" and seeking "medical treatment," but does not further specify his condition. The specific reference to "panic attacks" is from Carmen's filings in that case.

7. "hid himself ... this mania": From "Replies to Yeslam's numbered paragraphs," Court of First Instance, Geneva, translated and filed in Los Angeles C212648, op. cit. See also *Inside the Kingdom*, pp. 124 and 129.

8. "His wife seemed ... into a tree": Divorce Application, "As to Fact," Court of First Instance, Geneva, translated and filed in Los Angeles C212648, op. cit. "everything she could ... his business": "Replies to Yeslam's numbered paragraphs," ibid. Six weeks in Los Angeles, condition improved: "Declaration of Yeslam Mohammed Binladin," November 22, 1999, ibid.

9. "To dispose ... make money": From "Saudi Investment Company (SICO): An Emerging Financial Service Center," circa 1983, filed in *In Re Terrorist Attacks on September 11, 2001*, United States District Court, Southern District of New York, 03 MDL 1570.

10. Falken-owned Saudi Investment Company: "Reply Memorandum In Support of Defendant Yeslam Binladin's Motion," *In Re Terrorist Attacks*, ibid. Construction work in Sudan: In an affidavit submitted in *In Re Terrorist Attacks*, Omar Bin Laden described the formation "in the Jersey Channel Islands in the late 1980's" of a company called "Binladin

Overseas (Pvt. Ltd.)," which was "awarded a contract for the construction of the Port Sudan airport in the Sudan." Saudi Investment Company Panama Corp.: Panamanian filing supplied to author by Douglas Farah and Nine/Eleven Finding Answers Foundation. The incorporation papers are dated October 28, 1983. "Mohamed Binladin Organization Inc." of Panama: Farah and NEFA documents, ibid. The company filed incorporation papers on March 21, 1984.

11. "hundreds of marketing . . . our customers": From "Saudi Investment . . . Emerging Financial Service Center," op. cit. Stock holdings and turnover by the end of 1983, ibid.

12. Ibid.

13. DLJ introduced Yeslam to Tickle: Telephone interview with Charles Tickle, February 16, 2006. Saudi Investors, Inc., formed in Panama: NEFA documents, op. cit., and a prospectus for Saudi Investors filed in *In Re Terrorist Attacks*, op. cit. "Mohamed Binladin Family" and Richmond, Houston, project details: Saudi Investors prospectus, ibid. "A unique concept . . . purchasing power": "Saudi Investment . . . Emerging Financial Service Center," op. cit.

14. "always very professional . . . cared less": Interview with Tickle, op. cit.

15. "now, in effect . . . the princes": *Inside the Kingdom*, op. cit., pp. 111–12. "disagreements": Interview with Yeslam published in V.S.B. magazine, Geneva, December 2005, translated and filed in *In Re Terrorist Attacks*, op. cit.

16. Majid: *Inside the Kingdom*, op. cit., p. 113; Mishal: Ibid., p. 187.

17. Purchase price of Old Geneva building, including renovations: "Respondent's statement of defense and pleas," Court of First Instance, Geneva, translated and filed in Los Angeles C212648, op. cit. March 11 letter: Filed in *Christine Binladin v. Ibrahim Binladin*, Los Angeles County Superior Court, BD058156.

18. "he went through . . . intolerant and dogmatic": "Respondent's statement of defense and pleas," Court of First Instance, Geneva, translated and filed in Los Angeles C212648, op. cit. "taking him for a ride . . . any longer": Yeslam's "Divorce Application . . . As to Fact," ibid.

19. "They wanted . . . invest globally": Telephone interview with Auguste George James Sauter, July 15, 2005.

20. Moawalla, Falken Limited, computer system date: Regulatory filings of Russell Wood (Holdings) Limited and Russell Wood Limited, Companies House, London, 1987–1989.

21. All quotations from "Divorce Application" and "Respondent's statement of defense and pleas," Court of First Instance, Geneva, translated and filed in Los Angeles C212648, op. cit.

22. "burned all the hard disks": Interview with Sauter, op. cit. He said the Bin Ladens ultimately sued some of the stockbrokers involved to recover lost client funds; British court records of this type are closed to the public, and it was not possible to locate files that would confirm his recollection. "a breakdown in accounting controls": Russell Wood annual report, Companies House, London, 1988.

19. THE GRINDER

1. "Field Project Manager," board seats: *Who's Who in Saudi Arabia*, 1983–1984 edition. "who got . . . managed it": Interview with Mohamed Ashmawi, November 26, 2005 (RS).

2. "Where Salem ... process-oriented": Interview with Francis Hunnewell, August 9, 2006. "a very ...," "Yes, Salem": Interview with Michael Pochna, August 31, 2006.

3. Vespa scooter, Miami-Dade, "What kind of ... actually taste": Interview with a person who witnessed the conversation and who asked to not be otherwise identified. Bakr declined comment.

4. International students: *Ibis*, University of Miami yearbook, 1973 edition. Jewish students, pot survey, "Three things ... and pot": *Ibis*, 1972 edition.

5. "We never talked ... some money": Telephone interview Joaquin Avino, February 14, 2006. "a relatively ... university": Telephone interview with John Hall, March 8, 2006. Silk shirts and Cadillac Seville: Telephone interview with Jorge Rodriguez, March 8, 2006.

6. Suburban rambler, neighbors: Polk's *Miami South Suburban Directory*, a telephone book, lists Bakr and Haifa in its 1973 edition at 9435 SW 79th Avenue. Bresser's 1973 Cross-Index Directory lists that address as "Binladen Bakery," an apparent typo. The house is still there. Omar listed in Polk's in 1974 at 9143 SW 77th Avenue, Apartment B701; that building apparently has been torn down. Yahya also was listed at an address near the Miami-Dade North Campus in 1972, but the author could locate no one who remembered his time there. Haifa family background: Interviews with two people close to the family who asked to not be identified. "By no means": Interview with Rodriguez, op. cit.

7. "open minded ... bathing suits": Bin Ladin, *Inside the Kingdom*, pp. 80–81. "He is ... not necessary": Interview with a partner of the Bin Ladens who asked to not be identified.

8. The partner, not the same one as cited in the previous note, asked to not be identified. Bakr accompanied Osama: Interview with a senior Saudi official who asked to not be identified. Bakr declined comment.

9. Renovation details: Abbas, *Story of the Great Expansion*, pp. 3–9. "Many a time ... open-ended account": Ibid., in the foreword by Bakr Bin Laden.

10. "Sort of realignment ... wanted him gone": Interview with the former senior American official, who asked to not be identified. "Salem told ... his family": Interview with a business partner who asked to not be identified.

11. Azzam letter: "Rand: Early History of Al Qaeda Working Group, 2006."

20. THE ARMS BAZAAR

1. Interview with Thomas Dietrich, April 12, 2006. As indicated in the text, a second individual, a business partner of Salem's, separately confirmed that Osama had sent out messages to Salem asking for missiles, and that Salem went forward with the transaction through Dietrich's contacts.

2. "An increase ... staff": Quoted in Gunaratna, "Al Qaeda: Its Organizational Strengths and Weaknesses," 2006. Jawr battle: "The Story of the Arab Afghans," Anonymous, *Al-Sharq Al-Awsat*, December 12, 2004.

3. *Messages to the World*, op. cit., p. 150.

4. All quotations, interview with Deitrich, op. cit.

5. For one detailed account of this period of the war, see Coll, *Ghost Wars*, pp. 125–67.

6. Pillsbury's meetings and conclusions: Interview with Michael Pillsbury, May 2, 2006. In his memoir, *From the Shadows*, p. 349, former CIA director Robert Gates, referring to

the Arab volunteers in the Afghan war, wrote that the CIA "examined ways to increase their participation, perhaps in the form of some sort of 'international brigade,' but nothing came of it." No contemporary U.S. government documents describing this review have yet been declassified or otherwise published.

7. Salem's approaches to the Pentagon: Interviews with the business partner cited in note 1. "The problem . . . missiles": Interview with Dietrich, op. cit.

8. Ibid. A Heckler & Koch spokesman acknowledged that the firm had a department in the Middle East specializing in brokered arms sales, but declined any comment on the transactions reported in this book.

9. All quotations in this passage are from the interview with Dietrich, op. cit.

10. Simpson, *The Prince*, pp. 146–49.

11. Badeeb acknowledged purchasing SA-7 missiles: Interview with Badeeb, February 1, 2002. The two individuals familiar with evidence about the South African transactions are not the same sources cited earlier in these notes. One of them, Michael Elsner, an attorney representing victims of the September 11 attacks, said that he had interviewed an individual who acted as a translator at a meeting in Peshawar, at the Pearl Continental Hotel, attended by two South African military officers, as well as Osama and Sayyaf; they discussed weapons purchases and training, by this account. The second individual, who asked not to be identified, said he attended separate meetings in Jeddah in which Salem negotiated with South African suppliers to purchase arms that would be shipped to Osama in Pakistan.

12. "Americans . . . in Palestine": Lawrence (ed.), *Messages to the World*, p. 115. "For God's sake . . . issue here": Palestinian journalist Jamal Ismail in Bergen, *The Osama Bin Laden I Know*, p. 60.

13. This chronology and the numbers of followers at Lion's Den during 1986 are drawn from "Rand: Early History of Al Qaeda Working Group, 2006," and Gunaratna, op. cit.

14. Gunaratna, op. cit.

15. *Messages to the World*, op. cit., p. 48.

16. "very professional": Interview with Badeeb, op. cit. Contracts with Pakistani intelligence: Interview with a former U.S. official involved. Medina volunteers: "Early Al Qaeda Working Group," op. cit. Cairo visas: Interview with Michael Scheuer, former head of the Bin Laden unit at the CIA, July 5, 2005. Also *Al-Ahram* (Egypt), January 1, 2001. Peshawar construction projects for charities by Bin Laden companies: *Al-Ahram*, ibid.

17. Bearden: Quoted in *Frontline, Hunting Bin Laden*, 2001. "more practical": Harmony AFGP-2002-600094.

18. "History recounts . . . Russia": Lawrence (ed.) *Messages to the World*, op. cit., p. 147. "It's an attempt . . . tacit agreement": Ibid., pp. 87–88.

19. CIA logistics units provided cement and supplies: Interview with Peter Tomsen, former U.S. special envoy to the Afghan rebels, September 12, 2006. Haqqani was a unilateral: Interview with a former U.S. official involved. "hero . . . the Soviets": *Messages to the World*, op. cit., p. 151. For their part, CIA case officers recorded frequent accounts of the Arab volunteers who were increasingly active along the border, but they were not interested enough to accumulate lists of names or to track weapons shipments to them. They were much more focused on collecting intelligence about Spetsnaz assault tactics, information that might one day prove useful in a European war.

20. Charities named in *Al-Jihad* of December 1986: "Early Al Qaeda Working Group 2006," op. cit. "shy … pithy statements": Turki has spoken publicly many times about his encounters with Osama in Pakistan during this period, but this quotation is from a question-and-answer interview with *Der Spiegel*, March 8, 2004, FBIS translation.

21. "interesting figure": *Der Spiegel*, ibid. "Abdullah Azzam … sixth place": Letter from Turki to the author, April 22, 2005.

22. "It is … Saudi Arabia": Quoted in Bergen, *The Osama Bin Laden I Know*, p. 61, from an essay attributed to Al-Suri and published in 2004.

23. Badeeb's interview with Orbit Television, late 2001, tape supplied by Badeeb to the author and translated by The Language Doctors, Inc.

21. OFF THE BOOKS

1. Bath's guns, car, plane, investments: Property partition agreement, *Sandra C. Bath v. James R. Bath*, Harris County Court, 89-07180. In an affidavit of September 29, 1989, Bath affirmed that he was "President and sole director of Skyways, a company wholly owed by foreign nationals." He declined to identify the owners of Skyway; published media reports have identified Khalid Bin Mahfouz or his family as the controlling investors. Attorneys for Bin Mahfouz declined to comment.

2. How Bath met Lewis: Interview with Sheryl Johnson, September 8, 2005. Cadillac, money: Sandra Bath"s Fourth Amended Petition, *Bath v. Bath*, ibid. In an affidavit of September 5, 1991, Bath acknowledged "my affair with Mary Ellen Lewis" and that he had financed a company that she operated. In a court filing in that case, Bath's attorneys wrote that Bath "has agreed [to] assume that he is the biological father" of the Lewis child. The cards comparing their marriage to *Dallas:* Deposition testimony of Sandra Bath, ibid. How Sandra learned of the child: Interview with Johnson, op. cit. Drug allegations and denials: Bath's Second Amended Answer, ibid. "made threats … kill me": Bath's affidavit of April 20, 1990, ibid.

3. "indicated that … business associates": White pleadings, *Charles W. White v. NCNB Texas National Bank*, Harris County Court, 90-053147. White did not mention either Osama or Afghanistan in this earliest of his known accounts of Bath's alleged statements about CIA activities. Expanded comments to describe Bath's alleged air operations: Undated transcript of White's interview with the Canadian Broadcasting Corporation, circa 2006; White confirmed the accuracy of the transcript and reaffirmed his comments in a telephone interview with the author.

4. "paranoia … against him": Bath petition, *James R. Bath v. Charles W. White*, Harris County Court, 86-42551. "fantasy … agency": *Time*, October 28, 1991. "There"s all … participation": Unger, *House of Bush, House of Saud*, p. 34. Houston station: Coll, *Ghost Wars*, p. 314.

5. Interview with Sheryl Johnson, op. cit., and with a second individual who worked with Bath on aviation matters during this time.

6. McDonald flew from Jeddah to Riyadh aboard one of Salem's private jets on March 1, 1983, according to flight logs reviewed by the author. The log entry, in full, read: "Salem, Pizza, Congressman Larry McDonald, Georgia, plus two, plus money—Freeman." Jack and Anita Pizza and Robert and Gail Freeman were frequent fliers on Salem's planes;

they were friends and business partners. "Plus two" refers to two unidentified passengers who were probably traveling with McDonald. The origins of the money referred to and the purpose of McDonald's travel are unknown. Vinson and Elkins represented Salem: Interview with Charles Schwartz, May 12, 2005.

7. Certificate of Deposit, contact by Houston Police: White's pleadings in *Charles W. White v. NCNB Texas National Bank*, op. cit. Randa's estrangement: Interview with Gail Freeman, April 27, 2006.

8. "We have plenty . . . hereafter": Quoted in Bergen, *The Osama Bin Laden I Know*, pp. 51–52.

9. "Rand: Early History of Al Qaeda Working Group, 2006." Also, Bergen and Cruickshank, "How the Idea of Al Qaeda Was Conceived," 2006. Earliest known published account: Kim Cragin, "Early Al Qaeda Working Group."

10. "It was obvious . . . that party": Interview with Jamal Khashoggi, February 2, 2002.

11. *The Osama Bin Laden I Know*, op. cit. pp. 58–59.

12. *Meeting Osama Bin Laden,* Brook Lapping Productions, 2004.

13. Interview by Mohammed Al-Shafey, *Al-Sharq Al-Awsat*, April 30, 2006.

14. "was approached . . . other countries": E-mail statement from Bin Mahfouz attorneys at Kendall Freeman, London, to author, August 2007. At the time of the contribution, Al Qaeda had not yet been formed. "with the intention . . . U.S. Government": Second e-mail statement from Bin Mahfouz attorney Laurence Harris, managing partner, Kendall Freeman, London, to author, August 2007.

15. "I think Osama": *The Osama Bin Laden I Know*, p. 48.

22. THE PROPOSAL

1. "normal family . . . doing it": Interview with Bengt Johansson, October 3, 2006. Other friends, employees, and partners who described Salem"s girlfriends and marriage proposal in on-the-record interviews included Mohamed Ashmawi, Sabry Ghoneim, Thomas Dietrich, Anwar Khan, and Robert and Gail Freeman.

2. All quotations, including the note from "S," from an interview with Lynn Peghiny, February 7, 2006.

3. Carey family: Interview with a person close to the family, as well as biographical information from a family Web site, www.careyroots.com, examined and typed, May 9, 2007.

4. Interview with Peghiny, op. cit.

5. Ibid.

6. All quotations, ibid.

7. Interview with Gerald Auerbach, April 7, 2005.

8. All quotations, interview with Peghiny, op. cit.

9. Sheikha and Rafah on birthdays: Bin Laden, *Inside the Kingdom*, p. 104. Mona, Huda, and Randa in Europe: Flight logs and interviews with several people who went on the trips, including Thomas Dietrich, April 12, 2006.

10. "village idiot": *Inside the Kingdom*, p. 88. Los Angeles: Property records in Los Angeles County. Her fast driving: Interviews with two friends of Najiah who asked to not be identified.

11. Interviews with Robert and Gail Freeman, April 27, 2006.

12. All quotations, ibid.

13. "I paid you to smile!": Interview with Johansson, op. cit. "They were bitching . . . would say": Interview with Dietrich, op. cit.

14. Peter Theroux, *Sandstorms*, p. 114.

15. Strip mall, mining deal, cowboy movie: Interview with Wayne Fagan, May 10, 2005. London apartment with Muhammad Ali: Interview with Don Sowell, June 2, 2005.

16. All quotations, interview with Johansson, op. cit.

17. Interview with Jack Hinson, May 10, 2005.

18. Interview with Dietrich, op. cit., and with Salem's German assistant, Peter Blum, May 5, 2006.

19. All quotations, interview with Mohamed Ashmawi, November 26, 2005 (RS).

20. His temper: Interview with Ashmawi, ibid., as well as many other employees, partners, and friends. The Dubai episode: Interview with two people who were present.

21. All quotations, interview with Fagan, op. cit.

23. KITTY HAWK FIELD OF DREAMS

1. All quotations from an interview with a person familiar with the conversations, who asked to not be identified.

2. Wedding description and guests from interviews with eight people who attended, as well as photographs of the event.

3. Interview with Bengt Johansson, October 3, 2006. Swiss accounts: Interview with a friend of Salem who asked to not be identified.

4. Interview with the person cited, ibid., and with a second business partner of Salem's who asked to not be identified.

5. Flight logs reviewed by the author.

6. All quotations from an interview with Lynn Peghiny, February 7, 2006.

7. Ibid.

8. Interview with Gerald Auerbach, April 9, 2005.

9. All quotations from an interview with Jack Hinson, May 10, 2005.

10. History of Kitty Hawk: Interview with Earl Mayfield, April 9, 2005.

11. All quotations, interview with Hinson, op. cit.

12. The sequence of events before his flight: Interviews with Hinson and Mayfield, op. cit., and a third individual present. Salem's eyes teared: Interview with Thomas Dietrich, April 12, 2006. In addition to Dietrich, two other people who were particularly close to Salem said they believed that blurred vision caused by tears from the wind was the most likely cause of what unfolded at Kitty Hawk. There is no evidence to support alternative theories of either suicide or a disabling health event such as a heart attack or stroke. Wind speed: Written report of May 29, 1988, by Schertz Police Officer Lori Harris, who arrived at Kitty Hawk in a police patrol car at 3:34 P.M. Interview with Lori Harris, March 16, 2005.

13. Salem's flight trajectory: Interviews with Hinson, Mayfield, and the third individual,

op. cit. A fourth individual who viewed the videotape described the same sequence. The author was unable to locate a copy of the video, but several people who saw it all described the same sequence.

14. Notes from the ambulance run report provided to the author by Schertz Police Chief Steve Starr, examined and typed, April 8, 2005. The run report and the Harris police report describe witness accounts of how Salem was lifted from the ultralight by those who initially arrived and was given CPR.

24. WRITER-DIRECTOR-PRODUCER

1. "Mickey Mouse plane": Interview with Mohamed Ashmawi, November 26, 2005 (RS). Particular acuteness: Interview with a business partner who asked to not be identified. "family tragedy": Interview with ABC's *20/20*, broadcast March 29, 2002. Barbara Walters asked Abdullah what he recalled of Osama at the funeral. "I don't recall things because it was a family tragedy," he replied.

2. Interviews with two friends of Salem's who met the plane in Geneva.

3. Interview with one of the friends who was present.

4. "You haven't . . . him now": Interview with the friend, who asked to not be identified.

5. Interviews with two people present. For Hejazi and Wahhabi burial rituals, Yamani, *Cradle of Islam*, pp. 102–20. Bin Mahfouz declined to comment.

6. Buried with a child: Interviews with two people present. In an attempt to fact-check the reporting and interpretations in this book, I submitted to the Bin Ladens' principal American law firm, Jones Day, scores of specific questions and factual summaries for comment, correction, or clarification. Apart from several matters concerning the relationship between the family and Osama after he became radicalized, Jones Day responded to only one of these questions, involving the account here of the burial of a young girl with Salem. The letter offered a review of the appropriateness of such burial practices under Islamic law and appended an article from a humanities journal published in Helsinki in 1965, which described the existence of this practice in a Jordanian village. The Jones Day attorney who wrote the letter, Timothy J. Finn, stated that "we have not been able to confirm whether anything like this happened" in Salem's case, but then continued, "We have been told that Islamic custom does permit joint burial of an infant or small child who dies at the same time as an adult but that this is accomplished . . . by digging a notch at the foot of the adult grave where the child is laid to rest . . . both as [an] expression of community solidarity and, simply, as a convenience, since Islamic tradition requires immediate burial within 24 hours of death, with very simple or no grave markings. We have also found in Islamic tradition a little-known theological underpinning for this occasional practice to the effect that the angels of death will not treat the adult harshly in the presence of a child."

7. Osama was present: Abdullah Bin Laden, to *20/20*, op. cit., and interview with a second person close to the family, who asked to not be identified. "like a father . . . great deal": Transcript of interview with Khaled Batarfi, supplied to the author by Batarfi.

8. Ghalib worried about a conspiracy: Interview with Gerald Auerbach, May 11, 2005.

"Manner of Death: Accident," Bexar County, Office of the Medical Examiner, report 759–88. "was a big event": Interview with Jamal Khashoggi, March 17, 2006.

9. Date and place of Sama's birth: "Application for Appointment of Administrator," Bexar County probate proceeding, 91-PC-1012.

10. Bergen and Cruickshank, "How the Idea of Al Qaeda Was Conceived," citing an interview with Osama Rushdi, an Egyptian militant living in Peshawar at the time.

11. "Abdullah Azzam wanted . . . is welcome": Interview with Jamal Khashoggi, February 2, 2002. "from many different places . . . borders and walls": in Lawrence (ed.), *Messages to the World*, p. 96.

12. From transcripted interview published by *Al-Sharq Al-Awsat*, April 30, 2006.

13. All quotations, including those attributed to Banjshiri, come from Al-Surayhi. Bergen, *The Osama Bin Laden I Know*, p. 83.

14. The notes were seized by Bosnian authorities during a 2002 raid on an Islamic charity. Unclassified document sets have been released subsequently under the title, drawn from the originals, *"Tareekh Osama,"* or "Osama's History." The quotations here are from a meeting on August 11, 1988.

15. Ibid. The second meeting began on August 20.

16. *Messages to the World*, op. cit., pp. 119–20.

17. Interview with a former business partner and also with Peter Blum, who worked occasionally with Ghalib and his family, May 5, 2006.

18. Flight logs examined by the author.

19. "some cash": Interview with Gerald Auerbach, May 11, 2005. "They were almost . . . fences": Interview with Bengt Johansson, October 3, 2006. "the cash . . . camps": e-mail communication from Timothy J. Finn, November 24, 2007.

20. For an account of the assault on Jalalabad, see Coll, *Ghost Wars*, pp. 190–95. Night-vision equipment: "Lion's Breeding Grounds of the Arab Partisans in Afghanistan," 1991, "Rand: Early History of Al Qaeda Working Group, 2006." About one hundred: Bergen and Cruickshank, op. cit.

21. All quotations, interview with Jamal Khashoggi, February 2, 2002.

22. "At that point . . . Arab agents": *Messages to the World*, op. cit., p. 77. The first assassination plot in which Bin Laden is known to have been involved was an attempt on the life of the exiled king of Afghanistan, in 1991.

23. Badeeb, Orbit Television, late 2001, tape of interview supplied to the author by Badeeb, translated by The Language Doctors, Inc. Badeeb said, in full, "I suggested to [Osama] and the others to return to Saudi Arabia, since the task for which they came to Afghanistan was achieved. And in fact, [Osama] did return to the kingdom. We also began to thin out the presence of individuals on the Pakistani-Afghani borders who were involved in assistance. We did not have lists of names of individuals who came to Afghanistan. We believed that these people came and offered their services as a religious duty and thus we did not have any doubts about them."

24. Apple computers: Interview with Daniel Coleman, August 31, 2005. Coleman is a former agent with the Federal Bureau of Investigation, who worked on Bin Laden and Al Qaeda investigations for about ten years, beginning in 1995.

25. "Saudi is . . . reward them": Harmony AFGP-2002-60246. Several government investigators said in interviews that they believed the Golden Chain documents were cred-

ible and authentic. "Bin Laden brothers": "Government's Evidentiary Proffer . . ." in *United States of America v. Enaam Arnout*, United States District Court, Northern District of Illinois, 02-CR-892. "only a list . . . Al Qaeda supporters": Casey's Opinion on jurisdictional issues, *In Re Terrorist Attacks on September 11, 2001*, United States District Court, Southern District of New York, 03 MDL 1570, January 18, 2005. "I have never . . . any kind": Affidavit of Bakr Binladin, *In Re Terrorist Attacks*, sworn in Dubai, United Arab Emirates, January 25, 2006.

26. "a number of times . . . brother would": Interview with Jamal Khashoggi, March 17, 2006, op cit.

27. All quotations, ibid.

25. LUMP SUMS

1. The profile of Bakr here is drawn from interviews with fifteen business partners, employees, family members, government officials, and pilots who have known or worked closely with him.

2. "All his life . . . his brother": Interview with Sabry Ghoneim, a longtime Bin Laden employee in Cairo, November 14, 2005 (RS).

3. All quotations, interview with Yahia El Agaty, November 19, 2005 (RS).

4. The 2.27 percentage is listed in Ibrahim Bin Laden's "Schedule of Assets and Debts," as cited in "Declaration of Barbara L. Irshay," January 21, 1993, in *Christine Binladin v. Ibrahim Binladin*, Los Angeles County, BD058156. I have presumed that this is the ownership percentage of all male sons, and that female heirs own half as much, as provided by Islamic law.

5. "stocks that I inherited": Excerpted deposition testimony of Ibrahim Bin Laden, ibid. "Each beneficiary . . . clearing house": "Declaration of Linda Pergament Swift," May 24, 1993, ibid.

6. Al-Shammary (ed.), *Top 1000 Saudi Companies*, 1990. The directory listed the National Commercial Bank as the kingdom's eighth-largest business enterprise, with about $1.3 billion in annual revenue.

7. Interview with a Bin Laden business partner who asked to not be identified.

8. What the family told the FBI: Interview with Daniel Coleman, August 31, 2005. Coleman is a retired FBI agent who conducted interviews about these financial issues. The reorganization, Bakr's affidavit, the valuation of Osama's holdings circa 1993: Documents submitted by Bin Laden defendants in *In Re Terrorist Attacks on September 11, 2001*, United States District Court, Southern District of New York, 03 MDL 1570. That he owned about 2 percent of each firm: Osama's MBC holding is projected from Ibrahim's deposition testimony, op. cit. SBG holding of "about 2 percent" is disclosed by attorneys for the company in "Defendant Saudi Binladin Group's Reponse . . . To Plaintiffs' Objections . . . Dated July 26, 2007," p. 4, *In Re Terrorist Attacks*.

9. All quotations: Interview with Sabry Ghoneim, November 14, 2005 (RS).

10. "The amount received . . . $20 million": Associated Press, October 29, 2001. Yeslam's tax returns: Nine/Eleven Finding Answers Foundation documents, provided to the author by Douglas Farah. The 9/11 Commission investigation and findings: "Monograph on Terrorist Financing," National Commission on Terrorist Attacks Upon the United

States, Staff Report to the Commission by John Roth, Douglas Greenburg, Serena Wille, August 2004. He remained a partner: Bin Laden documents submitted in *In Re Terrorist Attacks*, ibid.

11. *In Re Terrorist Attacks* documents, ibid. These court filings by Bin Laden defendants affirm that Osama was a partner in both MBC and SBG after the reorganization, but they do not describe the size of Osama's SBG position.

12. No will, beneficiaries: Bexar County, Texas, probate case of Salem Bin Laden, 91-PC-1012.

13. "Deeds Issued by Shari'ah Courts, Registration No. 123, Submission No. 398," Abdul Moshen Bin Abdullah Al-Khayyal, President of the Jeddah Courts, translated and filed in *Ian Munro v. The Dee Howard Company*, Bexar County, Texas, 91-CI-00928.

14. Dietrich settlement: Interview with Thomas Dietrich, April 12, 2006. Bell Canada settlement: Interview with Michael Pochna, August 31, 2006. Shopping center: Interview with Wayne Fagan, May 10, 2005.

15. *Ian Munro v. The Dee Howard Company*, op. cit. Interview with Charles Schwartz, who represented Salem's estate, May 12, 2005. Also, interview with Keith Kaiser, who represented Howard, February 21, 2006.

16. "Financial Position . . . financial affairs": Letter from Bakr M. Binladin to Ian Munro, July 25, 1993, filed in *Ian Munro v. The Dee Howard Company*, ibid.

17. NCB settlement: Interview with Bengt Johansson, October 3, 2006, and a second individual who asked to not be identified. "He didn't . . . debts": Interview with Ghoneim, op. cit.

26. AMERICA IN MOTION

1. Attended USC, did not graduate: E-mail communication, James Grant, USC, March 1, 2006 Khalil majored in mechanical engineering and took classes between the autumn of 1975 and the autumn of 1980, before leaving without a degree. Profile of clothing, cars, habits, competition at card games: Interviews with three individuals who spent extensive time with him and who asked to not be identified, as well as with several neighbors who knew him less well. Aspects of his personality are also available from documents and deposition testimony in more than one dozen civil cases in which he or his companies were involved; see specific citations below.

2. Isabel: Interviews and court documents, ibid. Jonesboro Drive: Los Angeles County property records, examined and typed, June 28, 2005. $600,000 renovation: *Khalil Binladin and Isabel Binladin v. American Builders Association et al.*, Los Angeles County Superior Court, C663911.

3. As of mid-2007, Cappello was managing director of Cappello Capital Corporation, an international investment firm.

4. "If I don't know . . . say no": Interview with an individual who worked with Bin Laden. Business interests: Interviews cited in note 1.

5. Kabeltan Corporation, Carrollton building, Dividend Drive: Dallas County, Texas, property records, examined and typed, February 16, 2006; author's visits to properties. Cappello is listed as Kabeltan's president in Dallas County records of December 30, 1983. Kenny Rogers horse loan: Interviews with two individuals familiar with the transaction,

who asked to not be identified. These people differed slightly in their recollections of the loan amounts but described the deal and the profit margin in closely similar terms. A representative for Kenny Rogers did not respond to requests for comment.

6. Interviews with three individuals, op. cit. In a written declaration filed in *America in Motion Corporation and Khalil Binladin v. Ron R. Goldie et al.*, Los Angeles County Superior Court, WEC13994, Khalil identified Mark Love as an employee since 1985. BIN Corporation is identified in Dallas County property records as a "successor by merger" of Kabeltan Corporation.

7. Tax cases: *Dallas County v. Kabeltan Corp.*, Dallas County, Texas, 92-32136. Los Angeles County real property records document 99-1789705 describes a tax lien against Kabeltan, dating to 1986, involving a total liability of just over $172,000. See also 98-1432057, 97-1237072, 96-1849398, and 97-154966, which describe tax proceedings by Los Angeles County and the State of California against Kabeltan and BIN Corporation. Vituperative lawsuits: *Khalil Binladin and Isabel Bin Laden v. American Builders*, op. cit., and cross complaints.

8. Interviews with three individuals, op. cit. Frisaura said that Khalil Bin Laden was an honorable businessman, but that he would make no additional comment.

9. Leasing dispute history: *America in Motion Corp. v. Magnum Aircraft International*, Los Angeles County Superior Court, NWC043648. "a small corporation . . . $225,000 jet": Declaration of Darius Keaton, ibid., March 9, 1989. No judgment or settlement: E-mail communication from Kevin S. Marks, attorney for Clint Eastwood, September 7, 2007.

10. "a chartered accountant in Pakistan": Proposed Joint Statement of the case, Ron R. Goldie, *America in Motion and Khalil Binladin v. Ron R. Goldie*, op. cit. Also, Khan's statement of the case, Khalil's deposition testimony and declarations, ibid.

11. "an undivided . . . Massachusetts": Goldie proposed statement, ibid. Resun history: Company Web site, examined and typed, June 5, 2007. The company did not respond to a request for comment.

12. "Rebate": Excerpted deposition testimony of Khalil Bin Laden, ibid. "kick back": Letter from Ali-Khan to Khalil Bin Laden, February 28, 1989, ibid. Debt to Indosuez exceeded $3 million: Letter from Ali-Khan to Khalil Bin Laden, May 31, 1989, "Situation Report." Default: In excerpted deposition testimony, Mark Love acknowledges receipt of a default notice from Indosuez, although he describes this as "just a technical issue on behalf of the bank."

13. "loan": Letter from Ali-Khan to Bin Laden, May 26, 1989, "Re: Your Fax . . ." ibid. "my personal guarantee": Letter from Ali-Khan to Bin Laden, May 31, 1989, "Situation Report." "Please provide . . . a copy": Letter from Bin Laden to Ali-Khan, May 23, 1989, "Re: Your fax . . . " "The faxes . . . guaranteed": Letter from Khalil Bin Laden to Ali-Khan, date illegible, June 1989. All from court file, ibid.

14. "the $130,000 . . . by Khan": Declaration of Khalil Bin Laden, July 13, 1992, ibid. September 22, 1989: Los Angeles Police Department preliminary investigation report, ibid. "if this . . . this form":" Excerpted deposition testimony of Khalil Bin Laden, ibid.

15. *The People of the State of California v. Mussarat Ali Khan*, "Felony Complaint for Arrest Warrant." "possible international . . . in Paris": "Declaration for Bail Deviation," filed in *America in Motion Corporation and Khalil Binladin v. Ron R. Goldie et al.*, op. cit.

16. Declaration of Geoffrey Morson, ibid.

17. Declaration of Khalil Bin Laden, ibid.

18. "unable to leave . . . pay monies": Elizabeth Borges responses to interrogatories, *Isabel Binladin v. Elizabeth Borges*, Los Angeles County Superior Court, SCoo3124.

19. All quotations, Elizabeth Borges responses to interrogatories, ibid.

20. "slanderous . . . Saudi Arabian visas": Bin Laden complaint, September 5, 1990, ibid.

21. All quotations, ibid.

22. All quotations, Borges answer to the complaint, ibid.

23. Interview with an individual familiar with the transaction who asked to not be identified.

27. THE SWISS ACCOUNTS

1. The August 6 meeting has been described similarly, with slight variations, in a number of published accounts. Schwarzkopf on his knee: Freeman quoted in *The House of Saud*, Algeria Productions, 2004. See also Bronson, *Thicker Than Oil*, pp. 194–95; Clarke, *Against All Enemies*, pp. 57–59. Lippman, *Inside the Mirage*, pp. 300–1.

2. "Don't you think . . . take your point": Freeman, ibid. "Okay": Lippman, ibid.

3. "to increase . . . of Muslims": Lawrence (ed.), *Messages to the World*, pp. 198–99.

4. Family foundation, previous accounts in a Swiss bank: Interviews with international banking officials who asked to not be identified. The Swiss Bank Corporation account documents were submitted as exhibits by lawyers for the Bin Ladens in *In Re Terrorist Attacks on September 11, 2001*, United States District Court, Southern District of New York, 03 MDL 157. "Sub-accounts . . . invasion of Kuwait": Affidavit of Omar Bin Laden, January 25, 2006, *In Re Terrorist Attacks*.

5. All account document quotations, dates, financial transfers, from original account documents submitted by attorneys for the Bin Ladens in *In Re Terrorist Attacks*, ibid.

6. "has been forbidden . . . your economy": *Messages to the World*, op. cit., p. 167.

7. Interview with Khaled Batarfi, February 19, 2005.

8. Islamists in South Yemen: Interview with Dominic Simpson, former British intelligence officer who served in both Saudi Arabia and Yemen, May 17, 2002. "did have . . . funded everything": "Interview with Shaykh Al-Fadli On Aden-Abyan Islamic Army . . ." *Al-Quds Al-Arabi*, November 8, 2001, FBIS translation. See also "Yemen's Enduring Challenges . . ." *TerrorismMonitor*, Jamestown Foundation, Volume II, Issue 7, April 8, 2004, interview with former U.S. Treasury official Jonathan Winer.

9. "had reportedly asked . . . regime": *Against All Enemies*, op. cit., p. 59. "came to see me . . . not acceptable idea": Quoted in *Meeting Osama Bin Laden*, Brook Lapping Productions, 2004.

10. Badeeb: Interview with Orbit Television, tape provided by Badeeb to the author, translated by The Language Doctors, Inc. Raid on Bin Laden's farm: Sharaf Al-Din, *Bin Laden . . . the Arab Afghans*, pp. 52–53.

11. Coll, *Ghost Wars*, p. 222. Prince's identity: Osama says it was the "deputy minister," who at the time of the meeting would have been Abdul-Rahman, but at the time of Osama's statement, the deputy was Khalid Bin Sultan.

12. *Messages to the World*, op. cit., p. 257.

13. "This shy . . . changed": Quoted in *Meeting Osama Bin Laden*, op. cit.

14. Affidavit of Omar Bin Laden, *In Re Terrorist Attacks*, op. cit. All quotations from the

U.S. military are from documents submitted by Bin Laden attorneys in *In Re Terrorist Attacks*.

15. Al-Rasheed, *A History of Saudi Arabia*, p. 168.

16. Ibid., p. 167. Also, Fandy, *Saudi Arabia and the Politics of Dissent*, pp. 48–52.

17. "He apologized . . . peaceful way": Interview with Abdulaziz Al-Gasim, February 8, 2005.

18. Interview with Jamal Khashoggi, March 17, 2006. All quotations from Khashoggi, "To Be Strong by Spreading Fear," *Al Watan Al Arabi*, April 5, 2005.

19. May 1: *Messages to the World*, op. cit. p. 33. Left voluntarily: Affidavit of Bakr Bin Laden, *In Re Terrorist Attacks*, January 25, 2006. Sudan rentals, farm north of Khartoum, $250,000, Egyptian lawyer: Testimony of Jamal Al-Fadl, *United States of America v. Usama bin Laden et al.*, United States District Court, Southern District of New York, S 98 Cr. 539, February 6, 2001. "spent some time . . . economic activities": Interview with Khalil A. Khalil, February 10, 2005.

20. *Messages to the World*, pp. 49–50.

21. All Bruderlein quotations from Affidavit of Yves Bruderlein, *In Re Terrorist Attacks*, January 24, 2006, and "Minutes of a Witness Statement," The Office of the Swiss Federal Public Prosecutor, Bern, October 9, 2001, submitted as an exhibit in the same case.

22. Affidavit of Bakr Bin Laden, op. cit.

23. October 28 transfer: Account documents, op. cit., *In Re Terrorist Attacks*. Money went initially to Haider's custody: Interview with two individuals familiar with the transaction, who asked to not be identified. Last known use of Western banks: Michael Scheuer, writing as "Anonymous," the former chief of the CIA unit that tracked Osama's finances during the late 1990s, writes in *Through Our Enemies' Eyes*, p. 35: "My own pre–11 September 2001 research found no data showing that any money tied directly to Bin Laden had been located, blocked or seized in the West's [banking and financial] system."

28. A ROLLS-ROYCE IN THE RAIN

1. All quotations from the beginning of the chapter through "adequate" are from "Declaration of Christine Binladin," February 18, 1992, filed in *Christine Binladin v. Ibrahim Binladin*, BD058156, Los Angeles County Superior Court.

2. Ibrahim with Dodi Fayed: Interview with Jack Kayajanian, August 25, 2005; Kayajanian represented Christine after her divorce litigation resumed in 2002. Never filed a tax return: Christine's "Trial Brief," *Binladin v. Binladin*, op. cit. "a very . . . young lady": Telephone interview with Michael Balaban, June 15, 2005. Denim and Diamonds: Décor described in *Time*, March 15, 1993.

3. Interview with Balaban, ibid. Representatives for McCartney did not respond to requests for comment.

4. "In the end . . . pay for this' and Ibrahim's comments about work: Interview with an employee of the Bin Ladens who asked to not be identified.

5. An unsigned copy of the agreement was filed in *Binladin v. Binladin*, op. cit.

6. Christine's excerpted deposition testimony, ibid.

7. Consecrated under Islamic law: "Final Divorce Judgment," July 6, 1993, ibid. "and the wine . . . sight!": Freeman, "The Saudi Connection," unpublished manuscript.

8. All quotations in this passage from Ibrahim's excerpted deposition testimony, *Binladin v. Binladin*, op. cit.

9. "Declaration of Christine Binladin," December 1992, ibid.

10. "I see very . . . unhappy man": "Declaration of Ibrahim Binladin," December 22, 1992, ibid.

11. Christine's excerpted deposition testimony, op. cit.

12. "Declaration of Ibrahim Binladin," op. cit.

13. "She only started . . . from me": "Declaration of Ibrahim Binladin," ibid. "remained with . . . long enough": "Respondent's Memorandum of Points and Authorities For Trial," January 21, 1993, ibid.

29. THE CONSTRUCTION OF EXILE

1. Contract in 1989: Affidavit of Omar Bin Laden, January 25, 2006, *In Re Terrorist Attacks on September 11, 2001*, United States District Court, Southern District of New York, 03 MDL 1570. Contract price, role of Saudi Overseas Development Fund: *Okaz*, June 25, 1992, translated and filed in the same case by Bin Laden attorneys.

2. Testimony of Jamal Al-Fadl, *United States of America v. Usama bin Laden et al.*, United States District Court, Southern District of New York, S 98 Cr. 539, February 6, 2001.

3. Bosnia fundraiser: *Arab News*, July 6, 1992. Osama's team to Bosnia: "Former Bin Laden 'Bodyguard' Discusses 'Jihad' in Bosnia, Somalia," interview with Nasir Al-Bahri, *Al-Quds Al-Arabi*, March 24, 2005. "Gifts of charity . . . weapons": Harmony AFGP 2002-003214–Statement 18, "Tragedy of Bosnia and Deceit of Saudi Arabia," August 11, 1995.

4. Interview with a Bin Laden employee who asked to not be identified.

5. Al-Fadl testimony, February 6, 2001, op. cit.

6. "a new airport . . . joint venture": Clarke, *Against All Enemies*, p. 136. "built the Port Sudan airport": Bergen, *The Osama Bin Laden I Know*, pp. 122–23. "to the best . . . controlled by Osama": Affidavit of Omar Bin Laden, op. cit.

7. "This project . . . participated in it": *Okaz*, June 25, 1992.

8. "guest of honor": "Part One of Series of Reports on Bin Laden's Life in Sudan," *Al-Quds Al-Arabi*, November 24, 2001. "To the best . . . the Sudan": Affidavit of Omar Bin Laden, op. cit.

9. Bakr met with Osama during 1992: Affidavit of Bakr Bin Laden, January 25, 2006, *In Re Terrorist Attacks*, op. cit. "accompanied by . . . set": Letter to the author from Timothy J. Finn, October 31, 2007. "almost nine": Lawrence (ed.), *Messages to the World*, p. 55. "Late 1992 . . . States": Affidavit of Tareq Bin Laden, January 25, 2006, *In Re Terrorist Attacks*.

10. "became clear . . . refuse to return": Badeeb interview with Orbit Television circa late 2001, tape provided to the author by Badeeb, translated by The Language Doctors, Inc.

11. Interviews with two individuals who asked to not be identified. "I apologized . . . against them": *Messages to the World*, op. cit., p. 55.

12. "He was out of touch . . . so important": Interview with Jamal Khashoggi, March 17, 2006. Osama's Sudan activity: Al-Fadl testimony, op. cit.; *The Osama Bin Laden I Know*, op. cit., various testimony, pp. 126–32.

13. For example: "Global Network Provides Money, Haven," by Steve Coll and Steve

LeVine, *Washington Post*, August 3, 1993. Drawing upon LeVine's visit to Khartoum, where he unsuccessfully sought an interview with Bin Laden at his villa, the story reported: "Today Bin Laden lives in exile in a posh neighborhood of Khartoum, Sudan, building roads and airports for Sudan's new radical Islamic government, financing a lavish guest house for itinerant Arab veterans of the Afghan conflict and lecturing at times on revolutionary Islam, according to Sudanese businessmen, officials and diplomats." The story also made particular reference to the government of Egypt's antipathy toward Bin Laden and the exiled radicals he harbored in Sudan.

14. "Everything appeared . . . the regime": Fandy, *Saudi Arabia and the Politics of Dissent*, p. 119.

15. Ibid., p. 181.

16. Affidavit of Bakr Bin Laden, op. cit.

17. Ghalib's Al-Taqwa account and all quotations from documents filed in *In Re Terrorist Attacks*, op. cit. Ghalib's 1989 visit: See chapter 24. U.S. Treasury assessment: Letter from George B. Wolfe, Treasury deputy general counsel to Claude Nicati, office of the Swiss prosecutor general, January 4, 2002.

18. "To deprive . . . companies": Letter from Timothy J. Finn, op. cit. "Osama's . . . Middle East": Affidavit of Tareq Bin Laden, op. cit. "brother-to-brother": Interview with Khashoggi, op. cit. "With God's grace . . . go back": *Messages to the World*, op. cit., p. 55.

19. *Messages to the World*, ibid.

20. "take this money . . . other relatives": Interview with Abdulaziz Al-Gasim, February 8, 2005. Gasim said that in his work as an attorney, he had "seen legal papers, very secret, describing all this." About $9.9 million and all Bakr quotations: Affidavit of Bakr Bin Laden, op. cit. If, as court documents indicate, Osama owned about 2 percent of each of the two main family companies, and if the $10 million price of his shares reflected full value, this would mean the total market value of the Bin Laden enterprises in 1994 was approximately a combined $500 million.

21. *Al Nadwah*, February 20, 1994, translated and filed by Bin Laden attorneys, *In Re Terrorist Attacks*, op. cit.

22. Government announcement: *Riyadh Daily*, April 7, 1994. "never had access . . . control": "Defendant Saudi Binladin Group's Response to Plaintiffs' Objections . . . Dated July 26, 2007," *In Re Terrorist Attacks*, op. cit.

23. Al-Fawwaz's education: *Al Majallah*, March 14, 1999. Arrest, movements: Prosecutor's closing statements, *United States v. Usama Bin Laden et al.*, op. cit., May 1, 2001.

24. *Saudi Arabia and the Politics of Dissent*, op. cit., p. 181.

25. Ibid., p. 182.

26. The author is grateful to Bruce Hoffman, Kim Cragin, Nadia Oweidat, Sara Daly, Heather Gregg, and Anna Kasupski of the Early History of Al Qaeda Working Group for access to these texts from the "Harmony" collection, many of which were translated during 2006. "Supreme Council for Damage," Harmony AFGP 2002-003214–Statement 10, October 15, 1994.

27. "shady history . . . Muslims": Harmony AFGP 2002-003214–Statement 10.

28. "has a shady past . . . on its people": Harmony AFGP 2002-003214–Statement 13, "Prince

Salman and Charity Offerings in Ramadan," February 12, 1995. "tricksters": Ibid., Statement 16, "Prince Sultan and Flight Commissions," July 11, 1995. "hostile to Islam and Muslims": Ibid., Statement 18, "Tragedy of Bosnia and Deceit of Saudi Arabia," August 11, 1995.

29. Affidavit of Carmen Bin Laden, February 1, 2006, *In Re Terrorist Attacks*, op. cit.

30. Testimony of Jamal Al-Fadl, op. cit. "We had . . . his people": Quoted in Bergen and Cruickshank, "How the Idea of Al Qaeda Was Conceived . . . " 2006.

31. Harmony Statement 13, op. cit., February 12, 1995.

32. "she could not . . . hardship": *Al-Quds Al-Arabi*, March 30, 2005. "because my father . . . to my desires": *Al-Sharq Al-Awsat*, October 21, 2001. "avoided mentioning . . . hurt by him": *Al-Quds Al-Arabi*, March 30, 2005.

33. Khalifa: *Al-Sharq Al-Awsat*, May 4, 2002. Government put them on notice, donated to king's charities: Interview with a Bin Laden employee in Jeddah at the time, who asked to not be identified.

34. Affidavit of Omar Bin Laden, op. cit.

35. "I am tired . . . nostalgic I am": Hassan Al-Surayhi, *The Osama Bin Laden I Know*, op. cit. p. 126. Osama's interest in asylum in Britain was disclosed by Michael Howard, who was Home Secretary during the mid-1990s. *Times* (London) September 29, 2005.

36. "Emigration . . . Day of Judgment,' *Messages to the World*, op. cit., p. 19. "I tell you . . . pleasure of God": *Messages to the World*, p. 91.

30. HEDGE FUNDS

1. Interview with Chas Freeman, June 15, 2005, and with other officials who asked to not be identified.

2. Ibid.

3. Articles of incorporation filed by attorneys for Saudi Bin Laden Group in *In Re Terrorist Attacks on September 11, 2001*, United States District Court, Southern District of New York, 03 MDL 1570.

4. Interviews with former and current Bin Laden employees and partners who asked to not be identified.

5. Lucrative GE contracts: *Arab News*, April 18, 1996. *Saudi Gazette*, April 19, 1996. Party for Welch: Jane Mayer, *New Yorker*, November 12, 2001. Sarkissian office in New Jersey, Dallas-area projects: Interview with an individual familiar with the partnerships, who asked to not be identified. Directors of SBG (USA): Records submitted by Saudi Bin Laden Group, *In Re Terrorist Attacks*, op. cit.

6. Rihani's background: Interview with a colleague who asked to not be identified. His title, board service at Middle East Policy Council, Freeman as chairman: www.mepc.org, examined and typed, June 29, 2007.

7. A brother might open a travel agency, an American firm hired to inventory holdings: Interview with an individual close to the Saudi Bin Laden Group who asked to not be identified. "tank tops . . . denims . . ." and varied business lines: Saudi Bin Laden Group directory, from corporate Web site examined and printed by Peter Bergen prior to September 11, 2001. The author is grateful to Peter Bergen for access to these documents.

8. Loans to offshore companies: Russell Wood Limited filings, Companies House, London, 1996. The firm had outstanding loans to Celta Finance SA (117,669 pounds),

Tropiville BV (2,048,498 pounds), and Saudi Investment Company (International) BVI (1,772,304 pounds). "We are unable . . . all respects . . . ": Russell Wood Limited filings, Companies House, London, 1991. The auditor was Stoy Hayward. Securities and Futures Authority required: Russell Wood (Holdings) Limited filings, Companies House, 1997.

9. Moawalla background, Pilley: Russell Wood Limited filings, Companies House, London, 1987–1997. "You don't have a need": Interview with a former colleague of Moawalla who asked to not be identified.

10. Hotel rooms, appearance: Photographs examined by the author, interviews with three acquaintances of Shafiq. January 1958: Symphony Advisers Ltd. filings, Companies House, London, 2000. USF: Telephone interviews with Gary McDonald, March 15 and 16, 2006. Could hold his own: Interview with a colleague who asked to not be identified. Investment committee: Interview with a second business partner who asked to not be identified.

11. Briody, *The Iron Triangle*, pp. 1–89.

12. Ibid., pp. 69–80.

13. Raised $1.3 billion and California Public Employees: Ibid., p. 85; Soros: Ibid., p. 84.

14. Briody: Ibid., p. 145, quotes Basil Al-Rahim, an exiled Iraqi financier, saying that he brought the Bin Ladens into the Carlyle investment. The thrust of this account was confirmed by an individual familiar with the investment who asked to not be identified. The Bin Laden investment in Carlyle was about $2 million at the time it was sold in the autumn of 2001, but Briody's reporting suggests that the family may have made and cashed out larger investments during the 1990s. "knew them . . . favorite politician": Telephone interview with Charles Schwartz, September 20, 2006.

15. Saudi purchase, Middle East Broadcasting support: Interview with Tobin Beck, former UPI editor, October 12, 2005. "I don't appreciate . . . service": Interview with Arnaud de Borchgrave, March 10, 2005.

16. "clearly a man": Interview with Borchgrave, ibid.

17. Interviews with two family members and several Desert Bear neighbors who asked to not be identified.

18. The portrait is drawn from interviews with several former classmates and Abdullah's academic adviser. Range Rover: Telephone interview with Nada Abdelsater-Abusamra, January 2006 (RS). Near Beacon Street, Papa Razzi: Telephone interview with Lama Abu-Odeh, January 15, 2006 (RS).

19. "I would tease . . . you can tell me": All quotations from interview with Abu-Odeh, ibid.

20. Ibid.

21. "It could well be . . . feasible": Bin Laden, "Western Banking Practices . . . " p. 2.

22. "the academic . . . religion": Interview with Frank Vogel, December 2005 (RS).

23. "They were interested . . . Middle East": Interview with Vogel, ibid.

24. Interview with Andrew Hess, December 2005 (RS).

25. Ibid.

31. A TROJAN DESK

1. Car bomb: United States Senate Select Committee on Intelligence, staff report, September 12, 1996. Former Vinnell board member: Briody, *The Iron Triangle*, p. 67.

2. Christmas 1995, Bakr flew guests from America: Interview with Gerald Auerbach, May 11, 2005.

3. Interviews with several guests and members who have visited since the 1990s. The author visited the club as a guest more recently. 201 bedroom chalets and studios: Saudi Bin Laden Group Web site, pages examined and printed by Peter Bergen prior to September 11, 2001.

4. Interview with Auerbach, op. cit.

5. Ibrahim family real estate holdings: *Los Angeles Business Journal*, July 26, 1993, citing a press release from Newfield Enterprises International, a family holding company. "heart of hearts . . . next king": Interview with Wyche Fowler, June 1, 2005.

6. "abrupt, impulsive . . . popular": in Burdett (ed.), *Records of Saudi Arabia, 1966–1971, Volume 2: 1967, Part I.*

7. CIA request, all quotations from Scheuer: Interview with Michael Scheuer, July 5, 2005. Clarke on Yemen: Clarke, *Against All Enemies*, p. 59.

8. Interviews with four former U.S. officials familiar with the bugging incident and its aftermath. Robert Baer, a former CIA officer, in his book *Sleeping with the Devil*, apparently tried to disclose this incident publicly for the first time but had the material redacted by CIA censors, to whom he was required to submit his manuscript because of his previous government service. To show readers where censors had taken out material from his draft, Baer inserted black lines in his published book. On page 18, he wrote, "I often wondered why [Nayef] hated the U.S. so much." This sentence is followed by five redacted lines. (Baer was not a source for the disclosure here, so it is possible that he was trying to make a different point.)

32. THE AESTHETICS OF WORSHIP

1. Hammoudi, *A Season in Mecca*. "Through the window . . . firmament": pp. 74–75. "shop-windows . . . neon-lit boards": pp. 82–84. "'Modernity' ravaged everything": p. 111.

2. Ibid., pp. 109–15.

3. "deliberate desire": Ibid., p. 114. The $25 billion figure is regularly cited in press accounts, e.g., *Time*, October 7, 2001. The Bin Ladens themselves, in their self-published book *Story of the Great Expansion*, refer to "more than 50 billion Saudi riyals" in total spending, or at least $12 billion.

4. Prophet's Mosque about one-tenth the size of the Grand Mosque: Abbas, *Story of the Great Expansion*, p. 371. Other details of the projects, and their sequence, are drawn from this official Bin Laden company account.

5. Interview with Anwar Hassan, York International Corporation, October 13, 2005, and written briefing materials supplied to the author by Hassan and his colleagues.

6. All quotations from Hassan interview, ibid.

7. Angawi's background and "to preserve . . . holy cities": Interview with Sami Angawi, April 25, 2005.

8. Ibid.

9. "The largest . . . souls": Caudill, "Twlight of the Hejaz" (manuscript), pp. 74–75.

10. *Story of the Great Expansion*, op. cit., pp. 51–64.

11. Interview with Angawi, op. cit.

12. "This is where . . . heritage": Interview with a Jeddah professional who asked to not be identified.

13. Interview with Angawi, op. cit.

14. Ibid.

15. *Story of the Great Expansion*, op. cit., dedication by Bakr Bin Laden.

16. All quotations from "The Saudi Regime and Repeated Tragedies of the Pilgrims," Harmony AFGP 2002-003214, Statement 19.

33. ONE PHONE, ONE WORLD

1. *Independent* (London), May 18, 1998.

2. Whalen, "Communications Satellites: Making the Global Village Possible," www.hq.nasa.gov, examined and typed, July 17, 2006.

3. Around 1987, about $5 billion: *New York Times*, April 11, 2000. Motorola's fixed-price contract of about $3.5 billion: Securities and Exchange Commission, Iridium LLC, S-4 filing, July 21, 1997.

4. Swiss conference, "drop down . . . ": Telephone interview with F. Thomas Tuttle, July 19, 2006.

5. Trinford Investments: S-4 filing, op. cit., July 21, 1997. The two $40 million cash contributions are described in this document and by Tuttle, ibid., and a second former Iridium executive who asked to not be identified. Raised $3.46 billion: S-4, ibid. The final amount of equity investments may have been higher; it was supplemented by bank lending.

6. Iridium Middle East in Washington, Hassan at board meetings: Interviews with four former executives, three at Iridium, including Tuttle, who were familiar with the operation.

7. Johnny Walker sessions, and "has been ex-communicated": Interview with a former Iridium executive. Hassan's nocturnal habits were described in interviews by two former colleagues in the United States and several of his acquaintances in Beirut and Jeddah.

8. Major shareholder in Hard Rock Middle East: E-mail communication from Hard Rock spokesman, January 23, 2006. Slang, every pinball machine: Interview with a colleague in Beirut who asked to not be identified. Youth in Beirut, Layla, lived in hotels: Telephone interview with Layla Moussa, April 24, 2006 (RS). Cars, Al-Ittihad, Umm Kulsum: Interview with the Beirut colleague, op. cit., and a second Beirut acquaintance.

9. Opening night, list of paraphernalia: Interview with a colleague who attended; details posted on the restaurant's Web site, examined and typed by R.S., April 2006; site visit by R.S., April 2006.

10. Market size, 14 million wireless customers: S-4 filing, op. cit., July 21, 1997. Phones three thousand dollars, calls up to seven dollars per minute: *New York Times*, April 11, 2000.

11. "complete the telephone . . . very proud": *Washington Post*, August 21, 1999.

12. "I had a Mongolian": Interview with a former Iridium executive, who asked to not be identified. "What we had": Interview with Tuttle, op. cit.

13. S-4 filing, op. cit., July 21, 1997.

14. Transcript of Khaled Batarfi interview with Osama's mother, supplied to the author by Batarfi.

15. "Bin Laden 'Bodyguard' Details Al Qaeda's Time in Sudan, Move to Afghanistan," *Al-Quds Al-Arabi*, March 28, 2005. FBIS translation.

16. Public Broadcasting System translation. www.pbs.org/newshour/terrorism/international/fatwa_1996.html, examined and typed, July 10, 2007.

17. "Former Bin Laden 'Bodyguard' Discusses Al Qaeda Training Methods, 'Libraries,'" *Al-Quds Al-Arabi*, March 26, 2005. FBIS translation.

18. "What is . . . all and sundry": 'Bodyguard Interviewed on First Meeting With Bin Laden," *Al-Quds Al-Arabi*, March 26, 2005. FBIS translation.

19. Bergen, *The Osama Bin Laden I Know*, p. 165.

20. "like sort . . . a fish": Ibid., p. 181. "did not like . . . very late": "Bin Laden's Wife Interviewed . . . " *Al-Majallah*, March 10, 2002. FBIS translation.

21. Testimony of Detective Inspector Noel Feeney, *United States v. Usama Bin Laden et al.*, United States District Court, Southern District of New York, 98CR1023, March 27, 2001.

22. *The News* (Islamabad), June 16, 1998. English original, FBIS transmission.

23. Purchase November 1, 1996: Trial stipulations, *U.S. v. Usama Bin Laden et al.*, op. cit., March 27, 2001. Inmarsat history, market position: Interviews with two former Iridium executives.

24. Call records: *Sunday Times* (London), March 24, 2002, and *Newsweek*, February 25, 2002.

25. Interview with Michael Scheuer, July 5, 2005.

26. Scheure (as "Anonymous"), *Through Our Enemies' Eyes*, pp. 22–23.

27. Interview with Tuttle, op. cit. Statements to press: *Daily News* (New York), August 27, 1998. *Interspace*, September 9, 1998.

28. Only fifty-five thousand subscribers, write-offs of more than $2.5 billion: *New York Times*, April 11, 2000.

29. Department of Defense transcript, news briefing, December 8, 2000.

34. LAWYERS, GUNS, AND MONEY

1. Interview with Daniel Coleman, August 31, 2005.

2. That the Sudan files were very detailed: Interviews with two U.S. officials who read the files later. Two defectors in 1996, first introduction of the term "Al Qaeda": Interview with Coleman, ibid.

3. National Commission on Terrorist Attacks Upon the United States (the 9/11 Commission), "Monograph on Terrorist Financing," Staff Report to the Commission by John Roth, Douglas Greenburg, Serena Wille, August 2004, p. 35.

4. Scheuer's skepticism about money investigations: "Monograph on Terrorist Financing," ibid., p. 36. Also, interview with Michael Scheuer, July 5, 2005, and interview with Coleman, op. cit.

5. Interview with Coleman, op. cit. Griffin declined to comment.

6. "proper conversation . . . talking about": Interview with Coleman, op. cit.

7. All quotations from interview with Coleman. Urowsky declined to comment.

8. "at the senior . . . kind of trouble": All quotations from interview with Scheuer. Freeh declined to comment.

9. "They said . . . economic system": Ibid.

10. "Okay . . . establishments": Ibid.

11. Interviews with Wyche Fowler Jr., June 1, 2005, and John Brennan, September 13, 2006.

12. Ibid.

13. Investigators for the 9/11 Commission, after a thorough review of classified U.S. records, reported that neither the White House nor the intelligence community understood the details of Osama's inheritance until 1999 or 2000. It is possible, however, that some of this information surfaced earlier, at least in outline form; for instance, as part of Dan Coleman's early interviews with Osama's half-brothers. If so, the information never reached the National Security Council.

14. Interview with Brennan, op. cit.

15. "a decided reluctance . . . his brothers": Interview with Scheuer, op. cit.

16. Interviews with Fowler and Brennan, op. cit. Fowler also said, "One will recall that all the members of the Bin Laden family in the U.S. were allowed to return to Saudi Arabia in the days after September 11, which is because the FBI and the White House had cleared them of any terroristic activities, and because of the complete cooperation of the Bin Laden family in the three or four years preceding 9/11."

17. Inventory of CIA concerns: Interviews with four former U.S. officials familiar with the CIA's investigations, including Scheuer, op. cit. Khalfa used M.B.C. travel office: Affidavit of M.B.C. employee Eulalio Dela Pat. December 1, 2005, *In Re Terrorist Attacks*.

18. "Monograph on Terrorist Financing," op. cit., p. 39.

19. Interviews with three former U.S. officials involved in the discussions.

20. That Abdullah Bin Awadh of WAMY is a nephew of Osama: Affidavit of Omar M. Bin Laden, *In Re Terrorist Attacks on September 11, 2001*, United States District Court, Southern District of New York, 03 MDL 1570, January 25, 2006. The same information is also cited in "Supplemental Declaration In Support of Pre-Trial Detention," an affidavit by Bureau of Immigration and Customs Enforcement Senior Special Agent David Kane, filed in *U.S. v. Soliman S. Biheiri*, September 11, 2003; Kane attributes the information to an interview with Biheiri, who said he managed investments from Abdullah. None of these documents identifies which of Osama's half-brothers or half-sisters is Abdullah's parent, however. Two of Osama's half-sisters, Iman and Nur, are identified by Biheiri as investors in the same projects as Abdullah, according to Kane.

21. More than fifty offices, five continents: Kane affidavit, ibid. Abdullah's account of his activities, including all quotations from "the deliberate . . ." through "good word" are from "Saudi Arabia: Paper on Efforts to Promote Islam in U.S.," *Al-Sharq Al-Awsat*, October 19, 1997, FBIS translation. The quotations appear to be the journalist's paraphrase of Abdullah's remarks.

22. Kane affidavit, op. cit.

23. Interview with Coleman, op. cit.

24. Kane affidavit, op. cit. Also, notes from a Biheiri interrogation by Immigration and Customs Enforcement agents in June 2003, filed in Alexandria federal court: Notes from the transcript taken by *Washington Post* reporter Mary Beth Sheridan and generously shared with the author by her.

25. "has long acted": "Declaration in Support of Pre-Trial Detention," affidavit of David Kane, *United States of America v. Soliman S. Biheiri*, United States District Court, Eastern District of Virginia, 03-365-A. August 14, 2003. "indirect investment . . . on request": Letter from George B. Wolfe, Deputy General Counsel, U.S. Treasury Department, to Claude

Nicati, Office of the Swiss Prosecutor General, January 4, 2002. Ghalib's account history and lawsuit: Documents submitted in *In Re Terrorist Attacks*, op. cit. "seeking to put the bank out of business": "Defendant Saudi Bin Ladin Group's Response to Plaintiffs' Objections . . . Dated July 26, 2007," ibid.

26. An offshore entity controlled by Saudi Bin Laden Group: Declaration of Johann DeVilliers, Global Diamond chairman, *Mood v. Global Diamond Resources*, United States District Court, Southern District of California, 99cv01565. DeVilliers referred to the controlling entity as "The Bin Laden Group." He described Al-Qadi as a "principal of one of the Middle Eastern investors." Al-Qadi designation: http://www.ustreas.gov/offices/enforcement/ofac/sdn/sdnlist.txt. Examined and typed, July 16, 2007. "front": Citation quoted in *Chicago Tribune*, October 28, 2001. Al-Qadi denied, met Osama in 1980s: *Chicago Tribune*, ibid.; "Saudi Businessman on U.S. List . . . Dismisses Charge," *Al-Sharq Al-Awsat*, October 14, 2001, FBIS translation.

27. Scheuer, as "Anonymous," *Through Our Enemies' Eyes*, p. 34.

28. "lots of talk . . . been named": Interview with Dominic Simpson, May 17, 2002.

29. "always got . . . for him": Ibid. "generally turned away": "Monograph on Terrorist Financing," op. cit., pp. 17–18.

30. November 1998 CIA report, "reasonable estimate": "Monograph on Terrorist Financing," op. cit., p. 20. DIA report: Redacted and released, Judicial Watch, Inc.

31. "This is insane . . . from daddy": Clarke, *Against All Enemies*, p. 191.

32. Interviews with former U.S. officials.

33. The account of the meeting in Saudi Arabia is from several former U.S. officials. See also Clarke, op. cit., pp. 191–95, and "Monograph on Terrorist Financing," op. cit., which provide similar accounts.

34. Interviews with three U.S. officials and former officials familiar with the discussions.

35. For the details of what the Bin Ladens finally disclosed to Treasury, see also "Monograph on Terrorist Financing," op. cit., p. 20. This otherwise admirable study, in seeking to debunk the $300 million myth publicly, contains one dubious assertion, referring to Osama's forced sales of shares in 1994: "The Saudi freeze had the effect of divesting Bin Laden of what would otherwise have been a $300 million fortune." This is a considerable overstatement: even today, after inflation and growth in the Bin Laden empire, ownership of between 1 and 2 percent of the Bin Laden companies, as Osama seems to have possessed in 1994, would almost certainly be worth much less.

36. Interview with Coleman, op. cit.

37. "We presently . . . his cause": "Monograph on Terrorist Financing," op. cit., p. 18.

38. Interviews with two individuals who reviewed the FBI's pre-9/11 files on Bin Laden finances.

39. Interview with Coleman, op. cit., and a second senior former FBI official.

40. "hampered . . . disruption": "Monograph on Terrorist Financing," op. cit., p. 6. Africa $10,000, 9/11 about $400,000: Ibid., pp. 27–28.

41. Estimates of Al Qaeda budgeting, late 1990s: Ibid., pp. 18, 28. Omar's palace, mosque, shopping market: Author's visit to Kandahar, 2002. Even these Al Qaeda budget figures are at best approximations, little more than educated guesses. As the authors of the monograph, who systematically reviewed U.S. intelligence in this area, conceded, "There

is much the U.S. government did not know (and still does not know) about Bin Laden's resources and how Al Qaeda raises, moves, and spends its money."

35. BIN LADEN ISLAND

1. "There's only one sheikh . . . family": Interview with an individual close to the Bin Laden family, who asked to not be identified. The portrait of Bakr that follows is drawn primarily from interviews with this person and three other people, who asked to not be identified, who interacted with Bakr during this period.

2. Cairo, Kuala Lumpur, Amman Grand Hyatt: Saudi Bin Laden Group Web site pages printed by Peter Bergen in the summer of 2001 and shared with the author. United Medical Group: www.umgco.com, examined and typed, July 20, 2006.

3. Badging policy, severance policy: Saudi Bin Laden Group employment policy documents filed in *Mood v. Global Diamond Resources, et al.,* United States District Court, Southern District of California, 99cv01565.

4. Interviews with individuals close to the family who asked to not be identified.

5. Caudill, "Twilight in the Hejaz" (manuscript), pp. 138–39.

6. Agence France Presse, February 18, 2001; *Mail on Sunday* (London), February 18, 2001; *Observer* (London), February 18, 2001; *Press Association* (London), February 17, 2001.

7. Ibid. The exchange was reported in the same way by multiple British journalists, all of whom were traveling in Saudi Arabia with Prince Charles at the time and all of whom sourced the exchange to a person present at the event.

8. Preferred the plural "Faiths": *Daily Telegraph* (London), January 11, 2005. "misunderstandings . . . from Islam": "Islam and the West," Oxford Center for Islamic Studies, October 27, 1993.

9. *Press Association,* February 17, 2001, op. cit.; www.shell-me.com examined and typed, September 6, 2006.

10. Interviews with three individuals familiar with the contacts with State and Bush. Also Daniel Golden, James Bandler, Marcus Walker, *Wall Street Journal,* September 27, 2001.

11. Meetings with Carter, donations: E-mail communication from Deanna Congileo, the Carter Center, October 12, 2005. One of only two trips to the U.S. since 1973: Affidavit of Bakr Bin Laden, *In Re Terrorist Attacks on September 11, 2001,* United States District Court, Southern District of New York, 03 MDL 1570, January 25, 2006.

12. "for as long . . . acts of violence": Police report of Michele Smith filed in *Franklin Frisaura v. Regina Frisaura,* Orange County, Florida, DR97-3754. Examined and typed, January 24, 2006. Franklin Frisaura declined to comment.

13. All documents and quotations, ibid.

14. The Marina, Bin Laden Island: Interviews with visitors, including Yahia Agaty, November 19, 2005 (RS) and a second individual who asked to not be identified. Robin Shulman visited and photographed the resort.

15. *The 9/11 Commission Report,* p. 154.

16. "theater . . . superterrorist": Ibid.

17. Ibid., pp. 154–55.

18. Wedding video: *Meeting Osama Bin Laden*, Brook Lapping Productions, 2004. Four to five hundred guests, the scene: Zaidan in Bergen, *The Osama Bin Laden I Know*, pp. 255–56.
19. Ibid., p. 255.
20. Ibid., p. 256.
21. Ibid.

36. THE NAME

1. Interview with Jason Blum and Ricardo Pascetta, July 1, 2007 (KH). Interview with Ricardo Pascetta, June 2, 2007 (KH).
2. Interview with Blum, ibid.
3. "how horribile ... at her": Ibid. "violence ... Islam": Redacted FBI documents released and published by Judicial Watch as a result of its FOIA filings and lawsuit, *Judicial Watch v. Department of Homeland Security & Federal Bureau of Investigation*, United States District Court, District of Columbia, 04-1643 (RWR). The document describing the interview with Najiah, and quoting her, has redacted her name, but the context makes clear that it is her.
4. Interview with Blum, op. cit.
5. "The guy turned ... out of here": All quotations from interview with Blum, ibid. The circumstances of the flight crew's revolt were also described by Pascetta, op. cit.
6. The other groups of Saudi royals: Judicial Watch documents, op. cit. That Bandar did not discuss the flights with Bush, and "Those people ... no problem": Simpson, *The Prince*, pp. 314–16.
7. Interview with Fred Dutton, May 24, 2005. Dutton died about a month after this interview, on June 25, 2005, at the age of eighty-two.
8. "what to do ... bad apple": Interview with Dutton, ibid.
9. All quotations, ibid.
10. Ibid.
11. The meeting, "solicitous and kind": Interview with Chas Freeman, June 15, 2005.
12. Ibid.
13. Yeslam has given several similar interviews describing his experiences and thinking on September 11 and afterward. See, for example, *Dateline NBC*, broadcast July 9, 2004. The quotations here are from a published question-and-answer interview in *VSB*, Geneva, December 2005, translated and filed in *In Re Terrorist Attacks on September 11, 2001*, United States District Court, Southern District of New York, 03 MDL 1570.
14. "Bin Laden's half-brother condemns U.S. attacks," *Agence France Presse*, September 12, 2001.
15. "the possibility ... Saudi Arabia": *Dateline NBC*, op. cit.
16. "The strong ... Islamic faith": *Guardian* (London) September 21, 2001. "This is a criminal act ... who died": Interview with Sabry Ghoneim, November 14, 2005 (RS). "bloody Arabs": The author was present when the conversation occurred; the person who received the phone call relayed the language after hanging up.
17. "Even if I do not condone ... deserve it": Interview with Bassim Alim, February 21, 2005.

18. "a large amount . . . his family": From FBI documents released by Judicial Watch, op. cit.

19. Interview with Blum, op. cit.

20. Ibid.

21. Redactions in the FBI documents released to Judicial Watch make it difficult to be certain about the identity of the Washington passenger who was not interviewed. There were only five Washington passengers, however; of these, two were Shafiq and Akber Moawalla, who were clearly interviewed. Two others were college age. The fifth was Omar, who was then thirty-one years old.

22. Interviews with Blum and Pascetta, op. cit.

23. Ibid.

24. Ibid.

25. "Believe me . . . human being": *Boston Globe,* October 7, 2001.

26. *The Record* (Bergen County, NJ), September 27, 2001.

27. All quotations, ibid.

28. Lawrence (ed.), *Messages to the World,* pp. 111–12.

29. Ibid., pp. 117–22.

30. Ibid., pp. 124–25.

31. Hamud (ed.), *Osama Bin Laden,* pp. 75–79.

32. "a certain posture . . . corporation": Interview with Andrew Hess, December 2005 (RS).

33. *Sunday Telegraph* (London), December 16, 2001.

34. All quotations, ibid.

37. PUBLIC RELATIONS

1. The account of the delegation's trip and the exchange with Bakr Bin Laden is primarily from interviews with officials familiar with the Treasury Department's work during this period. See also "Testimony of R. Richard Newcomb, Director, Office of Foreign Assets Control, U.S. Department of Treasury Before the House Financial Services Subcommittee on Oversights and Investigations," June 16, 2004.

2. Interviews with two former U.S. officials involved in the discussions, who asked to not be identified.

3. Boston field office on September 11: *Boston Herald,* September 18, 2001. Other FBI investigations: Interviews with two former FBI officials and with several former Bin Laden partners and employees who were interviewed by the FBI or Department of Homeland Security investigators after September 11. FBI struggled with analysis: Declassified FBI files obtained by Judicial Watch show that much of the bureau's written analysis of the family's history and activity remained poorly developed.

4. Interviews with former Bin Laden partners and employees, and with former FBI officials, ibid. See chapter 24, footnote 19.

5. Telephone interview with Charles Tickle, February 16, 2006.

6. "couldn't help . . . a threat": Interview with Dale Watson, May 27, 2005. Interview with Dennis Lormel, May 25, 2005.

7. Interview with Lormel, ibid.

8. Interview with a former U.S. official who asked to not be identified.

9. Declassified e-mail obtained and released by Judicial Watch.

10. "who were emotional . . . the victims": Interview with Peri Bearman, December 2005 (RS). Fellowships suspended: E-mail communication from Frank Vogel, Harvard University.

11. "The family wasn't": Telephone interview with John McManus, February 13, 2006. Bakr's reaction: Interview with an individual who spoke with him, who asked to not be identified.

12. "is fully separated": *Wall Street Journal*, September 19, 2001. "a very honored name . . . cover": Associated Press, October 7, 2001.

13. Senior brothers did not go back: Interviews with two individuals close to the family who asked to not be identified. "I don't know . . . this way": Interview with Gail Freeman, April 27, 2006. Scotland Yard: Interview with an individual familiar with the incident, who asked to not be identified. London assault: *Express* (London) and *Sun* (London) August 16, 2002. German hotel: Interview with a second individual familiar with the incident.

14. Interview with a member of the Harley club, who asked to not be identified.

15. Transcript of *20/20* broadcast, March 15, 2002.

16. Interview with a person involved with the *20/20* broadcast who asked to not be identified. Barbara Walters did not respond to requests for comment.

17. Interview with Khaled Al-Maenna, February 20, 2005.

18. Interview with a person involved in the episode who asked to not be identified. Barbara Walters did not respond to requests for comment.

19. Broadcast transcript, op. cit.

38. BRANDS

1. Interview with Jack Kayajanian, August 25, 2005.

2. "I began . . . September 11": "Supplemental Declaration" of Ibrahim Bin Laden, September 30, 2002, filed in *Christine Binladin v. Ibrahim Binladin*, Los Angeles County Superior Court, BD058156.

3. Interview with Kayajanian, op. cit. Christine's financial condition from her Income and Expense Declaration, filed December 18, 2002, ibid.

4. Interview with Kayajanian, op. cit.

5. "my own safety . . . many individuals": Supplemental Declaration, September 30, 2002, op. cit.

6. Interview with Kayajanian, op. cit.

7. Much of the record concerning the custody struggle over Sibba that erupted in 2002 remains sealed, but the $4 million bond order is part of the public court file; it was an aspect of the court's rulings on custody issued October 4, 2002.

8. The attitude of Bakr and the brothers around him: Interview with two individuals close to the family, one of whom discussed the matter directly with Bakr; they asked to not be identified.

9. "I feel . . . like yours": Associated Press, December 23, 2005.

10. "The name . . . the ocean": *Wall Street Journal*, January 17, 2002.

11. "accepted moral standards": Associated Press, January 18, 2002. "insensitive": *Bloomberg News*, January 22, 2002. "I am not . . . a newspaper": *Time*, November 8, 2004.

12. Boutique, watches, perfume blends: Author's visit, December 2006. "shy, quiet . . . narrow legs": Marianne MacDonald, "O Brother, Where Art Thou?" *Evening Standard* (London) May 26, 2006.

13. All quotations, MacDonald, ibid.

39. SO WHAT?

1. "She's still . . . good to Sama": Interview with Sabry Ghoneim, November 14, 2005 (RS). Caroline remarried about eight years after Salem's death: Interview with a person close to the family who asked to not be identified.

2. The author is grateful to Robin Shulman for her enterprising field research, which brought her to the horse show where she made all of the observations and conducted all the interviews reflected in this section. Much of the descriptive language is also hers.

3. All quotations in this section, ibid. The brochure about Rabab was provided to Robin Shulman during her visit to Khaled's estate.

4. Interviews with General Fathy Fathalla and Manfred Baier, Cairo Airport Company, November 21, 2005 (RS).

5. "My father . . . camel again": Interview with Bengt Johansson, October 3, 2006.

6. Interview with an individual who discussed the issues with Yahya and who asked to not be identified.

7. *House of Saud*, coproduced by Martin Smith and Chris Durrance for *Frontline*, 2005.

8. "The B.A.E. files," by David Leigh and Rob Evans, *Guardian* (London), June 7, 2007.

9. "under . . . to Al Qaeda": from "First Amended Complaint" (the insurers' complaint), *In Re Terrorist Attacks on September 11, 2001*, United States District Court, Southern District of New York, 03 MDL 1570. Legal bills exceeded $10 million: Interview with a Saudi official who asked to not be identified.

10. Interviews with three people in the Orlando area who made inquiries about the property.

11. Abdulaziz Bin Bakr: *Gulf News*, November 18, 2006.

12. Interview with Anwar Hassan, October 13, 2005, and written materials provided by Hassan.

13. "were furious . . . themselves": Ibid.

14. *Worldwide Projects, Inc.*, July 1, 2003.

15. Economic City plans: *Al-Bawaba* (Saudi Arabia), December 21, 2005. "could either make . . . huge in scope": Interview with a Bin Laden executive who asked to not be identified.

16. *Washington Post*, October 14, 2005.

17. *Worldwide Projects, Inc.*, April 1, 2006.

40. IN EXILE

1. Author's visit, December 2005.

2. Brochure quotations from Fame materials obtained by the author. Abdullah's business

and lifestyle: Interviews with four colleagues and acquaintances in Jeddah, who asked to not be identified. See also "Bin Laden's Eldest Son Speaks . . ." *Al-Sharq Al-Awsat*, October 21, 2001.

3. At least twenty-three children: Associated Press, November 4, 2002. Arranged for at least one wife's departure: "Bin Laden's Wife Interviewed . . ." *Al-Majallah*, March 10, 2002. Yemeni wife home by December: *Al-Quds Al-Arabi*, December 29, 2001. Her return was confirmed by several Yemeni journalists during the author's visit to the country in March 2007.

4. "Saudi Interior Minister on Bin Laden's Sons . . ." *Al-Sharq Al-Awsat*, July 3, 2004.

5. "Osama did . . . the family": Quoted in Bergen, *The Osama Bin Laden I Know*, p. 384.

6. "Omar is wary . . . misses his father": *Times* (London), July 11, 2007. "Polygamy . . . she was forty": *Express* (London), July 16, 2007. *Sun* (London), September 20, 2007.

7. All quotations from "*Al-Majallah* Obtains Bin Laden's Will . . ." *Al-Majallah*, October 27, 2002, FBIS translation.

8. All quotations, ibid.

9. All quotations from Bergen, op. cit., p. 371.

10. "I am . . . whole world": Lawrence (ed.), *Messages to the World*, p. 208.

11. "a rare . . . world infidelity": "FBIS Report in Arabic," May 6, 2004.

12. Reward scheme: Ibid. "It is true . . . foreign one": *Messages to the World*, op. cit., p. 255.

13. "shows that . . . Islamic world": "FBIS Report," op. cit.

14. "The Americans . . . intellects": *Messages to the World*, op. cit., pp. 126–27.

15. "Some American . . . from you?": Ibid., pp. 161–62.

16. All quotations, Ibid., pp. 162–68.

17. "The swimmer . . . rain": BBC Monitoring, January 19, 2006.

18. "The freedom . . . America": *Messages to the World*, op. cit., p. 169.

19. "America . . . Zionist lobby": Ibid., p. 110. "the idiots . . . from a lion": "Bin Laden Calls Saudi Initiative 'High Treason' . . ." *Al-Quds Al-Arabi*, March 28, 2002.

20. "I miss . . . wolves": *Messages to the World*, op. cit., p. 248.

21. "that when . . . evil": Ibid., pp. 254–55.

22. "demonstrate . . . ugliness": Ibid., p. 194.

23. "underline . . . God Almighty": Ibid., p. 183. "war winners": Scheuer (as "Anonymous"), *Through Our Enemies' Eyes*, p. 66.

24. All quotations, BBC Monitoring, op. cit.

25. All quotations, ABC News transcript, abcnews.go.com/images/Politics/transcript2.pdf.

BIBLIOGRAPHY

BOOKS

ABBAS, HAMAD. *Story of the Great Expansion.* Jeddah: Saudi Bin Ladin Group, 1996.

ALFADL, SALEH S., ed. *The National Industries Directory.* Jeddah: Jeddah Chamber of Commerce and Industry, 1988.

ALGOSAIBI, GHAZI A. *Arabian Essays.* London: Kegan Paul, 1982.

ALIREZA, MARIANNE. *At the Drop of a Veil: The True Story of an American Woman's Years in a Saudi Harem.* Costa Mesa: Blind Owl Press, 2002.

AMIRAHMADI, HOOSHANG, AND NADER ENTESSAR, eds. *Reconstruction and Regional Diplomacy in the Persian Gulf.* London: Routledge, 1992.

ASAD, MUHAMMAD. *The Message of the Quran* (six volumes). Bristol: The Book Foundation, 2003.

ASLAN, REZA. *No God but God: The Origins, Evolution and Future of Islam.* New York: Random House, 2005.

BADEEB, SAEED M. *The Saudi-Egyptian Conflict over North Yemen, 1962–1970.* Boulder, CO: Westview Press, 1986.

BAER, ROBERT. *Sleeping with the Devil: How Washington Sold Our Soul for Saudi Crude.* New York: Crown Publishers, 2003.

AL-BARRAK, HOMOUD A., ed. *Commercial and Industrial Directory for the States of the Gulf Cooperation Council.* Riyadh: Dar Al-Mathhar for Publishing and Advertising, 1988.

BEATY, JONATHAN, AND S. C. GWYNE. *The Outlaw Bank: A Wild Ride into the Secret Heart of BCCI.* New York: Random House, 1993.

BELING, WILLARD A., ed. *King Faisal and the Modernisation of Saudi Arabia.* Boulder, CO: Westview Press, 1980.

BENJAMIN, DANIEL, AND STEVEN SIMON. *The Age of Sacred Terror.* New York: Random House, 2002.

BENT, THEODORE, AND MRS. THEODORE BENT. *Southern Arabia.* London: Smith, Elder & Co., 1900.

BERGEN, PETER L. *The Osama Bin Laden I Know: An Oral History of Al Qaeda's Leader.* New York: The Free Press, 2006.

———. *Holy War, Inc.: Inside the Secret World of Osama bin Laden.* New York: The Free Press, 2001.

BIDWELL, R. L., AND G. R. SMITH, eds. *Arabian and Isalimic Studies.* London: Longman Group Limited, 1983.

BIN LADIN, CARMEN. *Inside the Kingdom: My Life in Saudi Arabia.* New York: Warner Books, 2004.

BLANDFORD, LINDA. *Super-Wealth: The Secret Lives of the Oil Sheikhs.* New York: William Morrow, 1977.

BRADLEY, JOHN R. *Saudi Arabia Exposed.* New York: Palgrave Macmillan, 2005.

BRINKLEY, JOEL, AND STEPHEN ENGELBERG, eds. *Report of the Congressional Committees Investigating the Iran-Contra Affair, with the Minority View.* New York: Times Books, 1988.

BRIODY, DAN. *The Iron Triangle.* New York: John Wiley & Sons, 2003.

BRONSON, RACHEL. *Thicker Than Oil: America's Uneasy Partnership with Saudi Arabia.* New York: Oxford University Press, 2006.

BURCKHARDT, J. L. *Travels in Arabia.* London: Henry Colburn, 1829. Reprinted by Frank Cass and Co. Ltd., 1968.

BURTON, SIR RICHARD F. *Personal Narrative of a Pilgrimage to Al-Madinah and Meccah.* Toronto: Dover, 1893, 1964.

CARTER, J. R. L. *Merchant Families of Saudi Arabia.* London: Scorpion Publications, 1984.

CAUDILL, MARK R. *Twilight in the Kingdom.* Westport, CT: Praeger Security International, 2006.

CLARKE, RICHARD A. *Against All Enemies.* New York: The Free Press, 2004.

COLL, STEVE. *Ghost Wars: The Secret History of the CIA, Afghanistan, and Bin Laden, from the Soviet Invasion to September 10, 2001.* New York: Penguin Press, 2004.

DAWISHA, ADEED, ed. *Islam in Foreign Policy.* Cambridge: Cambridge University Press, 1983.

DEGAURY, GERALD. *Arabia Phoenix.* London: Kegan Paul, 1946, 2001.

AL-DIN, NABIL SHARAF. *Bin Laden: The Taliban, the Arab Afghans and the Fundamentalist Internationale.* Cairo: Maktabat Madbuli, 2002.

FANDY, MAMOUN. *Saudi Arabia and the Politics of Dissent.* New York: Palgrave Macmillan, 2001.

FIELD, MICHAEL. *Inside the Arab World.* London: John Murray, 1994.

————. *The Merchants: The Big Business Families of Saudi Arabia and the Gulf States.* Woodstock, NY: Overlook Press, 1985.

————. *A Hundred Million Dollars a Day.* London: Sidgwick and Jackson, 1975.

FINNIE, RICHARD. *Bechtel in Arab Lands.* San Francisco: Bechtel Corporation, 1958.

GAUHAR, ALTAF, ed. *The Challenge of Islam.* London: Islamic Council of Europe, 1976.

GERGES, FAWAZ A. *The Far Enemy: Why Jihad Went Global.* Cambridge: Cambridge University Press, 2005.

GLASSE, CYRIL. *The New Encyclopedia of Islam.* New York: AltaMira Press, 2002.

GROS, MARCEL. *Feisal of Arabia.* London: EMGE-Sepix, 1981.

HAFIZ, FAISAL A., AND SAMIR A. MURSHID, eds. *Who's Who in Saudi Arabia 1983–1984.* Jeddah: Tihama, 1984.

HALEEM, M. A. S. ABDEL, *The Qu'ran.* Oxford: Oxford University Press, 2004.

HAMMOUDI, ABDELLAH. *A Season in Mecca.* (Pascale Ghazaleh, tr.) New York: Hill and Wang, 2006.

HANSEN, ERIC. *Motoring with Mohammed: Journeys to Yemen and the Red Sea.* New York: Vintage Books, 1992.

HECKMAN, WOLF. *Hai fressen keine Deutschen (Sharks Don't Eat Germans).* Munich: F. A. Herbig Verlagsbuchhandlung, 1982.

HOLDEN, DAVID, AND RICHARD JOHNS. *The House of Saud: The Rise and Rule of the Most Powerful Dynasty in the Arab World.* New York: Holt, Rinehart and Winston, 1981.

HOURANI, ALBERT. *A History of the Arab Peoples.* London: Faber and Faber, 1992.

HOWARTH, DAVID. *The Desert King: A Life of Ibn Saud.* Beirut: Librairie du Liban, 1964.

INGRAMS, DOREEN. *A Time in Arabia.* London: John Murray, 1970.

IZZARD, MOLLY. *Freya Stark: A Biography.* London: Hodder & Stoughton, 1993.

———. *The Gulf: Arabia's Western Approaches.* London: John Murray, 1979.

KECHICHIAN, JOSEPH A. *Succession in Saudi Arabia.* New York: Palgrave Macmillan, 2001.

KOSTINER, JOSEPH. *The Making of Saudi Arabia, 1916–1936: From Chieftaincy to Monarchical State.* New York: Oxford University Press, 1993.

LACY, ROBERT. *The Kingdom: Arabia and the House of Saud.* New York: Avon, 1981.

LAWRENCE, BRUCE, ed. *Messages to the World: The Statements of Osama Bin Laden.* London: Verso, 2005.

LAWRENCE, T. E. *Seven Pillars of Wisdom.* New York: Anchor Books, 1926, 1991.

LIPPMAN, THOMAS W. *Inside the Mirage: America's Fragile Partnership with Saudi Arabia.* Boulder, CO: Westview Press, 2004.

LONG, DAVID E. *The Kingdom of Saudi Arabia.* Gainesville, FL: University Press of Florida, 1997.

MACK, JOHN E. *A Prince of Disorder.* Cambridge, MA: Harvard University Press, 2002.

MACKEY, SANDRA. *The Saudis: Inside the Desert Kingdom.* New York: W. W. Norton, 1987, 2002.

MACKINTOSH-SMITH, TIM. *Yemen: The Unknown Arabia.* New York: Overlook Press, 2000.

MANNAN, MOHAMMED ABDUL, ed. *Jeddah Commercial Directory.* Jeddah: Arab Circle Corporation, 1991, 1993.

NUSEIBEH, SAID, AND OLEG GRABAR. *The Dome of the Rock.* London: Thames and Hudson, date unknown.

PETERS, F. E. *The Hajj: The Muslim Pilgrimage to Mecca and the Holy Places.* Princeton, NJ: Princeton University Press, 1994.

———. *Jerusalem.* Princeton, NJ: Princeton University Press, 1985.

PHILLIPS, KEVIN. *American Dynasty: Aristocracy, Fortune, and the Politics of Deceit in the House of Bush.* New York: Penguin Books, 2004.

PRYCE-JONES, DAVID. *The Closed Circle: An Interpretation of the Arabs.* Chicago: Ivan R. Dee, 2002.

RANDAL, JONATHAN. *Osama: The Making of a Terrorist.* New York: Alfred A. Knopf, 2004.

AL-RASHEED, MADAWI. *A History of Saudi Arabia.* Cambridge: Cambridge University Press, 2002.

RISEN, JAMES. *State of War: The Secret History of the CIA and the Bush Administration.* New York: The Free Press, 2006.

RODENGEN, JEFFREY L. *The Legend of York International.* Fort Lauderdale, FL: Write Stuff Syndicate, 1997.

RUTHVEN, MALISE. *Fundamentalism: The Search for Meaning.* Oxford: Oxford University Press, 2004.

SADAT, ANWAR. *Those I Have Known.* London: Jonathan Cape, 1985.

SARHAN, SAMIR M. *Who's Who in Saudi Arabia 1976–1977.* Jeddah: Tihama, 1977.

SCHEUER, MICHAEL (as "Anonymous"). *Through Our Enemies' Eyes: Osama bin Laden, Radical Islam and the Future of America.* Washington, D.C.: Brasseys, 2002.

AL-SHAMMARY, MOHAMMED MUFARAH, ed. *Top 1000 Saudi Companies.* Al Khobar: International Information and Trading Services, 1990.

SHEEAN, VINCENT. *Faisal: The King and His Kingdom.* Tavistock, England: University Press of Arabia, 1975.

SIMPSON, WILLIAM. *The Prince.* New York: Regan Books, 2006.

STARK, FREYA. *The Southern Gates of Arabia: A Journey in the Hadhramaut.* London: John Murray, 1936.

STEFOFF, REBECCA. *Faisal.* New York: Chelsea House, 1989.

SURTEES, LAWRENCE. *Pa Bell.* Toronto: Random House of Canada, 1992.

SUSKIND, RON. *The One Percent Doctrine: Deep Inside America's Pursuit of Its Enemies Since 9/11.* New York: Simon & Schuster, 2006.

TEITELBAUM, JOSHUA. *Holier Than Thou: Saudi Arabia's Islamic Opposition.* Washington, D.C.: Washington Institute for Near East Policy, 2000.

THEROUX, PETER. *Sandstorms: Days and Nights in Arabia.* New York: W. W. Norton, 1990.

THOMAS, LOWELL. *With Lawrence in Arabia.* London: Prion, 2002.

TOAIMI, SALEH, ed. *Saudi Arabia Trade Directory 1981.* Jeddah: Council of Saudi Chambers of Commerce, 1981.

TROFIMOV, YAROSLAV. *Faith at War: A Journey on the Frontlines of Islam, from Baghdad to Timbuktu.* New York: Henry Holt and Co., 2005.

UNGER, CRAIG. *House of Bush, House of Saud: The Secret Relationship Between the World's Two Most Powerful Dynasties.* New York: Scribner, 2004.

VAN DER MEULEN, D. *The Wells of Ibn Saud.* New York: Frederick A. Praeger, 1957.

————. *Aden to the Hadhramaut: A Journey in South Arabia.* London: John Murray, 1947.

————. *Hadramaut: Some of Its Mysteries Unveiled.* Leiden, Netherlands: E. J. Brill Ltd., 1932.

VINK, STEVEN. *Daniel van der Meulen in Arabia Felix.* Amsterdam: Royal Tropical Institute, 2003.

WALLER, MARTIN, ed. *International Interior Design Review.* London: Andrew Martin International, 1998.

WOODWARD, BOB. *Veil: The Secret Wars of the CIA.* New York: Simon & Schuster, 1987.

WRIGHT, LAWRENCE. *The Looming Tower: Al Qaeda and the Road to 9/11.* New York: Alfred A. Knopf, 2006.

YAMANI, MAI. *Cradle of Islam: The Hijaz and the Quest for an Arabian Identity.* London: I. B. Tauris, 2004.

YOUNG, ARTHUR N. *Saudi Arabia: The Making of a Financial Giant.* New York: New York University Press, 1983.

AL-ZAYYAT, MONTASSER. *The Road to Al-Qaeda: The Story of Bin Laden's Right-Hand Man.* London: Pluto Press, 2004.

DOCUMENTS

BURDETT, A. L. P., ed. *Records of Saudi Arabia, 1966–1971,* volumes 1 and 2, London: Archive Editions, 2004.

COMBATING TERRORISM CENTER, UNITED STATES MILITARY ACADEMY: Selected Al Qaeda-related documents obtained during U.S. military battlefield operations in Afghanistan and elsewhere, translated and archived in the U.S. government's Harmony database, 2005–2006.

INGRAMS, DOREEN, AND LEILA INGRAMS, eds. *Records of Yemen, 1798–1960*, volumes 3–9, London: Archive Editions, 1993.

INGRAMS, W. H. *A Report on the Social, Economic and Political Condition of the Hadhramaut.* London: Colonial Office, 1936.

JARMAN, ROBERT L., ed. *The Jedda Diaries, 1919–1940*, volumes I–IV, collected British government documents from the Jedda legation. London: Archive Editions, 1990.

KORNBLUH, PETER, ed. *The Iran-Contra Affair: The Making of a Scandal, 1983–1988*, National Security Archive document set, George Washington University.

"The 9/11 COMMISSION REPORT: Final Report of the National Commission on Terrorist Attacks Upon the United States," July 2004. Washington, D.C.: Government Printing Office.

PROCEEDINGS OF THE EARLY HISTORY OF AL QAEDA WORKING GROUP, 2006–2007, Rand Corporation; Bruce Hoffman and Kim Cragin, co-directors; Daniel Byman, Martha Crenshaw, Peter Bergen, Lawrence Wright, Rohan Gunaratna, Nadia Oweidat, Sara Daly, Heather Gregg, Ann Kasupski, researchers and presenters.

RECORDS OF THE DEPARTMENT OF STATE, U.S. National Archives and Records Administration, College Park, Maryland.

RECORDS OF THE FEDERAL FOREIGN OFFICE, Federal Republic of Germany (West Germany), Berlin.

RECORDS OF THE FOREIGN OFFICE (later Foreign and Commonwealth Office), National Archives, Kew, Richmond, United Kingdom.

ROTH, JOHN, AND DOUGLAS GREENBURG, AND SERENA WILLE, "Monograph on Terrorist Financing," staff report to the commission, National Commission on Terrorist Attacks upon the United States (the 9/11 Commission).

RONALD REAGAN PRESIDENTIAL LIBRARY, National Archives and Records Administration, Simi Valley, California.

JOURNAL ARTICLES AND MANUSCRIPTS

ALANGARI, ABDULRAHMAN BIN MOHAMMED. "Mantaqat Qasr Alhgokm: The Development of the 20th Century," Conference on the Kingdom of Saudi Arabia, collected proceedings, January 1999: 237–336.

ALIREZA, MARIANNE. "The Late King Faisal: His Life, Personality and Methods of Government," Conference on the Kingdom of Saudi Arabia, collected proceedings, January 1999: 201–36.

AMIDHAR, ALI H. "International Succession Laws: Saudi Arabia," *Society of Trust and Estate Practioners*, issue 6, September 2004.

ARMITAGE, H. ST. J. B. "King Abdul Aziz and the English Connection: Captain William Shakespear and His Successors," Conference on the Kingdom of Saudi Arabia, collected proceedings, January 1999: 525–60.

BERGEN, PETER, AND PAUL CRUICKSHANK, "How the Idea of Al Qaeda Was Conceived," Rand Corporation, 2006.

BINLADEN, ABDULLAH M. "Western Banking Practices and Shari'a Law in Saudi Arabia," Cambridge, MA: Harvard University master's dissertation, 1992.

———. "Negotiability of Financial Instruments in Contemporary Financial Markets: An Islamic Legal Analysis," Cambridge, MA: Harvard University doctoral dissertation, 2000.

BLIGH, ALEXANDER. "The Interplay Between Opposition Activity and Recent Trends in the Arab World," in *Arabian Peninsula: Zone of Ferment*. Stanford, CA: Hoover Press Publication 287, 1984: 65–79.

CAUDILL, MARK A. *Twilight in the Hejaz: Dispatches from Western Arabia* (draft manuscript).

CORDESMAN, ANTHONY H., AND NAWAF OBAD. "Al Qaeda in Saudi Arabia: Asymmetric Threats and Islamist Extremists." Center for Strategic and International Studies, working draft: January 6, 2005.

DYAKOV, NIKOLAY N. "Arabia at the Turn of a New Age: Documents from the Historical Archives of St. Petersburg." Conference on the Kingdom of Saudi Arabia: 100 Years, collected proceedings, January 1999: 99–127.

FREEMAN, ROBERT. *The Saudi Connection* (unpublished manuscript).

GAUSE, F. GREGORY, III. "Be Careful What You Wish For: The Future of U.S.-Saudi Relations," *World Policy Journal*, volume 19, issue I, April 1, 2002: 37–50.

———. "Saudi Arabia over a Barrel," *Foreign Affairs*, May–June, 2000: 80 ff.

———. "The Middle East at a Crossroads," *Washington Quarterly*, volume 20, no. 1, Winter 1997: 143 ff.

———. "Yemeni Unity: Past and Future," *Middle East Journal*, vol. 42, no. 1, Winter 1988: 33–47.

———. "The Idea of Yemeni Unity," *Journal of Arab Affairs*, volume 6, no. 1, Spring 1987: 55–81.

———. "British and American Policies in the Persian Gulf, 1968–1973," *Review of International Studies*, vol. 11, no. 4, October 1985: 247–74.

GUNARATNA, ROHAN. "Al Qaeda: Its Organizational Strengths and Weaknesses with a Special Focus on the Pre-1996 Phase," Rand Corporation, 2006.

HO, ENGSENG. "Empire Through Diasporic Eyes: A View from the Other Boat," *Comparative Studies in Society and History*, vol. 46, no. 2, April, 2004: 210–46.

KATZ, MARK N. "U.S.-Yemen Relations and the War on Terror: A Portrait of Yemeni President Ali Abdullah Salih." *TerrorismMonitor*, Jamestown Foundation, volume II, issue 7, April 8, 2004: 7–9.

NASH, GEOFFREY P. "King Abdul Aziz ibn Saud and Amin al-Rihani: Some Notes on Al-Rihani's Anglo-American Diplomacy," Conference on the Kingdom of Saudi Arabia: 100 Years, collected proceedings, January 1999: 377–400.

NOVIKOV, EVGENII. "The Soviet Roots of Isalmic Militancy in Yemen." *TerrorismMonitor*, Jamestown Foundation, volume II, issue 7, April 8, 2004: 5–7.

PLATE, W. "Geographical and Historical Remarks on the Province of Hadramaut." *Original Papers Read Before the Syro-Egyptian Society of London*, volume I, part I, 1845.

AL-SALEH, FADIA SAUD. "Travels to Arabia During the Reign of King Abdul Aziz," Conference on the Kingdom of Saudi Arabia, collected proceedings, January 1999: 337–76.

ULPH, STEPHEN. "Shifting Sands: Al Qaeda and Tribal Gun-Running Along the Yemeni

Frontier." *TerrorismMonitor,* Jamestown Foundation, volume II, issue 7, April 8, 2004: 9–11.

WATKINS, ERIC. "Landscape of Shifting Alliances," *TerrorismMonitor,* Jamestown Foundation, volume II, issue 7, April 8, 2004: 3–5.

ZDANOWKI, JERZI. "King Abdulaziz in the Reports of the American Missionaries (1901–1921), Conference on the Kingdom of Saudi Arabia: 100 Years, collected proceedings, January 1999: 129–44.

COURT DOCUMENTS

Ali Khan Musarrat v. America in Motion Corp., Superior Court of California, Los Angeles County, C728912.

America in Motion Corp. v. Magnum Aircraft International, Superior Court of California, Los Angeles County, NWS043648.

America in Motion Corp. v. Ron R. Goldie, Superior Court of California, Los Angeles County, WEC13994.

America in Motion Corp. v. Steven McKim et al., Superior Court of California, Los Angeles County, C724395.

American Builder Association v. Khalil Binladin, Superior Court of California, Los Angeles County, WEC120274.

Ashton v. al Qaeda Islamic Army, United States District Court, Southern District of New York, 02Civ6977.

Bank of Beverly Hills v. Swiss American Financial, Superior Court of California, Los Angeles County, C685851.

Bank of California v. Alexander Cappello et al., Superior Court of California, Los Angeles County, C751115.

Barrera v. al Qaeda Islamic Army, United States District Court, Southern District of New York, 03Civ7036.

Binladen BSB Landscaping v. M. V. Nedloyd, 82 Civ. 1037 F. 2d 1006, 1012 (2d Cir. 1985).

Board of Managers of Flagship Wharf v. Sayeh, Suffolk Superior Court, Commonwealth of Massachusetts, SUCV1999-02657.

Burnett v. Al Baraka Inv. & Dev. Corp., United States District Court, Southern District of New York, 02Civ1616.

———, 03Civ5738.

Burnett Cos. Consolidated v. Jim Bath, Harris County Courts, Texas, 98-706743.

Carmen Bin Ladin v. Ibrahim Mohammed Bin Ladin, Superior Court of California, Los Angeles County, BC212648.

Charles White v. Skyways Aircraft Leasing, Harris County Courts, Texas, 90-53147.

Christine Binladin v. Ibrahim Binladin, Superior Court of California, Los Angeles County, BD058156.

Christine Hartunian v. Prestige Homes, Inc., Superior Court of California, Los Angeles County, SC055776.

Dallas County v. Kabeltan Corp., Dallas County Courts, Texas, 92-32136.

Ducharme v. Hunnewell, Supreme Judicial Court of Massachusetts, Norfolk, 411 Mass. 711; 585 N.E. 2d 321, 1992.

Federal Insurance v. Al Qaeda, United States District Court, Southern District of New York, 03Civ6978.

Franklin Frisaura v. Regina Frisaura, Orange County Courts, Florida, DR97-3754.

Frederic L. Nason v. Kabelton Corp., Superior Court of California, Los Angeles County, BC205378.

FSB Partner v. Khalil Binladin, Superior Court of California, Los Angeles County, LC000160.

Houston Independent School District v. Salha Binladen, Harris County Courts, Texas, 85-19835.

Ian Munro et al. v. the Dee Howard Co., Bexar County Courts, Texas, 91-CI-00928.

Ibrahim Bin Ladin et al. v. Paul Andrew Richley, Superior Court of California, Los Angeles County, WEC112956.

In Re: Estate of Salem Binladen, Deceased, Bexar County Courts, Texas, 91-PC-1012.

In Re: Franklin B. Frisaura, 97-9831, Chapter 7 bankruptcy proceeding, United States Federal Court, Central District of Florida.

In Re: Terrorist Attacks on September 11, United States District Court, Southern District of New York, 03 MDL 1570.

Isabel Binladin v. Elizabeth Borges, Superior Court of California, Los Angeles County, SC003124.

James R. Bath v. Charles W. (Bill) White, Harris County Courts, Texas, 89-42551.

James R. Bath v. Kim Frumkin, Harris County Courts, Texas, 99-36377.

John L. Laughlin et al. v. William E. King et al., Harris County Courts, Texas, 01-44577.

Judicial Watch v. Department of Homeland Security & Federal Bureau of Investigation, 04-1643 (RWR) Washington, D.C.

Justin Baldwin et al. v. Alexander Cappello et al., Superior Court of California, Los Angeles County, C658270.

Khalil Binladin v. American Builder Association, Superior Court of California, Los Angeles County, C663911.

——, SC002982.

Lansdowne Financial Services Ltd. v. Binladen Telecommunications Company Ltd., State of New York, 95 A.D. 2d 711; 463 N.Y.S. 2d 826; 1983.

Larson v. Macro International et al., United States District Court, Eastern District of Virginia (Newport News) 4:96-cv-00101-JCC.

Mary Ellen Lewis v. James R. Bath, Harris County Courts, Texas, 89-01780A.

Mouldi H. Sayeh v. Atlantic Bank and Trust Company, Suffolk Superior Court, Commonwealth of Massachusetts, 98-2532.

Petronella and Yarborough v. Charles W. (Bill) White, Harris County Courts, Texas, 99-724391.

Raida Binladin v. Morris Ziff, Superior Court of California, Los Angeles County, C645771.

Resolution Trust Corp. v. Express Park, Inc., Harris County Courts, Texas, 91-63093.

Salvo v. al Qaeda Islamic Army, United States District Court, Southern District of New York, 03Civ5071.

Sandra C. Bath v. James R. Bath, Harris County Courts, Texas, 89-07180.

Sparks Sandbach Kimberly v. Isabel Bayma, Superior Court of California, Los Angeles County, WEC080333.

Tremsky v. Osama bin Laden, United States District Court, Southern District of New York, 02Civ7300.

United States of America v. Enaam Arnout, United States District Court, Northern District of Illinois, 02-CR-892.

United States of America v. Oliver L. North, United States District Court, District of Columbia, 88-0080-02.

United States of America v. Soliman S. Biheiri, United States District Court, Eastern District of Virginia, Alexandria Division, 03-365-A.

United States of America v. Usama bin Laden et al., United States District Court, Southern District of New York, S 98 Cr. 539.

Vigilant Insurance v. Kingdom of Saudi Arabia, United States District Court, Southern District of New York, 03Civ8591.

FILMS AND TELEVISION

Abdulaziz, King Abdulaziz Foundation, 1999.

Death of a Principle, Panorama for BBC, 1996.

House of Saud, The, Algeria Productions, 2004.

House of Saud, coproduced by Martin Smith and Chris Durrance for *Frontline,* 2005.

Hunting Bin Laden, produced and directed by Martin Smith for *Frontline,* 2001.

In the Footsteps of Osama Bin Laden, Peter Bergen and Christiane Amanpour for CNN, 2006.

Meeting Osama Bin Laden, Brook Lapping Productions for WGBH Boston, 2004.

Sur Les Traces de Ben Laden, Christophe Brule for M6, 2005.

INDEX

Gates, Robert, 610*n*–11*n*

General Electric (GE), 178, 219, 419, 420, 541

Geneva, 189, 266, 267, 271–73, 318, 330, 382, 383, 480, 546, 549; Bin Laden accounts in, 371–72, 477, 540; 9/11 in, 522–23, 546

Geneva Accords, 334

Genthod, Yeslam's estate in, 266, 270, 272

Germany, 5, 23, 50, 320, 353, 542; engineers from, 93, 94, 99; Salem's performing in, 183–84; Saudi embassy of, 64, 65, 66, 86

Germany, Nazi, 33, 37, 41, 54, 484

Getty, J. Paul, 213

Ghandi, Ali Al-, 533–34

Ghanem, Alia, 74, 77, 150, 152, 462, 463, 597*n*; in London, 209; on Osama-Salem relationship, 332; on Osama's education, 140, 144; Osama's marriage and, 206–7; Osama's relationship with, 137, 138, 141–42, 211, 461, 482, 492, 511, 602*n*–3*n*; on Salem, 198; second marriage of, 137; Sudan visits of, 406, 415; weakness of, 251, 487

Ghanem, Hosam Aldin, 138

Ghanem, Soliman, 139

Ghanem family, 74–75, 77, 138, 588*n*

Gharn Bashireih, 19–21, 582*n*

Ghoneim, Sabry, 170, 252–53, 345, 350–51, 355, 523, 552

Ghosaibi, Ghazi Al-, 379

GID. *See* Saudi Arabia, intelligence of (GID)

gliders, of Salem, 172–73, 216

Global Diamond Resources, Inc., 486

globalization, 570; Bin Laden family and, 14, 15, 274, 503; telephones and, 453

Golden Chain, 342, 616*n*–17*n*

Goldie, Ron, 362

Goldstein, Steven, 529

golf carts, broken, 185

Gore, Al, 459, 490–91, 504

Govenco, 53

Grand Mosque, 83, 85, 86, 91, 225–31, 421, 431, 442, 446–49, 626*n*; siege at, 225–29, 231, 245, 246, 247, 266, 447, 604*n*

Grapevine, 466, 469

Gray, Linda, 10

Great Britain, 114, 501–4, 542–43, 565, 575, 631*n*; Abdulaziz's relations with, 33, 35, 41; asylum laws in, 410; Buraimi dispute and, 67, 588*n*; education and, 109–11, 123, 134, 143; Egypt's relations with, 70, 105, 144; Fahd's relations with, 160; Faisal as viewed by, 156; Hejaz Railway and, 95; intelligence of, 93, 487; medical treatment in, 209, 210,

602*n*; oil and, 37; Osama's calls to, 468; Philby's bitterness toward, 36, 37; Saudi embassy of, 54, 56; Saudi finances and, 47, 48; Saudi relations with, 33, 35, 41, 47, 48, 67, 115, 116, 289, 369, 416, 501–4, 557, 588*n*; Saudi road building and, 54–56; Sudan and, 143, 397; Suez Canal and, 70; U.S. relations with, 9; Wadi Doan and, 22–23, 24; *see also* England; London

Great Depression, 31, 41, 83

Greece, 103, 224, 309, 321, 457

Grey, David, 178, 242

Griffin, Philip, 418–22, 430, 474, 504

Guess, Stanley, 113

Gulf highway, 114, 593*n*

Gulf war, 375, 376, 380, 404, 436

gypsum, 65, 98

Hadhramawt region, 19–27, 125, 373, 575; emigration from, 15, 21, 25, 44, 65

Hadhramis, 19–27, 57, 73, 125, 131, 373, 507, 575; descended from Prophet Mohamed, 25, 137; in Jeddah, 26, 30, 65–66, 73, 249; Mohamed's marriages to, 47, 58; as money lenders, 50; reputation for entrepreneurialism of, 40, 67

hadiths, 146–47, 204

Hajj, 28, 81, 83, 116, 191, 250, 256, 280, 344, 438–40, 442, 443–44, 446–47, 483, 583*n*; Mohamed's sons and, 107, 139; origins of, 80–81; *see also* pilgrims

Hall, John, 278

HAMAS, 406

Hammerman, Bernie, 240

Hammerman Brothers, 240–41

Hammoudi, Abdellah, 439–42

Handy Encyclopedia of Contemporary Religions and Sects, A, 484

Haqqani, Jalaladin, 285, 290, 293–94

Haram Al-Sharif (Noble Sanctuary), 87

Hard Rock Cafe Middle East, Inc., 457–58

Hariri, Rafik, 105, 281

Harrington, George, 4–9, 293, 323

Harrington, Jim, 118–20, 593*n*

Harry, Prince, 502

Hartunian, Christine, 384–96, 601*n*; appearance of, 387, 389; celebrity name dropping of, 387; custody struggle of, 393–96, 546–48; Islamic conversion of, 388; lifestyle of, 384–85; prenuptial contract of, 388–89

Harvard Law School, 427–31

Harvard University, 430–31, 541